Employment Law

An Introduction

Employment Law

An Introduction

Third edition

Stephen Taylor

Astra Emir

OXFORD

UNIVERSITY PRESS

OXFORD
UNIVERSITY PRESS

Great Clarendon Street, Oxford OX2 6DP
United Kingdom

Oxford University Press is a department of the University of Oxford.
It furthers the University's objective of excellence in research, scholarship,
and education by publishing worldwide. Oxford is a registered trade mark of
Oxford University Press in the UK and in certain other countries

British Library Cataloguing in Publication Data
Data available

Library of Congress Cataloguing in Publication Data
Data available

ISBN 978-0-19-960489-0

Printed in Great Britain by
Ashford Colour Press Ltd, Gosport, Hampshire

This book is dedicated to our families.

How to use the Online Resource Centre

To support this textbook, there is a range of web-based content for students and registered lecturers.

www.oxfordtextbooks.co.uk/orc/taylor_emir3e/

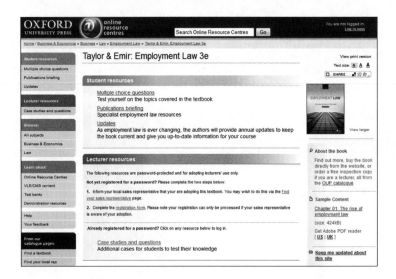

For students:

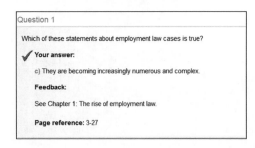

Self-test questions

A bank of interactive multiple choice questions provide instant feedback and assist you in independent self-study and revision.

INTERESTING RECENT CASES

The following are brief summaries of cases decided since the summer of 2010 that are notable, interesting or entertaining, confirming points or developing less significant new precedents. Some have significance for specific types of employment situation, others are simply curiosities:

* In Autoclenz v Belcher the Court of Appeal ruled that a group of car valeters were employees despite the presence of a substitution clause in their contracts (i.e.: permitting them to send someone else to work in their place) and a statement to the effect that there would be no mutuality of obligation. In practice, despite what these contractual terms said, the men were in an employment relationship and were therefore entitled to all employment rights.

* In Bateman et al v Asda the EAT made a somewhat contentious decision in favour of the employer. Asda had moved all staff onto a new pay structure without first securing their agreement. The defence was based

Bi-annual author updates

Updates from the authors ensure you are kept informed of the latest developments in employment law and provide wider contemporary context for chapter topics.

Publications briefing

Below are brief descriptions of significant books and articles on employment law and related subjects that have published recently.

Michael Duggan (2009): Equal Pay: Law & Practice. Jordon Publishing.

This is the latest in a series of books by Michael Duggan which examine key areas of employment law in detail. All cases of significance are discussed, the book comprising a first class and up to date commentary on equal pay law.

Jean-Michel Servais (2009): International Labour Law. Kluwer Publishing.

A new edition of the leading text on the International Labor Organisation's conventions and their practical impact. These cover employment rights and social security rights. The final section discusses problems of enforcement and possible ways forward.

Publications briefing

A directory of specialist employment law resources, selected by the authors, guide you towards areas of further reading to allow you to widen your knowledge of the subject.

For registered lecturers:

Taylor & Emir: Employment Law

CASE STUDY 1

A CASE OF QUESTIONABLE RECRUITMENT PRACTICES

The following short advertisement for a job at Southington NHS Primary Care Trust appears in a national newspaper and on the paper's internet recruitment site:

MANAGEMENT ACCOUNTANT

c £20,000 pa

Reporting to the Financial Controller, main duties will include:

Assisting in month end procedures, balance sheet reconciliation, control of cash flow, credit control, processing & dispatching invoices, preparing annual budgets, ensuring that any significant concerns are reported to the Financial Controller and deputising for the Financial Controller as required.

Case studies with questions

A bank of additional case studies are available to reinforce students' understanding of a topic and provide real world context. Each case study is accompanied by questions to encourage independent and critical thought.

TABLE OF CONTENTS

TABLE OF CASES

Foundations

The rise of employment law

Learning outcomes

By the end of this chapter you should be able to:

- identify the major fields that make up contemporary employment law;

- describe the development of UK employment law since 1965;

- explain why the UK has experienced a regulatory revolution in employment over recent years;

- distinguish between macro and micro-debates about employment law;

- put the case for and against existing and further regulation of the employment relationship.

Introduction

The past forty-five years have seen a revolution in employment relationships in the UK; a revolution to which all manner of economic, social, political and technological factors have contributed. Industries which once employed many millions of people manufacturing consumer goods, building ships, extracting coal, catching fish and farming the land have suffered substantial decline. In their place we have seen the growth of the retailing, media, hospitality, tourism, personal and financial services industries. These sectors too have seen revolutionary changes as small local branches have been closed down or forced out of business by larger nationally or regionally based operations offering a far more centralised and standardised approach to customer service. Many more people are now employed to work in call centres than there are employed in the car, steel and coal industries combined. Endless industrial restructuring means that mergers, acquisitions, strategic alliances, outsourcing, subcontracting and offshoring have become commonplace. Privatisation of public sector corporations has proceeded alongside the introduction of commercial disciplines to those public services that remain under central or local government control, leading to the employment of thousands of administrators who increasingly manage the professionals charged with delivering services to the public. Globalisation and technological developments have given rise to a world in which multi-national corporations wield terrific economic power and in which volatility has become the norm for organisations which once proudly dominated relatively stable national markets. Demographic developments have played their role too, creating tighter labour markets for higher-skilled workers. In most industries considerable up-skilling of jobs has occurred, a major growth having occurred in employment of the professional and managerial variety. Good social skills are in demand everywhere, and yet de-skilling has also been prevalent as technologically driven systems have reduced reliance on human brain power. More quietly, however, and less often commented on we have also seen a regulatory revolution whose impact as far as the employment relationship is concerned has been as significant as any of the developments cited in the above paragraph.

It is difficult to estimate the total cost of regulation to the UK economy with any degree of accuracy. A well-respected estimation is that published each year by the British Chambers of Commerce. In 2011, according to their measure, the total cumulative business costs associated with regulation introduced since 1998 was £76.8 billion (BCC, 2011), a figure that is based on the government's own published regulatory impact assessment exercises. Where these are unavailable, as is the case in some major areas of regulation such as the national minimum wage, they are not included. The real total cost of regulation, including indirect as well as direct costs is likely to be considerably higher. The Institute of Directors estimate for 2011 for the 'total administrative costs of regulation' was £112 billion (IOD, 2011).

A major division of this 'regulatory industry' is concerned with employment matters and there are few areas in which it has achieved faster growth in recent years. The number of applications made to UK employment tribunals is now regularly well in excess of 150,000 a year. This is twice or three times the number two decades ago (see Table 1.1), but is unsurprising when it is considered that there are now over eighty different types of claim that can be brought to a tribunal (Shackleton, 2005:128). In recent years the number

Table 1.1 Number of claims made annually to UK employment tribunals

1985/1986	38,590	1998/1999	91,913
1986/1987	38,395	1999/2000	103,935
1987/1988	30,510	2000/2001	130,408
1988/1989	29,304	2001/2002	112,227
1989/1990	34,703	2002/2003	98,617
1990/1991	43,244	2003/2004	115,042
1991/1992	67,448	2004/2005	86,181
1992/1993	71,821	2005/2006	115,042
1993/1994	71,661	2006/2007	132,577
1994/1995	80,061	2007/2008	189,300
1995/1996	108,827	2008/2009	151,028
1996/1997	88,910	2009/2010	236,100
1997/1998	80,435	2010/2011	218,100

Source: Employment Tribunal Service Annual Reports

of cases has risen sharply, as is always the case during periods of relatively high unemployment. Moreover, the cases themselves are becoming increasingly complex, often incorporating two or more types of claim in the same application and hence requiring more time either to settle or to hear. As a result, keeping on top of developments in employment law has become one of the most significant issues for managers, occupying increasing amounts of their time and energy. According to a survey of human resource managers carried out by the Chartered Institute of Personnel and Development (CIPD, 2002), two-thirds of HR specialists claimed to spend in excess of 20% of their time 'dealing with employment law issues', while a quarter reported that over 40% of their working days were spent in this way. In a further CIPD survey carried out five years later, 40% of HR professionals rated 'securing compliance with employment regulations' as one of their top five objectives, while 90% saw employment regulation as likely to become more important for their organisations in the future (CIPD, 2007).

The rise of employment law has also had a major impact on the legal profession, which even until fifteen years ago still tended to view employment as a poor relation of other areas of legal practice; something to avoid if you were serious about developing a legal career. It is now attracts many ambitious lawyers and is the source of substantial earnings. Sets of barristers' chambers and solicitors' firms specialise in employment law, the larger law firms developing their practices quickly in an increasingly competitive marketplace. Consultants specialising in employment law have also established themselves as major businesses in recent years, particularly where they provide easily understood, basic advice to small and medium-sized enterprises.

In this opening chapter, after defining some key terms, we focus on the two questions that are most commonly debated when people consider the revolution in employment regulation that has occurred in recent decades and its links with the other major trends in our business environment:

1. Why have we seen such a growth in the extent to which the employment relationship is regulated in the UK?

2. What are the advantages and disadvantages of increased employment regulation for the UK's economy and people?

In answering these questions we aim to introduce you to some of the major themes which underpin the evaluative material in this book. Later we will revisit these same arguments in different guises as we analyse specific areas of employment law from different perspectives. Here we take a broad brush view, considering the origins and impact of contemporary employment law as a whole.

 Activity 1.1

Consider the following statements. Which do you think are correct and which are false?

1 Most employment law concerns the relationship between trade unions and employers.

2 Modern UK employment law dates from the mid 1960s and early 1970s.

3 There is a long tradition of comprehensive employment regulation in the UK.

4 Employment law has largely developed as result of campaigns run by trade unions and other employee bodies.

5 Governments have used employment law in order to pursue wider economic objectives.

6 A strong economic case can be made both in favour of and against further regulation of the employment relationship.

Return to this activity once you have read the chapter to see how many of your answers were correct.

Fields of employment law

Employment law can be defined and sub-divided for the purposes of study in several ways. The most straightforward and useful from an employer's point of view involves a three-way division focusing on the regulation of the three types of relationship that are regulated by employment law. This approach is illustrated in Figure 1.1, the three relationships being:

1. the employer—employee relationship

2. the employer—trade union relationship

3. the trade union—member relationship.

The law governing the first of these three relationships is labelled 'individual employment law' and is the focus of the first five parts of this book. It encompasses dismissal law,

Figure 1.1 The three types of relationship regulated by employment law

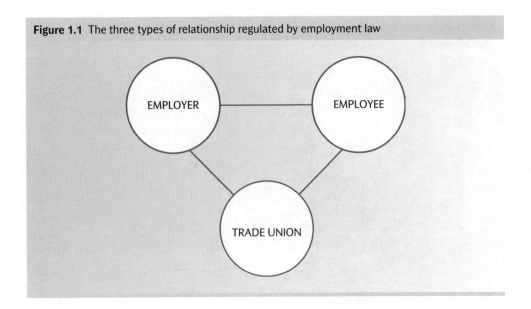

discrimination law, health and safety law and the various other rights that accrue to individual employees such as the national minimum wage, the right not to have unauthorised deductions made from wages and standard maternity rights. The second and third relationships are governed by collective employment law which we turn to in Part 6. The second includes law that protects the rights of employees to form and join trade unions, and requires collective consultation to take place in certain circumstances. Compulsory union recognition rules and regulations covering collective bargaining and the conduct of industrial action are also included. The third relationship, that between unions and their members, is also governed by a great deal of regulation which serves to limit the power of union officials to discipline members, to deny membership to individuals and more generally regulates the way trade unions must govern themselves.

While it is possible to make quite a clear division between collective and individual employment law, there are a number of areas which straddle the two. An example is redundancy law which is governed by individual employment legislation on the question of severance payments and selection issues, but by collective employment law when it comes to consultation requirements. The same is true of dismissals of strikers or for other trade union reasons. It must also be remembered, as Linda Dickens (2002) persuasively argues, that collective employment rights have the effect of underpinning and strengthening individual employment rights. This is because it is through membership of trade unions which are well-established in organisations that individual employees get advice about employment law and practical assistance in bringing claims. It tends to follow that employers are more careful to observe the law in unionised organisations than they are in union-free environments.

Another useful division can be made by separating out statutory rights from those that derive from the common law (see figure 1.2) We will cover this important distinction in greater detail in Chapter 2. For now you simply need to appreciate that by no means all

Figure 1.2 Divisions in employment rights

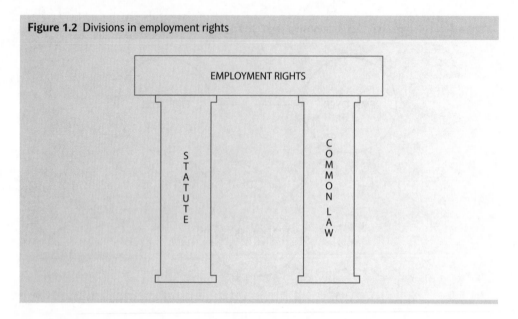

employment law is set out in Acts of Parliament, regulations issued under Acts or European Directives. While it is true that an increasing proportion takes the form of statutes, much is the creation of judges establishing precedents in the courts over centuries as cases have been brought before them. Very important areas of employment law fall into this category, the major examples being the law of contract and the law of negligence as it affects health and safety at work. Here again though, there is no clear cut division, because statutes frequently draw on common law precedents or are framed so as to build on established common law tests. An important example is introduced in Chapter 3 in the context of employment status. Nowhere in our statutes, despite their appearance in numerous pieces of legislation, are the terms 'employee' or 'worker' properly defined. Instead we are obliged to rely on established common law definitions and tests to establish whether or not a particular person fits into one or either category.

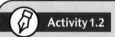 **Activity 1.2**

Here we have described the two most common ways in which employment law is divided for the purposes of study and practice. What other ways of dividing the field up would you suggest might be useful or appropriate?

The development of modern employment law

Prior to the 1960s and early 1970s the amount of law regulating the employment relationship in the UK was very limited. In contrast to most industrialised countries there were hardly any statutory codes setting minimum standards, let alone state agencies to enforce what law there was. The situation was famously summed up by Professor Otto Khan-Freund (1954:44) as follows:

> There is, perhaps, no major country in the world in which the law has played a less significant role in the shaping of industrial relations than in Great Britain and in which the law and legal profession have less to do with labour relations.

The only statutes of any importance covering employment matters put some restrictions on employers in respect of hours worked by women and children and defined minimum legal standards of health and safety practice. After the First World War wages councils were established requiring employers to ensure that everyone was employed on minimum sets of terms and conditions across the industry. However, only industries considered to be low-paying were included, and despite the system's expansion after the Second World War, only 12% of the working population were ever covered. Moreover, these councils were generally recognised to have done little in practice to raise wage levels in real terms (Davies & Freedland, 1993:30). The only other law was contained in the Truck Acts, which regulated when employers could lawfully make deductions from wages. Beyond this there was no regulation governing hours of work, minimum holiday entitlement or the level of pay. There were no statutory minimum notice periods, no law at all to protect people from discrimination on grounds of sex or race, and nothing to stop employers dismissing employees at will without any severance payments. Women who became pregnant had no rights as far as their work was concerned, while laws offering protection to employees on the transfer of a business or regulating what information employers could hold on file about them had not even been dreamt of.

Instead, contrary to the experience of most other countries, employment relations in the UK were governed by what Khan-Freund called the 'collective laissez-faire' system. This meant that the state largely stayed out of the employment relationship, pursuing a policy of voluntarism. The courts provided a means whereby individual contracts of employment could be enforced if broken by either the employer or the employee, but as to the content of these contracts there was no state involvement. Instead there was an assumption that individuals should be free to enter into whatever contractual arrangements they wished. What made the UK system work, and ensured that employers did not abuse the power that freedom to contract inevitably gave them, was the presence of strong trade unions with a mass membership and effective institutions of collective bargaining.

For much of the post-war period trade union density (ie, the proportion of the total workforce in membership) was between 40% and 50%. Union membership was, quite simply, the norm in all organisations of any size. Indeed, many operated closed shop arrangements whereby membership of a specific trade union was a condition of employment. By the time closed shop arrangements were outlawed in the 1980s over 5 million employees were affected (Dunn and Gennard, 1984). A far larger proportion of the workforce, including millions who were not union members, were covered by collective bargaining arrangements which effectively determined terms and conditions of employment across UK industry. In 1970 over 80% of the UK workforce were covered by such agreements negotiated by trade unions on their behalf. What is more, in most cases (60% or more) these were national-level collective agreements covering everyone working in an industry, all substantial organisations observing the minimum standards agreed by the employers' associations of which they were members (Brown et al, 2003).

To an extent the state encouraged the development of the collective laissez-faire system by providing a limited degree of protection for union officials and union members. Freedom of association existed to a great extent in practice, while unions enjoyed considerable freedom to organise industrial action, however much its results damaged an employers' business. But collective agreements remained, as they still do in the UK, binding in honour only and not legally enforceable.

In the years since the 1960s this situation has wholly changed. The law now plays a major and increasing role in determining not just how the collective employment relationship is managed, but also has a very major influence on all aspects of individual employment relationships. The first significant piece of modern employment law came in 1965 in the form of the Redundancy Payments Act. This ensured, for the first time, that reasonable severance payments were made to employees when they were laid off for economic reasons, the largest payments being made to the longest serving staff. A fledgling industrial tribunal system was set up to provide the means by which this law could be enforced. From 1971 it also gained responsibility for ruling in cases of unfair dismissal—new law which sought to ensure that employers could only dismiss employees for a good reason, and that they handled such dismissals in a reasonable manner. These two early pieces of employment legislation remain broadly in their original form on our statute books today. Later in the 1970s health and safety law was consolidated and expanded to cover all workplaces in the Health and Safety at Work Act 1974. This was closely followed by the introduction of sex discrimination and equal pay law in 1975 and by race discrimination law in 1976. Maternity rights were introduced by the Employment Protection Act 1975. In the 1980s, under the Thatcher governments, attention switched to collective employment law. Trade unions became increasingly regulated and the number of situations in which a union could lawfully organise a strike without impunity was substantially reduced. However, largely due to European directives, regulation of the individual employment relationship also continued to expand in the 1980s. Transfer of undertakings regulations were introduced from 1981, the scope of equal pay law was expanded in 1984 and new health and safety regulations concerning the usage of hazardous substances (including common cleaning fluids) came into operation from 1988. In the 1990s the Major government continued to legislate in order to restrict trade union power, also implementing important extensions to health and safety regulations as a result of European requirements. However, in terms of individual employment law, by far the most significant development was the passing in 1995 of the Disability Discrimination Act which has had a profound impact on the way that employers manage staff who have long-term illnesses, including their dismissal.

It is interesting to note that except in relatively minor ways each incoming government has refrained from repealing the employment legislation put in place by its predecessors. The Wilson government repealed many provisions contained in the Industrial Relations Act 1971, yet accepted unfair dismissal law in the form passed by the Heath government. The Conservative governments of 1979–1997 made no attempts to repeal sex or race discrimination laws and even kept on the statute books the right of unions to require employers to disclose information to them ahead of collective negotiations. Moreover, the regime of health and safety regulation established in 1974 was strengthened rather than weakened during these years. To a very great extent, the 'no repeal' approach was continued after the election of Labour governments in 1997, 2001 and 2005. While important reforms were made, the edifice of collective labour law established by the Thatcher and Major governments remained very much in place. Instead, the earlier law was kept and built upon, with an extraordinary quickening of the pace of new legislation until 2008 in response to the onset of recession. Between 1997 and 2007 new employment law included the national minimum wage, the working time regulations, substantial improvements to maternity rights and associated family-friendly laws, extensions to data protection law, new regulations on whistle-blowing, interception of e-mails and telephone calls by employers, protection for people employed on fixed-term and part-time contracts, compulsory union recognition in some circumstances, new requirements on employers to inform and consult, and the outlawing of discrimination on grounds of sexual orientation, religion or belief and age. Specific protection for agency workers was agreed in 2008 and came into effect in 2011.

The Coalition government elected in 2010 has also, by and large, decided against radical reform and is thus continuing the tradition of leaving in place the employment law created by its predecessor. We have seen some moves towards de-regulation (eg, the proposal to increase the qualifying period for unfair dismissal from one to two years from April 2012), but in other areas gentle tinkering is an accurate description of what has been done as far as de-regulation is concerned. In its first years the Coalition introduced, without substantial change, a number of significant measures that had been drawn up by its predecessor: the Equality Act 2010, the Agency Workers Regulations 2010 and reforms intended for future implementation contained in the Work and Families Act 2006 and the Pensions Act 2008. At the same time, significant new employment rights have either been introduced or are planned before 2015 (eg, the removal of the default retirement age, extensions to the right to request flexible working and major new paternity rights). The Coalition government has also continued its predecessor's policy of tightening up the rules on the employment of overseas workers by introducing caps on numbers.

In forty-five years we have therefore seen a total transformation in the extent to which the employment relationship in the UK is regulated. Collective laissez-faire, once held up proudly as a model approach, is now of only historical interest. In the vast majority of workplaces terms and conditions of employment and employment policies and practices owe far more to the requirements of the law than they do to any trade union negotiation. Regulation still does not quite play as big a role as it does across much of continental Europe. But while the traditions remain dissimilar, the essence of the UK system increasingly resembles that of France, Italy or Germany. 'Staying out' is the last thing that the state now does as far as the employment relationship is concerned.

 Activity 1.3

In 2001 a study was published by the then Department of Trade and Industry detailing the results of research into the substantial increase in employment tribunal claims lodged annually between 1985 and 1997 (see Table 1.1). The report's authors were Simon Burgess, Carol Propper and Deborah Wilson of Bristol University (DTI, 2001). They were interested in seeing whether reasons for the growth in tribunal applications generally could be established by focusing on the rate of increase of different types of claim. »

> The research established the following patterns:

- Discrimination claims had increased year on year as a proportion of the total number of claims. In other words between 1985 and 1997 there was a particularly fast growth in these types of claim.

- Unfair dismissal and redundancy claims had grown at a slower rate, rising more dramatically in the early 1990s before reducing somewhat.

- Claims for unlawful deduction of wages rose continually during this period, the number accelerating considerably after 1990.

Questions

1   Why do you think employees and ex-employees lodged twice as many tribunal claims in 1997 as they had in 1985?

2   What major social and economic trends do you think might account for the pattern of claims during this period?

3   What particular factors do you think might account for the fall in the number of unfair dismissal and redundancy claims after 1993?

Explaining the regulatory revolution

There are no simple explanations as to why the UK has, in one generation, so swiftly abandoned its long-established voluntarist approach to the regulation of employment relationship. The creation of our current regulatory structure has been carried out in a piecemeal fashion by governments with very different ideological stances and political priorities. At no stage has an overarching strategy been formulated which has gained cross-party or wide public support. Instead new regulation has been introduced in a step-by-step fashion, sometimes altering past approaches, but more commonly building up further layers to lie on top of the existing law. The absence of strategic direction, however, does not mean that the construction of the regulatory edifice has occurred by chance. There are several underlying factors which can be identified which, in combination, provide a convincing explanation for the regulatory regulation described above. We now discuss each of these in turn.

Europe

It is undoubtedly the case that UK membership of the EEC/EC/EU in the years since our accession in 1973 has had a profound effect on the nature and extent of employment regulation. Moreover, this has been particularly true of regulation introduced after the signing in 1997 of the Social Chapter of the Maastricht Treaty. As a result, a large and increasing proportion of UK employment law now has its origins in Europe and would in all likelihood not be on the statute books were it not for our membership of the European Union. The major examples are transfer of undertakings law, most consultation rights, protection from discrimination for people employed on fixed-term, part-time and agency contracts, working time regulation, discrimination law covering sexual orientation, religion or belief and age, the right to parental leave and data protection law. In addition, while not originating in Europe, other areas of employment law have been strengthened in important ways and their scope widened in order to meet European requirements. This is true of the law on equal pay, sex discrimination, race discrimination, disability discrimination and much statutory regulation of health and safety practice.

A number of EU initiatives in the employment field have been introduced despite the opposition of UK governments. There is a tendency, once the fight to prevent the passing of a directive in the Council of Ministers has been lost, for governments to defend the introduction of ensuing measures as being desirable or necessary. After all, ministers do not like admitting to having settled for less than they entered a negotiation hoping to achieve. But this tendency should not disguise the fact that much of the EU employment regulation introduced across all member states was originally opposed by the UK government, or failed to gain its enthusiastic support. Often, having failed to block original proposals, UK ministers succeed either in watering down or delaying its full impact before voting for a new directive. Critics of employment regulation often accuse governments of 'gold plating' EU directives by going further than is strictly required in order to comply. In fact a failure fully to transpose European directives is more common, leading to a situation in which amendments have to be made at a later date following rulings of the European Court of Justice. There are many examples that have occurred under both Labour and Conservative governments. The Blair government, for example sought to block the Information and Consultation Directive for several months in 2000 and 2001, successfully fighting to water down its practical effects so that it did not impose German-style works councils on all UK enterprises. Eventually ministers agreed to the Directive a day or two after the 2001 general election. Since their introduction in 1998 UK ministers have regularly had to fight hard to prevent substantial extensions to working time rights, including the removal of the opt-out system which is so widely used in Britain. Indeed the whole history of the working time regulations is one of UK government opposition to a Brussels-based initiative, the Major government going as far as to seek a European Court ruling to prevent their imposition on the UK. Earlier, in 1993, the Conservative government found itself introducing a major piece of employment legislation (The Trade Union Reform and Employment Rights Act) which gave effect to no fewer than seven European directives, most of which served to impair the achievement of its stated economic objectives. These included substantial extensions to transfer of undertakings rights which slowed down, and to an extent undermined, the government's flagship privatisation programme (Ewing, 1993). It is inconceivable that these measures would apply in the UK were it not for membership of the EU.

The decline of trade unions and collective bargaining

Another important underlying factor that helps to explain the abandonment of collective laissez-faire and its replacement with employment statutes has been the breakdown of the established collective bargaining system in the UK. Collective laissez-faire, without the collective ingredient would leave us with a world of employment ruled by the law of the jungle. Without the counter-balance of strong trade unions to ensure that employers do not abuse their power, major social injustices would occur. Moreover, in an increasingly competitive world economy, there would effectively be financial incentives to encourage shoddy treatment of the mass of employees who are readily replaced in their jobs. So to a considerable extent employment law has had to step in, to fill the gap left by the departure of the old-style unions.

The statistics on union decline are most striking. In 1979 union membership levels in the UK peaked at over 13 million people, representing 58% of the workforce. The figure now stands at just 6.5 million, representing around a quarter of all employed people (National Statistics, 2011). In 49% of workplaces employing over 25 people there are no union members at all (Kersley et al, 2006:110), while density among younger workers has fallen particularly sharply. Among the 25 to 34 year-old age group it is 24%, while only 10% of those aged 16 to 24 are members. Alongside this rapid decline we have seen huge reductions in the coverage of collective bargaining as the means by which most people's terms and conditions are determined. The proportion of the workforce covered by collective agreements has fallen from 80% in 1970 to just 22% now. In the private sector the percentage is just 11% (Kersley et al, 2006:19). More dramatic still has been the total collapse of national or industry-level bargaining from 60% in 1960 to just 7% today—almost all in the public sector and under attack from ministers with a decentralisation agenda (Kersley et al, 2006:184).

The whole premise of collective laissez-faire has thus disappeared. Employment law is quite clearly necessary now in a way that for most employees it was not in the immediate post-war period. Without it employers would be free to flout basic employment standards and to act inequitably at will. Furthermore, in many ways it provides a more satisfactory method of guaranteeing a measure of justice at work than collective laissez-faire because it covers almost everyone. Those working in small businesses which never have had to concern themselves with the presence of trade unions are thus now protected on the same basis as equivalents employed by larger enterprises.

Some important elements of modern employment law were introduced originally in order to help reduce the need for strikes to occur. The major example is unfair dismissal law which originally dates from 1971 when the government was especially concerned with the negative impact on productivity caused by localised, 'wild-cat' strikes precipitated by the apparently unjust dismissal of colleagues (Davies and Freedland, 1993:199–200). The most important single step in the development of contemporary employment law was thus taken specifically in order that the state should effectively replace the trade unions as the guarantor of the most basic of employment rights. In more recent years the trade union movement itself has been in the vanguard of campaigns to extend employment regulation, implicitly recognising as once it was loath to do, that it can no longer protect employees without the assistance of state institutions. This state of affairs is something governments have sought to encourage rather than discourage, deliberately (according to some analysts) building up individual legal entitlements in the workplace as a means of undermining established collective systems of regulation (see Colling, 2006).

Economic policy

Another major driver of increased employment regulation over the years has been the role it is perceived to play in helping governments to achieve their economic objectives. In the 1970s and 1980s a major concern of governments was how to curb the growing power of trade unions and, in particular, to reduce the number of days' work lost to strikes. Action of this kind was perceived as necessary in order to boost productivity in larger corporations (including many that were state-owned at this time), to encourage the economy to change in response to emerging global industrial trends and as part of the then always present 'fight against inflation'. Government responses took two forms, both of which involved the establishment of much new employment law. The Labour governments of the late 1960s and 1970s preferred on the whole to negotiate with trade unions in order to secure their acceptance of limited pay rises necessary in order to keep a lid on inflation. As part of this strategy employment legislation was introduced which offered protection to groups of employees. Equal pay law had its origins in such a strategy (Davies and Freedland, 2003:213), as did the legislation on pregnancy and maternity which formed part of the government's 'social contract' with the trade unions between 1974 and 1979. By contrast, Conservative governments historically took a confrontational approach. After 1979 their preferred method of reducing trade union power involved conspicuously fighting and defeating their 'enemy within' with considerable resolve. Part of the evolving strategy involved legislating to make it harder for unions to sustain industrial action over time (for example by banning secondary action and empowering the police to disperse pickets) and to maintain membership levels (eg, by ending closed shop arrangements). These more robust methods proved effective and so the law remained on the statute books under the reign of later Labour governments committed to supporting unions with 'fairness and not favours' and under that of the Coalition government.

The Conservative governments of 1979 to 1997 were also faced with the largest rates of unemployment to be suffered in Britain since the 1930s. Reducing unemployment and encouraging job creation was thus always a central aim of economic policy. As a result a perennial theme was the need to 'reduce the burdens on business', which led to a certain amount of de-regulation in the field of individual employment law. The qualifying period for unfair dismissal, for example, was raised to two years, while the wages councils first had their power curbed and were then abolished all together. Once unemployment began to fall in the later 1990s some new regulations were introduced (notably the Disability Discrimination Act), but there remained strong resistance to moving any faster in this direction for fear that doing so would reduce international competitiveness and hence to increased unemployment again.

The Labour governments of 1997–2010 initially faced a different economic situation. Unemployment fell to historically low levels, while increased female participation in the workforce had almost run its course. Most women now opted for a career rather than a full-time homemaking role, meaning that skills shortages rather than a surplus of labour supply posed the major economic threat. The government's response was to introduce employment legislation which had as part of its rationale the reduction of barriers which served to deter people who could work from doing so. It was partly about reducing the numbers of people who live on state benefits by encouraging them into work, and partly about providing incentives for people who have skills that could be placed at the disposal of the economy, but who were not currently working (such as young mothers, people claiming invalidity benefits and people who have opted to take early retirement). We thus saw the introduction of measures which sought to make work more attractive generally (eg, the national minimum wage) or which made it more possible for particular groups to work (eg, protection for part-time workers and the right of parents of young children to request flexible working arrangements).

A separate strand of economic policy that underpinned the Blair and Brown governments' policy agenda was their enthusiasm for partnership approaches to the management of employee relations. Partnership with employees became accepted as being the best way to promote productivity and growth and was thus actively encouraged via employment legislation. The introduction of compulsory union recognition was the most significant example.

During 2007 and 2008 as the economic fortunes of the country turned, heralding a period of recession and then much slower economic growth, government rhetoric switched again. De-regulation and simplification of employment law again became the leading objectives of government employment policy, the purpose being to help reduce costs and maintain high levels of employment. The Labour government did not propose that any major employment rights should be repealed. But the agenda switched from one in which further major

---

 Exhibit 1.1   **The Coalition Agreement**

The Conservative and Liberal Democrat election manifestos at the 2010 election differed in important respects on employment policy, and this was reflected in the Coalition Agreement that was subsequently negotiated when they formed their Coalition. While vague on detail, it provides us with a good general idea of the government's intentions as far as employment regulation is concerned through to 2015:

- The Coalition plans to phase out the 'default' retirement age of 65.
- The Coalition supports the need to introduce extended paternity leave along the lines proposed by the previous Labour government.
- The Coalition aims to retain the UK's 'opt-out' system from the 48-hour working week.
- The Coalition aims to extend the right to request flexible working.
- The Coalition is committed to ending 'gold-plating' of EU laws when transposing principles into UK laws.
- The Coalition plans to put an annual cap on the number of migrants from outside the EU entering the UK to work.

There was also a general commitment in the Coalition Agreement to 'review employment and workplace laws, for employers and employees, to ensure they maximise flexibility for both parties while protecting fairness and providing the competitive environment required for enterprise to thrive'.

In addition, the government committed itself during its first months in office to 'looking to promote gender equality on the boards of listed companies' and to regulating in order to deter the payment of 'unacceptable' bonuses in the financial sector.

Following its election, the government set up a number of reviews of policy that subsequently reported and made recommendations for change:

- Health and safety law under Lord Young
- Poverty and welfare under Frank Field MP
- Public sector pensions under John Hutton
- Public sector pay under Will Hutton

Over time it is likely that most of these recommendations will become the basis of future government policy in the field of employment.

regulation was planned, to one characterised by a desire to consolidate and to make existing regulation and enforcement mechanisms work better.

The same approach has been followed by the Coalition government since its election in 2010. Faced with slow economic growth and a need to cut the national deficit, it has had little alternative. Unable to cut taxes or to increase government spending as a means of promoting growth, it has had to seek out opportunities to cut business costs. Improvements to employment rights (eg, making it harder to mandatorily retire people and extensions to family-friendly regulations) have thus been combined with measures that reduce them somewhat (eg, extending the unfair dismissal qualifying period).

An age of regulation?

An interesting perspective on the regulatory revolution in the field of employment law involves seeing it as a small part of a more general trend towards the regulation of most aspects of corporate life during the past thirty years. Some argue that we are now living in an age of regulation in which government generally takes a far greater interest in how institutions are managed than was the case in past generations. Not only is this accepted by the electorate, it is expected. Cynics argue that such demands are largely a product of increased media scrutiny of government and other major public institutions. The first reaction of the news media whenever news of a scandal breaks, some kind of crisis occurs or a train crashes is to point the blame at an individual, the second is to call loudly and sanctimoniously for greater regulation. It is often a lazy and ill-considered response, but it has the desired effect as ministers are forced swiftly to announce new measures to extend regulation into some hitherto insufficiently regulated area of public life. The root cause of this trend is the breakdown that has occurred in the level of trust that the public have both in government and in managers of organisations. Michael Moran (2003) brilliantly analyses the dismantling since the 1970s of the prevalent voluntarist approaches in professions such as teaching and medicine, and in the financial institutions of the City of London. The same broad processes have also occurred in the world of pensions and more generally across all areas of corporate life. Moran sums up his central argument as follows:

> Had we examined the British system of self-regulation in the early 1970s, we would have noticed three things; that systems of self-regulation were central to the government of markets—for labour, services, and goods; that the British system was unique among leading capitalist nations in the extent to which it was run by private institutions beyond the reach of the state or the law; and that it was remarkable also in its stability, displaying cultures and institutional patterns that originated in the nineteenth century. Every one of those observations now has to be radically revised; the uniqueness of British self-regulation has declined dramatically; the private character of the most important part of the self-regulatory system has been transformed, to be replaced by tighter state controls; and the institutions and cultures bequeathed to us by the Victorians have either disappeared or are embattled. (Moran, 2003:7)

Could it be therefore that the development of employment law is simply part of this much broader shift towards a world in which we expect anything and everything to be regulated? This theory may not adequately explain each and every new piece of legislation, but it may well explain why for the most part regulation of the employment relationship has been so readily accepted by employers, employees and trade unions alike.

Political expediency

No analysis of the reasons for new legislation would be complete without recognition that governments often do things simply because they are politically popular with a constituency that is relied upon to help secure re-election. This is as true in the field of employment legislation as in any other and helps to explain the origin of much modern employment law. The early anti-discrimination measures were introduced not just because of a compelling case that they were needed, but because this case was powerfully put by lobby groups representing the interests of women and ethnic minorities (Davies and Freedland, 1993:381). Later, the anti-trade union legislation passed by the Thatcher governments, while vigorously contested by those who were adversely affected, served to enhance the government's popularity with the electorate in general. Indeed, given the significance of industrial relations issues in the months prior to the 1979 general election, to a great extent Margaret Thatcher was elected to cut down union power. The Blair and Brown governments too used employment law to shore up support among key constituencies. They advanced their regulatory agenda in a step-by-step fashion, consulting at length before legislating and not being afraid to reduce the radicalism of some original proposals. At each stage great care was taken not to alienate business supporters, even if this meant disappointing trade unions and other interest groups within the Labour Party. Hence, the National Minimum Wage was established, but set at a level way below that campaigned for by its supporters. Compulsory union recognition was introduced, but only where a union could clearly demonstrate a genuine demand for it on the part of the workforce. Then from time to time, in a calculated manner ministers introduced measures that were primarily designed to please the trade union constituency and thus help to ensure its continued support. The right for everyone to be represented by union officials at serious disciplinary and grievance hearings is a good example. Other measures, such as improvements in maternity rights and the introduction of paid paternity leave, were in part designed to enhance government popularity generally.

It will be harder for the Coalition government to court popularity by reforming employment regulation, because its hands are so tied by the economic challenges it faces. But it is surely significant that major extension of maternity and paternity rights appears to be planned for April 2015, just a month or so before ministers intend to hold the next general election.

  Activity 1.4

In April 2003, the then General secretary of the Trade Union Congress, John Monks, gave a lecture at Warwick University entitled 'A Eurovision at Work' (Monks, 2003). In this lecture he made a number of observations about the development of employment regulation and the way he would like to see it move on in the future. In the course of his lecture Mr Monks made the following points:

- All labour markets depend for their legitimacy on some form of regulation, achieved either via statute, collective bargaining or litigation on different forms of civil liability.
- There is a clear correlation between the decline of collective bargaining in the private sector and the increase in employment tribunal claims.   »

• The UK now faces a choice between an acceptance that employment rights depend entirely on the law and that enforcement depends on legal action, or a return to a system of collective bargaining based on a platform of basic statutory standards.

Questions

1 Why do labour markets need 'legitimacy' at all?

2 In what ways might John Monks' vision appeal to employers? What aspects of it might they find unattractive?

3 What weaknesses in John Monks' argument can be identified from an employee perspective?

Major debates about employment law

Throughout this book we will be assessing the pros and cons of different elements of employment law from a variety of perspectives. By its nature it is a field about which diverse views are held, leading to vigorous and sometimes quite complex debates. It is rarely possible to legislate in everyone's interests, because the employment relationship is one in which the two sides have different aims and objectives. Most new regulation favours the interests of employees and thus tends to be opposed to a degree by the representatives of employers. Conversely de-regulatory measures or those which reduce the freedom of manoeuvre enjoyed by trade unions tend to enjoy the support of employers and employer organisations. It is rare that a measure of general agreement is reached, and even where a broad principle gains wide acceptance, there is usually a debate between those who argue that specific legislation 'does not go far enough' and those who believe that it 'goes too far'.

Debates about employment law take two main forms. The first are focused on the detail of particular pieces of legislation and the way that they operate in practice. These are usefully labelled 'micro-debates'. The second are more principled, focusing on the overall impact of employment regulation on the UK's economy and working population. These we call 'macro-debates'. We will return many times to both as the book proceeds. For now our purpose is to introduce you to them in general terms.

 Activity 1.5

In 2006 the Confederation of British Industry, which represents larger private sector organisations in the main, published a report which argued for a number of reforms to different areas of employment law (CBI, 2006). We will return to consider some of their suggestions in the context of particular areas of employment regulation later in the book. Their many suggestions included the following:

• Permitting employers to require their workers to work over 48 hours a week, provided that on average they work below that number of hours when averaged over 52 weeks.

> • Permitting employers to negotiate changes to employee contracts when businesses are transferred provided that, taken in the round, the new terms are no less fvaourable than the old ones.

- Providing government-sponsored HR services to provide free advice on employment law issues to small firms that do not have access to in-house expertise.

- Greater powers for employment tribunals to strike out claims with little chance of success and to award costs against losing claimants who pursue such cases despite being advised of their low chance of success.

- Limiting the amount of new employment legislation to one bill per Parliament (ie, one every four or five years).

Question

What do you think of these proposals? Would they be workable in practice? What arguments could you make both for and against their adoption?

Sources: CBI (2006) and Wynn-Evans (2007)

Micro-debates

A number of criticisms are commonly made of areas of employment regulation which are essentially concerned with the detail rather than the broad principles or overall impact. Debates then hinge about what, if any, reforms are desirable and what their impact might be in practice. Some of the most common criticisms are as follows:

- It is often argued that some employment law fails to meet its own objectives in practice. It thus amounts to a burden for employers but fails to offer sufficient protection to employees. Equal pay law is often criticised in this way. Despite it being on the statute books for over thirty years, women's pay on average remains very much less than that of men.

- Another common criticism is that employment legislation is poorly drafted, lacking clarity and leaving both employers and employees confused about the precise nature of their rights. Too often the statutes fail to address central issues such as definitions of key terms. As a result clarity is only achieved after some years as cases come through the court system and precedents are made. A good example is the transfer of undertakings (TUPE) legislation, many aspects of which still remain unclear after thirty years of operation. New legislation, in particular, is often subject to this criticism because it takes several years sometimes before the courts get an opportunity to clarify the legal position in relation to types of business practice. Age discrimination law is a good example. It was introduced in December 2006, but at the time of writing (summer 2011), what practices are now unlawful and which are not is still not entirely clear because we do not yet know which the courts will ultimately judge to be justifiable in practice.

- Unnecessary complexity is a third common criticism, again leading to situations in which people are unsure of their rights. Employment status is a good example. As you will see when you read Chapter 3, deciding who is an 'employee', who is a 'worker' and who is 'genuinely self-employed' is often a difficult task for employment tribunals, let alone for employers and their staff. The law on industrial action is also often criticised for being unnecessarily complicated.

- Another common criticism concerns the way that perfectly good law is enforced. The complaint here is that employees who suffer because they are treated unlawfully cannot easily achieve satisfactory redress because of inadequate sanction. As a result there is no real deterrent effect, so employers do not fear continuing to act unlawfully. This usually occurs because the enforcement authorities are very limited in terms of any awards they can make, but it can also be because bringing a claim just causes more problems for individual employees than it is worth. Commentators often call for the introduction of more inspection regimes along the lines of those that already operate in the health and safety field as a means of improving enforcement.

- Finally some employment law can be criticised simply for being unjust in the way that it operates in practice. An example is the law of indirect discrimination which can be seen as operating unjustly from both the employer and employee perspectives. On the one hand it penalises employers who have no intention whatever of discriminating unlawfully, while on the other it allows employers to justify practices which have the effect of perpetuating social inequality.

Macro-debates

The other major debates about employment law are pitched at a more general level, focusing on the whole body of employment law rather than specific parts. Here it is possible to identify two opposite perspectives, one broadly in favour of employment regulation and the other broadly against. Protagonists who take the latter view tend to argue that regulation reduces economic competitiveness, makes it harder to create jobs and often has the effect of harming the interests of employees. Those who take the former view argue not only that modern employment law is necessary to protect employees against unjust acts perpetrated by employers, but that it also brings many positive economic benefits.

 Exhibit 1.2   **The principles of good regulation**

According to the Better Regulation Executive, now part of the Department for Business, Enterprise and Regulatory Reform, there are five key principles of good regulation:

1 **Transparency.** The case for a regulation should be clearly made and the purpose clearly communicated. Regulations should be simple and clear, and come with guidance in plain English.

2 **Accountability.** Regulators and enforcers should be clearly accountable to government and citizens and to parliaments and assemblies.

3 **Proportionality.** Any enforcement action should be in proportion to the risk, with penalties proportionate to the harm done.

4. **Consistency.** New regulations should be consistent with existing regulations. Enforcement agencies should apply regulations consistently across the country.

5. **Targeting.** Regulations should be aimed at the problem and avoid a scattergun approach. They should be reviewed from time to time to test whether they are still necessary and effective.

Source: www.bis.gov.uk

The most prominent critics of employment legislation are the organisations which represent employers' interests such as the Confederation of British Industry (CBI), the Institute of Directors (IOD), The Federation of Small Businesses and the Small Business Council (SBC). Some think-tanks, notably the Institute of Economic Affairs, also tend to take a negative, de-regulatory stance in their publications, as does the government's Better Regulation Taskforce.

The commonest complaints made by those who take a negative view about the current level of employment regulation relate to the costs of compliance. The CBI (2000:9), for example, calculated that the total cost to employers of implementing the National Minimum Wage and the Working Time Regulations amounted to over £10 billion. This kind of burden, it is argued, can only have the effect of reducing the competitiveness of UK organisations vis-à-vis those based elsewhere in the world. While it is accepted that the regulatory burden is higher still in most other EU countries, in a global economy competitors can be based anywhere. The result is slower economic growth than would otherwise be achieved, and less job creation. Moreover, where profit margins are tight, the outcome of additional regulation is net job losses. The same occurs when jobs are 'exported' from the UK to other countries in order to take advantage of lower wages and poorer terms and conditions of employment. The costs come in various different forms:

- Direct costs that employers are required to absorb resulting from new regulation. Recent examples include extensions in paid holiday entitlements, maternity pay and the need to make adjustments to accommodate the needs of disabled people.

- Knock-on costs that have to be absorbed when employees opt to exercise their employment rights. Examples are those associated with the employment of temporary staff to cover a period of parental leave or time taken to care for the needs of a dependent relative.

- Lost opportunity costs, largely made up of hours of management time spent understanding the implications of new regulation, finding out how to comply and then taking action to ensure that the organisation is complying.

- Litigation costs which have to be absorbed when an employee or ex-employee brings a claim. Even when the employer wins the case, there are substantial costs in the form of legal fees and management time spent preparing the case. A particular complaint is the way that most forms of litigation in the employment tribunal carry little or no equivalent financial risk for claimants.

A particular line of argument concerns the cost burden associated with employment law for small businesses, who it is argued should be exempted from some of the regulation. They are hit harder than larger organisations because they lack the flexibility, expertise and often the profit margins required to ensure compliance with all its aspects. Research carried out by the Small Business Council (2004) found that smaller employers had a very low knowledge of employment legislation and considered compliance a low priority vis-à-vis survival. Regulations were seen as being designed to meet the needs of larger employers and did not fit easily with the family-oriented, informal management approaches that are prevalent in many small businesses.

Aside from the cost-based arguments, other points are also frequently made by opponents of regulation. First they often put forward the view that improving employee rights can have a negative impact on employees. Regulation is counter-productive because employers will always look for ways of avoiding the need to comply. The most commonly cited example is the supposed disincentive employers now have to employ younger women:

> It is clear that many business people are very supportive of maternity benefits and rights (nearly a fifth of members provided more than the statutory maternity benefits in terms of leave or pay), but there is a clear warning from our survey. Already 45% of our members feel that such rights are a disincentive to hiring women of prime child-rearing age. If the regulations are made even more burdensome then employers will be even more reluctant to employ these women. (Lea, 2001:57)

Surveys of women who are pregnant back up this story. In 2005 the Equal Opportunities Commission surveyed 1000 women about their experiences at work when pregnant (EOC, 2005:10). They found that 45% had suffered some form of discrimination, while 7% (equating to around 30,000 women a year) had lost their jobs as a result of having become pregnant, mainly because they felt obliged to resign because they had been treated so badly. In 2008 Sir Alan Sugar, probably the most famous employer in the country, stated his belief that many employers in practice simply bin CVs that are sent to them by women of child-bearing age, arguing that it should be the responsibility of the state and not employers to bear the costs associated with the employment of mothers with young children (Daily Telegraph, 2008). Later in the same year the Chief Executive of the Equality and Human Rights Commission, Nicola Brewer, made a speech in which she suggested that increasing rights for parents, because they were in practice taken up in the main by women, had had the effect of 'reinforcing existing patterns of gender inequality' (Brewer, 2008:4).

The other major point that is commonly made concerns the tendency for new regulation to require a bureaucratic response from employers. Employment law, it is argued, imposes on organisations too great a need to centralise and standardise their policies and practices. Local management flexibility and informal management practices are lost as a result. This makes organisations less responsive not just to the needs of customers, but also to those of employees. The quality of working life is reduced because there is less scope for decision-making at the level of the local team. Instead power is placed in the hands of HR administrators who cannot understand the complex requirements or preferences of front-line managers.

On the other side of the debate stand the vast majority of academics who study and write about employment law, trade unions and left-leaning think tanks. The Institute of Employment Rights (IER) also regularly publishes papers which argue for greater regulation and which put alternative views to those of the employer organisations about the overall economic impact of employment law. The key points made by those who are broadly in favour of regulation are summarised very effectively by Davies (2009).

The most straightforward arguments in favour of employment regulation relate to social justice and basic human rights. The need for extensive law in this area is thus justified on the grounds that it is necessary to protect vulnerable workers from unjust, inequitable or negligent treatment by employers. Hence, health and safety law is necessary in order to provide employers with a strong incentive to ensure that their staff are not injured physically or psychologically as a result of their work, whilst unfair dismissal law ensures that longer serving employees cannot have their jobs (and livelihoods) terminated without good reason. The law on freedom of association, in protecting employees' right to join and form trade unions, helps to ensure that inequitable and unjust actions on the part of employers can be effectively resisted. In these areas employment law thus provides a measure of

Activity 1.6

In 2002 the government's Better Regulation Taskforce (now the Better Regulation Executive) published a report focusing on employment regulation. A total of twelve recommendations were made, most of which derived from a study of the impact of regulation on smaller businesses, a sector which accounts for '44% of all non-government employment and 37% of turnover'. It is impossible, according to the report, for employers in smaller enterprises to find time to read about all the regulations they have to comply with and run a business effectively. When approached, government officials themselves said it was impossible for them to know everything about employment regulation, yet this appears to be what is expected of employers. Three of the recommendations were as follows:

- Government should look for more alternatives to state regulation as a means of achieving its employment policies.

- Government should run a range of pilots, with different providers and funding methods, for a shared HR resource for small firms.

- Government should pilot a free or subsidised arbitration service for businesses with fewer than fifty employees. This would act as a cheaper and quicker alternative to Employment Tribunals as a means of settling legal disputes with employees.

Questions

1 What kind of alternatives to state regulation might be possible? How effective would they be in practice?

2 What would be the main advantages and disadvantages of the proposed 'shared HR Service' from the perspective of small businesses?

3 Why might small businesses object to the presence of an alternative arbitration service for them and their employees to use instead of employment tribunals?

security for employees in what would otherwise be an intolerably insecure world of work. Other regulations, such as those that make up discrimination law, protect individuals, but also serve a wider social purpose. In providing women and minority groups with a means of gaining redress when they suffer unfair discrimination, the law enhances their position in the labour market more generally and hence helps to reduce social injustices of great significance.

The economic case for employment regulation of the kind that we now have in the UK is harder to grasp and difficult to summarise succinctly. Three distinct strands of argument can be identified which are dealt with in greater detail by Deakin and Wilkinson (1996), IER (2000) and Davies (2009). The first concerns international competitiveness, it being argued that over the long term employment regulation enhances the competitive position of UK businesses, despite the short-term cost implications. In large part this is because, over the long term, skills shortages represent a major threat to UK prosperity. Any failure on the part of employers to recruit and retain sufficient numbers of qualified personnel to meet their human resource needs tends to mean a loss of international competitiveness. It follows that employers are more likely to guarantee their success over the long term if they provide workplaces in which people want to be employed and terms and conditions which make it worth their while to work.

It is easy to forget that millions of people who could work either in a full- or a part-time capacity are outside the workforce at any one time. The major groups are people who have chosen to take early retirement, women with young children, people who have caring roles, and people who consider themselves to be better off all-told by claiming state benefits of one kind or another rather than working. In addition there are hundreds of thousands of people who switch jobs regularly, taking time out from work in between jobs while they search for something more suitable. A good proportion of these people have skills which are not being placed at the disposal of the economy. Increasing employment standards and promoting flexible working through regulation serves to force employers to create jobs and packages which attract them back into the workforce, while also deterring others from leaving in the first place. By the same token, forcing up employment standards in this way helps to create a situation in which the UK is attractive as a destination for highly skilled migrant workers from overseas.

The second strand to the economic argument in favour of employment regulation is more controversial. This concerns the most appropriate type of economy that the UK needs to develop in order to guarantee its prosperity in the coming decades. The starting point is an acceptance of the view that the country will not prosper in the future if it seeks to compete internationally by cutting labour costs. Such a strategy is unsustainable when faced with competitors based in Eastern Europe and the developing countries who will always be in a position to undercut UK organisations on wage costs. Moreover, this will be the case whether or not the UK has a great deal of employment regulation. It thus follows that the economy needs to seek long-term competitive advantage by developing hi-tech and knowledge-intensive industries which offer products and services of the highest quality. Cost-based competition will still occur, but it will be achieved through the deployment of cutting-edge technologies which reduce the need for employees rather than by low wage costs. Employment regulation, it is argued, helps to push the economy in this direction by effectively outlawing low paid, low quality jobs and poor terms and conditions. It forces employers to seek alternative competitive strategies other than those based on cost. Creating more highly paid, specialised jobs gives employers a strong incentive to develop their people by investing in training and hence to retain those they have invested in for as long as possible. Employment law forms only one of the tools that governments have used to help transform the UK economy in this way. Education policy and research funding also play an important role, but employment regulation has often been justified on these grounds.

The third strand to the economic case concerns productivity. It is accepted by most economists and occupational psychologists that high levels of productivity, particularly in the service sector, are heavily associated with the effective management of people. Treating staff well enhances commitment, leads employees to maximise their efforts and is a necessary prerequisite for the achievement of excellence in terms of customer relationships. In a service economy demotivated and dissatisfied staff make effective competition difficult to attain, not least because employee turnover rates are too high to enable maximum efficiency to be achieved. Employment regulation, it is thus argued, helps to improve productivity by requiring employers to treat their people with dignity, respect and fairness. Linked to this is the view that partnership approaches to the management of the collective employment relationship serve to enhance productivity and organisational effectiveness. It follows that collective employment law which promotes partnership between employers and employees and which discourages the development of 'them and us' workplace cultures also plays its part in enhancing productivity. Much recent employment regulation has been explicitly justified by ministers in these terms.

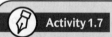 **Activity 1.7**

The view that increased employment regulation has benefited the economy is vigorously contested by some economists. One of the more prominent is J.R. Shackleton of Westminster University. The following quotations come from one of his recent contributions to this debate (Shackleton, 2005:140–142):

> Regulation reduces the ways in which firms can compete. Excessive regulation reduces the incentives to innovation, entrenches the market dominance of existing firms, and ultimately slows the economic growth on which our prosperity depends.
>
> Historically increases in employees' pay and improvements in other conditions of service have not come through government intervention, but as a result of economic growth resulting from entrepreneurial innovation and private investment by firms and individuals. Further improvements in working conditions and the continued generation of new job opportunities are more likely to continue if governments create a climate where such innovation and investment can occur. Such a climate surely places greater emphasis on allowing employers to reach voluntary agreements with their employees—and less on telling them exactly how to do so.
>
> We should not forget that there is a business case for being a 'good' employer. Such employers gain staff loyalty, enjoy reduced turnover and absenteeism, and benefit from higher productivity.

Questions

1 Which pieces of employment legislation might serve to reduce innovation or entrench the market dominance of existing firms?

2 To what extent do you agree that improved working conditions have historically come about as a result of economic growth?

3 Would we have more or less 'good' employment practice if the amount of regulation was to be reduced considerably?

An end to the era of regulation?

In recent years, to the manifest disappointment of those who favour tighter regulation on business (eg, Wedderburn, 2007), government ministers have sought to address the arguments put by representatives of businesses that the UK is over-regulated and that this is economically damaging. 2008, for example, saw the publication of a government report entitled 'Enterprise: unlocking the UK's talent' which was a statement of ministers' intent to seek ways of reducing the burden of regulation across all areas of business practice including employment matters. This followed the establishment in 2007 of another government initiative which committed a group of Whitehall departments to reducing the regulatory burdens they imposed on businesses by 25% before 2010.

Following the general election of 2010 and the forming of a Coalition government, ministers turned up the volume as far as de-regulatory rhetoric was concerned. Much trumpeted has been their intention to operate a policy of 'one in, one out' (OIOO) as far as new regulation is concerned, the ambition being to combine any new regulation with a programme of de-regulation that proceeds at the same pace. According to the Department for Business, Innovation and Skills (DBIS) the objectives of the policy are to:

- bear down on regulatory costs;
- get rid of laws that are no longer needed;
- bring about a culture change in the government's approach to regulation; and
- promote economic growth by delivering a positive outcome for business and civil society organisations.

The website goes on to explain that 'the introduction of the OIOO rule means that policy makers developing regulatory proposals must ensure they have identified the necessary deregulatory measures before submitting their Impact Assessments for scrutiny by the Regulatory Policy Committee (RPC)'. Moreover a body known as 'The Reducing Regulation Committee' has been set up to enforce the OIOO rule.

The extent to which such initiatives have had any real practical impact is, however, questionable. A survey of members of the Institute of Directors (IOD, 2007) found that 46% of respondents perceived government regulation to have become more demanding over the previous year, while 48% claimed to have seen no change. Only 1% reported having seeing an improvement. Similar findings were also reported in surveys undertaken by the Institute of Chartered Accountants and the National Audit Office (House of Commons, 2008) and by PriceWaterhouseCoopers (2008:14–15). The major CBI report entitled 'Lightening the Load' published in 2006 found that only 2% of its respondents were confident that the government would in practice deliver on its promises to de-regulate and to simplify the law (CBI, 2006).

In 2011 the Coalition government was widely criticised for failing, in practice, to meet its own commitment to 'one in one out', particularly in the area of employment regulation. And at the time of writing (summer 2011) it is difficult to argue with this assessment. No significant de-regulation has occurred to date while several new regulations have tended further to restrict the ability of employers to manage their workforces as they see fit. Not only have Coalition ministers introduced—without dilution—all the new employment regulation being planned by the former Labour government (eg, the Equality Act and the Agency Workers' Regulations), they have also restricted the ability of employers to hire workers from overseas or to operate a mandatory retirement policy. Moreover, of course, major reform of pensions, which will be particularly costly for smaller businesses, is going to be phased in between 2011 and 2015, while significant new paternity and maternity rights are planned for 2015.

Whatever government claims are made about regulation it would thus seem that those charged with complying need a lot more convincing that serious attempts to reduce their 'burden' really are being or are going to be introduced.

This perception is particularly true of employment regulation. Not only do employers believe it is increasingly unnecessary in terms of its extent and complexity, they also believe it to be having an ongoing negative impact. The problems remain most acute for small businesses. A survey by the Federation of Small Businesses reported that owners were fearful of employing more people due in part to 'the complexity of employment legislation' (32%), 'the overall burden of red tape and regulations' (31%) and 'the volume of employment legislation' (25%) (FSB, 2007). Similar views are expressed by senior managers of big organisations too as was shown in a survey of Chief Executives charged with running the world's largest corporations (PWC, 2008). Over-regulation was something that 'somewhat concerned' 37% of respondents and 'extremely concerned' a further 22%, making it one of the 'top three highest risks facing business'. The same survey showed that regulation had a major practical influence on decision-making and that employment law was seen as being one of the two major areas (along with taxation) that CEOs wanted governments to tackle as a matter of priority. As far as respondents from the UK and other EU countries were concerned, the need to reform employment law came top of the list ahead of all other concerns. The CBI (2006) also delivered quite a damning verdict on the existing body of employment regulation in the UK. Three-quarters of their respondents believed that complying with new employment rights was damaging their businesses while two-fifths stated that recent regulation in the field had harmed the UK's reputation 'as a place to do business'.

While it is highly questionable to argue that we are likely to see any really significant de-regulation in the employment area in the near future, it is much more likely that we will see a reduction in the pace at which new legislation reaches the statute book. This is certainly the message that politicians from across the political spectrum wish to put forward. The consensus view is that the period from 1997 to 2007 saw the creation of a framework of employment legislation that is now largely complete. While there remain one or two areas where existing law fails to offer adequate protection for some vulnerable groups, there are now no plans to extend rights further in any really significant ways. The coming years will thus largely see consolidation of existing employment rights and not the creation of new ones and we can thus conclude with some confidence that our regulatory revolution is now at an end.

CHAPTER SUMMARY

- British employment law, having been very lightly regulated in the past, has become very heavily regulated.
- Much of the more recent UK regulation has originated from the European Union.
- This regulation has been criticised and resisted by employers, who are concerned that it increases costs.
- It has, however, been welcomed by unions and workers, who believe that not only is it more socially just, but that it also increases productivity and therefore profits.

For updates and further materials, please see the online resource centre at www.oup.com.

REFERENCES

Better Regulation Taskforce (2002) *Employment Regulation: Striking a Balance*. London: Better Regulation Taskforce.

Brewer, N. (2008) Speech at the launch of the 'Working Better' consultation, 14th July.

British Chambers of Commerce (2011) *Burdens Barometer*. London: BCC.

Burgess S., Propper C. & Wilson D. (2001) *Explaining the Growth in the Number of Applications to Industrial Tribunals 1972–1997*. London: Department of Trade and Industry.

Chartered Institute of Personnel and Development (2002) *Employment Law: Survey Report.* London: CIPD.

Chartered Institute of Personnel and Development (2007) *The Changing HR Function. A Survey Report.* London: CIPD.

Colling, T. (2006) 'What space for unions on the floor of rights? Trade unions and the enforcement of stautory individual employment rights'. *Industrial Law Journal* 35.2 (p140–160).

Confederation of British Industry (2000) *Cutting through red tape: the impact of employment legislation.* London: CBI.

Confederation of British Industry (2006) *Lightening the Load: The need for employment law simplification.* London: CBI.

Cully M., Woodland S., O'Reilly A. and Dix G. (1999) *Britain at Work: As depicted by the 1998 Workplace Employee Relations Survey.* London: Routledge.

Daily Telegraph (2008) 'Sir Alan Sugar: Our children need enterprise', 2nd February.

Davies, A.C.L. (2009) *Perspectives on Labour Law*. Second Edition. Cambridge: Cambridge University Press.

Davies, P. & Freedland, M. (1993) *Labour Legislation and Public Policy*. Oxford: Oxford University Press.

Deakin, S. & Wilkinson, F. (1996) *Labour Standards—Essential to Economic and Social Progress*. London: Institute of Employment Rights.

Dickens, L. (2002) 'Individual statutory employment rights since 1997: constrained expansion'. *Employee Relations*, 24.6 (p619–637).

Dunn, S. & Gennard, J. (1984) *The Closed Shop in British Industry*. London: Macmillan.

Employment Tribunal Service (2008) *Annual Report and Accounts*. London: ETS.

Equal Opportunities Commission (2005) *Greater Expectations: Summary Final Report. EOC's Investigation into Pregnancy Discrimination.* London: EOC.

Ewing, K. (1993) 'Swimming with the tide: employment protection and the implementation of European labour law'. *Industrial Law Journal*, 22.3 (p165–180).

Federation of Small Businesses (2007) *Key Facts in Employment Law.* London: Federation of Small Businesses.

Grainger H. & Crowther M. (2007): *Trade Union Membership in 2006.* London: Department for Trade and Industry.

Grayson, D. & Hodges, A. (2001) *Everybody's Business: Managing Risks and Opportunities in Today's Global Society.* London: Dorling Kindersley.

House of Commons (2008) *Reducing the Cost of Complying with Regulations: The Delivery of the Administrative Burdens Reduction Programme 2007*. Comittee of Public Accounts. London: House of Commons.

Institute of Directors (2007) *Better Regulation—Getting Worse*. London: IOD.

Institute of Directors (2011) *Regulation Reckoner: Counting the Real Cost of Regulation*. London, IOD.

Institute of Employment Rights (2000) *Social Justice and Economic Efficiency*. London: Institute of Employment Rights.

Kersley B., Alpin C., Forth J., Bryson A., Bewley H., Dix G. & Oxenbridge S. (2006) *Inside the Workplace: Findings from the 2004 Workplace Employment Relations Survey.* Abingdon: Routledge.

Khan-Freund, O. (1954) 'Legal Framework' in A. Flanders and H. Clegg (eds) *The System of Industrial Relations in Great Britain*. Oxford: Blackwell.

Lea, R. (2001) *The Work-life Balance and All That: The Re-regulation of the Labour Market*. London: Institute of Directors.

Monks, J. (2003) 'A Eurovision at Work' *Warwick Papers in Industrial relations*, 70. Industrial Relations Research Unit: University of Warwick.

Moran, M. (2003) *The British Regulatory State: High Modernism and Hyper-innovation*. Oxford: Oxford University Press.

National Statistics (2011) *Trade Union Membership 2010*. London: HMSO.

PriceWaterhouseCoopers (2008) *Regulate & Collaborate: What is Success in a Connected World?* London: PWC.

Shackleton, J.R. (2005) 'Regulating the Labour Market' in P. Booth (ed): *Towards a Liberal Utopia?* London: Institute of Economic Affairs (p128–143).

Small Business Council (2004) *Evaluation of Government Employment Regulations and their Impact on Small Businesses*. London: SBC.

Waddington, J. (2003) 'Trade Union Organisation' in P. Edwards (ed) *Industrial Relations: Theory and Practice*. Second Edition. Oxford: Blackwell.

Wedderburn, B. (2007) 'Labour Law 2008: 40 Years On'. *Industrial Law Journal*, 36.4 (p397–424).

Wynn-Evans, C (2007) 'Bonfires of Red Tape?' *Industrial Law Journal*, 36.2 (p238–242).

ONLINE RESOURCE CENTRE

A range of online resources to help you through your employment law module have been developed by the author team. These include updates, self-test questions and sources for further reading. (www.oxfordtextbooks.co.uk/orc/taylor_emir3e)

Sources of employment law and institutions

2

Learning outcomes

By the end of this chapter you should be able to:

- understand the major sources of employment law in the UK and distinguish between them;

- explain the main principles governing the conduct of cases in the criminal and civil courts;

- list the main employment statutes;

- debate the strengths and weaknesses of law made via statute and statutory instrument;

- define the terms 'common law', 'contract' and 'tort';

- explain how European Union law is made and why it is sometimes controversial;

- assess the Human Rights Act 1998 and its implications for employment law;

- describe the UK court structure as it applies to employment law;

- explain the role played by employment tribunals and other judicial bodies;

- understand the role of the European Court of Justice in employment law;

- explain the role and function of the major quasi-legal bodies that form part of the UK employment law system.

Introduction

In order to understand employment law, to explain its workings to others and to give advice in situations where it may play a role in decision-making, it is necessary to understand where it comes from. Employment law in its various forms is 'made' by several different groups of people and institutions, often building on decisions made by others in the past. Which particular party makes a given piece of law determines to a large degree the rules under which it operates, the extent to which it is enforced in practice and the institutions responsible for enforcing it. In this second introductory chapter we focus first on the diverse sources of contemporary employment law, explaining some key terms and fundamental legal concepts on the way. In the second part our focus shifts to institutional arrangements, the court structure and the part played by quasi-legal bodies who play a role in the enforcement of employment law.

 Activity 2.1

Consider the following statements. Which do you think are correct and which are false?

a A great deal of contemporary employment law has been made by judges and not by Parliament.

b The judiciary can, in certain circumstances, overturn statutes that Parliament has approved.

c The law of Trust plays a major role in UK employment law.

d The criminal law plays less of a role in the employment field in the UK than in many other countries.

e The European Parliament is the major law-making institution in the European Union.

f The Human Rights Act 1998 has had a significant impact on employment law in the UK.

g Employment tribunals only deal with cases based on employment statutes.

h Appeals from the County Court are taken to the High Court.

i The House of Lords only hears cases of general public importance.

j ACAS operates a well-used arbitration scheme as an alternative to employment tribunal proceedings.

Return to this activity once you have read the chapter, to see how many of your answers were correct.

Overview

It is helpful when first exploring the sources of UK employment law to start by gaining an understanding of the main categories into which this big body of law can be divided. Figure 2.1 seeks to provide you with a mental map to help guide you through the rest of the material in the first part of this chapter. So we will start by briefly explaining each of the terms that features in the figure.

Figure 2.1 The main categories of employment law

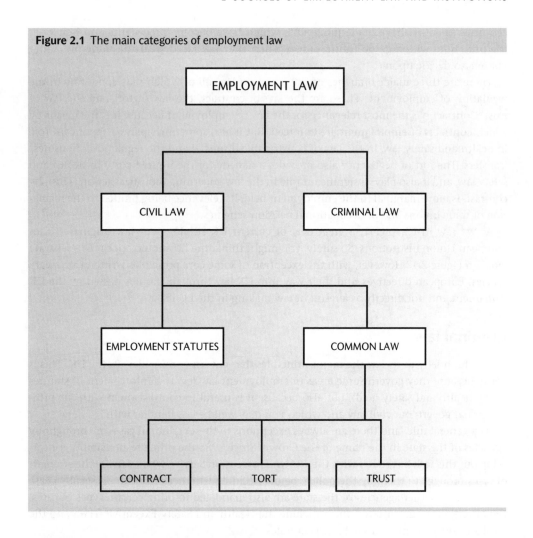

Working down from the top of the figure, the first major divide that can be identified is between the civil law and the criminal law. The latter plays a relatively peripheral role in the employment field, but is very significant in those areas which it does cover, such as health and safety, the employment of foreign nationals and the regulation of picketing during industrial disputes. In the UK, the vast majority of employment law falls into the civil law category, meaning that individual parties bring cases to court and seek redress in one form or another from other parties. Typically this involves an employee or former employee bringing a case against an employer.

The second major division illustrated in figure 2.1 is that between employment statutes and the common law. The former consist principally of Acts of Parliament or regulations issued under Acts which relate in some way to the employment field. Nowadays this is by far the biggest and most significant source of employment law, accounting for the majority of regulations which govern (or seek to govern) the conduct of the employment relationship. The common law, by contrast, is judge-made and has evolved over many centuries as courts have made judgments which have become precedents and hence set the principles which guide future judges when they are faced with the same or similar matters to decide upon.

There are three major branches of the common law, all of which play some role in the regulation of employment. These are the law of contract, the law of tort and the law of trust. Contract has the most relevance for the law of employment because it is the means by which contracts of employment are enforced. But it also sometimes plays a significant role in health and safety law, in the law of constructive dismissal and the regulation of business transfers. The tort of negligence also provides a remedy for the injured party in health and safety law, and it also plays a significant role in the law governing industrial action. Trust, by contrast, is more marginal in the employment field, its relevance being limited to the regulation of trade unions and of occupational pension schemes.

As we saw in Chapter 1, a great deal of current UK employment law originates from European Union institutions. So surely, you might think, the EU should appear as a separate 'box' on Figure 2.1? However, with the exception of some core principles written into treaty articles, European directives find their way into UK law through statutes passed by the UK Parliament and not directly as a result of law making in the EU itself.

Criminal law

It is useful briefly to review the major principles that govern criminal law in the UK. This is partly because they govern some areas of employment law (eg, the enforcement of statutes in the health and safety field), but also because it is useful to contrast them with the principles that govern our civil law and which you may well be less familiar with.

As a general rule (and there are always exceptions to these) criminal cases are brought by agencies of the state in the name of the Crown. Since 1985 the prime responsibility for carrying out this task has rested with the Crown Prosecution Service who evaluate the strength of cases brought to them by the police, before deciding whether or not to prosecute a case in the courts. Other agencies of the state are also mandated to bring certain types of cases. Importantly for our purposes these include the Health and Safety Executive (HSE) and the local authority health and safety inspectorates.

Relatively minor criminal cases come before the magistrates courts, the more serious before the Crown Courts. In the former the case is heard by lay magistrates, or a district judge, whose power to pass sentence is limited. In the Crown Court the case is heard by a judge, and a twelve-strong jury selected at random from the electoral register. The burden of proof is always on the prosecution to prove its case, so the defendant is presumed to be innocent unless and until proven to be guilty. The standard of proof, famously, is 'beyond reasonable doubt'. So unless the prosecution presents sufficiently strong evidence to back up its case, the magistrates or jury should acquit the accused of the offence. Moreover, in most criminal cases the prosecution is obliged to prove not only that the defendant (or defendants) committed the criminal act in question, but that they did so knowing that what they were doing was wrong, or reckless as to whether it was or not. Across much of the criminal law, showing that someone had a guilty mind (mens rea) is as important in establishing criminal liability as showing that they have committed an offence (actus reus). There are, however, a number of offences which do not require a mental element. These are called strict liability offences, and the defendant can be found guilty even if he did not know the details of the offence, so long as he was responsible for it. This is the case in many health and safety offences.

When a defendant is found guilty, the judge or magistrates who have heard the case pass sentence, the purpose of which is to punish the guilty person and to act as a deterrent to others. The payment of compensation to the victim is not the main aim of criminal proceedings—that is the remit of the civil courts, although criminal courts sometimes order the defendant to make a small payment as reparation. The punishments can range from fines (the state benefiting from any fines which are collected), community penalties, or prison sentences, which can be suspended in exceptional circumstances, and are only served when the individual concerned is found guilty of committing a further offence within a specified time period.

 Exhibit 2.1   **A view from the dock**

One of the most famous people in the UK to have been convicted of a criminal offence in an employment-related case is the actor Ricky Tomlinson who plays Jim Royle in the sitcom 'the Royle Family'. In 1973 he was tried along with several other strike organisers in Shrewsbury Crown Court following their arrest while picketing at a construction site. He was found guilty of unlawful assembly, affray and conspiracy to intimidate other workers and cause criminal damage. He was sentenced to two years in prison.

The description of the strike, the trial and his subsequent period in jail form a major part of his autobiography, providing an excellent description of what it feels like to be accused, tried and sentenced. The fact that he genuinely believed himself to be innocent and expected to be acquitted make these passages in the book all the more interesting, and raise questions about justice and the law as applied during episodes of industrial action.

Civil law

While agencies of the state frequently bring civil actions and, more often, are required to defend their actions in the civil courts, the majority of cases are brought by private individuals or institutions against other private parties. The purpose is to persuade the relevant court that the defending party (the respondent or defendant) has committed an unlawful act and that a detriment has been suffered as a result by the claimant (sometimes known as the plaintiff). When a case is successful, it is common for the losing party to be required to pay compensation to the party which has suffered a detriment, but compensation is by no means the only outcome in civil courts. Sometimes people merely seek a declaration of their legal rights or that an unlawful act has been committed (eg, a declaration that someone has been unfairly dismissed). Injunctions are also sometimes sought as is the case when an employer goes to court in order to prevent an unlawful strike from going ahead as planned. In some unfair dismissal cases the aim of the claimant is to be reinstated in a job, while other claimants are simply looking for an order that their employer should be required to provide them with information (eg, a statement of their main terms and conditions of employment).

Whatever the remedy, its purpose is to compensate or 'put right' a wrong, and not to punish the party which has been found to have committed the unlawful act.

In the civil courts the burden of proof can vary, in that different parties have to prove different elements of the case depending on the area of law concerned. In most situations it is for the claimant to prove his or her case, there thus being an assumption of 'innocence' as far as the respondent is concerned when proceedings begin. This situation, however, is sometimes reversed as is the case in unfair dismissal law where it is for the employer to satisfy the tribunal that the main reason for the dismissal was one which is considered fair under the law. The varying burden of proof can be illustrated by discrimination cases, where it is for the claimant to show facts from which it might be reasonably presumed that an act of unlawful discrimination has taken place. But once that has been achieved, the burden of proof shifts across to the respondent to show that no such act was actually committed. Importantly, the standard of proof in the civil courts is not 'beyond reasonable doubt' but simply 'on the balance of probabilities'—a far lesser hurdle for the claimant to jump than is faced by the prosecution in a criminal case.

 Exhibit 2.2   **Variation in the standard of proof**

The difference in the standard of proof that applies in the civil and criminal courts can sometimes confuse people who apparently find themselves treated differently by different courts in respect of the same incident.

For example, it is not uncommon for a case to come before an employment tribunal the result of which hinges on whether or not a potentially criminal act has been committed. This is the case when an employer suspects an employee of theft and dismisses him, or when an employee resigns because she claims to have been physically assaulted by a manager. In such cases a criminal prosecution will typically take place alongside the civil action. In such circumstances it is common for the criminal case to be heard first, simply because the waiting times for employment tribunal cases in most parts of the country are now frequently in excess of nine months or even a year.

The situation can thus arise in which someone is acquitted of the criminal offence in the magistrates court because the prosecution was unable to prove their case 'beyond reasonable doubt' and yet be on the losing side in the employment tribunal.

There may well be insufficient evidence to show that an employee has stolen something or that a manager has assaulted someone to satisfy a criminal court, but enough to allow an employment tribunal to conclude that the employer acted reasonably in concluding that it was more likely than not that the theft or assault did take place.

Employment legislation

Legislation in the UK is encompassed both by Acts of Parliament, known as 'statutes', and delegated legislation where the power is given to ministers to set out rules in certain areas. These are referred to as 'regulations'.

Employment statutes, in the form of Acts of Parliament, account for the lion's share of modern employment law. These are statutes that have become law having passed through both Houses of Parliament and gained Royal assent. A major piece of employment legislation comes onto the statute books every two or three years. The most important current Acts that impact on the employment relationship or trade union affairs are as follows:

The Health & Safety at Work Act 1974

The Rehabilitation of Offenders Act 1974

The Public Order Act 1986

The Trade Union and Labour Relations (Consolidation) Act 1992

The Pensions Act 1995

The Employment Rights Act 1996

The National Minimum Wage Act 1998

The Employment Relations Act 1999

The Employment Act 2002

The Work and Families Act 2006

The Employment Act 2008

The Equality Act 2010

From time to time a number of separate Acts are brought together into a single statute and hence effectively 'reissued' in a more user-friendly form. When such a process involves no substantive changes, the result is a consolidation Act like the 1992 Act on trade unions and labour relations. This consolidated the principles that had previously been set out in a series of separate Employment Acts passed during the 1980s. The Employment Rights Act 1996 also contains a great deal of consolidated material, including the law covering unfair dismissal and the unlawful deduction of wages which had previously been covered in other Acts. The most recent example was the Equality Act 2010 which, while containing significant new law, also served to consolidate under one roof several long-standing pieces of legislation such as the Equal pay Act 1970, the Sex Discrimination Act 1975, the Race Relations Act 1976 and the Disability Discrimination Act 1995.

In the employment field, the government is increasingly making use of its right to issue delegated or subordinate legislation. This occurs when an Act is presented to Parliament which sets out the broad principles of a new or reformed area of law, but also gives ministers the right to issue much more detailed regulations on how these principles are to be implemented in practice. The regulations are then presented to Parliament for approval, but are not debated in full over many days as is the case with a major new Act. This mechanism has the advantage of allowing the government to implement different parts of its new legislation in stages, consulting with interested parties before final detailed drafts of new regulations are issued. Recent examples include the Additional Paternity Leave and Pay Regulations 2010. In practice the government has little alternative. If Parliament were to debate every aspect of all new employment law in full, it would have little time left to consider other more significant measures.

More controversially the practice has now been adopted of implementing major new pieces of legislation originating in the European Union by regulation rather than through the passing of a full Act. Hence we have statutory instruments such as the Transfer of

Undertakings (Protection of Employment) Regulations 2006, the Working Time Regulations 1998, the Part-time Workers (Prevention of Less Favourable Treatment) Regulations 2000, and, most recently, the Agency Workers Regulations 2010. These are not subjected to proper parliamentary scrutiny and, as a result, have sometimes attracted criticism for being poorly thought through. It is only once test cases reach the higher courts and terms are fully defined by the judges that employers and employees can know what their true legal position is. This also happens with full Acts of Parliament which may need further clarification.

Unusually in the UK we do not have a written constitution which defines the powers of ministers, Parliament or indeed the Queen. As a result it is not the role of any court to interpret the constitution. In countries which do have such arrangements, such as the USA and France, the Supreme Court can overrule executive or legislative institutions when it considers them to be acting unconstitutionally. This is not the case in the UK, where the principle has long been established that Parliament is sovereign. No court, therefore, can overturn or alter the meaning of an Act of Parliament. Only Parliament itself can alter its own previous decisions. People often challenge ministerial decisions in court using a process called 'judicial review', but the aim in such cases is to challenge an interpretation of the law, not the law itself.

However, there are very limited circumstances, such as those under the Human Rights Act, in which courts can effectively overturn rules which are enshrined in statutory instruments—ie, regulations issued under Acts of Parliament. This occurs when a regulation is subjected to judicial review and found to go beyond what is actually authorised by the Act under which it has been issued.

 **Activity 2.2**

Many people argue that the UK should have a written constitution like most other countries which defines precisely what are the powers of the Prime Minister, the Cabinet, The House of Commons, the House of Lords, the Queen and the courts. It would follow that there would be a need for some form of constitutional court to interpret the constitution when people disagreed about its meaning or its applicability in certain situations as is the case in the USA.

Questions

1   Why do you think the UK has never drawn up a formal written constitution?

2   What in your view would be the major advantages and disadvantages of committing our constitutional principles to paper?

Codes of practice

Employers seeking to ensure that they do not face legal action and win any cases they are involved in must take care to follow the prescriptions of codes of practice as well as statutes and statutory instruments. These have statutory force and are approved by Parliament, but they do not form part of the law.

Organisations which breach one of the codes of practice relating to employment are not acting unlawfully. However, when a case does come before a court or tribunal, the contents and principles of the code are used as the standard to judge whether or not an employer has acted reasonably. The most important is the ACAS Code of Practice on discipline at work. This sets out what an employer ought to do when disciplining an employee. It recommends a system of warnings, formal hearings, appeals and the circumstances in which an employee being disciplined can exercise his or her right to be accompanied at a disciplinary hearing (see Chapter 5). Failing to follow the code when terminating a contract does not mean that an employer has unfairly dismissed someone. However, if the case comes before a tribunal, this failure will go against the employer unless a very convincing argument can be put forward to explain it.

Some statutory codes of practice are issued by government alongside new Acts in order to help people to understand their meaning. A well-known example was the Code of Practice on Picketing issued with the Employment Act 1980 which recommended a maximum number of six pickets on any entrance to a workplace during an industrial dispute. Other codes are issued by the Health and Safety Executive and the Equality and Human Rights Commission (see below).

Statutory interpretation

However carefully drafted a statute is (and many in the employment field are poorly drafted) it is impossible for the draftsmen to foresee every type of situation that will arise when the law is applied in practice in the workplace. The precise meaning of terms will be unclear and it will not always be obvious what principles are and are not being put into law by the Act. You will be introduced to many examples later in the book. Some of the more problematic issues arising from unclear drafting in recent years have included the definition of 'disability' in the Disability Discrimination Act 1995 (now found in the Equality Act 2010) and the definition of several fundamental terms in the Transfer of Undertakings (Protection of Employment) Regulations 1981 and 1986. Clarification of the meaning of such terms and of how parts of a statute are to be interpreted in the future comes when the judges have to reach decisions when faced with actual cases.

The process of statutory interpretation is not, however, done on a whim. The judges take great care to apply long-established rules when making these decisions. They are obliged, for example, to take account of the Interpretation Act 1978 which sets out some general rules of statutory interpretation. Here it is stated that references to 'he' and 'him' in statutes should always be taken to include 'she' and 'her' too, while the word 'person' can always be taken to include a company as well as an individual human being. In addition, the judges always take account of several other long-established rules such as 'noscitur a sociis' which requires the meaning of a word to be decided with reference to the context in which it is used. In more recent years they have had to take care to ensure that their interpretation of UK law does not conflict in any way with an established principle of EU law.

The common law

The common law has evolved and developed over a thousand years or so, having its origins in the codification of English law according to the customs of the time by William the Conqueror in the eleventh century. This is law which has not been made by Parliament, but has instead been honed by generations of judges hearing cases and passing judgment on them. These decisions enter the law through the doctrine of precedent which means that all courts are bound to follow the decisions and apply any legal principles set by courts that are further up the hierarchy. So once a judge or group of judges sitting in one of the higher courts has passed judgment, their decisions are binding on the lower courts whenever similar cases are presented before them. Parliament can of course, if it wishes to, override any common law principle by passing a statute. But where it has chosen not to do so, the common law stands as the law of the land, and continues to evolve year on year as new types of situation are presented for consideration by the judiciary.

Contract

A contract is basically an agreement between the people involved, and it can be either in writing or oral, although the details of it may be hard to prove in court if it is not in writing. The law of contract forms a major part of the common law and clearly plays a central role in modern employment law. This is because, despite the presence of dozens of employment statutes that restrict an employer's freedom of action, at base the employment relationship remains contractual in nature. Anyone who takes up employment is forming a contractual relationship with their employer, whether or not this is put in writing. The terms of the contract are then binding on both parties and cannot be altered unilaterally. If one side (either employer or employee) alters the contract without the consent of the other and a detriment is caused as a result, this constitutes an unlawful breach. The wronged party can thus go to court to ask that the contract be restored and that compensation for any losses suffered as a result of the breach should be paid. Actions of this kind are brought regularly when employers cut pay or holiday entitlement, or try to force new contracts on their employees without agreement.

However, there is much more to the law of contract than straightforward righting obvious breaches of a contract of employment. This is because over the centuries judges have decided that all contracts of employment in the UK contain certain 'implied terms'. These are deemed to be present despite the fact that they are not usually written expressly into contracts. They include all manner of common law duties which employers are said to owe to their employees and vice versa. We will cover this in much more detail later in the book (see Chapter 8), but it is important at this stage to flag the significance of implied terms. Examples include the duty of care and the duty to maintain safe systems of working. Where an employer fails in such a duty a breach of these implied terms has occurred, and if someone gets injured as a result, they can go to court and invoke the law of contract in order to secure compensation. Another significant duty on both employers and employees is the duty to maintain a relationship of mutual trust and confidence. Recent case law has shown that a bullying approach on the part of managers can be construed as breaching this duty. Then there is the duty of employers to hear reasonable grievances brought to them by their employees. A refusal to listen or to treat a reasonable grievance seriously is a breach of an implied term and hence an unlawful breach of contract.

The law of contract has also come to play a fundamental role in cases of constructive dismissal—where an employee resigns as a direct result of unreasonable conduct on the part of his/her employer. This is because the test used to establish whether or not an employee was entitled to resign and claim some form of compensation is contractual. The question asked by the tribunal is 'Did the employer's action constitute a repudiation of the contract?' If the answer is yes, then the resignation is treated as if it were an unfair dismissal, and compensation may be required to be paid.

Tort

The law of tort also forms part of our common law and plays a role in employment law too. A tort is best described as a 'civil wrong'—the civil law equivalent of a crime. A party who commits a tort and causes a detriment to another party as a result can find itself being sued for compensation. There are numerous torts, some more generally well known than others. Examples are negligence, defamation, nuisance, deceit, libel, conspiracy and trespass. Of these by far the most significant generally, and particularly in the employment field, is negligence. This is because it is the basis of many personal injury claims brought against employers who have allowed (albeit unintentionally) employees to get hurt. The law of defamation can also be invoked, for example, when an employer writes a reference which is unfair, untrue and causes someone to lose out on appointment to a new job.

The other major area of employment law in which tort plays a significant role is in the law on industrial action (see Chapter 29). This is because trade unions and their officers find it hard to avoid committing certain torts when organising and prosecuting industrial action. As a result the law gives them immunity from prosecution in respect of certain torts providing their action is lawful in other respects.

The European dimension

Increasingly the European Union is a major source of new employment law. In recent years European competence has extended into many areas, many of which were hitherto unregulated in the UK, the major examples being transfer of undertakings law, working time regulations, data protection rules, collective consultation arrangements and a wide range of anti-discriminatory measures. However, the involvement of the EU in UK employment law has occurred for as long as the UK has been a member. Sex discrimination, for example, has long been an area of EU competence, the principle that men and women should be paid equally for carrying out work of equal value being written into the Treaty of Rome and being the subject of a European Directive thirty-five years ago. The same is true of health and safety law, which has developed according to principles laid down by the EU since the late 1980s. The acceleration in recent years has occurred because the Social Chapter of the Maastricht Treaty (signed by the UK in 1997) is concerned with harmonising elements of social policy across all member states, including the regulation of employment practices.

The vast majority of EU employment law comes in the form of directives agreed by the Council of Ministers and endorsed by the European Parliament. European directives set out core principles rather than detailed codes of law. Once agreed, each member state has a limited amount of time (typically three or four years) to give effect to the principles of the directive through their national legal systems. In the UK this means that legislation is passed as and when necessary to ensure that the directive forms part of our employment law. Sometimes, because there is already extensive legislation on a topic in place, the government needs only to introduce a relatively short bill in order to ensure compliance. This occurred in 2004 when new measures were introduced to bring existing UK law on disability discrimination in line with the expectations of the EU directive. Other directives require major new sets of regulations because they establish principles or cover areas which are new as far as EU employment law is concerned. Examples are the Working Time Directive and the Directives outlawing discrimination on grounds of sexual orientation and belief.

Much of the law which originates in the EU is uncontroversial and is welcomed by employer and employee organisations alike. This has been true in the case of many health and safety measures and directives dealing with discrimination on grounds of sex, race and national origin. Other directives have proved to be more divisive and have actively been opposed by sizeable groups of UK business people and employers' associations. The Working Time Directive has been, and continues to be, something of a running sore, while many organisations find the EU's data protection rules to be no more or less than a costly and unnecessary waste of resources.

Directives are particularly controversial when they are introduced without enthusiasm by a UK government that would never have passed equivalent legislation unless required to do so under the terms of a European treaty. This was certainly true of the Working Time Directive which was effectively forced on the UK in the teeth of governmental opposition, but it is also true of other directives which were only agreed to once the UK found itself unable to block them. The Information and Consultation Directive is a good example.

Figure 2.2 summarises the various stages in the EU law-making process. Central is the role of the Council of Ministers which effectively controls what does and what does not become law. This consists of a representative from each member state. When employment matters are being decided, it is the employment or industry minister from each country who will attend. Each representative then casts however many votes their country has allotted to it. The precise weighting of voting power alters from time to time as new members join the

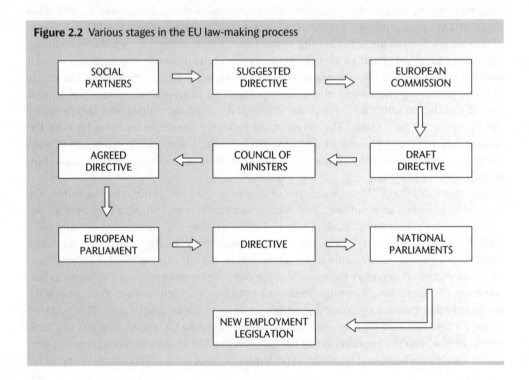

Figure 2.2 Various stages in the EU law-making process

Union and new treaties are agreed. But the number broadly reflects population size. Social measures such as those covering employment are passed by the Council of Ministers on a qualified majority basis, meaning that a draft directive becomes a 'real live' directive once it has been passed in the Council of Ministers with around a 75% majority of the vote. This system permits four or five countries to get together to form a blocking minority to prevent a measure passing. The UK is regularly part of attempts to block new EU legislation and often succeeds with its allies in watering measures down somewhat so as to make them more palatable for UK employers. Once agreed by the Council, the European Parliament votes on proposals, and provided it passes them, a directive becomes EU law.

As far as the private sector is concerned there then follows a wait of a number of years before the directive is introduced into UK law. But public sector employers have to be more careful. This is because directives, once agreed, often have 'direct effect' as far as public authorities are concerned. In principle, therefore, an employee in such an organisation can bring a legal action if he or she believes their employer to have breached the principles of a directive. This is not widely known and rarely occurs in practice, but the prudent public sector manager must bear in mind the real if unlikely possibility that an employee might exercise this right.

The Human Rights Act 1998

The final source of law we cover in this chapter is the European Convention on Human Rights, wrongly assumed by many to be a product of the European Union, but which in fact comes from the Council of Europe. This is a different body, which is wholly separate from the Union, having as signatories several countries which have remained outside the EU. The Convention was developed after the Second World War, coming into force in 1953. The European Court of Human Rights (based in Strasbourg) was established by the Council of Europe as a forum to which citizens of signatory countries could bring complaints when they perceived that laws were in contravention of the Convention. Over the years relatively few cases were taken and even when successful created no binding requirement on the government to alter the offending statutes. The main deterrents were the time it took to get a decision out of the court (about five years) and the costs associated with the bringing of a claim (around £30,000 according to the government).

This situation led to the passing in 1998 of the Human Rights Act, which came into effect in 2000. Henceforth, for the first time, the European Convention on Human Rights has been formally incorporated into UK law. The Act has three main purposes:

1. It allows UK citizens to challenge legislation in the home courts, obviating the need to mount a case in Strasbourg. If successful a declaration can be made by a judge to state that a particular statute is in contravention of the Convention. This places pressure on government to take action, but does not compel ministers to repeal or amend laws.

2. It requires all UK courts to interpret statute and the common law in line with the convention (see the section on statutory interpretation above), and this may include overturning previous judgments if they are found to be less compatible with the Convention than other interpretations.

3. It makes it unlawful for any public authority to act in a manner which is incompatible with the Convention.

Table 2.1 Current allocation of votes in the Council of Ministers

Member State	Votes allocated	Member State	Votes allocated
Germany	29	Austria	10
United Kingdom	29	Bulgaria	10
France	29	Slovakia	7
Italy	29	Denmark	7
Spain	27	Finland	7
Poland	27	Ireland	7
Romania	14	Lithuania	7
Netherlands	13	Latvia	4
Greece	12	Slovenia	4
Czech Republic	12	Estonia	4
Belgium	12	Cyprus	4
Hungary	12	Luxembourg	4
Portugal	12	Malta	3
Sweden	10		

Total = 345

Qualified majority = 258

Blocking minority = 88

The Convention itself is a relatively short document containing eighteen articles which set out a list of fundamental human rights such as the right to life, the right not to be tortured, freedom of expression, the right to marriage, education, liberty and security. It also contains specific provisions outlawing the death penalty except in times of war.

When the Act was first passed a great deal of excitement was generated among employment lawyers and analysts who believed that it would, once in force, have a profound impact on the future evolution of the regulation of employment. All manner of possible new interpretations of existing law were suggested. Particular interest was focused on Article 6 (the right to a fair trial) which some thought may have consequences for employers' disciplinary procedures, Article 8 (the right to respect for private and family life) which was thought to render unlawful employer practices such as listening into phone calls and recording e-mails, and Article 11 (the right to freedom of assembly and association) which was believed to sound the death bell for the UK's restrictive laws on industrial action.

In practice, certainly as far as employment law is concerned, the practical effect of the Human Rights Act has been almost negligible. Legal arguments have been deployed, but rejected in every case where a long-standing principle of employment law has been challenged. That said, it is still early days, and relatively few cases based on Convention articles have yet to find their way up to the higher courts. Employers must therefore be wary and must not assume that because the Act has had little impact to date, it does not mean that it will not in the future.

Exhibit 2.3   **Legal representation at internal disciplinary hearings**

R (on the application of G) v Governors of X School

This important Court of Appeal judgment was overturned by the Supreme Court in late June 2011. In so doing, not for the first time, a judicial interpretation of the law based on the Human Rights Act ultimately failed to become established.

Until 2009, as a general rule, employees had no right to bring a legal representative with them when they attended a disciplinary hearing.

However, thanks to the rulings in this case and another (*Kulkarni v Milton Keynes Hospital NHS Foundation Trust* (2009) IRLR 829), this position changed in 2009.

The *Kulkarni* case concerned a part-qualified doctor who was disciplined after a patient complained that he had placed his stethoscope inside her underwear without first getting her to consent.

Because the outcome of the case could, if it went against the claimant, have led to a situation in which he could not practise as a doctor in the UK, he asked that he might be permitted legal representation at the disciplinary hearing. The request was turned down.

The outcome of this case, which went in favour of Dr Kilkarni, hinged on the detail of his contract and of the Trust's policies. However, in passing judgment the Court of Appeal dealt (via *obiter* comments) with the general issue, and it is this part of the judgment which has significance for certain types of organisations.

Unusually we saw here the application in a UK employment case of principles derived from the European Convention on Human Rights. The Court of Appeal made reference to a Belgian case that was decided in the European Court of Human Rights in 1982 in making its *obiter* judgment.

Article 6 of the Convention concerns the right to a fair trial. The judgment confirms that the right to legal representation does not apply in a conventional disciplinary hearing which may lead to the loss of a job. However, where the potential outcome would be *in effect* the loss of a career (ie, the loss of a right to practise a as a member of a profession), then Article 6 can apply.

The *R v X* case concerned a music teacher who was alleged to have kissed a fifteen-year-old boy. Here the High Court, and subsequently the Court of Appeal, found that legal representation should have been available to the claimant at all stages in the disciplinary process because the outcome could have been a ban from working in any educational institution on the direction of the Secretary of State.

Thanks to the Supreme Court this is now no longer good law. It said that Article 6 should not have been interpreted as extending to internal disciplinary hearings.

 Activity 2.3   *Pay v Lancashire Probation Service*

Mr Pay was employed as a probation officer, carrying out a role which involved him working extensively with sex offenders. However, in his spare time, he also acted as director of a company which sold products related to 'bondage, domination and sado-masochism' over the internet. He also appeared in performances at 'hedonist and fetish clubs', photographs of which were posted on the internet. »

» When his employers discovered the nature of his spare time activities, they dismissed him. Mr Pay then brought a claim of unfair dismissal to an employment tribunal, arguing that his spare-time activities should be of no concern to his employers provided that they did not affect his work. He lost his case. The tribunal concluded that the Lancashire Probation Service had acted quite reasonably in dismissing him.

Mr Pay then appealed the case to the Employment Appeals Tribunal (EAT), basing his claim on Articles 8 and 10 of the European Convention on Human Rights. These protect the right to respect for private life and the right to freedom of expression. Mr Pay lost his appeal.

Questions

1 The outcome of Mr Pay's appeal would be considered by most to amount to common sense, but was it legally correct in your view?

2 Write down the major strands of the legal case you would have presented to the EAT had you been representing (a) Mr Pay and (b) the Lancashire Probation Service.

You may find it helpful and interesting to read the judgment on the EAT's website.

The court structure

Figure 2.3 illustrates the structure of the court system as it relates to employment matters. Cases are started, and usually end too, in one of the three courts at the base of the figure—the County Court, the High Court and the employment tribunal. Which one depends partly on the type of case which is being brought and partly on the level of damages or compensation that is being sought. It is possible for the losing party to get leave to appeal a decision and to take an appeal to the next court up the ladder of authority. Appeals from employment tribunals are taken to the Employment Appeal Tribunal (EAT), and hence to the Court of Appeal. Appeals from both the High Court and County Court are taken directly to the Court of Appeal. In rare cases litigation continues and cases are appealed beyond the Court of Appeal to the Supreme Court (formerly the House of Lords). This is where cases which do not concern European Law cease, the judgment of the Supreme Court being final. However, where the matter concerns an interpretation of European law (ie, a treaty article or a European directive), a further appeal beyond the Supreme Court to the European Court of Justice is possible. Importantly, as a rule, appeals in the civil court system can only be based on issues of law and not of fact. This means that leave to appeal will not be granted simply because the losing side dislikes the interpretation of the lower court on the question of what happened when or about who said what to whom. If you do not think that the court has done justice to the evidence you put before it, there is no possibility of an appeal. To appeal you need to be able to show that the court concerned may have misinterpreted the law in some way or applied it wrongly.

Employment tribunals

Employment tribunals hear cases which have at their root a claim that an employment statute has been breached (see above). The vast majority of the employment statutes are enforceable only in the employment tribunal. So this is the forum which decides three-quarters of the law we describe and analyse in this book.

Figure 2.3 The structure of the court system as it relates to employment law

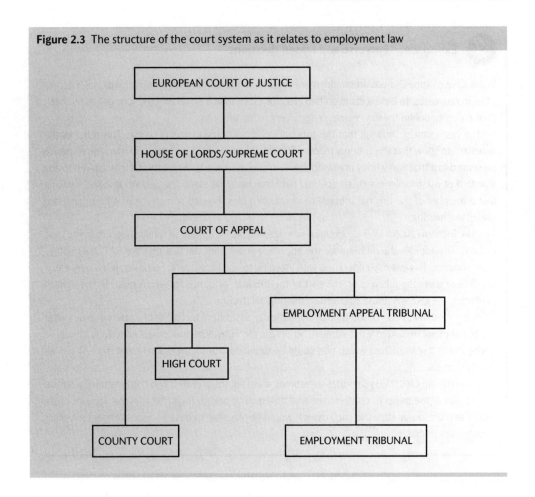

Until 1998, employment tribunals were known as 'industrial tribunals', the name which they had been known by from their establishment in the 1960s. They began with limited powers to hear specialised cases relating to the now long-defunct training levies system established in 1964. Since then, step by step, as employment law itself has developed via statutes employment tribunals have grown in importance (see Chapter 1). Each new piece of employment legislation expands the numbers of types of claim that they can hear, while the development of the case law makes their task increasingly complex. Despite a recent increase in the number of situations in which a case can be heard by an employment judge 'sitting alone', the large majority of full hearings take place in front of a panel of three people—a judge and two 'lay' or 'wing' members.

There are over 100 full-time employment judges and over 200 part-time judges. Until 2007 they were known as employment tribunal chairmen, many of whom (despite the masculine title) were women. They sit at twenty-one centres around the country. All are lawyers of at least seven years' standing, most of whom have considerable experience of employment law either as barristers or solicitors. They have the same status as County Court and Crown Court judges and enjoy the same remuneration, but they do not wear the wigs and

Exhibit 2.4   **Perverse and biased decisions**

In the case of appeals from an employment tribunal to the Employment Appeal Tribunal it is possible, in rare cases, to base a claim on two grounds other than a belief that the former has misinterpreted or misapplied the law. However, they very rarely succeed.

The first involves showing that the tribunal's original decision was perverse. This requires the
appellant to show that the tribunal made a finding of fact or made an inference from the evidence
presented to it that was wholly unreasonable—so unreasonable that no tribunal that aspired to any
standard of reasonableness could possibly have reached that view. The second involves showing
that a member of the original tribunal demonstrated bias through something that he or she said
during the hearing.

Cunningham (2005:313–316) explains why these types of appeal so rarely succeed. In the case
of perversity appeals the problem for the appellant arises from the fact that the EAT does not re-
hear evidence. It is entirely concerned with listening to legal argument. So unless it is a very clear-
cut case of unreasonableness on the part of the tribunal, evidence for which exists in the written
judgment, the EAT will refuse to overturn the original decision.

In the case of appeals based on bias the difficulty arises from a conflict of evidence about what
a tribunal member said in what context. So unless the individual concerned effectively admits to
having made a remark from which bias could be deduced, it is highly unlikely that the EAT will allow the appeal.

Cunningham (2005:315) says that sometimes a written tribunal decision demonstrates a refusal
on the part of the panel to contemplate that a particular person might be lying on account of seniority or professional status. In such cases it would be plausible to base an appeal either on a claim
of perversity or bias.

---

gowns worn by the judiciary in these other courts. Chairmen are appointed by the Justice
Secretary, or in Scotland, by the Lord President of the Court of Session. Lay members, by
contrast, are appointed for their industrial rather than their legal expertise. They apply for
their positions via written applications to the Tribunals Service (which advertises for people
periodically) and, if successful, are appointed either to the employers' list or the employees'
list. There are around 2000 lay members at any one time (Deakin and Morris, 2001:86).
They serve on a part-time basis for a modest fee. Many are retired or semi-retired managers
or trade union officials, but those who are employed have the right to take several days off
work each year in order to carry out their tribunal duties. The role of the lay members can be
most significant, for example in assessing what actions of an employer should be accepted
as 'reasonable' or appropriate given its size and resources. In theory it is quite possible for an
employment tribunal to reach a majority decision in a case, one of its three members dis-
senting. Moreover, this is conceivable where the judge (ie, the legally qualified member) is
the dissenter. In practice, however, it is a rare occurrence.

Aside from statutory matters, employment tribunals can also hear breach of contract
cases if the claimant is no longer employed by the respondent, but can only award damages
of up to £25,000. Until 1994 this was not the case, leaving applicants who had both been
unfairly dismissed and short-changed contractually on their dismissals in the position of

having to bring two separate claims to two different courts. In *Sajid v Sussex Muslim Society* (2001) it was established that someone seeking more than £25,000 for breach of contract can have their claim heard in the employment tribunal, be awarded £25,000, and then launch a separate claim for the balance in either the County or the High Court.

When they were originally established, employment tribunals were intended to be relatively informal fora for the settling of disputes. Davies and Freedland (1993:164) argue that their origin was as 'court substitutes' rather than as full-blown courts, although in practice this has never actually been achieved. When they were first established, except in complex cases, it was not anticipated that parties would need to be legally represented when appearing before a tribunal. Instead it was hoped that they would be 'of easy access to workers and employers' and that they would provide 'a speedy means of settling disputes with less formality and expense than might be entailed if disputes were to go to the courts'.

Some of these original aspirations remain present in the way that employment tribunals now operate, but it has been clear for many years now that they operate as courts of law in all but name. Parties are frequently represented by lawyers, but can choose simply to represent themselves or can appoint anyone else they wish to represent them. Trade union officials, HR managers, representatives from Citizens' Advice Bureaux and family friends commonly undertake the role of representative in tribunals—a situation which is not permitted in the County or High Courts. Moreover, a bias towards informality and accessibility is written into the tribunals' rules of procedure. There are no formal rules of evidence applied in the employment tribunal, meaning for example that hearsay evidence can be heard and taken account of when a decision is made. Legal language is avoided, judges taking great care to explain the law and its practical implications to the parties, as well as making sure that everyone understands the procedures being followed.

In practice the extent to which informality is achieved depends to a great extent on the complexity of the case and on whether one or both sides are represented by legally qualified people. Where both sides are legally represented judges assume familiarity with the law, court etiquette and with tribunal procedure, and often show considerable impatience with representatives who fail to meet their expectations in this respect. On the other hand, when there are no legal representatives present, great care is taken to explain everything in layman's language, the judge necessarily taking a far more pro-active role in questioning witnesses and in ensuring that all relevant evidence is properly presented. Achieving fairness is harder when one party is legally represented (normally the employer) and the other is not. In such cases the judges strive for fairness by assisting as far as is reasonable the unrepresented party to put their case over fully and properly.

 Activity 2.4 **The overriding objective**

Since 2001 employment tribunals have been required formally to focus on achieving an 'overriding objective'. According to Manley and Heslop (2004:6) the current version of the relevant regulation reads as follows:

1 The overriding objective of these regulations and the rules in Schedules 1, 2, 3, 4 and 5 is to enable tribunals and chairmen to deal with cases justly.

»

2 Dealing with a case justly includes, so far as is practicable:

   a) ensuring that the parties are on an equal footing;

   b) dealing with the case in ways which are proportionate to the complexity or importance of the issues;

   c) ensuring that it is dealt with expeditiously and fairly; and

   d) saving expense.

3 A tribunal or chairman shall seek to give effect to the overriding objective when it or he:

   a) exercises any power given to it or him by these regulations or in the rules in Schedules 1, 2, 3, 4 and 5; or

   b) interprets these regulations or any rule in Schedules 1, 2, 3, 4 and 5.

4 The parties shall assist the tribunal or chairman to further the overriding objective.

Questions

1 What do you think tribunals can do to help ensure that the requirements of regulation 2a are met when one party is represented by a lawyer and the other is unrepresented?

2 What are the implications of regulation 4 for parties whose case is weak in some respect?

3 What conflicts do you think might arise between meeting both regulations 2c and 2d?

The Employment Appeal Tribunal

The Employment Appeal Tribunal (EAT) was established in 1975 to hear appeals from employment tribunals and of decisions made by the Certification Officer (see below). It is based in London and Edinburgh and hears around 1,000 appeals a year. The EAT is constituted in a similar way to employment tribunals, consisting for the vast majority of cases of a three-person panel. It is chaired by a High Court judge, the lay members being appointed jointly by the Tribunals Service. In practice they are experienced names taken from the employer and employee lists described above.

Appeals to the EAT must be made within forty-two days (ie, six weeks) of the original ET decision being made (or sent in the post if judgment has been reserved). Most are all then listed for a preliminary hearing at which the appellant has to convince the judge that a strong argument can be made in support of the view that the original employment tribunal was guilty of either a 'misdirection, misapplication or misunderstanding' of the law. The case will then either be dismissed or allowed to proceed to a full hearing.

The EAT never hears evidence. It simply reads the original tribunal decision and written submissions provided by the parties in support of their view about whether or not it erred in law. Oral submissions are also heard, the EAT asking questions to clarify its understanding and to test legal arguments. There are four possible outcomes:

1. The EAT agrees with the original employment tribunal ruling and refuses the appeal.

2. The EAT overturns the original employment tribunal ruling and allows the appeal.

3. The EAT makes a ruling on a point of law and remits the case back to the original employment tribunal.

4. The EAT makes a ruling on a point of law and remits the case to a differently constituted employment tribunal.

It is necessary sometimes to remit a case back down to the employment tribunal because evidence needs to be heard or re-heard in the light of the legal position that the EAT has established. Decisions of the EAT are binding on all employment tribunals and on itself, although the English and Scottish EATs are not apparently bound by one another's decisions (Upex et al, 2004:17).

The County Court and the High Court

Employment law cases are not always heard in the employment tribunal. All common law matters with the exception of the breach of contract claims that tribunals can now hear are presented either in the County Court or in the High Court. This includes claims in tort (negligence, conspiracy, defamation, etc), most breach of contract claims and cases concerning the law of trust. The most common employment-related cases to be heard in these courts concern health and safety, personal injury claims always being heard in the first instance in either the County or the High Court. Which case is heard by which court is determined mainly by reference to the size of the damages being sought. At present the High Court can only hear cases for which damages in excess of £15,000 are being sought, but it is possible for the county courts to hear these cases too. For personal injuries claims the equivalent limit is £50,000. In any case judges in the High Court can transfer a case to the County Court (and vice versa) in response to an application from one of the parties or of its own volition (Bailey et al, 2002:94–97). However, certain types of claim are always taken to the High Court, an example being that of an employer seeking an injunction to prevent a planned strike from proceeding (see Chapter 29).

There are 220 county courts in which cases are heard by judges assigned to one of sixty county court circuits. They hear all manner of civil cases including issues relating to the law of contract and tort, the vast majority of their work having nothing whatever to do with employment law. The High Court deals both with civil claims and acts as a court of appeal in criminal matters. There are three divisions to which High Court judges are assigned (the Chancery, Queen's Bench and Family divisions). The Queen's Bench division deals with most employment-related cases, including personal injury claims, but it is to the Chancery courts that claims relating to the law of trust are taken. The Queen's Bench division is headed by the Lord Chief Justice, cases being decided by one of seventy-five to eighty High Court judges sitting in either London or at one of twenty-seven regional centres.

Rights of audience are a great deal more restricted in the county courts than in the employment tribunal. Unless the claimant is willing and able to represent themselves, it is necessary to hire a solicitor or barrister to do so. In the case of the High Court rights the role of representation is restricted to barristers and a specialised group of solicitors who have applied for and gained rights of audience. In practice this means that litigation in these courts is a good deal more expensive for most parties than is the case in the employment tribunal.

The Court of Appeal and the Court of Session

Around thirty-five Lords Justices of Appeal, headed by the Master of the Rolls, are responsible for hearing cases that are appealed from the EAT, the County Courts or the High Court to the Court of Appeal. The judges sit in panels of three, reaching their decisions either on a unanimous or a majority basis. In reading case reports the Court of Appeal judges are always referred to with the suffix 'LJ' after their names for 'Lord Justice'. In the case of the Master of the Rolls the suffix 'MR' is used. Cases are always heard in London.

In Scotland appeals are taken to the Court of Session in Edinburgh rather than to the Court of Appeal. Cases there can be heard by panels of five judges, but the quorum and usual number is three. The Court of Session is headed by the Lord President. Further appeals, as is the case with the Court of Appeal, are to the Supreme Court.

The Supreme Court

The Supreme Court is the highest (and last) court of appeal as far as matters relating to UK law are concerned. Cases are heard by twelve Justices of the Supreme Court sitting in panels of three, five or seven.

The Supreme Court came into existence in 2009. Before that its functions were carried out by the Law Lords sitting in the House of Lords. While the name changed in 2009 along with the location at which cases are heard, only very limited changes were made to the role played by the House of Lords/Supreme Court in our legal system.

It is particularly important to appreciate that judgments made before 2009 by the House of Lords remain in place, and throughout this book we will make reference to leading cases decided by the House of Lords. You need to remember that these judgments have the same significance as those made in more recent years by the Supreme Court.

The Supreme Court hear a few dozen cases each year. They made fifty-eight judgments in 2010, of which only two or three had any significance for employment. Moreover, cases are only presented when the Justices consider that the points of law they raise are of 'general public importance'. In practice this means that the Supreme Court makes decisions only when there is some confusion or doubt surrounding the correct interpretation of a significant legal issue. Their judgments thus tend to have the effect of simplifying the law and tend to make life easier for employers, employees and lawyers alike.

 Exhibit 2.5   *Murray v Foyle Meats*

A good example of a House of Lords judgment which helped employers and employees alike by simplifying the law was made in 1999 in the case of *Murray v Foyle Meats*.

Until 1999 redundancy law was a great deal more complex than it now is. This was because the courts had reached rather different and sometime complex judgments about what should happen in various types of situation. For example, it is common for someone to do different work in their day-to-day working lives than is described in the contract of employment. Is it fair to make them redundant when the work they are doing ceases but that described in the contract continues? Similarly what should happen in a multi-site organisation where one workplace closes but individual contracts state that employees may be required to work at any number of sites if required? Is it fair to restrict redundancies to people working in the one place? The answers to these questions were unclear because different courts had made slightly different judgments in similar (if distinguishable) types of cases.   »

> In the case of *Murray v Foyle Meats Ltd* (1999) the House of Lords ruled that courts faced with redundancy issues should simply ask three questions.

1 Has the employee been dismissed?

2 Has there been an actual or prospective diminution in the need for employees to carry out work of a particular kind?

3 Is the dismissal wholly or mainly attributable to this state of affairs?

If the answer to all three is 'yes' then in principle it is a lawful redundancy.

The European Court of Justice

Officially known as the Court of Justice of the European Communities, the European Court of Justice (ECJ) decides questions of European law. It has no jurisdiction to hear other cases, but can overrule the decisions of the supreme courts in member states such as the House of Lords if they concern EU treaty articles, directives or regulations. The ECJ sits in Luxembourg and comprises a judge from each of the member states. Except where the government of a member state or the European commission is prosecuted in the court, the ECJ itself does not technically impose decisions on the courts that sit beneath it across the European Union. Instead matters are referred to it by lower courts and an opinion on the correct or proper interpretation of EU law requested. Although it takes some time (a year or more) for the opinion to be forthcoming, the case that has given rise to the issue is then decided by whichever court originally referred it to the ECJ. As far as UK employment law is concerned, which court refers a matter to the ECJ is very important, because the ruling only becomes a binding precedent on courts that are lower down the tree than the one which actually makes the decision. Hence if a matter is referred directly to the ECJ by an employment tribunal, the subsequent ruling will only definitely apply to the particular case the tribunal is considering. Other tribunals, and more importantly higher courts in the UK system, are not bound by the ECJ's interpretation. Only if the Supreme Court makes a reference to the ECJ and subsequently applies the ruling in its decision in a case, is the ECJ's interpretation of the law binding on all the UK courts.

Precedent

It is important to understand that once a higher court makes a ruling on a legal issue it becomes binding on courts lower down the hierarchy. It thus sets a precedent which then must be followed or applied in subsequent cases. Most courts are not bound by precedents made at the same level in the system. So an employment tribunal need not follow a precedent set by another employment tribunal. But it would be required to follow a relevant precedent that had been set by the Employment Appeals Tribunal. The Court of Appeal operates its own rules which mean that it, unlike all the other courts, cannot overturn its own precedents. High Court rulings are considered to be binding on the county courts. Precedents set by the European Court of Justice are binding on all lower courts, except where the ECJ offers an opinion which subsequently informs the judgment of a lower court. Precedents which are not binding may nonetheless be considered 'persuasive'. This means that someone representing one or other party in a case may quote the precedent and the reasoning behind it in the hope that another court at the same level will take it on board.

Quasi-legal institutions

In addition to the courts, there are a range of other institutions which play a role in enforcing employment law in one way or another. We will look at each in more detail later in the book. Our purpose here is to introduce each briefly and to state how it fits into the broader employment law structure.

ACAS

ACAS stands for the Advisory, Conciliation and Arbitration Service. It has several distinct functions in the UK's employment law system. It is funded by government but is independent, being accountable to its own council nominated in part by the Trade Union Congress (TUC) and the Confederation of British Industry (CBI). When it was originally established in 1974 most of ACAS's activity concerned arbitrating and conciliating in industrial disputes. Nowadays it is its other functions which have become more prominent.

1. ACAS provides a range of advisory services, including an employment law telephone helpline and various publications, and runs various training events. The helpline is free and very useful indeed for employers and employees alike. Charges are made for most of its other advisory activities.

2. ACAS has drawn up and publishes three codes of practice which are updated from time to time. The first concerns the handling of disciplinary and grievance issues in the workplace, the second concerns the disclosure of information by managers to unions during collective negotiations, while the third focuses on the granting of time off to union officials and their members to carry out union duties or activities. These are statutory codes. As a result, whilst breaching one of the codes does not itself constitute an unlawful act, the codes are used by tribunals and other bodies as the standard against which an employer's reasonableness or unreasonableness is judged.

3. Since 2001 ACAS has operated an alternative method of settling unfair dismissal and flexible working cases to the conventional route provided by employment tribunals—the Alternative Dispute Resolution procedure. If both parties agree, the case will be considered and decided by an ACAS arbitrator rather than taken before an employment tribunal. According to Chapman et al (2003:7) the advantages are 'speed, cost, privacy and greater informality'. However, whether or not this is true, the scheme has not proved popular in practice. By 2011 only sixty cases had been disposed of this way (Lockton, 2011:17).

4. The most important role played by ACAS as far as employment law is concerned is in conciliating individual cases. ACAS conciliators receive copies of all claim forms that are sent to the Employment Tribunal Service and all the response forms sent in by employers. They then contact the parties and mediate with the aim of encouraging an out-of-court settlement. In this they have considerable success. Around 100,000 cases lodged with tribunals are withdrawn or settled each year ahead of a full hearing, often on the advice of or with the active help of ACAS conciliators.

ACAS has other functions too of less direct relevance to employment law. Chief among these is its role in helping to settle collective industrial disputes either through conciliation or arbitration.

The Central Arbitration Committee (CAC)

Like ACAS the CAC is a publicly funded but independent body, and it also dates originally from the mid-1970s. Chaired by a High Court Judge, it operates like a court in many ways, having jurisdiction in certain specific areas of collective employment law. During the 1980s and 1990s it had a peripheral role, being responsible for dealing with around forty disputes each year relating to the information that employers are required to disclose to union officials to enable effective collective bargaining to take place. The CAC still deals with these cases, but it has had added to its brief, since 1999, responsibility for dealing with compulsory trade union recognition claims, and since 2004, disputes relating to the Information and Consultation Regulations (see Chapter 28). The CAC first tries to conciliate in the cases put before it, making a legally binding adjudication if no voluntary settlement can be agreed.

The Equality and Human Rights Commission (EHRC)

The EHRC was established in 2007 following the merger of the three separate commissions that had operated for some years previously: the Equal Opportunities Commission (EOC), the Commission for Racial Equality (CRE) and the Disability Rights Commission (DRC). The new Commission has similar powers and duties but a much wider remit, covering all areas of discrimination law and the wider field of human rights generally. Its interests extend well beyond the confines of employment practice. The Commission conducts enquiries, funds research and advises ministers on all aspects of discrimination and diversity both in the workplace and in general. But it also plays several further specific roles in the employment law system:

1. It is empowered to bring cases against employers who it considers are acting unlawfully—for example by publishing discriminatory job advertisements.

2. It undertakes formal investigations when it believes that an employer is persistently acting unlawfully in respect of discrimination law.

3. It brings cases against the UK government and taking them up to the ECJ if necessary in order to force amendments to the law. This usually occurs when the Commission believes that the government has failed fully to implement an EU directive.

4. It funds test cases, providing legal advice and representation to claimants in order to push the law forward in their areas of concern.

5. Like ACAS the Commission issues statutory codes of practice which employment tribunals are bound to take into account when deciding relevant cases.

6. More generally the Commission provides advice on discrimination law to employers, employees and job applicants.

(It should be noted that the previous commissions published codes of guidance in their respective areas, which are still in use and available on the EHRC website)

Activity 2.5 *Equal Opportunities Commission v Secretary Of State for Trade and Industry*

In 2007 the Equal Opportunities Commission, one of the predecessor bodies that later merged to form the Equality and Human Rights Commission, took the UK government to court, alleging that Parliament had not fully implemented a European directive in the area of sex discrimination at work (The Equal Treatment Amendment directive 2002). The case was brought against the Secretary of State for Trade and Industry, a department which also changed its identity and is now the Department for Business, Innovation and Skills (DBIS). The case was heard in the High Court.

The case was complex, dealing with a series of issues relating in the main to the law on sexual harassment and maternity leave. The outcome was a victory on the majority of points for the EOC. Had it wished to, the government could have appealed the judgment and argued its case again before the Court of Appeal and subsequently, if necessary, before the House of Lords and the European Court of Justice. In the event, however, ministers conceded and stated that they would bring forward new amending legislation. This promise was honoured in the form of the Sex Discrimination (Amendment) Regulations which came into force on 6 April and 5 October 2008.

The measures were significant. For example, they mean that in the case of babies born on or after 5 October 2008 mothers have been able to retain all their contractual rights with the exception of pay during the whole period of maternity leave. They also mean that someone can now base a case of sexual harassment on a situation in which they have not been targeted for harassment as an individual—working in an environment which is hostile in a sexual way is sufficient. Thirdly, the new regulations make employers responsible when a member of staff is harassed sexually by 'a third party' such as a customer or supplier, rather than just a fellow employee as was often the case previously.

Questions

1   What reasons do you think might have caused the government to concede on these points rather than to appeal the case up through the hierarchy of courts?

2   What possible advantages do you think might have occured from the government's point of view, had an appeal been launched?

3   Why do you think governments get themselves into situations like this whereby legislation has to be amended after it has originally been passed simply because the initial law is later found not to meet EU requirements?

The Health and Safety Executive (HSE)

Until 2007 there were two bodies with responsibility for the regulation of health and safety management in the UK. The Health and Safety Commission (HSC) determined policy and published codes of practice and advice, while the Health and Safety Executive was responsible for law enforcement. The two bodies have now been merged. The new HSE thus both makes and enforces the law. Importantly, it employs teams of inspectors who have considerable statutory powers. They are required to undertake spot-inspections on employers' premises and will, if they are unhappy with what they see, issue improvement notices or prohibition notices requiring an employer to make improvements. You will read a great deal more about the role played by inspectors in Chapter 24.

The Information Commissioner

The Information Commissioner has the major role in enforcing data protection legislation. Employers are supposed to make an annual return to his office, naming their designated 'data controller' and setting out the types of data they hold on their employees. Complaints about breaches of data protection law are investigated by the commissioner's staff, and if necessary, he has the power to require employers to comply with his rulings. The Information Commissioner has issued four codes of practice to date on various aspects of data protection law which employers are expected to comply with.

The Certification Officer

The Certification Officer has various roles to play in relation to trade union affairs. Importantly he determines which bodies are and which are not to be officially 'listed' as trade unions. For bodies that are included on his list important legal privileges accrue such as the right to organise lawful strikes. He also plays an important role in the authorisation of trade union mergers and de-mergers and is responsible for investigating and ruling on complaints received from trade union members about the way they run their internal affairs.

CHAPTER SUMMARY

- The criminal law plays a marginal but significant part in employment regulation. It has a central role in health and safety law and immigration law. Most employment law in the UK is civil law.

- The source of most employment law is statutes—Acts of Parliament and sets of regulations issued by government ministers under Acts. Most EU law is introduced into UK law through statutes. Cases relating to employment statutes are mostly brought to employment tribunals.

- The common law is judge-made. It has evolved over centuries as cases are brought to court and appealed up through the court hierarchy. The laws of contract, trust and tort all play a part in the regulation of employment. Most cases relating to common law matters are brought to the County Court or the High Court.

- Cases can be appealed to the Employment Appeals Tribunal (EAT) and on to the Court of Appeal, the Supreme Court and, if the matter concerns EU law, to the European Court of Justice.

- There are a range of other institutions which play an important role in the employment law system. Examples are the Advisory, Conciliation and Arbitration Service (ACAS), the Equality and Human Rights Commission (EHRC) and the Health and Safety Executive (HSE).

REFERENCES

Bailey S.H., Ching J.P.L., Gunn M.J. and Ormerod D.C. (2002) *The Modern English Legal System*. Fourth Edition. London: Sweet & Maxwell.

Chapman C., Gibson J. & Hardy, S. (2003) *ADR in Employment Law*. London: Cavendish.

Cunningham, N. (2005) *Employment Tribunal Claims*. London: Legal Action Group.

Davies, P. & Freedland, M. (1993) *Labour Legislation and Public Policy*. Oxford: Oxford University Press.

Deakin, S. and Morris, G. (2001) *Labour Law*. Third Edition. London: Butterworth.

Lockton, D. (2011) *Q&A Employment Law 2011–12*. London: Routledge.

Manley, I. & Heslop, E. (2004) *Employment Tribunals: A Practical Guide*. London: The Law Society.

Tomlinson, R. (2003) *Ricky*. London: Time Warner.

Upex R., Benny R. & Hardy S. (2004) *Labour Law*. Oxford: Oxford University Press.

ONLINE RESOURCE CENTRE

A range of online resources to help you through your employment law module have been developed by the author team. These include updates, self-test questions and sources for further reading. (www.oxfordtextbooks.co.uk/orc/taylor_emir3e)

Barriers to employment rights

Learning outcomes

By the end of this chapter you should be able to:

- distinguish between a 'contract of service' and a 'contract for services';

- explain the origin and legal significance of 'the worker category';

- state which statutory rights apply to all 'workers' and which only apply to 'employees';

- identify the main groups who are and who are not typically considered 'employees';

- explain the evolution of the legal tests used to decide cases in this field;

- advise on the specific position of casual workers, homeworkers, office holders, agency workers and sub-contractors;

- critically evaluate suggested reforms in the law on employment status;

- state which employment rights can only be accessed by employees who have completed a defined period of continuous service;

- explain how employment tribunals approach disputes between employers and employees relating to continuity of employment;

- give advice about hiring people from outside the European Union and the application of regulations concerning their employment;

- explain the significance of employment tribunal time limits for claimants and respondents;

- advise on the situations in which time limits can and can not be extended.

Introduction

It is often, but wrongly, assumed that UK employment law gives equal protection to everyone who could reasonably be considered to be working for an employer. In fact, this is far from being the case. A substantial minority of people who work for private firms, companies and public sector organisations do not enjoy the protection of employment law in some significant respects. As a result, it is often the position that before a court or tribunal is able to hear a claimant's case it must first be satisfied that it has the jurisdiction to make a ruling.

While various groups are sometimes excluded from protection under specific statutes (notably the police, members of the armed forces and a somewhat obscure group known as 'share fishermen'), there are three types of situation that commonly arise and which deny people the opportunity to bring their claims to court:

1. when a claimant is not considered to be an employee;

2. when a claimant is not considered to be a worker;

3. when a claimant (who is an employee) has not completed sufficient continuous service with their employer; and

4. when a claimant is found not to be working legally in the UK.

In addition, employment tribunals operate quite strict limits on how soon after someone is dismissed or suffers from an instance of unlawful discrimination they make a claim if they want it to be heard. For most tribunal jurisdictions this time limit is set at three months, meaning that after this period has passed a claim cannot be considered because it is 'out of time'. In practice this rule can also act as a fifth type of barrier preventing people from accessing their employment rights. In this chapter we focus on these five types of situation.

 Activity 3.1

Read the following paragraphs and try to answer the questions that follow. If you return to the activity again when you have finished reading the chapter, you should be able to give full and accurate answers to the questions.

1   Mike is a gifted musician who makes a living via three part-time occupations. Most of his evenings are taken up with teaching pupils on a freelance basis at his own flat. While some of them find out about him from his previous pupils, most are sent to him by an agency. Mike's afternoons are mainly spent playing the piano in the lounge of a large London hotel. When he is too busy (on rare occasions) he sub-contracts this work to friends and pays them his fee. In addition, on Monday and Wednesday mornings he works as a music teacher in a primary school, where he also undertakes playground and some administrative duties. He has made his living this way for over seven years, approximately a third of his income coming from each activity. He sends invoices each month to the hotel, but is paid through the payroll at the primary school like »

» any other teacher. The agency from which most of his private pupils come collects fees on his behalf and sends these on to him less a 10% fee. Without any warning he now receives a letter from the hotel stating that his services are no longer required as a result of a cost-cutting drive. The letter asks him to submit a final invoice for payment and thanks him for his services.

2 Julie works as a tour guide accompanying coach-loads of American tourists as they travel around Europe. The company she works for hires her on a tour by tour basis, paying her a basic daily fee which she supplements with extensive tips and commissions. At the end of each tour she submits a claim and is paid her fee in cash. No tax is deducted by the company. In practice, during the summer season, one tour follows on directly from another, meaning that she is employed continually from April to October. However, in the winter months employment is more erratic. The precise number of weeks worked varies each winter, but on average the tours take up 50% of her time. She has no other job. After five years a complaint is received from a group Julie has escorted complaining of rudeness and inefficiency on her part. As a result she is offered no further work by the company.

Questions

1 What legal rights does Mike have as far as employment law is concerned in respect of his employment at the school, at the hotel and in his freelance teaching work?

2 What further information would you need in order to advise him about whether or not legal action would be appropriate or likely to succeed following his 'dismissal' from the job at the hotel?

3 What potential barriers stand in Julie's way were she to consider bringing a claim of unfair dismissal? Which issues would you expect an employment tribunal to consider before allowing her case to proceed?

Employment status

The law on employment status is far from straightforward. It is often messy and confusing, leaving people unsure of the extent to which they do or do not in fact have various employment rights. The growth of atypical employment in recent decades (homeworking, agency working, casual employment, etc) means that more and more people now fall into a grey area somewhere between employment and self-employment. Some features of their working arrangements are similar or even identical to those of employees, while in other respects they have more in common with independent contractors. Are these people entitled to the full protection of employment law, to some but not all of it or to none of it at all? The answer, as matters currently stand, depends on the particular facts of each individual case.

Painter & Holmes (2002:50) are far from being alone in their view that the current situation is highly unsatisfactory because 'the only guidance on the question in the legislation is so completely circular as to be absolutely useless'. Many have argued that reform in this area is overdue and the government has indicated a possible preparedness to make changes at some future stage. However, as yet the law remains unreformed. This is because while desirable, it is very difficult in practice to define exactly what is and what is not an 'employee'. What is more, there are few obvious overseas models to study or to imitate, as all jurisdictions in the industrialised world have long struggled to resolve the same basic issues (see Engels, 2001 & Casale, 2011).

While the lack of clarity in this fundamental area of employment law is disturbing, from the students' perspective it is a useful subject to study and to come to grips with at an early stage in a course. This is because the law on employment status illustrates very effectively the interplay of the different sources of law we discussed in the previous chapter. The law in this area has evolved over hundreds of years (see Deakin, 2007) and continues to evolve today as economic circumstances and political priorities change. Recent statutory definitions have been laid on top of longer established common law foundations, European law also playing a significant role in shaping the current position. Employment tribunals and courts are required to consider both the wording of legislation and various tests established as precedents in earlier cases when considering whether or not particular individuals can or cannot pursue their cases.

Dependent employees and independent contractors

Over the past century and a half the courts have developed various common law tests to determine whether or not someone is an employee and hence entitled to the full range of employment protection rights. This process has involved the establishment of 'a binary divide' between two distinct types of employment status, under which people are either defined as being dependent employees or independent contractors. The notion of a division of the workforce into these two categories has a long history. According to Freedland (2003:20) it is possible to trace them right back to Roman law, while Engels (2001) shows that they remain prevalent in the employment law of most countries.

When deciding in which of these two categories an individual should be classed, the court or tribunal is obliged to decide which of two types of contractual arrangement best describes the one that it is faced with:

- a contract of service

or

- a contract for services.

The first suggests that the applicant is (or was) working in a subordinate role which in some sense puts them under the control of an employer. The relationship is thus a modern day equivalent to that of a master and servant: the employer gives instructions which, provided

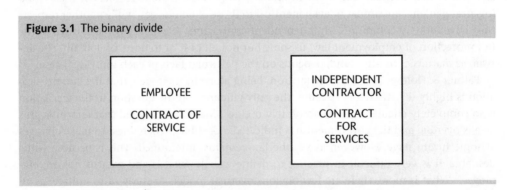

Figure 3.1 The binary divide

EMPLOYEE

CONTRACT OF SERVICE

INDEPENDENT CONTRACTOR

CONTRACT FOR SERVICES

they are reasonable and within the terms of the contract, the worker is obliged to obey. If a tribunal finds this to be the case, then it will conclude that the claimant is an employee and is entitled to the full range of statutory employment rights. The same is true of a County or High Court action. Employment status depends on the nature of the relationship being found to be consistent with 'a contract of service'. If this is not the case, the relationship is considered to be founded on 'a contract for services' in which there is no subordination of the master-servant type. In such circumstances the applicant is deemed to have more in common with a self-employed contractor. He or she is not therefore entitled to the full range of rights (including the right not to be unfairly dismissed) which are only available to employees working under contracts of service.

In most cases, of course, the issue of employment status is not a matter of dispute between the parties. It is clear, and always has been from the start of their relationship, that someone is either an employee working under a contract of service or a self-employed person, in business on their own account, and working under a contract for services. A secretary who is on a large company's payroll who reports to and takes orders on a daily basis from a manager is in all likelihood working under a contract of service. On the other hand, a plumber who is sourced using Yellow Pages and is subsequently employed for a few weeks to carry out a major maintenance job before sending in an invoice would clearly be working under a contract for services. The problem lies in settling the position of the various groups who fall into the grey area in between the two categories. These people constitute a surprisingly large and growing proportion of the UK workforce:

> It was estimated that around 64% of respondents were clearly employees and 5% were clearly self-employed. This left 30% who had an employment status that, on first inspection, had elements of uncertainty and was not completely clear. They were made up of two groups: those defining themselves as self-employed, but who were not directors or partners in their own business, and who did not employ others; and those defining themselves as employees who had some type of non-standard working pattern or classified their jobs as non-permanent. (Burchell et al, 1999:86)

The worker category

The picture has been complicated somewhat in recent years by the passing of employment statutes, often with a European origin, that include *some* independent contractors as well as employees within their remit. While the precise terminology used varies from one statute to another, for most practical purposes the same groups are included. This has become known as the 'worker category'. It is intended to extend some (but by no means all) fundamental employment rights beyond the ranks of employees working under a contract of service to those identified above as falling into the grey area between employment and 'out and out' self-employment. The major statutory rights which apply to workers and only to employees are identified in Exhibit 3.1. Until recently no employment rights at all had been granted to genuinely self-employed people. Where they had a case, it could not be heard in the employment tribunal, making litigation a more expensive and risky prospect. However, this changed in December 2003 with the introduction into UK law of EU directives covering discrimination on grounds of sexual orientation and religion or belief, in 2006 with the advent of age discrimination law and in 2010 was further extended across a wide range of

Figure 3.2 The worker category

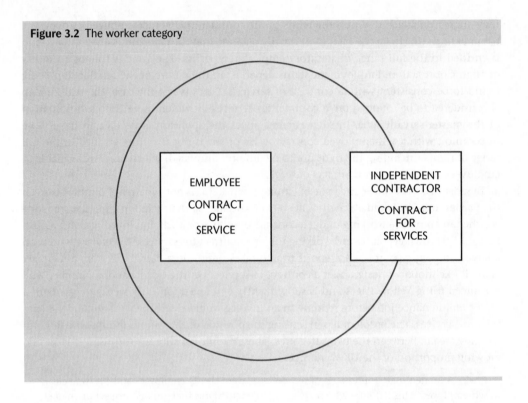

'protected characteristics' thanks to the Equality Act. The UK's employment regulations on these matters specifically include self-employed people.

What this means is that we now effectively have three categories of employment status rather than the traditional two. First, we have dependent employees who are able to claim the full range of employment rights. Secondly, we have independent contractors who are classed as workers. They are able to benefit from some employment rights, but remain excluded from some of the most fundamental. Finally we have a group that can be labelled 'genuinely self-employed'. They are independent contractors who fall outside the worker category and thus enjoy only limited employment rights.

Exhibit 3.1 lists the major employment protection rights that apply to workers and employees respectively, but it is important to recognise that the core binary divide between employees and independent contractors has important implications that go well beyond the allocation of statutory employment rights:

- Employees enjoy more common law employment rights such as the duty to maintain a relationship of mutual trust and confidence, or the general duty of care that all employers owe to all employees (see Chapter 8).

- Employers owe employees a higher duty under health and safety law than is the case with independent contractors (see Chapter 25).

- Employers are held in law to be vicariously liable for the actions of their employees (not always independent contractors) while they are at work. This has significance both in health and safety law (see Chapter 25) and in cases of unlawful harassment (see Chapter 11).

- Tax and national insurance arrangements are different for employees and independent contractors. Tax schedules are different in many cases (E for employees and D for independent contractors), permitting the latter more scope for deducting tax to take account of expenses incurred as part of their work. Employees pay higher NI contributions (Class 1) than independent contractors (Class 2), but also get better benefits as a result, such as statutory sick pay (see Chapter 21). Employers only pay national insurance contributions in respect of employees, not independent contractors.

 Exhibit 3.1 **Major statutory employment rights enforceable in employment tribunals**

Those which apply to all employed and self employed persons

- discrimination on grounds of sex, race, sexual orientation, disability, belief and age,

Those which apply to workers but not to other independent contractors

- equal pay for equal work
- limitations on unauthorised deductions from pay
- basic health and safety rights
- the national minimum wage
- working time rights
- data protection rights
- time off for family emergencies
- most transfer of undertakings (TUPE) rights

Those which accrue to employees from the start of their employment

- right to a Section 1 statement (ie, a statement setting out main terms and conditions)
- right to itemised pay statements
- statutory sick pay (SSP)
- time off for public duties
- fifty-two weeks' maternity leave
- the main trade union rights
- minimum notice periods
- right to request flexible working

Those which accrue to employees over time

- statutory maternity pay (after six months)
- paternity leave (after six months)
- unfair dismissal rights (after one year)
- parental leave (after one year)
- the right to a permanent contract (after four years)

- Employers are legally obliged to insure themselves against liability towards employees and apprentices. They are not compelled to do so in respect of independent contractors.
- In the absence of a written agreement that states otherwise, employers are deemed in law to be the owners of any copyright relating to work carried out by their employees in the course of their employment. This is not the case with independent contractors.

Establishing employee status

How then do we establish whether or not someone is an employee or an independent contractor? Unfortunately the answer is far from straightforward. Moreover, it is important to understand that the answer may be different in relation to the same individual depending on the purpose for which the question is being asked. It is quite possible, for example, to be considered an employee for taxation purposes (and thus to pay Class 1 national insurance contributions and have one's tax deducted at source) and yet to be an independent contractor as far as employment rights are concerned. Many agency workers are in this position. The reverse position is also possible although a good deal less common in practice.

The employment statutes provide little or no assistance. The Employment Rights Act 1996, which is the current source of much of the employment law that applies only to 'employees', defines the term as follows:

an individual who has entered into or works under (or, where the employment has ceased, worked under) a contract of employment (section 230(1)).

It then goes on to define the term 'contract of employment' as meaning:

a contract of service or apprenticeship, whether express or implied, and (if it is express) whether oral or in writing (section 230(2)).

The Trade Union and Labour Relations (Consolidation) Act 1992, the other major source of statutory employment rights, incorporates a similar definition:

In this Act 'contract of employment' means a contract of service or of apprenticeship, 'employee' means an individual who has entered into or works under (or, where the employment has ceased, worked under) a contract of employment, and 'employer', in relation to an employee, means any person by whom the employee is (or, where employment has ceased, was) employed. (section 295(1)).

Parliament, in passing these statutes, was thus effectively allowing the courts to apply and to further develop their own established common law definitions about the meaning of the term 'contract of service' and to apply these when deciding whether or not a particular individual is entitled to have his or her statutory claim heard.

Over more than a century the courts have developed a variety of different tests to apply when deciding whether or not someone works under a contract of service as opposed to a contract for services. Deakin and Morris (2009:133–144) identify four major tests that the courts have at some time applied either separately or in combination.

The control test

This is the longest established of the four, being the accepted approach taken by the courts throughout the late nineteenth and early twentieth centuries. It requires the court to inquire about the extent of supervision. To what extent does the individual concerned work under the direction of the employer? To what extent does the individual have control over their own work? Who decides what work is done, when it is done and where it is done? Is the individual required to obey the orders of the employer? The more evidence of control that is provided to the court or tribunal, the more likely it is to decide that the individual concerned is an employee working under a contract of service.

The integration test

In the post-war period a new test was evolved which focused on the extent to which the work performed by an individual was fully integrated into the core activities of the employing organisation. Is the work performed done as an integral part of the business? Or is it only accessory to it? Is the individual included within the remit of personnel policies such as disciplinary and grievance procedures? Are they entitled to join any occupational pension scheme or provided with other benefits that form part of a standard package of terms and conditions? The more integrated the individual's work is, the more likely it is that he or she is (or was) working under a contract of service.

The economic reality test

This test looks at the issue of employee status from the opposite angle. Instead of focusing on the detail of the relationship between the supposed employee and employer, it asks how far it can be said that the individual is 'in business on his own account'. In other words, it looks for evidence of self-employment rather than employment. All manner of factors can be taken into account here. What are the payment methods used? Is tax deducted at source? Is money transferred through a payroll or are invoices sent by the individual? Who owns and/or maintains the equipment that is used to carry out the work? Who has the power to fix or approve the time of holidays? Are holidays paid? Is sick pay paid? Is the individual free to provide a substitute to carry out the work in his or her absence? Does the individual take any personal financial risk, for example if work is completed late? The more evidence of economic independence that is found, the less likely it is that a contract of service exists (or existed).

The mutuality of obligation test

The fourth test has been given particular emphasis in the most recent cases and is perhaps harder to understand fully. It is explained by Deakin and Morris (2001:162) as follows:

> With reference to the employment contract, 'mutuality of obligation' has a specific meaning which refers to the presence of mutual commitments to maintain the employment relationship in being over a period of time. While, at its most basic level, the contract of employment is a contract to serve in return for wages, every contract of employment contains, in addition, a *second tier of obligation* consisting of mutual promises of future performance.

Central is the idea that the individual concerned must be required to accept work that is offered by the employer. If it is possible for the individual to turn down an offer of work and not suffer a detriment as a result, then mutuality of obligation does not exist. If on the other hand a worker who refuses an offer of work finds that no further such offers are made in the future, then mutuality of obligation probably does exist. This is because there is evidence that the employer, at least, expected the relationship to be ongoing. The employer committed itself to providing work and expected that the individual would take whatever work was offered. The more evidence there is of mutuality of obligation, and the longer such arrangements have been in place, the more likely it is that the court or tribunal will find that a contract of service exists.

The multiple test

What has evolved over the years is a situation in which the courts look at all these tests, and sometimes at other relevant factors too, when deciding whether someone is employed under a contract of services or a contract for services. In effect a multiple test is now used which involves the court asking a variety of different questions such as those set out above as a means of establishing, in the round and on the balance of probabilities, whether or not someone has the status of an employee for the purposes of employment law. In some cases there are several factors on each side of the equation, making it very difficult to reach a fair judgment.

The multiple test was effectively established in 1968 in the case of *Ready Mixed Concrete (South East) v Minister of Pensions and National Insurance* in which the following formulation was advanced by MacKenna J:

A contract of service exists if three conditions are fulfilled:

i) The servant agrees that, in consideration of a wage or other remuneration, he will provide his own work and skill in the performance of some task for his master.

ii) He agrees, expressly or impliedly, that in the performance of that service he will be subject to the other's control in a sufficient degree to make that other master.

iii) The other provisions of the contract are consistent with its being a contract of service.

Since then, this formulation has been approved on several occasions by the Court of Appeal and more recently by the House of Lords in *Carmichael v National Power* (2000) and so is now accepted as setting out the approach which tribunals and courts must follow.

It is important to note that the decision in the *Ready Mixed Concrete* case is not prescriptive about exactly which factors a tribunal should take into account when reaching its own decision in a particular case. Mackenna J went on to give some examples of the kind of factors that might be significant and which he had in mind under point iii (above), but he did not say which were to be considered in any case, nor did he give any advice about the weighting of different factors. These questions are thus left to the tribunals to decide for themselves. Incidentally, later case law has clearly established that the label the parties themselves use to describe their relationship should be just one factor among the many that the multiple test should encompass. It is no more or less significant or decisive than the others.

In *Montgomery v Johnson Underwood Ltd* (2001) the Court of Appeal again quoted Mackenna J's formulation in the *Ready Mixed Concrete* case with approval, also quoting other recent decisions including that by the House of Lords in *Carmichael v National Power* (2000). In this case the court made it clear that two factors should be treated as being the 'irreducible minimum by way of legal requirement for a contract of employment to exist', namely control and mutuality of obligation. These two tests have thus now been given a new prominence over and above the other two (integration and economic reality) and any other factors that a tribunal might wish to consider. In short this means that the multiple test must still be applied, but that without clear evidence of employer control over an individual's work and of mutuality of obligation, tribunals must find that no contract of service exits (or existed). An interesting and controversial application of the multiple test is described in Exhibit 3.2.

Exhibit 3.2   *O'Kelly v Trusthouse Forte plc* **(1984)**

In this controversial case the Court of Appeal found that a group of wine waiters employed to work on a casual basis at a hotel were not employed under contracts of service and were thus not entitled to bring claims of unfair dismissal against their former employer. The men concerned worked as 'regular casuals'. They had no fixed hours of work, being called in whenever the permanent staff employed by the hotel were unable to cope with a large banqueting function and required additional assistance. The men were paid a set hourly rate for the work they did through the hotel payroll, tax and national insurance deducted in the same way as other employees. When at the hotel they worked under the direction of banqueting managers and wore uniforms supplied to them. On average they were employed for between thirty and forty hours a week and none had any other job.

When the men became shop stewards of a union and began to recruit members among hotel staff they were offered no further work. They thus brought claims of unfair dismissal to an industrial tribunal on the grounds that they had been unlawfully dismissed for a trade union reason (see Chapter 27).

In considering the case, the tribunal applied the multiple test by identifying a number of factors which suggested the contract was one 'of service' and others which suggested it was 'for services'. Burchell et al (1999:10) list the factors that were considered in this case under three headings:

1 Factors consistent with employee status:

- a lack of financial investment by the applicants in the business
- holiday pay was paid, as well as an incentive based on past service
- the men worked under the control of managers when in the hotel
- the payment of wages weekly in arrears, with deductions being made, through the payroll

2 Factors not inconsistent with employee status:

- the men were only paid for the work they actually performed (ie, no guaranteed weekly pay)
- no regular working hours
- the men were excluded from company sick pay and pension schemes

3 Factors inconsistent with employee status:

- contracts terminable on either side without notice
- the applicants had the right to refuse work
- the company was under no obligation to provide work
- both parties considered the men to be independent contractors (including the men themselves)
- it was recognised custom and practice in the industry to treat casual workers as employed under contracts of service

The tribunal, in finding for the hotel company, placed particular weight on mutuality of obligation, but did consider the other factors too. The Employment Appeals Tribunal then overturned this decision, finding that on balance the factors suggested a contract of service. The Court of Appeal then restored the original tribunal decision on the grounds that it had not in any way erred in its application or interpretation of the law.

Activity 3.2

Oak's Brewery operates a chain of thirty traditional pubs in the south west of England. Over 150 permanent staff are employed, together with a further seventy-five part-timers who work on a casual basis. This latter group provide cover when permanent employees are away because of sickness or holidays. They are also called upon to work odd shifts during the summer period when many of the pubs become busier than usual.

Assume that you have been asked by the brewery's HR Director to prepare a short report outlining the company's existing legal obligations towards the seventy-five casual workers. She also wants you to state how this would change were the brewery to put its relationship with the casual staff on a more formal basis by offering them full contracts of employment.

What would you include in your report?

Establishing worker status

The second major division that exists in terms of determining who has access to employment rights and who does not is that between independent contractors who are considered to be 'workers' and those who are not because they are 'genuinely self-employed'. This is significant only in as far as it establishes whether or not an individual benefits from specific forms of statutory protection (see Exhibit 3.1). In itself, as matters currently stand, there are no wider implications as far as common law rights are concerned.

The term 'worker' appears in several EU directives and has principally entered UK employment law through that route. Employment statutes which are considered to fall within areas of European competence (see Chapter 2) thus generally extend their remit beyond dependent employees working under contracts of service to include independent contractors who are in some form of employment relationship. However, in addition, four significant pieces of UK legislation which do not have a European origin have also been framed to cover 'workers' whether or not they are employed under contracts of service. These are the right to be paid the national minimum wage, the right not to have unlawful deductions made from pay packets (see Chapter 21), the right to be accompanied at a serious disciplinary or grievance hearing (see Chapter 27) and rights under the Public Interest Disclosure Act 1998 (see Chapter 22).

Two different forms of words appear in the statutes. While some commentators (eg, Freedland, 2003:25–26) worry that they may one day be found to mean something different, it is generally agreed that for practical purposes they mean essentially the same thing. The first formation is as follows:

> a contract of service or apprenticeship *or any other contract personally to execute any work or labour.*

These words define the scope of most discrimination law, appearing in the Equality Act 2010, having previously been used to define the scope of rights set out in the Equal Pay Act 1970 (section 1(6)(a)), the Sex Discrimination Act 1975 (section 82(1)), the Race Relations Act 1976 (section 78(1)) and the Disability Discrimination Act 1995 (section 68(1)).

The second form of words is used in the National Minimum Wage Act 1998 (section 54(3)), the Working Time Regulations 1998 (regulation 2.1) and in Part 2 of the Employment Rights Act 1996 (section 230(3)). These are as follows:

> In this Act 'worker' (except in the phrases 'shop worker' and 'betting worker') means an individual who has entered into or works under (or where the employment has ceased, worked under)—
>
> a) a contract of employment or
> b) any other contract, whether express or implied and (if it is express) whether oral or in writing, whereby the individual undertakes to do or perform personally any work or services for another party to the contract whose status is not by virtue of the contract of a client or customer of any profession or business undertaking carried on by the individual;
>
> and any reference to a worker's contract shall be construed accordingly.

Deakin (2001:147) sums up what this means in practice very succinctly:

> With the 'worker', the crucial dividing line is now between those who are economically dependent on the business or undertaking of another (whether they are employees or not), on the one hand, and those who contract through their own business, on the other. This excludes from the 'worker' category three groups: those who do not contract to provide personal services (this leaves out those who contract to supply only a certain end product); those who contract as professionals; and more importantly for present purposes, those who have an undertaking of their own through which they contract with a 'client' or 'customer'.

Essentially, establishing whether someone is a worker or is genuinely self-employed involves applying the economic reality test described above in isolation. The fundamental questions that need to be asked are:

1. is this person in business on their own account? and
2. is this person working for an employer or for a client/customer?

Two cases illustrate how the courts have gone about making this distinction. The first is *Smith (National Minimum Wage Compliance Officer of the Inland Revenue) v Hewitson and another t/a Executive Coach Catering Services* (2001) in which the EAT decided that a group of people were not entitled to the national minimum wage because they were *not* workers. The men and women in question were 'employed' by a catering company to act as stewards on board National Express coaches. They brought their own food supplies and sold these at profit to passengers on the coaches. In this respect their work resembled that of a genuinely self-employed person, there being a degree of financial risk involved for the stewards. However, other features of the arrangement had more in common with those of 'workers'. The stewards were obliged to wear a set uniform (which they hired) and were also obliged to work to an agreed roster if and when they accepted work.

In the case of *Byrne Brothers (Formwork) Ltd v Baird and others* (2002) the EAT came to a different decision when considering whether or not a group of sub-contractors working in the construction industry were entitled to rights under the Working Time Regulations. It was decided that these people were not genuinely self-employed and were instead dependent workers. They had worked for the same employer for some time, they had few if any special-ist skills, they were fully integrated into the workforce, used the employer's equipment and took no economic risk themselves. The only factor that pointed the other way was a 'limited power to appoint substitutes' to work in their place on days when they themselves could not or would not work. The EAT decided that this power 'was not inconsistent with an obliga-tion to provide personal service' because for the vast majority of the time a personal service was in fact provided.

Until a good deal more case law relating to 'worker status' reaches the higher courts, it will not be possible to set out clear guiding principles that managers and legal advisors can use to establish an individual's likely status. However, the broad direction of judgments is becoming clear. Earnshaw et al (2002:11) suggest that it involves making a basic distinction between:

1. an individual who performs services for another

and

2. an individual who provides a service.

The former is a worker; the latter is someone who is genuinely self-employed.

Affected groups

Having set out the principles of the law in this area as it has evolved, we now turn to its practical consequences for the growing number of atypical workers who commonly fall into the 'grey areas' between self-employment, worker status and employee status. The position of the major groups is briefly discussed below.

Casual workers

Hundreds of thousands of people work on a casual basis, often in pubs and restaurants, com-ing in to cover a shift as and when they are required. For some the work is very irregular or limited to a particular season such as the Christmas period. Others work on a casual basis for the same employer over many years, coming in when regular staff are unable to work or when the outlet is especially busy. Sometimes they work at short notice, sometimes they work the same regular weekly hours.

Their position, according to the recent case law, rests heavily on whether or not mutu-ality of obligation exists. If the casual worker is able to turn offers of work down and still reasonably expect to receive further offers in the future then it can now be said with some confidence that he/she is not as an employee for the purposes of employment law. The same is true of any arrangement, whether in writing or not, in which the employer is under no obligation to offer work and the staff are under no obligation to accept it.

Although the principle has been less commonly tested in the courts, it is apparent that most casual staff would be classed as 'workers' for employment law purposes. The organisa-tions they work for by and large control their activities when they are at work and act as employers rather than as customers. They are at work to perform a service on behalf of the employer and not to provide a service to the employer.

Activity 3.3 *Carmichael and another v National Power plc (1999)*

In November 1989 Mrs Carmichael and Mrs Leese applied for jobs at Blythe Power Stations in Northumberland as tour guides. The job required them to 'supervise parties of visitors on pre-selected tour routes around the power station site'. The work was part-time but had no fixed hours. Instead the women would be called whenever parties of tourists were expected and were paid on an hourly basis by credit transfer, tax and national insurance being deducted. Their pay increased in accordance with the terms of the relevant collective agreement and they were invited to apply for shares in National Power on the same basis as other employees when the company was privatised. They did not, however, receive sick pay or holiday pay, and were not entitled to join the company pension scheme. Nor were they party to the company's discipline and grievance procedures. In some weeks they worked as many as twenty-five hours, in others as few as four hours. It was made clear to them in their offer letters that the employment was being offered 'on a casual as required basis' and that formal training would be provided.

In 1995 they asked their employer to provide them with written particulars of their terms and conditions of employment (ie, a section 1 statement). This request was refused on the grounds that they were not employees working under contracts of service and that they were not therefore legally entitled to such a statement. The women disagreed with this and so decided to make an application to an industrial tribunal (now known as employment tribunals).

They were unsuccessful at the tribunal on the grounds that their case 'founders on the rock of absence of mutuality'. On several occasions both women had turned down offers of work, only to be invited to attend again in future weeks. They had not been disciplined for refusing these offers. They then appealed first to the Employment Appeals Tribunal (EAT), who also found in favour of the employer, and then to the Court of Appeal.

At this stage the women were successful. The Court of Appeal found, by a majority, that there was mutuality of obligation via an 'umbrella contract' because 'there was an obligation to accept and perform some reasonable amount of work for the power station'. Moreover, most other features of the relationship were consistent with a contract of service.

The employer then appealed to the House of Lords and won the case. The industrial tribunal had, according to their Lordships, made the right decision in the first place. The offer letters and acceptances 'did no more than provide a framework for a series of successive ad hoc contracts of service or for services which the parties might subsequently make', and therefore 'when they were not working as guides they were not in any contractual relationship' with the employer.

Questions

1 Why do you think the parties decided, at considerable cost, to pursue a case that concerned the right to receive a statement of terms and conditions right up to the House of Lords? Why did they not settle the matter at an earlier stage?

2 Why do you think the judgment of the House of Lords in this case was controversial and the subject of much adverse criticism in the press?

3 Do you think that the law is right to place so much emphasis on mutuality of obligation when deciding whether or not someone is an employee? What alternative approaches would you prefer to see taken?

Sub-contractors employed on a long-term basis

When a self-employed person, such as an IT specialist, is employed for three or four months on a sub-contracted or freelance basis, the relationship is unlikely to constitute a contract of service. The IT specialist is hired on a self-employed basis to carry out a particular programme of work.

Such people are also likely to be 'genuinely self-employed' and to see themselves as being in business on their own account. They are providing a service for a client and not performing a service on behalf of an employer. But what happens when the relationship becomes more long-term, particularly if it is exclusive? What is the situation after six months, a year or three years? Does the 'IT contractor' ever become an 'IT worker' or even an 'IT employee' and, if so, when exactly?

The answer is that it is quite possible in theory for status to change as the reality of the relationship changes, notwithstanding the existence of written agreements employing someone on a self-employed basis. This was the conclusion of the EAT in *Byrne Brothers (Formwork) Ltd v Baird* (2002) which concerned labour only contractors working in the building trade. The court decided that they were in effect 'workers' despite having signed contracts which clearly identified them as working on a self-employed basis and paying tax as self-employed persons. Central were the findings that the men provided a personal service (ie, performed the job themselves) and secondly that they were not 'carrying on a business undertaking'. Factors of relevance in determining this second point were the degree of exclusivity (was the contractor obliged to work for the one employer for an indefinite or significant period?), the extent to which control was exercised over their work and whether or not payment was made on a time basis.

Homeworkers

It was once thought that the advent of internet technologies would make us into a nation of homeworkers or 'teleworkers' as we took the opportunity to avoid commuting into offices and based ourselves at home for much of the working week instead. This has not happened in practice, but a small and growing minority of the UK workforce (around 3%) do now work wholly or mainly from home. In many cases they work exclusively for one employer, carrying out duties that could equally well be done in an office or factory and may previously have been. Others work for long periods for one or two clients. What is their employment status? Do they have the same employment rights as anyone else would doing similar work on an employer's premises?

The answer appears to be yes. When reaching a decision about their status the same tests are applied to homeworkers as to any other group whose status is ambiguous, but the courts have been more willing to find that homeworkers are employees than has been the case with other atypical groups. This was so in *Airfix Footwear v Cope* (1978) and in *Nethermere (St Neots) Ltd v Taverna* (1984) in which individuals who had long-standing relationships with single employers were found to be employed under contracts of service. Despite working away from their respective factories, the same level of quality control was exercised and there was found to be mutuality of obligation.

Office holders

Many people who fall into this category hold offices which are paid but which only take up a relatively small part of their working lives. They may sit as trustees on a board or hold some public office as a member of a quango, or serve on tribunals or as arbitrators. Trade union officials are office holders, as are clergymen. The world of education employs office holders to act as examiners and moderators of various kinds, while non-executive directors are employed to advise and oversee the activities of all the major corporations. Police officers are still considered to be office holders, while as a result of legal action in the 1980s, this is no longer true of prison officers. Some of these people derive either all or a fair proportion of their income from such offices, but what is their employment status?

It is possible for office holders to be employees, provided the usual tests outlined above apply, but the case law suggests that in most cases they do not work under contracts of service. In some cases (eg, non-executive directors) this is because they are not subject to the control of the employer in any way, in others it is because the appointment is to 'be something' rather than to 'do something' and that no contract of employment therefore exists. Antell (2002) states that most office holders, in practice, are not employees. Most, however, are treated as such for tax and national insurance purposes.

Whether or not office holders are workers depends on whether or not they work under a contract. If the work is paid and has been offered by an employer and accepted by the office holder, then a contract will normally exist, but this is not always the case. People who are elected to an office will not usually have a contract, the same being true of ministers of religion (with the exception of employed ministers such as hospital chaplains). These latter groups have very little protection in employment law terms, working neither under contracts of service nor contracts for services. Some are nonetheless protected to an extent through other pieces of legislation such as the Police Act 1996 and the Companies Acts of 1985 and 2006, or through procedural arrangements set up by their organisations. The Church of England, for example, announced in 2004 that it was henceforth going to observe unfair dismissal provisions in respect of its clergy. Public officials are able to apply for judicial review of decisions made by government bodies that have adversely affected them.

Agency workers

Temping agencies of one kind or another have expanded rapidly in recent years, moving into areas well beyond the traditional provision of secretarial and clerical staff. Nurse banks have become significant businesses as have agencies who supply other highly qualified personnel on a temporary basis. These organisations are subject to a great deal of regulation, but what is the position of the temps themselves as regards basic employment rights? Are they employees or just workers? And if they are employees, who is their employer, is it the agency that supplies them and pays their weekly wages, or is it the organisation which directs their day-to-day work?

The precise legal position has been unclear for some time and remains confusing. There has been a huge amount of case law in this area in recent years leaving employers, agencies and the people who work for them uncertain about what rights they have. The fundamental problem arises from the fact that it is the agency which contracts with the workers/employees but it is not the agency which controls their day-to-day work. Control is exercised by the client (referred to in employment law as the 'end user') who has a contract with the agency, but not with the worker/employee. Over the years the courts have applied themselves to resolving this problem and have come out with apparently different decisions in different cases. In 2008, however, thanks to a ruling by the Court of Appeal in *James v Greenwich Borough Council*, a degree of much needed clarity was restored.

The confusion started in 2002. Until then agency workers had not succeeded in showing that they could be employees working under contracts of service. They were, however, generally able to establish 'worker' status, sometimes in respect of the agency and sometimes of the client depending on the facts. In *Montgomery v Johnson Underwood Ltd* (2002), the Court of Appeal appeared to decide that an agency worker had no contract with either the agency or the client company for which she actually worked (Freedland, 2003:34). In law she thus met the definition of a 'worker' but had no employer against whom she could bring her case. This appeared to put at least some agency workers outside the protection of all employment legislation which does not specifically include them (including the Working Time Regulations and the National Minimum Wage Act). The situation was then thrown into further confusion by the decision of the Court of Appeal in *Brook Street Bureau Ltd v Dacas* (2004) in which one of the judges stated in his ruling that there *could* be circumstances in which an agency worker was the *employee* of an end-user and that it could not simply be assumed that all agency staff were not employed under contracts of service by the client organisations in which they actually performed their work.

Following the *Dacas* case a series of cases came before the courts, some being appealed to the EAT and Court of Appeal, litigants trying to establish in exactly what circumstances agency staff could be said to be employees of the end-users they worked for. Most of these cases concerned the right not to be unfairly dismissed, involving situations where workers provided by agencies had clocked up over a year's service with the one client and were then dismissed summarily without notice. While the courts found in favour of the agency staff in one or two cases (eg, *Cable & Wireless Plc v Muscat* (2006)), in most cases the employer won. Finally in 2008 the Court of Appeal got an opportunity to clarify some of these issues. The judgment in *James v Greenwich Borough Council* distinguished the facts of the various earlier cases that had caused confusion. Here the judges ruled clearly that a typical triangular agency relationship in which an agency supplies a client organisation with a member of staff cannot lead to an employment relationship existing between the worker and the end-user. This will only be the case in unusual circumstances such as those that applied in Mr Muscat's case where the agency worker had previously worked in the capacity of an employee for the end-user for many years before returning on an agency basis.

The *James* ruling was deeply disappointing for those who campaign for more rights for agency workers—a growing group who often do not enjoy anything like as many employment rights as the employees they usually work alongside. Their position has been improved to an extent by the Agency Workers Regulations 2010 which give effect in the UK to the European Union's Temporary Workers Directive. It gives agency workers the same rights as permanent employees whom they work alongside in respect of their pay, working time, holiday and maternity leave, once they have completed twelve weeks' work with an end-user. However, their overall employment status does not change as a result of these regulations. It thus remains the case that agency workers, except in unusual circumstances, do not qualify for unfair dismissal rights however long they remain continuously employed by the same end-user.

Exhibit 3.3   **Who is the employer?**

It is not just agency workers who often experience confusion in identifying exactly who they work for and what responsibilities are owed to them by whom (if at all). Earnshaw et al (2002) and Stone (2004) describe several other types of situation in which the question of who exactly is the employer is blurred:

- Situations in which a public sector organisation outsources services such as cleaning and catering to private sector companies. The staff often work under the direction of managers employed by the public authority, despite being employed by a private company.

- Private finance initiatives involve public and private sector organisations working in partnership to deliver large-scale capital projects. Once built, the new hospital, prison or road is owned by a private sector consortium which recoups some of its investment by charging the public authority for cleaning, maintenance or administration services. Situations can thus arise in which employees of a private company take orders from managers of the public authority, who also judge their individual performance.

- Call centre operations in which individual staff are assigned to carry out a service on behalf of a particular client over a prolonged period. They work in the call centre which employs them, but carry out work for a client to specifications set and monitored by the client. Indeed, in many cases, it is a requirement that the client's customers believe the call centre staff to be part of that company.

- Multi-employer sites such as airports in which people employed for hundreds of different separate organisations work alongside one another, the operating systems being managed and overseen by the airport's management. A very high degree of co-ordination is necessary. But who has ultimate authority to dismiss someone (for a security breach for example)? Who is responsible for health and safety? Who judges an employee's performance?

- Franchise operations involve a large organisation permitting individuals or smaller companies to operate its branches according to tightly defined specifications. Restaurants, pubs and post offices are frequently run by franchisees who pay a fee for the privilege. But are franchisees employees, workers or self-employed people? And who employs their staff?

Trainees

People who are taken on in a training capacity form another group about whom there is significant ambiguity. Those who are employed under a formal contract of 'apprenticeship' are not employees but nonetheless enjoy most of the same statutory protection (see IDS, 2008). But there are thousands of people employed by organisations under other forms of training contract. Many owe their positions to government youth training schemes, but are paid a basic wage by the employer for whom they work. Do they enjoy all the major employment rights or just those that are provided for workers? Or is it possible that they are neither workers nor employees?

The answer, in most cases, appears to be that they are neither workers nor employees. In the case of those placed with an employer under a government scheme, the courts have decided that the rules of the relationship are determined by state agencies and can thus not be considered to amount to contracts agreed between the trainee and the employer (see Deakin & Morris, 2003:169–170). Outside the government schemes the position is less clear cut, but in a further prominent case (*Edmonds v Lawson* (2000)), it was also found that the trainee (in this case a pupil barrister) was neither an employee nor a worker, and was thus not entitled to the national minimum wage. The Court of Appeal held that there was no mutuality of obligation and that any work she carried out for the members of her set of chambers was done in the capacity of a professional working for a client. There was no worker's contract, just a training contract.

Trainees, however, are not denied all employment rights. Despite their ambiguous contractual status they are specifically covered by the Working Time Regulations, health and safety law and much discrimination law.

Reforming the law on employment status

The law as it currently stands in this area is clearly most unsatisfactory. With the growth of service industries and knowledge work more and more people find that they derive some, if not all of their income, from atypical forms of employment. Outsourcing, sub-contracting and agency working are all becoming more common, meaning that a greater proportion of the population each year falls into one of two categories:

1. jobs which fall into the 'grey area' between employment and self-employment described above

2. jobs for which it is not clear exactly who is the employer, and hence against whom legal action could be taken.

The law, while developing steadily over many years, has not kept pace with these more far-reaching, contemporary labour market developments. We thus have a situation in which we are increasingly obliged to apply in the modern context principles of employment law formulated to meet the requirements of a past era.

As a result major groups within the workforce are left unsure of exactly which, if any, of the major employment rights apply to them. For employers there is also considerable uncertainty. In many cases they cannot know what legal obligations they have taken on when they hire someone. What is written on the contract or letter of appointment, as we have seen from the case law, can mean little or nothing when a court comes to decide whether an individual is to be classed as an employee, worker or self-employed person. The same is also true of the taxation arrangements. This can give rise to a situation in which even the best of employers, seeking to meet all their legal obligations, can unwittingly find themselves to have acted unlawfully.

More worryingly is the potential for some employers to take advantage of the confused situation and exploit it to their own unfair advantage. Harvey (2001) analyses the way that, in his view, this has happened in the construction industry over many years. The practice of employing builders and other workers via sub-contractors on 'bogus' self-employed contracts has very serious consequences which Harvey describes as 'scandalous'. First, there are losses to the Exchequer that derive from the way that builders are wrongly categorised as self-employed contractors and hence not subject to employer national insurance contributions and able to take advantage of tax rules that are not available to employed persons. Harvey estimates the total direct annual loss to the Treasury to be around £1.5 billion. Secondly, the practice means that workers are effectively denied significant employment rights such as those deriving from unfair dismissal law because they perceive that they are not themselves qualified to bring claims. Thirdly, the fact that so many construction workers are classed as self-employed means that accidents involving them frequently go unrecorded and are thus not reported to the Health and Safety Executive. Harvey (2001:9–10) claims that nineteen out of every twenty workplace accidents involving self-employed construction workers are never recorded because legal responsibility for doing so rests with self-employed persons themselves and not with the construction firm that employs them. Moreover, because these people are self-employed they have no right to industrial compensation for any injuries that they sustain at work.

Above all though, the major defect with the status quo as far as the law on employment status is concerned is simply that millions of working people who are to all intents and purposes in a dependent employment relationship and are not in reality 'independent contractors' are denied the same standard statutory and contractual employment rights that are enjoyed by the majority of the working population. Most casual workers can never claim unfair dismissal, however long they have served their employers and however just their claim might be. Agency workers are denied the right to take paid maternity leave, parental leave or even the right to request to work flexibly simply because, in most cases, they are not considered to be dependent employees. Many office holders and trainees have no basic employment rights at all beyond those recently introduced as a result of the EU directives on age, sexual orientation and religion or belief.

Government intentions

At one stage it appeared as if the government had every intention of reforming this area of employment law. In the 'Fairness at Work' white paper published by the incoming Blair government in 1998 it was acknowledged that the coverage of individual employment rights in the UK did not reflect 'the modern world of work'. Indeed, the early employment legislation passed by the government, such as the Working Time Regulations 1998 and the National Minimum Wage Act 1998, specifically included all 'workers' rather than just 'employees' within its remit. Then in the Employment Relations Act 1999 a section was included which permits the Secretary of State to extend *by regulation* the coverage of existing statutory employment rights to groups who have hitherto been uncovered. This means that ministers could in the future, without the need to take fresh legislation through Parliament, simply declare particular groups to be 'employees' or 'workers' for the purposes of employment law. Ministers commissioned a report into the issue in 2001, but brought forward no proposals (Wedderburn, 2007:410). As of 2011 it remained the case that no extensions of employment rights to groups in the 'worker category' had been introduced and no proposals to do so were anywhere on ministerial agendas.

Indeed, in recent years we have seen a return to regulations which are limited in their scope to employees only. The right to request flexible working arrangements, the right to take parental leave and rights for fixed-term employees are conspicuous examples.

The reasons for governmental caution in this area were effectively conveyed in a 'discussion document on employment status in relation to statutory employment rights' published by the then Department of Trade and Industry in 2002. Here it was suggested that employment rights must not be extended so much as to reduce the willingness of employers to create atypical jobs such as those discussed above. Ministers then and now regularly express concern that if too many employment rights are given to groups such as casual workers, office holders, trainees and agency workers, then the growth of these kinds of jobs will be threatened. This would be damaging for the economy both because it could lead to increased unemployment, and because such jobs are perceived to attract people into the labour market (particularly parents of younger children) who might otherwise choose not to work. Moreover, they are concerned that existing atypical workers who enjoy a greater degree of flexibility at work because of their contractual arrangements might be required to work less flexibly or to demonstrate greater commitment were they to be re-designated 'employees' and given commensurate employment rights. Aside from these, there are the usual concerns about the cost burden for industry and for small businesses in particular.

 **Activity 3.4**

To what extent do you agree with the concerns that have been identified by the government about the possible practical implications of extending employment rights to uncovered groups?

Would fewer new jobs be created? Would employers require people to work less flexibly and show greater commitment? Would it result in problematic cost increases for employers?

Prescriptions for reform

Labour law academics have long called for reform of the law on employment status, but have tended to differ somewhat in their views about the extent and nature of the changes that are necessary or desirable. It is useful to consider the various prescriptions that have been put forward as falling within two broad schools of thought that can be labelled 'moderate' and 'radical'.

The moderate proposals essentially involve extending to all *workers* most, if not all, the statutory employment rights that are currently available only to *employees*. Deakin (2001:150–151) argues for a step-by-step approach, starting with those which can be described as constituting accepted human rights. Top of his list is protection from unfair dismissal for 'inadmissible reasons' (see Chapter 12). Many of these (eg, dismissals on grounds of pregnancy, race or disability) already apply to people in the 'worker category' through anti-discrimination legislation, but some do not. Notable examples are dismissals on grounds of trade union membership, official industrial action and spent convictions. Deakin goes on to argue for the extension to all workers of rights 'which do not depend in any way upon regularity and length of service'. These include the national minimum wage and working time rights, which already apply in principle to most people in the worker category, and the full range of health and safety rights, which do not.

Wholesale extension of employment rights beyond employees to encompass a wider group would involve retaining the principle of a binary divide between those who are and those who are not protected, but shifting the boundary so that it is no longer focused around the division between a 'contract of service' and a 'contract for services'. Instead, it is commonly argued, the divide should clearly be between those who are either dependent or semi-dependent on an employer and those who are genuinely in business on their own account (ie, quite clearly self-employed). Freedland (2003: 27–35 & 2006) and Freedland and Kountouris (2011) call for the replacement of the notion of a 'contract of service' with that of a 'personal employment contract' or 'personal work nexus' which is defined as 'comprising contracts for employment or work to be carried out normally in person and not in the conduct of an independent business or professional practice'. In practice this would encompass those currently located in the worker category as well as those working under contracts of service.

Harvey (2001:52) and Collins et al (2001:180) agree that the line should be drawn between economic dependence and independence, the coverage of employment law 'ending' at this point and commercial law taking over as the basis for the regulation of relationships. Harvey goes on to argue that the legal test that should be used to establish on which side of the line an individual falls should be an extended version of the 'economic reality test' described above. He suggests that existing HMRC rules already provide a list of questions that could be used for this purpose. The result would be a situation in which almost anyone who was not genuinely self-employed (eg, office holders, trainees, casual workers, agency workers, sub-contractors) would gain the full range of basic employment rights currently restricted only to 'employees'.

More radical proposals for change include the case made by Davies and Freedland (2000:278–281) for an extension of some employment rights beyond the ranks of employees and a group they refer to as 'employee-like' (ie, workers) to encompass some self-employed people as well. In particular, they argue that basic protection from discrimination on unlawful grounds and the health and safety statutes are just as necessary to protect self-employed people as they are for dependent workers. The authors focus on these areas of employment law on the grounds that 'in both cases the existence of a dependent work relationship does not form a crucial part of the arguments in favour of the imposition of liability'. Davies and Freedland acknowledge that extending employment law beyond the ranks of employed persons would be problematic, but argue that procedurally labour law courts are well placed, because of their experience, to make decisions in these fields.

More radical still are the ideas discussed by Supiot (2001:50–52) and Collins (2003:42–45) which involve profound 're-institutionalisation' of the employment relationship, and indeed of employment law. These and other authors are effectively calling for the abandonment of systems of employment law which are built on the foundation of the employment contract. Collins et al (1991:180–181) put the case for reform as follows:

> The major source of the difficulty in determining the proper scope of employment regulation is the flexibility accorded by freedom of contract for the parties to shape their economic relation in any way that they wish. To hire people through the labour market, there is no requirement to adopt a standard form arrangement, or even to comply with a few different models. The effect is that regulation is always chasing the variety of contractual forms in order to achieve the desired scope of application.

Instead, it is argued that the state, through statutes, codes of practice and definitions of minimum standards, should define exactly what constitutes an employment relationship. Terms and conditions, instead of being determined by the parties through a contract, would effectively be determined by the law. An employer offering an individual a job would thus be mandated to honour not their contractual agreement, but a set of standards defined in employment law.

Advocates of this approach acknowledge that 'a one size fits all approach' in which a single set of labour standards and rules governed all employment relationships would be impractical for many organisations and industries in which different norms have been established over decades. Some flexibility would thus be necessary. One approach advocated by Collins (2003) would involve the state setting the core standards, but allowing organisations to derogate partially and to establish their own alternatives through some form of collective agreement. This already happens to an extent in the case of the parental leave and working time regulations (see Chapters 20 and 26) where the government has drawn up a default scheme which sets out how the regulations should be applied in the absence of a workplace agreement that puts in place some alternative.

Another possibility would be for the state, through employment legislation, to define a number of different types of employment relationship, each with its own minimum standards with which all would be required to comply. The French system, in which everyone is hired into one of five categories, has moved in this direction (see Perulli, 2011). Workers in France are either classed as being 'continuously employed', 'fixed-term employees', 'temporary employees' (which includes agency workers), 'trainees' or 'independents'. In each case employers are obliged to adhere to detailed codes setting out required standards. Finally, Collins et al (2001:181) suggest that an alternative approach might simply involve prohibiting certain forms of contractual relationship, otherwise allowing employers and employees full scope to reach their own agreements as at present.

 Activity 3.5

Look back through the chapter at the facts and decisions in the cases of *O'Kelly*, *Carmichael* and *Edmonds*.

Questions

1 Which of these do you think would have had a different outcome if the economic reality test had been applied in isolation?

2 To what extent do you agree that the other tests of employment status (control, integration and mutuality of obligation) should be abandoned when determining whether or not someone should have access to statutory employment rights?

Multiple employer scenarios

Where employees (or workers) work in environments in which they are subject to the control of more than one organisation (see Exhibit 3.3) the problem is less one of employment status and more one of determining which, if any, of the employers who direct their work carry legal responsibility as far as employment law is concerned. A possible solution to this confusing state of affairs which would ensure that all were properly protected would involve designating both (or all three/four) employers as jointly responsible. If the reality of the situation is that someone has more than one employer, then surely that should be reflected in the regulatory arrangements. An interesting possible approach is advocated by Earnshaw et al (2002:43–4):

> We could indeed envisage that the answer to the question 'Who is the employer?' should depend on the reason for the question being asked. For instance, if the question arises because an employee has been injured at work, the person who should be deemed to be the employer is the one who has greater control over the working environment and input into devising the relevant systems of work. If, on the other hand, the employee seeks redress in respect of the loss of his or her job, one should consider not only who has the right to discipline, but who in reality has the greater influence over that person's job tenure.

Freedland (2003:40) also addresses this issue. His suggested approach would involve each employer being designated as responsible for one of four functions and thus taking responsibility for any legal claim that might arise in relation to these. The four are as follows:

1. engaging workers for employment and terminating their employment;
2. remunerating workers and providing them with other benefits of employment;
3. managing the employment relation and the process of work; and
4. using the worker's services in a process of production or service provision.

For example, where an agency worker worked for some time in a host organisation it could be established that the agency was the employer as far as functions 1 and 2 were concerned, but that the host organisation was the employer in respect of functions 3 and 4. It would then follow that a claim of unfair dismissal or unlawful deduction of wages would be brought against the agency, but that a personal injury claim or a claim of sexual harassment would be brought against the host organisation.

Deakin (2007) has argued for the establishment of a new 'conceptual alphabet' to help achieve a situation in which employers in agency or other multi-employer scenarios can

 Activity 3.6 *Motorola Ltd v Davidson and Melville Craig Group Ltd*

In a decision that ran against the trend in cases about agency workers, the EAT found against Motorola in this case. The facts were as follows:

Mr Davidson worked as a mobile telephone repairer. He was hired by an agency called Melville Craig who employed him on a 'contract for services' basis and paid him a salary when he was working for their clients. Melville Craig assigned Mr Davidson to work for Motorola, which he did for some years. He used Motorola's tools in carrying out his duties, wore a Motorola uniform and worked under their managers' control. When he wanted to take holidays he agreed this with his Motorola supervisor, to whom he was told to take any grievances he might have. The contract between Motorola and Melville Craig gave the client the right to 'return' Mr Davidson if his work was deemed by them to be 'unsatisfactory'. When later his conduct was called into question, Motorola informed both Mr Davidson and Melville Craig that his assignment would be terminated with immediate effect.

Mr Davidson then brought a case of unfair dismissal against Motorola. The company's defence was based on the claim that as Melville Craig was Mr Davidson's legal employer they were not liable. Mr Davidson won his claim at the employment tribunal and subsequently in the EAT. Motorola was found to have exerted sufficient control over Mr Davidson for it to be classed as his employer.

Questions

1 To what extent do you agree that the EAT's decision in this case was fair in all the circumstances?

2 Why do you think Mr Davidson chose to bring his claim for unfair dismissal against Motorola, given that his contract was clearly with Melville Craig?

3 Were the law on multiple employer scenarios to be changed along the lines advocated by Earnshaw et al (2002), Freedland (2003) and Deakin (2007), how might the outcome of future cases like this one be affected?

know exactly what their areas of responsibility are. He points out that in areas of health and safety law this principle has already been established, there being different duties placed in law on 'principals' (ie, agents) and 'users of labour'. Were this to prove too complex—it would after all require the redrafting of many Acts of Parliament and other statutory instruments—Deakin (2007) suggests that two or more employing entities could simply be made jointly and severally liable.

Continuity of employment

The length of time for which a claimant has been continuously employed in the same employment is legally significant for three reasons. First, and most importantly for our purposes in this chapter, there are some employment rights enforced in employment tribunals that are only available to employees who have completed six months, a year or four years' service with their employers. Secondly, the length of continuous service claimants have completed is used to calculate the level of compensation they are awarded if they win unfair dismissal cases. Finally, redundancy payments are also calculated according to length of service with the employer who is making the redundancies. The major employment rights that require continuity of employment are the following:

- a week's notice—requires one month's service
- request flexible working—requires six months' service
- statutory maternity pay (SMP)—requires six months' service
- paternity leave—requires six months' service
- adoption leave—requires six months' service
- unfair dismissal—requires twelve months' service (2 years after April 2012)
- parental leave—requires twelve months' service
- statutory redundancy payments—require two years' service
- fixed-term contract becomes permanent—requires four years' service

The substance of each of these employment rights will be discussed later in the book. Our focus here is purely on how the law defines and interprets the requirement for continuity of employment itself.

There are three major legal issues that tribunals sometimes need to consider:

1. disputes over the date at which a period of employment started or ended
2. questions about the maintenance of continuity when the employer changes
3. issues about the maintenance of continuity when there are breaks in service.

The first two of these are straightforward and can be explained concisely. The third is more complex and involved, much depending on the reasons for and the length of a particular break in service. We will now look at each in turn.

Start and end dates

In the absence of any written evidence to confirm when someone's employment started, and where the two parties in a case disagree about the precise date, an employment tribunal simply listens to the evidence put forward on each side and decides who (claimant or respondent) it is

Exhibit 3.4   **Unfair dismissal—the one-year rule**

Ever since unfair dismissal law first came onto our statute books in 1971 there has been disagreement about how long the qualifying period should be—that is the length of continuous service that an employee must have completed before being able to claim.

Over the years it has varied, being six months for a period in the late 1970s, then two years and then one year. During the 1980s part-timers had to wait five years before they were able to bring an unfair dismissal claim.

At the time of writing (2011) the government is consulting on the question of whether the qualifying period should go back to two years. This will happen from April 2012.

The main argument made for extending the period is that doing so removes a significant disincentive for employers (particularly small ones) to hire staff. The one-year rule, it is believed, served to keep unemployment higher than it could be while also deterring employers from growing their businesses.

The main arguments agianst change and retaining the one-year rule are based on social justice. Why should an employer be free to dismiss at will and destroy someone's livelihood when they have demonstrated competence in their roles over a period of several months. In most other EU countries, after all, a period of just three or six months is the most common that is used.

Interestingly, however, an argument can be put from the employees' perspective in favour of moving back to a two-year qualifying period. This is based on the perception that many employers now routinely dismiss people after eleven months' service when they have yet to decide whether or not the individual concerned will make a good long-term employee. There is a tendency in such situations to err on the side of caution and dismiss before unfair dismissal rights kick in at the twelve-month mark. Such employees would have longer to prove themselves under a two-year rule.

more inclined to believe. The burden of proof in such cases is on the employee/ex-employee, so the assumption is that claimants do not have sufficient continuity of service unless they can satisfy the tribunal, on the balance of probabilities, that they do.

Another type of situation that arises from time to time is when an offer letter or contract of employment states that the employment started on a particular date, but that work actually began on a different date. It may be in the interests either of the claimant or the respondent to make such a claim, because it may lengthen or shorten the time that has passed since the contractual start date. According to IDS (2001:5) the principle in cases such as this was established by the EAT in *General of the Salvation Army v Dewesbury* (1984) in which, due to a bank holiday weekend, there was a discrepancy between Ms Dewesbury's actual start date and the date on which her employment was stated to have started in her offer letter. The decision was that the relevant date should be the day on which the contract started to run, namely the date in the offer letter and not the one she actually began to start work. It mattered a great deal in this case because it meant that Ms Dewesbury was permitted to pursue her claim of unfair dismissal. She had not worked for twelve months at the time of her dismissal, but she had been employed under a contract of service for twelve months at that point.

The date a job ended can also be significant, and hence an issue of dispute, in unfair dismissal cases and when the size of a redundancy payment is to be calculated. For unfair dismissal the key phrase is 'the effective date of termination' which means the date the employment came to an end, not the date on which work ceased. So where someone leaves early, for example, because they have accumulated holiday, or where they are given notice, the effective date is the day on which the contract comes to an end—even if they actually stopped turning up for work some weeks earlier. The only exception to this is in cases of gross misconduct when a contract is lawfully terminated without notice. In such cases the effective date of termination is the date on which the employee was actually dismissed. In the case of redundancy payments the key phrase is 'the relevant date' which will usually be the same as the 'effective date of termination' but can differ in one or two types of situation. An example is a situation in which redundant employees leave without working their contractual notice. We deal with this and other related issues in Chapter 6.

Employer changes

Under normal circumstances when an employee leaves one employment and starts another, whether or not there is a break in service, continuity of employment is broken and the clock starts ticking again as far as gaining access to the above employment rights is concerned. But there are some exceptions to this general rule which affect many people.

The most important exception concerns associated companies. Employees moving from employer to employer within a group of companies enjoy continuity of service provided they move directly from the one job and into the other. What is important is that the two companies concerned are controlled by the same party. So movement between two companies both of which are controlled by a third company is covered, as is movement from a subsidiary to a controlling company or vice versa. In the first of these two situations the controlling party does not have to be a company for continuity to be protected, but will be in the vast majority of cases. There is extensive case law on what type of bodies are to be considered 'companies' for the purposes of this law. The situation is somewhat complex because in some circumstances the courts have moved away from their earlier established view that only limited companies are covered. Partnerships and overseas subsidiaries of one kind or another are now included (see IDS, 2001:105–114).

It is clear that local authorities, health authorities and NHS Trusts are not 'companies' and that movement between these types of public body does not bring with it continuity of employment except in relatively few situations. Different statutes have an impact here, specifying in what circumstances continuity should be preserved in the public sector. An example is where health service employees move from trust to trust in order to complete a programme of professional training. Continuity is also preserved when teachers move from school to school within the same local education authority. Moreover, for the purposes of redundancy payments only, continuity is preserved when employees move jobs from one local government employer to another.

The other major type of situation in which continuity is preserved despite a change in employer occurs when an employing organisation, or part of an employing organisation (business, partnership, public sector body or whatever) changes hands. The identity of the employer may change in such circumstances, but the Transfer of Undertakings (Protection of Employment) (TUPE) Regulations ensure that the employees' former service prior to the take-over is recognised as far as employment rights are concerned. The law on TUPE is notoriously complex, as we will see in Chapter 23, and there are some situations in which the precise position as regards continuity of employment is not clear. However, it is safe to conclude at this stage that continuity does continue as of right when employees transfer along with the body which employs them from one controlling body to another.

Breaks in service

It is common for two periods of employment with the same employer to be interrupted by a break in service of some kind. The effect on someone's continuity of employment, and hence their ability to claim core employment rights, varies depending on the particular circumstances. It is possible to identify three distinct categories of impact as far as continuity is concerned. These are illustrated in Figure 3.3. The first (Situation A) is one in which continuity continues but in which the period of absence does not 'count' towards the total. A break of two months during a period of twelve months' service is thus treated by the law as if it were just ten months' continuous service. The period of the break is thus effectively deducted from the total length of service.

The second category (Situation B) is one in which continuity continues despite the break in service and in which the relevant period of absence also counts as employment for legal purposes. The law thus treats the break in service as if it had not happened at all. Finally there is Situation C in which the break in service represents a clean break in service. One contract ends and another starts after the break comes to an end.

Situation A is the rarest of the three, applying principally when employees go on strike. If subsequently it is necessary to determine whether or not someone can claim unfair dismissal, or if a redundancy payment has to be calculated, the approach used is simply to assume that the employment began later than it actually did. So if an employee was on strike for three months in the middle of his first year's service, he is treated as if he has only completed nine months in that employment come the anniversary of his start date. He will thus only be eligible to bring a claim of unfair dismissal to an employment tribunal after completing fifteen months of service. According to IDS (2001: 69–70) exactly the same situation applies when an employee is a member of the reserve forces and is called up for military service. The Reserve Forces (Safeguard of Employment) Act 1985 ensures that reservists come back into the same employment following

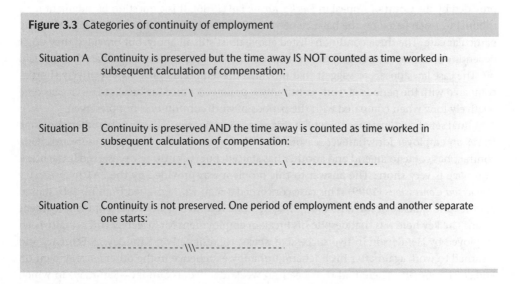

Figure 3.3 Categories of continuity of employment

Situation A   Continuity is preserved but the time away IS NOT counted as time worked in subsequent calculation of compensation:

Situation B   Continuity is preserved AND the time away is counted as time worked in subsequent calculations of compensation:

Situation C   Continuity is not preserved. One period of employment ends and another separate one starts:

a period of call-up with their continuity preserved, but without the weeks they were away being counted in the calculation of any subsequent redundancy payments.

Situation B is very common. It applies, for example, during periods of maternity leave or most periods of sickness because the contract of employment remains in place. Occasionally, however, employees will either resign or be dismissed due to ill health and then be rehired a few weeks later when they have fully recovered. In such situations, provided the absence is caused by an illness, continuity of employment is preserved for up to twenty-six weeks. So, provided the employment restarts within six months, the law effectively treats the absence as not having occurred as far as continuity rights are concerned.

The legal position is more complex in cases of temporary lay-offs when an employee is temporarily dismissed because there is insufficient work available to do, but is rehired a few weeks or months later. The rule here (section 212(3)b of the Employment Rights Act 1996) is that continuity is preserved provided three conditions are in place:

1. the lay-off is due to a 'cessation of work', by which is meant there is insufficient work for the person concerned to perform
2. this cessation is known to be temporary
3. the reason for the employee's absence is the cessation in work.

Interestingly the same approach is taken when someone is hired on a succession of fixed-term contracts with breaks during periods in which there is no work to perform. The leading case here is *Ford v Warwickshire County Council* (1983) in which a teacher was employed for nine years on a series of temporary contracts. Each September Mrs Ford was hired only for the academic year, effectively being laid off the following July. In this case the House of Lords ruled that for the purposes of her employment rights she had been employed continuously for nine years and not for just nine months.

Matters are less predictable when the pattern of work is less regular and the gaps in employment longer than was the case in *Ford v Warwickshire County Council*. What happens when over a duration of some years a person is *intermittently* employed by one employer when there is work to do, but regularly laid off for periods of time when the work ceases? The answer was provided by the Court of Appeal in *Flack v Kodak Ltd* (1986). It is a question of judgment for a tribunal to reach based on the balance between periods of work and periods of lay-off in any particular case. The three conditions listed above must still all apply, but provided they do, it depends on employees working over the given time for rather more time than they are laid off. The case law appears to suggest that provided the temporary breaks are relatively short as compared with the periods of work, continuity is preserved. Once the breaks in service become relatively long when compared with the periods of work continuity is not preserved.

A final set of circumstances in which this area of law has significance arises when someone leaves an employer for whatever reason but is then rehired relatively soon afterwards. One contract has come to an end and another has started, but is continuity preserved if the break in service is very short? The answer to this problem was provided by the EAT in *Sweeney v Henderson Concessions* (1999). This case concerned a man who resigned from his job, started another and quickly decided he didn't like it. So he returned swiftly to his old employment again. The key here was that despite his break in employment Mr Sweeney had actually been employed by Henderson in two successive weeks. He resigned on Saturday 15 February and returned to work again after his brief and unhappy experience in the other employment on Friday 21 February. There had thus been no week (defined as Sunday—Saturday) in which

Mr Sweeney had not been under contract to work with the same employer. Continuity was thus preserved. It would seem clear therefore that breaks of less than a fortnight do not breach continuity, even if someone clearly resigns. After two weeks it could not be said that a resignee had been under contract during two successive weeks, so Situation C would apply and continuity of employment would not be preserved.

Situation B also applies where someone is dismissed, subsequently wins a claim of unfair dismissal and is either reinstated or re-engaged. In such circumstances the victorious claimant returns to work with their original contract intact and honoured. The law treats them as if they had been employed all along.

 Activity 3.7 *Clifton v James Motor Company*

Mr Clifton, a motor mechanic was employed by the James Motor Company from September 1992 until April 1995. However, during this period he was absent from work for a period of twelve weeks during which time he served a prison sentence. He was rehired on his release, but dismissed eight months later.

The tribunal found that the period of imprisonment constituted a break in service. Mr Clifton's original contract came to an end when he was sentenced and a new contract started when he was released. He could not therefore claim unfair dismissal because he had not completed a sufficient period of continuous service at the time he was dismissed.

Questions

1 Do you consider the tribunal's decision to have been fair?

2 What if Mr Clifton had been wrongly accused, held on remand and then found 'not guilty' of the offence he was charged with?

3 Why did section 212(3)b of the Employment Rights Act not operate to ensure that Mr Clifton's continuity of employment was preserved?

Tribunal time limits

The fourth barrier that sometimes comes down and has the effect of preventing an employment tribunal case from being heard relates to the time limits that apply in each of the main areas of jurisdiction. The precise details vary from case to case, but for most common types of tribunal case the time limit is three calendar months. This means that unless some relatively unusual factor applies, claimants are ruled 'out of time' if they do not submit their claim forms to the Employment Tribunal Service within three months of the incident about which they are complaining. In the case of unfair dismissal and redundancy payment claims it is on 'the effective date of termination' that the clock starts ticking. In the case of most discrimination law it is three months from the day on which the discriminatory act that the employee is complaining about took place. For equal pay matters a time limit of six months applies.

It is possible for the time limits to be extended, but historically tribunals have been reluctant to do so. In unfair dismissal cases late claims can only be accepted and go forward to a hearing if the claimant can satisfy the tribunal that it was 'not reasonably practicable' to have returned the claim form any earlier. As a rule ignorance of the existence of time limits is not an acceptable justification, particularly when claimants have access to advice from trade unions, citizens advice bureaux or other bodies. The leading case on this issue is *Palmer and Saunders v Southend-on-Sea Borough Council* (1984) in which the Court of Appeal said that the term 'reasonably practicable' fell somewhere between 'reasonable' and 'physically practicable' and that if it was 'reasonably feasible' for the claimants to have got their applications in on time, then time limits should not be extended. Illness is one possible reason, ignorance that an unlawful act has occurred is another.

In discrimination law the grounds for extension are less restrictive, but still quite difficult to meet in practice. Tribunals have more discretion than in unfair dismissal cases in that they can allow an extension if in their view 'it is just and equitable' to do so, taking account of the individual circumstances of the case. Where discrimination is ongoing over a period of time (as in an equal pay case) it is not necessary to bring the claim soon after the inequality first occurs; provided some act of unlawful discrimination has occurred within the relevant time limit the case can be heard. The same is true of a series of connected acts such as might be the case when someone is subjected to ongoing sexual harassment over a period of time.

A more recent development is an apparent softening of the previously quite hard line taken with claimants whose applications arrived late because they had received poor advice from their legal advisors. Some case law suggests that such situations are more likely to fall into the 'not reasonably practicable' category than used to be the case. For example, in *Marks and Spencer v Williams-Ryan* (2005), the Court of Appeal held that it was acceptable for a tribunal to hear a late claim where the claimant had received misleading or insufficient advice about the time limits that applied. In this case Mrs Williams-Ryan had been under the impression that she had to exhaust all Marks and Spencer's internal appeal mechanisms before she could bring a tribunal claim in respect of her dismissal. The same is true of discrimination claims. In *Chohan v Derby Law Centre* (2004) the EAT reached a similar conclusion where poor legal advice had been given and that was the reason for the late arrival of the claim form (Javid, 2005). However, in the absence of such reasons, a hard line is taken. In two cases in 2007 employment tribunals ruled that claim forms had been delivered 'out of time'. In one case the claim form reached the Employment Tribunal Service web server eighty-eight seconds after midnight on the final day, in another it was just eight seconds late.

 Activity 3.8   *Machine Tool Industry Research Association v Simpson (1988)*

Mrs Simpson was employed as a typist by the MTI Research Association. At the time of her dismissal she was informed in writing that it was for reasons of redundancy.

It is lawful for employers to make employees redundant provided there is a genuine reduction in the need for employees to do the work they are performing. In this case the company waited for three months before hiring a new typist to fill Mrs Simpson's old job.

Mrs Simpson heard that this had happened and realised that she had probably not been dismissed for reasons of redundancy at all. She therefore made an application for unfair dismissal.

Her claim arrived in the tribunal offices three months and three days after her effective date of termination. She was permitted by the tribunal to proceed with her case.   »

» **Questions**

1 What arguments do you think Mrs Simpson and her representatives were able to show that it was 'not reasonably practicable' for her to have got her claim in on time?

2 Do you agree with the tribunal's decision in this case?

3 How far do you agree that a three-month time limit should normally apply after which cases are ruled out of time?

4 Why should a six-year limit not apply for tribunal claims as is the case with most common law claims brought in the County Court or High Court?

Overseas workers

Another group of workers who have no employment rights are those who are employed to work in the UK unlawfully. The law in this area has changed quite radically over recent years, the government requiring employers to take a much greater role than was previously the case in preventing the unlawful employment of non-EU nationals. The relevant legislation is contained in the Immigration, Asylum and Nationality Act 2006 which applies to all immigrants entering the UK after 29 February 2008.

This Act introduced major changes. Before it came into effect a long-established and quite complex set of rules applied which gave employers considerable freedom to recruit migrant workers with relatively few legal risks. This is no longer the case. The new system is simpler to understand, but carries many more and greater risks for employers who fail to comply, even unwittingly.

The most significant change was in the area of enforcement, a new authority having been created called the UK Border Agency whose inspectors have wide powers including the ability to fine employers who are not complying with the regulations. On-the-spot inspections are now a feature of the Border Agency's work to check that employers and migrant workers are complying with the conditions. Fixed-penalty 'fines' (known as 'civil penalties') can now be levied where employers recruit illegal migrant workers through negligence. The maximum is £10,000 per illegal worker. In addition a new criminal offence has been created for employers who *knowingly* employ illegal migrant workers, punishable with a jail term of up to two years and/or an unlimited fine.

When a Border Agency official issues a fixed-penalty notice, the recipient either has to pay up within twenty-eight days or appeal. The main basis for a successful appeal is an ability to demonstrate that:

1. pre-employment checks have been carried out to establish a right to work in the UK

2. where someone does not have an indefinite right to work in the UK, twelve-monthly checks have been carried out to establish that the right is continuing.

This requires that the employer takes copies of relevant documents and takes reasonable steps to verify that they are genuine and not forged. The Regulations make reference to two lists of documents that employers can collect and copy when establishing the right to work in the UK. List A contains documents which prove a right to stay and work in the UK indefinitely. List B contains documents which prove a right to work in the UK, but with restrictions. To avoid penalties employers thus have to check the credentials of workers who do not have indefinite leave to remain in the UK every twelve months—and demonstrate that they have done so.

Citizens of EU countries that joined the Union prior to January 2007 are permitted to work in the UK without a permit. However, people from countries acceding in 2004 must in most cases register with the government under its Worker Registration Scheme and then apply for a residence permit after completing a year's continuous service with a UK employer. Work permits are not required by people coming from countries in the European Economic Area (EEA) but not in the EU (such as Norway and Switzerland), citizens of British Overseas Territories (eg, Gibraltar) or people from commonwealth states whose parents or grandparents were born in the UK. Spouses of UK citizens who retain an overseas nationality can also work in the UK without a permit.

For everyone else a points-based scheme now applies, making it a great deal easier for someone in their early twenties with a higher degree, savings, good English and a high existing salary to obtain a permit than someone who is older, poorer and less highly educated. The scheme also involves the government maintaining a list of professions entitled the 'National Shortage Occupation List' where there are skills shortages (updated periodically and published on the UKBA website). These attract sufficient points to enable people to enter the country.

The intention is that non-EEA low-skilled workers, or those whose skills are not in sufficiently short supply in the UK (and are hence not on the UKBA's shortage list), will have no possibility of entering the UK legally to work, except on a temporary basis to carry out specific roles. The new scheme classifies all applicants into five 'tiers':

- Tier 1:   Highly skilled migrants—people with particular qualifications will be allowed into the UK as of right
- Tier 2:   Skilled workers with a job offer to fill shortages in the UK labour market
- Tier 3:   Low-skilled workers needed to fill specific temporary labour shortages
- Tier 4:   Overseas students
- Tier 5:   Youth mobility and temporary workers: people allowed to work in the UK for a limited period of time to satisfy primarily non-economic objectives (eg, people on 'working holidays', musicians, actors, etc).

Tier 1 people are free to enter the UK and look for a job once they are here. For the others, it is necessary to secure employment before entry, which means in the vast majority of cases an employer acting as 'sponsor'. Employers wishing to employ people from overseas in Tiers 2 and 5 who are not EEA citizens must now first be licensed by the new 'order and Immigration Agency.' Tier 3 is not currently in operation.

Once licensed an employer will be able to issue would-be migrants with a 'certificate of sponsorship' which will allow them to apply for 'prior entry clearance'. It currently takes around six weeks to obtain a licence. The costs vary depending on the size of the organisation from £300 up to £1000. Loss or suspension of a licence will be the punishment if employers fail to inform the authorities when a migrant worker breaches their conditions of entry.

Another new requirement requires that vacancies are advertised locally before an overseas recruit is hired. Jobs paying over £40,000 a year must be advertised for at least one week and those paying under £40,000 for at least two weeks. Where the ads are placed varies from profession to profession, codes of practice for these being available on the BIA website.

There is also a duty placed on employers of migrant workers to inform the BIA within nineteen working days if:

- a worker does not turn up on the first day of work;
- a worker is absent without authorisation for ten days or more; or
- the worker's employment comes to an end.

Failure to comply can also result in the loss of a certificate of sponsorship.

In November 2010 the government announced its intention to cap immigration from outside the EU from April 2011. Once the requisite numbers have entered the UK each month, no more will be permitted to enter until the following month. The caps for 2011–12 are as follows:

- Tier 1: 21,700
- Tier 2: 20,700

One thousand more will be admitted under a new 'exceptionally talented' category.

Future caps for the other tiers, including overseas students, were yet to be finalised at the time of writing (summer 2011).

CHAPTER SUMMARY

- It is untrue to state that employment law applies to all workers on the same basis.
- Significant employment rights, notably the right not to be unfairly dismissed, apply only to people who work under a 'contract of service'.
- A variety of quite complex tests have been developed over the decades to establish who is an 'employee' and who is a 'worker', and hence which employment rights apply in each individual case.
- Some employment rights only accrue after an employee has completed a set number of months' or years' continuous service. Some breaks in service have the effect of ending a period of continuous employment, while others do not.
- As a general rule employment tribunal claims are judged 'out of time' if they are submitted more than three months after the incident that is the subject of the complaint.
- Since 2008 a new regime has applied for the employment of workers from outside the European Economic Area. This places considerable onus on employers both to ensure and to be in a position to demonstrate that its workers are legally employed.

For updates and further materials, please see the online resource centre at www.oup.com.

REFERENCES

Antell, J. (2002) *Employment Status: A guide to taxation and workers' rights.* London: Butterworth.

Burchell B., Deakin S. and Honey S. (1999) *The Employment Status of Individuals in Non-standard Employment.* London: Department of Trade and Industry.

Casale, G. (2011) (ed) *The Employment Relationship: A Comparative Overview.* Oxford: Hart Publishing.

Collins H., Ewing K.D. and McColgan A. (2001) *Labour Law: text and materials.* Oxford: Hart Publishing.

Davies, P. and Freedland, M. (2000) 'Employees, workers and the autonomy of labour law' in H. Collins, P. Davies and R. Rideout (eds): *Legal Regulation of the Employment Relation.* London: Kluwer Law International.

Deakin, S. (2001) 'Employment protection and the employment relationship: adapting the traditional model?' in K. Ewing (ed): *Employment Rights at Work: Reviewing the Employment Relations Act 1999.* London: Institute of Employment Rights.

Deakin, S. (2007) 'Does the "Personal Employment Contract" provide a basis for the reunification of employment law?' *Industrial Law Journal* 36.1 (p68–83).

Deakin, S. and Morris, G. (2001) *Labour Law.* Third Edition. London: Butterworths.

Deakin, S. and Morris, G. (2009) *Labour Law.* Fifth Edition. Oxford: Hart Publishing.

Department of Trade and Industry (2002*) Discussion document on employment status in relation to employment rights.* London: DTI.

Earnshaw J., Rubery J. and Cooke F.L. (2002) *Who is the Employer?* London: Institute of Employment Rights.

Engels, C. (2001) 'Subordinate employees or self-employed workers' in R. Blanpain and C. Engels (eds): *Comparative Labour Law and Industrial Relations in Industrialized Market Economies.* The Hague: Kluwer.

Freedland, M. (2003) *The Personal Employment Contract.* Oxford: Oxford University Press.

Freedland, M. (2006) 'From the contract of employment to the personal work nexus' *Industrial Law Journal* 35.1 (p1–29).

Freedland, M. (2011) 'Legal characterization of personal work relations' in G. Davidov & B. Langille (eds): *The Idea of Labour Law.* Oxford: Oxford University Press.

Harvey, M. (2001) *Undermining Construction: The corrosive effects of false self-employment.* London: Institute of Employment Rights.

IDS (2001) *Continuity of Employment.* London: Incomes Data Services.

IDS (2008) 'Apprenticeships, internships and work experience' *IDS Brief 855.* June.

Javid, M (2005) 'Time for some good advice' *People Management*, 19 May (p19).

McDonald, K. (2002) 'Workers and Employees' *IRS Employment Review* 761, October. London: Industrial Relations Services.

Painter, R. and Holmes, A. (2002) *Cases and Materials on Employment Law.* Fourth Edition. Oxford: Oxford University Press.

Perulli, A. (2011) 'Subordinate, Autonomous and Economically Dependent Work: A comparative analysis of selected European countries' in G. Casale (ed): *The Employment Relationship: A Comparative Overview.* Oxford: Hart Publishing.

Stone, K.V.W. (2004) *From Widgets to Digits: Employment regulation for the changing workplace.* Cambridge: Cambridge University Press.

Supiot, A. (2001) *Beyond Employment: Changes in work and the future of labour law in Europe.* Oxford: Oxford University Press.

Wedderburn, B. (2007) 'Labour Law 2008: 40 Years On' *Industrial Law Journal* 36.4 (p397–424).

ONLINE RESOURCE CENTRE

A range of online resources to help you through your employment law module have been developed by the author team. These include updates, self-test questions and sources for further reading. (www.oxfordtextbooks.co.uk/orc/taylor_emir3e)

The contract of employment

PART II

Unfair dismissal—reasons and remedies

4

Learning outcomes

By the end of this chapter you should be able to:

- set out the three main legal questions that employment tribunals may need to answer when faced with a case of unfair dismissal;

- distinguish between 'unfair dismissal', 'wrongful dismissal' and 'constructive dismissal';

- state which groups of workers are excluded from unfair dismissal law;

- explain the approach taken by tribunals when it is unclear whether someone has been dismissed or has resigned;

- advise on which category a particular dismissal falls into—automatically fair, automatically unfair or potentially fair;

- explain how the tribunals treat cases differently depending into which of the three categories a particular dismissal falls;

- give advice about the calculation of awards in unfair dismissal cases;

- evaluate the effectiveness of remedies in unfair dismissal law.

Introduction

In Part II of the book we focus on various aspects of the contract of employment. Later in Chapters 7, 8 and 9 we will introduce the law of contract (part of the common law) and the concept of a breach of contract. In Chapters 4, 5 and 6, by contrast, we focus on the major way that employment statutes limit the freedom of employers to terminate contracts of employment through the application of the law of unfair dismissal.

Around one and a half million workers in the UK are technically dismissed from their jobs each year (Fitzner 2006:17), but these are not always unexpected or unwelcomed by employees. A good number of dismissals are redundancies (with compensation and often voluntary), retirements and the consequence of fixed-term contracts coming to an end. Nonetheless tens of thousands of dismissed employees feel sufficiently aggrieved about their position to bring formal legal action by taking an unfair dismissal claim to an employment tribunal. Around one in seven dismissals result in a tribunal claim (Knight & Latreille, 2000:541), giving the Employment Tribunal Service between 40,000 and 60,000 cases to manage each year. This is a rather greater number of cases than are brought under any other employment tribunal jurisdiction. Legal action is common because the law of unfair dismissal is a well-established and widely understood legal right. It was first established in the Industrial Relations Act 1971, yet despite the addition of many amendments and refinements in the years since then, retains its original structure and operates according to exactly the same principles. Most of unfair dismissal law is now found in the Employment Rights Act 1996.

When faced with a claim of unfair dismissal the tribunal may be required to address three separate questions:

1. Is the claimant entitled in law to pursue his/her claim?

2. Was the main reason for the dismissal potentially lawful?

3. Did the employer handle the dismissal in a reasonable fashion?

Interestingly the burden of proof switches for each question. It is for ex-employees to show that they are entitled to bring their claims and it is for employers to satisfy the tribunal that the reasons for the dismissal were lawful. The burden of proof becomes neutral (ie, is on neither side) when the third question is being considered. However, question 2 is only ever asked if the answer to question 1 is 'yes', and question 3 is not asked unless the answer to question 2 is 'yes'. If the answer to question 1 is 'no', the employer wins the case. By contrast, if the answer to question 2 is 'no' then the ex-employee wins the case.

 Activity 4.1

Assume that you have just started working as a Human Resources manager in a large retail company (ABC Ltd). It is concerned at the number of employment tribunal applications which ex-employees are bringing after having been dismissed. Until now the firm's policy has been to settle all cases, often at considerable cost, so as to avoid wasting the time and trouble associated with preparing and attending tribunals. You are asked to review policy in this area as a matter of priority.   »

» On your arrival at your desk you are given a file listing some recent dismissal cases and the amount of money paid to the individual by way of compensation. All were employees working under contracts of service. The following items are included:

Name	Length of service	Nature of complaint	Settlement
Angela Andrews	2 years	Sacked while on maternity leave. Replaced by a male employee.	£15,000
Brenda Butcher	6 months	Sacked shortly after she stated that she was gay.	£10,000
Charles Cooper	11 months	Sacked after joining a trade union.	£10,000
Dave Drake	3 years	Required to take retirement to allow for the promotion of a younger colleague at the age of 67.	£15,000
Elizabeth Evans	5 years	Sacked, after repeated warnings about her tendency to express racist opinions.	£10,000

State which of these settlements in your view were necessary to avoid employment tribunal cases and which were not. Briefly explain the reasoning behind your choices. What further information would you need to give definitive advice?

Return to this activity once you have read the chapter, to see how many of your answers were correct.

In this chapter we are going to discuss the first two of these three questions. The issue of reasonableness is the focus of Chapter 5, while in Chapter 6 we move on to look at issues relating to redundancy and insolvency in greater detail.

Terminology

It is helpful at the start of our chapters on dismissal issues to start by distinguishing between three different types of dismissal claim that are commonly brought to employment tribunals. People often get confused between the three and use their labels interchangeably, but they are in fact three very different kinds of situation.

Unfair dismissal

This is a dismissal which occurs in breach of statute. The reasons for the dismissal or the manner in which it was handled by the employer fall short of the standards expected by the law as expressed in the Employment Rights Act 1996 and in other statutes. This is the area of law we discuss in this and the subsequent two chapters.

Wrongful dismissal

This is a dismissal in breach of contract. In dismissing an employee the employer did not follow its legal obligations as expressed in the dismissed employee's contract of employment. We discuss wrongful dismissal in detail in Chapter 9.

Constructive dismissal

This is a resignation rather than a dismissal, but it is a resignation that occurs in response to the employer's decision to breach the contract of employment. In such circumstances the law treats the resignation as if it were a dismissal. Constructive dismissal is also discussed in Chapter 9.

Is the claimant entitled to pursue a claim?

There are a number of reasons which will lead a tribunal to strike out a claim of unfair dismissal or to find against the claimant at an early stage in proceedings. Some of them were covered extensively in Chapter 3:

- where the claimant was not employed under a contract of service at the time of the dismissal (ie, was not an employee)
- where the claimant had not completed a year's continuous service with his/her employer or an associated employer at the time of the dismissal (NB, this does not apply in the case of automatically unfair dismissals—see below)
- where the claimant failed to submit his/her claim within three months of the effective date of termination (or by a later date set by a tribunal) when it would have been reasonably practicable to do so.

In addition, there are certain defined groups of employees who despite working under contracts of employment are not generally able to bring claims of unfair dismissal. The major groups are as follows:

- employees in the police service
- members of the armed forces
- share fishermen and fisherwomen
- people who work wholly outside Great Britain (except in very unusual circumstances)
- people employed under illegal contracts of employment (see Chapter 7).

Has there been a dismissal?

Unless a dismissal has actually occurred, it is not possible for a claimant to pursue a claim of unfair dismissal. You would be forgiven for thinking that this was a straightforward matter. Surely it is apparent whether or not someone has been fired? Unfortunately for the employment tribunals this is not the case. There are plenty of circumstances in which it is not clear whether or not a dismissal has occurred, whether the employee resigned or whether the two parties simply agreed that their relationship should come to an end. Moreover, it is often in the interests of the parties to a case to argue that terminations in such 'grey areas' either do or do not constitute dismissals. Employers will try to argue that there was no dismissal, while ex-employees will seek to persuade tribunals that they were dismissed. So this is a preliminary issue which tribunals commonly have to determine before a case of unfair dismissal can proceed.

Sections 95(1) and 95(2) of the Employment Rights Act 1996 sets out four situations in which a dismissal occurs in UK law, and hence in which a claim of unfair dismissal can be pursued:

- where a contract of employment is terminated, with or without notice, by the employer
- where a fixed-term contract comes to an end and is not renewed

- where the employee resigns by reason of the employer's conduct (ie, a constructive dismissal situation)
- where an employee resigns during his/her contractual period of notice after having received notice from the employer.

Problems most commonly arise where the facts of a case are contested in respect of the first of these three types of dismissal situation. It is rare, after all, for an employer to dismiss someone in writing without first having informed them verbally. They may confirm a verbal dismissal in writing after the event, but that still does not always mean that an actual dismissal has occurred. What happens, for example, when imprecise language is used and people are left unsure about whether or not they have been dismissed? What about situations where managers appear to dismiss 'in the heat of the moment' during a row, but claim not really to have meant it? And what about situations in which someone appears to have resigned but subsequently returns to work only to find that they are not welcome and are told to go away again?

There is no statute that helps tribunals reach decisions in these kinds of cases. Instead they have to exercise their judgment given the evidence presented to them. There is, however, some useful case law to draw on, a good starting point being the EAT's ruling in *Tanner v DT Kean* (1978), quoted by Deakin and Morris (2009:405):

> ...the test which has to be applied in cases of this kind is along these lines. Were the words spoken those of dismissal, that is to say, were they intended to bring the contract of employment to an end? What was the employer's intention? In answering that a relevant, and perhaps the most important question is how would a reasonable employee, in all the circumstances, have understood what the employer intended by what he said and did?

Tribunals are thus required to look at all the circumstances in cases where it is unclear whether or not a dismissal has occurred and not just at the words used to terminate the relationship. The meaning of the words is then considered in the light of the circumstances and a test of reasonableness applied. IDS (2005:4) show how this approach is taken in practice, giving the example of the case of *Westwell v Crampton t/a CK Haulage and Distribution* (1996). Here the manager of a road haulage company told an employee on the telephone that he should return his truck and then 'fuck off back home'. In itself the EAT held that these words did not constitute a dismissal as they were uttered in the heat of the moment. The reasonable employee would interpret this as an appeal to get out of his way temporarily and not permanently. However, subsequent behaviour on the part of the manager involving making a v-sign to the employee was held by the tribunal as evidence that a dismissal had in fact occurred. In other cases of a similar type tribunals have decided that no dismissal has occurred on the grounds that the use of such language is normal in the environment concerned and could not reasonably be taken to indicate that a dismissal was intended.

The same broad approach is taken in situations where someone resigns in the heat of the moment (or appears to), then later regrets it and returns to work. Everything depends on the circumstances. According to IDS (2010:6) the leading case here is *Sothern v Franks Charlesly and Co* (1981) in which the Court of Appeal found that an employee had resigned because the language used had been unambiguous and there were no reasonable grounds that might suggest that the employee had intended otherwise. However, in this case the Court of Appeal took the opportunity to state that there are situations in which someone might say that they were leaving yet reasonably be understood by their employer not really to mean it. These would include 'heat of the moment' statements or 'idle words spoken under emotional stress which the employer knew or ought to have known were not meant to be taken seriously'. The Court of Appeal also warned that the law should look favourably on ex-employees in situations in which an employer is 'anxious to be rid of an employee' and hence 'seizes upon her words and gives them a meaning which she did not intend'. Subsequent cases have involved tribunals taking account of resignees' mental states and the extent to which they were suffering from stress at the time they resigned.

Another type of case involves the employer making an assumption that an employee has resigned because of their actions or inactions. Examples from the case law include situations in which employees fail to return from holiday on the expected date, 'disappear' for a few days or refuse to communicate with the employer when off sick despite the employer sending letters. The outcome of these cases also varies depending on the wider circumstances of each case, the test that is applied being one of reasonableness. If a tribunal considers that given all relevant circumstances a reasonable employer would not make the assumption that the employee had resigned, then a refusal to permit the employee to continue to work constitutes a dismissal.

Finally, it is important to point out that a resignation which is obtained by an employer either through force or deception will be considered to be a dismissal in law. Forced resignations are common. These occur when an employer gives an employee the chance to resign ahead of a dismissal—an opportunity to jump before being pushed. It is sometimes done in the erroneous belief that an unfair dismissal claim will be avoided, and sometimes more

 Activity 4.2   *Kwik-Fit (GB) Ltd v Lineham* **(1992)**

In this case an employee (Mr Lineham) got into an argument with fellow employees during the working day. Tempers flared to such an extent that Mr Lineham was given a formal warning which he regarded as being 'humiliating'. He then stormed out, flinging his keys down and using impolite language. The next day he turned up for work as usual, only to be told that it had been assumed that he had resigned on the previous day. The employment tribunal found that this amounted to a dismissal and not a resignation. The decision was subsequently approved in principle by the EAT. However, they said that it was not necessary for an employer to check whether or not the 'resignation' was genuine or not. A reasonable employer would simply avoid jumping to hasty conclusions and would not seize the opportunity provided by such situations to be rid of a troublesome employee without the need formally to dismiss.

Questions

1   What specific factors do you think would account for the decision of the employment tribunal in this case?

2   Do you think the outcome would have been different if Mr Lineham had returned to work several days later?

3   How far do you agree with the ruling that employers are not under any duty to check the employee's true intentions in cases such as this before assuming that a resignation had occurred?

charitably in order to avoid a situation in which someone has a dismissal on their employment record. Either way it is still a dismissal as far as the tribunals are concerned and can thus lead to an unfair dismissal hearing. Less common are situations in which an employee is deceived into resigning. This sometimes occurs in the run up to redundancies in order to avoid the need to make severance payments. Employees are tricked into resigning their jobs and accepting others at the last minute. When such situations are orchestrated by employers, the tribunals find them to amount to dismissals.

What was the main reason for the dismissal?

In most cases a tribunal is not required to satisfy itself that the claimant has a right to bring his/her claim because this point is not contested by the employer. Only if one of the types of situation described above applies is the question ever given consideration. In typical unfair dismissal cases the tribunal thus starts by focusing its attention on the reason or reasons for the dismissal. At this stage the burden of proof is on the employer to show that the reason was genuinely one of those for which it is potentially lawful to dismiss. A failure to do so leads to a finding in favour of the claimant.

Employers will usually set out the reasons for the dismissal in their notice of response (the ET3 form) that they complete and return to the tribunal once a claim has been lodged. While there is no longer a specific requirement to do so, employers are well advised to state the reason for the dismissal when explaining their grounds for resisting the claim. Moreover, the Employment Rights Act 1996 gives all dismissed employees a right to receive from their ex-employers a written statement of the reasons for their dismissal. Except in the case of women who are pregnant or taking maternity leave there is no requirement on employers to issue a statement of the reasons unless they are asked to provide one, but they must reply to any request within fourteen days if asked to do so.

It is very much in the employers' interests to set out the exact reasons for the dismissal in one of these ways, and to take care to ensure that the reasons given are entirely consistent with those set out in writing elsewhere, for example in a letter confirming a dismissal. Inconsistency or ambiguity of any kind, and particularly attempts to introduce 'new' reasons at a later time (eg, in evidence given to the tribunal at the hearing), can be exploited by claimants' representatives as a means of showing that the real reason for the dismissal was unfair and hence unlawful.

The Employment Rights Act 1996, together with various other statutes define three categories of reasons for dismissal, the outcome of any case depending to a great extent on which of the three categories a particular dismissal is found to fall into. The three categories are as follows:

- automatically fair reasons
- automatically unfair reasons
- potentially fair reasons.

If the main reason for the dismissal is found to be 'automatically fair' the employer wins. If it is 'automatically unfair' the former employee wins. If it is 'potentially fair' the tribunal goes on to ask the further third question we identified at the beginning of this chapter about 'reasonableness'. In the case of potentially fair dismissals it is thus the way that the dismissal was handled that effectively determines the outcome of the case.

Automatically fair reasons

There are now only two automatically fair reasons for dismissal and these are relatively rare occurrences. The first is for reasons of national security. Section 10(1) of the Employment Rights Act 1996 reads as follows:

> If it is shown that the action complained of was taken for the purpose of safeguarding national security the employment tribunal shall dismiss the complaint.

Moreover, special regulations apply when a tribunal is constituted to hear claims of this kind. They include permitting a minister to direct that hearings are held in private, that the identity of witnesses is concealed and that the reasons for any decision are kept secret (Duggan 1999:293–4).

The other automatically fair reason for dismissal concerns *unofficial* industrial action. We will deal with this in greater detail in Chapter 29. For now it is sufficient simply to state that unofficial industrial action occurs when workers organise it themselves at a local level without the sanction of a listed trade union. The relevant law is contained in section 237 of the Trade Union and Labour Relations (Consolidation) Act 1992. Quite simply, if a dismissal takes place while an employee is taking unofficial industrial action *'an employee has no right to complain of unfair dismissal'*. This formulation means that the fact that the employee is taking industrial action need not necessarily be the main reason for the dismissal. Provided the real reason for the dismissal is not 'automatically unfair', it is possible to dismiss almost anyone selectively in such circumstances without risk. For example, long-serving employees who are relatively poor performers can be fired, as can the organisers of the unofficial action. There is no requirement to follow any procedure or to act consistently because the employer's reasonableness in handling the dismissal will never be considered by a tribunal. Understandably this provision has attracted a great deal of criticism from trade unions and other bodies representing employee interests.

Automatically unfair reasons

In contrast to the list of automatically fair reasons, the list of automatically unfair reasons for dismissal has grown steadily in recent years. However, as we will see, the extensions have not always been made on exactly the same basis. As a result this area of the law is more complicated than used to be the case and can be somewhat misleading. Moreover, there is no single source of law which sets out all the automatically unfair reasons for dismissal. Instead these rights are found in several different statutes and statutory instruments. The list, as of 2012, is as follows:

- Dismissal for a reason relating to pregnancy or maternity
- Dismissal for a health and safety reason (eg, refusing to work in unsafe conditions)
- Dismissal because of a spent conviction
- Dismissal for refusing to work on a Sunday (retail and betting workers only)
- Dismissal for a trade union reason
- Dismissal for taking official industrial action (during the first twelve weeks of the action)
- Dismissal in contravention of the part-time workers or fixed-term employees regulations.

- Dismissal for undertaking duties as an occupational pension fund trustee, employee representative, member of a European Works Council or in connection with jury service.

- Dismissal for asserting a statutory right (including rights exercised under the Employment Rights Act, as well as those connected with the Working Time Regulations, the National Minimum Wage Regulations, the Public Interest Disclosure Act and the Information and Consultation of Employees Regulations; the right to request flexible working, the right to time off for dependents, the right to adoptive, parental or paternity leave, the right to be accompanied at disciplinary and grievance hearings and the claiming of working tax credits).

- Dismissal for a reason connected with the Transfer of an Undertaking in the absence of a valid economic, technical or organisational reason.

Detailed discussion of most of these reasons is beyond the scope of this chapter. We will deal with each (eg, spent convictions, maternity, part-time and fixed-term working) in the appropriate context later on. For now, it is the general principles of automatically unfair dismissals that we need to focus on.

The major factor which distinguishes a dismissal for an automatically fair reason from a dismissal for a potentially fair reason is the absence of any potential defences for employers to deploy in the employment tribunal. A dismissal which is found to have occurred chiefly for one of the reasons on the above list is always unfair. However reasonable the employer believes that it has been, whatever justification it would like to put forward for its actions, the tribunal must find for the claimant. Quite simply, it is unlawful in *any* circumstances to dismiss an employee for an automatically unfair reason.

The other important distinguishing factor is that in most cases of automatically unfair dismissal there is no requirement to have completed a year's continuous service at the time of the dismissal. In other words, all employees have the right not to be dismissed for an automatically unfair reason from the first day of their employment. In the case of qualifying conditions there are two exceptions:

- transfer of undertakings,
- spent convictions

In these situations tribunals can only hear cases brought by employees with over twelve months' service at the date of dismissal.

However, it is important to remember that it remains the case that only employees are able to claim unfair dismissal. Other categories of 'worker' (see Chapter 3) do not have the right to bring a claim even if they are dismissed for an automatically unfair reason. People in such circumstances may well have a good claim under discrimination law or under another statute, but they are not entitled to bring unfair dismissal claims. For example, a casual worker who is not working under a contract of service but who is dismissed because she is pregnant or because she has complained that she is being paid below the national minimum wage can seek legal redress— she just can't claim unfair dismissal. The same is true of all employees and workers who are dismissed for unlawful reasons that are not explicitly included on this list. Dismissing a woman because she is a woman, or a gay person, or a member of a racial or religious minority for these reasons is in effect 'automatically unfair'. But redress has to be sought under other statutes.

Exhibit 4.1

Professor Hugh Collins of the London School of Economics (2004: 74–78) strongly argues that the law in the area of dismissals for automatically unfair reasons needs to be strengthened. In his opinion it is important that the law recognises that a 'double wrong' is being committed by employers who dismiss for such reasons. Not only is the dismissal unfair, but some other legal right is also being violated at the same time. A greater level of deterrence is thus needed as is the case in many other countries in similar types of dismissal situation.

Collins suggests the following:

1. That compensation levels when claimants win cases of this kind be substantially increased over and above those paid in other cases of unfair dismissal. There should be punitive damages in addition to damages which compensate the former employee for economic loss.

2. It should be possible for employees to obtain injunctions to prevent a dismissal from going ahead if it is for an automatically unfair reason.

3. It should be possible for employees dismissed for *any* automatically unfair reason to claim interim relief in the way that those dismissed for trade union reasons currently can. This would involve a tribunal chairman assessing the claim within a few days of its receipt and requiring employers to provide a measure of compensation up front, ahead of a full hearing, in situations where the claimant's case appears strong.

In addition, Collins argues for a wide extension of the number of reasons for dismissal that are classified as 'automatically unfair'. He believes that there are too many anomalies in the current list, particularly the way that some forms of unlawful discrimination are included while others are not. His suggestion is that the European Union's Charter of Fundamental Rights is an appropriate standard to use. A dismissal which breached any of these core civil and political rights included in the Charter would thus be both automatically unfair and involve the employer paying some form of punitive damages to the employee or employees concerned.

Potentially fair reasons

The final category of dismissals recognised by unfair dismissal law is 'potentially fair'—the category into which most dismissals fall in practice. Here the outcome of any tribunal case depends on how the employer handled the dismissal, the requirement being that the employer acted 'reasonably'. It is thus only in potentially fair cases that the third of the three questions we identified at the beginning of this chapter is asked. We will focus in detail on the meaning of the term 'reasonableness' in this context in Chapter 5. For now it is simply necessary to set out the potentially fair reasons and to define those that are not self-explanatory. The Employment Rights Act 1999 lists five potentially fair reasons. A sixth was added in the Employment Relations Act 1999 (amended in 2004). A further potentially fair reason was effectively added to the list during the course of 2006. This brings the total to seven:

- Capability
- Conduct

- Redundancy
- Statutory Bar
- Some other substantial reason
- Engagement in *official* industrial action (after the first twelve weeks of the action)
- In connection with the transfer of an undertaking where a valid economic, technical or organisational reason applies (see Chapter 23).

Capability covers both poor performance in a job and ill health. The statutory bar category relates to situations in which an employer believes it would be unlawful to continue employing an individual in their current job, for example when a work permit runs out. Some other substantial reason is an ill-defined category that has attracted much criticism from commentators. Its presence in the statutes permits employers to come to a tribunal and argue that their reason for dismissing the employee in question was fair in all the circumstances despite it not being 'listed' as fair or potentially fair in the Act. We will assess what this has meant in practice in Chapter 5 along with dismissals on grounds of capability and conduct. Redundancy is covered in Chapter 6 and official industrial action in Chapter 29.

Other reasons

While the three 'lists' of reasons contained in the statutes cover a good majority of the reasons that employers have for dismissing people, there remain plenty of possible reasons that are not listed. Some of these can, as we will see in Chapter 5, be defended under the 'some other substantial reason' heading, but what about reasons that are not substantial by any definition of the word? What is the legal position of a person who is dismissed because he or she is irritating to work with, smelly, fat or excessively hairy?

The answer is that all these other reasons can effectively be characterised under a fourth heading which we might label 'ordinarily unfair'. That is to say that it is unfair to dismiss for these reasons in law, but only when the dismissed person:

- has completed a year's continuous service
- is an employee working under a full contract of employment
- is not excluded from bringing an unfair dismissal claim for another of the reasons set out above.

 Activity 4.3 **Gender and unfair dismissal**

Knight and Latreille (2001) reported the results of research they carried out into 'gender effects' in unfair dismissal cases dealt with during 1990 and 1991. Their findings were striking and somewhat perplexing:

- 69% of unfair dismissal cases are brought by men
- 71% of cases that reach a full hearing are brought by men
- Women are considerably more likely to be *offered* a settlement by their employers prior to the tribunal hearing »

- 51% of cases brought by women resulted in a settlement, compared to only 44% in the case of male claimants
- 49% of the women won their cases
- Only 37% of men won their cases
- Men represented themselves at the hearing in 34% of cases, for women the figure was only 19%
- Women won 57% of cases in which they represented themselves, the figure for men was 36%
- Compensation levels were found to be very similar, all things considered, as between victorious female and male claimants.

The researchers were unable to find any clear explanation for the relative success of women v men at unfair dismissal hearings. They suggest that it could be as a result of chivalry on the part of predominantly male tribunal panels, or because women are treated more harshly by their employers and thus come to court with stronger cases. It is also possible that women are more frequently unfairly dismissed than men because they are a good deal less likely to be members of trade unions, and hence less well placed to resist dismissal at the time it occurs.

Questions

1 What do you think of the possible explanations advanced by Knight and Latreille to explain their research findings?

2 What other explanations do you think could be advanced and why?

Remedies

When a claimant wins an unfair dismissal case there are four possible outcomes: reinstatement, re-engagement, compensation and a declaration that a dismissal was unfair. In practice the third of these, compensation, is by far the most common outcome.

Re-instatement involves the ex-employee returning to his or her previous job, with full back pay, pension rights and any seniority-related increments honoured. In every respect the employee has to be treated as if he or she had never been dismissed. Re-engagement also involves the ex-employee being taken back into employment by the employer, but not necessarily into exactly the same job or on the same terms and conditions. The precise terms of re-engagement orders inevitably vary from case to case, but the key principle is that the new position should be both 'comparable' to the previous job and 'suitable'.

Reinstatement and re-engagement are very rare in practice, accounting for less than 1% of all unfair dismissal cases which proceed to a hearing. The Employment Tribunal Service's annual report for 2010–11 records eight instances during that year (Ministry of Justice, 2011). This is partly because relatively few employees request these remedies in the first place and partly because employers are able successfully to argue that it would be impractical to reinstate or re-engage. Given the length of time which typically passes between a dismissal and a tribunal hearing (six months to a year) it is common for employers to have replaced the person concerned and they can thus plausibly claim that there is no vacancy. Alternatively an employer can argue that the personal relationship between managers, or indeed colleagues, and the dismissed employee has deteriorated to such a level that it would be impractical to re-engage or reinstate. Loss of confidence in the employee can also form the basis of successful appeals by employers who wish to resist reinstatement (IDS, 2010:530–1). In any case, at the end of the day, an employment tribunal cannot force an employer to reinstate or re-engage anyone. Where an order to do so is refused by an employer the penalty is simply a limited amount of additional compensation. The amount of such 'additional awards' is somewhere between twenty-six weeks' and fifty-two weeks' pay subject (in 2011) to a cap of £400 per week. This means that the maximum additional award that can be made by a tribunal is £20,800.

 Exhibit 4.2   **Reinstatements**

The most common situation in which full re-instatements occur following an unfair dismissal case is when an employer has dismissed a group of employees before re-hiring them immediately on new terms and conditions. As we will see in Chapter 7, this is a method that can be used entirely lawfully in order to alter contractual terms, but it carries considerable risks from a legal perspective. As a rule it is defended in the tribunal under the 'some other substantial reason' heading. And because that is a potentially fair reason for dismissal, it is open to the tribunal to find it unfair in law on the grounds that the employer handled it unreasonably. When this occurs it is hard for the employer to argue that it would be impracticable to reinstate or that confidence has been lost. The claimants are, after all, still usually employed and in the same jobs. In such cases reinstatement thus means reinstatement of previous terms and conditions of employment.

Compensation is what most ex-employees are looking for, and is what they get in the vast majority of unfair dismissal cases that they win. There are usually two headings under which compensation is calculated—the basic award and the compensatory award—but in exceptional cases additional awards are made. Basic awards are calculated in the same way as statutory redundancy payments, the maximum figures rising broadly in line with inflation from 1 February each year. At the time of writing (2011) the basic award is calculated as follows:

- one-and-a-half week's pay for every year of service completed over the age of forty-one
- one week's pay for every year of service completed between twenty-two and forty-one
- half a week's pay for every year of service completed between eighteen and twenty-two.

These are all subject to a limit of a maximum of £400 per week and twenty years' service. This means that the maximum possible basic award in typical unfair dismissal cases is £12,000. Basic awards are sometimes reduced to take account of redundancy payments already received or when a claimant is found unreasonably to have refused an offer of reinstatement.

Compensatory awards vary in size depending on the circumstances of the case. They are intended to compensate the claimant for financial losses sustained as a result of the dismissal.

They are not intended to punish the employer in any way. The maximum limit on compensatory awards was substantially raised from £12,000 to £50,000 in October 1999. As of

2011, it stands at £68,400. Early on in the evolution of unfair dismissal law clear 'heads of loss' were established for employment tribunals to consider when calculating compensatory awards (*Norton Tool Co v Tewson* (1972)). These have been refined somewhat in the years since then, but remain broadly similar. According to IDS (2010:563) the current 'heads' are as follows:

- immediate loss of earnings (ie, lost pay between the dismissal and the tribunal hearing)
- future loss of earnings (ie, estimated likely losses following the hearing)
- expenses (ie, costs incurred due to the dismissal such as those associated with making job applications—legal costs are not included)
- loss of statutory employment protection rights (eg, inability to claim maternity leave or unfair dismissal in the future until over a year's service has been completed with a new employer)
- loss of pension rights (calculated according to established formulae).

The amounts awarded vary hugely depending on how well paid an individual claimant is, how quickly they have managed to find another job and what pension losses have been sustained. However, awards are often reduced substantially. There are a number of situations in which this occurs:

1. Where the claimant has failed to mitigate his/her losses sufficiently—for example by failing to try to find alternative employment following the dismissal.
2. To take account of social security payments such as unemployment benefit received by the claimant.
3. Where claimants are found to have contributed to an extent to their own dismissals.

A finding of contributory fault is not at all uncommon. Tribunals are required either to find that a dismissal is fair or unfair. There is no middle way available to allow a 'sharing of the blame' between employer and employee in the finding itself. However, the fact that an employee's conduct contributed in some measure to a dismissal which was nonetheless unfair in law can be reflected in the compensation awarded. Tribunals are guided in this area by the ruling in *Nelson v BBC* (1980) in which the Court of Appeal set out a three stage test to be applied:

Question 1:   Was the employee culpable or blameworthy?

Question 2:   Did the employee's actions cause or contribute to the dismissal?

Question 3:   Is it just and equitable in the circumstances to reduce the award?

If the answer to these questions is yes a deduction is made, the amount being assessed on a percentage basis. So if the tribunal finds that a claimant was 50% to blame for his or her own dismissal, the award is reduced by 50%. In some cases a tribunal will find that a dismissal is unfair in law (frequently when there have been procedural deficiencies), but that the claimant is nonetheless 100% responsible for their own fate. In such circumstances no award is made and all that happens is that a declaration is issued stating that the dismissal was unfair. We will deal with these issues in more detail in the next chapter.

It is also common for so-called 'Polkey reductions' to be made, named after the famous case *Polkey v Dayton Services* (1988). These occur when, for example, a tribunal judges a dismissal to have been unfair on procedural grounds, but accepts that had a proper procedure been followed, dismissal would nonetheless have been the final outcome.

Finally, there are one or types of cases in which the statutory limit on compensatory awards is lifted. These are where a dismissal occurs for one of three automatically unfair reasons:

- refusal to work in unsafe conditions
- carrying out the duties of a health and safety representative
- the employee made a 'protected disclosure' under the terms of the Public Interest Disclosure Act (see Chapter 22).

Under the terms of the Employment Act 2008 further adjustments to compensation can be made. The two relevant sections concern the level of compensation paid to victorious claimants in a wide variety of employment tribunal cases, but have had their biggest practical impact in cases of unfair dismissal. The first reads as follows:

> If, in the case of proceedings to which this section applies, it appears to the employment tribunal that—
>
> (a) the claim to which the proceedings relate concerns a matter to which a relevant Code of Practice applies,
>
> (b) the employer has failed to comply with that Code in relation to that matter, and
>
> (c) that failure was unreasonable,
>
> the employment tribunal may, if it considers it just and equitable in all the circumstances to do so, increase any award it makes to the employee by no more than 25%.

In the context of unfair dismissal this means that employers who dismiss without having complied with the requirements of the ACAS Code of Practice on 'Discipline at Work' are likely to be required to pay an uplifted award by way of compensation to the dismissed person. You will read about the contents of this Code of Practice in Chapter 5.

A second section in the Employment Act 2008 reads as follows:

> If, in the case of proceedings to which this section applies, it appears to the employment tribunal that—
>
> (a) the claim to which the proceedings relate concerns a matter to which a relevant Code of Practice applies,
>
> (b) the employee has failed to comply with that Code in relation to that matter, and
>
> (c) that failure was unreasonable,
>
> the employment tribunal may, if it considers it just and equitable in all the circumstances to do so, reduce any award it makes to the employee by no more than 25%.

This raises the possibility that dismissed employees who win their tribunal cases, but who have not themselves fully complied with the expectations of the ACAS Code of Practice, may see a considerable reduction made in the compensation they would otherwise have received. This may well happen, for example, where an employer offers someone the right to appeal against the decision to dismiss them, but where they do not take advantage of this invitation.

> **Exhibit 4.3   *Dunnachie v Kingston upon Hull District Council* (2004)**
>
> *Dunnachie v Kingston upon Hull City Council* was a dismissal case in which Mr Dunnachie was fired following a prolonged period in which he had been treated poorly and had suffered a nervous breakdown. Following his dismissal he had a loss of confidence and was unable to take up a new job with equivalent pay and status to that which he had lost. Mr Dunnachie won his case, but what was significant about it was that he succeeded in winning compensation not just for financial loss (as is usual) but also an additional sum of £10,000 for injury to feelings.
>
> Injury to feelings awards have long formed part of the compensation paid to winning applicants in discrimination cases, but they had not hitherto been awarded in unfair dismissal cases.
>
> The legal basis for the change was a series of remarks made by Lord Hoffman in his judgment in a wrongful dismissal case (*Johnson v Unisys* (2001)). He said in passing that he could not see why in principle 'distress, humiliation, damage to reputation in the community or to family life' should not be compensated in unfair dismissal awards.
>
> In November 2003 the case was heard by the Court of Appeal and decided by a majority of two to one in Mr Dunnachie's favour. However in July 2004 this ruling was overturned on a further appeal to the House of Lords. So the position now is as it has been for many years. Compensation in unfair dismissal cases is only for financial losses sustained as a direct result of the dismissal.

Debates on remedies in unfair dismissal cases

One of the chief criticisms made of unfair dismissal law is that the remedies available to victorious claimants are inadequate, and that employers are thus not properly deterred from dismissing an employee unfairly. And the figures released each year by the Employment Tribunal Service confirm that awards in most cases are pretty low. In 2010–11, for example, the average award made in cases of unfair dismissal was £8,924, the median figure being just £4,591 (Ministry of Justice, 2011). Despite the raising of the cap on compensatory awards in 1999 to £50,000, the figures show that it is very rare indeed for claimants to win sums of this order. Only 153 awards of over £30,000 were made in 2010–11, just 6% of the total).

This has two major effects:

1. Employers who might otherwise think twice about dismissing someone conclude that the amount of possible compensation is affordable. They thus go ahead and dismiss unfairly, or in the full knowledge that the dismissal is probably unfair in law.

2. Dismissed employees who might otherwise bring claims decide that the money, time and effort it would cost them are too great when compared with the likely award they could win if they won their cases.

The result is a situation in which the law of unfair dismissal too often fails to meet its objectives. It does not, in practice, ensure that unjust dismissals do not take place.

A number of commentators have suggested reforms to aspects of unfair dismissal law that would have the effect of improving the deterrent effect (eg, Lewis, 1999; McMullen, 2003; Collins, 2004:66–73 and Collins, 2010:181–82). The major suggestions put forward are the following:

- Removing the various caps on compensation levels. Basic and additional awards would thus be calculated according to a person's actual weekly pay and not limited to £400 per week, while compensatory awards could be as high as was necessary fully to compensate for all financial losses sustained.

- Parliament could overturn the *Dunnachie* ruling (see Exhibit 4.3), requiring tribunals to make awards that compensated for loss of dignity, injury to feelings or stress associated with the dismissal as well as financial loss. This would be easy to implement in practice because the principles for calculating appropriate awards of this kind are already well established in discrimination law.

- Deductions to take account of failure to mitigate losses could cease so that a punitive as well as a compensatory element was introduced.

- Reinstatement or re-employment orders should be made more frequently, with higher penalties for non-compliance. Lewis (1999:184) proposes that a trial period system be introduced whereby the employee is reinstated for four weeks, and a decision made at the end of this period about whether the employment should continue or compensation be made.

An argument against such reforms is that they would result in a great deal more litigation and that this is costly for the tax payer. However, it can equally well be argued that higher compensation would mean that employers took greater care to ensure that they acted lawfully in the first place and gave their ex-employees no reason to pursue a claim.

 Activity 4.4   Compensation for dismissal in other EU countries

Unfair dismissal law in most other EU countries is a good deal tougher on employers than is the case in the UK. Qualifying periods are a good deal less than a year (three to six months is typical) and compensation levels are higher.

- In Spain forty-five days pay per year of service are payable when an employee is unfairly dismissed.

- In France unfairly dismissed employees with more than two years' service cannot be awarded less than six months' pay.

- In Germany the average severance payment is two to three weeks' pay per year of service.

- In Italy reinstatement is the usual outcome of an unfair dismissal case. Employers who refuse to comply are required to pay the ex-employee up to fifteen months' salary.

- In Sweden compensation levels rise depending on length of service. For employees with less than five years' service, sixteen months' pay is awarded where dismissals are found to be 'without cause'. For those with over ten years' service the award is thirty-two months' pay—this figure rises to forty-eight months' pay in the case of workers who are over sixty.

Questions

1 What do you think are the major advantages and disadvantages of these high compensation levels from the perspective of employers, employees and government?

2 What, if any, impact do you think the compensation levels have on the amount of overseas inward investment these countries can attract?

3 How far and in what ways would you like to see UK law on remedies in unfair dismissal cases reformed?

CHAPTER SUMMARY

- When faced with an unfair dismissal claim an employment tribunal may need to ask three questions in the following order: is the claimant entitled to bring the case? what was the main reason for the dismissal? and did the employer act reasonably in carrying out the dismissal?

- If no dismissal took place, except in the case of constructive dismissals, there is no case to answer.

- The statutes provide lists of reasons for dismissal classed as 'automatically fair', 'automatically unfair' and 'potentially fair'.

- In the case of automatically unfair dismissals, there is no defence. In most cases there is also no one-year service requirement.

- In the case of potentially fair dismissals the outcome depends on the extent to which the employer is found to have acted reasonably when dismissing.

- Most victorious claimants in unfair dismissal cases seek compensation. Levels of compensation in the UK are rather lower than in most EU countries.

For updates and further materials, please see the online resource centre at www.oup.com.

REFERENCES

Collins, H. (2004) *Nine Proposals for the Reform of the Law on Unfair Dismissal*. London: Institute of Employment Rights.

Collins, H. (2010) *Employment Law*. Second Edition. Oxford: Oxford University Press.

Deakin, S. & Morris, G. (2009) *Labour Law*. Fifth Edition. Oxford: Hart Publishing.

Duggan, M. (1999) *Unfair Dismissal: Law, Practice and Guidance*. Welwyn Garden City: CLT Professional Publishing.

Fitzner, G. (2006) *How have Employees Fared? Recent UK Trends*. Employment Relations Research Series 56. London: DBERR.

IDS (2005) *Unfair Dismissal: Employment Law Handbook*. London: Incomes Data Services.

IDS (2010) *Unfair Dismissal: Employment Law Handbook*. London: Incomes Data Services.

Knight, K.G. & Latreille, P.L. (2000) 'Discipline, Dismissals and Complaints to Employment Tribunals' *British Journal of Industrial Relations* 38.4 (p533).

Knight, K.G. & Latreille, P.L. (2001) 'Gender Effects in British Unfair Dismissal Hearings'. *Industrial and Labor Relations Review* 54.4 (p816)

Lewis, D (1999) 'Re-employment as a remedy for unfair dismissal: How can the culture be changed'. *Industrial Law Journal* 28.2 (p183).

McMullen, J. (2003) 'Practice Points: Unfair Dismissals: Time for a Rethink' *Law Society Gazette,* July.

Ministry of Justice (2011) *Employment Tribunals and EAT Statistics*. 2010–11. London: Ministry of Justice.

ONLINE RESOURCE CENTRE

 A range of online resources to help you through your employment law module have been developed by the author team. These include updates, self-test questions and sources for further reading. (www.oxfordtextbooks.co.uk/orc/taylor_emir3e)

Unfair dismissal—reasonableness

Learning outcomes

By the end of this chapter you should be able to:

- define the term 'reasonableness' as it is used in unfair dismissal cases;

- explain the significance of procedure, consistency and mitigating circumstances in assessing 'reasonableness';

- advise on how employers should handle breaches of conduct in workplaces;

- distinguish between 'gross misconduct' and 'ordinary misconduct';

- advise on lawful means of dismissing employees whose performance is poor;

- outline the expectations of the law in the dismissal of employees on ill health grounds;

- debate the merits of the presence in unfair dismissal law of the 'some other substantial reason' category;

- discuss the major critiques of UK dismissal law.

Introduction

In Chapter 4 we introduced the law of unfair dismissal and explored its framework. The various different reasons for dismissal that feature in employment statutes were described and the way the law treats each assessed. In Chapter 4 we explained that in the case of potentially fair dismissals (ie, those for reasons of conduct, capability, redundancy, etc) tribunals make their decision about whether or not a dismissal is fair or unfair depending on their assessment of how reasonably the employer handled the dismissal. This involves asking the third of the three questions that are asked in unfair dismissal cases:

Did the employer handle the dismissal in a reasonable manner?

If the answer is 'yes', then the dismissal is fair, if it is 'no', then it is unfair and the issue of an appropriate remedy is considered by the tribunal.

In this chapter we explore this concept of 'reasonableness' in detail. We explain how it has evolved over the decades and why the way it is interpreted by the courts remains highly controversial. In particular we focus on how the courts have determined what does and what does not constitute a fair dismissal on grounds of misconduct, poor performance and ill health. Later we introduce and assess some of the major debates about unfair dismissal law more generally. Issues relating specifically to redundancies are discussed in Chapter 6.

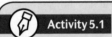 **Activity 5.1**

Assume that you have recently been appointed as HR Manager in a company which operates a small chain of up-market clothing boutiques. Until your appointment there has been nobody employed with the CIPD or any legal qualifications, hiring and firing decisions being taken by individual store managers.

On your first day you discover that three employment tribunal cases are pending. In each a former employee is bringing a claim. Your boss, the Operations Director, is keen to fight each case in order to deter future dismissed staff from bringing cases. You are sceptical, believing that there is no point in pursuing a case you are likely to lose and that ensuing poor publicity could damage the business.

The basic facts in each of the three cases are as follows:

1   Patricia Button had completed two years' service at the time of her dismissal. She was fired when she was off sick for the fourth time in as many months. The absences were for a variety of anxiety-related medical complaints. Prior to her dismissal she had been told on a number of occasions by her manager that her absence record was unsatisfactory.

2   Paul Collar was a warehouseman with fifteen years' service when he was summarily dismissed on grounds of gross misconduct. One day he returned from his lunch break the worse for drink. Later, while trying to sober up, he dropped a cup of black coffee over an open box of white lingerie. The total cost of the damage caused was £150. Paul said that he would pay this, but his offer was refused.

> **3** Antonia Flare was a store manager with three years' service. She was summarily dismissed after three members of her team complained about her management style. She was said to be very negative in her approach, continually criticising her staff and never giving any positive feedback. They said that she was impossible to please. Everything they said and did, even their mannerisms, were the subject of endless censure. They stated that if she was not sacked they would leave.
>
> What are likely to be the major legal issues on which the outcome of each of these cases will hinge? What further information would you need to know in order to make a judgement about whether to recommend settling each case ahead of an employment tribunal hearing and why?
>
> Return to this activity once you have read the chapter, to see how many of your answers were correct.

The band of reasonable responses test

When considering whether or not dismissals for potentially fair reasons are fair, the test the tribunals use is one of 'reasonableness'. But they do not ask themselves whether or not the dismissal was reasonable in general terms, nor do they judge the employer's actions against what they themselves would have done in the same situation. 'Reasonableness' in unfair dismissal is not analogous in any way to 'good practice' on the part of managers, and in the case of misconduct dismissals there is no expectation at all that employers should adhere to anything similar to a legal standard of proof when deciding whether or not to dismiss. Instead, the law allows employers a good deal more latitude.

The test that is used is known as 'the band of reasonable responses' test which was first articulated by the Court of Appeal under Lord Denning in *British Leyland (UK) Ltd v Swift* (1981) and then further developed by the EAT in *Iceland Frozen Foods Ltd v Jones* (1983). This means that the tribunal is only required to satisfy itself that the employer's actions (in dismissing the employee) 'fell within the band of reasonable responses'. In practice, the tribunal must thus ask itself the following question:

Is it possible to characterise the employers' actions as being 'reasonable'?

The use of this test means that the tribunal must not make its judgment according to what it or any supposed man or woman in the street would have done itself when faced with the same situation as was faced by the employer. Instead it must simply ask whether or not the action taken by the employer *could* be construed as being that of a reasonable employer.

What is 'reasonable' in any one particular case will also in part be determined by 'the size and resources' of the employer concerned. Tribunals expect higher standards from larger companies and public sector employers with HR departments, experience of handling disciplinary issues and access to legal advice than they do from small businesses employing a handful of employees. There is no clear division made between 'large' and 'small' employers when considering resources. Each case is judged on its merits and tribunals can take different approaches. However, in the authors' experience businesses employing in excess of 100 to 200 people are generally expected by tribunals to act according to the same broad standards as the largest organisations.

Exhibit 5.1   *Haddon* and *Madden*

For a short period between October 1999 and May 2000 the long-established 'band of reasonable re-sponses test' was briefly abandoned. This happened as a result of a judgment made in the case of *Had-don v Van de Bergh Foods* (1999). This case provides a useful and interesting illustration of the types of problems that tribunals can face when determining whether or not a dismissal was reasonable in law.

Mr Haddon had worked for the respondent company for fifteen years at the time of his dismiss-al, and on the day in question had attended with his wife a celebratory meal held at the workplace at which he was presented with a long service award. However, following the meal Mr Haddon did not return to work the remainder of his shift (about one and a half hours) as he had been asked to do. Instead he continued celebrating the long service award elsewhere. He was fired on the grounds that he had deliberately disobeyed a reasonable management instruction.

The tribunal that heard the case stated that in its view Mr Haddon's dismissal had been 'harsh in the extreme', but that it was nonetheless fair in law. This was because the employer's actions did fall within 'the band of reasonable responses'. It could be said that the dismissal was the ac-tion of a reasonable employer. Treating a long-serving employer in such a way might generally be considered to be unfair, but it was lawful because the employer was consistent in its application of well-established and well-communicated workplace rules.

Mr Haddon appealed his case, where he was fortunate to come before the then President of the EAT (Lord Justice Morison) shortly before his retirement. The EAT took the opportunity both to over-turn the tribunal's judgment in Mr Haddon's case and to overturn the band of reasonable responses test in the process. In many situations, Morison said, an employer could be said to be acting reasonably whether the employee concerned was or was not dismissed. Moreover, in applying the band of reason-able responses test, tribunals often made perverse decisions, accepting as 'reasonable' the actions of employers whose approach was at one 'extreme end' of the possible band of reasonable responses.

For a few months after this employment tribunals appeared happily to abandon the band of reason-able responses test. Instead they started making decisions on the basis of whether they thought the em-ployer had acted reasonably in more general terms, applying their own views about what was and was not reasonable in particular circumstances. This was all well and good, but it did not mask the fact that the EAT in Mr Haddon's case had acted above its own authority. This was because the band of reason-able responses test, though originally invented in the EAT, had subsequently been explicitly approved on several occasions by the Court of Appeal, whose rulings are binding on all lower courts including the EAT. So a few months later, when the first opportunity to do so arose, the EAT (under a new President) put the band of reasonable responses test back. This was achieved in the case of *HSBC Bank v Madden* (2000) which concerned the summary dismissal of a bank clerk on suspicion of a minor fraud. There was some evidence to link Mr Madden with the theft of some debit cards, but no solid proof that he had been involved. What was more, his previous record of service for the bank was unblemished.

Taking its lead from the *Haddon* case, the tribunal substituted its own views for those of the em-ployer, concluding that if faced with the same set of circumstances it would not have dismissed. As a result Mr Madden's dismissal was unreasonable and hence unfair in law. The case was appealed to the EAT and found to be fair. The bank's actions could be described as falling within a band of reasonable responses. This ruling was subsequently confirmed by the Court of Appeal which took the opportunity to state that in the *Haddon* case the EAT had made '*an unwarranted departure from binding authority*'.

Sources: Collins et al (2001:570–75), Deakin and Morris (2010:445–6)

Nowhere in either statute or in the case law is 'reasonableness' as it applies in unfair dismissal law fully defined. There is no checklist of factors set out that tribunals (and indeed employers) can follow when making decisions in this area. However, over the years some fairly solid standards have evolved which the tribunals are obliged to consider when deciding whether or not a dismissal should be found fair or unfair. It is possible to identify three such standards which are generally applied—the procedure used, the consistency of the employer and the issue of whether dismissal was an appropriate sanction in the circumstances. We introduce each of these briefly now, going on to refer to their detailed practical consequences later in the context of specific types of dismissal.

Procedure

It has been firmly established for many years now that the extent to which an acceptable procedure was used in carrying out a dismissal is a central determinant of whether or not it was reasonable. In the case of dismissals on grounds of poor conduct, redundancy and poor performance, in particular, cases frequently turn on this issue.

The centrality of procedure was established in probably the most significant employment law case ever to be determined by the courts—*Polkey v AE Deyton Services* (1988). Here the House of Lords stated that unless it was established by the tribunal that a proper procedure had been used in carrying out the dismissal, it must be found unfair by the tribunal. Moreover, this was true even where individual employees had clearly contributed in large measure to their own dismissals. In such cases, according to *Polkey*, the dismissal was to be judged unfair, but any compensation reduced (perhaps even by 100%) to reflect contributory fault or the chances that the dismissal would have been fair had a proper procedure been used.

Prior to the *Polkey* judgment it had been common for employers to justify their failure to dismiss using a proper procedure (including their own established procedures) by claiming that to have done so would have made no difference to the final outcome. This defence was found to be acceptable by the EAT in *British Labour Pump Co Ltd v Byrne* (1979). It was effectively overturned by *Polkey* and since then the courts have only very rarely found dismissals fair in situations where customary procedures were not followed. Where they have it is because the employer has been able to satisfy them, as is permitted under *Polkey*, that following a proper procedure would have been either 'futile' or 'utterly useless'.

Between 2004 and 2009 a short-lived set of regulations known as the Statutory Disputes Resolution Procedures were in force. These required employers to dismiss in line with a basic three-step procedure. Where this was found not to have occurred the dismissal was declared by tribunals to be automatically unfair and compensation uplifted by 10%–50%. These Regulations were repealed after a government review led by Michael Gibbons found that they were not, as had been anticipated, helping to reduce the number of cases coming to tribunal. As of 2009, therefore, we have returned to the position that had long been established prior to 2004. A failure to follow procedure is now simply a major factor taken into account when assessing whether or not a dismissal for a 'potentially fair' reason is or is not unfair in law. It no longer determines whether or not a dismissal is 'automatically unfair'.

Consistency

A further well-established criterion that tribunals must take into account when making judgements about reasonableness is whether or not the employer has treated its employees consistently. It is thus unlawful to dismiss one person for a reason, while failing to dismiss another whose situation is very similar. It is common for claimants, for example, to admit to having committed an act of misconduct, but to argue that their subsequent dismissal was unfair because others have been allowed to get away with similar conduct in the past. Case law on the dismissal of (official) strikers gives particular weight to consistency. All must be treated alike. If some are dismissed while others are kept on, their dismissals will be judged unfair on grounds of inconsistent treatment (see Chapter 29).

The significance of consistency derives from section 98(4) of the Employment Rights Act which requires tribunals to judge reasonableness '*in accordance with equity and the substantial merits of the case*'—wording which was used as the source of the judgment in the leading case on consistency (*Post Office v Fennell* (1981)). Here the Court of Appeal made it quite clear that unless their actions could be effectively justified, employers must not treat one employee more leniently than another in the same circumstances. Subsequent cases have stressed that employers are permitted a degree of flexibility in how they meet the requirement to act consistently, but the general principle still holds true and can be decisive where two employees are in the same position but only one is fired. The position is neatly summed up by IDS (2005:88):

> Employers, while retaining flexibility of response to employee behaviour, have to act reasonably in the sanctions they choose to apply. Any change of punishment policy without warning; any dismissal of faults previously condoned; or any unjustified difference in treatment of employees in similar positions will help to make the dismissal unfair.

 Activity 5.2   *Proctor v British Gypsum Ltd* (1992)

Mr Proctor was employed as a foreman by the British Gypsum company. He was summarily dismissed from this job after one of his subordinates claimed to have been assaulted by him.

In his defence, Mr Proctor presented evidence to show firstly that he had been provoked, and secondly that in the past employees had not been dismissed for rather more serious incidents of fighting and assault. He therefore claimed that the employer had acted unreasonably in summarily dismissing him—on grounds of inconsistency. Moreover, his previous record of conduct had been impeccable.

The employer claimed that the other incidents had occurred some time previously and that their policy on such matters had toughened in the years since. They also claimed that Mr Proctor's position as a foreman made his case materially different.

The employer won the case.

Questions

1 Why should the fact that Mr Proctor was a foreman make his case 'materially different'?

2 Why do you think Mr Proctor was unsuccessful in persuading the tribunal to take decisive account of his impeccable past disciplinary record and the provocation he suffered?

3 Under what circumstances do you think it is fair for an employer to defend itself in cases of disparity of treatment by arguing that it has recently tightened up its procedures? In what circumstances would such a defence be unfair in your view?

Mitigating circumstances

Employers are not just able in some circumstances to take a flexible approach to the requirement to act consistently when dismissing, there are occasions on which a failure to act flexibly when it would be just to do so can render a dismissal unfair. This occurs when there are mitigating circumstances apparent which any reasonable employer would take account of. IDS (2010:97) illustrate this with the example of *Merseyside Passenger Executive v Millington* (1989) which concerned a breach of an organisation's rules by three employees. In this case Mr Millington and two colleagues were 'caught' by a manager in a pub at lunchtime. All were summarily dismissed because they had broken a long-established and well-communicated ban on all employees entering licensed premises while on duty. Yet there were differences between the cases. Two of the men were drinking at the time they were discovered. Mr Millington, on the other hand, was only eating his lunch. The EAT ruled that in applying the rule in a blanket fashion without taking account of the differences in the respective actions of the three men rendered Mr Millington's dismissal unfair. In other cases courts and tribunals have found disciplinary dismissals to be unfair because employers failed to take account of a long unblemished record of service. In the case of poor work performance, it is a failure to take proper account of mitigating circumstances that originate in employees' home lives which can lead to a finding of unfair dismissal.

In such cases tribunals may come to the conclusion that an alternative, lesser sanction such as a formal warning or holding back a promotion would be more appropriate, or that such a possibility should at least have been considered by the employer. This was the ruling in *P v Nottinghamshire County Council* (1992) in which the Court of Appeal stated that the employer should have considered whether redeployment of an employee rather than dismissal might have been more appropriate following his conviction for a criminal offence. A factor of significance in this case was the fact that the employer was a large local authority with redeployment opportunities. Its 'size and resources' were thus taken into account by the court in coming to a decision about the reasonableness of its actions.

Misconduct dismissals

A dismissal on grounds of misconduct occurs when an employee breaches an employer's rules. This is classed as a potentially fair reason for dismissal, so a particular case will be judged fair or unfair depending on the employer's reasonableness in the circumstances. In deciding cases tribunals have used as their standard yardstick ACAS's Code of Practice 'Discipline at Work'. Employers who follow this code and can show that they have done so, are very likely to win their cases should they need to defend them in court. It is helpful to consider the law in this area under two separate headings—dismissals on grounds of gross misconduct and those for ordinary misconduct.

Gross misconduct

The term 'gross misconduct' does not feature in any statute, although it has been a concept used in the common law for many decades. It is defined in the ACAS Code of Practice as constituting acts of misconduct on the part of employees which 'are so serious in themselves or have such serious consequences that they may call for dismissal without notice for a first offence'. No more precise definition is given, although the ACAS code does give a list of examples that 'might' be included. The implication is that an employee who is guilty of a serious breach of one of these can, in principle, lawfully be summarily dismissed on grounds of misconduct. In the previous edition of the ACAS code eleven examples were given:

- theft, fraud and deliberate falsification of records
- physical violence
- serious bullying or harassment
- deliberate damage to property
- serious insubordination
- misuse of an organisation's property or name
- bringing the employer into serious disrepute
- serious incapability whilst on duty brought on by alcohol or illegal drugs
- serious negligence which causes or might cause unacceptable loss, damage or injury
- serious infringement of health and safety rules
- serious breach of confidence.

ACAS state quite clearly that this is a list of examples and that it is by no means exhaustive. They also make it clear that what does and what does not constitute 'gross misconduct' in any particular workplace is for employers to determine 'in the light of their own particular circumstances'.

In practice the law thus allows employers very considerable freedom (many would argue too much freedom) to decide for themselves what 'counts' as gross misconduct in their own workplace. Hence food manufacturers commonly make eating the produce gross misconduct (problematic for workers in chocolate factories), while in hospitals it is usual that drug errors (ie, giving the wrong dose or the wrong drug to a patient) are treated in the same way. Drinking any form of alcoholic beverage during a shift is treated as gross misconduct in some professions (eg, airline pilots), while moderate drinking at lunchtime, for example, will be of no consequence at all in some others. What matters crucially is that whatever rules are decided upon, employers are only safe to dismiss someone who is in breach of them if the rules have been properly communicated. A dismissal is generally unfair if someone is dismissed summarily for an offence he or she did not know was classed as gross misconduct. As a result it is vital that the rules are written down in some form of disciplinary policy and then communicated effectively to all employees. A staff handbook given to all new employees is a common way of communicating house rules, but it can also be done via an intranet site to which employees' attention is drawn. Only in the case of offences that very clearly amount to gross misconduct in any reasonable employer's eyes is it lawful to dismiss without first warning employees that summary termination of the contract is the punishment they can expect to receive if they are found to have committed the offence (see Exhibit 5.2).

In recent years it appears that the EAT has started to take a rather more employer-friendly line when hearing appeals that relate to dismissals on grounds of gross misconduct. For example in *Weston Recovery Services v Fisher* (2010) it was decided that even though an employee was found by a tribunal not to have been guilty of an act of gross misconduct (some seats in a minibus were not properly secured after he had borrowed it), it should nonetheless have found his summary dismissal to be fair.

Exhibit 5.2   **Misuse of the internet**

In *Parr v Derwentside District Council* (1998), Mr Parr was summarily dismissed having been caught by his employers accessing pornography from his computer while at work. He claimed that he had visited the site concerned by accident, had got himself stuck in it and had subsequently 'revisited it only because he was disturbed by the prospect that entry could easily be made by children'. His claim for unfair dismissal failed because the employers had used a fair procedure and because they were able to show that Mr Parr had broken established codes of conduct.

By contrast, in *Dunn v IBM UK Ltd* (1998), a summary dismissal occurring in similar circumstances was found to fall outside the band of reasonable responses. In this case the employers were found not to have investigated the matter properly and not to have convened a fair disciplinary hearing—the whole matter was handled far too hastily. Moreover, there was no company policy on internet usage for Mr Dunn to have broken and he was unaware that he had done anything that would be construed as gross misconduct. He won his case, but had his compensation reduced by 50% on the grounds that he was partly responsible for his own dismissal.

In a third case, *Humphries v VH Barnett & Co* (1998), a tribunal stated that in normal circumstances the act of accessing pornography from the internet while at work should not be construed as gross misconduct unless such a policy was made clear to employees and established as a workplace rule. However, in this case, the tribunal decided that the pictures downloaded were so obscene that Mr Humphries could be legitimately treated as having committed an act of gross misconduct.

Source: IDS (1999)

Essentially the EAT appears to have decided that 'gross misconduct' and what it represents does not need to play a part in justifying summary dismissals. All that matters is that the employer's actions satisfy the *Burchell* test (see below), that it gets its dismissal right procedurally and more generally acts within 'the band of reasonable responses'. This ruling therefore appears to take little account of the ACAS Code of Practice or its accompanying guidance on what should and should not 'count' as gross misconduct.

Ordinary misconduct

An employee is guilty of an act of ordinary misconduct if their breach of the rules is minor, unintentional, or if a breach of the rule itself cannot be described as 'serious breach of contractual terms'. What is and is not treated as ordinary misconduct will vary from workplace to workplace. Persistent lateness or rudeness would be common examples as would minor acts of insubordination and minor breaches of health and safety rules. Some organisations have clear rules about matters such as the use of headed notepaper by employees, or the use of telephones for private calls. Others do not. Dress codes are an issue in some workplaces as are rules on smoking, in others employees are freer to do as they please. For some employers uttering criticisms of management policies and practices in a public arena would be seen as amounting to misconduct, in others employees are able to make such criticisms of their own employer without suffering any sanctions. As with gross misconduct, what constitutes misconduct of any kind is determined by employers in the light of their own circumstances. Provided employees know about these rules, they cannot subsequently have cause to complain if they breach them and get punished for doing so.

Ordinary misconduct differs from gross misconduct in that it does not lead to summary dismissal. It is not reasonable to dismiss for a 'first offence'. Instead a formal warning is issued by the employer, a dismissal only taking place subsequently on a second or even a third breach of the rules on the part of the same employee.

It is considered good practice to give formal warnings a 'shelf-life' of a year or six months, after which the record is wiped clean and the warning removed from the employee's file. There is no legal requirement to do this. As far as the law is concerned a warning can stay on an employee's file indefinitely—provided of course that all are treated consistently. However, most case law makes it clear that where employers do give warnings shelf-lives, these must be adhered to.

 Activity 5.3 *Airbus UK Ltd v Webb* **(2008)**

In this case Mr Webb and four colleagues were caught by a supervisor watching TV in a locker room when they should have been working. All five men were charged with gross misconduct and found guilty following an investigation. However, only Mr Webb was summarily dismissed. The other four were given final written warnings. This was because they, unlike Mr Webb, had clean disciplinary records. He, by contrast had previously been given a final written warning for misusing company equipment. What made the case contentious was the fact that Mr Webb's previous warning had been time-limited and had expired. He thus claimed that it should not have been taken into account and that he had been unfairly dismissed.

Mr Webb won his case at the employment tribunal and subsequently at the EAT. The dismissal would not have occurred had the employer not taken into account an expired warning and hence was unfair. The Court of Appeal overturned these judgments and found in favour of Airbus. They said that there was nothing in existing case law which said it was automatically unreasonable for an employer to take account of an expired warning. In some circumstances it might be reasonable. It is 'good practice' to disregard expired warnings, but not necessarily unreasonable in law if an employer fails to do so. In this case Mr Webb had been given 'a second chance' following one instance of gross misconduct. There was no inconsistency because his four colleagues were now being given the same 'second chance'.

The ACAS disciplinary procedure

ACAS makes a number of recommendations in its code, such as the advantage of having separate misconduct and incapability procedures and the advantages of training people in their use, which do not amount to requirements on employers. However, in other areas ACAS sets firm procedural expectations which employers must follow if they wish to maximise the chances that a dismissal on grounds of misconduct will be judged 'reasonable' by a tribunal. The most significant features are as follows:

1. Employers are expected to have written rules and procedures which they apply when dealing with cases. These should be fair, transparent and well communicated to staff.

2. Matters should be dealt with promptly and consistently.

3. The following steps must be taken as far as procedure is concerned:

- Establish the facts of each case
- Inform the employee of the problem
- Hold a meeting with the employee to discuss the problem
- Allow the employee to be accompanied at the meeting by a work colleague or trade union official
- Decide on appropriate action
- Provide employees with an opportunity to appeal.

It is important to remember that the ACAS code effectively sets out a minimum acceptable procedure. Where an organisation has more elaborate procedures in place those must be used when dismissing, unless of course, the member of staff concerned is not an employee with a year's continuous service.

ACAS recommends suspension on full pay while a serious accusation of gross misconduct is investigated and the use of formal 'oral warnings' in the case of minor infringements. Written warnings, including final written warnings, are recommended in more serious cases and in situations where earlier oral warnings have not had the desired impact. Disciplinary hearings should be held before written warnings are be issued, employees who are accused of misconduct given every opportunity to defend themselves.

The right to be accompanied

A relatively recent addition to the law in this area concerns the right for employees to be accompanied at any serious disciplinary or grievance hearing. The current law was introduced as part of the Employment Relations Act 1999 and was significantly amended in the Employment Relations Act 2004. There is thus now a right for all workers to be accompanied either by a trade union official or a work colleague and for the companion to 'put the worker's case, sum up the case, respond on the worker's behalf to any views expressed and confer with the worker during the hearing'. Companions can also now ask and answer questions on behalf of the accused employee. It is important to note that the right to be accompanied by a trade union official exists irrespective of whether or not trade unions are recognised in the workplace concerned. This legal right is covered in more detail in Chapter 27.

The *Burchell* case

Aside from the ACAS procedure described above, it is very common for the representatives of the parties at an unfair dismissal hearing in the employment tribunal to make reference to the decision of the EAT in *British Home Stores Ltd v Burchell* (1980), like the *Polkey* case a landmark ruling in the development of unfair dismissal law. Here the EAT took the opportunity to set out a three-stage test for tribunals to apply when faced with a misconduct dismissal:

1. Did the employer genuinely believe that the claimant was guilty of misconduct?

2. Were there reasonable grounds in his (ie, the employer's) mind on which to sustain this belief?

3. At the point at which the belief was formed, had the employer carried out as much investigation into the matter as was reasonable in the circumstances?

If the answer to any of these questions is found to be 'no', it is likely that the ex-employee will win his or her claim of unfair dismissal. It is thus essential for employers to carry out a full and thorough investigation into someone's alleged misconduct before making a final decision about whether to dismiss them. The investigations do not have to be exhaustive, but it is necessary, for example, to take witness statements from anyone who was present when an incident occurred or who might have evidence that is relevant. Taking one person's word for something, or even two or three people's word, when others could also shed light on a matter can render a dismissal unfair.

The other crucial feature of the *Burchell* ruling is the way in which it releases employers from the need to have irrefutable proof of misconduct on the part of an employee before taking disciplinary action, including dismissal. All the employer needs to show is that at the time the decision was taken to dismiss, it genuinely and reasonably believed that the employee concerned was guilty of misconduct.

According to IDS (2010:215), the only circumstances in which the courts find misconduct dismissals fair in situations where employers have not formed 'a genuine belief of guilt on reasonable grounds after reasonable investigation' is when a group of employees come under suspicion and it is impossible to discover which of them actually committed the offence. This occurs in cases of theft, damage to property or where one of several employees provoked a fight. According to the Court of Appeal ruling in *Monie v Coral Racing Ltd* (1981) in circumstances where one employee is responsible for an act of misconduct, but in which despite investigation the culprit cannot be identified, it is reasonable for the whole group to be dismissed on the basis of 'reasonable suspicion short of actual belief'.

 Activity 5.4

Last month Paul was sacked from his job as a porter in a large four-star hotel located in central London. He had worked in the hotel on a full-time basis for four years. He blames himself for the dismissal and thinks that he probably deserved to be sacked given his conduct. He had reported for duty one afternoon having drunk four pints of strong ale in a pub at lunch time. He had then apparently sworn loudly at a colleague in front of several hotel guests. When reprimanded about this incident by the head porter he had told him to 'piss off' and was seen punching him on the left jaw. He had been summarily dismissed there and then without notice.

To his surprise Paul has found out from a friend that his dismissal might in fact be classed in law as being unfair. He thus completes the relevant documentation and sends an unfair dismissal claim to his local employment tribunal office.

Assume that you are the HR manager in the hotel at which Paul was employed. When Paul's unfair dismissal claim is received the general manager asks your advice.

Questions

1   What course of action would you recommend was taken and why?

2   Were no action to be taken and a tribunal case heard, what would you expect the outcome to be and why?

Dismissals on grounds of poor performance

The Employee Relations Act 1996 lists lack of 'capability' as a potentially fair reason for dismissal, defining the term as covering 'skill, aptitude, health or any other physical or mental quality'. In practice, however, the law has somewhat different expectations of employers vis-à-vis dismissal on grounds of ill health and on grounds of poor work performance. It thus makes sense to look at these two common reasons for dismissal separately.

While poor work performance is never easy for managers to deal with from a human point of view, the requirements of the law are straightforward and well established. It is essentially dealt with in the same way as ordinary misconduct, which is just as well as it is by no means easy always to distinguish between minor acts of misconduct and poor work performance. For example employees who are persistently late or indolent, or who fail to meet standards set by managers may be falling short of expectations because they 'won't' do so and not because they 'can't'. Fortunately, from a management point of view, fine distinctions of this kind do not have to be made. ACAS specifically includes reference to poor work performance in its Code of Practice on 'Discipline at Work' and this is the standard that tribunals use to judge the actions of employers when poor performance dismissals come before them. Indeed, ACAS specifically define 'disciplinary situations' as including both 'misconduct and/or poor performance'. Either way, the approach taken is essentially the same. And the courts have long accepted that this is the approach that employers should use:

Stage 1: A full investigation of the employee's performance is carried out in order to identify the problem.

Stage 2: A warning is issued to the employee stating what the consequences of a failure to improve will be.

Stage 3: The employee should be given a fair opportunity to improve.

It is now a requirement that these steps are taken formally, and it makes sense for employers to make sure that each stage is documented. Importantly, a formal hearing needs to be held at which the employee can be represented and at which he/she has every opportunity to explain or indeed to challenge the allegations, and if necessary to appeal the decision. Aside from procedural requirements, the same other tests are also used to establish reasonableness—has the employer acted consistently and have mitigating circumstances been taken into account?

A finding of fair dismissal on grounds of poor performance thus occurs when an employer can show that the problem was identified and explained to the employee, at least one and (for larger employers) two formal warnings have been given and a fair opportunity to improve given following the issuing of each warning. Where the problem is genuinely one of incapability, ACAS state that *'the worker should, wherever practicable, be assisted through training or coaching and given time to reach the required standard'*.

This is all very well in theory, but in practice the requirements of the law in this area can be criticised on a number of grounds. A major problem is the length of time that it takes to dismiss someone who is genuinely incapable of reaching the standards of work that an employer requires.

This is less of an issue with lower-skilled jobs, but with more senior or well-paid people it can take many months or even years to dismiss fairly on grounds of poor performance. This is because tribunals expect to see that under-performing employees have been given a fair period of time to improve their standard of work. In addition to that the need to show that coaching, training or additional support has been provided makes the process costly.

These problems are made worse by the formality required of both the ACAS procedure and the statutory disciplinary and dismissal procedures. In practice, any experienced human resource manager knows when presented with the case of an incapable employee that it may well end up as a dismissal. We know in theory that an improvement in performance is possible, but that in practice it is highly unlikely simply because the employee concerned is incapable of raising their game. As a result, the interests of the organisation require that moves are made directly to organise a formal hearing at which a representative can be present and which results in the issuing of a formal warning. It would be nice to be able to attempt to tackle the issue informally first, but time is not on the employers' side in most cases. As a result a negative, past-focused disciplinary approach is taken from the start, when good management practice would suggest that a better way of tackling poor performance is to take a positive, informal and forward-looking approach. Positively motivating people and giving them self-belief often involves saying things to them that you do not really believe. It may require a manager, for example, to give someone a far more positive appraisal than is genuinely deserved. But doing so in a situation in which a dismissal may result is not a good idea because the documentation can later be brought to a tribunal by an aggrieved ex-employee in support of an unfair dismissal allegation. The reason that good practice in performance management is not followed is thus purely and simply because the law requires that a contrary approach is taken.

The law in this area is thus bad for employers, but also bad for employees who are under-performing. It is the one area of dismissal law in which there is a genuine tension between the principles of the law and principles of effective management. As a result it is the area of dismissal law that employers most commonly seek to sidestep or ignore. The process required is so long, tortuous and unpleasant, that managers avoid it. In some organisations, particularly in the public sector, this means that poor performance is not properly tackled at all. Instead of confronting performance issues, sub-standard performers are carried by others, shifted from department to department or just allowed to get away with it. Elsewhere, where commercial pressures require a quick solution to a performance issue, other approaches are taken. It is common, for example, for redundancy situations to be 'created' as a means of dispensing quickly with the services of a poor performer or for employees simply to be dismissed with a pay-off and a compromise agreement to prevent them bringing legal action. A third approach is a great deal less pleasant, is certainly unethical, but on the face of it (at least) is lawful. This involves finding sufficient fault in someone's performance so as to have a case, albeit very thin, for suspending them on grounds of suspected gross misconduct. Unscrupulous employers then keep the person suspended for many weeks or even months while they undertake an elaborate investigation. They will often hold an investigatory interview or two with the person concerned at which a highly unpleasant approach is taken in the questioning, and will commonly forbid them from contacting any work colleagues at all. In these ways huge pressure is placed on people, their managers calculating that they will resign rather than go through with a disciplinary hearing. Most do so, giving the organisation what it wants. But those who don't and decide to fight their cases find that they are not dismissed at the end of their hearings, but instead re-deployed to another part of the organisation and issued with a final warning.

Another legal principle relating to dismissals for poor performance was decided early on in the development of dismissal law and has not changed since. What should happen when the employer and ex-employee genuinely disagree about whether or not a claimant's performance in the job was sub-standard or not? This is a very common situation, particularly when sales figures, customer ratings or pupils' exam results are used as the yardstick. To what extent are poor figures due to poor performance or to other factors? The answer to this question was provided by the Court of Appeal in *Alidair v Taylor* (1978). Here a two-stage test was developed:

1. At the time of the dismissal did the employer genuinely believe that the employee was incapable of satisfactorily performing the job?
2. Did the employer have reasonable grounds for this belief?

This was an important judgment in that it stated clearly that it is for employers and not tribunals to establish what is a satisfactory standard of performance in any workplace. Secondly, tribunals are not required to reach any kind of objective judgment about whether or not an employee's work performance was or was not sub-standard. What matters is whether the employer genuinely believed that the employee was under-performing at the time of the dismissal and that some good evidence to support this can be provided.

Dismissals on grounds of ill health

Dismissals on grounds of ill health—usually resulting in absence—fall into two categories. Each is treated differently by tribunals, and must in practice be treated differently by employers too. The first is a situation in which an employee is off sick for a long period of time due to medical reasons. The second is where an employee's record of attendance is unacceptably poor either because of a single underlying medical condition or due to a number of different, unrelated illnesses.

Long-term illness

The way that dismissals on grounds of long-term, medical conditions should be handled is well established and clear. Since 1996, however, a degree of additional complexity has been introduced thanks to the introduction of disability discrimination law (see Chapter 13). The way that employers need to treat illnesses which fall within the purview of the Equality Act 2010 (previously the Disability Discrimination Act) is different than is the case with those which are not, but the general approach required was determined in cases heard long before 1996.

Dismissing people on grounds of ill health is a highly unpleasant activity, but it is one which managers are obliged to carry through from time to time. Employees who cannot fulfil their contracts and are not likely to be able to in the near future cannot be kept on indefinitely and at some point an employer has to bring the relationship to an end.

Such situations, unlike misconduct and poor performance, are no longer covered by ACAS in its Code of Practice. However, some very useful guidance used to be included which effectively set out the expectations of tribunals when judging reasonableness:

> Where the absence is due to medically certified illness the issue becomes one of capability and employers should take a sympathetic and considerate approach to these sort of absences. In deciding what action to take in these cases employers will need to take into account, the likelihood of an improvement in health and subsequent attendance (based where appropriate on

professional medical advice), the availability of suitable alternative work, the effect of past and likely future absences on the organisation, how similar situations have been handled in the past and whether the illness is a result of a disability as defined in the Disability Discrimination Act 1995 (now the Equality Act 2010).

The disability discrimination provisions in the Equality Act are likely to apply in most cases of long-term illness because most medical conditions of this nature meet the definition of disability set out in the Act, namely *'a physical or mental impairment which has a substantial and long-term adverse effect on an employee's ability to carry out normal day-to-day activities'*. Almost all seriously debilitating illnesses which have already lasted for a year or could reasonably be expected to do so fall into this category. The exceptions are conditions which are serious and prevent employees from carrying out particular aspects of their jobs, but which nonetheless do not prevent them from carrying out 'normal day-to-day activities'.

In the case of the illnesses which do not amount to disabilities, the law effectively requires employers to take the following steps:

- regularly consult with the employee about their illness and the likely date at which they will be able to return to work
- base decisions on whatever medical evidence can be obtained from the employee's own doctors, a company doctor or the organisation's own occupational health services
- discuss the possibility of alternative employment in the organisation with the employee
- discuss the possibility of a staged return to work, perhaps starting on a part-time basis
- warn sick employees that their contracts will be terminated if they are unable to return to work by a particular date
- act consistently in the way that all employees are treated.

Employees who are sick do not always provide their managers with full medical reports, while busy doctors are understandably reluctant to write extensive letters to employers. In particular medical practitioners tend to be resistant to estimating when a return to work is likely, and this includes doctors employed by the organisation concerned. Managers tend to get vague and unhelpful answers to letters asking for such information. Decisions about whether to dismiss or not are thus often necessarily taken without full knowledge of the medical condition in question or the likely long-term prognosis. The tribunals accept this. Employers are not expected to make medical decisions, only management decisions. What matters is that all reasonable attempts have been made to gather the relevant facts before making a decision about whether to dismiss. A dismissal on medical grounds is likely to be found to be unfair if it emerges that an employer did not first seek all the available medical information. Relying on GPs' letters, when specialist consultants' reports are available or soon will be, is likely to render a dismissal unfair. By contrast, where an employee refuses to provide medical information, or unreasonably refuses to be examined by a company doctor or one employed by an occupational health service, tribunals find in favour of employers if a dismissal subsequently takes place.

The requirements in the case of illnesses which fall within the ambit of disability discrimination law are the same, but there is also an additional requirement. Here it is not enough simply to consult with the employee about likely return dates and the possibility of an alternative job. Instead the employer is under a duty to see whether any 'reasonable adjustments' could be made to working practices or policies in order that an incapacitated employee could return to work. This might well include changing hours of work, adjusting job content, altering the place at which some or all of the work is carried out and redeploying staff into jobs without requiring them to compete with others for a role which they could carry out. Dismissing without first giving full and serious consideration to the possibility of 'reasonable adjustment' or failing to make such adjustments when they could be made is likely to mean that the organisation is both unfairly dismissing and breaching disability discrimination law. In practical terms this is hugely important because the level of compensation that is available to claimants under the Equality Act is much greater than that which can be awarded under unfair dismissal law. It is therefore imperative from an employer's point of view that consideration of possible reasonable adjustment is taken seriously and is fully documented prior to any dismissal.

An important question to which the case law provides no clear answers concerns the length of time that someone must be absent due to ill health before it becomes reasonable to dismiss them. The approach taken by the law on this point is to leave it to tribunals to evaluate given the particular circumstances of the case before them. A number of factors are taken into consideration, the most important of which is the size and resources of the employer concerned. The larger and better funded the organisation, the longer it is expected to wait before dismissing someone who is suffering from a long-term illness. This is because large organisations are able to cover for absence more easily than smaller ones. In the public sector and in many larger private corporations it is common for employees to benefit from full pay while off sick for six months and then from half pay for a further six months. After a year pay stops, and this is commonly the point at which the decision to dismiss takes place. As a general approach this is regarded as reasonable by tribunals, provided of course that it is consistently followed. However, the case law makes it clear that there are circumstances in which it would be unfair to dismiss at a set trigger point like this (eg, when a recovery on the part of the employee is imminent) and also circumstances in which an earlier dismissal could be fair (eg, when the employee's absence cannot effectively be covered by others). Because senior managers are harder to replace satisfactorily on a temporary basis than junior staff, tribunals recognise that earlier dismissals are more justifiable in their case.

In small firms it is usually possible to justify dismissals at a far earlier stage, particularly where business genuinely suffers due to the illness of a key individual. In such cases, where no recovery is expected in the near future, tribunals have found dismissals to be fair after two or three months of absence.

Regular short-term absences

The position with employees who have bad absence records depends on whether or not there is an underlying medical condition that is causing the absences. If there is then employers must treat the matter as they would a long-term absence. There is a need to consult, to warn, to take decisions in the light of medical evidence and to consider possible alternative employment opportunities that would result in less absence. It is often possible, for example, to provide people suffering from back problems with duties that minimise their pain. Similarly those suffering from serious depression, can be relieved of high-pressure activities that they are finding problems coping with. Importantly, of course, reasonable adjustments *must* be made before deciding to dismiss in circumstances where the illness meets the definition of a disability in the Equality Act.

The situation is wholly different where there is no underlying medical condition and where an unacceptable absence record is explained with reference to different ailments. Even where these are covered by doctors' notes and do not appear to be accounted for by employees taking 'sickies', the case law has established that a dismissal is fair in principle purely on grounds of insufficient attendance. This position was robustly confirmed by the Court of Appeal in *Wilson v Post Office* (2000) in which an employee was found to have been fairly dismissed due to his failure to meet the requirements of an attendance policy agreed between his employer and its trade union.

Procedure in such cases is central. Employers need to be able to show that they have formally warned the employee about his or her attendance and then given him or her a sufficient period of time to improve. It is common for employees in such circumstances to be set a target attendance rate to meet which is equivalent to the average rate for the division or department in which they work. If they fail to meet this over the ensuing months, it is reasonable for the employer to give a final warning, or where the absence record is particularly poor, to dismiss.

 Exhibit 5.3   *International Sports Co Ltd v Thompson* (1980)

Ms Thompson was employed for a period of eighteen months before her dismissal at a time when the qualifying period for unfair dismissal rights was one year. During that time she was absent for a total of ninety-six days (ie, around 25% of the time). With the exception of her final period of absence which lasted one month, the rest was taken in short periods of one or two days. For the most part her illnesses were covered by medical certificates, but there was no apparent link between them. Doctor's notes referred separately to dizziness, anxiety, nerves, bronchitis, viral infections, cystitis, althrugia of the knee, dyspepsia and flatulence.

Ms Thompson was warned that her absence record was unacceptable on three occasions, but no formal medical examination was carried out prior to her dismissal. This was because the company doctor saw no point in doing so given that the illnesses were unrelated and transient.

Ms Thompson claimed that she had been unfairly dismissed on grounds of illness as no proper medical investigation had been undertaken. The tribunal found in Mrs Thomson's favour, but this was overturned by the EAT on appeal. The employer had investigated her medical record fairly, had allowed her plenty of opportunity to state her case and had given clear warnings that dismissal would result if her attendance did not improve. This was therefore a fair dismissal.

Some other substantial reason

Since its inception one of the most controversial aspects of unfair dismissal law has been the presence in the list of potentially fair reasons of a catch-all general category of dismissals labelled 'some other substantial reason'. In theory it makes sense for employers to be able to come before a tribunal and argue that their reason for dismissing someone was reasonable despite it not being one of the common reasons for dismissal specifically covered by the Employment Rights Act 1996.

The criticisms that many commentators make does not concern SOSR in principle, but SOSR in practice. This is because over the years its presence has led to some rulings which appear to be far too favourable to employers. Examples include the dismissal of a man employed at a children's camp simply because he was discovered to be gay (*Saunders v Scottish National Camps Association Ltd* (1980)), the dismissal of a woman because she developed a 'personality clash' with some of her work colleagues (*Treganowan v Robert Knee and Co Ltd* (1975)), the dismissal of a woman because she was married to a man who had been dismissed (*Kelman v GJ Oram* (1983)) and, more recently, the dismissal of a probation officer because in his spare time he ran a company which sold products for use by sadomasochists (*Pay v Lancashire Probation Service* (2004)).

Such cases are, however, by their nature rare. According to IDS (2010:351) SOSR is most commonly used in more reasonable circumstances:

- when an employee refuses to agree to a change in terms and conditions in circumstances where it is considered necessary by managers
- when a re-organisation takes place which results in dismissals which do not meet the statutory definition of a 'redundancy'
- when a third party (usually a major customer) pressurises an employer to dismiss someone
- when a fixed-term contract comes to an end and it is not possible to re-employ someone
- in a transfer of undertakings case where there is an 'economic, technical or organisational' reason to justify the dismissal.

It is also important to remember that no dismissal for one of these reasons is going to be found to be 'automatically fair'. They fall firmly within the 'potentially fair' category and are thus judged according to the 'band of reasonable responses test'.

Mandatory retirements

Between 2006 and 2011 employers were able to make use of a specific procedure before forcing someone to retire at the age of 65 or at a later set retirement age. A failure to follow this procedure rendered a dismissal unfair. As a result of the repeal of the law in this area, as of October 2011 it has no longer been the case that an employer has been able to avoid unfairly dismissing someone who is mandatorily retired simply by following a legally mandated procedure.

Interestingly, however, mandatory retirement can still be justified under age discrimination law (see Chapter 12) if the employer can show that its practice amounts to a 'proportionate means of achieving a legitimate aim'. This raises some most interesting questions about the future of mandatory retirement policies, and these are questions that have not been resolved at the time of writing (summer 2011). In short, what we appear now to have is a situation in which mandatory retirement is considered unlawful under UK unfair dismissal law, but lawful (if it can be objectively justified) under EU age discrimination law.

One possibility is that employers will in the future argue that mandatory retirement is lawful by justifying it under the 'some other substantial reason category'. This would involve arguing that if a mandatory retirement policy is objectively justified in age discrimination law, it should also be considered to be reasonable under unfair dismissal law. It will be interesting to see how these issues are settled over the next few years.

Activity 5.5   Married couples who work for competitor companies

In *Simmons v SD Graphics* (1979) Mrs Simmons was employed as a secretary in a small company. She had access to confidential information regarding clients of the firm. Her husband was also employed by SD Graphics. He left to take up a position as a sales director with a direct competitor. SD Graphics were concerned that Mrs Simmons might pass confidential information to her husband, thus damaging the firm's market position. They therefore dismissed her. While admitting that her job gave her access to commercially sensitive information which would damage the firm if disclosed to her husband, she denied having passed any information on and stated that she would not do so. In defending their action, the firm said that the risk was too great and that they had thus acted reasonably in dismissing her. The tribunal found in favour of the employer, as did the EAT when the case was appealed.

In *Skyrail Oceanic Ltd t/a Goodmos Tours v Coleman* (1980) Mrs Coleman was dismissed by a travel agent when she married a man employed by a rival company. She had access to confidential information, but had given an undertaking to her employer that she would not pass this on to her husband. At the time of her dismissal no evidence was produced that she had leaked any information. The tribunal found the dismissal unfair, and on appeal to the EAT this finding was confirmed. It would have been fairer, according to the ruling, for the employer to have warned her that she would be dismissed if she divulged any information to her husband.

Questions

1   Why is the ruling in the *Simmons* case cited frequently as an example of why SOSR is interpreted unfairly?

2   What differences between the circumstances of these two cases do you think might account for the different outcomes?

3   How far do you think the outcome of cases like this might be different if the two people concerned are parent and child or unmarried partners? Why?

Critiques of the law on reasonableness

Employee perspectives

The most common, major critique of unfair dismissal law made by academics relates to the band of reasonable responses test we outlined above. Most argue that it has the effect of allowing employers to dismiss in circumstances where they should not. Collins (2010:179) is particularly critical of tribunal decisions which find dismissals to have been 'harsh but fair'. Surely, he asks, if a dismissal is harsh it should not be found to be fair in law? The whole point of unfair dismissal law is that it should deter employers from acting harshly.

According to Anderman (2004: 122–126), the UK courts are wedded to the band of reasonable responses test because it is in accordance with the long-held assumption in our company law that employers have exclusive 'property rights' over the jobs in organisations—the jobs, along with the companies are owned by shareholders. This assumption underlies the law in most Anglo-Saxon countries with common law traditions, there being a long-standing reluctance on the part of judicial systems to interfere with this position. In the USA the doctrine of 'employment at will' is followed, whereby there is no statutory protection whatever for employees who are dismissed unless the termination of a contract breaches some other law such as sex or race discrimination. In the majority of European jurisdictions employees do not enjoy full property rights over their jobs, in so far as they cannot be bought and sold like other forms of property, but the law starts with the assumption that employers are not the sole owners. It is frequently the case (as in Germany) that decisions to dismiss, like other significant decisions in an enterprise, are taken jointly by managers and representatives of a works council. In Italy, according to Anderman, the norm following a finding of unfair dismissal from a firm employing more than fifteen workers is for employees to be reinstated in their old jobs, while in the Netherlands it is considered unlawful to dismiss until a local state official has assessed the case and sanctioned termination of the contract. In these ways employment law ensures that employers and employees both, to a degree, have property rights in the jobs that make up the organisation.

In the UK a middle way between the US and European approaches has been adopted through the development of the band of reasonable responses test. Jobs in an organisation remain the property of employers, but restrictions are placed on their ability to abuse their power by acting in a wholly unreasonable manner. The problem is that this position has the effect of allowing employers to act somewhat unreasonably and certainly unfairly by the standards of good industrial practice. It is thus argued that the courts need to accept that their role may involve interfering with employers' sole property rights in employment and that they may from time to time have to judge 'reasonableness' according to another more restrictive test. This is not such a big step when it is considered that far more restrictive tests are already placed on employers in the field of discrimination law.

Different commentators argue in favour of somewhat different approaches. Hepple (1992: 95), for example, proposes a simple test of 'just cause' under which 'the substantive interests of management and the employee would be equally considered'. Ewing (1996:304) advocates a more complex approach which would involve five criteria for judging whether or not a dismissal is reasonable:

- risk of harm to the employer's business,
- the resources of the employer,
- proportionality,
- consistency,
- reasonableness in the circumstances.

Collins (2004:39–40 and 2010: 176–79) suggests that the test used to determine reasonableness in unfair dismissal law should be similar to that now used in cases of indirect discrimination in discrimination claims (see Chapters 10–17)—that of proportionality:

> Under such a test, the tribunal must ask whether the employer is genuinely pursuing a legitimate interest in dismissing the employee, and if so, whether the dismissal was a necessary and proportionate means to achieve that legitimate objective in the circumstances of the case. The employer would be required to show that the employee's continued employment was posing a significant problem for the business operation, and that the sanction of dismissal, as opposed to lesser disciplinary action, was both necessary and a proportionate response.

Activity 5.6

Go back and look again at the facts of the various cases we have described in this chapter in Activity and Exhibit boxes. We suggest that you consider the cases of *Haddon, Madden, Proctor, Parr, Dunn, Humphries, Thompson, Webb, Simmons* and *Coleman*. In each case try to apply the test of proportionality suggested by Collins.

Questions

1   How easy did you find it to apply the proportionality test, given the very limited facts you had to work with?

2   In which of the cases was the outcome the same as it was using the band of reasonable responses test, and in which was it different?

3   Having applied the proportionality test in practice, how far would you agree with Collins that it achieves a fairer balance between the interests of employers and employees than the band of reasonable responses test?

Employer perspectives

Larger employers and their organisations have rarely complained about unfair dismissal law and appear to have, in the main, no major problems with the range of reasonable responses test. Critiques from an employer perspective have thus overwhelmingly come from the small firms sector. Analysis of employment tribunal statistics persistently shows that small firms are much more likely than larger organisations to have claims for unfair dismissal made against them and, subsequently, are considerably more likely to lose these cases (Earnshaw et al, 2000: 63–64). This long-standing and continuing situation has led many to argue that the law favours larger employers. In particular it is often said that the assumptions in unfair dismissal law about what constitutes 'a reasonable response' do not fairly reflect the reality of management in small companies.

The major criticism relates to the apparent preference of unfair dismissal law for formality over informality. Where, as in large organisations, bureaucratic systems are used as part and parcel of the management process, ensuring consistency and adherence to management strategies, this is not so in most small companies—particularly those which are run by owner-managers. While now somewhat dated, the following quotation from Westrip (1986:196) articulates this small business perspective effectively:

> ... the underlying motivation for many owner-managers was the need to 'attain and preserve independence', with personal satisfaction ranking as a high priority, often at the expense of rationality. Thus, where the desire for autonomy and self-esteem are dominant goals, he tends to adopt a highly personalised style of management, sometimes paternalistic, often autocratic. Resistant to delegating decision-making, he is less likely to consult with colleagues or discuss the perceived problems with the employee before taking the decision to dismiss. Since personal characteristics of employees often appear more important to the owner-manager than skill level, previous training or formal qualifications, any perceived deterioration is unlikely to be tolerated. Priding himself on an informal and flexible form of management, the owner-manager may be inconsistent in the standards he applies, not only to different individuals but

with the same employee over a period of time. In short, personnel management in the small firm is likely to be very different to the approach adopted in larger concerns, with a far greater likelihood of the owner-manager dismissing at a whim.

Because of this preference for informality, there are particular problems in small firms meeting the procedural requirements needed in order to win cases of unfair dismissal for potentially fair reasons. Earnshaw et al (2000) found that moving on from informal approaches to the first stage of a formal disciplinary procedure was seen by employees as 'an indication that they had already decided to dismiss' and that this was only done, in practice, to 'go through the motions' or 'cover their tracks' in case a tribunal claim was lodged later. However, at the same time, leaving it until after informal approaches have been tried and failed also left employers vulnerable to accusations that the decision to dismiss had already been taken before a formal hearing had taken place or that insufficient time and effort had been put into investigating the circumstances of an individual case ahead of a hearing.

A number of surveys have been carried out looking at the experiences of small firms in employment tribunals (eg, Earnshaw et al, 2000; Marlow, 2002 and Small Business Council, 2004). While in all cases the views expressed were mainly negative, there is little evidence that owner-managers allow the threat of tribunal claims to alter their approaches to any great extent. They prefer informality and will not allow unfair dismissal law to interfere with this preference. Moreover, there is no general support for the proposition that small firms should be exempted from unfair dismissal law. Instead the view from the small firm sector is that tribunals should adjust their assumptions so as to take greater account of their needs and practices. What is 'reasonable' in a small firm should not be defined in the same way as what is 'reasonable' in a large firm. Tribunals should not expect formality and should be tolerant of a degree of inconsistency resulting from flexible management styles. Moreover, they should accept that it is inevitable that a manager in a small firm is going to have made up his or her mind about the outcome of a formal hearing before it takes place. In short, far greater consideration should be given by tribunals than is currently the case to the relative 'size and resources' of the respondent in each case.

One way of helping to achieve this would be to ensure that the lay members hearing unfair dismissal cases brought against small employers (or at least one of them) has some experience of working in the small-firm sector. But this would only be of partial assistance because the tests that tribunals are obliged to use when deciding cases are well established and approved by the EAT and the higher courts. The solution to the small-firm problem might thus, paradoxically, be the same as the solution to the 'harsh but fair' problem identified above. What is needed is a move away from the band of reasonable responses test, towards one which gives tribunals far more freedom to determine for themselves, given all the facts of the particular case before them, whether on balance the dismissal was 'fair'.

CHAPTER SUMMARY

- In the case of potentially fair dismissals the outcome of the case rests on the application of 'the band of reasonable responses test'. This requires the tribunal to judge whether or not the employer's actions when dismissing the claimant could be described as being those of a reasonable employer.

- Reasonableness is principally determined with reference to the procedure used, consistency of treatment as between different employees and the extent to which any mitigating circumstances were taken into account.

- When an employee is guilty of an act of gross misconduct, it is lawful for an employer to dismiss summarily without notice. However, the law imposes quite stringent tests to establish whether or not an act of gross misconduct has taken place. If not, it is expected that at least one warning will be given before dismissal is contemplated.

- Warnings are also necessary when an employer dismisses on grounds of poor performance or ill health. In the case of ill health dismissal care must be taken both to act reasonably and to meet the expectations of the Equality Act.

For updates and further materials, please see the online resource centre at www.oup.com.

REFERENCES

Anderman, S. (2004) 'Termination of Employment: whose property rights?' in C. Barnard, S. Deakin & G. Morris (eds): *The Future of Labour Law*. Oxford: Hart Publishing.

Angell, T. (2005) 'Polkey: dead or alive?' *New Law Journal*, April.

Collins, H. (2004) *Nine Proposals for the Reform of the Law on Unfair Dismissal*. London: Institute of Employment Rights.

Collins, H. (2010) *Employment Law*. Second Edition Oxford: Oxford University Press.

Collins H., Ewing K. & McColgan A. (2001) *Labour Law: Text and Materials*. Oxford: Hart Publishing.

Deakin, S. and Morris, G. (2009) *Labour Law*. Fifth Edition. London: Butterworths.

Duggan, M. (1999) *Unfair Dismissal: Law, Practice and Guidance*. Welwyn Garden City: CLT Professional Publishing.

Earnshaw J., Marchington M. & Goodman J. (2000) 'Unfair to whom? Discipline and dismissal in small establishments' *Industrial Relations Journal* 31.1 (p62).

Ewing, K. (ed) *Working Life: A new perspective on labour law*. London: Lawrence & Wishart/Institute of Employment Rights.

Hepple, B. (1992) 'The Rise and Fall of Unfair Dismissal' in W McCarthy (ed) *Legal Intervention in Industrial Relations: Gains and Losses*. Oxford: Blackwell.

IDS (1999) 'Downloading Pornography'. IDS Brief 637, May. London: Incomes Data Services.

IDS (2005) *Unfair Dismissal: Employment Law Handbook*. London: Incomes Data Services.

IDS (2010) *Unfair Dismissal: Employment Law Handbook*. London: Incomes Data Services.

Marlow, S. (2002) 'Regulating labour management in small firms' *Human Resource Management Journal* 12.3 (p25).

Small Business Council (2004) *Evaluation of Government Employment Regulations and their Impact on Small Business*. London: HMSO.

Westrip, A. (1986) 'Small Firms Policy: The Case of Employment Legislation' in J. Curran, J. Stanworth & D. Watkins (eds): *The Survival of the Small Firm*, Volume 2. Aldershot: Gower.

ONLINE RESOURCE CENTRE

A range of online resources to help you through your employment law module have been developed by the author team. These include updates, self-test questions and sources for further reading. (www.oxfordtextbooks.co.uk/orc/taylor_emir3e)

Redundancy

Learning outcomes

By the end of this chapter you should be able to:

- define the term 'redundancy' and explain why different definitions are used in different parts of UK redundancy law;

- advise employers on how to go about establishing a pool of employees who are 'at risk' of redundancy;

- devise a lawful method for selecting employees for redundancy;

- ensure that an organisation complies with its duty to consult individually and collectively before making people redundant;

- calculate statutory and contractual redundancy payments;

- advise managers and employees about the rights of people who are serving their redundancy notices before receiving their severance payments;

- explain the position vis-à-vis redundancy payments for people employed by insolvent companies;

- comment on the debate about UK redundancy law being a 'soft touch' in comparison with the law in many other EU countries.

Introduction

Redundancy is one of the potentially fair reasons for dismissal listed in unfair dismissal law. As a result, whether or not a particular redundancy is lawful depends on the reasonableness with which the dismissal is handled by the employer. The procedure used must be fair and all employees must be treated consistently for this to be the case. In this respect redundancy law is straightforward both to understand, and from a management point of view, to abide by in practice. However, as a topic area it is in fact quite complex and not always easy to grasp. This is partly because of the way redundancy law has evolved over the past thirty years, EU obligations forcing the UK to alter its statutes regularly, and partly because it is quite possible for an employer to dismiss people for economic reasons without technically making redundancies. Further complexity arises from the requirement for employers to pay redundant employees compensation in the form of a redundancy payment when they

---

 Activity 6.1

After several years of expanding on the back of healthy profits, the firm you work for has had a bad year. Aggressive marketing and innovative product development on the part of a competitor has reduced sales of your products to new customers, while several major existing clients have also been attracted by your rival. It is necessary to cut costs in order to ensure that the firm remains in the black in the coming financial year. At the same time, however, senior managers need to hire some new staff to develop product lines which will attract customers back in the future. The board of directors approves a plan which will reduce the staff in administrative functions across the business by 20%. You are asked to make one of the two accounts administrators who work in your department redundant. But who should it be?

Sue is the longer serving of the two employees, having been employed in her role for over twenty years. The redundancy payment she would be entitled to would be sizeable, but she has a disabled husband and two children to provide for. At her age she might find it difficult to find a new job quickly.

Julian, by contrast, is young, single and has only been employed by the firm for two years. But he is the better performer of the two by a considerable margin. His absence record is impeccable, whereas Sue's is poor, and he has obvious potential for promotion into a more senior role fairly soon. Julian is also more popular than Sue among colleagues and managers because he is so much more cheerful and helpful to people.

Questions

1 What criteria do you think should be used to make the decision about which of the two accounts administrators should be made redundant?

2 How would you go forward procedurally?

3 What further information would you require in order to ensure that the redundancy was carried out lawfully?

Return to this activity once you have read the chapter, to see how many of your answers were correct.

dismiss for this reason. As a result a good deal of the case law relates to situations in which employees want to be made redundant in order to claim their payment, but in which they have instead been retained by their employers in some capacity. Redundancy law becomes more complex still in the case of insolvencies when there may or may not be sufficient funds available to make redundancy payments.

Defining redundancy

We are in the strange and rather unsatisfactory position at present of having in our statutes two effective definitions of the term 'redundancy'. The first, which we use for unfair dismissal and redundancy payments purposes, dates from the Redundancy Payments Act 1965. It is now found in the Employment Rights Act 1996. The second definition derives from European law and is used when questions of collective consultation in redundancy situations are being decided. This is broader than the established UK definition, effectively including all dismissals which are for economic reasons and are thus not related to the actions or inactions of individual employees.

The established UK definition is apparently not designed to make life easy for employers and employees. It is as follows:

a) The fact that an employer has ceased, or intends to cease—

   i) to carry on the business for the purposes of which the employee was employed, or

   ii) has ceased or intends to cease, to carry on that business in the place where the employee was so employed.

   or

b) The fact that the requirements of that business—

   i) for employees to carry out work of a particular kind, or

   ii) for employees to carry out work of a particular kind at the place where the employee was so employed, have ceased or diminished or are expected to diminish.

(Employment Rights Act 1996 (section 139(1))

In practice this means that a redundancy situation is one of the following:

- a business is closing
- a workplace is closing
- there is a diminishing need for employees to do particular kinds of work in an organisation.

If one of these three conditions is not the cause of a dismissal, in law it is not a redundancy. Central, therefore, is a reduction in headcount. Fewer people must be required either in a business, a workplace or in a particular area of work for a redundancy situation to be created. As a result, dismissals which occur for economic reasons, but which fall outside this definition, are not redundancies and do not give the employees concerned the right to claim redundancy payments. This often happens when employers restructure their enterprises or re-organise the allocation of work in order to achieve greater efficiency or to deliver a changed business strategy. The result may well be the dismissal of individual staff, but if there has been no diminution of 'work of a particular kind' it is not a redundancy.

As far as unfair dismissal is concerned such re-organisations are treated by tribunals, at least in principle, as 'some other substantial reason'. Like bona fide redundancies they thus fall into the 'potentially fair' category and will be judged as fair provided the employer has acted within the band of reasonable responses. The same is true of situations in which employees are dismissed for failing to agree to, or adapt to, the requirements of a re-organisation. Provided a particular employee's 'sphere of employment' does not change, if he or she does not adapt to new procedures or practices, any subsequent dismissal is not for redundancy. As long as it is carried out fairly in terms of procedure, it will be fair in law and will not give rise to the right to a redundancy payment.

 Activity 6.2   *Vaux and Associated Breweries v Ward* **(1968)**

One of the earliest, most notorious and most widely quoted cases about redundancy dates from 1968 and concerned the fate of a middle-aged barmaid called Mrs Ward.

Mrs Ward worked as a barmaid in a hotel run by the Vaux Brewery. Here, the management decided to refurbish the pub and re-open with different decor and style of service. As part of the re-branding it was decided to replace the existing bar staff with bunny girls. Both Mrs Ward and the managers agreed that she was unsuited to the new uniforms. There were no other jobs available which were suitable for her. However, instead of allowing her to continue in the bar job, she was dismissed.

As this occurred before the days of unfair dismissal law, Mrs Ward was unable to challenge the legality of the dismissal itself as she would now be able to, nor could she bring a sex discrimination claim of any kind as that only became possible in 1975. But she did take legal action in order to try to secure for herself a redundancy payment.

When the case was heard before an industrial tribunal Mrs Ward won. The two lay members outvoted the chairman and made her the award. However, on appeal the company won their case. Mrs Ward was not entitled to a redundancy payment.

Question

1   Why did Mrs Ward lose her case?

2   What significance might this ruling have at your workplace?

3   Should the law be altered to help people in this type of situation?

4   How might the definition of 'redundancy' be re-written to achieve this purpose?

Until 1999 redundancy law was a great deal more complex than it now is. This was because the courts had reached rather different and sometime complex judgments about what should happen in various types of situation:

1. For example, it is common for someone to do different work in their day-to-day working lives than is described in the contract of employment. Is it fair to make them redundant when the work they are doing ceases but that described in the contract continues?

2. Similarly what should happen in a multi-site organisation where one workplace closes but individual contracts state that employees may be required to work at any number of sites if required? Is it fair to restrict redundancies to people working in the one place?

3. A third thorny issue is bumping (also known as transferring redundancies). Is it fair to sack person A when their job is not redundant, in order to retain person B whose job is becoming redundant?

The amount of complexity was hugely reduced by the House of Lords in its judgment in *Murray v Foyle Meats Ltd* (1999). Here it was ruled that what mattered for the purposes of a lawful redundancy was what the individual concerned actually did in his/her job. If there was a difference between their actual work and what their contracts of employment define as their work, it is the actual situation that the courts must look at. But, very helpfully, the judgment goes further than this. The law lords said that when faced with a situation in which parties dispute the existence of a redundancy situation three questions must be asked. If the answer to all three is 'yes' then it is a redundancy. Whether it is lawful or not, of course, depends on the procedure used. The three questions are as follows:

1. Has the employee been dismissed?

2. Has there been an actual or prospective diminution in the need for employees to carry out work of a particular kind?

3. Is the dismissal wholly or mainly attributable to this state of affairs?

This is a most significant ruling—one of the most important in UK employment law. Whether or not it is helpful for employers or employees depends on the circumstances. It makes it easier for employers to make people redundant lawfully, but at the same time it increases the number of situations in which dismissed employees can claim redundancy payments as of right. Moreover, it strongly appears to suggest that bumping redundancies is a lawful practice—at least in principle. Employers can retain the services of valued individuals whose jobs are going by switching them into jobs that are remaining and dismissing, instead, the holders of those jobs. This does not mean that bumping can lawfully occur without applying the core principles of a fair procedure and consistent treatment of all employees, but it is lawful provided those other matters are correctly handled (see McMullen, 2011 for an excellent discussion of this issue).

Bennett (2002:146) heaps praise on the House of Lords for its decision in *Murray v Foyle Meats* on the grounds that their judgment *'reflects the ordinary meaning of the words'* in the statute and does not put any gloss on them. As a result, he argues, the law now achieves what it was created to achieve, namely greater mobility in employment. He contrasts this state of affairs with that which applies in the case of the 'band of reasonable responses' test used more generally across unfair dismissal law:

> The range test is a gloss, which distorts the statute, ignores what is fair to an employee and makes a finding of unfairness unlikely. In addition, it does not achieve the purpose of the legislation of having an impartial decision on the dismissal and thus justice is not seen to be done.

Bennet looks forward to the day when the House of Lords has the opportunity to consider the band of reasonable responses test, hoping that in doing so it might take a leaf out of its own book and apply the same gloss-free reasoning that they did in *Murray v Foyle Meats*.

Redundancy selection

The law does not specify the procedure that employers should use to effect redundancies. However, in practice, in order to meet its requirements employers are obliged to comply with a long-established two-stage approach. The first stage involves identifying those who are 'at risk' of redundancy or the 'pool of employees' from which the redundancies will come. This stage is necessary because it allows employers to comply with the consultation requirements (outlined below) which require discussion at an early opportunity with those 'who *may* be affected' by the dismissals. Identifying a suitable pool is also helpful from a management point of view in that it allows an organisation to state up front who is not going to be affected by the redundancies. This reduces the degree to which morale-reducing rumours spread across members of a workforce who have no need to worry about their own personal positions. The second stage then involves selecting from the pool of people who are 'at risk' those who are actually going to be given notice and be made redundant.

There is no discernible principle in the case law that favours either big or small pools. The courts have made it quite clear in a succession of rulings over many years that each case must be considered on its merits and that there can thus be no judicially approved guidelines for employers to follow. Employers can thus draw their boundaries around the at risk group widely or can take a more restrictive approach. Everything depends on particular circumstances. If redundancies are only going to affect one division or one group of staff, it makes sense only to include them in the pool. Alternatively if a more general downsizing exercise is taking place which cuts across divisions or departments, it is probably wise to include almost everyone. All that the law requires is that the employer is able to show that some clear, objective rationale was consistently applied at the time that the pool was idenitified. The great danger lies in unreasonably limiting a pool to a specific group, when in practice it is not distinguished in any meaningful way from another group which is excluded from the pool. In particular, tribunals take a dim view of processes which exclude favoured individuals from a pool without good reason. It would, for example, be blatantly inconsistent (and hence outside the band of reasonable responses) to exclude the managing director's secretary from a pool of 'at risk' employees which included all other secretaries in the organisation. IDS (2008:205) cite the case of *Hendy Banks City Print Ltd v Fairbrother* (2004) to illustrate the dangers associated with an overly restrictive pool. Here the only staff included in the pool were those who had been trained to use a particular machine which was no longer going to be used. Other staff, most of whom were less experienced than those who were included in the pool, were excluded despite the fact that two-thirds of the work the two groups performed was identical. The tribunal, and subsequently the EAT too, declared the redundancies unfair.

When it comes to selecting individuals from the pool to make redundant there are in practice three approaches which are lawful in principle. These effectively give employers a considerable degree of flexibility. The three are last-in-first-out (LIFO), points-based systems and selection-based systems. What matters legally is how each of these is carried through in practice. In *British Aerospace v Green* (1995) the Court of Appeal said that there are two bases for challenging a selection procedure in a tribunal:

1. *'a challenge to the fairness of the system of selection which the employer adopted, including the criteria for redundancy, safeguards against bias and the extent of consultation'*.

2. *'a challenge to the fairness of the manner in which the system was applied in practice'*.

LIFO

Last-in-first-out used to be almost always used by UK employers (Muir 1996:18). This was partly because it was the approach favoured by trade unions in an era when they had substantial influence over redundancy selection processes and partly because until 1994 tribunals were obliged to find redundancies *automatically unfair* if selection occurred 'outside an agreed or customary procedure'. Except in special cases, employers were thus obliged to follow the same approaches they had used in the past, and this was invariably LIFO.

Last-in-first-out has a number of advantages. First, of course, it is the least expensive approach to take. Because longer-serving employees are entitled to higher redundancy payments than colleagues who have only joined the organisation relatively recently, a great deal of money can be saved by dismissing those with the fewest years of service under their belts. It is also administratively straightforward and hence less expensive in terms of management time than the other possible approaches. Thirdly it is straightforward and means that everyone knows where they stand. The uncertainties associated with the alternative procedures when seen from the employees' perspective are thus avoided. Finally LIFO is objective and hence feels fair. The likelihood of dissent manifesting itself in the form of industrial action, reduced levels of performance or employment tribunal cases is thus minimised.

Set against these advantages, though, is one major disadvantage. LIFO invariably means that good performers are made redundant (albeit cheaply) while poorer but longer-serving colleagues keep their jobs. This problem is compounded by the fact that many of those who retain their jobs would actually like to go, while colleagues who are keen to stay have their contracts terminated. For these reasons LIFO is a lot rarer now than it was ten or twenty years ago.

There is also a question mark over the extent to which LIFO complies with age discrimination law. This is a potential issue because it invariably favours older employees and disfavours younger ones. At the time of writing (summer 2011) a case on this precise issue has yet to reach one of the higher courts. We can, however, draw some guidance from *Rolls Royce plc v Unite* (2009) in which the Court of Appeal ruled that the use of length of service to determine redundancy selection was capable of amounting to age discrimination, but that in this case at least it was nonetheless justified as '*a proportionate means of achieving a legitimate aim*'. Importantly the *Rolls Royce* case concerned the use of service length as one of a number of selection criteria, so this was not a 'pure' LIFO situation. Moreover, a factor taken into account by the court was the fact that the redundancy selection procedure used at Rolls Royce had been negotiated with a recognised trade union who supported its continued use.

Points systems

The second lawful approach to take to redundancy selection is a great deal more complicated. It involves taking a range of criteria into account and scoring each employee in the pool against these. The number of points awarded in the case of each is then added up, and those who have the lowest scores are dismissed. Any number of criteria could be used, but it is important that they are justifiable on business grounds and not irrational or whimsical in any way. Pulling names out of a hat or basing decisions on star signs will not impress tribunals.

Great care also has to be taken not to use criteria that would fall foul of discrimination law and render the redundancies automatically unfair. The more common criteria used, according to IDS (2001:7) are the following:

- attendance records
- disciplinary records
- performance/quality of work
- attitude
- skills/competencies
- versatility/adaptability
- qualifications
- experience
- customer focus
- length of service.

LIFO is thus still a factor in many systems that are used, but it is not decisive. Duggan (1999:249–250) and IDS (2008:209–213) cite instances in which other factors have been used by employers and found to be lawful by tribunals. Examples are physical fitness, future potential and loyalty as judged by participation or non-participation in industrial action. Age was found to be a fair criterion in the past, but is now likely to be unlawful as a result of the introduction of age discrimination law in 2006. How significant each factor is will depend on the weighting it is given vis-à-vis the others, and this will in part determine its fairness in a tribunal's eyes. Over-emphasising absence records, for example, at the expense of other factors could be seen as lacking fairness. Moreover, of course, absence caused as a result of pregnancy or because of a disability that is covered by the Equality Act must be discounted if sickness records are to be included.

With points systems the overriding consideration that employers need to take into account is the need both to apply the criteria objectively and to be seen to be doing so. Consistency too is vital if a possible finding of unfair dismissal is to be avoided.

 Exhibit 6.1   *Pinewood Repro Ltd v Page* **(2010)**

This is an important case with implications for employers who use matrix-type or points-based scoring systems to select employees in a pool for redundancy. Here the employer used a variety of criteria, some subjective in nature, others more objective (absence rates, productivity, etc). One of the subjective criteria was 'flexibility'.

Mr Page scored very poorly on 'flexibility' and during his consultation meetings he asked why this was. No answer was given. He was not therefore in a position to challenge the score he had been given.

Subsequently, having been made redundant, Mr Page brought an unfair dismissal claim to the tribunal and won. The employer had not consulted fully because it had not shared with Mr Page the reasoning behind his low score on a subjective measure. Mr Page won again when the case was appealed to the EAT.

Selection systems

The third approach that is considered fair in principle involves taking a fundamentally different approach than is the case with the first two. Here the starting point is to draw up the organisational structure that will be in place following the redundancies. The scope of each job is determined and the selection criteria drawn up. Employees in the pool are then invited to apply for the jobs in the structure. Those who do not have the required skills or attributes to apply, together with those whose applications are unsuccessful are then made redundant.

In order to be lawful the employer needs to be able to satisfy the tribunal that the criteria were fair and objective and fairly applied in practice. It is wise to make and retain detailed notes from interviews so that objectivity can be proved to have been applied in court if necessary.

 Exhibit 6.2   **Good practice and the law**

There are a number of myths about redundancy law which are very commonly believed. These stem from a confusion on many people's part between what constitutes good practice in the handling of redundancies and what is strictly necessary in order to comply with the law. Achieving the latter is a good deal less onerous from the employer's point of view than achieving the former.

For example, asking for volunteers during a redundancy programme is not a legal requirement. Failing to do so will in no way mean that a tribunal will find the employer's actions to have been unreasonable. The same is true of the provision of outplacement services. Hiring consultants to provide training in job-seeking skills and practical careers advice for people at risk of redundancy is helpful and ethically very justifiable. But it is not a legal requirement—even for the largest and best-resourced organisations.

Good practice guides also tend to stress the importance for managers of communicating information concerning redundancies in a sensitive, appropriate and carefully planned way. This has great advantages because it stops the perpetration of rumours in a workplace which can easily end up reducing morale, or even in some cases, precipitating resignations from good performers who would in all likelihood be retained in any event. These too are not legal requirements.

That said, of course, in a general sense it must be the case that the employer which does take these steps and can show that good practice has been followed, is going to appear far more professional and reasonable in the eyes of a court than one who has not. Good practice therefore is not a legal requirement, but it could be of assistance to an employer which finds itself having to defend the procedures it adopted in front of an employment tribunal.

Consultation requirements

Aside from fair and objective selection, the other major procedural requirements relate to the duty to consult with affected employees prior to redundancies taking effect. Here a distinction has to be made between individual redundancies (where small numbers are dismissed) and collective redundancies which involve the termination of large numbers of contracts. The law is quite specific about where the boundary between the two lies—it is when it is proposed that twenty or more employees are to be made redundant within a period of ninety days.

Collective consultation

Collective consultation procedures, unlike the rest of redundancy law, derive from European law. The requirements are set out in the Collective Redundancies & Transfer of Undertakings (Protection of Employment) (Amendment) Regulations 1999—the most recent in a line of statutes designed to bring UK law into line with EU requirements in this field. The key points in these Regulations are as follows:

- Consultation has to occur at the earliest practicable opportunity, but has to happen in any event:
  - thirty days before the first dismissal takes effect if twenty to one hundred are being made redundant
  - ninety days before if over one hundred are being made redundant.
- Where a trade union is recognised employers must consult with this union, irrespective of how many affected employees are union members.
- Where more than one recognised trade union represents staff in affected groups, all must be consulted with.
- Where no trade union is recognised consultation must take place with 'appropriate representatives' of the affected workforce—this can be existing elected reps (eg, staff association officers).
- If there are no elected staff representatives, time and facilities must be made available to allow an election to take place.
- The employer can decide how many elected reps there need to be, but sufficient numbers must be elected to represent the interests of all affected employees.
- Consultation must cover the following topics:
  - ways to avoid/minimise the number of dismissals
  - ways of mitigating the consequences of the dismissals.
- To back this up various pieces of information (known as written particulars) must be given in writing by the employer to the elected reps/TU officials to enable meaningful consultation to take place.

In *UK Coal Mining Ltd v NUM* (2007) a significant new interpretation of the law on collective consultation was established. The case concerned the failure of management to consult properly over the closure of a colliery in Northumberland where 329 employees were made redundant. The employer stated that the closure was for health and safety reasons due to flooding when in actual fact economics had played a major role in the decision. Consultation arrangements were generally inadequate, but the significant legal point concerned the refusal of managers to provide the union with copies of the documents (geologist's report, hydrologist's report, risk assessments, etc) which they claimed demonstrated that the pit had to be closed for health and safety reasons. In other words, while meaningful consultation took place about ways of mitigating the planned redundancies, there was no consultation about the reasons that the redundancies were necessary in the first place. Managers claimed that they had no duty under law to consult about that basic decision, only about the consequences of it.

The managers were right in so far as the leading UK case on this question (*R v British Coal Corporation and another ex parte Vardy and others* (1993)) did indeed say that the reasons for redundancies need not be consulted on. However, the *Vardy* case pre-dates a change in the law dating from 1995 in the form of the Collective Redundancies and Transfer of Undertakings (Protection of Employment) (Amendment) Regulations. These specifically require consultation about 'ways of avoiding dismissals'.

The EAT's judgment in this case states that where a business or workplace is to be closed, and it is known at the time such a proposal is made that redundancies are likely to be caused as a result, the closure itself and the reasons for it should be the subject of consultation. Moreover, and importantly, this consultation should take place from the point at which the employer first proposes to close a workplace. The law thus now requires that the collective consultation stage in the redundancy process is triggered at a rather earlier point than was previously the case.

There is a defence that can be deployed by employers who fail to consult collectively, known as the 'special circumstances' defence. Here, the claim is made that special circumstances arose, outside the control of the employer, that prevented it from consulting collectively. However, in practice the courts have interpreted this narrowly. The circumstances really do have to be 'special', 'outside the employer's control' and such as to 'prevent' consultation from occurring in order to provide an effective defence.

For the purposes of these Regulations the term 'consultation' means entering into meaningful discussions in good faith. Consulting is not the same as negotiating, and the employer is in no way required to reach a formal agreement with staff representatives during consultation. But there must be a serious attempt made to reach agreement. If this is impossible to achieve, as it often will be, legal obligations will have been met provided talks were held and common ground sought.

It has always been common practice in the UK for employers to issue redundancy notices to employees during the consultation process and to continue consulting after this point has been reached. However, according to IDS (2008:274), this is no longer lawful. In *Junk v Wolfgang Kuhnel* (2003) the European Court stated that consultation must have a clear end point as well as a start point. It ends, apparently when an agreement has either been reached or not. Moreover, the redundancies themselves occur at the point at which notice is given to individuals, and not at the point that the contract actually comes to an end. It is thus now the case that employers are under an obligation to complete their consultations (either with or without agreement) before they issue termination notices.

When an employer fails to consult collectively according to requirements set out above a complaint can be taken to an employment tribunal. Where the issue relates to a failure to consult properly with a recognised trade union, the trade union brings the case. Where it relates to a failure on the employer's part to consult properly with employee representatives (ie, where no union is recognised) it is the rep or reps who bring the case. Where it relates to a failure to arrange the election of employee reps any affected employee can bring the case. In each case a collective complaint is made to an employment tribunal listing the names of the employees who have been affected by the failure to consult in accordance with statutory requirements (normally those who have been made redundant). Then, if the tribunal finds that the complaint is well founded a 'protective award' is made. This is a week's pay (capped at £400—this figure increasing in February each year) multiplied by a number of weeks determined by the tribunal. The greater the employer's failings, the more weeks' pay the tribunal will award. Ninety days (ie, thirteen weeks or so) is the maximum award that can be made. In *Evans & Or v Permacell Finesse Limited* (2008) the EAT took the opportunity to state that the purpose of protective awards in cases such as this was to punish employers for failing to consult and not just to compensate individual employees for their losses. There is thus no reason why the level of an award should be limited to thirty weeks' pay when fewer than a hundred people are made redundant at the same time.

When collective redundancies take place (ie, over twenty in the same ninety-day period) the Secretary of State for Business, Innovation and Skills (DBIS) must be formally notified using the HR1 form. Notification must occur, at the latest, at the same thirty-day and ninety-day trigger points that exist for consultation to begin and must occur before any termination notices are issued to employees. Failure to comply with this requirement, or to co-operate with the DBIS when it approaches the employer to ask for further information, is a criminal offence. Fines of up to £5000 can be levied on organisations which do not comply.

Individual consultation

Notwithstanding the requirement in EU law to undertake meaningful consultation with employee representatives before making redundancies, there remains an additional requirement in UK law to consult with the affected individuals. This applies in all redundancy situations including those in which fewer than twenty are being dismissed in a ninety-day period and must occur even if parallel collective consultation is being carried out at the same time with employee representatives.

There is a great deal of case law on this obligation, but it does not greatly help in clarifying exactly what the employer is required to do. Consultation with individuals must be 'adequate' if the dismissal is not to be unfair, but what 'adequate' means varies from situation to situation and is, according to the EAT, *'a question of fact and degree for an employment tribunal to consider'* (*Mugford v Midland Bank PLC* (1997)). Nonetheless the following can be concluded from a reading of the case law:

- It is necessary to warn people at an early stage that their jobs may be redundant. Employers ought, therefore, to consult individually with people who are identified as being 'at risk' of redundancy and not just with those who are definitely going to be made redundant.

- Employees must be consulted with about their selection for redundancy. They should be given the opportunity to challenge this and formerly appeal against it.

- The opportunity should be taken to discuss possible alternative employment in the organisation.

- The right to be accompanied by a trade union official or work colleague does not apply to redundancy consultation meetings.

Lewis (2001:80) cites the case of *King v Eaton* (1996), in which the Court of Session in Scotland helped to clarify requirements on individual consultation somewhat by creating the following test: Was the employee *'given a fair and proper opportunity to understand the matters that are subject to consultation, express a view and have that view properly considered?'*.

There is no specific remedy available for a failure to consult individually as there is in the case of collective consultation (ie, a protective award). Instead the failing is simply taken into account by a tribunal when assessing the fairness or unfairness of the dismissal. Failure to consult fully is usually seen as being a serious procedural error on the part of an employer, and hence means that the dismissal fails the 'band of reasonable responses' test. In itself it is thus sufficient to result in a finding of unfair dismissal.

 Activity 6.3   **Why are there so many redundancy cases?**

Lewis (2001) undertook an in-depth analysis of all the cases reported in Industrial Relations Law Reports (IRLR) between 1987 and 1996, identifying all of those which related to organisational change in some shape or form. He found 328 cases that had generated, between them, 547 separate legal issues to be determined. As IRLR only reports the decisions of the higher courts (ie, not employment tribunals) this means that during this nine-year period the EAT, Court of Appeal and other higher courts made rulings on an average of over sixty change-related legal issues each year. Of these, Lewis found, 42% related to redundancy—by far the highest single category. This finding was surprising given that redundancy law is so well established.

Questions

1   Why do you think there is so much litigation about redundancy matters generally?

2   What factors might account for the large number of cases during this particular period?

3   Can you identify any changes to redundancy law at this time that might account for so many appeals on points of law to the higher courts?

Redundancy payments

Employees with more than two years' continuous service are entitled to receive redundancy payments when they are dismissed. Income tax does not need to be paid on such payments up to a threshold level which is currently set at £30,000. The law sets a statutory minimum redundancy payment which must be paid in the absence of a more generous contractual scheme. In practice most larger employers, including public sector organisations, have in place contractual arrangements which are more generous than the statutory scheme.

Statutory redundancy payments

Minimum statutory redundancy payments are calculated as follows:

- one-and-a-half weeks' pay for each completed year of service over the age of forty-one

- one week's pay for each completed year of service between twenty-two and forty-one

- half a week's pay between eighteen and twenty-two

subject to maximum of:

- twenty years
- £400 (this figure rises on 1 February each year).

The biggest possible payment at present under the statutory scheme is therefore £12,000. These age-related criteria were retained after 2006 when age discrimination law was introduced. However, the opportunity was taken at this time to abolish the laws which permitted employers to avoid paying compensation to those who were made redundant having passed the age of 65 and the system which reduced payments by a twelfth for each completed calendar month after an employee was past their sixty-fourth birthday.

The date for calculating the number of years' completed service is the effective date of termination (ie, the date the dismissal actually takes effect). In making their calculations employers often fail to take account of statutory minimum notice periods (one week for every completed year of service up to twelve). In the case of longer serving staff, this can frequently mean that a further year of service has been completed at the point of termination, thus entitling them to a higher redundancy payment.

Contractual redundancy payments

In most cases entitlement to severance pay which is higher than the statutory minimum is stated clearly in employees' contracts of employment. Alternatively it is incorporated unambiguously through a collective agreement or staff handbook. From time to time, in the absence of any written or verbal agreement, tribunals are required to establish whether or not there is nonetheless an entitlement to an enhanced payment implied in employees' contracts. This occurs where it can be established that it is 'custom and practice' in the organisation to pay enhanced rates. We will look in more detail at implied terms of a contract in Chapter 8.

Enhanced redundancy payment schemes typically award two weeks' pay per year of service and do not place a cap on the amount of a week's pay that can be taken into consideration. This means that even quite modest earners with a few years of service under their belts can look forward to redundancy payments that are in excess of £20,000 or £30,000. When it is considered that tax is only paid on payments that are over £30,000, it is not difficult to understand why employees are often very happy to be made redundant—particularly when they have skills that are in demand from other employers. Enhanced schemes of this kind do not breach age discrimination law provided they mirror the statutory scheme in terms of the age ranges and offer a straight multiplication of the number of weeks' pay on which compensation is based. Other forms of design which include age-based criteria may breach the principles of age discrimination law, but they may still be lawful if the employer can objectively justify its particular scheme.

Exhibit 6.3   **Retirement windfalls**

In *Woodcock v Cumbria Primary Care Trust* (2010) the employer sped up Mr Woodcock's redundancy, dismissing him before completing a full redundancy consultation. The reason was to sack him before he accrued entitlement to an enhanced pension. In other words they got rid of him early to save the costs associated with paying him a pension that he would otherwise have been due in addition to his redundancy payment. The justification offered was thus largely to achieve financial savings. Mr Woodcock would have received a 'windfall' had he got both the redundancy payment and the enhanced pension.

The employer won the case both in the tribunal and again subsequently at the EAT. Windfall avoidance was found to be a potential justification for indirect age discrimination.

A similar situation arose in *Kraft Foods v Hastie* (2010), although here the situation was a more common one. The employer had a scheme in place that tapered redundancy payments downwards as employees approached retirement. Again the purpose was to avoid paying 'windfalls' in the form of large redundancy payments to staff who were due to retire soon on a pension. Mr Hastie's redundancy payment was capped at a sum equal to that he would have earned had he continued to work until sixty-five. The EAT agreed with the employer that this policy represented 'a proportionate means of achieving a legitimate aim'.

However, the ECJ's ruling in a Danish case called *Ingeniorforeningen i Danmark/Andersen v Region Syddanmark* (2011) casts some doubt on how long these UK precedents will remain good law. This case relates specifically to a Danish law which stipulates that employers can avoid paying redundancy payments when the people they dismiss are due to receive a pension paid for by the employer—ie, prevents entitlement to a double payment/'windfall'.

Here the ECJ found against the Danish government. It said that employees should have the right to waive the pension and continue working if they wish to. Denying such a person their severance payment amounts to age discrimination which is not justifiable.

Resignation before termination

An interesting but rather complicated feature of redundancy law concerns the position of employees who resign in order to take up alternative employment while working under notice of redundancy. In principle, provided such people are working what is known as an 'obligitory period of notice', they can resign before the date at which their contracts are due to terminate and still claim a redundancy payment. The 'obligitory period' is defined by the Employment Rights Act 1996 as the longer period of either:

- the notice period in the individual's contract of employment

or

- the statutory minimum notice period to which all employees are entitled (ie, one week for each year of continuous service up to a maximum of twelve).

There is a caveat however. The employer can object and insist that the employee continues working until the final day of the contract. If this request is put in writing, and the employee nevertheless leaves early, the right to a redundancy payment can be lost. The law requires that the employee does not unreasonably refuse to continue working, and this is not defined in statute. The reasonableness of each particular case is thus left for employment tribunals to determine on the facts before them.

Alternative job offers

A further aspect of redundancy law concerns situations in which employees who are under notice of redundancy are offered work by their employers. This may be a continuation of the existing contract (ie, effectively a rescinding of the redundancy), or more commonly a new contract to carry out a different job—perhaps at another location. Some employees will be pleased to receive such an offer, but many are not because they would prefer to have their contracts terminated and to claim a redundancy payment. As a result it is often the case that employees refuse such offers.

Under the Employment Rights Act 1996, provided the alternative job being offered by the employer is suitable and provided it starts within four weeks of the existing contract coming to an end, employees lose the right to a redundancy payment if they do not take up such offers. However, a job is only considered to be 'suitable' if it is the same or similar to the current job and in the same or a nearby location. An employer can also offer a redundant employee some other job which is different from the existing one or is in a more distant location, but here the legal position in respect of redundancy payments is slightly different. The employee is effectively obliged to try carrying out the job during a trial period which must be four weeks long, but can be for longer if this is agreed. At the end of this period a decision must be taken about the long-term suitability of the new position. If the employee reasonably turns down the offer of continued employment, a redundancy payment can be claimed (calculated as if the employment terminated before the trial period began). If on the other

---

 Exhibit 6.4   *Taylor v Kent CC* (1969)

Mr Taylor was employed as the headmaster of a boys' school. The council decided to merge it with a neighbouring girls' school and to appoint the headmistress as overall head of the merged unit. Mr Taylor's job was thus redundant.

However, instead of laying him off, the council offered Mr Taylor a new post as a 'mobile teacher', working in different schools undertaking different assignments as and when required. His salary level was to remain the same—ie, the headmaster's rate even though much of the work would be that of a less senior teacher.

He refused the offer on the grounds that his status was being reduced and that the work he would be doing in the new job was not equivalent. He therefore claimed a redundancy payment.

The council argued that the offer was reasonable, the work suitable to his qualifications and the pay identical to that paid under his current contract. He was not therefore entitled to claim redundancy.

The court decided that the work being offered was not 'substantially equivalent' and that Mr Taylor had not acted unreasonably. He was therefore entitled to receive a redundancy payment.

hand the employee unreasonably refuses to continue working no redundancy payment can be claimed. What is and what is not 'reasonable' varies hugely from case to case and is often dependent on an individual's particular personal circumstances. As a result the tribunals do not tend to apply specific tests. It is, however, clear that the new job must be pretty similar in nature in order for the employer to be able to avoid paying the redundancy payment.

Insolvency

Redundancies often occur because a company has become insolvent. In such circumstances it is frequently the case that there are insufficient funds available to pay redundancy payments that are due or that full contractual entitlements by way of severance payments cannot be honoured. What happens when a company becomes insolvent is governed by the Insolvency Act 1986, the vast majority of which does not relate to employment issues at all. Readers looking for a good summary of this law written for non-specialists will find one in Owens (2001: Chapter 31).

Various types of action can be taken when a company becomes insolvent. Sometimes it will be wound up or liquidated straight away, but it is more common for receivers to be appointed first in order to manage the company's debts and to try to keep it going (or parts of it going). From an employment law point of view there are thus two separate situations that can arise once a company is declared insolvent:

1. Receivership. This occurs when a company can no longer meet its financial obligations. It is taken over by receivers appointed by a court who decide what steps to take. They may sell the company as a going concern, they may sell parts of it or they may wind it up. At this stage the company still exists along with contracts of employment.

2. Liquidation. This occurs when the receiver decides that the company is not viable and cannot be sold (either in full or in part) as a going concern. The company is wound up and its assets sold off to pay its creditors. Once liquidation has occurred the company ceases to exist, so no contracts of employment exist either. All employees are thus redundant.

Ex-employees are treated as preferential creditors and are thus first in the queue when debts are recovered on the sale of assets. However this only applies in respect of wages and other payments owed:

- for work undertaken in the past four months
- to a maximum of £800.

Where there are insufficient funds to meet liabilities to employees, the receiver will provide IP1 and IP2 forms on which claims can be made to the DBERR for compensation from the National Insurance Fund. The current limits on payments are as follows:

- eight weeks' pay up to a maximum of £400 per week
- Holiday pay due in respect of the previous twelve months (up to six weeks and £400)
- Pay in lieu of notice where applicable up to statutory maximimum of twelve weeks (also subject to £400 limit).

It can take some months for payments from the National Insurance Fund to be made. This is because all claims are assessed carefully and are refused wherever there are grounds to do so. If the department believes that the employer (or a successor company) and not the state

---

 Exhibit 6.5   *Secretary of State for Employment v Spence et al* **(1986)**

A group of men were employed by a company called Spencer and Sons Ltd which became insolvent. They were all made redundant by the receiver at 11.00am on 28 November 1983. At 2.00pm on the same day, the business was sold to another company.

On 29 November all the men who had been made redundant the previous day were re-employed by the new owners on the same terms and conditions as formerly. The men believed that they were entitled to redundancy payments because they had been made redundant—albeit only for an afternoon. However, because the vendor was insolvent, they could only bring their claim to the Secretary of State for Employment, asking that payments be made to them from the National Insurance Fund.

Their claim was rejected on the grounds that they had been employed in the same undertaking 'immediately before' it was transferred to a new owner. Under TUPE regulations therefore, they transferred with the business. There was thus no entitlement to a redundancy payment.

The Secretary of State lost this case at tribunal, at the EAT and then at the Court of Appeal. The men had been made redundant. They did have a claim under TUPE against the vendor as this firm was insolvent. Therefore the National Insurance Fund was obliged to stump up.

 Activity 6.4   **UK redundancy law—a soft touch?**

Over many years UK redundancy law has been criticised by commentators and particularly by trade unions for being too relaxed in comparison with the approach adopted in many European countries (see Smith, 1996; Brown, 2001; Evason & Broussal, 2001). Procedural requirements are less involved in the UK, it is argued, while statutory severance payments are less.

Particular criticism is reserved for consultation requirements, as has long been the case despite a great deal of legislative amendment over the years. In practice critics argue that employers are able to get away with 'sham consultations', going through the motions of talking to employees and their representatives only after decisions have been made and without any intention whatever of taking account of any counter proposals advanced during the consultation process.

In most continental countries this is not possible. In some, notably Germany and the Scandinavian countries, works councils are involved from early on in discussions about possible redundancies and have a very real influence over such decisions. In France, consultation requirements are similar, but failure to comply fully can lead to imprisonment of senior managers. More significantly, French employee groups can go to court before redundancies take effect and get an injunction postponing them until such time as the employer complies with the law. The same European directives govern what happens as regards consultation across all member states, but they have been far more rigorously applied elsewhere than in the UK.   »

>> The effect, according to many commentators, is that international organisations have a strong incentive to make their British workers redundant rather than those they employ elsewhere in Europe. UK operations are always downsized first, simply because it is cheaper and easier to achieve quickly. This claim is then typically associated with a call to increase regulation in the UK so as to bring it into line with the rest of Europe.

Successive governments, however, have taken a different view. The light-touch approach has always been favoured and continues to be applied (see Chapter 28 on consultation requirements more generally). The arguments advanced in favour of this are as follows:

- the UK attracts much more inward investment from overseas than other EU countries because it has relatively relaxed redundancy law

- critics of UK redundancy law tend to overstate their case about differences between the position vis-à-vis other EU countries

- flexible labour markets and high job mobility are required by modern economies and result in lower unemployment over the long term.

Questions

1 To what extent do you agree with the case for a continuation of a light-touch approach to redundancy law in the UK?

2 What would be the impact in practice of:

   a) allowing employees to postpone redundancies via injunctions where employers did not consult with them properly?

   b) actively involving employee representatives in decision-making about redundancies?

is actually responsible for paying up then they will refuse to pay. Appeals against such decisions are taken to employment tribunals and must be submitted within three months of the date at which the DBIS refused to pay compensation. In such situations redundant employees are frequently in the difficult position of needing to make a tribunal application naming both their ex-employer and the Secretary of State as respondents. The tribunal will then have to decide which, if either party, is responsible for making the payments.

CHAPTER SUMMARY

- Redundancy is a common form of 'potentially fair' dismissal. It is defined slightly differently in UK and EU law, but it generally occurs when an employer reduces its workforce for economic reasons.

- It is important, if redundancies are to be lawful, that a pool of potential selectees is established and that sufficient consultation is carried out with these employees and (if more than twenty are to be dismissed together) with their representatives.

- There are three lawful ways in which selection for redundancy can be achieved: last-in-first-out, points-based approaches and employee selection processes.

- Redundancy payments must be equal to the statutory minimum and are often higher due to additional contractual arrangements which are more generous. Notice periods must also be honoured.

- UK redundancy law is often criticised because it is less procedurally cumbersome and requires employers to compensate less than is the case in other larger EU countries. This tends to mean that multi-national corporations dismiss their UK employees before counterparts elsewhere in Europe.

For updates and further materials, please see the online resource centre at www.oup.com.

REFERENCES

Bennett, M. (2002) 'Interpreting unfair dismissal and redundancy payments law: the judicial reluctance to disapprove employer decisions to dismiss' *Statute Law Review* 23.1 (p135).

Brown, K. (2001) 'CBI attacks unions over redundancy law myths' *Financial Times*, 4 May.

Duggan, M. (1999) *Unfair Dismissal: Law, practice and guidance*. London: CLT Professional Publishing.

Evason J. & Broussal D. (2001) 'Vive la difference?' *People Management*, 17 May (p18).

IDS (2001) Managing Redundancy. *IDS Study Plus*, Autumn. London: Incomes Data Services.

IDS (2005) 'Collective redundancy consultation'. *IDS Brief 780*. May. London: Incomes Data Services.

IDS (2008) *Redundancy*. London: Incomes Data Services.

Lewis, P. (2001) 'Legal aspects of employment change and their implications for management' *Industrial Relations Journal* 32.1 (p71).

McMullen, J. (2011) *Redundancy: The Law and Practice*. Third Edition. Oxford: Oxford University Press.

Owens, K. (2001) *Law for Non-Law Students*. Third Edition. London: Cavendish Publishing.

Smith, S. (1996) 'Europe's poor relation' *Computer Weekly*, 12 September (p36)

ONLINE RESOURCE CENTRE

A range of online resources to help you through your employment law module have been developed by the author team. These include updates, self-test questions and sources for further reading. (www.oxfordtextbooks.co.uk/orc/taylor_emir3e)

Contractual employment rights

7

Learning outcomes

By the end of this chapter you should be able to:

- explain the principles of the law of contract as it applies to employment;

- set out the conditions that need to be in place for a contract of employment to be formed;

- give advice about the main issues that arise concerning the law of contract in the recruitment and selection process;

- draw up a statement of written particulars of employment;

- identify the main situations in which employers can vary or adjust contracts without gaining the consent of employees;

- develop strategies for pushing through necessary contractual changes when employees resist the changes.

Introduction

Until now this book has primarily been concerned with the statutory regulation of the employment relationship—the requirements and expectations of Acts of Parliament and other statutory instruments. We will return to further statutory issues later, but first it is necessary to focus on employment law which comes from another source altogether. The law of contract is part of the common law which we introduced in Chapter 2. It is made by judges rather than Parliament as cases come before them and decisions about new types of situation are reached. Through the doctrine of precedent, decisions on points of law made by a court are binding on all the courts that lie beneath it in the hierarchy. So the law of contract has evolved steadily over centuries as people have appealed cases up through the court system. What makes it interesting, but also somewhat unpredictable, is that the common law continues to evolve all the time. Steadily, as cases come before them, the judges articulate new doctrines and principles, so that over time it becomes possible to trace clear lines of direction in judicial thinking. As a result it makes sense to identify ways in which the law of contract 'is currently developing' and to debate the significance of such trends.

In this chapter we introduce the basic principles of the law of contract as they apply to contracts of employment. We focus in particular on issues relating to the formation and

---

 Activity 7.1

Wellbeing PLC is a private healthcare company operating forty nursing homes at various locations in the north west of England. It has grown quickly by taking over existing family-run businesses which have then been amalgamated into the centrally-run Wellbeing operation.

The company employs over 1200 people in total, of whom 300 are qualified nurses. The company is finding it increasingly difficult both to recruit and retain nurses of the required calibre. It has found some success in its attempts to recruit from abroad, but is unable to pay sufficient rates to retain them for more than a few months. The managing director is thus considering ways of reducing the company's reliance on this group of employees.

Local authority regulations prevent private nursing homes from operating without a qualified nurse on duty at all times. At present each nurse is contracted to work at only one named home, which does not allow for much operational flexibility. It would therefore be useful for the company to require its existing nurses to work at any one of its premises as and when a need arises. This will reduce the total number of qualified nurses required.

The managing director asks you to advise her about the legal implications of the proposed changes.

1   How should she go about reaching a situation in which each nurse can be required to work at any home run by the group?

2   What options does she have?

3   What further information would you need to know in order to give accurate advice?

    Return to this activity once you have read the chapter, to see if your answers were correct.

variation of employment contracts and on how these are enforced in practice. We also cover the statutory requirement to inform employees of the major terms and conditions of their employment. In the next chapter we introduce the concept of 'the implied term' and explain the growing significance of implied terms of contract in employment law.

Introduction to contractual rights

By definition, as we explained in Chapter 3, all employees work under a contract of employment. They would not be 'employees' and would not have the full range of statutory employment rights if they were not working under contracts of employment. Yet it is common to hear people say that they do not have contracts. By this they mean that they do not have written contracts setting out their terms and conditions which they and their employers have signed—a very common situation in the UK—but this does not mean that they do not have contracts.

In law a contract of employment is simply an agreement between two parties which sets out the terms and conditions under which an individual is employed to work. It thus exists whether or not it is in written form. In fact a contract can be formed very easily and very quickly through a brief exchange of letters, by e-mail, on the telephone, on a handshake or in casual conversation. Indeed, contracts can even be formed implicitly through custom and practice if two parties act as if they have a contractual relationship for long enough.

Too much informality can be problematic, because it means that employers and employees may have subtly (or even significantly) different understandings about what constitutes their agreed terms and conditions of employment. This can lead to disputes and sometimes to legal action. There is usually some evidence in written form for the court or tribunal to use in reaching a judgment about what the contract contains, but this is sometimes limited to an offer letter or a brief statement of working conditions set out by the employer, but which the employee has never specifically agreed. In such situations it is necessary to rely on verbal testimony about what exactly was agreed at the time the relationship was formed and on evidence of what actually happens in practice on a day-to-day basis in the organisation concerned.

The law of contract plays an important role in employment law for the following reasons:

- a contract of employment is enforceable in court,
- where one party breaches an established contract, and the other suffers a detriment as a result, it is possible for the latter to sue the former for damages,
- terms and conditions, once agreed, cannot be changed by either party without the other's agreement,
- where the employer breaches the contract in a fundamental way it is possible for employees to resign and have their resignation treated as a dismissal by a tribunal (ie, constructive dismissal).

However, it is not only a question of enforcing the agreed terms of contract. In addition to these express terms, contracts of employment are also deemed to contain implied terms. Often these exist even though they have not been expressly agreed by the two parties. Some implied terms are specific to a particular workplace, while others are deemed by the courts to be present in all contracts of employment. The duty of care which all employers owe all employees is an important example of a generally applicable implied term. It forms the basis of a lot of the health and safety law that we will be discussing in Part V. We will focus in depth on implied terms in Chapter 8. For now it is important simply to remember that a breach of implied terms, in principle, is treated in the same way by the courts as a breach of the express terms with which we are mainly concerned in this chapter.

Forming contracts of employment

The law on the formation of contracts of employment derives from general rules relating to the formation of any kind of contract. Many argue that this is unsatisfactory because the employment relationship is fundamentally different in nature from any other kind of commercial relationship. In employment, one party is subordinate to the other while their power relationship is very uneven. But as matters stand the same basic legal principles apply when someone offers and takes up a job as when they buy a car or employ a plumber to install a new boiler.

The position in English law is that the following five conditions must be in place for a contract to be formed. Once they are in place, a contract exists along with all the legal rights and obligations that follow:

1. an unconditional offer
2. an unconditional acceptance
3. an intention to form a legally binding agreement
4. consideration
5. certainty.

The need for offers of employment and acceptances to be unambiguous and unconditional can be very significant. It is, for example, common for job applicants to be offered positions 'subject to satisfactory references', 'subject to successful application for a work permit' or 'subject to a medical examination'. What is more, it is not uncommon for the employment actually to start before references have been received or before a report of a clean bill of health has been sent. In law this leaves new starters in a precarious position, because there is no contract in place that is legally enforceable until such time as the offer of employment is confirmed as being unconditional. It is thus highly risky to resign a job in order to take up another until your new employer confirms that the required references have been received or the medical examination passed.

An intention to form a legally binding relationship is assumed to be in place whenever a job is offered and accepted. However, problems sometimes arise when family members or close friends work for one another. In such circumstances it is not always clear that there was an intention to form a legal as opposed to a personal relationship. If the court decides there was not, then no contract can be enforced and no-one can have the benefit of any contractual employment rights (let alone statutory employment rights). Certainty simply means that the courts must be able to identify the key terms. If they cannot then they have to declare it 'void for uncertainty'.

Consideration is payment or payment in kind. In English common law a contract is seen as a bargain. No contract can thus exist unless both parties gain something and give up something. So voluntary work (unless rewarded in kind) can never be considered to constitute an employment relationship and its terms and conditions cannot thus be enforced in court. According to Aikin (2001:12) Scottish law varies in this respect. In Scotland there has to be 'causa' rather than 'consideration'. This is a wider concept which includes the intention to create some form of moral obligation, so north of the border it is possible, in principle, for voluntary workers to work under contracts of employment and to enjoy some contractual rights.

Provided these five conditions are present, in 99% of situations, there is a contract of employment in existence whatever it is called and whatever people perceive their position to be. However, there are one or two relatively unusual situations in which a contract is deemed to be void and cannot thus be enforced:

1. Where one of the parties to the contract was 'of unsound mind' at the time it was formed.

2. Where the contract has an illegal purpose or is 'tainted by illegality'. A common example is where a contract is formed with an immigrant who does not have the required work permit. Contracts which are set up in such a way as to defraud HM Revenue and Customs are also illegal and hence unenforceable.

3. Where a contract has been 'frustrated' as can be the case when an employee is absent due to incapacity or imprisonment for twenty-six weeks or more.

Special rules apply in the case of contracts agreed with minors (defined as people under the age of eighteen) in order to protect them from undue exploitation. A contract made with a minor is valid (ie, deemed by the courts to exist) but only in so far as it is for the minor's benefit and operates in their interests. Any term which does not operate in the interests of the minor, such as long-notice provisions or a requirement to work at night, is void as far as the courts are concerned. Once you are eighteen there is no such protection, and provided a contract is not actually illegal, in principle you are bound by what you sign up to.

 Exhibit 7.1 **Holding employees to their contracts**

It is commonly believed by employers that if there is a clear and unambiguous term in a contract of employment, they have the right to require the employee concerned to comply with it. As a result employers think that they can effectively give themselves very considerable leeway to treat employees as they wish by writing a great deal of flexibility into their contracts. Bonus payments thus become 'discretionary', contracts contain mobility clauses and other types of flexibility clause giving employers the right to alter people's working lives in all kinds of ways, and restrictive covenants are inserted to deter people from leaving to join a competitor.

However, as Smith (2004) shows; 'modern employment law is now moving away from classic contract law principles', and 'rules and approaches are being developed that may be used by a »

» court to limit, or even prevent altogether, unfair or unconscionable exercises of powers apparently unambiguously bestowed on employers by the contract'.

What we are seeing is a steady move in the case law towards a situation in which a distinction is made between, on the one hand, the right conferred on an employer in a contract to force an employee to do something against his/her will, and on the other, the decision taken by the employer to exercise that right. If the employer acts unreasonably in exercising its discretion to activate a term in a contract, then the court may well find in favour of an employee who suffers a detriment as a result. As Smith (2004) points out, the courts have stopped short of creating a clear duty on the part of employers to exercise contractual power reasonably; we have now got a 'situation in practice which is not a million miles from such a principle'.

For example, many contracts contain mobility clauses which give employers the right to redeploy staff to any of their UK sites. That means that an employee based in Birmingham can in principle be moved to Edinburgh. But that does not mean that the employer can say to this person on a Friday afternoon 'as of next week you are working in Scotland'.

The same is true of situations in which employers exercise the discretion that they give themselves in contracts to award 'nil bonuses' to staff, sometimes as a punitive measure or when people leave. Recent case law has found some such decisions to be 'perverse' in nature, the courts ruling that no reasonable employer could come to such a decision in the circumstances of particular cases.

Recruitment

An interesting area of law that gives rise to some confusion concerns the status in legal terms of promises made or assurances given during recruitment which the employer subsequently fails to honour. Is it a breach of contract, for example, if a job advertisement states that monthly remuneration will vary with sales, but that pay will average £25,000 a year, and this turns out to have been a serious overestimate? What if a candidate is promised a sizeable bonus on completion of a satisfactory six-month probation period, but this does not materialise in practice? Are these examples of breaches of contract or not?

The answer depends on when any promise was made. Because the law views contracts of employment like any other commercial contract, a job advertisement is generally considered to be 'an invitation to treat' and does not therefore, in itself, create legal obligations (Leighton & O'Donnell, 1995:29). Making dishonest statements in a recruitment advertisement may well fall foul of the Misrepresentation Act 1973, but if the person subsequently accepts a job under false pretences they cannot claim that the employer has breached their contract of employment. The situation can be different in the case of promises made at interview. Here we are past inviting people 'to treat' and are into a negotiation phase. Any clear assurances made thus do become part of the contract of employment and must be honoured. Employers therefore need to take care not to give any guarantees at interview about earnings or benefits such as company cars or career development opportunities that they cannot honour in practice.

Making the offer

It is not always clear who in an organisation has the authority to make offers of employment. Sometimes a relatively junior manager will carry out interviews or will simply see people informally and make a verbal offer of employment. But what happens if a more senior manager then decides that someone else is going to get the job or that no offer will be made after all? Many organisations require appointments to be ratified centrally before they are confirmed in writing, but the position can be confused in practice. The answer here is that legal relations are formed if the above conditions are in place—unambiguous offer, unambiguous acceptance, etc. Unless a candidate is told that the appointment needs to be ratified by a senior manager and will have to be confirmed in writing, a contract exists. In law, as is the case with sexual harassment, employers are vicariously liable for the actions of their employees, and that includes a junior manager overstepping his/her authority by making job offers.

A slightly different situation concerns the position of recruitment agents. Can they make offers of employment on the employer's behalf which are subsequently binding on the employer? Here everything depends on the contract that the agent has with the employer. If that gives the agent the right to make offers, then the employer cannot subsequently decide that they do not wish to employ people to whom offers have been made. It is therefore essential, from an employer's point of view, that it agrees terms with its agents which are clear on this matter. It is tempting when dealing with agencies to avoid close scrutiny of the lengthy and sometimes impenetrably phrased statements of terms and conditions provided by the agent.

When does the contract start?

A contract exists, and legal obligations are thus owed, from the point at which unconditional acceptance is communicated to the employer, unless it is post-dated. Withdrawal after this point thus constitutes a breach of contract. Leighton & O'Donnell (1995:33–34) describe a number of situations in which confusion can, however, arise. For example, what is the legal position when an acceptance is communicated via a message left by telephone or e-mail? What happens if a letter accepting a job is lost in the post? The answer is that the law is rather confused on these matters. In the case of acceptances by post, it would appear that the legal relationship comes into being at the point at which the letter is dropped into the letter box. By contrast, with faxes, it is the point at which the fax communicating acceptance is actually received which triggers the start of a contractual relationship.

 Activity 7.2

Assume that you work as an HR officer in an NHS Trust. One Monday morning three people arrive at the hospital believing that they are due to start new jobs working in the outpatients' reception area. All claim to have been appointed by the manager, Mrs Daze. Unfortunately there is only one job available. The three people are Miss Keene, Mr Reddy and Mrs Hackney.

The facts of the case are as follows.

The receptionist's job was advertised two months earlier in the local newspaper, generating a large number of applications. Six candidates were interviewed. One of these, Miss Keene, was offered the job verbally at the interview subject to the provision of two suitable references from past employers. No references were subsequently sent to the hospital, but Miss Keene has brought one excellent reference with her on what she thinks is her first day. »

> ➤ Three weeks after the interviews, Mrs Daze assumed that Miss Keene had withdrawn because no references had been received. She therefore phoned Mr Reddy and offered him the job. He said he would think about it. She subsequently wrote to him confirming the offer. She then heard nothing and assumed he was not interested. However, Mr Reddy claims that he received the letter and replied to it on the same day. He has copies of the correspondence with him and is claiming that his reply must have got lost in the post.
>
> The need for a new receptionist was now becoming acute, so last week Mrs Daze contacted Mrs Hackney, her third choice for the job. Mrs Hackney said that she would accept the job if she was offered a slightly higher rate of pay than was discussed at interview. Mrs Daze said that she would look into this possibility, but in the meantime sent written confirmation of her offer quoting the original salary in the post. This letter arrived on Thursday of last week. Mrs Hackney arrived for work this morning stating that she was now prepared to accept the original offer.
>
> 1 Explain the legal issues that are of relevance to this case.
>
> 2 Given the facts provided, which of the three candidates would you recommend was asked to go home and which would you ask to complete a 'new starters' form?

Written particulars of employment

Until 1993 employers were under no legal obligation to set out in writing for their employees the main terms and conditions under which they were employed. This changed, thanks to a European directive, and the relevant law is now found in the Employment Rights Act 1996. The right is for employees (not all workers) to receive what is known legally as a section one statement and what is more generally known as their 'written particulars of employment' within eight weeks of commencing employment. The written particulars must cover the following in a single document:

- the names of the employer and employee between whom a contractual relationship has been formed
- the date the employment commenced
- the job title or a brief description of the work concerned
- the amount of pay
- the dates on which pay will be received
- details of bonuses or commission to be paid
- the hours of work
- holiday and holiday pay entitlements
- the place of work.

Employees have also to receive other documentation which can be incorporated into the principal statement described above or can be sent separately. These are the following:

- sick pay arrangements and other terms and conditions relating to sickness
- notice periods for both employer and employee

- details of any occupational pension arrangements
- the anticipated duration of the contract, if it is temporary
- details of any collective agreements which govern the terms and conditions of employment.

For employees working abroad, there is an additional requirement to state the length of the period to be spent overseas and the currency in which payments will be made. Any extra allowances or benefits that are provided for overseas workers have also to be included. Finally, and importantly, written particulars must always include details of relevant disciplinary and grievance procedures. Details of the entire procedural arrangements do not need to be included, but all employees must be informed of where they can access these details. Until 2004 there was a requirement on employers to issue a section one statement during the first eight weeks of employment even if they had already informed the employee of everything in some other document such as a written contract of employment. This requirement has now been dropped. So, provided all employees are given all the above information, no special written particulars need to be issued.

Moreover, until 2004 legal incentives to persuade employers to comply with the requirement to issue written particulars were extremely weak. As a result the extent of non-compliance among UK employers has always been high. All an employee who was not provided with written particulars could do was to ask an employment tribunal to require that a statement was issued. This remains the case, but an additional incentive was introduced under regulations that form part of the Employment Act 2002. These include a right for employment tribunals to award compensation of between two and four weeks' pay to anyone who wins a case of another kind and is found not to have been issued with the written particulars. The same remedy is available to those who have not been informed of important changes that mean that their original statements are now out of date. It can be argued that this still represents an inadequate sanction, and that many smaller employers continue to ignore the legal requirement as a result.

It is important to stress that a section one statement is not the same thing as a written contract of employment. It is quite possible for somebody's contract of employment to differ in some respects from the terms and conditions set out in a section one statement. This is because a particular manager may offer a particular individual a job on specific, non-standard terms. In such cases, provided the employee concerned can satisfy the court that their contract is different in a key respect, the employer cannot rely on the written particulars they have issued to defend themselves in a breach of contract claim. That does not mean to say, however, that a section one statement is irrelevant when it comes to the law of contract. While not itself constituting a contract, even when signed by an employee and returned for filing, it remains a useful statement of the employer's view of what the contract itself contains. And if the employee fails to complain that the written particulars issued are inaccurate at the time they are issued, it is going to be hard later to sustain the claim that the contract actually contains rather different terms.

It is important to note that the requirement to give information about disciplinary and grievance procedures in written particulars of employment does not mean that such procedures themselves form part of the contract of employment. Most employers, very sensibly, prefer to ensure that disciplinary and grievance procedures are definitely not contractual so that they cannot be accused of acting unlawfully if they do not follow their own procedures to the letter. However, employees do effectively have a contractual right to be informed where they can find out about disciplinary and grievance procedures.

 Exhibit 7.2   *Robertson & Jackson v British Gas Corporation* (1983)

Mr Robertson and his colleague Mr Jackson had been employed by British Gas as meter readers for some years. At the time of their appointment their offer letters stated that '*incentive bonus scheme conditions will apply to meter reading and collection work*'.

This conflicted with the statement of terms and conditions issued to them once in their jobs (ie, the section one statement) which said that incentive payments depended on agreements made with the trade unions using established collective bargaining machinery, and that these might change from time to time.

Subsequently the collective agreement was altered and the bonus payments stopped.

The two men claimed that this amounted to breach of contract. They had accepted their jobs on the understanding that bonus payments would be made. They therefore claimed the payments.

The company argued that the section one statement was the authoritative document. Moreover, both men had signed to confirm that they had received their copies of the statement and had read its contents.

The Court of Appeal found against British Gas and for Mr Robertson and Mr Jackson. The offer letters pre-dated the section one statements and thus established their terms and conditions of employment. These had not been changed with their agreement, so they were entitled to the unpaid bonus payments.

 Activity 7.3

You are employed as a human resources officer in a call centre operation in Yorkshire. It is early September and one of your employees, Dick Young, comes to see you about his holiday entitlement. He has asked his team manager for three days off next week but has had his request turned down on the grounds that he has already used up all his holidays for the current year. He has been studying various pieces of documentation he has been sent over the years, but is still very confused about his position. He has taken thirty days' holiday so far this year including the eight bank holidays. He shows you the following items:

- His offer letter (dated January 2010) states that he is entitled to thirty days' holiday per year.

- A document headed 'Statement of Terms and Conditions' (dated March 2010) which states that employees are entitled to 'twenty-five days holiday per year in addition to all eight public (bank) holidays'. »

- A copy of the company's staff handbook (dated January 2011) which states that all employees are entitled to twenty-two days' holiday per year. On the first page of the handbook it is stated that its contents 'form part of employees contracts of employment'.

- A letter (dated March 2012) informing him that the holiday entitlement for employees is to rise to twenty-four days per year in line with the requirements of the Working Time Regulations.

- A print-off from the company's intranet site which states that the 'holiday year' runs from 1 October to 30 September.

Questions

1   What is the significance of each of these documents as far as Dick's contract of employment is concerned?

2   Which should take precedence over the others and why?

3   Is Dick entitled to take three further days off next week or not?

Varying contracts

The more organisations are subject to change and the more varied working life becomes, the more situations arise in which an employer needs to alter or adjust the terms and conditions under which their employees are employed. But just as a contract is formed by the agreement of two parties to its terms, the contract cannot simply be altered by one party without the other agreeing. In law the employer cannot unilaterally alter the contract of employment without the agreement of the employee, no more than the employee can do so without first gaining the consent of the employer.

In most cases alteration of a contract is not contentious. The employer makes a proposal to make a variation and the employee agrees. The most common examples are the award of pay rises and promotions, but there are countless other relatively minor changes to job duties and responsibilities that get made all the time with consent. In a minority of cases, however, employees reject proposals to change their contracts—particularly where they are going to suffer economically as a result. The main situations where there is resistance concern the following:

- changes in work location
- altered hours of work
- the introduction of new technology
- changes to systems for determining payment
- changes to work duties
- the introduction of new policies (eg, dress codes).

In any of these situations an employee who does not wish to accept the proposed changes can, in principle, say so and may be legally entitled not to accept. If the employer nonetheless forces through the changes without the employee's agreement the following kinds of legal action can follow:

1. the employee can sue for damages,
2. the employee can ask for a declaration stating that the contract has been breached and must be put back,
3. the employee can ask for an interlocutory injunction preventing the employer from making the proposed changes,
4. the employee can resign and claim constructive dismissal.

In practice, however, employers do vary the terms of contracts from time to time and do not face legal action as a result. In a fast-changing business environment it would be difficult for many to survive if they did not. So how is it done? First, there are a number of ways in which employers give themselves (knowingly or not) the right to make reasonable changes. The following are the major ways in which this occurs.

Flexibility clauses

By far the best approach, from an employer's point of view, is to include within a written contract, offer letter or other statement of terms and conditions, clauses which provide for flexibility. This is simply done by including a clause which says that the employer reserves the right to make reasonable changes to certain terms and conditions should business needs require this.

If this is construed too broadly, there is a danger that good potential employees will not sign, but if it is too narrow it is of little use in terms of allowing flexibility. Many contracts list the areas in which changes may be made—job duties, work location, job title, hours of work, payment arrangements and so forth. Aikin (2001:73) suggests that a 'narrow but changeable term' is often a good way of building in sufficient flexibility. She gives the following example by way of illustration:

> You are employed to work at St Luke's House, but the company reserves the right to relocate you to any other establishment in the London and South East region on a temporary or permanent basis.

When making use of flexibility clauses it is always important to remember that any discretion to make changes to employees' terms and conditions is applied reasonably (see Exhibit 7.1 above). Giving oneself the right to make changes does not mean that employees can be treated unreasonably or without due care in terms of the *manner* with which management's discretion is exercised. Giving notice and consulting ahead of time are indications of reasonableness on an employer's part.

Birmingham City Council v Wetherill and others (2007) concerned the employer's decision to take advantage of a clause in employment contracts which allowed it to alter a car-user allowance unilaterally. According to the Court of Appeal, however, this did not mean that the council had the right to exercise its right to vary '*for an improper purpose, capriciously or arbitrarily, or in a way in which no reasonable employer, acting reasonably would exercise it*'. This is a most interesting judgment which appears to be creating a test analogous to the 'band of reasonable responses' used in unfair dismissal cases when judging employers' actions in this field.

Collective agreements

Where trade unions are recognised and collective bargaining occurs it is highly likely that changes to employment contracts will be negotiated from time to time. This is perfectly acceptable in law provided employees are informed clearly that a particular collective agreement is incorporated into their individual contracts of employment. This is usually done in an offer letter which states, for example, that pay, hours and holiday entitlements are determined through negotiation with a particular trade union or with reference to a named local or national collective agreement. The fact that individual employees may well choose not to join the union, or may leave it during the course of their employment, does not alter this position. Collective agreements generally apply across a whole workforce (or entire group of employees) irrespective of whether everyone is a signed up member of the relevant union. Effectively, in such cases, the contract of employment creates a situation in which the union acts as the agent of all relevant employees.

When collective agreements come to an end, perhaps as a result of de-recognition of the union, the terms and conditions set out in the most recently negotiated version of the collective agreement remain in place. Management cannot simply issue new terms and conditions to replace those already agreed, although they can negotiate changes with individuals that relate only to their own contracts, and can of course proceed to establish new terms and conditions by agreement.

Technical variations

When new technology is brought in and employees are asked to continue carrying out existing duties in a different way using new tools, provided training is given the courts regard this as quite reasonable. The leading case is *Cresswell et al v Inland Revenue* (1984) which concerned the computerisation of PAYE records. The court ruled no breach of contract had occurred because the employees were merely being asked to adapt to a new method of carrying out the same job. The following quotation from the judge in this case is clear:

> although doubtless all of us, being conservative by nature, desire nothing better than to be left to deepen our accustomed ruts, and hate change, a tax officer has no right to remain in perpetuity doing one defined type of work in one particular way.

Changes required by statute

From time to time laws are passed which effectively require employers to make changes to contracts of employment. The Working Time Regulations have been the most prominent example in recent years, causing employers to rewrite terms and conditions relating to rest breaks, night work and annual leave entitlement. In some organisations the fixed-term employees and part-time workers' regulations have led to contractual changes, as have new rules on asylum and immigration. Interestingly, during the fire fighters' dispute in 2003 the government threatened to force through contractual changes by statute if the strikers did not sign an agreement.

Custom and practice

Where it is custom and practice for contractual changes of a particular type to be made, employers can sometimes show that they have a legal right to make such changes. Custom and practice can never be used to overrule expressly agreed terms, but in the absence of anything agreed, the employer can argue that the parties have clearly demonstrated through their conduct over a period of time that a right to change terms exists. This tends to occur in the absence of any written terms and conditions and where changes in job duties or locations are regular, common and generally accepted in the place of work. In order to win a case the employer is required to show that the practice is 'reasonable, certain and well-known'. This is not at all easy, and many cases fail. For example, in *International Packaging Corporation (UK) Ltd v Balfour* (2003) the employer reduced hours without agreement, claiming that because there had been previous agreements with the workforce to take such action, custom and practice now gave the employer the right to vary hours unilaterally. The court rejected the argument. By contrast, an example of a case where the employer successfully won on this point is *General Transport Services v Henry* (2001). Here there was a collective agreement but it had never expressly been incorporated into individual contracts of employment. Here too management reduced hours of work, but only with the agreement of the trade union. Some employees went to court to argue that because the collective agreement was not con-tractual there was no right for managers to reduce hours without first gaining the consent of individual employees. The court ruled in favour of the employer, because acceptance of changes negotiated with the union in the past meant that this could be construed as custom and practice.

Acceptance through practice

Where alteration is not 'authorised' in the contract, the employer can seek to impose it unilaterally, in the hope/anticipation that employees will accept it. This occurs when em-ployees continue working, under the new term, without protesting in any way, for a number of weeks. If they later complain, the employer can argue that they have implicitly accepted the change through their actions—they acted as if it was accepted—this is quite acceptable to the courts as evidence of its acceptance.

Importantly however, a change cannot be deemed to be accepted by everyone just be-cause a majority of employees accept it. Even if 99% do—and 1% don't—the 1% have every right to hold out against the changes, to refuse new working practices and to reject the new terms. It is also quite clear that merely working on does not constitute acceptance. Employees can work on 'under protest' by signaling clearly that they do not accept the changes. If this is the case the employer cannot say that there has been acceptance through practice.

No detriment is suffered

While it is not strictly necessary to show that a detriment has been suffered in order to win a breach of contract claim, the claimant must be able to show that they have clearly suf-fered materially, physically or emotionally in a real way in order to win anything by way of damages. In practice this means that employers can often make minor changes to terms and conditions which have no adverse impact at all without fearing legal action. The same is evidently true of changes which actually have the effect of improving an employee's posi-tion, like a pay rise.

Activity 7.4

You work as an HR manager in a small, long-established food manufacturing company. Three hundred staff are employed on a single site close to the centre of Manchester. Some weeks ago the company's owner received an excellent offer for the factory buildings and has announced her intention of relocating to a new purpose-built site in Warrington. The move entails no job losses, but it will mean considerably longer commuting times for many employees. No written contracts of employment have ever been issued to employees at the company, although most were sent formal letters of appointment offering positions based at the Manchester city centre site. The company recognises a trade union and has bargained with it about pay, hours and holidays for many years.

1 What are the main implications of the proposed move from the point of view of employment law?

2 What further information would you need in order to give accurate advice?

3 What course of action would you advise is taken to ensure that subsequent litigation is avoided?

Pushing through contractual changes

Sometimes it is necessary for managers to try to push through contractual changes in situations where none of the above circumstances apply. Of course it may be possible simply to gain agreement and move on, but wherever employees believe themselves to be suffering a detriment as a result of proposed changes, managers are highly likely to come across perfectly legitimate resistance. However strong the manager believes the business case for change to be, some people are likely to find it a good deal less compelling and to insist, quite reasonably from their perspective, on their contractual rights. Where this is the case there are two courses of action that are usually followed. Both carry a degree of risk and are likely to have a negative impact on employee relations, so they are usually last resorts. Litigation is common, and so as a result there is a good deal of case law available to help guide management actions.

Paying sweeteners

The first approach that employers tend to prefer involves making some form of payment to staff who accept new terms and conditions of employment. The fairest way to do this is to make an offer to all staff of a lump-sum payment to 'buy out' old contracts and replace them with new ones. Some employers offer higher payments to longer-serving staff, while others prefer to offer a single sum to all employees concerned. In order to encourage a speedy response from the maximum number, it is common to make an offer which is available until a deadline date.

Such an approach is entirely lawful except where individual employees are approached and effectively bribed to move off terms and conditions that have been negotiated with a recognised trade union and on to individual contracts of employment. Paying sweeteners to those who signed individual contracts in place of collectively bargained terms and conditions was sanctioned by the House of Lords in the *Associated Newspapers* and *Associated*

Ports cases in 1995. The Employment Relations Act 1999 then backed up their interpretation. The Lords' judgment was then criticised by the European Court of Human Rights,
and was amended in 2004 to make unlawful all inducements aimed at persuading people
to refrain from union membership or participation in union activities such as collective
bargaining.

Where sweeteners are lawfully offered it is often the case that a proportion of employees
will reject the payment and will instead state that they prefer to remain on their existing
terms and conditions. It is important to remember that they have every right in law to
take this view and that they cannot be forced to accept new terms and conditions against
their will. Sometimes employers faced with resistance from a relatively small group will
increase the sum they are offering in a bid to buy over more people. This is entirely lawful,
but can have serious adverse employee relations consequences. Those who accepted the
lower, original sum tend to resent the higher payments. An alternative is to leave matters
as they are, appointing all new starters on the new terms and conditions, so that over
time the number remaining employed on the old contracts reduces steadily. Provided the
contracts in question permit it, it is possible to freeze pay for those on old contracts, so
that over time there is an incentive to transfer across. Indeed, some employers take this
approach from the start. Instead of offering payments to switch over, they simply say that
those on old contracts will have their pay frozen. This is ethically dubious and may well
lead to serious loss of trust with the workforce, but it is lawful in principle—provided of
course that in the process the National Minimum Wage Regulations and equal pay laws
are not breached.

Dismissing and rehiring

A more drastic measure which can only ever be used when other alternatives have been ex-
hausted involves dismissing people who refuse to accept new terms and conditions and then
rehiring them, instantly, on new terms. This is done with an explicit guarantee that accrued
rights and continuity of employment will not be affected (see Chapter 3). This approach is
more often threatened than actually carried out, because most employees will wish to avoid
being dismissed, even if it is technically for a few minutes, but it is sometimes necessary to
go the whole way and carry out dismissals of this kind.

The risk, of course, derives from the fact that any dismissal of employees in the qualifying
group could lead to claims of unfair dismissal being brought. Some people will not accept
the offer of re-employment and will instead take their cases to an employment tribunal.
In such situations it is possible for the employer successfully to defend the claim, but only
where the right steps are taken prior to the dismissals going ahead.

The defence deployed is that the dismissals are for 'some other substantial reason'—one of
the potentially fair reasons for dismissal permitted under the Employment Rights Act 1996.
This means, of course, that the reasonableness of the employer's actions determine whether
or not the dismissal is fair in law. Olga Aikin (2001:83–90) sets out her view, based on an
analysis of the case law, of what an employer needs to do in order to satisfy a tribunal that its
actions fell within the band of reasonable responses. She recommends the following:

1. It is necessary to show that there is a 'genuine organisational need' for the contractual
   change to take place. So a full, reasoned explanation must be given. It is not necessary to
   show that organisational survival depends on the changes taking place, but merely that
   the changes will be genuinely 'beneficial' for the organisation.

2. If collective dismissals are going to occur these fall within the European definition of 'redundancy' because they are for economic and not personal reasons. As a result consultation must take place ahead of time in just the same way as occurs in the case of redundancies as defined in UK law (see Chapter 6 for an explanation of this distinction).

3. The employer must be able to justify as reasonable any offers made to employees in the form of sweeteners (see above) before moving to dismiss. The bigger the proportion of employees who have accepted, the better the chance that the tribunal will judge any offer made to have been 'reasonable'. Moreover, the new terms themselves must be reasonable.

4. The employer must be able to show that it informed employees fully of the situation and gave them time to make a decision about whether to accept the new contracts or not.

5. Dismissals should be with full notice and with any outstanding payments made.

Consistency of treatment as between different employees in the same situation is also necessary if a finding of unfair dismissal is to be avoided. So it is important to ensure that all employees who do not accept your sweetener and refuse to move on to new contracts are included in the dismissal/rehire programme on the same terms.

Finally, it is important to point out that none of the above applies if the reason for either the dismissals, or indeed the initial change in contracts, is related to the transfer of an undertaking (ie, a merger, acquisition or the transfer of any part of one employing organisation to another). Such situations are covered by a whole different area of employment law (TUPE) which we cover in detail in Chapter 23.

 Exhibit 7.3 **Burdett-Coutts v Hertfordshire County Council (1984)**

This case concerned a group of school dinner ladies whose employer believed there was no alternative, if jobs were to be preserved, for them to accept new terms and conditions of service. The proposed changes were complex, including changes in the number of weeks' work each year and alterations to the payment system. The net result was a reduction in both hours and pay. Negotiations with the relevant union were held but did not lead to agreement. Consequently a letter was sent to each individual giving 'detailed notice of the variations in your contract of service'. The letter went on to set out the amendments proposed by the council.

> This letter is the formal notice of these changes in your contract of service which take effect on 31.3.83. I do hope you will understand why the County Council have to change your conditions of service as set out above, as a means of preserving both the school meals service and employment. I hope you will continue in the school meal's service.

The reaction of the dinner ladies was to state clearly that they were unhappy about the new terms, which were wholly unacceptable to them. Nevertheless, 31 March came, and they turned up to work in the usual manner. The next pay packets were then found to be lower than previously as they had been calculated using the new method. At this point the ladies sued the employer for breach of contract, claiming the difference that was owed to them. The case came to court some months later, with the women claiming full back-pay to 31 March 1983.

The dinner ladies won their claim. The employer had breached their contracts by forcing through a change without their consent. The employer's defence that its letter constituted a dismissal and rehire was roundly dismissed by the court. Full back-pay was awarded.

Activity 7.5

Assume that you have recently taken up a position as an HR manager in a jewelry manufacturing company. Four hundred staff are employed on a single site. The same terms and conditions of employment have been in place for many years. No trade union is recognised.

Soon after you take up your position it becomes clear that the firm is in financial difficulty and that it will only continue in business if it can reduce its costs substantially. In order to achieve this without the need to make redundancies, it is proposed that all staff take a pay cut of 10% and that new job descriptions are issued to permit the achievement of more flexible working practices.

1   What are the main legal issues that need to be taken into consideration in putting these proposals into effect?

2   Given a desire to avoid legal actions, how would you advise the managing director to proceed?

The Unfair Contract Terms Act 1977

The Unfair Contract Terms Act (UCTA) is a statute which allows a party to a contract to ask a court to rule that a term is void if it unreasonably excludes or limits liability for:

1. death or personal injury

or

2. breach of contract or *'rendering performance substantially different from that which was reasonably expected of the contracting party'*.

This piece of legislation was not intended to regulate employment contracts—except in Scotland where it clearly does have such an effect. In England and Wales the use of the term 'consumer' in the Act has meant that it has almost exclusively been used to settle disputes in the wider commercial field. However, in 2000 the High Court ruled in *Brigden v American Express Bank Ltd* that employees could, in principle, be considered to be 'consumers'. Here, Mr Brigden had been summarily dismissed without the use of a disciplinary procedure which had been incorporated into his contract. It happened because there was also an express term allowing the employer to dismiss on grounds of gross misconduct without using the procedure in the first two years of service. The court ruled that this second term breached UCTA.

More recently, however, in *Keen v Commerzbank AG* (2007) the Court of Appeal decided that it found the High Court's judgment in the *Brigden* case to be unsatisfactory. For the time being, therefore, it appears that attempts to extend the scope of the Unfair Contract Terms Act into the employment arena in England and Wales have come to a halt.

CHAPTER SUMMARY

• Everyone who is employed has a contract of employment. In many cases this is not written and some of its terms may be unclear. Once established the contract is binding on both parties and its terms can, if necessary, be enforced in court.

- A contract is established when an unconditional offer of employment is unconditionally accepted. Once in existence, in principle, neither party can alter its terms without the consent of the other.
- Employers are required under EU law to provide new employees with written particulars of their main terms and conditions within their first eight weeks.
- Employers do, in practice, make changes in contracts from time to time. This is possible, for example, through flexibility clauses.
- When contractual changes are genuinely necessary for good business reasons and when employees refuse to accept the change after a reasonable payment has been offered, it is usually lawful for employers to dismiss them and rehire instantly on new terms and conditions.

For updates and further materials, please see the online resource centre at www.oup.com.

REFERENCES

Aikin, O. (2001) *Drawing Up Employment Contracts*. Third Edition. London: Chartered Institute of Personnel and Development.

Leighton, P. & O'Donnell, A. (1995) *The New Employment Contract: Using Employment Contracts Effectively*. London: Nicholas Brealey Publishing.

Smith I. (2004) 'You signed the contract ...' *New Law Journal*, 9 January.

ONLINE RESOURCE CENTRE

A range of online resources to help you through your employment law module have been developed by the author team. These include updates, self-test questions and sources for further reading. (www.oxfordtextbooks.co.uk/orc/taylor_emir3e)

Implied terms

8

Learning outcomes

By the end of this chapter you should be able to:

- distinguish between different types of contractual term;

- state which type of term takes precedence when two are incompatible;

- explain in what circumstances courts can imply terms into individual contracts of employment;

- outline the major implied duties that employers and employees owe to one another;

- explain the significance of the development of the implied duty to maintain a relationship of mutual trust and confidence;

- give advice about which court a claim for breach of contract can be taken to;

- set out the different remedies that can be obtained through breach of contract proceedings.

Introduction

In the last chapter we introduced the principles of the law as they apply to contracts of employment. For the most part our focus was on the express terms which the employer and employee agree when their relationship is established and which may subsequently be varied. In this chapter we move on to look at the terms which are implied into contracts of employment. This means that they are deemed to be present by a court despite never having been explicitly agreed or even discussed by the employer or employee. This is quite a complex and widely misunderstood area of employment law, but one which is becoming increasingly important as the law evolves over time.

We begin by setting out the different types of implied term and differentiate these from other types of terms, before going on to explore the major implied terms and their significance. We focus in particular on the duty to maintain a relationship of mutual trust and confidence as this is the area in which the most significant recent legal developments have occurred. After this we consider situations in which implied terms conflict with express terms, before discussing procedural issues in breach of contract cases.

 Activity 8.1

Joanne Steele is employed as a personal assistant to the managing director of a medium-sized business, Jason Blunt. She is highly paid in the job, having been personally chosen by Mr Blunt when temping at the company four years ago. He pays her well but treats her badly.

- He always refers to her by her second name, usually with the prefix 'f***ing' in front of it— as in 'F***ing Steele—get your fat arse into my office now'.

- On several occasions he has asked her humiliating personal questions in front of groups of male colleagues.

- He frequently requires her to work long hours, refusing to allow her to leave the office before him in the evenings.

- Her workload has increased steadily throughout her time at the company so that she is now regularly working for sixty hours a week.

- Whenever she complains and asks for assistance, promises are made about future increased staffing levels, but no assistant is ever appointed.

- When she handed in her notice last year, she was persuaded to stay on with a pay rise and a promise to provide future assistance. These did not materialise.

- In recent months Joanne has become depressed due to the pressure of her work and has been prescribed medication by her doctor. She has continued to work while taking these drugs.

Joanne asks you to advise her about her legal position. What type of legal action might she be able to bring? What would be the legal basis of her claim? To which court should she take her claim? What would be her chances of success?

Return to this activity once you have read the chapter, to see how many of your answers were correct.

Types of contractual terms

There is no concise, clear or generally agreed categorisation of the different types of terms that can make up a contract of employment. Writers differ somewhat in the way that they label different types of terms. A useful four-way categorisation is provided by IDS (2009:77–78) which we shall adopt for the purposes of this chapter. The four types are as follows:

Express terms

These are the terms that are agreed by the parties up front, although they may be changed over time with agreement (see Chapter 7). Typically they will include the most significant terms such as the rate of pay, the job title, the location where the work will occur, holiday entitlement and notice provisions. They may be agreed either in writing or orally.

Incorporated terms

These are terms which are set out in documents such as staff handbooks, lists of workplace rules or collective agreements. They are not agreed between the employer and employee individually, but are explicitly incorporated into individual contracts of employment. Hence, when someone starts a job in the public sector they typically receive an offer letter which makes explicit reference to the collective agreement which covers their job. As a result, where the relevant trade union negotiates a change to terms and conditions for the workforce *as a whole*, each individual contract is adjusted accordingly.

Statutory terms

These are terms which are deemed by the courts to be present in all contracts of employment because they concern employment rights created by statutes. They are terms which have been given to all employees by Parliament and which cannot be 'signed away' by individual employees. An example is the equality clause which all contracts of employment contain thanks to the Equal Pay Act 1970. Another is the right not to be required to work more hours in a week than are permitted under the Working Time Regulations 1998 (see Chapter 26)—a term that was declared present in all contracts of employment in the case of *Barber & others v RJB Mining* (1999).

Implied terms

These are terms which are not agreed by the parties, but which are nonetheless found to be present in a contract of employment. There are two major types of implied terms. Some are general and are considered present in all contracts of employment. These are often known as implied or common law duties. Some are owed by employers to employees, some by employees to employers, while others are owed to both by both. The second type of implied terms applies only to a particular contract or to contracts in a particular workplace. In the absence of there being any clear express term about (for example) hours of work, the court implies such a term by taking evidence about what happens in practice. We will focus on this second type of implied term next, before moving on to focus on generally applicable implied duties.

A hierarchy of terms

What happens when there is a conflict between an express term and an implied term? Or between a statutory term and an incorporated term? Can one type 'trump' another? The answer is generally that they can and that there is, in effect, a hierarchy of different types of terms which determines which overrides another when two appear to conflict. This is as follows:

1. statutory term
2. express term
3. incorporated term
4. implied term.

However, great care must be taken not to apply this hierarchy in a manner which is too formulaic. While it is true that in most cases an individual cannot 'sign away' statutory rights by agreeing expressly to do so, there are one or two situations in which this can happen. A good example is the right of employers to require would-be employees to sign 'opt-out' agreements in respect of the Working Time Regulations 1998 (see Chapter 26). Moreover, of course, it is quite possible for any employer to reach a general agreement with a departing employee barring the taking of legal action as part of a severance settlement. In signing such an agreement, employees are effectively signing away (via express terms) their rights to bring tribunal claims relating to breaches of statutory terms, including the equality clause.

As a general rule express terms override implied terms, but as we explained in Chapter 7, the courts are increasingly willing to make a distinction between an express term and a management decision to exercise discretion in enforcing an express term. The latter (ie, the management action) can then be found to be a breach of an implied term such as the duty of care or the duty to maintain a relationship of mutual trust and confidence.

Implying terms into individual contracts

It is important to appreciate that the courts are reluctant to imply terms into a contract of employment and apply quite restrictive tests before doing so. Moreover it will only ever be done if there is no express term, or at least no *agreed* express term setting out what was the intention of the parties in establishing their contractual relationship. This is not an area in which a general test of 'reasonableness', 'objective justification' or 'proportionality' applies as in other areas of employment law that we have discussed. IDS (2009:85) usefully set out the situations in which, according to the case law, terms can be implied. These are as follows:

- when a term is a necessary part of the type of contract that the parties have agreed to make
- when a term is necessary in order to give business efficacy to a contract
- where it is custom and practice to include a term in contracts of the kind in question
- where an intention on the part of the parties to include a term is demonstrated by their actions in practice
- where a term is so obvious that it must have been the intention of the parties to include it in the contract.

In addition, Lindsay (2001) states that conventionally a term can only be implied if 'it is capable of clear expression' and is 'reasonable and equitable'.

The term 'business efficacy' requires some explanation. Essentially it means workability. If a contractual relationship cannot work in practice in the absence of a particular term, and no relevant express term exists, then the court will read one in so as to make the contract effective in practice. According to Duggan (2003), two long-established legal tests are still used by the courts when deciding whether or not to 'read in' an implied term. The first was formulated by Lord Scrutton in a Court of Appeal judgment made as long ago as 1918 (*Reigate v Union Manufacturing Limited*):

> The first thing is to see what the parties have expressed in the contract; and then an implied term is not to be added because the Court thinks it would have been reasonable to have inserted it in the contract. A term can only be implied if it is necessary in the business sense to give efficacy to the contract; that is, it is such a term that it can confidently be said that if at the time the contract was being negotiated someone had said to the parties, 'What will happen in such a case', they would both have replied 'Of course, so and so will happen; we did not trouble to say that; it is too clear'. Unless the Court comes to such a conclusion as that, it ought not to imply a term which the parties themselves have not expressed.

A slightly different test, which appears charming and eccentric nowadays, was developed a few years later by Lord McKinnon in *Shirlaw v Southern Foundries* (1926). This is known as the officious bystander test because the court puts itself in the position of a nosy onlooker observing the parties making their contract:

> if while the parties were making their bargain, an officious bystander were to suggest some express provision for it in the agreement, they would testily suppress him with a common 'oh, of course'. At least it is true, I think, that if a term were never implied by a judge unless it could pass that test, he could not be held to be wrong.

Most recent cases concern work location, as this is a matter which is often not clarified in offer letters or other documents establishing contracts of employment, and may well appear so obvious to both parties that it is not specifically agreed at the time a contract is formed. What then happens if a company relocates, or closes one workplace and wishes to transfer its workers to another? What happens if an organisation simply wants its staff to work flexibly across a number of sites and not to remain based in just one? The answer appears to vary depending on the type of job—the question being asked 'what is necessary to make the contract work in practice?'. IDS (2009:88–90) give two contrasting examples to illustrate this point.

Courtauld's Northern Spinning Ltd v Sibson & another (1988) concerned the closure of a depot from which the employees concerned worked as HGV drivers. The company closed this depot and asked the men to work instead from another which was within 'reasonable daily reach' of their homes. There was no express mobility clause in the contract, so the court was asked to imply one. The Court of Appeal thus asked itself what would have been agreed between the drivers and Courtaulds at the time their relationship began had the question of a possible future need to change depots been addressed. They concluded that an agreement to move depots would have been included. The fact that as HGV drivers the men spent most of their time away from the depot anyway was significant as it meant that the precise location of the depot was relatively unimportant.

In another case, however, a different conclusion was reached. Ms Aparau worked as a checkout supervisor in an Iceland retail outlet (*Aparau v Iceland Frozen Foods plc* (1996)). The company decided that it wished to deploy its supervisors flexibly across all its London stores, but Ms Aparau refused to work anywhere except at the store that she had always worked in. There was no express term concerning work location in her contract. The EAT decided that it could not imply a mobility clause into the contract. This was not necessary to give business efficacy to the contract.

Custom and practice is another common basis for reading in implied terms. The leading case here is *Sagar v H Ridehalgh & Son Ltd* (1931) in which a worker in a Lancashire cotton mill had some of his wages deducted for poor workmanship. As there was no express term in his contract permitting deductions of this kind, he sued his employer for breach of contract. The mill owners argued that the right to deduct wages in these circumstances should be implied because the rule had been applied in their business for over thirty years and was common practice in over 85% of all Lancashire cotton mills. The court doubted Mr Sagar's claim that he himself did not know of the practice, and so decided that the term should be implied. Nowadays Mr Sagar would win his claim because statutes passed by Parliament since the 1930s prohibit employers from making deductions unless employees agree to rules ahead of time (see Chapter 21). But the custom and practice principle still applies. The test used is that in order to be implied as a term in a contract, the practice in question must be 'reasonable, notorious and certain'. IDS (2001:92) define this as follows:

> It must be fair and not arbitrary or capricious ... it must be generally established and well-known and it must be clear-cut.

Over the years a number of cases have been appealed to the higher courts and have been reported, there often being an apparent overlap between those which are based on custom and practice and those based on the actions of the parties in practice. Most concern wage deductions, non-payment of established bonuses or disputes over hours of work. A good example is *Dean v Eastbourne Fishermen's & Boatmen's Protection Society* (1977). Here a man worked over several years for an organisation despite no express term relating to hours of work ever having been agreed. Subsequently, a dispute arose about what hours Mr Dean could be required to work. The court took evidence from the parties about what hours had actually been worked in practice and decided to rule that these should form the implied term. Another case quoted by Duggan (2003:200) is *Scott v Victor Blagen (Barking) Limited* (1982) in which a maintenance fitter challenged his employer's right to require him to continue working at weekends, despite the fact that he had done so for over twelve years. In the absence of any express term, the EAT ruled that weekend working should be implied in the contract because it was clearly custom and practice in this employment relationship. Other cases, however, favour employees, particularly where employers seek to alter job duties fundamentally irrespective of how long an individual employee has been performing a particular job role. In the absence of express terms setting out what job duties are or permitting changes to be made, it is considered to be breach of contract to make alterations to a job without first securing agreement.

The requirement that a practice should be notorious in order for it to be an implied-term contract is particularly relevant in the case of discretionary payments. Of course it is preferable for employers to make it clear in writing whether or not a bonus payment of some description is discretionary or a contractual right. But where this is not done and where no express term exists, problems can occur if discretionary payments are always made in practice when a certain set of circumstances applies. An employee who is denied a payment can then claim that their contract has been breached because it is custom and practice to pay in these circumstances. The extent to which employers can exercise discretion in withholding commonly paid bonuses or supplements depends on how well publicised, and hence 'notorious', the practice is within the organisation. If it well known to all employees and paid every year or every month in practice, it is difficult for the employer to argue that it should not be implied as a contractual right through custom and practice.

 Activity 8.2   *Morley v Heritage plc* **(1993)**

Mr Morley was employed as a finance director. His written contract stated that he was entitled to four weeks paid holiday each year, the holiday year commencing on 1 January.

He resigned from his job in October 1989, having only taken two days holiday that year. He asked his employer for thirteen days accrued holiday pay—the balance of what he was entitled to, but his request was turned down. The employer said that in resigning he was giving up his entitlement to accrued holiday.

There were no documents outlining company policy on this matter, no precedents to rely on and no express terms to clarify the contractual position.

Mr Morley sued the company for breach of contract, arguing that the right to pay in lieu should be construed as an implied term. He lost his case.

1   What legal tests would the court have applied when deciding Mr Morley's case?

2   To what extent do you consider the outcome to have been fair?

3   What could the employer have done differently in order to avoid having to defend itself in court?

Implied duties

Many employers and most employees are wholly unaware of the existence within *all* employment contracts of terms labelled 'implied' duties or 'common law duties'. Yet breach of such a duty by either the employee or the employer is considered just as much a breach of contract as the breach of an express term. It can thus form the basis of serious disciplinary action on the part of the employer, or in some circumstances to a claim for damages being made against an employee. Alternatively, breach of contract or constructive dismissal proceedings may be brought by an employee against an employer.

This is an area of employment law which is developing at a steady pace. Implied duties are the creation of judges, and new ones are created from time to time as test cases are taken up through the court hierarchy. Moreover, court rulings regularly result in the further development or 'fleshing out' of longer-established implied duties which may only have been the subject of a handful of claims previously. A detailed exploration of all the implied duties is beyond the scope of this book. This chapter would run to hundreds of pages if we were to attempt such an exercise. Instead we set out below a list of the major examples, going on to focus on some of the more significant implied duties in more detail. One or two, such as the duty of care and the duty of fidelity are covered in greater detail later in the book in relation to other topic areas.

The major duties owed by employees to employers are the following:

- to co-operate
- to obey instructions
- to exercise reasonable care and skill
- to act in good faith and fidelity.

The major duties owed by employers to employees are the following:

- a general duty of care
- to pay agreed wages
- to provide work
- not to treat employees in an arbitrary or vindictive manner
- to provide support to employees (eg, proper training in duties, etc)
- to provide safe systems of work
- to inform employees of important decisions
- to indemnify (ie, against any expenses incurred)
- to take account of legitimate grievances
- to provide a suitable working environment
- to provide references
- not to conduct a corrupt or dishonest business.

In addition, both employees and employers owe a duty to one another to maintain a relationship of mutual trust and confidence, while ex-employees retain, after leaving, a general duty of fidelity to their former employers (see Chapter 22).

 Activity 8.3   *W.A. Goold (Pearmark) v McConnell* **(1995)**

Mr McConnell and his colleague, Mr Richmond, were employed as jewelry salesmen and paid on a salary plus commission basis. In 1994 the employer decided to alter the approach and methods employed to sell the company's products. The initiative did not succeed and the commission earned by the two men dropped substantially.

Soon after the changes were made, the men raised a complaint with their manager, but he said that nothing could be done immediately. Some weeks later they again complained but nothing was done. Finally they tried to take the matter up with the company chairman, Mr Goold, but were not given an appointment to meet with him. They thus resigned and claimed constructive dismissal. They won their case.

1 On what basis do you think they won?

2 To what extent do you agree that this was a just outcome?

The duty to obey instructions

In entering into a contract of employment, as was explained in Chapter 3, the employee is agreeing to a relationship characterised by subservience. It follows that a general duty to obey an employer's instructions forms a central part of the contract. In principle, therefore, a failure to do so is a breach of contract and can lead to dismissal.

However, the law restricts to some extent the duty to obey in significant respects and employees are thus effectively able to justify a refusal to obey in some circumstances. An important example is where the management instruction does not itself fall within the terms of the employee's contract of employment. This principle was established as long ago as 1862 in the case of *Price v Mouat* where the judges ruled that a highly paid employee could not be required to undertake unskilled manual work. The other situations in which the case law states that employees can refuse to obey are as follows:

- where obeying might put personal safety at risk
- where the instruction is illegal
- where the employer acts in bad faith in giving the instruction.

This last situation arose in the well-publicised case of *Macari v Celtic Football and Athletic Company Ltd* (1999) when the football manager Lou Macari brought proceedings against Celtic Football Club. He had refused to comply with his employer's request that he should move house so that he lived within a forty-five radius of Glasgow, and was dismissed as a result. Mr Macari claimed that the order to move house had been made in bad faith purely in order to put additional pressure on him and hence to bring about a situation in which he could be dismissed. He lost his case, but in giving judgment Lord Caplin stated that in principle an instruction given by an employer which aimed to embarrass or harm an employee could be justifiably refused.

The duty to exercise reasonable care and skill

This mainly relates to skilled employees or those undertaking professional duties. There are situations in which carelessness or negligence on the part of the employee can lead to substantial losses being sustained by the employer and which can lead to legal action. Another case from the nineteenth century established the principle (*Harmer v Cornelius* (1858)). Duggan (2003:208–209) quotes the following key passage from the judgment:

> When a skilled labourer, artisan or artist is employed, there is on his part an implied warranty that he is of skill reasonably competent to the task he undertakes.... Thus, if an apothecary, a watch-maker, or an attorney be employed for reward, they impliedly undertake to possess and exercise reasonable care and skill in their several arts. The public profession of an art is a representation and undertaking to all the world that the professor possesses the requisite ability and skill.

A more recent case was *Janata Bank v Ahmed* (1981). Here a bank manager had negligently lent money to customers who were in no position to repay it. The bank successfully sued its former manager for £36,000 on the grounds that he had not exercised reasonable care when carrying out his job.

It is important to remember, in this context, that the principle of vicarious liability always applies in the employment relationship. The employer is liable in law for the actions of employees. Customers or other employees who suffer a detriment because of the incompetence of an employee thus bring their cases against the employer. However, this does not mean that there are no circumstances in which the employer can seek to recover the damages from the employee who has caused the problem in the first place.

The duty to provide work

You might think that a failure on the part of an employer to give any work for an employee to do would not cause many employees to take legal action. Being paid not to work is a situation that many would quite like to be in. But there are situations in which it can cause a detriment to an employee and lead to litigation. Where this occurs the claim made is breach of contract under the implied duty to provide work.

The cases mainly fall into two categories. On the one hand there are situations in which a lack of work causes a reduction in income, for example when a good deal of someone's pay is derived from piecework or from sales commission. The other is where being deprived of the ability to exercise a skill regularly or frequently itself causes financial loss. This latter situation has long applied to actors and actresses who are denied publicity when hired to play a leading role and then demoted to the position of understudy. But recent cases have extended the principle into other fields too, and particularly to situations in which employees are suspended or placed on 'garden leave' for some months and are thus denied the opportunity to make regular use of certain skills. IDS (2009:108) give the example of *William Hill Organisation v Tucker* (1999) to illustrate this principle. Here a senior dealer who specialised in spreadbetting was asked not to work his notice, but to remain at home instead for a number of months before taking up his new job with a competitor. Mr Tucker won his case.

The duty to provide support

An implied term that is rarely invoked and which remains unknown to many employment lawyers is the duty to provide reasonable support. To date only a handful of cases have been heard and these have not been appealed beyond the EAT. So there is a great deal of scope for further development of the duty in the future. At present, according to IDS (2009:110) it is uncertain whether or not a failure on the part of an employer to provide the tools needed to do a job properly can be construed as a breach of contract. There is no question that it could be if the result is a health and safety risk, but otherwise it would appear from the current case law that this does not constitute a breach.

The duty to provide support therefore applies principally to the deployment of sufficient staff to enable a body of work to be carried out effectively and to situations in which employees do not get co-operation from subordinates or colleagues. Both these factors played a part in one of the first cases to be decided following the creation of the implied term by the EAT in the late 1970s. In *Seligman & Latz Ltd v McHugh* (1979) a hairdresser found herself unable to carry out her work properly following the resignation of her assistant. Other assistants were employed, but were not willing to help her sufficiently. This was ruled to be a breach of contract. Mrs McHugh could not carry out her job without further support, and this was not provided by her employers.

Exhibit 8.1   *Whitbread PLC/Thresher v Gullyes* **(1992)**

Mrs Gullyes had been employed as branch manager in a Thresher off-licence for four years—a job she carried out with conspicuous success. Indeed, so successful was she, that the company offered her a new position in a larger branch which had substantial staff and operational problems. She was reluctant to accept the promotion, but allowed herself to be persuaded against her better judgment.

On arrival at the new shop, she encountered a variety of problems. Staff were difficult to supervise and there were high turnover and absence rates. She soon found herself working over seventy hours a week.

After a few weeks she went away on holiday. She then returned to find that, in her absence, the area manager had transferred her two most effective assistants to other branches. At this point, realising that she would not be able to cope, she requested an immediate transfer to another branch. When this was refused she resigned and brought a claim of constructive dismissal. She won her case. There had been a breach by the employer of the implied duty to provide support.

The duty of fidelity

We will focus on this implied term in more detail in Chapter 22 in the context of restrictive covenants and the protection of confidential information. Here it is only necessary to note that all employees are under a duty not to compete against their own employers or to act in a way that is calculated to harm their employers' interests. This means that there will almost always be a breach of contract on the part of an employee who takes part in industrial action, even according to IDS (2009:103) when the action taken simply involves withdrawal of goodwill. However, this does not mean that it is lawful to sack anyone who goes on strike. As we will see in Chapter 29, statutes ensure that employers are very restricted when it comes to dismissing people who take industrial action. Docking strikers' pay is the major sanction that is used in practice to reflect the fact that industrial action amounts to a breach of contract.

Mutual trust and confidence

The recent development by the courts of the implied term of mutual trust and confidence has been highly significant. What is more, as each year goes by it is further developed in ways which can have major consequences for employers and employees. Several commentators (eg, Brodie, 2001), as well as the President of the EAT himself (Lindsay, 2001) have written at length speculating about how its impact may further spread in the future to cover a great range of situations that can arise in the employment relationship. Their view is that we are still only at the beginning of what could be a long journey in new directions as far as its future is concerned.

There is some debate about exactly when a duty on employers and employees to maintain a relationship of mutual trust and confidence was first found to amount to an implied term, but it is clear that it became well established in cases that were decided from the late 1970s onwards. In *Courtaulds Northern Textiles v Andrew* (1979) the EAT ruled that:

it was an implied term of the contract that the employers would not, without reasonable and proper cause, conduct themselves in a manner calculated or likely to destroy or seriously damage the relationship of confidence and trust between the parties.

This principle was eventually approved by the House of Lords in *Malik & Another v Bank of Credit and Commerce International* (1997), and is thus now fully established as far as employer conduct towards employees is concerned. The same is true of employee conduct, but here it is the law of unfair dismissal which has been the focus of developments. In *Neary v Dean of Westminster* (1999) it was established that *'conduct amounting to gross misconduct justifying dismissal must so undermine the trust and confidence which is inherent in the particular contract of employment that the master should no longer be required to retain the servant in his employment'*.

Mutual trust and confidence is the most significant of the implied duties because of its very general nature and because it can be applied in so many different situations. Brodie (2001) also argues that its emergence represents a breakthrough in the development of employment law in that it has involved the courts recognising that the employment relationship is more than a financial one. It is also, for most people, a source of identity, dignity, self-worth and important personal relationships. These human factors are now explicitly acknowledged in our law by virtue of the fact that it is unlawful for an employer to undermine the trust and confidence of its employees.

It is important to point out, however, that the duty to maintain a relationship of mutual trust and confidence is not the same thing as a duty on employers to act reasonably. The law does not place a general obligation on employers to be reasonable in their treatment of employees. Reasonableness is a significant concept in dismissal law and in some other areas of employment law, but in general day-to-day dealings with employees, employers can be unreasonable without breaching the contract of employment. The same is true of the way that employees conduct their relationship with their employers. Being unreasonable in itself does not amount to a breach of mutual trust and confidence and should not lead to summary dismissal on grounds of gross misconduct. The conduct, on either side, must effectively be *intolerable* in nature for there to be a breach.

Because of its wide applicability in practice, it is not easy to summarise succinctly the implications of mutual trust and confidence from an employer's point of view. Duggan (2003) gives useful summaries of the major cases in which rulings on points of legal principle have been made in favour of both employers and employees. The following lists of examples come from his book and from cases reported in more recent years.

Situations in which a breach of the implied term *has* been found to have occurred:

- where an employee was required to undergo a medical examination without reasonable cause
- where an employer withdrew a loan it had used to encourage an employee to relocate to a different region of the country
- where a manager told a fellow employee that his PA was 'an intolerable bitch on a Monday morning'
- where an employer reported an employee to the police without due cause
- where an employee suffered a detriment because of an annual performance appraisal which she was not shown

- where an employee was accused of dishonesty without good grounds
- where an employee lost her continuity of employment (and hence her right to claim unfair dismissal) because she was induced into resigning a job and joining a non-associated company
- where improved terms and conditions were offered to all employees in a business except one
- where a teacher was unjustly suspended following allegations of sexual misconduct
- where an employer failed to take all reasonable steps to ensure the continuation of sickness benefits by an insurance company
- where disciplinary charges were investigated by a panel which was not independent as required by the employer's procedures.

Situations in which a breach of the implied term *has not* been found to have occurred:

- where an employee was 'unsettled' by a relocation to a new part of the country
- where an employer suggested that an employee should look for a new job
- where employees resigned before being transferred to a new employer on the grounds that they believed their contracts would not be honoured in full
- where an employer had negligently (not deliberately) misled employees about future job security.

Ultimately the extent to which unprofessional and unpleasant conduct on the part of a manager constitutes a breach of trust and confidence is a matter of judgement for the tribunal. Much depends on the facts of particular cases, and opinion will inevitably therefore differ. An extraordinary example was recently reported when the EAT overturned an earlier tribunal ruling in the case of *Parsons v Bristol Street Fourth Investments Ltd t/a Bristol Street Motors* (2008). This concerned a highly eccentric manager called Mr Lawrence who humiliated his employees in various subtle and not so subtle ways. Mr Parsons, the claimant, had been grabbed by the testicles, had been given what is known in footballing circles as 'the hairdryer treatment', and had been given nicknames such as 'the old parsonage' and 'old git'. Mr Lawrence was also found guilty of 'engaging in dangerous behaviour in the workplace including the use of an air gun, a mini-motorbike and a go-cart'. The employment tribunal found that these actions did not constitute a breach of the duty to maintain a relationship of mutual trust and confidence because that was not Mr Lawrence's intention. The EAT overturned them, saying that intention was irrelevant. If the net result is a breach of trust and confidence then a breach has occurred.

A further major principle was established by the House of Lords in *Johnson v Unisys* (2001). Here it was decided that the implied term of mutual trust and confidence does not extend to cover the manner of a dismissal. This means that employees who are harshly treated in the way that they are dismissed can only claim against their employers through the law of unfair dismissal (ie, statute). They cannot claim additional damages for breach of contract as well. This principle was then extended by the Court of Appeal in *Eastwood v Magnox Electric plc* (2002) to cover the whole course of events leading up to a dismissal, and not just the dismissal itself.

An important consequence of the *Malik* case (see above) is that the employer's conduct need not be expressly directed at an individual employee for there to be a breach of the implied term. In this case Mr Malik complained that his career prospects had been seriously damaged because he had worked for a corrupt business. He had suffered a detriment because his managers had acted dishonestly, although they had not treated him poorly in any personal sense. Acts of omission as well as acts of commission on the part of an employer can thus amount to breaches of implied terms.

The most recent developments in this field of litigation concern bullying of employees by managers. There is nothing new about the principle that arbitrary or capricious behaviour on the part of an employer can amount to a breach of trust and confidence. The EAT decided as long ago as 1990 (in *Hilton International Hotels v Protopapa*) that rebuking someone in a humiliating or degrading manner constituted a breach of the implied term. But a reasonably recent case hit the headlines and thus has made managers, trade union officials and employees much more aware of their rights in this area. This was the Court of Appeal judgment in

---

 Exhibit 8.2 Waiving the right to a relationship of mutual trust and confidence

In his article examining various aspects of the implied term of mutual trust and confidence, the President of the EAT Mr Justice Lindsay (2001) makes an interesting observation.

If it is true, he argues, that express terms override implied terms when the two are inconsistent, surely it would be possible in principle for an employer to write an express term into a contract of employment which excludes any duty of mutual trust and confidence. Lindsay goes as far as to suggest the following formulation for such an express term:

> The term described in Malik v BCCI as the implied term as to confidence and trust and any term representing the same in English or Scottish law shall form no part whatsoever of this contract and neither the company nor the above-named employee shall owe to the other the obligations which would otherwise arise thereunder.

Lindsay concludes that such a term would probably not be enforceable, unless negotiated with a trade union, because it could be argued that the waiver was not 'freely arrived at on the basis of adequate information'. But he is hesitant in reaching this conclusion.

He also argues that it is improbable that an employer would include an express term such as this in a contract. As time goes on, however, and the term is found to apply in more and more situations, it is possible to envisage circumstances in which firms such as Cantor Fitzgerald might prefer to exclude the term than run the risk of paying out further large sums by way of compensation to very highly paid employees.

Barmes (2006) points out that in the case of other significant implied terms, such as the duties that relate to health and safety, statute ensures that employers cannot override the duty by establishing an express term which has such an effect. Any such clause is void under the Unfair Contract Terms Act 1977. She thus argues in favour of a general statute *'specifying that terms implied by law could not be excluded by agreement.'*

Horkulak v Cantor Fitzgerald International (2004) in which a senior manager used threatening and abusive language to a subordinate. The publicity arose because damages were assessed at £900,000.

Procedural matters in breach of contract cases

There are two further issues to consider briefly. First the question of which court breach of contract cases are taken to, and secondly the types of remedy that are available.

Which court?

Until 1994 all cases relating to breaches of contract were heard in the County Court or the High Court and not in the employment tribunal, the latter's area of jurisdiction extending only to statutory employment rights. Since then employment tribunals have been able to deal with breach of contract issues which are *'outstanding on the termination of the employee's employment'*. In practice this covers a large percentage of the claims that are brought, but it still leaves out many situations in which employees (and employers) bring cases alleging breach of contract. Another restriction is that tribunals can only award damages of up to £25,000. Where bigger sums are being sought, the case must be taken to the County Court or (if over £50,000) to the High Court. Tribunals are also barred from considering claims that relate to personal injury, live-in accommodation, intellectual property rights or covenants in restraint of trade. Even if these arise on the termination of employment, claims must be taken to the County or High Courts.

Employers can only bring counter-claims to the employment tribunal. They cannot originate proceedings there. So they can only sue an ex-employee for damages (because the claim must relate to the termination of someone's employment) once proceedings have already been initiated by the person concerned.

Often in the case of breach of contract claims litigants have a choice about which court they wish to take their case to. Just because employment tribunals *can* hear cases in certain circumstances, this does not mean that they are the *only* forum in which such cases can be pursued. It is open to claimants to take their case to the County Court instead if they wish to. Indeed, because the three-month time limit applies in the case of employment tribunal claims, those who are out of time have no choice but to take their cases to the County Court. What is clear, however, is that the same claim cannot be pursued in both types of court. You cannot try again in the County Court once an employment tribunal has ruled against you. Nor can you go to the tribunal, win £25,000 and then pursue the case again in the County Court in order to to secure additional compensation (*Fraser v Hilmad Ltd* (2006)).

Remedies

Damages to recover financial loss are the most commonly sought type of remedy in breach of contract cases. In some circumstances damages can also be claimed for psychiatric injury and also for 'stigma' where individual reputations are adversely affected by former association with a dishonest or corrupt employer. Reductions can be made to reflect payments already received from the employer and failure on the part of claimants to mitigate their losses.

Other types of remedy that can be applied for are declarations of rights and injunctions to restrain an employer from taking an action in breach of contract, such as dismissing someone. The latter, according to Duggan (2003:497–509) are unusual, because the courts are reluctant to force an employer to continue employing an employee in whom confidence has been lost. However, there are cases where injunctions have been awarded in such circumstances. These occur when there is no loss of confidence, damages would not be an appropriate remedy and the injunction has the effect of giving the employee statutory protection of some kind (see *Hill v Parsons & Co Ltd* (1971)).

CHAPTER SUMMARY

- There are four major types of term which are found in contracts of employment: express terms, implied terms, statutory terms and incorporated terms. When there is a difference between them, as a rule, express terms trump implied terms and statutory terms trump express terms.

- In the absence of any clear agreement about the nature of key terms in an individual contract, a court will imply terms by establishing the nature of custom and practice in the relationship and in the workplace more generally. This involves applying the 'business efficacy' test or the 'officious bystander' test.

- A range of further terms are implied into all contracts of employment because, over time, the courts have created 'common law duties'. These include the duty of fidelity, the duty of care and the duty to maintain a relationship of mutual trust and confidence.

- The evolution of the duty to maintain a relationship of mutual trust and confidence is one of the most significant contemporary developments in employment law.

For updates and further materials, please see the online resource centre at www.oup.com.

REFERENCES

Barmes, L. (2006) 'Common law implied terms and behavioural standards at work' *Industrial Law Journal* 36.1.

Brodie, D. (2001) 'Mutual trust and the values of the employment contract' *Industrial Law Journal* 30 (p84).

Duggan, M. (2003) *Wrongful Dismissal and Breach of Contract: Law, Practice and Precedents.* Welwyn Garden City: Emis Professional Publishing.

IDS (2009) *Contracts of Employment.* London: Incomes Data Services.

Lindsay, J. (2001) 'The implied term of trust and confidence' *Industrial Law Journal* 30 (p1).

ONLINE RESOURCE CENTRE

A range of online resources to help you through your employment law module have been developed by the author team. These include updates, self-test questions and sources for further reading. (www.oxfordtextbooks.co.uk/orc/taylor_emir3e)

Wrongful and constructive dismissal

Learning outcomes

By the end of this chapter you should be able to:

- define 'wrongful dismissal' and distinguish it from 'unfair dismissal';
- set out the most common situations in which wrongful dismissals occur;
- explain why some groups of employees bring wrongful dismissal cases in preference to unfair dismissal cases;
- advise on the different remedies that can be ordered when a claimant wins a wrongful dismissal case;
- outline the test used by tribunals to determine whether or not a constructive dismissal has occurred;
- give advice about the significance of the timing of a resignation in constructive dismissal claims;
- assess when a constructive dismissal is fair and when it is unfair;
- distinguish between constructive dismissals and forced resignations.

Introduction

In this final chapter of Part II we turn to look in more detail at two areas of employment law to which we have already referred in earlier chapters. We start with an exploration of wrongful dismissal law, which has for many decades provided employees who are dismissed in breach of their contracts with the opportunity to apply to a court for damages. In recent decades wrongful dismissal has been superceded to an extent by unfair dismissal law which provides a more satisfactory remedy for most who are unlawfully dismissed. But there are circumstances in which the longer-established law continues to play a role, and it is on these that we focus in the first part of this chapter. We move on to look in depth at constructive dismissal law, which appears to become more and more significant each year as precedents are set and more people become aware of the possibilities it offers when they resign from their jobs as a direct result of suffering unacceptable treatment from their managers.

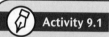 **Activity 9.1**

Consider the following statements. Which do you think are correct and which are false?

1 A wrongful dismissal occurs when an employer dismisses an employee for an unlawful reason.

2 Wrongful dismissal claims are commonly brought by employees who have completed less than a year's service with their employers when they are dismissed.

3 There is no right to be reinstated when an ex-employee wins a wrongful dismissal claim.

4 It is common for employees to be granted injunctions preventing their dismissals from taking effect.

5 A constructive dismissal occurs when an employer acts unreasonably towards an employee, causing him or her to resign.

6 It is possible to be reasonably constructively dismissed.

7 A common type of constructive dismissal is when an employer gives someone an opportunity to resign before dismissing them.

Return to this activity once you have read the chapter, to see how many of your answers were correct.

Wrongful dismissal situations

Because a wrongful dismissal is a breach of contract, claimants can pursue their claims either in an employment tribunal or in the County Court. Wrongful dismissal occurs most often when someone is dismissed without being given the notice they are entitled to under their contract of employment. The manner of the dismissal thus breaches the contract. However, this is not the only situation in which a wrongful dismissal can occur. Any dismissal in breach of contract can potentially amount to a wrongful dismissal and can entitle the employee concerned to claim damages. In most of these situations, however, the employer can deploy a defence of justification. The three most common situations concern the following:

Inadequate notice

Under statute (the Employment Rights Act 1996) all employees with over one month's continuous service have a right to minimum periods of notice when their contracts are terminated. The only exception applies when they have committed an act of gross misconduct which justifies summary dismissal (see Chapter 5). The statutory right is to a week's notice for each year of service up to a maximum of twelve years (six years of service thus gives a right to six weeks' notice). However, contracts of employment frequently include provision for more notice. Four weeks or one month is typical for all employees from the first day of employment, while more senior employees are often required to give (and are also entitled to receive) three months, six months or even a year's notice. Dismissing people without giving the required notice (provided there is no justification by way of gross misconduct) is thus a breach of contract and a wrongful dismissal. In many cases employers do not require people who are dismissed to work their notice period, but pay a salary in lieu of notice. This is acceptable as far as the law is concerned.

Contractual termination procedures

It is not uncommon (if perhaps unwise) for employers to incorporate into their contracts of employment the procedures they use when dismissing people or making them redundant. This usually occurs because the procedures concerned form part of a collective agreement or because they are set out in a staff handbook which is expressly incorporated into each employee's contract. Normally these procedures simply set out what is required in statute (warnings, hearings, right to be accompanied, appeal to a more senior manager, etc), but they can go further than is required under unfair dismissal law. If so it is possible that a breach of the contractual procedure constitutes a wrongful dismissal, even if the dismissal is lawful under unfair dismissal or redundancy law. Significantly, of course, in principle contractual procedures apply to all an organisation's employees whether or not they qualify for unfair dismissal rights.

Temporary and fixed-term contracts

From time to time employers employ people on fixed-term contracts which specify an end date, but which contain no additional provision for notice. This is done in an attempt to bind the employee to work until the contract expires. A variation of the same principle is a contract which specifies no end date, but which states that the contract will continue until a particular task or project is satisfactorily completed. Dismissal before the expiry of such a contract, in the absence of any other notice provisions, is thus a breach of contract and is covered by the law of wrongful dismissal. Here too, though, the employer can justify a dismissal without notice on grounds of gross misconduct.

 Exhibit 9.1   **PILON clauses**

One way in which the law of wrongful dismissal is somewhat confusing relates to situations in which a contract clearly states that payment in lieu of notice (PILON) will be paid if the employer terminates it without adequate notice. Technically when this happens there is no breach of contract »

» in the act of dismissal and hence no wrongful dismissal at common law. But it makes no real practical difference because the employee concerned receives in notice payments what they would have been awarded in damages by a court or tribunal.

However, there have been cases in which no pay in lieu of notice is paid on the dismissal of an employee with such a term in his or her contract. Here the Court of Appeal has ruled that the termination itself is still lawful (*Abrahams v Performing Rights Society* (1995)) and that there is thus no right for the employee concerned to claim damages for breach of contract. Instead the debt must be recovered as a 'liquidated sum under the contract.' On the surface this appears to be a purely technical distinction, but it has some significant consequences:

1 No breach of contract has occurred, so the matter cannot be dealt with by an employment tribunal.

2 There is no duty for employees concerned to mitigate their losses by seeking alternative employment during the period of notice that they are not being required to work.

3 Because the contract has been terminated lawfully, any duties it places on the organisation's former employees (such as restrictive covenants) remain binding. Ex-staff are normally freed from such obligations when their contracts are breached by their employers.

Sources: Duggan (2001:341), Yew (2005:249), IDS (2009:355–356)

Who might bring a wrongful dismissal case?

It is important to remember that the wrongful and unfair dismissal regimes operate entirely separately, the former deriving from the common law, the latter from employment statutes. Unfair dismissal law concerns the reasons for a dismissal and the reasonableness of the employer in carrying out the dismissal. By contrast, wrongful dismissal relates solely to whether or not in dismissing someone an employer breaches their contract. It is thus quite possible to be wrongfully dismissed but not unfairly dismissed, unfairly dismissed but not wrongly dismissed or indeed both wrongly and unfairly dismissed at the same time. This occurs particularly where a statutory procedure is incorporated into an individual contract of employment. However, where a dismissal is both wrongful and unfair for the same reason, in practice it is to the law of unfair dismissal which employees generally turn because the compensation they stand to gain tends to be higher. Moreover, where a dismissal is found to be unfair in circumstances where inadequate notice has been given, the unpaid weeks or months of salary are recoverable under unfair dismissal law, without there being a need to bring an additional wrongful dismissal claim. This typically occurs when an employer summarily dismisses when the employee concerned has not committed an act of gross misconduct. Claims of both wrongful and unfair dismissal can be brought, but there is no real advantage to be gained by bringing the wrongful dismissal claim because more compensation is payable under unfair dismissal law.

To a considerable extent, therefore, unfair dismissal law supercedes the longer-established wrongful dismissal law. Indeed, unfair dismissal law was largely introduced because it was considered that inadequate protection was given to employees by wrongful dismissal law (Deakin and Morris, 2009:355). So who does benefit from bringing a wrongful dismissal claim, and why is this law still of relevance for employers and employees? The answer is those groups of employees who either do not qualify to bring an unfair dismissal claim or who are seeking higher levels of compensation than can be paid under unfair dismissal law—in 2011, a basic award of £12,000 and a compensatory award of £68,400 (see Chapter 4). IDS (2009:358) give the following examples:

- where the employee is highly paid and is dismissed without their full contractual notice or without use of a contractual disciplinary or redundancy procedure
- where the employee has not yet completed a year's continuous service
- where the employee does not qualify for unfair dismissal due to being in employment which is not covered (eg, police, armed forces, share fishermen, etc)
- where the employee's compensation under unfair dismissal law might well be considerably reduced to reflect contributory fault (eg, someone who is dismissed without proper procedure but is heavily responsible for his/her own fate by virtue of poor conduct)
- where the employee is out of time as far as presenting their unfair dismissal case to an employment tribunal is concerned, and opts instead to pursue a wrongful dismissal claim in the County Court (where a six-year limit applies).

It is also quite possible, of course, that someone may have a claim of wrongful dismissal despite the dismissal being fair as far as unfair dismissal is concerned. This happens when an employer acts reasonably in dismissing someone for a potentially or automatically fair reason (see Chapter 4), but simply gives or pays inadequate notice.

Remedies in wrongful dismissal cases

Except in the case of well-paid people with long periods of notice in their contracts, the amount of damages that can be won through the law of wrongful dismissal is low. This is because the purpose of the courts in making awards is to put the employee back to where they would have been financially had they been dismissed in accordance with their contracts. It is not to compensate them for having been dismissed per se. There is thus no right to reinstatement, or general compensation for losses sustained as a result of the unlawful dismissal, only a right to claim damages for wages lost:

- during the proper notice period
- during the remainder of a fixed-term contract
- during the period which the court judges to be necessary to have completed a proper contractual disciplinary procedure.

Damages are then commonly reduced by a suitable amount to take account of the following:

- the fact that the claimant found a new job
- former employees' failure to mitigate their losses by looking for another job
- the fact that some payment (albeit unsatisfactory) has been received
- any statutory payments (eg, for unfair dismissal or social security payments) that have been received.

The low level of damages is an aspect of wrongful dismissal law that has been heavily criticised by commentators. It is persuasively argued that they are often far too small to act as a deterrent that might prevent an employer from acting unlawfully. They are also too low in most cases to make it worth an ex-employee's while to pursue a case. Deakin and Morris (2009: 388) show that in other countries which have similar common law systems, the courts have shown a willingness to develop far more generous approaches to the awarding of damages on dismissal than the 'minimal compensation' available in the UK. This is particularly true of the USA where the absence of any equivalent to the UK's unfair dismissal law means that breach of contract is the only means of legal redress employees who are 'unlawfully discharged' can obtain. As a result there has been considerable development of the common law in this area in a number of states, an implied term of 'good faith and fair dealing' being created to give a degree of protection to employees who are arbitrarily dismissed. Dismissed employees have also made effective use of defamation law in the USA to claim extensive damages when they have been falsely accused of poor conduct or performance when having their contracts terminated. Moreover, in the USA and elsewhere, because collective agreements are legally enforceable, breaches of dismissal procedures amount to breaches of contract in most unionised organisations.

The House of Lords had an opportunity to award damages above and beyond compensation for basic financial loss in the important case of *Johnson v Unisys Ltd* (2001) and decided not to do so. They ruled that it would be inappropriate for them to duplicate in the common law a statutory right that already existed (ie, unfair dismissal law), and which was subject to clear limits by way of compensation and access prescribed by Parliament. They therefore decided that when an employee was dismissed in breach of contract no damages should be awarded to compensate for the manner of the dismissal, however poorly the employee concerned was treated and however unjust the reason for the dismissal. The implied term of mutual trust and confidence (see Chapter 8) hence now can only apply to the actions or inactions of employers and employees during an employment relationship which is ongoing. It is not possible to sustain a claim for damages based on the argument that the implied term was breached in the act of dismissal.

When an employee is dismissed without the employer following a contractual disciplinary or redundancy procedure the tribunal makes a judgement about how long it would have taken the employer to dismiss in line with the procedure. They then add to this period the proper notice period in calculating the total damages to be awarded. The approach is best explained with an example. In *Dietmann v Brent London Borough Council* (1988) a woman who was entitled to eight weeks' notice under her contract was summarily dismissed for alleged gross misconduct. No disciplinary hearing was held, despite the incorporation into her contract of a full disciplinary procedure. Ms Dietmann won her claim. There had been no gross misconduct and she should not have been summarily dismissed without notice. The Court of Appeal ruled that the employer would have taken eight weeks to dismiss her using the contractual disciplinary procedure (ie, the time taken to investigate the allegation fully, hold a hearing, consider the employee's case, make a decision, allow an appeal, etc). As a result the damages awarded amounted to sixteen weeks' pay—eight weeks' notice plus the eight weeks that it would have taken to dismiss her lawfully.

The *Raspin*, *Harper* and *Wise Group* cases

In *Raspin v United News Shops* (1999) an employee was summarily dismissed after she had been accused of stealing from her employers. However, she was not given a proper opportunity to answer the charge because no detailed allegation was ever put to her. The employer claimed that it was basing her dismissal on a security video, but this was not shown to Mrs Raspin, thus denying her the opportunity to put her side of the case. The employer believed it was acting lawfully because it dismissed Mrs Raspin three weeks before she would have completed twelve months' service and would thus have been able to bring an unfair dismissal claim. However, they neglected to take account of the fact that their disciplinary procedure had been incorporated into Mrs Raspin's contract. The EAT was thus able to rule that had this term of the contract been observed and a proper, full disciplinary procedure followed, Mrs Raspin would not have been dismissed until after she had completed a year's service. This is because the process of investigating the alleged misconduct, allowing her to answer the allegations properly and to appeal would necessarily have taken more than three weeks. She was therefore awarded damages, not just to cover pay for the weeks that would have been needed to carry through a proper procedure, but also for 'loss of the chance' to claim unfair dismissal.

Raspin v United News Shops is an important ruling with major consequences for employers who seek to terminate contracts just before unfair dismissal rights kick in, but has it effectively been overruled by the House of Lords in *Johnson v Unisys Ltd* (2001)? There is a degree of confusion about this question because of the Court of Appeal's ruling in another case, *Harper v Virgin Net Ltd* (2003). Here an employee was summarily dismissed on grounds of gross misconduct thirty-three days before she would have been able to claim unfair dismissal. She won her subsequent claim of wrongful dismissal on the grounds that she had not committed an act of gross misconduct and should therefore have been dismissed with the three months' notice stipulated in her contract. The employment tribunal also awarded her a large sum by way of compensation for loss of the chance to claim unfair dismissal. However, Ms Harper's case was different from Mrs Raspin's in that there was no contractual disciplinary procedure. She thus relied purely on the three-month notice period that formed part of her contract. Had she been given three months' notice and not been summarily dismissed, she argued, she would have completed twelve months' service at the date that her contract terminated and would then have been able to bring a case of unfair dismissal. Not so according to the EAT. The House of Lords in *Johnson* had precluded any award of damages in wrongful dismissal cases to compensate for the manner of dismissal. Ms Harper could not thus be awarded any compensation for 'loss of chance'.

At the time it was widely argued that the ruling in the *Harper* case need not mean that the *Raspin* ruling has also been overruled. A distinction could be made between loss of chance claims that are based on notice periods alone (like Harper's) and those which are based on a failure to follow a contractual disciplinary procedure (like Raspin's). Because a disciplinary procedure pre-dates a decision to dismiss, the breach of contract does not strictly speaking occur at the point of termination. It follows that the *Johnson* ruling should not cover these situations. This argument, however, did not impress the EAT in *Wise Group v Mitchell* (2005). Here, with some apparent reluctance, it judged that damages for wrongful dismissal could not include sums relating to the loss of the chance to bring an unfair dismissal case. The *Raspin* judgment is thus no longer good law.

Injunctions and declarations

The courts are reluctant to provide any other remedy but compensation to employees who win wrongful dismissal claims. This is because they do not see it as their role to force an employer to continue employing someone against its will, any more than an employee should be forced to continue working for an employer he or she wishes to leave. But, in principle there is no reason why injunctions cannot be awarded to stop a dismissal from taking place in the first place and no reason why a court cannot make a declaration which clarifies that a dismissal was unlawful, even if no damages can be awarded in the particular case (for example, because the employee found a better-paid job the day after the dismissal).

Injunctions to prevent dismissals are only rarely awarded. The main condition is that there must have been no breakdown of trust and confidence between the employer and the employee, which is unusual when a dismissal is about to occur. More recent cases appear to have relaxed this criterion somewhat in favour of a test based on workability. If granting the injunction would leave in place a 'workable' situation, it can be given. The following are examples given by IDS (2009:401–410) of successful attempts on the part of employees to secure injunctions preventing dismissals from taking effect:

- where an employee would have gained an important new statutory right preventing his dismissal had he been given the correct contractual notice
- where a social worker was dismissed for refusing to transfer to new duties that fell outside his contract
- where an employer admitted dismissing a senior employee in breach of its disciplinary procedure
- where an employer proposed to make long-serving employees redundant instead of following its contractual last-in-first-out selection procedure.

However, there are also examples of cases where injunctions have been sought and not awarded:

- where an employer threatened employees with dismissal if they did not undertake to refrain from taking part in a strike that was being organised by others
- where an employee was unreasonably suspended during an investigation into his apparent unprofessional conduct.

A further reason that the award of an injunction is rare is that in order to gain one, the employee must clearly refuse to accept the employer's breach. In other words, either verbally or in writing, when being dismissed, the employee must say *'in dismissing me you are breaching my contract of employment, I do not accept your breach'*. Otherwise the employee is deemed to have accepted the breach and can only claim damages. The same is true when people seek declarations of their rights when they are wrongfully dismissed. This too is rare, but can occur when an employer dismisses and in the process breaches its own contractual disciplinary procedures. In such circumstances an employee under notice of termination can seek a declaration from a court which states that a dismissal is null and void. If an employee is working his/her notice, this will have the effect of forcing the employer to retract a dismissal and to start again using the procedure that is stipulated in the contract. One would have thought that declarations of this sort would be most commonly sought and granted in redundancy cases where individuals are put under notice of redundancy and continue to work for some weeks or months before their contracts are actually terminated. However, no such case is recorded by IDS (2009) or by Duggan (2003) in their extensive surveys of the case law in this field.

 Activity 9.2

John works as an accountant in a marketing company. He has been employed there for nine months. He spends a high proportion of his time supervising the introduction of a new IT accounting system. All line managers need to be trained in its use and the required software needs to be installed and tested before the system 'goes live' in a few weeks' time. John is concerned that this is not going to be achieved because insufficient resources have been allocated to the project. He complains to his boss, the company's finance director, but is told that he has been given more than enough time and staff support to carry out the introduction of the new software, and that it is his fault that it is slipping behind schedule. John is greatly angered by this meeting. He believes that his boss is trying to set him up as a scapegoat for the failure of the project, when the main fault lies with the FD himself. As a result John goes to speak to the managing director who listens to what he has to say and says that he will give it full consideration.

The next day the finance director calls John into his office, bawls him out for speaking to the managing director behind his back and announces that he will be terminating John's contract of employment without notice as soon as the planned deadline date for the operation of the new system passes. The FD advises John to get himself another job lined up for the following day if he does not think the deadline will be met. John knows that there is no way the system will be ready by this date.

John has no written contract of employment, but was told at his interview that his notice period would be three months. The date on which the new system is supposed to 'go live', and on which he now expects to be dismissed is five weeks before he will have completed a year's service with the company. He comes to you, as a friend, to ask if such a dismissal would be unlawful and whether there is anything he can do to resist it?

Questions

1   If he was to be dismissed on the day the system is supposed to go live, which of the following claims might he be able to bring successfully, and why?

   a) wrongful dismissal

   b) unfair dismissal

   c) an injunction preventing the dismissal from taking effect?

2   How would you advise him to proceed now?

Constructive dismissal

A constructive dismissal is defined in the Employment Rights Act 1996 as a situation in which:

> the employee terminates the contract under which he is employed (with or without notice) in circumstances in which he is entitled to terminate it without notice by reason of the employer's conduct.

It is thus a resignation and not a dismissal, but one which takes place because of unacceptable conduct on the part of the employer concerned. Constructive dismissal originates from 1971 when it was introduced as part of the legislation creating the law of unfair dismissal. The intention was to make quite sure that employers could not effectively get around the requirements of unfair dismissal law by treating any employees they wanted to fire so badly that they would resign without needing to be dismissed. This was achieved by including within the statute the above clause, ensuring that resignations which occurred in such circumstances would be treated by the tribunals as if they were dismissals and that they would be subjected to the same scrutiny as would any potentially unfair dismissal. As a result, only those who can bring claims of unfair dismissal (ie, employees with over a year's continuous service) are entitled to bring claims of constructive dismissal. Moreover, the heads of compensation for constructive dismissal are the same as for unfair dismissal.

Constructive dismissal is therefore part of unfair dismissal law and is a creature of statute and not of the common law. So why include it in a chapter about breaches of contract? The answer is that the test that is now used to establish whether or not a constructive dismissal has occurred concerns the contract of employment. It is not enough for the ex-employee to show that the employer acted unreasonably. To prove constructive dismissal the employer must have acted in such a way as to breach the employee's contract in a fundamental way. The test was established by the Court of Appeal in one of the most significant judgments there has ever been in UK employment law—*Western Excavating (ECC) Ltd v Sharp* (1978). It was set out by Lord Denning as follows:

> If the employer is guilty of conduct which is a significant breach going to the root of the contract of employment, or which shows that the employer no longer intends to be bound by one or more of the essential terms of the contract, then the employee is entitled to treat himself as discharged from any further performance. If he does so, then he terminates the contract by reason of the employer's conduct. He is constructively dismissed.

In fact, since 1978 three essential conditions have had to be in place for a resignation to constitute a constructive dismissal:

1. The employer must, through its actions, be in actual or anticipatory breach of the contract of employment.
2. The employee must decide to resign shortly after the breach.
3. The employee must resign because of this breach.

The most problematic aspect of the test is that which requires a tribunal to judge whether or not a breach of contract is sufficiently 'fundamental' to permit it to find that a constructive dismissal has occurred. The judgment in the *Western Excavating* case suggests that relatively minor or trivial breaches on the part of an employer are insufficient because they do not 'go to the root of the contract'. To cause a constructive dismissal a breach must be repudiatory in nature. That is to say that the employer has repudiated or renounced the contract through its actions. Yet, according to IDS (2005:4) the test that is used by the courts takes no account of the employer's motives at all, focusing almost exclusively on the impact its actions have on the employee. If the employee suffers a serious detriment and this results from some form of breach of contract, it is a usually found to amount to constructive dismissal. The case law has, by and large, been very helpful to employees. Indeed, according to many commentators (eg, Anderman 2000), the years since 1978 have seen the development, in practice, of a test that is as close to one of 'reasonableness' as it is to one of 'fundamental breaches':

> In all such cases, we see examples of the judges stretching the concept of a contractual test to allow the statutory provision of constructive dismissal to extend to cases of seriously unreasonable conduct or serious mistreatment by employers.

This has occurred in a number of ways. First, the courts have included within their definition of a 'repudiatory breach' breaches of express terms that could well be seen as falling short of the test set out in *Western Excavating v Sharp*. For example, any cut in pay, even if it is quite a trivial sum, appears to count as a 'fundamental breach'. It is even the case when payments are made in full but a few days late, or when a bonus payment over and above the monthly salary is not paid on time. The same is true of changes to job duties which are not authorised via a flexibility clause, changes to hours of work and even the switching of responsibility for higher-status projects from one individual to another. Secondly, as was described in Chapter 8, we have seen since 1978 very extensive development of implied terms by the courts. Indeed, many of these have either been created or have further evolved during the course of appeals in constructive dismissal cases. This is true, for example, of the duty to take proper and timely account of employees' legitimate grievances, the duty to provide a suitable working environment and, especially, of the duty to maintain a relationship of mutual trust and confidence. Finally, and perhaps most importantly of all, we have seen the development of 'the last straw' doctrine in constructive dismissal law which enables ex-employees to base their claims on a series of relatively minor breaches on the part of their employers.

After *Western Excavating v Sharp* (1978), the second most important constructive dismissal judgment was that of *Lewis v Motorworld Garages* (1985) in which the last straw doctrine was given approval by the Court of Appeal. Here Mr Lewis had been subjected over a period of time to a number of wholly unjustified actions by his employers, which he believed were intended to push him into resigning:

- he was demoted for 'poor performance'
- he was given a smaller and less pleasant office to work in
- he was subjected to a series of petty criticisms—all of which he claimed were unjustified and involved singling him out for criticism
- he was given a written warning.

The first of these represented a repudiatory breach on its own, but Mr Lewis had not brought his claim within three months of this occurring, so he could not base it on that point alone. However, he succeeded in establishing that the cumulative effect of the later minor breaches amounted to a fundamental breach of the implied duty to maintain a relationship of mutual trust and confidence. As a result, any employer who acts unreasonably towards an employee over a period of time is now at risk of losing a constructive dismissal claim if the individual resigns for that reason.

Despite the tendency for tribunals to find in favour of former employees on the question of whether a breach is or is not fundamental, it is important to point out that the claimant is by no means successful in all cases. This is particularly so when the issue is clouded to an extent with fault on both sides. A good example is *Evans v Deen City Farm* (1997) (quoted by IDS, 2005:19).

This case concerned the actions of an employee who took the decision to put a piglet down without first consulting a vet. The motives were good, but this constituted a breach of the organisation's rules. Ms Evans wrongly recorded that the animal had died of natural causes, and when the deception was discovered some time later, she was issued with a final written warning. However, the employer also placed details of the disciplinary proceedings on a staff notice board— an act which itself breached the requirement for confidentiality included in the organisation's disciplinary procedure. As the procedure was contractual, Ms Evans was able to resign and claim constructive dismissal. She lost her case both at the tribunal and subsequently at the EAT on the grounds that the employer's breach of confidence in this case was not sufficiently fundamental to amount to a repudiatory breach. It is difficult not to suspect that a different outcome would have occurred had Ms Evans herself not breached her employer's rules in quite a serious way before the employer breached her right to confidentiality.

Activity 9.3 *Stanley Cole (Wainfleet) Ltd v Sheridan* (2003)

After five years' service with her employer during which time she had never been given any formal warnings for poor conduct or performance, Mrs Sheridan was involved in an argument with a fellow employee. Because this upset her so much, she left the company's premises for a period of an hour and a half—a period that included her lunch break. She had done this without permission. The response of the employer was to carry out a disciplinary investigation and to issue her with a final written warning.

Mrs Sheridan then successfully applied for a new job and resigned. She then claimed constructive dismissal and won her case both at the employment tribunal and subsequently at the EAT.

Questions

1 In what way do you think the employer fundamentally breached Mrs Sheridan's contract of employment in issuing her with a final written warning?

2 Why do you think that the issue of Mrs Sheridan having obtained another job was a significant factor in the employer's defence?

3 To what extent do you agree with the employment tribunal and EAT that the obtaining of a new job was irrelevant to the finding of constructive dismissal?

Anticipatory breaches

As constructive dismissal law has developed, it has become clear that an employee who resigns before a breach of contract has actually occurred can still win a case. This happens when it is shown that the employer is intent on breaching the contract and is therefore found to have been 'in anticipatory breach'. However, it is important to note that this will only apply where an employer has very clearly signalled an intention to change terms and conditions or job duties without first seeking agreement. Employees who resign because they believe that a breach is about to occur or because proposals have been made, but are yet to be finalised, are unlikely to be able to win their claims. IDS (2005:5) state that no more or less than 'a clear and unequivocal statement' of an intent to breach a contract is necessary in order to sustain a case of constructive dismissal. The great danger for an employee, therefore, is that a resignation occurs too early before it becomes certain that a breach is about to take place.

Timing of the resignation

Resignations can also come too late. Employees who wait too long after a breach has occurred before resigning are leaving themselves open to the claim that the real reason for their resignation was not the breach, but something else entirely—such as a desire to find another job. The longer the delay, the more likely it is that a tribunal will find that in continuing to work without resigning, the employee was affirming the contract and effectively accepting the employer's breach. There is no set time, but the case law suggests that a delay of more than a month or so, especially when wages are being claimed, is strong evidence of an acceptance. This is certainly true of situations in which employees have waited a number of months before resigning.

Much, in practice, depends on other factors such as what action short of resigning the employee took before taking the decision to leave. It is possible, as we saw in Chapter 17, for employees to state clearly that they do not accept the employer's breach and that they are going to continue to work 'under protest'. This will be acceptable in terms of protecting the right to bring a constructive dismissal claim for a few weeks or months while a formal grievance is dealt with, but after that continuation of employment is taken as indicating that the contract has been affirmed. The leading case here is *WE Cox Turner (International) Ltd v Crook* (1981), in which the claimant 'worked under protest' for six months following his receipt of a final written warning for a disciplinary offence. During this time correspondence was exchanged between the parties' solicitors, but no resolution of the dispute was reached. At this point Mr Crook's solicitor sent a letter of ultimatum, stating that unless the written warning was withdrawn, Mr Crook would resign and claim constructive dismissal. The employer clearly stated that there would be no withdrawal. Mr Crook then waited a further month before resigning. He lost his case. In waiting so long, and in particular waiting a month after having received a clear statement of the employer's refusal to withdraw his warning, Mr Crook had affirmed the breach.

 Exhibit 9.2   ***Buckland v Bournemouth University Higher Education Corporation* (2009)**

In this case the Court of Appeal cleared up two areas of confusion that emanated from judgments of lower courts pointing in different directions. The case concerned a professor who resigned after a set of exams he had marked (many being failed) were re-marked in order to secure a higher pass rate without consulting him. Professor Buckland subsequently made a formal complaint to the university's 'executive group' who set up an enquiry which vindicated the professor and criticised his manager. In any event, concerned that his integrity had been questioned, Professor Buckland decided to resign and claim constructive dismissal. »

>> The university defended itself on two counts:

1 Even though there had been a breach of trust and confidence, its actions were nonetheless justified as falling within the band of reasonable responses.

and

2 In setting up an inquiry which vindicated Professor Buckland the University had 'cured' its initial
breach.

On both counts the Court of Appeal found against the University and for Professor Buckland.
Repudiatory breaches cannot subsequently be 'cured' and the band of reasonable responses test is
irrelevant to the question of whether or not a repudiatory breach has or has not occurred.

Procedure in constructive dismissal cases

In effect, constructive dismissal cases are unfair dismissal cases 'with a twist'. Procedurally the
tribunals therefore treat them in broadly the same way and the remedies are the same too.

In Chapter 4 we described the three stages that a tribunal can go through when considering a case of unfair dismissal. The same is true of constructive dismissal cases, the same three
basic questions being asked in the following order:

1. Is the claimant entitled to bring the case?

2. What was the reason for the dismissal?

3. Did the employer act reasonably in treating this as a reason for dismissal?

The burden of proof shifts in the same way from employer to employee to neutrality.
However, what makes constructive dismissal cases different is the significance of the first
question. In unfair dismissal proceedings it is often unnecessary to ask it at all. Both sides will
normally accept that the individual concerned is in one of the qualifying groups (ie, an employee with over a year's continuous service) and that a dismissal has occurred. The tribunal
thus starts with the second question about the reason for the dismissal. With a constructive
dismissal claim the question of whether or not a dismissal has occurred is fundamental and
will often (although not always) determine the final outcome. The employer will invariably
argue that the resignation was not for reason of any fundamental breach on its part, while the
former employee will argue that it was, and that it thus amounts to a constructive dismissal
situation. Importantly, the burden of proof is on the claimant to show that this is so.

In many cases proceedings come to an end at this point. Either there was or there was not
a constructive dismissal. But because these are unfair dismissal cases, it remains open to an
employer who has been found to have constructively dismissed an employee to argue that
its actions were nonetheless reasonable in the circumstances. This requires the respondent
to undertake a course of action known as 'pleading in the alternative' or deploying two apparently contradictory defences one after the other. The employer starts by arguing that no
dismissal has occurred (ie, it was not its fundamental breach that led to the resignation), but
if it loses on this point it changes tack and argues that the dismissal was justified on grounds
of reasonableness. In order to do this, the employer needs to set out its intention to plead in
the alternative in its notice of response (ie when completing its ET3 form).

In theory it is possible to base a defence of reasonableness on any of the potentially fair reasons for dismissal defined in unfair dismissal law (see Chapter 5). It is simply a question of showing that the breach of contract was for a reason related to the capability of the employee, his or her conduct, a redundancy situation, etc. However such approaches rarely lead to a finding in favour of the employer. This is because in breaching the contract the employer will almost invariably have acted 'unreasonably' as well, so the dismissal will be unfair. The major exceptions are the following types of situation:

- where an employee is demoted after committing an act of gross misconduct (ie, when the employer would be entitled to summarily dismiss, but chooses to give the employee a further chance)

- where an employee's duties are changed as a result of genuine poor performance and a detriment is suffered as a result

- where an employee is redeployed to other duties during a genuine redundancy situation.

The other type of situation in which fair constructive dismissals occur concerns business re-organisations and situations in which employers force through changes in terms and conditions for necessary business reasons. As far as unfair dismissal law is concerned this comes under the heading of 'some other substantial reason'. We explained how the defence is deployed and gave some examples in Chapter 8 under the heading 'dismissing and rehiring'. The principle is the same with constructive dismissals in which employees resign when required to change their terms and conditions instead of being dismissed with a view to being rehired on new terms and conditions. Just as with an actual dismissal, issues relating to procedures adopted and consistency play a central role in determining the outcome.

It is therefore possible to be fairly constructively dismissed, but only in relatively unusual circumstances. The employer needs to show that:

1. it re-organised for a good business reason and that this necessitated changing employees' contracts,

2. people were consulted, warned and treated equitably,

3. some employees or one employee then refused to accept the new terms and conditions, preferring to resign and claim constructive dismissal.

Most of the examples in the case law concern changes to job descriptions, disputes over the precise scope of mobility clauses and situations in which employers either cut hours or increase them without also increasing pay. In all such cases, provided the employer genuinely needs to make the changes, consults fully and considers alternatives, subsequent claims of constructive dismissal are likely to fail when they come before a tribunal.

 Exhibit 9.3   *Pickles v JS Sainsbury plc* (1982)

Mrs Pickles was employed as a canteen assistant at a Sainsbury's supermarket. She worked the night shift, preparing meals for the people working overnight preparing the store for the following day's trading. In this job she worked alone without any direct supervision, and as a result was paid a premium hourly rate. »

>> Unfortunately, Mrs Pickles' co-workers did not like the food she cooked for them. The employers took steps to try to improve her cooking and consulted her and her union representative fully when dealing with the complaints made about it. But in the end it was decided to move her onto a day shift where she would work as part of a team and would receive proper supervision. This meant that she lost her premium hourly rate of pay. Her response was to resign and claim constructive dismissal.

The tribunal decided that this was an example of a fair constructive dismissal. The employer had breached Mrs Pickles' contract and she had resigned directly in response. But the reason for the breach was Mrs Pickles' capability. The employer had handled the matter reasonably and was thus justified in its defence.

Forced resignations

Finally in this chapter it is necessary to reiterate the distinction made in law between a constructive dismissal and a forced resignation. The former, as we have seen, is a voluntary resignation by an employee in direct response to a breach of contract (actual or anticipated) on the part of their employer. A forced resignation is a different beast altogether. This occurs where an employer says 'if you do not resign we will sack you'. An employer may say this to allow someone an opportunity to leave with an apparently unblemished employment record, or simply to avoid the need to waste everybody's time by taking someone through a painful disciplinary hearing whose outcome is not in doubt. Less scrupulous and ill-informed employers force resignations because they think, wrongly, that this will protect them from a subsequent unfair dismissal claim.

It is important to appreciate that forced resignations are treated in law as if they were actual dismissals. They are not considered to be constructive dismissals. This has significant implications from the point of view of former employees bringing cases to tribunal. They are greatly helped by the lack of a need, as there would be if it was a constructive dismissal situation, to prove that a fundamental breach on the part of the employer has occurred. It is far easier to show, on the balance of probabilities that pressure was placed on them to resign.

Remedies in constructive dismissal cases

When someone wins a constructive dismissal claim, the remedies are exactly the same as in standard unfair dismissal cases. The matter is simply treated as if the employee had been unfairly dismissed. The purpose of the compensatory award is to put the claimant back financially where he/she would have been had the dismissal not occurred, a basic award also being made and calculated on the same basis as a statutory redundancy payment. It is highly unlikely that someone would wish to be reinstated or re-engaged, having resigned from their job, but in theory there is no reason why they should not ask to be reinstated on the terms and conditions that pre-dated the employer's breach. Deductions can be made to reflect contributory fault, as in unfair dismissal cases, but this happens very rarely. No damages are available to take account of injury to feelings or psychiatric injury.

CHAPTER SUMMARY

- A wrongful dismissal occurs when the manner in which an employer dismisses an employee breaches the contract of employment. Cases are much rarer than they used to be before the advent of unfair dismissal law in the 1970s.

- Wrongful dismissal cases now tend to be brought by employees who have completed less than a year's service or who earn high salaries and are seeking more compensation than is available under unfair dismissal law.

- The most common types of wrongful dismissal are dismissals with inadequate notice and dismissals which do not follow contractual disciplinary procedures.

- Constructive dismissals are resignations. This law forms part of unfair dismissal law and is designed to ensure that employers cannot avoid it by treating people so badly that they resign before being dismissed.

- The test that is used to establish whether or not a constructive dismissal has occurred is a contractual one. The employee must resign as a result of and shortly after an actual or anticipated repudiatory breach by the employer has occurred. This can be a breach of implied terms as well as express terms.

- It is possible for employers to defend themselves in constructive dismissal claims using the defence of reasonableness established in unfair dismissal law.

For updates and further materials, please see the online resource centre at www.oup.com

REFERENCES

Anderman, S. (2000) 'The interpretation of protective employment statutes and contracts of employment' *Industrial Law Journal* 29 (p223).

Deakin, S. and Morris, G. (2005) *Labour Law*. Fourth Edition. Oxford: Hart Publishing.

Duggan, M. (2003) *Wrongful Dismissal and Breach of Contract: Law, Practice and Precedents*. Welwyn Garden City: Emis Professional Publishing.

IDS (2005) *Constructive Dismissal*. Employment Law Supplement. London: Incomes Data Services.

IDS (2009) *Contracts of Employment*. London: Incomes Data Services.

Yew (2004) 'Recipe for chaos?' *New Law Journal* 154.

Yew, J. (2005) *Dismissals: Law and Practice*. London: The Law Society.

ONLINE RESOURCE CENTRE

A range of online resources to help you through your employment law module have been developed by the author team. These include updates, self-test questions and sources for further reading. (www.oxfordtextbooks.co.uk/orc/taylor_emir3e)

Discrimination law

PART III

Introducing discrimination law

Learning outcomes

By the end of this chapter you should be able to:

- set out the grounds on which anti-discrimination cases can be taken to tribunal;

- advise on the major differences in the way the law treats the different grounds;

- explain the current aims and development of European Union law in the discrimination field;

- debate the merits of discrimination law in general terms;

- assess the cases for and against major reform of UK discrimination law.

Introduction

The following seven chapters deal with specific areas of discrimination law, explaining them, setting out the background and introducing the key debates that exist about how the law operates and how it might be improved in the future. Our purpose in this chapter is to introduce the field in general terms, to explain why it takes the form it does, and to summarise the critical arguments that are most commonly advanced concerning the whole body of anti-discrimination legislation.

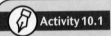 **Activity 10.1**

Consider the following statements. Which do you think are correct and which are false?

1   Discrimination law covers fewer people now than was the case twenty years ago.

2   Directives of the European Union have been a major source of recent discrimination law.

3   Positive discrimination is unlawful in the UK.

4   Many commentators advocate the case for the abolition of discrimination law on the grounds that it harms the people it is supposed to protect.

5   A strong case can be made for requiring employers to take positive action to create genuine equality of opportunity.

6   Employment tribunals often force employers to alter their practices so as to make them less discriminatory.

Return to this activity once you have read the chapter, to see how many of your answers were correct.

The scope of discrimination law

The scope of anti-discrimination law in the UK has expanded in the past twenty years. Prior to 1996 there was fairly comprehensive protection provided for those discriminated against because of their sex or race, and limited protection afforded to trade union members and ex-offenders. The situation is now wholly different. The full list of grounds for which anti-discrimination claims of some kind can be brought, together with an indication of the chapters in which each is discussed, is provided in Table 10.1.

 **Activity 10.2**

In Table 10.1 there are eighteen different grounds listed under which some form of discrimination claim can be taken to an employment tribunal.

Questions

1   What other grounds do you think ought to be included on the list and why?

2   Are there any you would like to see removed from the list?

3   What would the arguments be for and against an approach which simply outlawed the causing of *any detriment* to a worker on *any grounds* that did not constitute a necessary business reason?

Table 10.1 The scope of discrimination law

sex	(chapter 16)	religion or belief	(chapter 15)
marital status	(chapter 17)	age	(chapter 12)
pregnancy/maternity	(chapter 17)	fixed-term contracts	(chapter 19)
transsexuality	(chapter 17)	part-time contracts	(chapter 19)
race	(chapter 14)	agency workers	(chapter 19)
ethnicity	(chapter 14)	ex-offenders	(chapter 19)
national origin	(chapter 14)	trade union membership	(chapter 27)
disability	(chapter 13)	non-trade union membership	(chapter 27)
sexual orientation	(chapter 17)	trade union activity	(chapter 27)

Source: World Bank; Eurostat

As matters stand, however, these diverse areas of discrimination law function in very different ways. Despite the consolidation of much discrimination law into the Equality Act 2010, this is by no means a coherent body of law operating according to standard principles. The drawback is of course that staff, and indeed managers, do not always know where they stand. The advantage is that each piece of relevant legislation is framed pragmatically to achieve a reasonably fair balance between the interests of employers and members of the various protected groups. From a student's point of view the diversity of principles provides a feasible and potentially fruitful way of critically analysing discrimination law. So as you read on we would urge you to give some thought to the arguments for and against applying the principles that apply in one area (eg, disability discrimination law) to another (eg, sex discrimination law) and vice versa. The major ways in which the approaches vary are the following:

Sources

Some discrimination law has a UK origin, cases being determined only in the UK courts. As yet these are not covered by EU law and appeals cannot therefore be made to the European Court of Justice. Law protecting ex-offenders, trade unionists and non-unionists falls into this category, as does much of the law protecting transsexuals from discrimnation and that which offers protection on grounds of pregnancy and marital status. A second category is law which has a UK origin but which has, in the years since it was introduced, fallen within the scope of European competence. The law on sex discrimination, equal pay, race discrimination and disability discrimination falls into this category. Here there are sometimes question marks over how fully the original UK law has been amended to meet the requirements of the relevant directives. Finally there is law which both originates in the EU and has been introduced into UK law as a result of European directives. The law covering discrimination on grounds of age, sexual orientation, religion or belief, agency workers, fixed-term and part-time work make up this third category.

Coverage

Discrimination law also varies in terms of its coverage. In the case of most of the grounds listed in Table 10.1 all workers are covered, as well as job applicants and former employees. The latter group generally only bring cases when they are unfairly given poor references or indeed refused a reference at all by an ex-employer. But some anti-discrimination law is restricted only to employees (see Chapter 3 for material on the difference between 'employees' and 'workers'), effectively cutting out a sizeable proportion of the workforce. This is true of the fixed-term employees regulations, for example, and of law protecting people from discrimination on trade union grounds, although in the latter case job applicants are protected to an extent.

Defences

An important area of difference between different areas of discrimination law concerns the extent to which employers are able to deploy defences when they are found to have discriminated and the nature of these defences. Under some of the headings employers are given a general right to defend their actions through objective justification—the precise formulation now being 'a proportionate means of achieving a legitimate aim'. This effectively means that it is lawful to discriminate, provided a good and genuine business reason lies behind the decision. Such is true of the fixed-term employees and part-time workers regulations. It is also generally the case when an employer discriminates indirectly, for example, by maintaining a practice which inadvertently favours one group over another (such as men over women). In other fields of discrimination law defences are available, but they are a great deal more restricted in nature. This is true, for example, of the material factor defence in equal pay law (see Chapter 18), of the occupational requirement defence that operates in several areas of discrimination law and of the circumstances in which people can be mandatorily retired under age discrimination law (Chapter 12). In disability discrimination law, by contrast, it is only permissible for employers to discriminate once they have first given full consideration to how they might reasonably alter their working practices or environments to meet the needs of individuals suffering from disabilities. This is an interesting approach, but is not one that has been used in the case of the other areas of anti-discrimination law. For many forms of direct discrimination there is no defence available. It is simply unlawful to discriminate for that reason—end of story. With the rare exception of one or two health and safety situations, such as the case when a woman is discriminated against on grounds of pregnancy, it is simply unlawful to discriminate for that reason.

Positive discrimination

Positive discrimination (also called 'affirmative action') involves actively discriminating in favour of a group which is under-represented in a workforce either generally or at more senior levels. Another way in which UK discrimination law varies is in the extent to which positive discrimination is permitted. Until recently in sex and race discrimination law, with one significant exception and in one other relatively rare type of situation (the selection of Parliamentary candidates), it had long been established that positive discrimination was unlawful. This was simply because an act of positive discrimination in favour of women or members of ethnic minorities was by definition an act against men or white people. While the motives behind the discrimination may be ethical and entirely well-intentioned, the act itself was considered unlawful because it discriminated on grounds of sex or race—and this is precisely what the law is seeking to deter employers from doing. As a general rule it remains the case that positive discrimination is unlawful when in doing so another group is discriminated against. But, as you will see in Chapter 11, under the Equality Act 2010 it has now become lawful to discriminate in favour of an under-represented group in certain quite narrowly defined situations.

However, discriminating in favour of a protected group does not always lead to discrimination against another protected group. This is true, for example, of disability discrimination law. As a result it has always been quite lawful to discriminate in favour of disabled people because the law does not extend any protection to able-bodied people. Discriminating against someone because he/she does not suffer from a disability is entirely lawful.

 Exhibit 10.1   Positive action

While 'positive discrimination' reamins unlawful across much of UK discrimination law, 'positive action' is permitted. The distinction between the two can sometimes be hard to draw, but 'positive action' essentially stops short of actual discrimination. Common forms of positive action which are lawful include the following:

- putting equal opportunities statements in recruitment advertisements,

- offering training courses to meet the needs of women or members of ethnic minorities who aspire to be managers,

- offering assistance to women returning to work after a period spent raising children.

Under European law positive action is encouraged, and in some circumstances forms of affirmative action which would be unlawful in the UK have been accepted by the European Court when hearing appeals from other member states. For example in *Re Badek* (2000) the court ruled that it was lawful to reserve half the places on a training course for women and also to ensure that as many women as men were placed on shortlists for jobs wherever possible.

The Equal Treatment Framework Directive

In November 2000 the Council of Ministers of the European Union unanimously agreed Directive 2000/78/EC '*establishing a general framework for equal treatment in employment and occupation*'. The Directive specified that its provisions were to be introduced into national law by all member states stage by stage. Some measures had to be in place by 2 December 2003, the final date for effective implementation being 2 December 2006. This is therefore the timetable to which the UK government, like others across the EU, complied with between 2000 and 2006—a period in which a very great amount of new discrimination law came onto our statute books.

The Equal Treatment Framework Directive required all EU member states to extend the established principles of sex and race discrimination law to four new fields:

- sexual orientation
- religion or belief
- disability
- age.

As a result, since 2006, the UK like all the other member states has had in place a pretty comprehensive set of anti-discrimination laws covering six core areas (the four listed above plus sex and race) which operate along similar principles. In particular, the Framework Directive helps to ensure that four distinct types of claim can be brought to court under each of the six headings. These are as follows:

- Direct discrimination (when an individual or group of people are directly discriminated against because of their sex, race, disability, age, sexual orientation or religion/belief)
- Indirect discrimination (when an apparently neutral 'provision, criterion or practice' puts members of a protected group at a comparative disadvantage)
- Victimisation (when an employer treats workers adversely because they have either made a complaint or taken legal action aimed at enforcing their right to equal treatment on the above grounds)
- Harassment (when a worker suffers from unwanted conduct related to the above grounds which violates dignity or creates 'an intimidating, hostile, degrading, humiliating or offensive environment')

The scope of the Directive is also set out. This also has the effect in practice of standardising to a degree the extent to which individuals are protected when it comes to discrimination on these six grounds. The scope covers access to employment (including recruitment and selection criteria), promotion, working conditions, pay, dismissal, access to training, retraining, work experience and 'vocational guidance'. It also specifically covers membership and involvement in the activities of professional bodies, trade unions and any other 'organisation of workers'.

As a result of this Directive (and others updating EU law on sex and race discrimination) a great deal of new anti-discrimination law has been introduced recently in the UK with the aim of bringing the law into line with EU expectations. Wholly new law has been passed to ensure compliance with EU requirements in the fields of discrimination on grounds of age, sexual orientation and religion or belief, while amendments have been made to existing UK statutes on sex, race and disability discrimination to ensure compliance with the relevant directives. Importantly, the law is still only really beginning to develop in some of these areas—sexual orientation, religion or belief and age in particular—as it takes several years from when a new right is first introduced for test cases on points of principle to be appealed to the higher courts.

Debates about discrimination law

In the subsequent chapters we will be outlining some of the major debates about specific aspects of current discrimination law. You will see that this is a controversial field in which people have widely differing views both about questions of principle and the practicalities of effective enforcement. Here our intention is to introduce you briefly to some of the more general issues in discrimination law about which opinions vary, focusing on the major critiques advanced by leading authors in the field.

Arguments against anti-discrimination law

It is useful to start by pointing out that some commentators argue strongly against the extension of anti-discrimination law and, in some cases, for its wholesale repeal. The most notable exponent of this position is Richard Epstein (1992 & 2002), but others have also contributed significantly to its development (see Davies, 2009:118–120). Three distinct arguments are commonly advanced, each of which has itself been the subject of much criticism.

The first derives from an acceptance of neo-classical economic theory. Anti-discrimination laws are unnecessary, it is argued, because discrimination in the workplace on any grounds that are unrelated to someone's ability to perform a job is economically inefficient. In a competitive marketplace it thus follows that organisations which discriminate unfairly will suffer economically over the long term. The discrimination will thus be eliminated, over time, by the operation of the market. The proper role of the state must thus be to ensure that a free market for goods, services and labour operates. Davies (2009:120) summarises the case very succinctly by drawing on the work of GS Becker:

> Discrimination is a 'taste' or preference for which employers are willing to pay. For example, a homophobic employer might be willing to pay an extra £2 per hour (called a 'discrimination coefficient') in order to obtain a workforce made up entirely of heterosexuals. This might mean paying £10 an hour to heterosexual workers but only hiring a gay or lesbian worker if he or she was willing to accept less than £8 an hour. According to Becker, this situation is not sustainable over the longer term. The employer's products must compete in the market. A non-discriminating competitor could easily take advantage by employing gay and lesbian workers at £8 an hour. The competitor's products would be cheaper and would ultimately drive the discriminating firm out of the market.

A further economic argument focuses on corporate reputation generally. Here it is argued that employers cannot afford to discriminate even if they wish to because their market share would be adversely affected as a result of customer disapproval. An extension of the argument focuses specifically on labour market reputation. The most able employees will not want to work for an employer that discriminates unfairly. So not only is the potential pool of staff reduced by the absence of the group against whom the employer is discriminating, but others are also disinclined to apply for jobs/stay in jobs too. Epstein (2002:38) makes the point starkly by asking 'What if McDonalds announced that it would have no women in its senior management? How long would it be before it was unable to attract able men to work for it?'

The second major strand to the argument advanced by opponents of anti-discrimination legislation is that in reducing the efficiency of the operation of free markets, the law actually causes harm. Moreover, the people most harmed are often those which the law sets out to protect. This occurs, according to Epstein (2002:8) because *'by raising production costs and distorting business decisions, it lowers per capita incomes'*. In other words, because discrimination law (like most employment law) reduces employers' flexibility and increases their costs, the result is a less successful economy than we would otherwise have. This means lower incomes and, potentially, higher unemployment. Hence it follows, in Epstein's words, that 'equal opportunity' leads in practice to 'less opportunity'. Invariably, he argues, managers have a more accurate view about what is best for their organisations than government regulators. In a world of free competition they should be allowed to get on with managing their businesses as they see fit. Government interference in the form of anti-discrimination law simply serves to decrease organisational competitiveness and wealth-creating capacity.

The third strand of the argument is philosophical rather than economic. Ultimately it involves an acceptance of the primacy of liberty over equality when these two principles are in conflict. At the end of the day, according to Epstein (1992:498–499), it is just right that individuals and corporations should be able to contract with whosoever they want on whatever terms they want:

> Our strong tradition of freedom of speech, which allows persons to say thoughtless and hurtful things about the symbols held dear by others ... is eminently defensible even though these hurts are real to the persons who bear them. The decision to keep off represents a profound social judgment that the business of weighing and trading symbolic meanings is one in which the state should never inject its collective judgment. What is true about speech itself should carry over into other laws, even those with manifest symbolic import. Their adoption or rejection should depend on their capacity to allow individuals to develop a sphere of personal control in which they can lead their own lives.

This philosophical position, backed by the belief that discrimination law does more economic harm than good leads Epstein to advance the bold and highly unfashionable view that the law should protect the right of 'every individual or group to refuse to contract or associate with, or to otherwise discriminate for or against any other group or individual for whatever reasons they see fit, including without limitation, race, creed, sex, religion, age, disability, marital status, or sexual orientation' (Epstein, 2002:11).

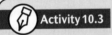 **Activity 10.3**

Epstein's theories have been the subject of a great deal of criticism, and it is not difficult to advance quite strong and emotionally charged arguments against him. Surely he is advocating a situation in which it is lawful for an organisation to select for redundancy anyone who is disabled, gay or female? He is arguing in favour of return to a world in which an employer can lawfully state that 'no Jews need apply' in a job advertisement? Yet there is some logic in his argument that discrimination law ends up causing more harm than good.

Questions

1   To what extent do you think that Epstein's basic assumptions are questionable?

2   Can you develop three arguments that answer each of the three strands we have identified that make up the case against discrimination law?

Broadening the scope of discrimination law

At the beginning of this chapter we set out a list of grounds on which discrimination is, to some extent at least, unlawful in UK workplaces. Later we set out the scope of the European Union's most recent equal treatment directives in the area of discrimination law. The number of groups covered is now a great deal more than it was a few years ago, but there is a case that is often made for further extension. Indeed, many commentators go as far as to say that there should be no defined list of grounds. Instead all unjust discrimination by employers should be outlawed in some shape or form.

There is an interesting debate about whether or not any core philosophical principle can be identified which can be used to justify which grounds for discrimination should be lawful or unlawful. Davies (2009:124–125) raises the possibility of 'immutability' being used as the underpinning principle, by which is meant characteristics which an individual is unable to change, or can only change with some difficulty. Under this formulation discrimination on grounds of sex, race, disability, age and sexual orientation would be unlawful, but protection for people on trade union grounds would not be provided. Ex-offenders probably would be included on the grounds that once gained a criminal record is 'immutable', but fixed and part-time workers would be excluded. Religion or belief could either be included in the list of grounds or not, depending on how readily changeable more deeply held convictions are considered to be. The problem with the adoption of such a principle is that it might lead to the extension of anti-discrimination law to all kinds of groups who are currently unprotected, and who would probably not be considered by most to require state protection. Discrimination against ugly people or people with strong regional accents might become unlawful, for example, or indeed against obese people (notwithstanding the theoretical availability of crash diets, elocution lessons and plastic surgery). In the case of regional accents there is a very real issue. In 2008 a survey of employers carried out by the law consultancy Peninsula revealed that 76% happily admitted to having discriminated against people with regional accents at the recruitment stage, applicants from Birmingham and Liverpool being the most unfortunate (Berry, 2008). It appears, according to research carried out by Workman and Smith (THE, 2008) that these accents are strongly associated in people's minds with perceptions of low intelligence, criminality and untrustworthiness.

Fredman (2002:67) suggests two different possible approaches. The first is that the groups who should be protected are those who for one reason or another suffer from 'political powerlessness'. The key criterion for inclusion within the scope of anti-discrimination law might thus simply be that a particular group needs to be included because it is suffering unjustly through being excluded. The problem here though, according to Fredman, is that rights are only extended on the say-so of the majority as represented by political parties or by judges who come from politically powerful groups. For this reason, paradoxically it is only once a minority group is politically powerful enough to convince the majority that it needs protection from discrimination that protection will be extended. For this reason sexual orientation was only added to the list of grounds in 2003, despite gay and lesbian people having suffered from discrimination in the workplace for decades. To have passed such a law in 1973 or even 1983 would have been a very difficult prospect simply because it would have been politically unacceptable to the majority. The second suggestion made by Fredman is that a list of groups should be agreed between governments of all developed countries and that these should be set out in an international treaty. But surely this too would make extensions to some groups who suffer unjustly from discrimination difficult to achieve? At the end of the day political pragmatism rather than principle simply has to prevail.

Hellman (2008) also addresses the possibility of pinning down a general theory of discrimination. She investigates various possible ways in which such a theory could be constructed. For example, she looks into the possibility of defining unlawful discrimination as being motivated by prejudice or grounded in stereotypes. She goes on to consider whether a departure from merit-based decision-making could form the basis of a general principle. In each case she finds problems. Eventually she concludes that the key factor that should determine whether or not an act of discrimination is unlawful should be the extent that it demeans the people who are adversely affected by it.

Which groups who are not currently covered by anti-discrimination law might have a case for inclusion? A number of commentators have made suggestions here. One group which currently has many legal rights, but no comprehensive coverage in anti-discrimination law is people with responsibility for the care of dependants (ie, young children, elderly relatives or disabled people).

A strong case can be put for any unjustified discrimination against people in this position to be made unlawful. Other extensions that are frequently mooted include political opinion (as opposed to philosophical belief which is already covered) and social origin (Hepple et al, 2000:42), both of which are included in the relevant international labour standard alongside several of the existing grounds for discrimination outlawed in the UK (see Ben-Israel 1998:253). Article 14 of the European Convention of Human Rights goes a good deal further and is deliberately not exhaustive. It covers 'sex, race, colour, language, religion, political or other opinion, national or social origin, association with a national minority, property, birth or other status'.

The inclusion of 'other status' is attractive to many commentators who would like to see a far less closely defined list of grounds in our legislation. Fredman (2002:67–68) goes as far as to argue in favour of an approach that does not list any categories at all, but which simply

---

 Exhibit 10.2

In 2007 Personnel Today surveyed HR professionals about what were the personal characteristics in respect of which it is still considered socially acceptable to tease people. The results suggest that there are still plenty of situations in which people are commonly harassed at work, a good number of which could give rise to legal action. However, because it is socially accepted that teasing on these grounds continues, victims are reluctant to make formal complaints of any kind at all.

Ginger hair	81%	Large ears	61%
Blonde hair	75%	Large nose	58%
Regional accent	74%	Glasses	57%
Baldness	72%	Small breasts	49%
Eccentric dress sense	70%	Underweight	46%
Shortness	70%	Body odour	45%
Overweight	65%	Bad teeth	40%
Unusual name	65%	Speech impediment	40%
Tallness	63%	Acne	38%
Large breasts	63%	Dandruff	29%

guarantees equality before the law and leaves it up to the judges to decide what grounds for discrimination are and are not to be considered unlawful. This is attractive in principle, but in practice would mean that employers and employees would not know where they stood until test cases were decided in the higher courts. Moreover it could conceivably lead to a situation in which groups were given protection despite this being contrary to public opinion, or indeed the public interest. People discriminated against for holding racist or other extreme political opinions might be protected, for example, as might people with undesirable sexual preferences—the very groups the 2003 regulations on sexual orientation and religion or belief were framed to exclude.

Complexity

Another frequently argued criticism of UK employment law relates to its complexity. Many commentators argue that this is unnecessary and undesirable because it means that neither employers nor employees can always be certain of their precise legal position. Employers are left unsure about whether a particular course of action is or is not unlawful, while employees and job applicants are left not knowing whether or not they have a strong case that might be worth pursuing in an employment tribunal.

For many years prominent campaigners argued the case for a consolidation of all discrimination law into a single Act of Parliament. Consolidation was one of the major recommendations made by a panel chaired by Bob Hepple in 2000 in its 'Independent Review of the Enforcement of UK Anti-Discrimination Legislation' (see Hepple et al, 2000). Their call was subsequently echoed by the Institute of Employment Rights (2002:57–73 and 2003:6–7) and is a cause that had wide support among trade unions over many years. Hepple argued that there should be 'clear, consistent and easily intelligible standards' set in a framework which is 'effective, efficient and equitable, aimed at encouraging personal responsibility and self-generating efforts to promote equality'. A second argument in favour was always that a single equality act would make it a great deal easier for people who wished to bring multiple claims (eg, someone who believes she has been discriminated against because she is a woman *and* black).

However, campaigners also saw the consolidation of equality law into a single act as an opportunity to improve protection for vulnerable and under-represented groups in significant ways. This would occur through a process of 'upward harmonisation' whereby the same sets of principles could govern all the major grounds of discrimination—a change that would have the effect, in practice, of extending across all discrimination law the most comprehensive rights that have applied only in the field of sex discrimination.

In recent years government has taken action which moves some way to meeting the demands of campaigners for less complexity in discrimination law, but progress has been limited and has not involved any serious attempt at upward harmonisation. In 2007, for example, we saw the establishment of the Equality and Human Rights Commission, replacing the three previous commissions and, at the same time, extending the scope of the remit beyond sex, race and disability to cover age, sexual orientation and religion and belief too, as well as human rights more generally. Then in 2008 a new equality bill was brought before Parliament which subsequently became, after a fair amount of amendment, the Equality Act 2010 (see Chapter 11). This has consolidated all the major discrimination regulations into a single statute and has also both simplified and harmonised the language in which the rights are expressed. It has also extended some rights and employer duties, mostly in order to bring UK statutes in line with decisions of the European Court of Justice. However, the

Equality Act did not hugely extend employment rights or create new ones, although some genuine advances were made in the area of disability discrimination. Moreover, it did not represent any general attempt to harmonise the principles that underpin the different types of discrimination that are covered by the law. For those who want to see greater employment rights the passing of this Act into law thus represented a lost opportunity and a disappointing continuation of the 'piecemeal and patchwork' approach that characterised legislative progress in the field of discrimination for the previous forty years (see Dickens 2007).

Formal equality v substantive equality

Critics of UK discrimination law have also long advanced the case for more fundamental reforms which would alter the principles on which the law is based away from those of 'formal equality' (also labelled 'equality as consistency') and towards 'substantive equality'. With one or two minor exceptions (eg, the fixed-term employee regulations and a requirement on public sector bodies to promote equality in limited ways), the focus of UK law is on deterring discrimination. The aim of the law is to help ensure that members of one group are not treated less favourably than those of another group in the same or equivalent circumstances. This is what is meant by formal equality. Employers are obliged in law to treat people *consistently* whether they are men or women, black or white, young or old, disabled or able-bodied. This has the effect of reducing injustice, but it also has serious limitations. For example, because the law is only concerned with achieving equality of treatment, it permits employers to harmonise downwards as a means of achieving equality. Fredman (2011:8) sums the position up as follows:

> (The law) requires only that two similarly situated individuals be treated alike. This means that there is no difference in principle between treating two such people equally badly, and treating them equally well. There is no substantive underpinning. For example, it has been held that if an employer harasses both men and women, then there is no discrimination on grounds of sex because they are both treated equally badly. Similarly, equal pay laws are of no benefit to a low paid woman if the only similarly situated male comparator is equally badly paid.

A law based on formal equality is also limited in that it provides no assistance to members of groups who cannot ever be 'similarly situated' because they are socially disadvantaged in a general sense. A disabled person, for example, might be turned down for a job not because of his disability, but because he does not have as much relevant experience in the role as another able-bodied candidate. That would be entirely lawful, irrespective of the fact that the reason the person in question has not achieved the experience is because of his disability. The same is often true in equal pay matters. A woman may genuinely be paid less than a man doing work of equal value because she has fewer years of experience. This is lawful, but the law takes no account (or requires employers to take no account) of the fact that she has fewer years of experience because she had a break from work for five years in order to bring up two young children.

For these reasons commentators advocate a shift towards law which is based on the principles of 'substantive equality'. The aim of the law should be to help achieve genuine equality and not simply to root out discrimination. There are two types of substantive equality that are commonly identified:

- equality of opportunity

and

- equality of results.

The former is focused on ensuring that everyone participates in the labour market on a 'level-playing field' and that all groups are given the same basic opportunities to gain jobs, to benefit from training and work experience and to achieve promotion. Fredman (2011:14) prefers the metaphor of a running race, arguing that equality of opportunity requires that everyone begins together at the same starting point and that none are weighed down with unnecessary baggage. In practical legal terms this means that employers should be required to take action which has the effect of ensuring that all compete on the same terms. Compensation thus needs to be made for those who are disadvantaged because of their gender, race, age, sexuality or other equivalent characteristic. This definitely requires positive action and may also require positive discrimination. As we explained earlier in this chapter, positive discrimination is unlawful in the UK in most areas of discrimination law. Positive action is not unlawful, but there is no duty placed on an employer to take steps of this kind.

Equality of results is a principle which goes further still, envisaging law which actively seeks to bring about social outcomes which are fair and which is not simply about removing obstacles that hinder the progress made by disadvantaged groups. The aim should thus be to achieve equal representation of men and women at senior levels in businesses or proportionate representation of ethnic minorities in the police force. Achieving this quickly would necessitate quite radical forms of positive discrimination. Employers might, for example, be required to reserve certain numbers of jobs at different levels in their organisations for members of disadvantaged groups.

The whole focus of discrimination law would change. It would be highly controversial partly because it would challenge the vested interests of powerful groups, but also because it would inevitably result in promotions for people who were not the best qualified to undertake the role. But it would certainly help to create genuine social equality very quickly. Some countries have moved in this direction to an extent, passing laws which guarantee equality of representation in the civil service, for example, or more generally across the public sector. This is the case, for example, in India where strenuous attempts have been made to reduce discrimination suffered by members of lower castes. Moreover, as Fredman (2011:143–145) points out, the same is true of the fair employment legislation that operates in Northern Ireland. This places a positive duty on employers to promote fair participation as between Catholics and Protestants 'where disparities are apparent even though there is no proof that the employer was guilty of unlawful discrimination'.

A major problem with the existing discrimination law in the UK, so its critics argue, is not just that it places no serious duty on employers to take action which eliminates discrimination, but that it actually helps to entrench inequality:

> The concept of equality as 'equal treatment' resonates with notions of assimilation (to a male, white, heterosexual norm) and integration rather than recognition and valuing of difference. It has thwarted employers (such as the police) seeking to increase representation or attainment of disadvantaged groups by positive action. Dickens (2007:474)

Moreover, according to some, discrimination law is failing to evolve alongside other developments in the working environment, the result being less rather than more protection for disadvantaged groups. In Chapter 3 we discussed the way that as far as the law on race, sex and disability is concerned, self-employed people have far fewer rights and find them much harder to enforce than is the case with people who fall into the 'worker' or 'employee' categories. Yet it is among women in particular that self-employment has grown most quickly. In many cases, however, these women are not running small businesses, but are in reality dependent on an employer for their work. They are homeworkers, agency temps, freelancers, franchisees, and hence perceive themselves to be outside the protection of discrimination law even if, in reality, a case could be made in some circumstances for them to be included (Fudge, 2006). The result in practice is thus a situation in which the law provides protection to fewer women than used to be the case.

Activity 10.4 Representation of women in Parliament

At the UK 2010 general election 650 Members of Parliament were elected, of whom 507 were men and 143 women. This represents a female election rate of just 22%. In the House of Lords in January 2011 there were 181 women out of a total of 833 peers (an ennoblement rate of 21.7%). Women are better represented than they were twenty years ago, but this is due in large part to the highly controversial, if lawful, practice adopted by the Labour Party of imposing 'all women shortlists' on constituency associations where the seat is likely to be won by the Labour candidate. The Conservative Party has not gone this far, but it does now ensure that equal numbers of men and women are on the final shortlist of people from whom candidates in each constituency are selected.

Questions

1 How would you characterise the system for selecting parliamentary candidates—is it based on principles of 'formal equality', 'substantive equality' or a mixture of the two?

2 What principles do you think should underpin this system and why?

3 What would be the major advantages and disadvantages of a system in which a quota of seats in either the House of Commons or the House of Lords were reserved for women, members of different ethnic minorities, disabled people, gay people and young people?

4 To what extent would you like to see employers restricted in similar ways when recruiting people and why?

Enforcement

The final substantial critique of discrimination law that is frequently developed concerns the way it is enforced. This helps ensure, according to critics, that its social impact is necessarily limited and that inequality continues despite the presence of such law on our statute books for more than thirty years. Three features of the system are particularly questioned:

1. Employers are only held to account for their actions in the courts when an individual who believes he or she has suffered from unlawful discrimination takes a case to an employment tribunal.

2. In order to win a case it is sometimes necessary for the claimant to cite a comparator who has received or would receive more favourable treatment in similar circumstances.

3. Once a case is won any remedy imposed by the tribunal only applies to the individual who has brought the case. Others in the same employment must also bring similar cases if they are to achieve the same outcome.

On all three counts it is possible to argue for a different approach to be adopted. In the case of the first criticism the alternative approach most commonly mooted is to bring into existence a government-funded inspectorate operating either at national or regional level. Equality inspectors would be mandated with the task of checking that employers were not discriminating unlawfully and could carry out inspections of some sort when complaints were made to them. Some argue that such an institution would be toothless unless it had the power to force changes to be made and levy fines itself and that it should therefore be far more than a body which brings cases to tribunal on behalf of groups of employees. Whilst this would represent a radical departure from existing UK practice, it can be plausibly argued that no less a solution is required if socially disadvantaged groups are not to remain disadvantaged for generations to come. Moreover, of course, there is a fully functioning and reasonably successful model of such a system already operating in the field of health and safety law on which an equality inspectorate of some description could be based. Cost provides is the major argument against moving in this direction.

An alternative way forward proposed by Hugh Collins (2003:73–75) is to move towards what he labels 'participatory self-regulation' in the area of equality. Just as organisations are required to consult with health and safety committees, he suggests there should be equal opportunities committees in workplaces with which consultation is required by law. Such a system would be 'likely in itself to promote respect for diversity and inclusiveness, and at the same time to facilitate minority groups in asserting and defining their particular needs'.

A third suggestion has the advantage that it would cost government relatively little, but might well be a great deal more effective than the measure proposed by Collins. Dickens (2007:484–485) argues that government should make much more use of its 'procurement power' than it currently does, by which she means making decisions about which companies should be awarded contracts in part on the basis of their record on discrimination and equality. Those who wanted to do business with governmental and local government bodies would thus have to demonstrate what action they were taking to promote equality if they were to be successful. The impact could be substantial when it is considered that around £100 billion a year is spent by the public sector procuring goods and services from the private sector.

The argument about claimants having to cite a comparator is a little more complex. As matters stand in some areas of discrimination law (eg, equal pay, fixed-term employment, part-time employment and trade union-based discrimination) it is necessary for the claimant to name a 'real living' comparator in a similar situation who is being paid more or has been treated more favourably. If there is no equivalent comparator available, the case cannot proceed. In most other areas of discrimination law a comparator is required, but this can if necessary be a hypothetical comparator. So, for example, a woman who is discriminated against can compare herself with a hypothetical man and base her case on the argument that she would have received more favourable treatment had she not been female. This approach greatly improves the position of claimants, but some argue that it should not be a requirement to have a comparator at all and that the whole concept of discrimination law based on comparators is unreasonable. This is because the law makes the assumption that the comparator is 'normal' and the claimant abnormal. Fredman (2011:9) quotes Catherine MacKennon's (1987:34) view of the issue, written from a feminist perspective:

> Concealed is the substantive way in which man has become the measure of all things. Under the sameness standard, women are measured according to our correspondence with man ... Gender neutrality is thus simply the male standard.

The same is true of race discrimination law (the 'norm' is white) and discrimination on grounds of sexual orientation (the 'norm' is heterosexual).

This becomes a major stumbling block when the reasons that underlie discrimination do not equally apply to the white, male heterosexual 'norm'. An example would be a woman who could not comply with a requirement to work in the evenings because she has childcare responsibilities. As a result she is not promoted or is discouraged from applying for promotion. The accepted norm, in such a case, is a man with equivalent childcare responsibilities, and it is with him (or a hypothetical version of him) that the woman would need to compare herself were she to bring a tribunal claim. It would be more satisfactory, according to many, for her simply to base a claim on the fact that she had suffered a detriment because she had children she needed to care for. There should be no need to go through a process of presenting statistical evidence to back up the claim that fewer women than men are able to comply with the organisation's expectations. The law has effectively moved in this direction in the case of pregnancy—it has had to because men cannot become pregnant. For a period the approach used was for a pregnant woman to compare herself to a sick man. Faced with such a case the tribunal would ask 'was she treated less favourably than a sick man either was or would be in similar circumstances'? But this approach has now been abandoned. Effectively the question asked now simply relates to pregnancy—would the woman have been treated differently had she not been pregnant? The need for a male norm as comparator has thus gone. Taking the same approach across discrimination law would remove obstacles and help promote greater equality. But it would also add greatly to the restrictions placed on employers by the law, and as such it would be politically controversial.

The third major problem with existing approaches to enforcement is simply that under the UK system individual claimants bring cases on their own behalf, and if they win their cases, the remedies won apply only to them. People frequently bring group claims, but the fact remains that only those who actually bring the case benefit from winning it. This is not the case in many other countries. For example, in the United States, courts are able to place 'mandatory injunctions' on employers requiring an employer to alter its practices if they are found to have been unlawfully discriminatory. Failure to comply with such an injunction has major financial consequences. In the UK, by contrast, employment tribunals have no power to issue injunctions of any sort. All they can do is make recommendations and, in the case of discrimination claims, award compensation to individuals who bring cases to them. So for example, where a woman wins a sexual harassment claim, the remedy will take the form of compensation. The tribunal might recommend that the employer takes steps to tighten up its policies and procedures, or disciplines the perpetrator, but it cannot force these recommendations on the employer. In such a situation it is more likely that the employer will congratulate itself on only having had to pay out limited compensation to the victim and carry on as before, the perpetrator remaining in post and in a position to harass again. The same is true in equal pay cases. The spoils (in this case accumulated back pay) only go to the victors in a tribunal case. There is no requirement placed on the employer to pay equally in the future.

A plausible case can thus be made to strengthen the power of tribunals to require employers to 'put right the wrong' as well as awarding compensation to those who have suffered as a result of unlawful practices.

In this section we have briefly summarised some of the major critiques of existing discrimination law, also presenting some suggested ways forward for the future. The suggestions have included the following:

- extending general protection from discrimination to all unfair grounds
- requiring employers to take positive action
- encouraging employers to positively discriminate
- establishing an equality inspectorate with statutory powers
- requiring employers to consult with equality committees in their workplaces
- giving tribunals the power to issue mandatory injunctions.

Questions

1 Which of these do you think would have the greatest practical impact as a means of improving the position of under-represented or socially disadvantaged groups?

2 Which would have the least practical impact?

3 Which would be most objected to by employers?

4 If you were able to impose one of these measures on all employers in the UK, which would you choose and why?

CHAPTER SUMMARY

- The scope of anti-discrimination law has widened very considerably over the past twenty years, principally as a result of new EU law protecting people from discrimination on grounds such as age, sexual orientation, religion and fixed-term or part-time status.

- Different areas of discrimination law vary in respect of the types and extent of defences that are possible when it is alleged that an act of unlawful discrimination has taken place. How far positive discrimination is lawful also varies.

- Some argue that anti-discrimination law tends in practice to harm the people it sets out to protect by distorting the market and discouraging the hiring of under-represented groups.

- There is much debate about whether it is possible to establish a general principle to help define who exactly should be protected by discrimination law, in what ways and on what basis.

- Critics of contemporary discrimination law attack the way that it stops short of forcing employers to establish equality of outcome, preferring instead merely to encourage equality of opportunity.

- Critics also find much fault with enforcement regimes, particularly the way that the law requires comparators (real or hypothetical) to be cited by claimants.

For updates and further materials, please see the online resource centre at www.oup.com.

REFERENCES

Ben-Israel, R. (1998) 'Equality and the prohibition of discrimination in employment' in R. Blanpain and C. Engels (eds): *Comparative Labour Law and Industrial Relations in Industrialized Market Economies*. London: Kluwer Law International.

Berry, M. (2008) 'Accent discrimination hits record levels' *Personnel Today*, 24 June.

Collins, H. (2003) *Employment Law*. Oxford: Oxford University Press.

Davies, A.C.L. (2009) *Perspectives on Labour Law*. Second Edition. Cambridge: Cambridge University Press.

Dickens, L. (2007) 'The road is long: Thirty years of equality legislation in Britain' *British Journal of Industrial Relations* 45.3 (p463–494).

Epstein, R.A. (1992) *Forbidden Grounds: The case against employment discrimination laws*. Cambridge, Massachusetts: Harvard University Press.

Epstein, R.A. (2002) *Equal Opportunity or More Opportunity? The good thing about discrimination*. London: Civitas.

Fredman, S. (2011) *Discrimination Law*. Second Edition. Oxford: Oxford University Press.

Fudge, J. (2006) 'Self-employment, women and precarious work: The scope of labour protection' in J. Fudge & R. Owens (eds): *Precarious Work, Women and the New Economy*. Oxford: Hart Publishing.

Hellman, D. (2008) *When is Discrimination Wrong?* Cambridge, Massacheusetts: Harvard University Press.

Hepple B., Coussey M. & Choudhury T. (2000) *Equality: A New Framework: Report of the Independent Review of the Enforcement of UK Anti-Discrimination Legislation*. Oxford: Hart Publishing.

Institute of Employment Rights (2002) *A Charter of Workers' Rights*. Edited by K. Ewing and J. Hendy. London: IER.

Institute of Employment Rights (2003) *Achieving Equality at Work*. Edited by Aileen McColgan. London: IER.

MacKennon, C. (1987) *Feminism Unmodified*. Cambridge, Massachusetts: Harvard University Press.

Personnel Today (2007) 'In the eye of the beholder? When does teasing at work become harassment?' *Personnel Today*, 13 June.

Times Higher Education (2008) 'Yorkshire lasses shine brighter' *THE*, 10 April.

ONLINE RESOURCE CENTRE

A range of online resources to help you through your employment law module have been developed by the author team. These include updates, self-test questions and sources for further reading. (www.oxfordtextbooks.co.uk/orc/taylor_emir3e)

The Equality Act 2010: key concepts

11

Learning outcomes

By the end of this chapter you should be able to:

- list which characteristics are protected by discrimination law;

- state what kind of conduct is prohibited;

- define the term 'direct discrimination' and explain its meaning in practice;

- say what is meant by indirect discrimination and differentiate it from direct discrimination;

- set out what defences are open to an employer if discrimination is alleged;

- define harassment and the situations in which it applies;

- define the term 'victimisation' and explain its practical significance;

- understand the remedies that are available in discrimination cases and state when each is awarded;

- assess the merits of the cases put forward by the two sides in the debate about justification in cases of direct sex discrimination.

Introduction

There has been some sort of discrimination law in the United Kingdom since the 1960s, with the introduction of the first race relations Acts, followed by sex discrimination and equal pay legislation in the 1970s, disability in the 1990s and religion, sexual orientation and age in the 2000s. As Wadham points out:

> before the introduction of the Equality Act, we had more than 100 different sets of equality legislation amassed in 35 Acts, 52 statutory instruments, 13 codes of practice and 16 European directives. (Wadham, 2011)

The legislation was often of its time—for example the sex legislation did not include pregnancy or sexual orientation, and much time and money was spent trying to persuade judges that it did, with results as we shall see in forthcoming chapters.

 Exhibit 11.1   **The main legislation in force prior to the Equality Act 2010**

Equal Pay Act 1970

Sex Discrimination Act 1975 (This included sex and marital status, and was later amended to include pregnancy and gender reassignment.)

Race Relations Act 1976

Disability Discrimination Act 1995

Employment Equality (Religion and Belief) Regulations 2003

Employment Equality (Sexual Orientation) Regulations 2003

Employment Equality (Age Regulations) 2006

In addition to the main legislation listed above, there were a number of other statutes and statutory instruments that tinkered with various issues, and which were sometimes difficult to keep up with. This proliferation of legislation became unwieldy, and at times had definitions that were not quite consistent (such as those for indirect discrimination in relation to sex and race).

As mentioned in the previous chapter, there were discussions for many years about whether this discrimination law should be collated into one statute. This was eventually done in the final days of the Labour government in 2010, with the passing of the Equality Act, which has now been mostly brought into force by the Coalition government.

The main purpose of the Equality Act is not to make new law, but rather to harmonise the myriad of statutes and regulations that previously combined to make the body of discrimination law. The Act therefore brings all the disparate legislation together, and purports to establish a consistent body of anti-discrimination law. Although this has been welcomed by many, there has also been some criticism, which we shall look at later.

Such harmonisation of definitions and getting rid of arbitrary distinctions has, Hepple argues, *'generally levelled up protection against indirect discrimination across the board, and have*

Exhibit 11.2   **The purpose of the Equality Act**

The Act, while being huge in terms of its volume, creates precious few new employment rights of any great significance. For the most part it is simply concerned with:

- consolidating diverse pieces of equality legislation into one single statute,

- ensuring that our statutes catch up with recent developments in the case law, and particularly decisions of the European Court of Justice,

- harmonising the terminology that is used across different areas of equality law,

- clarifying the law in areas where things have not always been so clear in the past.

extended protection against victimisation' by removing the need for a comparator, as well as no longer a need to prove less favourable treatment for pregnancy and maternity discrimination. (Hepple, 2011)

Unlike many other English statutes, the Equality Act also has a comprehensive set of explanatory notes, which have been praised by Lord Lester QC, the veteran campaigner on human rights and discrimination. He states that they are 'so clear and comprehensive that they serve in themselves as a practical guide on the policy and content of the Act' (Hepple, 2011: Foreword). These notes can therefore be very helpful in understanding the intentions of Parliament, and will undoubtedly be of great use to lawyers, judges and students.

As part of the harmonisation, the Equality Act effectively sets discrimination law out into two lists—protected characteristics and prohibited conduct. We shall look briefly at these in this chapter, and then consider in more detail each characteristic and the conduct prohibited in relation to it in following chapters.

Cases decided under the old legislation will be referred to as they will often still be valid, at least until the courts build up a new body of case law. In addition, while the remit of this book is employment law only, some non-employment cases will also be referred to, as discrimination law is in most cases wider than just in the employment field.

Who is covered by the Act?

The previous law applied to employment in Great Britain, but the Equality Act does not specify, so that tribunals can decide if there is sufficient connection with Britain in each case.

The law covers both applicants for employment and those already in employment. The protection continues after the employment has come to an end in certain cases such as victimisation. Also, the definition of employee is a wide one for the purposes of this Act, in that it covers workers and the self-employed who personally carry out services under a contract. (*Harvey* calls it employment 'in a loose sense', para 553.)

An employer cannot discriminate:

- in the arrangements he makes for deciding who will be offered employment (including advertisements and interview arrangements)

- in the terms that employment is offered

- by refusing or deliberately omitting to offer the employment
- in the way that he affords access to opportunities for promotion, transfer, training or other benefits
- by dismissing the person or subjecting her to any other detriment.

Protected characteristics

The characteristics are listed in alphabetical order in section 4 of the Act as:

- age
- disability
- gender reassignment
- marriage and civil partnership
- pregnancy and maternity
- race
- religion or belief
- sex
- sexual orientation.

In a schedule to the Act it also provides for equal pay.

It is important to remember that all these, apart from disability and pregnancy are *symmetrical*. In other words, sex discrimination applies to men and women, age discrimination applies to older and younger people, etc.

(In previous editions of this book we considered the protected characteristics more or less in the order that they came into force, but in the following chapters we will mostly follow the order that they appear in the Act, although the sex-related characteristics such as pregnancy, etc will follow on from the sex discrimination chapter for the sake of clarity).

Prohibited conduct

There are a number of types of conduct prohibited by the Equality Act which relate to most of the protected characteristics. The main ones that we shall consider in this chapter are:

- direct discrimination (including discrimination by association and perception)
- combined/dual discrimination
- indirect discrimination
- harassment
- harassment by a third party
- victimisation.

Most of these were found in the previous legislation, albeit not always drafted consistently, leading to arbitrary distinctions. The slightly different wording of some definitions also changes the law in some ways, as will be seen below. The rest of the prohibited conduct applies to specific types of protected characteristics (such as disability) and will be dealt with in those chapters.

Direct discrimination

Direct discrimination is what most people think of when they think of discrimination. They think of someone being treated less well than other people because of a particular characteristic, such as their sex or their race.

The definition is set out in section 13 of the Equality Act, and is when a person (A) treats another person (B) less favourably than he treats or would treat someone else (C), because of a protected characteristic.

This is effectively a two-stage test. First you have to look at whether the discriminatory treatment was *less favourable* treatment than had been given to someone else, and then you have to consider whether it was *because* of the protected characteristic. Direct discrimination cannot therefore be proved simply by showing applies to all the protected characteristics.

'Less favourably'

Discrimination law does not cover someone simply because they are treated badly. An employer can treat all his staff badly—that would not be discrimination, it would be treating people equally, albeit badly. Discrimination cannot therefore be proved simply by showing that someone is treated badly because of their protected characteristic.

The complainant therefore has to show that the treatment was less favourable than treatment given to someone else in similar circumstances who did not have that characteristic. In other words, they have to show less favourable treatment, not just unfavourable treatment. The person that a complainant compares themselves to is known as the 'comparator', and can be either a real or a hypothetical person.

The retention in the Equality Act of the need for a comparator for most characteristics has been criticised by some commentators, and the law on direct discrimination has therefore been described as a 'levelling down' by Hepple, allowing people to be treated equally badly (Hepple, 2011:55).

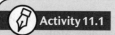

Activity 11.1

1   Do you think that the law should prohibit employers from simply treating people badly because of their protected characteristics? Give reasons for your answer.

2   If you do, how would the law work in practice?

Choosing a comparator can be important to the outcome of a case (as can be seen in the historic cases dealing with pregnancy and sexual orientation, which will be looked at in later chapters). The comparison must be 'like with like', and the comparator (who can be either a real person or a hypothetical one) must be someone who shares all the relevant circumstances and attributes of the claimant, such as the same employer, etc, but not the protected characteristic of the person claiming discrimination. So, for example, the comparator for a woman would be a man, the comparator of someone who is gay would be someone who is not gay, and so on.

Dress codes

Treating someone less favourably does not mean treating them differently. You can treat someone comparably, but differently, and this would not be discriminatory. This is best illustrated with the cases that relate to dress codes, which we shall consider in more detail in later chapters.

Let us take, for example, an employer who wishes to have particular standards of dress between men and women, such as requiring men to have short hair and allowing women to have long hair tied back. This is certainly treating them differently, but it is not treating men less favourably. The reason is that the employer is seeking to impose conventional dress on his employees, and so is in effect treating his employees the same, in accordance with the standards of the day. Provided the same standards are imposed equally the dress code will not amount to unlawful discrimination. There may be a difference of treatment but it is not less favourable. We will look at this further in other chapters.

'because of'

The definition in the old law was 'on grounds of' a protected characteristic, which led to a lot of argument on what it meant. The judges developed tests which can be seen in the old cases, such as the 'but for' test and the 'reason why' test. The Equality Act has clarified this by using simple language—if someone was treated less favourably than someone else *because of* a characteristic then they will have been discriminated against.

The words 'because of' have, however, meant in practice that direct discrimination has been widened, and that issues such as 'associative discrimination' and 'perceived discrimination' are now covered, and will be dealt with later in this chapter.

Motive

When people think of discrimination, they often get an image of a person deliberately treating someone badly because they don't like their race, etc. In law, however, there does not have to be a conscious motivation to discriminate. As Lord Nicholls said in the House of Lords case of *Nagarajan v London Regional Transport* (1999) (in relation to a race discrimination case):

> All human beings have preconceptions, beliefs, attitudes and prejudices on many subjects. It is part of our make-up. Moreover, we do not always recognise our own prejudices. Many people are unable, or unwilling, to admit even to themselves that actions of theirs may be racially motivated. An employer may genuinely believe that the reason why he rejected an applicant had nothing to do with the applicant's race. After careful and thorough investigation of a claim members of an employment tribunal may decide that the proper inference to be drawn from the evidence is that, whether the employer realised it at the time or not, race was the reason why he acted as he did.

The motive for less favourable treatment is therefore not relevant, otherwise the law would not be able to overcome people being stereotyped or being subjected to assumptions. So, for example, if the reason that a woman is not given a job is because the employer thinks that she might prefer to stay at home with her children, or he thinks it is not a nice job for a woman to have to do, or he feels that the man would fit in better with the people who were already employed by him, it would still be direct discrimination.

> **Activity 11.2** *Amnesty International v Ahmed* **(2009)**
>
> A woman working for Amnesty International was not given the post of 'Sudan researcher' because her ethnic origin was northern Sudanese. Because of this Amnesty genuinely believed that there would be a conflict of interest which would increase the safety risk for herself and others.
>
> The EAT said that there was direct discrimination on the ground of her ethnic origin, even though the reason for Amnesty's decision was concern about her safety.
>
> **Question**
>
> 1 Read the debate below about justification of direct discrimination, then come back to this question. Do you agree with the EAT's decision or with Amnesty's actions? Give reasons for your answer.

The fact that the difference in treatment is only minor is also irrelevant. The case of *Peake v Automotive Products* (1977) concerned a factory in the 1970s where the female workers were allowed to leave work five minutes before the men. One of the men, Mr Peake, complained that he was being treated less favourably than the women because he had to work an extra five minutes per day.

The employers argued that this was a concession to the women, rather than discrimination against the men. They explained that the main reason was a chivalrous one, to avoid women being jostled and crushed as some 4,000 employees left the factory at the end of the shift.

The EAT decided that Mr Peake was being treated less favourably than the women, and that this was on the grounds of his sex. They also said that although it was a minor detriment, that made no difference to the law.

Irrelevance of alleged discriminator's characteristics

A person can discriminate against someone even if he shares the same characteristic. The characteristics of the discriminator are therefore irrelevant, and the Equality Act says this specifically. In the past, this was only clear in relation to religion or belief, but has now been extended to all characteristics.

Justification of direct discrimination

Apart from a few exceptions, direct discrimination cannot be justified. This means that an employer cannot give an excuse or reason for the less favourable treatment, even if it is done with a good intention. If someone is treated less favourably because of a protected characteristic then that will be direct discrimination, no matter what the excuse, unless it comes within one of the exceptions set out in the Act.

The first of these exceptions relates to age discrimination. The Equality Act states that potential age discrimination can be justifiable if the employer can show the justification is 'a proportionate means of meeting a legitimate aim'. This means that if the employer has an objective reason for his actions, and this reason is reasonable, then he can justify what might otherwise appear to be a discriminatory action. An important use that an employer would have for this is if he wishes to set a retirement age for his employees.

The second exception set out in the Act is that of Occupational Requirements.

Occupational requirements (ORs)

These used to be known as Genuine Occupational Requirements or Genuine Occupational Qualifications, depending on which piece of legislation was being considered. They apply where it is essential that a person has a particular characteristic for a particular job, such as a black male actor playing the part of Othello.

The requirement must be crucial to the post, and not merely one of several important factors. It also must not be a sham or pretext. In addition, applying the requirement must be 'proportionate so as to achieve a legitimate aim' (as with age discrimination). If an employer can prove this, then he can treat people differently.

The explanatory notes to the Act give the following examples:

- The need for authenticity or realism might require someone of a particular race, sex or age for acting roles (such as in the Othello example above, or an old man to play Falstaff) or modelling jobs.

- Considerations of privacy or decency might require a public changing room or lavatory attendant to be of the same sex as those using the facilities.

- An organisation for deaf people might legitimately employ a deaf person who uses British sign language to work as a counsellor to other deaf people whose first or preferred language is BSL.

- Unemployed Muslim women might not take advantage of the services of an outreach worker to help them find employment if they were provided by a man, so a woman would be required.

- A counsellor working with victims of rape might have to be a woman and not a transsexual person, even if she has a gender recognition certificate, in order to avoid causing them further distress.

- There are also specific exceptions for religions, but only if being of that religion or belief is a requirement for the work. For example, a Catholic priest can be required to be a man, but a requirement that a church accountant should not be gay would not be covered, as his sexuality is nothing to do with how he performs his job.

The employer is allowed to apply an OR

- in the arrangements made for recruiting for the job
- by refusing or deliberately omitting to offer the job
- in the way access is afforded to opportunities for promotion or transfer to the job or for training for the job or by refusing or deliberately omitting to offer such opportunities.

Other types of direct discrimination

The wording of direct discrimination in the Equality Act changed slightly from the former definition in most of the old legislation. Instead of the less favourable treatment being 'on grounds of' a particular person's protected characteristic, it is now 'because of' a characteristic. Because the definition does not refer to the protected characteristic of any particular person (whereas before it was the characteristic of the person being discriminated against, 'B') this has allowed new types of direct discrimination to be read into the legislation. These are associative discrimination and perceptive discrimination.

Associative discrimination

Associative discrimination is where someone is discriminated against because of someone else that he is associated with. For example, if a woman is not given a job because her husband is a Muslim, then this would be associative religious discrimination.

Such discrimination by association was found by the courts in *Coleman v Attridge Law* (2010) in relation to disability discrimination, but the Equality Act has extended this to most other forms of protected characteristic. It does not apply, however, in cases of marital status/ civil partnership and pregnancy and maternity. Therefore if, for example, someone lives with a married couple, that does not provide him with grounds to complain to a tribunal if he is discriminated against on that basis. It therefore has to be the 'victim' of the discrimination, not anyone else, who is the married person or civil partner.

Perceptive discrimination

Another 'new' type of direct discrimination is that of perceptive discrimination. This is where the discrimination occurs because the discriminator believes that the person has a particular characteristic, even though he does not. Again, under the old law, the judges started trying to bring in perceptive discrimination, such as in the case of *English v Thomas Sanderson Blinds* (2008), where the Court of Appeal said that homophobic abuse towards a man who was not gay, and whom the alleged harassers did not believe was gay, could still be harassment on the grounds of sexual orientation.

Deterred discrimination

The Equality definition of direct discrimination contains the words 'than he treats or *would treat* others'. Selwyn states that this therefore leaves it open to a person to claim 'deterred discrimination'. Such discrimination would occur, for example, if an employer advertises a job, but gives an indication that a person who has a particular protected characteristic would not be considered for a post, if someone can show that he had genuinely intended to apply for the post, and was suitably qualified for it, but was deterred from applying because of the indication. (Selwyn, 2010:129).

 Activity 11.3

An advertising agency advertises for 'young, dynamic people' to join their new office in Cheltenham. John, a fifty-year-old man who had been aware that the office was to open and was looking forward to applying, sees the advert and is upset that he is too old to apply. Is this discrimination? If so, what kind?

Dual or combined discrimination

This is a new element in discrimination law. It had been due to come into force in April 2011, but the Coalition government put it on hold. It is not known how long this will last, or if indeed the provision will ever be brought into force. In the event that it might be, it is important to consider it in our look at the Equality Act.

Dual discrimination is when a person can bring a claim on the basis that they have two of the protected characteristics and that is why they have been discriminated against. It was drafted in order to protect people who would not succeed just on proving one of the characteristics. For example, if someone is discriminated against because she is a black woman, but there would have been no discrimination if she were a white woman or a black man, then her only claim would be a combined discrimination one.

The protected characteristics that can be combined are:

- age
- disability
- gender reassignment
- race
- religion or belief
- sex
- sexual orientation.

An example given in the notes to the Act is that of a black woman who has been passed over for promotion to work on reception. The reason is because her employer thinks black women do not perform well in customer service roles.

The employer has a white woman and a black man doing similar work in reception, and so the black woman cannot succeed on a claim based only on race or only on sex. If the discrimination was because of race, the employer could say he employed a black person in reception. If it was because of sex, the employer could say that he employed a woman in reception.

The only option the black woman has, therefore, is to claim combined discrimination on the basis that she is a black woman, because of her employer's prejudice against black women. The comparator would be someone who is not black or a woman, ie, not a black woman.

Indirect discrimination

Direct discrimination is what most people think of when they think of discrimination. They have in mind a deliberate action taken against someone because of their sex or race, etc. The law, however, prohibits another kind of less obvious discrimination known as 'indirect discrimination'. This is where the employer may not even realise that he is discriminating, but is in fact doing something that makes it more difficult for one group of people to comply with than another. This is also a type of discrimination, and applies to all kinds of protected characteristic apart from pregnancy and maternity.

This type of discrimination originated in the United States, and is the reflection in British law of the American concept of disparate impact, which arose in the USA decision of *Griggs v Duke Power Co* (1971). In the original Sex Discrimination Bill in the early 1970s, the intention was to outlaw only direct discrimination. The then Home Secretary, Roy Jenkins, visited the USA, however, and gained an understanding of the importance of prohibiting indirect discrimination in the fight to eradicate discrimination. He came home declaring that *'the Bill would be too narrow if it were confined to direct discrimination'*.

The definition of indirect discrimination as set out in section 19 of the Equality Act harmonises the different versions that existed in the previous legislation. It now states that a person indirectly discriminates against another if (to paraphrase):

1. He applies a provision, criterion or practice to someone who has a protected characteristic.
2. The provision, etc also applies to people who do not have the particular protected characteristic.
3. When the provision is applied it puts (or would put) people who have the particular protected characteristic at a disadvantage compared with the people who do not.
4. It puts (or would put) an individual person with that characteristic at a disadvantage.
5. It cannot be shown that it is a proportionate means of achieving a legitimate aim.

This last criterion shows that indirect discrimination can be justified, which is one of the major differences from direct discrimination.

In short, it will be indirect discrimination if an employer has a policy (which the law calls a 'provision, criterion or practice') which he applies in the same way to everyone, but which has an effect which puts one group of people, for example women, at a disadvantage. These have been referred to as the 'winning group' and the 'losing group' (Forshaw and Pilgerstorfer, 2008:348). If it can be shown that this puts an individual person at a disadvantage too, then this would be unlawful unless the employer can justify it.

An example is if the employer requires his staff to work unsociable hours as this would disadvantage women who usually have more childcare commitments than men, or not allowing staff to have beards as this would put Sikh men at a disadvantage. Such policies would be discriminatory unless the employer has an objective justification for them.

This was the situation in the case of *London Underground v Edwards* (1995), where Mrs Edwards, a single parent with a young child, was employed as an underground train driver. London Underground announced a new shift system which she would have found difficult to do because of her child, and this was found to be indirect discrimination.

The law also allows for deterred discrimination, in the same way as for direct discrimination—so if someone is deterred from doing something, such as applying for a job, because a policy which would be applied would put him at a disadvantage, then this could also be indirect discrimination. To use the example above, if the employer advertised a job and said that the applicant would have to work different shifts, this could potentially be indirect discrimination because it would put women at a disadvantage, unless the employer could justify it.

Therefore, even though what the employer might be doing is not a deliberate measure, if it is an unjustifiable practice that stands in the way of, for example, women achieving equal opportunities to men, and it puts women at a disadvantage, then it is discriminatory.

Provision, criterion or practice
The provision, criterion or practice will have to be applied to everyone equally, regardless of any characteristic. It can be something which appears to be innocent enough, until one looks at the effect of it. For example, in a sex discrimination situation, the employer could advertise for an employee who is over six feet tall. On the face of it, he is saying that he will accept both men and women if they come within the criterion. It is therefore a 'provision, criterion or practice' which has been applied to men and women alike, but in practice it will disadvantage women compared to men, as fewer women are over six feet tall, and so come within the criterion.

Under the old definition, which required a disproportionate impact, the tribunal had to consider what counted as a larger proportion, and what the pool of comparison was. This was a comparative exercise, and usually required statistical evidence to prove the proportion. This was costly and difficult, especially if the pool chosen for the statistics was different to the one the tribunal decided to use.

All that needs to be shown for the current test is that a provision puts or would put someone belonging to the claimant's group at a particular disadvantage when compared to others. It is not necessary to have statistical evidence, and there can be hypothetical comparisons. This is broader, and so appears to make it easier for the claimant to establish a case without having to provide statistical evidence, but this remains to be seen from new case law.

Justification

In direct discrimination cases there is no defence of justification (aside from the ORs and age discrimination), but where indirect discrimination has been found to have taken place it is possible for the employer to defend himself. In other words, indirect discrimination can be lawful if, and only if, the employer, who has the burden of proof, is able to justify the provision that has caused the situation. In order to justify, the employer has to show that the provision is 'a proportionate means of achieving a legitimate aim'.

Lord Justice Mummery in the case of *R (on the application of Elias) v Secretary of State for Defence* (2006) set out some guidelines in relation to how to determine if the justification is proportionate. He said that the provision must correspond to a real need of the employer, and it must be appropriate and necessary with a view to achieving that objective. The need must be weighed against the seriousness of the detriment to the disadvantaged group. He set out the test for proportionality as:

1. Is the objective sufficiently important to justify limiting the fundamental right to equality?

2. Is the measure rationally connected to the objective?

3. Are the means no more than necessary to achieve the objective?

IDS explains the test in the following way:

> The employer has to show that he has carried out a balancing exercise, weighing the business's need to impose the PCP [provision, criterion or practice] against the discriminatory effect of the PCP and, in doing so, must put forward cogent evidence tipping the scales in favour of his argument: generalisations will not be acceptable. This process requires the employer critically and objectively to evaluate his business decisions where discrimination is obvious or likely. (IDS, 2008:110)

 Exhibit 11.3   **Direct v indirect discrimination**

Lady Hale in the *JFS* case (2010) said:

> The basic difference between direct and indirect discrimination is plain: see Mummery LJ in *R (Elias) v Secretary of State for Defence* [2006] EWCA 1293, [2006] 1 WLR 3213, para 119. The rule against direct discrimination aims to achieve formal equality of treatment: there must be no less favourable treatment between otherwise similarly situated people on grounds of colour, race, nationality, or ethnic or national origins. Indirect discrimination looks beyond formal equality towards a more substantive equality of results: criteria which appear »

>> neutral on their face may have a disproportionately adverse impact upon people of a particular colour, race, nationality or ethnic or national origins.

Direct and indirect discrimination are mutually exclusive. You cannot have both at once. As Mummery LJ explained in Elias at para 117 *'the conditions of liability, the available defences to liability and the available defences to remedies differ'*. The main difference between them is that direct discrimination cannot be justified. Indirect discrimination can be justified if it is a proportionate means of achieving a legitimate aim.

Harassment

The previous law on harassment was quite piecemeal, being found in various cases and bits of statute, many of which were inconsistent and difficult to follow. The Equality Act has harmonised these, and now defines three types of harassment in section 26 of the Act.

1. The first type applies to all the protected characteristics apart from pregnancy and maternity, and marriage and civil partnership. It is similar to the previous definitions of harassment, in that it consists of unwanted conduct which is related to a protected characteristic and has the purpose or effect of creating an intimidating, hostile, degrading, humiliating or offensive environment for the complainant or violating his or her dignity.

   It is therefore behaviour which is related to sex, race, etc and makes the person who hears it feel intimidated, offended or degraded. Examples of such behaviour could be physical abuse, offensive language, racist jokes and banter, etc.

   In the past, harassment law had to be 'on grounds of', and as such covered only the person who was the subject of the unwanted conduct, but it is now only 'related to a protected characteristic'. The notes to the Equality Act make it clear that this is therefore wider. The example given is of a white worker who sees a black colleague being subjected to racially abusive language. This white worker could show harassment against herself if the language used against her black colleague also causes an offensive environment for her.

2. The second type of harassment is specifically sexual harassment. This consists of unwanted conduct of a sexual nature or related to gender reassignment which has the same purpose or effect as the first kind of harassment.

   An example given in the notes to the Act is of an employer who displayed any material of a sexual nature, such as a topless calendar. This could amount to harassment of his employees if this makes the workplace an offensive place to work for any employee, whether male or female.

3. The third type is treating someone less favourably than someone else because he or she has previously either submitted to or rejected conduct of a sexual nature or related to sex or gender reassignment.

   The example given here is of a shopkeeper who propositions one of his shop assistants. She rejects his advances and is then turned down for promotion. She believes that she would have got the promotion if she had accepted her employer's advances, and so she would have a claim of harassment.

When deciding whether an intimidating, hostile, etc environment has been created, the perception of the person making the complaint must be taken into account, as well as the other circumstances of the case, and whether it was reasonable for the conduct to have that effect.

The claimant does not have to be the direct recipient of the unwanted conduct. They could simply be witness to someone else's harassment. If the environment at work is degrading, humiliating, hostile, threatening or offensive it can be felt by all those working in it, even those who are not specifically the targets of the conduct, and the law allows such people to bring an action even if the direct victim chooses not to do so himself. The law also protects against harassment based on association or perception.

Third party harassment

In the case law previous to the Equality Act, there was also at times confusion as to whether there was what is known as 'third party harassment'. This is where someone else, not the employer or another employee, but perhaps a client of a customer, harasses the claimant, and this applies to all the protected characteristics apart from marriage/civil partnership and pregnancy and maternity.

This was established as law in the case of *Burton and Rhule v De Vere Hotels* (1997), then overruled by another case, before being reinstated some years later. Two black waitresses, Freda Burton and Sonia Rhule, were working at a hotel where the comedian Bernard Manning was speaking at a dinner. He made very racially offensive remarks, and made the two waitresses the subject of some of his comments. It was found by the court that the event was under the control of the employers, and they could have brought an end to it, or could have withdrawn the waitresses if things became unpleasant. They were therefore liable for third party harassment.

The Equality Act, in section 40, now covers this specifically in employment situations. The section forbids harassment of an employee/applicant by an employer, and says that harassment by third parties also counts as harassment by an employer.

For third party harassment to be found against an employer:

- the harassment must have occurred on at least two previous occasions (although not necessarily by the same harasser or suffering the same type of harassment);
- the employer must be aware that it has taken place; and
- the employer must have failed to take reasonable steps to prevent it from happening again.

This has been criticised for being more stringent than the test in Burton, because it effectively brings in a 'three strikes and out' test (Hepple, 2011:82), and makes it harder to prove. It was put into the statute so that there would be fewer cases and therefore it would be less of a burden on employers, and this is also the reason why, although it came into force in October 2010, the Chancellor indicated in the 2011 Budget that there would be a consultation as to whether this provision should be removed. The future for this type of harassment is therefore uncertain. It is unclear whether, if it is repealed, judges will be able to find a way to reinstate the test in *Burton v De Vere Hotels*.

Defences

In harassment cases the doctrine of vicarious liability applies. This means that the case can be brought against the employer as well as, or instead of, the actual perpetrator of the harassment. This is the case because employers are deemed in law to be responsible for the actions of their employees while they are at work.

It is possible for an employer to mount a defence by claiming that vicarious liability does not apply in a particular case. There are two types of defence that can be deployed:

(a) The employer can show that it took all reasonable steps to prevent the act from occurring and that it acted promptly to deal effectively with the complaint as soon as it was drawn to a manager's attention.

(b) The employer can show that the act did not occur 'during the course of employment'.

The first hinges on the existence of harassment policies, dissemination and training and the fact that the employer took immediate action when informed (eg, suspension, full investigation, appropriate disciplinary action, etc). In the context of the second defence, office parties and social events organised by employees are considered to occur 'during the course of employment' even when they take place on other premises.

Victimisation

The last type of prohibited conduct is known as victimisation. This term is used in law a great deal more narrowly than it is in day-to-day conversational English, and relates to a specific type of situation in the workplace.

The law states that victimisation is intended to cover the situation where the employer, on the grounds of any of the protected characteristics, subjects a person to a detriment because he or she:

(a) brings proceedings under the Equality Act,

(b) gives evidence or information in connection with proceedings,

(c) does any other thing for the purpose of or in connection with the Act

(d) makes an allegation that another person has contravened the Act.

This is different to the former definition of victimisation because there is no longer any need for a comparator.

This is intended to cover the situation where the employer treats the complainant unfavourably because the complainant has had the temerity to, or the employer suspects that he/she is about to, exercise a right under the Act, or support someone else in doing so.

If a person therefore makes a complaint about discrimination, or supports someone else in their complaint, and does this 'in good faith' (in other words not maliciously) in relation to a false complaint, then they are protected from being victimised.

Positive action

In the previous chapter, we discussed formal equality versus substantive equality. Hepple describes direct discrimination as being based on formal equality, in other words ensuring that everyone is treated the same, albeit possibly equally badly. Indirect discrimination is said to be an attempt at substantive equality, trying to make sure that there is equality of opportunity as well as equality of results.

There are other parts of the Act that try to further the idea of substantive equality, such as the public sector duty to promote equality (which is outside the scope of this book), and the idea of positive action.

As we saw in the previous chapter, there is a difference between positive action and positive discrimination. One is lawful, and the other is not.

There are two kinds of positive action that can be taken, set out in sections 158 and 159 of the Equality Act. The first one is known as the general exception relating to positive action measures. It existed before the Act came into force, and is referred to in the previous chapter. It is where the employer can do things such as offering training courses to meet the needs of women or members of ethnic minorities who aspire to be managers, or offering assistance to women returning to work after a period spent raising children.

The second type of positive action relates to recruitment and promotion only and is the kind that was decided by the ECJ to be lawful in the case of *Marschall v Land Nordrhein-Westfalen* (1995), and is now enshrined in the Equality Act. This allows for positive action when an employer is deciding whether to recruit or promote someone with a protected characteristic which is under-represented in the workforce. He can only do so, however, in two very limited circumstances where the candidates are equally qualified. So, for example, if an employer has a shortlist after interview of a white person and a black person who are both equally qualified and with similar experience, he can lawfully employ the black person if black people are under-represented in his workforce. If, however, the white person was better qualified for the role than the black person, then the employer would not be able to favour the black person simply because of their race.

Burden of proof

A person who believes they have been discriminated against can bring an action in the employment tribunal. This has to be done within three months of the discriminatory act complained of.

In general, the claimant has to prove the case that they bring. The EU in the Burden of Proof Directive recognised, however, the difficulty of proving discrimination, and the idea of the reversed burden of proof was established. The Equality Act has extended this to all forms of discrimination because of a protected characteristic.

There are two stages in proving a case. First, the claimant has to prove, on a balance of probabilities, the facts from which a tribunal *could* decide, in the absence of any other explanation, that the respondent has contravened the Equality Act.

If the claimant proves these facts, then the burden of proof 'shifts' to the respondent, who has to prove, again on a balance of probabilities, that he did not contravene the Act.

Remedies

If discrimination is proved, there are a number of remedies that can be awarded. Remedies are considered in Chapter 30, but we shall look at them briefly here in the context of discrimination cases.

Remedies are set out in section 124 of the Equality Act. A claimant can ask for one of three remedies if discrimination is found by the tribunal:

1. A declaration. This can occur in dress code cases for example, where all the claimant is looking for is the right to dress in a particular way in future.

2. A recommendation to the employer which will have the effect of removing the discrimination. This often happens, for example, in sexual harassment cases where a recommendation is made to separate two individuals who work in the same location. This used to be just in relation to the complainant, but the Explanatory Notes to the Act suggest that the power could be used for the benefit of other people.

3. Compensation. This is the most common remedy, and is currently unlimited in discrimination cases, although the Coalition government have suggested that it might be limited in the future. The compensation can include injury to feelings, and there are guidelines for the tribunal as to how much to award, as set out in Chapter 30.

   Compensation is the usual outcome in cases of discriminatory treatment, either because a financial loss has been sustained (for example, following a dismissal or a failure to be recruited), or because there has been a very real injury to feelings (for example in harassment cases).

Debates

There are a number of debates about certain sections of the Equality Act, and whether the law went far enough, or indeed too far. These will be considered in later chapters on particular protected characteristics. Here, we will concentrate on the issue of confusing direct and indirect discrimination.

Direct or Indirect discrimination?

On the face of it, direct and indirect discrimination are very different things. However, they can often be confused, even by the courts. This is important, because if a tribunal decides that a case is one of direct discrimination, and the case is proved, the tribunal is obliged to find in favour of the claimant. The employer is not permitted to defend its actions, because no defence is possible.

By contrast, if the discrimination is found to be of the indirect variety, the employer is given the opportunity to defend itself by putting forward an objective justification.

Sometimes, the courts appear deliberately to decide if something is direct or indirect discrimination, so that account can be taken of the defence of justification, or not as the case may be. One example that we shall look at below is that of the case of *James v Eastleigh Borough Council* (1990).

In a study carried out in 2000, Hepple, Coussey and Choudhury sought views on whether direct discrimination should be allowed to be justified. The overwhelming response was that it should not (Hepple, Coussey and Choudhury, 2000: para 2.43). Bob Hepple's own belief (writing in the context of sex discrimination) is that such a course of action *'would seriously undermine the conceptual framework which is necessary to prevent gender-stereotyping of women and men'* (Hepple 1994:48).

In 2002, Bowers and Moran suggested that legislators should look again at the law, and break the 'taboo' by allowing direct discrimination to be justified. They argued that because legislation which prohibited direct discrimination against part-time workers and those on fixed-term contracts allowed a justification defence (and of course this is now also the case in relation to age discrimination), then there is a basis for allowing justification in general direct discrimination too.

They cite in particular the case of *James v Eastleigh* arguing that the difficulties that the judges had in trying to fit it into the legislation led to an 'unpalatable conclusion' that they felt 'compelled to reach' because of the limitations of the statute (Bowers and Moran, 2002:

Activity 11.4   *James v Eastleigh Borough Council* (1990)

Read the following case which deals with direct and indirect discrimination, and try to answer the questions which come after it. This is not an employment case, but it established important principles which apply in the employment field.

Eastleigh Council charged 75 pence admission to its swimming pools but allowed free swimming 'for children under three years of age and persons who have reached the state pension age'.

In November 1985, Mr James and his wife were both aged sixty-one. He was retired from employment. In accordance with the council's policy, when they went to the swimming pool, since she had reached the state pensionable age which was then sixty for women, she did not have to pay, but as he had not reached the then state pensionable age sixty-five for men, he did have to pay the admission fee. With the support of what was then the Equal Opportunities Commission, Mr James claimed that he had been discriminated against on grounds of sex.

It is clear that he was treated less favourably than his wife, but the question that fell to be decided was 'was the less favourable treatment on the grounds of his sex?' In other words, did it amount to unjustifiable direct sex discrimination?

The Court of Appeal said that it was indirect discrimination because the condition relating to men and women was applied equally to men and women. They agreed with the council's argument that, since it was the council's aim to aid the needy rather than give preference to one sex over the other, any adverse impact was indirect discrimination, and therefore capable of being justified.

The case was appealed to the House of Lords, who decided, on a 3:2 majority, that in fact it was not indirect discrimination, but direct discrimination on the grounds of his sex, and therefore the motive was irrelevant. Lord Goff encapsulated the test as: '*would the complainant have received the same treatment from the defendant 'but for' his or her sex?*'

This meant that the practice could not be justified, and was therefore discriminatory.

Questions

1   Why do you think that Mr James and the EOC were prepared to go all the way to the House of Lords to decide whether he should have to pay 75 pence in order to go swimming?

2   Do you agree with the majority of the House of Lords that this was direct discrimination?

3   If not, was the Court of Appeal correct to say that it was justifiable indirect discrimination?

316–317). If they had been allowed to say that it was direct discrimination and could be justified, there would have been a much clearer outcome.

The article uses in its defence an earlier discredited decision in which Lord Denning effectively tried to say that good motives were acceptable in direct discrimination, and a European case in which the European Commission argued fruitlessly that there should be a defence of justification for direct discrimination. Bowers and Moran say that if the courts had the power to look at the motives of the employer, then this would clarify the law, and that employers could take into account financial motives such as the views of their customers when deciding whether to discriminate.

These arguments raised in the *Industrial Law Journal* were firmly rebutted in a later article in the same journal by Gill and Monaghan (2003), who believe that one of the strengths of UK discrimination law is that there is a distinction between direct and indirect discrimination, and that the former cannot be justified.

They point out that direct discrimination is based on personal characteristics, such as gender, whereas indirect discrimination is not personal, but has an incidental effect. They follow this through by stating that discrimination against fixed-term workers and part-timers is also not personal, but based on their job status. An additional point that they omit to make is that the statutory prohibition of discrimination against fixed-term and part-time workers is effectively a formalised form of the judicial decisions about indirect discrimination, as such workers tend to be women, and that as indirect discrimination, this would have been justifiable in any event. It is the fact that direct discrimination is personal that makes it '*undermine the dignity of the worker*' (Gill and Monaghan 2003:119). This can be seen clearly by the fact that until recently, damages were not awarded for cases of indirect discrimination, only direct discrimination, although this is not mentioned in the article.

Gill and Monaghan point to the inherent danger of Bower's and Moran's idea of allowing employers to justify direct discrimination on economic grounds, by saying that this would lead to more discrimination, because the more prejudiced the customers, the more justified the discrimination would be, as the employer would be able to say that he was just following the diktats of his business (Gill and Monaghan 2003:120).

Since then, the Supreme Court Judge Lord Phillips has weighed in on the argument in the *Jewish Free School* case (2010) (discussed in more detail in Chapter 17), by suggesting

there may well be a defect in our law of discrimination. In contrast to the law in many countries, where English law forbids direct discrimination it provides no defence of justification. It is not easy to envisage justification for discriminating against a minority racial group. Such discrimination is almost inevitably the result of irrational prejudice or ill-will. But it is possible to envisage circumstances where giving preference to a minority racial group will be justified. Giving preference to cater for the special needs of a minority will not normally involve any prejudice or ill-will towards the majority. Yet a policy which directly favours one racial group will be held to constitute racial discrimination against all who are not members of that group.

The Equality Act has kept the law as it was in terms of no justification of direct discrimination (apart from age discrimination), although it has made it easier to prove indirect discrimination.

Exhibit 11.4

The main changes made by the Equality Act 2010 are:

1 Discrimination against people on grounds of gender reassignment and pregnancy/maternity were explicitly added to the existing list of 'protected characteristics'.

2 The requirement for gender reassignment to be occurring 'under medical supervision' at the point of discrimination in order for an individual to be able to bring a claim has been removed.

3 The wording of the definition of direct discrimination has been changed from 'on grounds of' to 'because of'. This means that associative and perceptive discrimination in respect of all the protected grounds are now included.

4 The need for a comparator in victimisation claims has been removed.

5 The principle of indirect discrimination, long established in the fields of sex and race discrimination and present in the more recent discrimination laws, has been extended to cover disability discrimination.

6 The highly controversial '*Malcolm* judgment' has been overturned with the creation of a new type of disability discrimination labelled 'discrimination arising from disability'. There is therefore now no requirement for a disabled person to establish that they have been treated less favourably than any comparator.

7 The statutory definition of a 'disability' has been amended so that there is no longer a need to show that someone's impairment affects one of eight named 'bodily functions'.

8 The Act clarified a confusion in the previous law by stating that an employer will not be committing an act of disability discrimination if at the time it could not reasonably have been expected to know about an employee's disability.

9 Equal pay law has been amended in mainly minor ways to make it more easily understood and to bring occupational pensions fully within its remit. 'Comparators' are now 'colleagues' while 'genuine material factors' are now simply 'material factors'.

10 The Act seeks to increase the power of employment tribunals to make recommendations about an employer's practices in rulings on discrimination matters so that they apply across a whole workforce and not just the individual claimants.

11 The Act includes specific reference to 'third party harassment'.

CHAPTER SUMMARY

- The Equality Act has brought together all the previous discrimination legislation and put it under one statute.

- The Act lists discrimination under headings of protected characteristics and prohibited conduct.

- Direct discrimination cannot be justified.

- There are exceptions to direct discrimination called occupational requirements, but these can only be used if essential to the role.

- Indirect discrimination can be justified if it is a proportionate means of achieving a legitimate aim.

- There are three different kinds of harassment, only one of which is of general application.

- There is no longer any need for a comparator in cases of victimisation.

REFERENCES

ACAS (2011) 'The Equality Act—What's new for employers?' London: Advisory, Conciliation and Arbitration Service.

Bowers, J. and Moran, E. (2002) 'Justification in sex discrimination law: breaking the taboo' *Industrial Law Journal* 31.4.

Explanatory Notes to the Equality Act 2010.

Forshaw, S. and Pilgerstorfer, M. 'Direct and indirect discrimination: Is there something in between?' *Industrial Law Journal* 37.4.

Gill, T. and Monaghan, K. (2003) 'Justification in sex discrimination law: taboo upheld' *Industrial Law Journal* 32.2.

Harvey on Industrial Relations and Employment Law. Butterworths: London (1972–present) (looseleaf).

Hepple, B. (1994) 'Can direct discrimination be justified?' *Equal Opportunities Review* 48.

Hepple, B. (2011) *Equality: The New Legal Framework*. Oxford: Hart Publishing.

Hepple, B., Coussey M. and Choudhury T. (2000) *Equality: A New Framework*. Oxford: Hart Publishing.

IDS (2008) *Employment Law Handbook*. Thomson Publishing.

IDS (2010) *Equality Act 2010*. Thomson Publishing.

Selwyn, N. (2011) *Selwyn's Law of Employment*. Oxford: Oxford University Press.

Wadham, J. (2010) 'New equality landscape' 160 *New Law Journal* 1482.

ONLINE RESOURCE CENTRE

A range of online resources to help you through your employment law module have been developed by the author team. These include updates, self-test questions and sources for further reading. (www.oxfordtextbooks.co.uk/orc/taylor_emir3e)

Age discrimination

Learning outcomes

By the end of this chapter you should be able to:

- participate in debates about the aims of age discrimination law;
- discuss the extent to which these are achieved in practice by legislation;
- state how and when an employer can retire an employee;
- advise employers what steps they must take to comply with the law on age discrimination.

Introduction

While sex and race discrimination legislation have been with us for several decades, and disability discrimination since the 1995 Disability Discrimination Act, it was not until the European Union enacted Framework Directive 2000/78/EC, following on from the Treaty of Amsterdam in 1997, that further areas of discrimination were covered. These were religion, sexual orientation and age. The Employment Equality (Age) Regulations came into force in 2006, and age is now a protected characteristic in the Equality Act. Even though it was the last characteristic to be prohibited, it is rapidly becoming one of the most litigated areas of discrimination law. The tribunal statistics in 2010–2011 show that age discrimination cases rose by almost a third from the previous year, to 6,800 cases a year, and that they are now the third most litigated type of discrimination, after sex and disability (Chamberlain, 2011).

Activity 12.1

Consider the following situations and state whether the employers' actions are lawful. Give reasons for your answer. When you have finished reading the chapter, come back to this activity and see how many of your answers were correct.

1 A youth club advertises for a youth club leader who is less than twenty-eight years of age and who is able to work in the evenings.

2 Alfred is sixty-five. His employer retires him because the employer believes that sixty-five is an appropriate retirement age for all occupations.

3 Maya is nineteen. She is refused a job because her employer does not think that a nineteen-year-old would have the experience required.

History and background

Age discrimination was described by the former Trade and Industry Secretary Patricia Hewitt as *'the last bastion of lawful unfair discrimination in the workplace'*. Hepple states that it became a major social demand because of longer life spans, longer periods of retirement, and the decline in pension provision (Hepple 2011:29). It has been unlawful in the UK since October 2006 when the last part of the Framework Directive was implemented into domestic legislation.

The main impetus for the outlawing of age discrimination lies in changing demographics. The population of the UK and of the EU is an ageing one, as healthcare and living standards have improved and people are living longer, while for a long time fewer babies were being born. The April 2000 report *Winning the Generation Game* states that:

> projections suggest that the working age population will start declining in almost all EU countries by 2015, by when the population aged 55–64 will have risen to 22 per cent of the total compared to just 16 per cent now. These trends are starting to cause serious alarm about the future supply of labour.

More recent figures published by the Office for National Statistics found that over the past twenty-five years, the number of people aged over sixty-five has risen dramatically, whereas those younger than sixteen has fallen (Mid-year population estimates, Office for National Statistics, www.statistics.gov.uk accessed 2011).

It may be that these alarms had some part in leading to the agreement to implement age discrimination legislation. The aim may well in part be to increase the numbers of older people in the workplace, rather than a respect for rights and equality. Indeed, the view of Colm O'Cinneide is that '*much of the political and legal response to age discrimination across the EU has been driven by a utilitarian approach, with the emphasis being on patching up the labour market rather than adopting a rights based approach*' (O'Cinneide, 2003). This argument is furthered by Sargeant, who comments that the then government, in its consultation on how the then Regulations should be drafted, took on board many of the wishes of employers, and that this has diluted the impact of the Regulations and put limitations on their effectiveness (Sargeant, 2006). It would thus appear that it is most likely that the impetus behind the Age Regulations, and therefore the age part of the Equality Act, is economic rather than social.

In the past, a number of cases were brought under other branches of legislation, in cases where age is a factor. Examples are cases such as *Price v Civil Service Commission* (1978), where the court found that imposing an age requirement of seventeen to twenty-eight was indirect sex discrimination against women who had taken time off to have children. This is not satisfactory, however, as only indirect discrimination can be argued. Moreover, it does not cover all situations, as was seen in the case of *Rutherford and Bentley v Secretary of State for Trade and Industry* (2004), in which the appellants' argument that the upper age limit for bringing a claim of unfair dismissal or redundancy under the Employment Rights Act was indirectly discriminatory was dismissed by the Court of Appeal.

One aim of prohibiting age discrimination given by the then Labour government is to provide choice to workers. As Alan Johnson, then Trade and Industry Secretary, said '*It's all about choice—not work till you drop but choose when you stop*'. This was echoed by the Coalition in its response to the consultation on the abolition of the default retirement age: '*These changes do not mean that individuals can no longer retire at 65—simply that the timing of that retirement becomes a matter of choice rather than compulsion.*'

It remains to be seen whether the legislation will have the required effect and will work in practice. In 2010 figures published by the Department of Communities and Local Government as part of the Citizenship Survey: 2009–2010 show that ageism is still the biggest single reason for discrimination in recruitment. 4 per cent of all workers aged fifty and over—estimated to be in excess of 300,000—say they have been refused a job because of their age in the past five years (Berry, 2010).

Protected characteristic

The Equality Act applies to people of every age—not just old people. It is equally important to protect younger people as older ones because people make assumptions about their limited ability, or may be worried that clients may not like having a younger person dealing with them. This is as much age discrimination as not employing a fifty-year-old because he or she is not apparently as dynamic-looking as a twenty-five-year-old person. The idea is that people should be judged on merit and not assumptions or stereotypes. The Equality Act also makes clear that it is not just a person's age that is protected from discrimination, but also a person's age group, so, for example, there can be no discrimination against someone who falls within the 'over fifties' age group, or 'those aged forty-five to fifty'. This is quite widely defined, and appears to allow the claimant to define the disadvantaged age group as he or she wishes.

 Exhibit 12.1   *Wilkinson v Springwell Engineering Limited* **(2007)**

Leanne Wilkinson was a nineteen-year-old admin assistant. She was dismissed from her job at Springwell Engineering in Newcastle because she was too young, and the firm wanted an older person with more experience. The employer said that the dismissal was based on capability, but the employment tribunal found that there was no evidence that she lacked in performance. They also found that the employer had expressly stated that they were dismissing the claimant because she was too young for the job. The employment tribunal also stated however that, even if such a statement had not been made, discrimination could be inferred from the employer's stereotypical assumption that a link exists between age, experience and capability.

Prohibited conduct

The Equality Act makes illegal all forms of prohibited conduct on grounds of age discrimination, including associated, perceived and deterred discrimination.

 **Activity 12.2**

Brian is thirty-eight. He works for an internet company. Brian is also the main carer for his elderly father. He is refused time off to help take his father to hospital. He feels that this is discriminatory, and points out that another employee was recently given time off to go to the dentist in work hours.
   Is this discrimination? If so, what kind?

Direct discrimination

This is set out in section 13 of the Act. Direct discrimination is less favourable treatment because of someone's age, for example, deciding not to employ or dismiss someone, refusing training or promotion or retiring them before the employer's usual retirement age. Unlike direct discrimination in most other types of discrimination, however, direct discrimination because of age can be objectively justified. If, therefore, an employer can show that the treatment of the person is a proportionate means of achieving a legitimate aim, then this treatment would not amount to discrimination.

There have been a number of other examples of justification being allowed by the courts, the most notable being in the ECJ. In the case of *Palacios de la Villa v Cortefiel el Servicios SA* (2008), for example, the ECJ said that a Spanish law allowing compulsory retirement on the grounds of age was not discriminatory, as it was justified as an appropriate and necessary means of checking unemployment and encouraging recruitment.

Like other types of prohibited conduct, direct discrimination on grounds of age requires a comparator. This would be a person who is not of that person's age or age group, and can be real or hypothetical.

Indirect discrimination

Indirect discrimination because of age is covered by section 19 of the Equality Act. Examples of areas in which indirect discrimination can arise include selection criteria, policies, benefits, employment rules or any other practices which, although they are applied to all employees, have the effect of disadvantaging people of a particular age, unless this can be justified. Selwyn (2011:140) suggests that the aim of such indirect age discrimination is aimed at disguised age barriers, not barriers that stem from retirement, and uses the case of *Homer v Chief Constable of West Yorkshire Police* (2010) to illustrate this. In that case, it was a requirement that the post holder should have a law degree. The claimant was sixty-one years old, and could not comply with that requirement before he retired. His claim of indirect discrimination failed. It was held by the Court of Appeal that the particular disadvantage suffered by him stemmed from the fact that his working life would have come to an end before he could qualify, and thus was an inevitable result of age, and that therefore it was not discriminatory. This is a case which we would submit is quite limited on its facts. It is due to be the first age indirect discrimination case to be heard in the Supreme Court.

Harassment and victimisation

This applies as the section 26 harassment, as well as harassment by third parties under section 40. Victimisation is prohibited under section 27 as is discrimination in employment under section 39.

Exceptions and exemptions

There were a number of exceptions in the original Regulations, which were criticised by Sargeant because there were so many of them that he suggested they effectively legitimised some aspects of age discrimination at work (Sargeant, 2006). These are generally preserved in the new law. In addition to occupational requirements, which should of course only apply in very limited circumstances, the law allows for a number of other exceptions. These are matters such as pay related to retirement, the national minimum wage, and benefits based on length of service.

Occupational requirements

This is in Schedule 9 to the Act, and for age discrimination an example of this could be where a play is being staged and an elderly person is required to play King Lear. The ECJ considered this in the case of *Wolf v Stadt Frankfurt am Main* (2010), where it decided that a requirement that applicants for jobs in the fire service should be under the age of thirty was justifiable as a genuine and occupational requirement. They noted that the fire-fighting and rescue duties were only carried out by younger officers, and that recruitment at an older age would have the consequences that too large a number of firemen could not be assigned to the most physically demanding duties.

This has been a somewhat controversial decision, with IDS describing it as a surprising result (IDS, 2010:227). Their view is that EU law may be becoming less stringent on the question of what may be accepted as an occupational requirement. In this case, the requirement was found to be justified because the kind of work required a high level of physical capacity, and the argument that such capacity inevitably declines with age appeared to be accepted. In other words, as IDS points out, the ECJ allowed the employer to rely on age as an indicator of physical fitness.

IDS also points to another reason why this case is controversial, which is that the parties argued that there was an occupational requirement. There was no need for this, as the Directive allows age discrimination to be objectively justified, and the occupational requirement is intended to be reserved for exceptional cases. If the same reasoning is applied to other types of prohibited conduct, OR might permit the application of a lower age limit to women, or even the exclusion of women from the fire service altogether, on the ground that they are not as physically strong as men (IDS, 2010:227).

Dismissal for reason of retirement

This is enshrined in Schedule 9, Part 2 of the Act, and allows for an employer to set a retirement age that he can objectively justify. Until October 2011, there was a default retirement

---

 Exhibit 12.2　　**The 'Heyday Case' (R (Age UK) v Secretary of State for BIS (2009))**

This was a case brought by Age Concern, which challenged the default retirement age. It went all the way up to the ECJ, which found that the default retirement age of sixty-five can be justified and is therefore lawful, but that there was a 'compelling case' for raising or removing it.

In order to show that the default retirement age was justified, the government had to show that the reason for having it was to meet a legitimate social policy aim, and that this was proportionate. The aim was to maintain confidence in the labour market, and this was found to be legitimate and proportionate by the ECJ.

It was however pointed out by the court that the default retirement age did not require employers to dismiss employees at the relevant age, but rather it allowed them to do so. The court also said that the retirement age was designed to give employer and employees certainty for planning purposes.

The case was then sent back to the High Court, where the judge, Mr Justice Blake, decided that the introduction of the default retirement age in the Age Regulations 2006 had been lawful, but he also gave a strong message to the government that there is a 'compelling case' that the default retirement age should either be raised or removed as a result of the review that the government had pledged to hold.

He said that, 'in view of the changed economic circumstances, and the generally recognised problems that a longer living population created for the social security system' had the default retirement age been introduced in 2009, rather than in 2006, he would have found that the default retirement age was not a proportionate way of maintaining confidence in the labour market. However, the default retirement age had been introduced when the country was in a different economic climate. The judge also indicated that the government's proposed changes strongly influenced his decision not to make a ruling that the legislation should be reconsidered.

The default retirement age has been abolished since this decision.

age of sixty-five. Provided an employer followed the set procedure, he could lawfully retire an employee at sixty-five without having to give any reason, or having to justify the retirement. This has now been abolished, together with the special procedures that accompanied it, but this does not mean that an employer can never retire an employee. An employer can set his own retirement age, but only if he can show that there is an objective reason for it. The former age limit of sixty-five was called the 'default retirement age', and the latter is often referred to as the 'employer-justified retirement age'.

The default retirement age was abolished by the Coalition government as one of the measures taken to allow people to work for longer, and so ease the strain on the economy (as well as the choice argument discussed above). The abolition came into force in April 2011, with transitional arrangements until October 2011. It is expected that case law in relation to the employer-justified retirement age will increase now that the default retirement age is no longer in use. Up to now, the employer-justified retirement age has tended to be used only in exceptional circumstances in which an employer has a retirement age under sixty-five (ACAS, 2011). ACAS gives as an example posts in the emergency services which require a significant level of physical fitness or other occupations requiring exceptional mental and/or physical fitness such as air traffic controllers (also such as in the *Wolf* case referred to earlier).

The employer-justified retirement age up to now has also been used where the default retirement age has not applied, such as in a partnership, as in the case of *Seldon v Clarkson Wright and Jakes* (2010), which is discussed in further detail below.

In order to justify a retirement age, an employer has to show that it is objectively justified. This means two things—first of all that there is a legitimate aim in setting that particular retirement age, such as workforce planning (ACAS gives examples as the need for business to recruit, retain and provide promotion opportunities and effectively manage succession), or for health and safety reasons, such as in the fire-fighter case referred to above. Once the legitimate aim is established, the second aspect is for the employer to show that setting that particular retirement age is a proportionate means of achieving that aim.

 Exhibit 12.3   *Seldon v Clarkson Wright and Jakes* (2010)

This was a case that concerned the retirement of a partner in a solicitors' firm. There was a policy for partners of the firm to retire at the age of sixty-five. This was set out in the partnership agreement.

Mr Seldon was a partner who did not want to retire at sixty-five, and so brought a claim to a tribunal. The tribunal found that the retirement age was justified. He appealed to the EAT, which reversed the tribunal decision. It made the following points:

1   The tribunal was correct to find that it was a legitimate aim to ensure that associate solicitors have the opportunity to become a partner after a reasonable period (referred to as the 'dead men's shoes' aim).

2   It was also a legitimate aim to facilitate the planning of the partnership and the workforce across individual departments.   »

> **3** The EAT found, however, that a third aim of maintaining the friendly culture of a law firm by avoiding confrontation with underperforming partners close to retirement was not legitimate (referred to as the 'collegiality' aim). The EAT said that suggesting that partners of or around the age of sixty-five are more likely to underperform involves a stereotypical assumption and the law firm produced no evidence that partners of that age have particular performance difficulties.
>
> Mr Seldon then took his case to the Court of Appeal. By this time the *Heyday* decision referred to above had been decided. The Court of Appeal agreed with the EAT and dismissed his appeal. They disagreed with Mr Seldon and accepted that there could be a legitimate aim of 'dead men's shoes'. They accepted that an employer or partnership may have slightly mixed motives, but said that if the aim is to provide employment prospects for young people and encourage them to seek employment by holding out good promotion prospects, then that is consistent with social policy.
>
> The court also found against Mr Seldon's argument and disagreed with the Court of Appeal in relation to the 'collegiality' aim. They said that an aim intended to produce a happy workplace has to be consistent with the social policy justification for the Regulations. It can be a legitimate aim to have a cut-off age after which individuals are required to retire to avoid forcing an assessment of a person's falling-off in performance, thus maintaining a confrontation-free workplace.
>
> At the time of writing (summer 2011), Mr Seldon had been given leave to appeal to the Supreme Court, and the decision is awaited. Please check the updates on our online resource centre (see end of chapter) for further information.

Although the set procedure that accompanied the default retirement age has been abolished, it is still important to have a fair procedure. Employees should be given proper notice of the retirement age and the fact that it is approaching, and any request to stay on should be considered on its merits, although it is important to make sure that consistency is maintained between employees.

Service-related benefits

It is often a standard feature of employment that pay and benefits improve as the employment continues. This would inevitably amount to indirect age discrimination as older workers are more likely to have completed more service than younger workers, and so there is a specific exemption for this in Schedule 9 to the Act to ensure that an employer does not have to justify paying or providing fewer benefits to a worker with less service than a comparator.

If the length of service exceeds five years, the exception applies only if the employer can show that the reason the criterion was used was to fulfil a business need of the undertaking, for example, by encouraging loyalty or motivation, or rewarding the experience of some or all of his workers.

In other words, if an employee has been employed for less than five years, he can complain if he is not given a benefit based on long service where another employee has been given that benefit. An employer can defend himself by showing the 'business need' as described.

Some examples given in the notes to the Act are:

- An employer's pay system includes an annual move up a pay spine, or a requirement that a certain amount of time must elapse before an employee is entitled to be a member of an employee benefits scheme. Provided that the pay spine or time it takes to get the benefit is no longer than five years or can be justified the exception will apply.

- An employer's terms and conditions relating to annual leave entitlement provide that employees are entitled to an additional five days' leave after ten years' of service. Such an entitlement needs to be justified as reasonably fulfilling a business need.

Enhanced redundancy payments

The statutory redundancy scheme requires an employer to make a redundancy payment based on age, length of service and weekly pay, as described in Chapter 6. If an employer has an enhanced scheme which is based on the statutory scheme, but which offers more generous terms, this is permitted and would not be discriminatory. An example is *Rolls Royce v Unite the Union* (2009), which found that length of service was a lawful criterion for selection for redundancy since it achieved a legitimate aim by a proportionate means.

Further exemptions

There are further exemptions in the legislation. The first is in relation to the national minimum wage (which provides different levels of payment based on age). If the employer bases his pay structure on the national minimum wage legislation, then this would be acceptable. The government's intention in doing this was ostensibly to protect young workers, and promote their employment, because if they are cheaper, businesses may be more likely to employ them, and less likely to make them redundant. Other exemptions are those covering life assurance, childcare benefits (an employer can, for example, use the age of a child to provide crèche facilities) and pension benefits.

 Exhibit 12.4

The Chartered Institute of Personnel and Development (CIPD) suggests that employers consider the following good practice when seeking to avoid discriminating on grounds of age.

Advertising—Age, age-related criteria or age ranges should not be used in advertisements other than to encourage applications from age groups which do not usually apply. Where this is the case, it should be clearly stated.

Application forms—It is desirable to state that age criteria will not be taken into account in employment decisions but used only for monitoring purposes. This information should be asked for in a 'tear-off' section of the application form and be kept separate from the application process.

Interviews—Interviewers and those concerned with selection must not be subjective on the basis of physical characteristics and unfounded assumptions.

Medical advice—An individual's age should not be used to make judgements about their abilities or fitness. Where such a judgement is required, an occupational health or medical practitioner should be consulted.

Reward—Pay and terms of employment should not be based on age-related criteria, but should reflect the value of individual contributions and standards of job performance.

Training and development—Should be open to all employees as there is the potential to waste talent if particular age groups, eg, those near retirement, are automatically excluded from training and development programmes.

>> **Retention and redundancy**—When releasing employees, the organisation's future needs for knowledge, skills and competencies should be taken into account.

Alternatives to redundancy should be considered, such as shorter hours, part-time working, contractual arrangements, secondments and perhaps employment breaks.

Retirement—Research from CIPD indicates that many older workers would welcome an opportunity:

- for phased retirement
- for flexible working
- to work beyond the normal retirement age
- to work on a self-employed basis
- to work in the voluntary sector.

Organisations should also consider the advantages of using retirees as mentors to pass on experience and develop other employees through use of their knowledge and expertise. See www.cipd.co.uk

There is also excellent guidance available from ACAS (ACAS, 2006).

Debates

Although the law covers all the main elements of direct discrimination, indirect discrimination, harassment and victimisation, age discrimination is different from other forms of discrimination legislation in that it does not first identify a characteristic of a minority group and then remove that factor from the decision-making process, but rather it has a quality common to all (ie, age), and seeks only to prevent reliance on it for purposes that are 'illegitimate' or if the consequences of doing so are 'disproportionate'. This has been described as an uncertainty at the core of the Regulations, because it is unclear '*what form of equality*' the Regulations are intended to bring (Swift, 2006). Is it formal or substantive? This would further appear to support the view that the legislation is 'utilitarian' and business-oriented, rather than being based on principles of equality. The number of exceptions and the fact that direct age discrimination can be justified would also go to support that position.

CHAPTER SUMMARY

- Direct age discrimination, unlike other protected characteristics, can be justified.
- There is no longer a default retirement age in the UK.
- If an employer wishes to retire an employee at a particular age, he has to have objective reasons for choosing that age.
- Unlike other protected characteristics, there are a number of other exceptions, such as length of service benefits, which have been kept from the Age Regulations of 2006.

REFERENCES

ACAS (2006) *Age and the workplace: putting the employment equality (age) regulations 2006 into practice*. London: Advisory, Conciliation and Arbitration Service.

ACAS (2011) *Working without the DRA*. London: Advisory, Conciliation and Arbitration Service.

Berry, M. (2010) 'Age discrimination warning for growing numbers of older workers' *Personnel Today*, 26 July.

BIS (2011) 'Phasing out the default retirement age: Government Response to Consultation'.

Chamberlain (2011) 'Age discrimination claims up by one third' *Personnel Today*, 1 July.

Hepple, B. (2011) *Equality, The New Legal Framework*. Oxford: Hart Publishing.

O'Cinneide, C. (2003) 'Comparative European Perspectives on Age Discrimination Legislation' in S. Fredman & S. Spencer (eds): *Age as an Equality Issue: Legal and Policy Perspectives*. Oxford: Hart Publishing.

Office for National Statistics (2011) 'Mid-year population estimates', www.statistics.gov.uk, accessed 7 August 2011.

Performance and Innovation Unit (2000) *Winning the Generation Game* (available at www.number-10.gov.uk).

Rubenstein, M. (2002) 'Golden Threads Among the Silver: Principles for Age Discrimination Law' *Equal Opportunities Review* 115, March 2003.

Sargeant, M. (2004) 'Age discrimination in employment in further and higher education' *Education Law Journal* 91.

Sargeant, M. (2006) 'The Employment Equality (Age) Regulations 2006: a legitimisation of age discrimination in employment' *Industrial Law Journal* 35 (p209).

Selwyn, N. (2011) *Selwyn's Law of Employment*. Oxford: Oxford University Press.

Swift, J. (2006) 'Justifying age discrimination' *Industrial Law Journal* 35 (p 228).

ONLINE RESOURCE CENTRE

A range of online resources to help you through your employment law module have been developed by the author team. These include updates, self-test questions and sources for further reading. (www.oxfordtextbooks.co.uk/orc/taylor_emir3e)

Disability discrimination

Learning outcomes

By the end of this chapter you should be able to:

- trace the history of disability discrimination legislation in the UK;

- define the term 'disability' and explain its component elements;

- say what is meant by discrimination arising from disability;

- state what 'reasonable adjustments' are and what steps an employer is expected to take in accommodating them;

- set out when an employer is permitted to ask a candidate about his health; and

- explain and discuss the two models of disability.

Introduction

In terms of its practical effect on employers, the introduction of comprehensive disability discrimination law in 1996 represented a significant extension of employment legislation. Widely criticised at the time of its introduction, disability discrimination law remains controversial, despite the passing of several pieces of amending legislation in the years since. For disability campaigners it falls well short of the full and proper provision they have long campaigned for. Moreover, they can cite legislation in other countries such as the USA which provides more substantial protection without damaging economic efficiency. Smaller employers tend to take the opposite view, arguing that disability discrimination law can severely limit the flexibility they require to compete effectively. Lawyers criticised the original DDA for being unclear about key issues and for being sloppily drafted, but this has recently been harmonised with other areas in the Equality Act. A more recent line of criticism relates to the contention of many that UK law in this field still falls well short of European expectations despite the introduction of amendments designed to bring it into line with the relevant EU directives. Nonetheless it remains the case that the disability discrimination law has had a major impact, particularly as regards the way that employers deal with staff who fall seriously ill. Thousands of claims have been brought under the Act and very substantial sums of money won by victorious claimants, making it one of the most litigated areas of discrimination law. This is not therefore an area of law that any employer can afford to ignore.

 Activity 13.1

Read the following paragraphs and try to answer the questions that follow. If you return to the activity again when you have finished reading the chapter, you should be able to give full and accurate answers to the questions.

John Smith is employed as a sales manager at PQS Ltd, a company which manufactures soft drinks. He is one of a team of sales personnel whose job involves expanding the company's customer base and trying to interest existing customers in increasing the quantity of goods they buy. About half of John's time is spent on the road visiting clients and attending sales events; he is based in his office the rest of the time.

Last week the company's sales director telephoned you in your capacity as personnel manager to ask your advice. He tells you that John Smith has developed a medical condition which results in him suffering from occasional epileptic fits. He is taking medication to control his condition and will probably make a full recovery over the course of a year or two. In the meantime, however, John is banned from driving and has been told to avoid stressful situations.

The sales director believes that the company cannot continue to employ John because his job involves both driving and stressful situations.

Questions

1 What are the main legal implications that arise from the situation outlined above?

2 What course of action would you recommend was taken?

Historical background

Disability discrimination took much longer to outlaw than discrimination on grounds of sex or race, and it was not until 1995 that the original Disability Discrimination Act was enacted in Britain, although it was clear that many people needed its protection. It is estimated that there are about 14 million disabled adults in the UK, and even by 2010, fifteen years after the passing of the DDA, only 21% of disabled men were employed full time, compared with two-thirds of men who are not disabled (National Equality Panel, quoted in Hepple, 2011:32). In December 2010 a study by the Office for National Statistics found that more than half of disabled people would like to work more (quoted in Gilbert, 2010). The Life Opportunities Survey by the Office for Disability Issues found that people with disabilities were twice as likely as others not to be able to work (quoted in Paton, 2011).

As Baroness Hollis of Heigham (then Parliamentary Under-Secretary of State, Department for Work and Pensions) said during the debate in the House of Lords prior to the passing of the Disability Discrimination Act 2005:

> Disabled people face greater difficulties than most. They encounter institutional ignorance and misunderstanding, individual prejudice and the all-too-familiar barriers to access in every walk of life. That can have a devastating effect on their opportunities and self-esteem.

There was initially some attempt at legislating during the Second World War, as an attempt to assist the many disabled servicemen that were returning from the battlefields. This resulted in the Disabled Persons (Employment) Act 1944. The main purpose of that Act was to set up a registration system for the disabled, and established a quota of 3% disabled employees for employers of twenty or more, making it a criminal offence for such employers not to comply. It also established a reserved occupations scheme, whereby some jobs were to be kept especially for registered disabled people. Only two occupations were in fact reserved—those of electric lift attendant and car park attendant—which reinforced the impression that disabled people were only capable of low-grade and low-paid employment. Although this statute was a step in the right direction, its effect was minor, because of limitations in the way that it was drafted. Many people did not register as disabled, feeling that it was a stigma to do so. Moreover, employers could easily apply for exemptions, and so the legislation was hardly ever enforced.

After those early years, disability rights campaigners became more vociferous, and other countries such as the United States, Australia and New Zealand led the way, which gave more impetus to those campaigning for change in the UK and resulted in the DDA 1995. This statute was described in the case of *Clark v TDG t/a Novacold* (1999), the first Court of Appeal decision relating to the statute, as '*a revolutionary Act, aimed at the integration of disabled people into society and, in particular, into the country's workforce*'.

Despite its efforts to combat discrimination, there were several aspects of the Act that initially attracted disapproval. Employers thought that it was too restrictive, while disability groups were of the opinion that it did not go far enough. The statute itself was badly drafted and was described by Lord Lester as being '*riddled with vague, slippery and elusive exceptions, making it so full of holes that it is more like a colander than a binding code*'.

The 1995 Act was later the subject of a number of amendments, culminating in the Equality Act 2010. These have not obliterated entirely all the complaints about the legislation, but as Lord Justice Mummery said in *Clark v TDG t/a Novacold* (1999):

Anyone who thinks that there is an easy way of achieving a sensible, workable and fair balance between the different interests of disabled persons, of employers and of able-bodied workers, in harmony with the wider public interests in an economically efficient workforce, in access to employment, in equal treatment of workers and in standards of fairness at work, has probably not given much serious thought to the problem.

He also described the DDA as *'an unusually complex piece of legislation which poses novel questions of interpretation'*. This was echoed by Lord Bingham in *London Borough of Lewisham v Malcolm* (2008), calling it:

an ambitious and complex Act, seeking . . . to prevent disabled people being treated disadvantageously because of their disability. It sought to do this in a primarily negative way, by proscribing as unlawful certain acts of discrimination in several fields.

Notwithstanding criticism of the details of the legislation, it has had a substantial effect on employment law in Britain. The legislation has many imperfections, but it is a great deal better in achieving a degree of justice than its predecessor, the 1944 Act. The major effect has been in the area of ill health dismissals. Whereas previously it was not unlawful to dismiss someone for this reason, now, if the complainant comes within the definition of a disabled person, it can only be lawful to dismiss him because of his disability where reasonable adjustments cannot be made in order to accommodate his needs. This has led to a wholesale change in employer practice and must have benefited hundreds of thousands of workers.

Protected characteristic

One of the major differences between the law relating to disability discrimination and other areas of discrimination, such as sex and race, is the fact that the disability law is not symmetrical. In other words it only protects disabled people, whereas the protected characteristic of sex, for example, can be used by both men and women. The reason for this lies in the ethos behind the statute. As Lady Hale said in the case of *Archibald v Fife* in 2004, the then Disability Discrimination Act was concerned with addressing the needs of disabled people, whereas the Sex Discrimination and Race Relations Acts wanted everyone to be treated equally. The DDA focused on the reason for the treatment, rather than just comparing disabled with non-disabled:

. . . this legislation is different from the Sex Discrimination Act 1975 and the Race Relations Act 1976. In the latter two, men and women or black and white, as the case may be, are opposite sides of the same coin. Each is to be treated in the same way. Treating men more favourably than women discriminates against women. Treating women more favourably discriminates against men. Pregnancy apart, the differences between the genders are generally regarded as irrelevant. The 1995 Act, however, does not regard the differences between disabled people and others as irrelevant. It does not expect each to be treated in the same way. It expects reasonable adjustments to be made to cater for the special needs of disabled people. It necessarily entails an element of more favourable treatment.

This also means that it is not unlawful to have positive measures to improve things for disabled people.

Definition of disability

Guidance to the definition of disability is set out in section 6 of the Equality Act. In essence, someone has a disability if they have a physical or mental impairment, and this impairment has a substantial and long-term adverse effect on their ability to carry out normal day-to-day activities.

Not being able to show that they are disabled is the main hurdle at which many claimants fall. Most disabled people are not visibly disabled, and the EAT (in *Goodwin v The Patent Office* (1999)) said that tribunals should not have '*a stereotypical image of a person in a wheelchair*' in mind when deciding if someone is disabled. They should, instead, look at each of the elements, and decide:

- Does the applicant have an impairment that is either mental or physical?
- Does this impairment affect his ability to carry out normal day-to-day activities and does it have an adverse effect?
- Is the adverse effect long-term?
- Is the adverse effect substantial?

There has been substantial litigation on exactly what each of the elements of discrimination means. Schedule 1 to the Act gives further guidance, as does the accompanying Code of Practice by the Office for Disability Issues.

Physical or mental impairment

The disability has to be present at the time of the alleged discrimination. The court has to decide whether, looking at all the evidence, including the medical evidence, the applicant has an impairment. In relation to mental impairments, there used to be a requirement that this had to be a clinically recognised illness, but that is no longer necessary. With disability, it is very important that each case is looked at on its own facts.

It is the effects of the impairment which need to be considered when deciding if someone is disabled, rather than the underlying conditions themselves. The Code gives the following example:

> A woman has obesity which gives rise to impairments such as mobility restrictions and breathing difficulties. She is unable to walk more than 50 yards without having to rest.

Some people, such as those with cancer, HIV infection and multiple sclerosis will be treated as being disabled from the time that they are diagnosed. People who are registered blind or partially sighted also do not have to show substantial adverse effect etc.

The Code sets out a number of conditions which are not to be treated as impairments. These are addictions to alcohol, nicotine etc (unless the substance is medically prescribed), hayfever, or certain personality disorders such as pyromania, kleptomania, exhibitionism or a tendency to abuse others. If a condition such as an addiction to alcohol were to lead to something else, such as depression and liver damage, however, those would be treated as impairments. As stated above, however, each case should be looked at on its own facts.

An example given by the Code is:

> A young man has Attention Deficit Hyperactivity Disorder (ADHD) which manifests itself in a number of ways, one of which is exhibitionism. The disorder, as an impairment which

has a substantial and long-term adverse effect on the young person's ability to carry out normal day-to-day activities, would be a disability for the purposes of the Act. However, the young man is not entitled to the protection of the Act in relation to any discrimination he experiences as a consequence of his exhibitionism because that is an excluded condition under the Act.

A severe disfigurement can also count as an impairment, but not those which are deliberately acquired, such as tattoos.

Substantial and long-term

'Substantial' has been described as 'more than minor or trivial'. 'Long-term' means that the condition has lasted, or is expected to last, at least twelve months. This includes previous disabilities. If an impairment ceases to have a substantial adverse effect on a person's ability to carry out normal day-to-day activities, but is likely to recur, then it will be treated as continuing.

An impairment might not have a substantial adverse effect on a person's ability to undertake a particular day-to-day activity in isolation, but its effects on more than one activity, taken together, could result in an overall substantial adverse effect.

An example of this given in the Code is that of a person whose impairment causes breathing difficulties and who may, as a result, experience minor effects on the ability to carry out a number of activities such as getting washed and dressed, preparing a meal, or travelling on public transport. Taken together, however, the cumulative result would amount to a substantial adverse effect on his or her ability to carry out these normal day-to-day activities.

Medical treatment

If the impairment, which would otherwise have a substantial adverse effect, is being treated by means of continuing medical treatment, this treatment is to be ignored in deciding if a person is disabled or not, but it is for him to provide medical evidence to show that he falls within that category. (Note that a person who wears glasses to correct his eyesight does not count as disabled, but a person who is registered blind or partially sighted does.)

Normal day-to-day activities

Before the coming into force of the Equality Act, the Disability Discrimination Act set out a guide as to what normal day-to-day activities meant. This was a list of items, which were mobility, dexterity, physical co-ordination, continence, the ability to lift, carry or otherwise move everyday objects, speech, hearing or eyesight, memory or ability to concentrate, learn or understand, and the perception of the risk of physical danger.

This list is no longer set out in the legislation, because the view was taken by Parliament that such limitations were no longer necessary (Selwyn, 2011)

Deciding whether something affects normal day-to-day activities is something for the tribunal to decide, using its common sense, looking at what the claimant cannot do, or can only do with difficulty. It remains the case, however, that someone cannot be classed as 'disabled' under the Equality Act if they cannot play football or climb a mountain—those are not day-to-day activities. As a result, where an element of a job cannot be performed owing to a medical condition of some kind, but where that task is not within the scope of a 'normal day-to-day activity' then a claim relating to discrimination on such grounds will fail. A good example of a case like this is *Quinlan v B&Q plc* (1997). The facts were as follows:

In 1997 Mr Quinlan was dismissed from his job as an assistant working at a garden centre after seven days because he refused to carry out the heavy lifting work that formed a part of the job. He would not do this because he had had open heart surgery some ten years previously and had been told that lifting heavy weights might injure his health. He brought a claim to a tribunal under the Disability Discrimination Act arguing that it would have been reasonable for the employer to omit from his work the requirement to lift heavy weights, and that his dismissal was thus unlawful. He lost his case on the grounds that he was not disabled under the terms of the Act. This was because lifting heavy weights was not found to constitute 'a normal day-to-day activity'. He could only have succeeded had his illness not allowed him to lift everyday objects. He therefore failed at the first hurdle of proving that he was disabled.

Prohibited conduct

Like other discrimination legislation, disability discrimination law applies to job applicants and workers as well as employees. The Disability Discrimination Act originally allowed for only two types of action on the part of employees.

The first was adverse treatment for a disability-related reason (which is broadly equivalent to direct discrimination), for which the DDA allowed justification.

The second type of case could be brought where an employer failed to make reasonable adjustments in order to accommodate the needs of a disabled person. This positive duty on the employer still exists, and will be looked at in the next section.

The original DDA, however, contained no specific outlawing of direct or indirect discrimination. It had been thought that this would not be necessary given the concepts of disability-related discrimination and reasonable adjustments, which Parliament thought would cover the necessary situations.

Direct discrimination was later added, and now the Equality Act has also added a general prohibition against indirect discrimination. Disability-related discrimination has also been amended and is now described as 'discrimination arising from disability', for reasons which we will discuss below.

The Equality Act now covers the following in relation to disability:

- direct discrimination (including associative and perceptive discrimination)
- indirect discrimination
- harassment
- victimisation
- discrimination arising from disability
- duty to make reasonable adjustments
- enquiries about disability and health.

Direct and indirect discrimination, harassment and victimisation all follow a similar pattern to other protected characteristics.

Direct discrimination

Unlike other forms of protected characteristic, direct discrimination because of disability is not symmetrical, and so cannot be used by someone who is not disabled. This also means that positive measures taken to help disabled people cannot be discriminatory against non-disabled people.

An example of direct discrimination (given by the former Disability Rights Commission) is that of a disabled woman in a wheelchair who applies for a job. She can do the job just as well as any other applicant, but the employer wrongly assumes that the wheelchair will cause an obstruction in the office. He therefore gives the job to a person who is no more suitable for the job but who is not a wheelchair-user. This would be direct discrimination, because she has been treated in this way because of her disability.

The comparator in cases of direct disability discrimination would be someone who does not have the particular disability of the claimant and whose circumstances are the same, or there is no material difference between them.

It must be remembered the employer cannot justify the treatment, except if an occupational qualification exists. If it does not, and the treatment is less favourable, because of the disability, then the discrimination is made out and the employer loses the case.

There can also be direct discrimination because of the person's association with a disabled person, or because the employer perceives him or her to be disabled.

Direct, indirect, harassment and victimisation are all described in more detail in Chapter 11. In this chapter we will concentrate on the two disability-specific concepts of discrimination arising from disability and the duty to make reasonable adjustments.

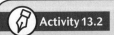 **Activity 13.2**

An employee develops cancer, and has to have several weeks off work within a three-month period for treatment. The employer does not consider him for promotion, because he feels that he cannot rely on the person being available when required, particularly if his condition deteriorates. He gives the promotion to another employee, who does not have cancer, but who is slightly more junior.

Questions

1 Is this discrimination?

2 Is it disability-related or direct discrimination?

3 Who would be the comparator and why?

4 Can the employer justify his treatment of the employee with cancer?

5 If the employer did not know of the reason for the absence, would your answer be any different?

Discrimination arising from disability

This is set out in section 15 of the Equality Act, and is established if a person treats a disabled person unfavourably because of something that arises in consequence of that person's disability. As this refers to 'unfavourable' rather than 'less favourable treatment', it requires no comparator. The employer can justify it if he can show that the treatment is a proportionate means of achieving a legitimate aim.

A reason arising from disability could, for example, be dismissing a disabled person who is often late because he lacks mobility and finds it difficult to get to work using public transport. The action is not taken because he is disabled, but rather because he is late.

The lateness, however, arises from his disability. There is no need to look for a comparator, and therefore it is not relevant if other non-disabled workers would have been dismissed for the same reason.

Section 15(2) of the Equality Act states that there will be no discrimination arising from disability if the employer shows that he did not, and could not reasonably have been expected to know, that B had the disability.

Justification

The treatment will not amount to discrimination if it is a proportionate means of achieving a legitimate aim, for example, if it is done because of health and safety reasons. An example of this is *Lane Group plc v Farmiloe* (2003). In this case the claimant worked in a warehouse. He could not wear safety boots because he suffered from psoriasis. A local authority health and safety officer required him to wear safety boots, and threatened enforcement action if he failed to do so. The employers approached various footwear manufacturers, but none could provide anything suitable. As there was no other employment available for him, he was dismissed. This was acceptable because health and safety law overrode the principles behind the then DDA (and this would also apply to the Equality Act).

Another example, which was given in the original Code to the DDA, is that of a person with severe back pain who is unable to bend over, who applies for a job as a carpet fitter. The employer would be justified if he refused him the job, because he would not be able to fit carpets, which is the essential requirement of the job. This would be justified as the reason he is rejected is a substantial one and is clearly material to the circumstances.

Justification will not be possible if the circumstances also show that the employer is under a duty to make reasonable adjustments in relation to the disabled person but has failed to comply with that duty. If the reasonable adjustment would have made a difference, then the justification defence is not open to the employer. We shall look at reasonable adjustments later in this chapter.

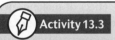 **Activity 13.3**

A woman with dyslexia applies for a job as an administrator. She does not disclose her condition on the application form, and fails a letter-typing test because of her bad spelling (although she has a spell check program on her computer). Apart from her spelling, she would be an excellent, practical administrator, although it would take her longer to read documents. The employer refuses to employ her because accuracy is an important part of the job. She claims disability discrimination.

Questions

1   Has she been treated less favourably than someone who would not have failed the test (ie, was she subjected to less favourable treatment because of her disability?)

2   Would your answer be any different if she had disclosed the dyslexia on her application form?

3   Can the employer justify this because spelling is essential for her job?

4   When you have read the section about the duty to make reasonable adjustments, consider whether there would be any that the employer would be expected to make in these circumstances.

Novacold v Malcolm

A provision similar to section 15 but not identical was in the original DDA. Unlike the current section, it referred to 'less favourable treatment' and therefore required a comparator. The leading case on this had been that of *Clark v TDG t/a Novacold* (1999). Mr Clark suffered an injury which left him unable to walk properly, and so was absent from his manual job for some time. The employer, having no alternative work for him, dismissed him and he claimed disability discrimination.

The Court of Appeal said that the correct comparator was someone to whom the reason for the treatment did not apply. In other words, the reason for the dismissal was that Mr Clark was unable to perform the main function of his job. They said that the correct comparator was therefore someone who was able to perform those functions, and this person would not have been dismissed (the question of justification is a separate one to be decided at the end of the reasoning). This decision arguably made it much easier for a disabled person to show less favourable treatment as he only had to show that someone who did not behave in the same way would not have been dismissed. The court came to this conclusion because they said it was inappropriate to use the same kind of comparison in disability cases that one would use, for example, for sex and race cases.

This was law for many years, but then in 2008 the House of Lords decided the case of *London Borough of Lewisham v Malcolm* (2008). This was not an employment case, but the principles still apply. Malcolm was the secure tenant of a property owned by Lewisham. He sublet the property without Lewisham's consent, at a time when his schizophrenia was untreated, which he probably would not have done had it not been for his mental illness. He was served notice to quit. Up until this point, the council had not known that Malcolm was schizophrenic.

According to *Novacold* the appropriate comparator here would have been a person who had not illegally sublet the flat. The House of Lords decided that this was incorrect, and that instead the comparator should be a non-disabled person who had illegally sublet the flat. To put this in an employment context, the person off on long-term sickness would now have to show that he or she had been treated differently from someone who has been off sick for the same length of time but not because of a disability. The decision therefore had the effect of making such discrimination almost impossible for the employee to prove, and caused a great deal of uproar.

The trouble with the case of *Malcolm* is that the judges tried to do a comparative test in the same way as would be done for other forms of discrimination. Disability is different, however, as Hepple points out (generally, and not specifically in relation to *Malcolm*). He says that disability differs significantly from other protected characteristics, because

> The differences between men and women (pregnancy apart), Black and White people, persons with different sexual orientations or of different faiths or age groups are generally treated as irrelevant. But the law does not expect disabled people to be treated in exactly the same way as those who are not disabled. The reason for this is that formal equality, comparing a disabled person with others, would not result in genuinely equal treatment or equality of outcomes. (Hepple 2011:72)

This is perhaps the reason for the uproar, as it meant that the DDA therefore offered much weaker protection after *Malcolm*. In the Equality Act, therefore, Parliament took the opportunity to replace 'disability-related' discrimination with 'discrimination arising from disability', which does not require a comparator, so that the effect of *Malcolm* could be negated and the same situation could not occur again.

Duty to make reasonable adjustments

This is set out in section 20 of the Equality Act, and consists of three requirements.

(a) Where a provision, criterion or practice puts a disabled person at a substantial disadvantage compared with non-disabled people, the employer has to take such steps as are reasonable to avoid the disadvantage.

(b) Where a physical feature puts a disabled person at a substantial disadvantage compared with non-disabled people, the employer then has a duty to take such steps as are reasonable to avoid the disadvantage.

(c) Where a disabled person would, but for the provision of an auxiliary aid, be put at a disadvantage compared to non-disabled people, then the employer has a duty to take such steps as are reasonable to provide the auxiliary aid.

Unlike the previous legislation on this matter, the failure to make reasonable adjustments can no longer be justified.

This can be seen as a type of indirect discrimination, but one that also imposes a positive duty on an employer to ensure that disabled people are not put to substantial disadvantage by either the employer's practices or his premises.

We shall look at each of these below, together with possible steps an employer could take.

Provision, criterion or practice

These can be, for example, arrangements for offering employment, terms and conditions of employment, benefits etc, determining to whom employment should be offered and arrangements for interviews. Such steps that an employer could take are:

- allocating some of the disabled person's duties to another person,
- transferring him to fill an existing vacancy,
- altering his hours of working or training, such as allowing part-time working, or giving the disabled person extra breaks,
- allowing him to be absent during working or training hours for rehabilitation, assessment or treatment,
- giving, or arranging for, training or mentoring (whether for the disabled person or any other person),
- modifying procedures for testing or assessment,
- providing a reader or interpreter,
- providing supervision or other support.

Physical feature

These are such things as the design and construction of buildings (including access to and exit from buildings) and any fittings, furniture or equipment on the premises. (Of course, it should be remembered that if the employer provides services to the public, it will also have a duty to make its premises physically accessible to them. This is a separate matter to the duty owed to employees, and comes under a different part of the DDA.)

Such steps an employer could take are:

- making adjustments to premises, such as widening a doorway, or providing a ramp for a wheelchair user,
- assigning the disabled person to a different place of work or training, for example, transferring him to another building, or another floor which is more easily accessible.

Auxiliary aid
Steps an employer could take are:

- acquiring or modifying equipment, such as a large screen for a visually impaired person or an adapted telephone for someone with a hearing impairment, or a special chair for someone with back problems;
- modifying instructions or reference manuals, for example, providing them in Braille or on audio tape.

The statute, does, however, emphasise that the steps that an employer is required to take should be reasonable, and so one should look at matters such as:

- the extent to which taking the step would assist the disabled person,
- the extent to which it is practicable for the employer to take the step,
- the financial and other costs which would be incurred by him in taking the step and the extent to which taking it would disrupt any of his activities,
- the extent of his financial and other resources,
- the nature of his activities and the size of his undertaking.

The duty applies to job applicants as well as employees. The employer is not subject to this duty if he does not know and could not reasonably be expected to know that the job applicant has a disability or that an employee is likely to be put at a disadvantage because of one of the three matters mentioned above.

Activity 13.4 *Archibald v Fife Council* (2004)

Mrs Archibald was employed as a road sweeper by the local council. As a result of a minor operation going wrong, she became disabled and could no longer do her job. The council, accepting that it had a duty to make reasonable adjustments, went to some lengths to find her another job, one which was not manual, within the local authority. It sent her on a number of computer and administrative courses to equip her with appropriate skills.

The council had a rule that before a person could be appointed to a job, he or she had to do a competitive interview. Although she was automatically shortlisted for about 100 jobs, Mrs Archibald did not pass any interview, and felt that it was because she was moving from a manual job. She argued that the council should simply have transferred her to a sedentary job, without the requirement for an interview, so long as she could show that she was qualified and suitable for the job in question, and that this would have been a reasonable adjustment for the council to have to make.

» Lord Hope, in the House of Lords, said that the duty to make reasonable adjustments

. . . is not simply a duty to make adjustments. The making of adjustments is not an end in itself. The end is reached when the disabled person is no longer at a substantial disadvantage, in comparison with persons who are not disabled, by reason of any arrangements made by or on behalf of the employer.

The House of Lords also said that there was a positive discrimination element to the DDA, and that an employer may have to treat a disabled person more favourably than a non-disabled person. Because the original tribunal had not considered the point, it sent the case back to them to decide if the council's duties were reasonable.

Questions

1   If you had been sitting on the tribunal panel, what would your decision have been?

2   Do you think that the council discharged its duty, or should it have done more to find Mrs Archibald a job?

Comparator

As can be seen in the *Archibald* example above, the comparison is to be made with a person who does not have the disability and therefore who is not prevented from carrying out the essential functions of his job.

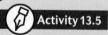 **Activity 13.5**

In the example given above, of a disabled man who found it difficult to keep the hours requested by his employer, and was dismissed for being consistently late, would the employer be justified in dismissing him?

Would there be any reasonable adjustments that the employer could be expected to make in his case?

Would your answer be any different if the employer were not aware of the man's disability, and assumed that it was just an inability to get up on time in the morning?

Enquiries about disability and health

The Equality Act contains a new provision in section 60 which prohibits an employer from asking a candidate about their health before offering work or placing them on a shortlist.

The employer would not be in breach of the section merely by asking about the person's health, but if he *relies* on this information then he might be in breach. In other words it depends on the reason for asking the applicant about his health. The employer is allowed to ask about health if the question is necessary for the purpose of:

(a) Establishing whether the applicant will be able to comply with a requirement to undergo an assessment, designed to give an indication of the applicant's suitability for the work concerned, or whether there would be a duty on the employer to make reasonable adjustments in connection with the requirement to undergo an assessment (in other words the employer is checking if he needs to make any adjustments before a candidate comes for interview).

(b) Establishing whether the applicant will be able to carry out a function that is intrinsic to the work concerned.

(c) Monitoring diversity in the range of persons applying to the employer for work.

(d) Establishing whether the employer can take lawful positive action under section 159 of the Equality Act.

(e) If there is a work requirement to have a particular disability, ascertaining if the applicant has that particular disability. The requirement must be an occupational requirement and its application must be a proportionate means of achieving a legitimate aim.

Section 60(5) says that if an employer does ask questions about health, then this can be used as a fact from which the tribunal can decide that the employer was being discriminatory. Therefore if an employer does ask health-related questions of job applicants, he runs the risk that that a tribunal might later draw an inference that a particular applicant was not offered a job because of their disability. This does not mean that a tribunal is obliged to draw an inference and has to decide that there is discrimination, but only that it is a fact that the tribunal can take into account. An employer who can show the staff who dealt with the replies to a health-related question had no input into the decision-making process (for example, if it was on a separate form that went to a different department) should still be able to show that there was no discrimination.

Activity 13.6

Clarkson and Co advertise for computer programmers. Part of the application form contains a section asking whether the applicant has a disability that requires the employer to make any adjustments prior to the interview.

Jeremy applies for the job. On his application form he discloses that he walks with two sticks, and that he will need to have step-free access to the premises.

Clarkson and Co read this on the application form. They decide that it would be difficult if an employee had two sticks, because other people might trip on them, and they therefore decide not to interview Jeremy.

Questions

1 Are Clarkson and Co permitted to ask the question in relation to whether they need to make any adjustments for interview purposes?

2 Are they permitted to rely on the answer when making the decision not to interview Jeremy?

3 What difficulties does Jeremy face in proving his case? What might assist him?

A medical or social model of disability?

As well as criticisms in the way that the statute is drafted, particularly in the way that disability is defined, there is a vigorous ongoing debate as to whether the correct model of disability has been used as a basis for the legislation. The two models are known as the medical model and the social model. According to the medical model upon which the British disability laws are generally seen to be based, disability is viewed as a *problem* for the individual disabled person. Claimants are required to show that they are disabled according to a particular definition in the statute. The ethos is that it is a personal problem and unrelated to external factors. The social model is much wider, and

> recognises that the circumstances of people with disabilities and the discrimination they face, are socially created phenomena which are not directly related to their impairments per se . . . the problem is not in the impairment itself, but rather is one which results from the structures, practices and attitudes that prevent the person from exercising his or her capabilities. (European Commission Communication to the Council and European Parliament— quoted in Wells, 2003:253).

In other words, the social model views disability not just as the narrow problem of one individual person, but a problem arising as a result of the relationship between the individual and society. Such a model would, its proponents say, be a better way of providing equal opportunities for all disabled people.

Wells (2003) points out that the fact that the medical concept is used under the Disability Discrimination Act (and has now been continued in the Equality Act) serves to limit the protection of the Act, particularly because of the difficulty in establishing that a particular person is disabled. She cites research showing that 16% of claims were rejected because the tribunal found that the applicant was not disabled, and that this was the most common reason for DDA claims to fail. She suggests that the social model is a better one and regrets that the changes made to the DDA pursuant to the Framework Directive did not incorporate this—despite the fact that in her view the Framework Directive itself can be regarded as leaning towards a social model.

Wells states that there are three issues that arise with the use of the medical model in the Disability Discrimination Act:

1. The narrow definition and interpretation by the courts of disability means that some people, who might otherwise be regarded as disabled, are excluded because they fail to establish that they come within the definition. The complexity and the technical nature of the procedure may also have an effect on deterring disabled people from pursuing applications.

2. The emphasis in the medical model is on what is wrong with the person and what he cannot do, and placing the focus on this impairment and requiring substantial evidence may perpetuate the labelling and stigma faced by disabled people in the labour market.

3. The use of the medical model means that other people who have some disability, such as a hearing difficulty, but which is not substantial enough to come within the definition, can still be discriminated against, but they will have no remedy.

This approach, although it may seem attractive in terms of rights and opportunities, may not however be practical to enforce in the courts. It is one thing to have laudable statements of aims, and attempts to change people's attitudes, but quite another to give the courts and tribunals a set of rules that can easily be applied. Whittle (2002) tries to find a middle route. His view is that having a concept of impairment is necessary for a definition, but that having a definition does not necessarily mean that legislation cannot be based on the social model. He does, however, think that there should be some safeguards:

> 1) it is crucial that the legislative concept of impairment does not (a) incorporate the phraseology that will encourage an assessment as to the extent of an individual's functional limitations and (b) ignore the social dimension to disability

2) the concept of impairment must be defined in a comprehensive manner to ensure that the question for the judiciary is more to do with whether an individual's past, present, future of perceived impairment constitutes an appropriate disability for the purposes of the law. (Whittle, 2002:323)

Despite the above arguments, it could be said that the DDA does incorporate some element of the social model, in that it provides for a duty to make reasonable adjustments (albeit that the employer has to be aware of the person's disability, which dilutes the social aspect). As stated in the Code:

The concept of discrimination in the Act reflects an understanding that functional limitations arising from disabled people's impairments do not inevitably restrict their ability to participate fully in society. Rather than the limitations of an impairment, it is often environmental factors (such as the structure of a building, or an employer's working practices) which unnecessarily lead to these social restrictions. This principle underpins the duty to make reasonable adjustments.

CHAPTER SUMMARY

- Disability discrimination is different to other types of discrimination.
- Discrimination arising from disability is different to direct discrimination on grounds of sex and race, and can be justified.
- Direct discrimination because of disability cannot be justified.
- Employers have a duty to make reasonable adjustments to avoid discriminating against disabled people.
- Disability can refer to a physical or mental impairment.

REFERENCES

Gilbert, H. (2010) 'Employers urged to help disabled workers' *Personnel Today*, 10 December.

Hepple, B. (2011) *Equality: The new legal framework*. Oxford, Hart Publishing.

Office For Disability Issues (2011) 'Equality Act 2010 Guidance'.

Paton, N. (2011) 'Government research shows major barriers for disabled' *Occupational Health Magazine*, 01 January.

Selwyn, N. (2011) *Selwyn's Law of Employment*. Oxford: Oxford University Press.

Wells, K. (2003) 'The impact of the Framework Employment Directive on UK disability discrimination law' *Industrial Law Journal* 32 (p253).

Whittle, S. (2002) 'The Framework Directive for Equal Treatment in Employment and Occupation: an analysis from a disability rights perspective' *Employment Law Review* 303.

ONLINE RESOURCE CENTRE

A range of online resources to help you through your employment law module have been developed by the author team. These include updates, self-test questions and sources for further reading. (www.oxfordtextbooks.co.uk/orc/taylor_emir3e)

Race discrimination · 14

Learning outcomes

After reading this chapter you should be able to:

- explain the reasons for the introduction of race discrimination law in the UK;

- state the meaning of 'race' and what the definition includes;

- give examples of 'direct race discrimination';

- differentiate between direct and indirect race discrimination;

- set out when an occupational requirement can apply in race cases;

- set out how an employer can defend itself when it has been found to have discriminated indirectly on grounds of race;

- define the term 'victimisation' in the context of race discrimination law and explain its practical significance.

Introduction

In terms of its basic principles the law in the UK on race discrimination operates on the same lines as most other types of discrimination covered by the Equality Act.

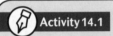 **Activity 14.1**

Read the following paragraph and try to answer the questions that follow. If you return to the activity again when you have finished reading the chapter, you should be able to give full and accurate answers to the questions.

Assume that you are employed as an advisor in a human resource consultancy. While all kinds of advice and training is offered by your firm, much of its work involves giving basic legal advice to owners and managers of small businesses by telephone. During your first two months you are contacted by several clients faced with potential race discrimination issues. The following are some examples:

1   A Lebanese restaurant owner wants to know if she can advertise for Lebanese chefs and waiting staff.

2   A Manchester-based printer recently advertised a job, but only received one application. It was from a Welsh person. He would prefer to employ someone local and wants to re-advertise.

3   A care home manager recently won a tribunal case in which one of her staff claimed he had suffered racial harassment. A patient had used some racially offensive language when speaking to him. Is it safe for her now to dismiss this man given that he has completed less than a year's service?

Your boss requires you to make brief notes setting out the advice you give to each client who contacts you and your reasons. This is then retained in the relevant files. What notes would you write in connection with each of the above cases?

Historical background

Immigration is not a recent trend. There have been ethnic communities in Britain for many years. The British population has been contributed to by a number of waves of immigrants arriving from overseas, such as long-standing black communities in sea ports like Cardiff and Liverpool, the Irish who arrived in the nineteenth century, the Jews, those from the Caribbean who answered the call for more workers after the Second World War, people from the Indian sub-continent who left after the partition of India, followed by the South Asians expelled from East Africa, down to the recent arrivals from Eastern Europe and other countries around the world. The waves of migration have created a culturally and linguistically diverse society, and one which needs the assistance of discrimination legislation if it is to allow all to have equality in their opportunities in life.

It was only in the latter part of the twentieth century, however, that any legislation was brought in to protect the members of those communities from the discrimination that they faced. Such migrants tended to be in the lowest paid jobs, and live in cheap, low quality housing (Jones, 1996:61), whilst experiencing a high degree of exploitation, discrimination and marginalisation ... Although by the 1970s African-Carribbean and Asian people worked in a broader range of occupations than before, these were still jobs that were 'deemed fit' for ethnic minorities rather than white workers (Solomos and Back, 1996: 67-69).

The white paper published prior to the Race Relations Act 1976 saw that there was a:

> ... familiar cycle of cumulative disadvantage by which relatively low paid or low status jobs for the first generation of immigrants go hand in hand with poor and overcrowded living conditions, and a depressed environment. If, for example, job opportunities, educational facilities, housing and environmental conditions are all poor, the next generation will grow up less well equipped to deal with the difficulties facing them. The wheel then comes full circle ... (HMSO, 1975: para 11)

Legal background

There were originally attempts to deal with this in the 1960s, first with the setting up of welfare agencies and then with the Race Relations Act 1965. This outlawed discrimination in places of public resort, such as hotels and restaurants, and made it a criminal offence to stir up racial hatred. The Act also set up the Race Relations Board, whose duty it was to look at complaints of race discrimination.

One of the main problems with this Act was its limited coverage. A major omission was that it did not cover discrimination in employment law. The Race Relations Act 1968 attempted to solve the problems of its predecessor by widening the remit to include employment, housing and the provision of goods and services. However, this was still not entirely satisfactory. If a person was aggrieved by such discrimination, he could not go to court or tribunal. His only recourse was to complain to the Board, who would then investigate. Only after conciliation had been tried and had not succeeded could the matter be referred to a court. This was not an effective way of dealing with discrimination, and by 1975 only one employment case had in fact reached the courts. In addition, the only type of discrimination that was outlawed was direct discrimination. As Brown (1986:51) says:

> it had become apparent that direct discrimination was not always at the heart of racial disadvantage: regulations, policies and practices of organisations often discriminated indirectly against ethnic minorities, and the Act lacked any provision for dealing with these cases.

This is what Lord Scarman, in his report on the riots of the 1980s, called 'unwitting' or unconscious' racism.

The example of the USA race relations legislation led to campaigners in the UK to intensify their efforts, and eventually, in 1976, the Race Relations Act that we knew for many years was passed. This introduced a right of individual petition to the courts and the prohibition of indirect as well as direct discrimination.

Although society and attitudes are now very different than they were in the 1970s, the problem of racism has not been entirely eradicated. In 1994 McCrudden pointed out that almost twenty years after the coming into force of the RRA 1976: '*Despite the legislation . . . and despite relatively favourable interpretation by the higher courts there remain high levels of racial discrimination in contemporary Britain.*' (McCrudden 1994: 451)

The report of Lord Macpherson, who conducted the inquiry into the Stephen Lawrence murder, concluded there was deep, entrenched 'institutional racism' within the police service in 1999. Such stories continue in the press today, and show that, despite the change in attitudes for many, there is still an underlying problem.

The Race Relations Act 1976

The Race Relations Act 1976 was modelled very closely on the Sex Discrimination Act of the previous year, and many of its provisions were mirror images of its sister act. Most of the principles were the same, and the courts tended to use the case law under one statute to assist in the interpretation of the other. The main difference was that the Sex Discrimination Act was from the beginning an area of European competence, whereas until 2003 the Race Relations Act was a matter for the UK courts alone. This meant that in some areas, European legislation was able to develop the sex discrimination law rather further. When race did become an area of European competence after the Treaty of Amsterdam, not all the elements that exist in UK law were prohibited, such as colour or nationality, so this led to parallel definitions (for example two different definitions of indirect discrimination depending on what type of race discrimination it was) which were quite confusing. This has now been harmonised by the Equality Act.

Protected characteristic

The Act protects those who are discriminated against because of their 'race'. Race includes:

- colour;
- nationality;
- ethnic or national origins.

Also included is 'racial group', and this can be made up of two or more distinct racial groups, for example 'Black British'.

Most of the elements of 'race' are self-explanatory. Nationality refers to citizenship, but is a separate concept from national origins, which can include Welsh, Scottish or English. Such people are a national group, but not an ethnic one. National origins has been quite narrowly interpreted, with case law saying that just because a person was born abroad without any reference to place or country of origin, this is not discrimination. Hepple argues that 'this runs counter to the aims of the legislation by making it possible to discriminate against ill-defined groups such as 'immigrants' or 'asylum-seekers' or 'foreigners.'

Activity 14.2

When Gordon Brown became Prime Minister, he came up with the slogan of 'British Jobs for British workers'. Mackenzie Ltd think this is a great idea, as they are based in an area where racial tensions are high, and there is high white unemployment. They think if the government had it as a policy then it would be fine to follow it and show their patriotism. They therefore reject an application from Marco, an Italian man, although he is the best qualified for the job. Marco takes them to an employment tribunal, claiming race discrimination.

Do you think he can establish his case? Can the company use Gordon Brown's statement as justification?

When you have read to the end of the chapter return to this question and see if your answer is still the same.

The aspect which has generated the most litigation, however, has been that of 'ethnic origins'. One of the main reasons for this is the fact that, until 2003, there was no law prohibiting discrimination on grounds of religion, and 'ethnic origins' was used by the courts to protect some religious groups by terming them racial groups. The main case where this issue arose was *Mandla v Dowell Lee* (1983) in the House of Lords. In that case, Lord Fraser set out the essential characteristics of 'ethnic origins' as being:

- a long shared history, of which the group is conscious as distinguishing it from other groups, and the memory of which it keeps alive;
- a cultural tradition of its own, including family and social customs and manners, often but not necessarily associated with religious observance.

Other, non-essential but relevant characteristics could be:

- either a common geographical origin, or descent from a small number of common ancestors;
- a common language, not necessarily peculiar to the group;
- a common literature peculiar to that group;
- a common religion different from that of neighbouring groups or from the general community surrounding it;
- being a minority or being an oppressed or a dominant group within a larger community, eg, a conquered people and their conquerors might both be ethnic groups.

By using this definition of 'ethnic origins', the courts were able to extend the meaning of the term 'racial group' to Jews and Sikhs, and so give them protection at a time when people had no remedy if discriminated on grounds of their religion. This did not, however, extend to Muslims, or some other groups such as Rastafarians because their religions were not limited to members of a particular ethnic group. Gypsies, however, did come within the definition of 'ethnic origins', and so were protected as a racial group.

The definition of race says that 'race includes...' It was previously an exhaustive definition, but this is no longer the case, and thus may allow the courts some leeway, for example to include caste (IDS, 2011). The Equality Act does not specifically include 'caste' as an aspect of 'race', but has made provision for this to be outlawed by amending regulations if, for example, the Home Secretary feels that there is a need for it.

The reason it was not included is that it was not felt that there was a need to do so, although a study is being done as to its necessity. At the time of writing, however (autumn 2011) a tribunal case in Coventry concerning caste discrimination in relation to a person of the Dalit caste (previously sometimes known as 'Untouchable') is being argued (*Begraj v Heer Manak Solicitors*), but it is likely that this will work its way through the appeal process before a legal basis is established. It is our current view that it is unlikely that race will be taken to include caste without specific amendment of the legislation, precisely because there is special mention of including it at a later date in the Act. It can therefore be argued that the fact that Parliament specifically did not include it in the Equality Act means that the Act specifically allows for the possibility of amendment. There is, however, uncertainty on this point, which will only be resolved either in the appeal courts, or if the government decide to make the amendment.

Exhibit 14.1   **The *JLS* case**

A Jewish boy had a father who was Jewish by birth, and a mother who became Jewish when she converted to Judaism. They attended the Progressive Jewish Synagogue, where people are held to be Jewish because of their faith, rather than their origin.

He applied to go to the Jewish school in North London, which is run by Orthodox Jews, and is very oversubscribed. Here, the entry requirement was for children who were Jewish according to the Orthodox rules, in other words if their mother was Jewish by birth.

Children of atheists and Christians were also admitted to the school, if their mothers were born to Jewish families, because 'the child of a Jewish mother is automatically and inalienably Jewish' (Lord Phillips in the Supreme Court). This particular boy was not permitted to attend the school, as in the school's Orthodox view his mother was not Jewish.

The boy argued that the school's application of this 'matrilineal test' discriminated against him on grounds of his ethnic origin, even if the motive behind that discrimination was religious. It was argued that there was a distinction between a Jew as a member of an ethnic group, as defined in Mandla, and a Jew according to Orthodox religious principles. This was therefore essentially an argument between faith and ethnicity.

The Supreme Court decided, by a majority, that there had been race discrimination on grounds of ethnic origin. This is a difficult decision, as can be seen from the fact that the judges were split 5/4. It is interesting to note, however that Lord Phillips said:

> there may well be a defect in our law of discrimination. In contrast to the law in many countries, where English law forbids direct discrimination it provides no defence of justification. It is not easy to envisage justification for discriminating against a minority racial group. Such discrimination is almost inevitably the result of irrational prejudice or ill-will. But it is possible to envisage circumstances where giving preference to a minority racial group will be justified. Giving preference to cater for the special needs of a minority will not normally involve any prejudice or ill-will towards the majority. Yet a policy which directly favours one racial group will be held to constitute racial discrimination against all who are not members of that group.

This fits in with the debates looked at in Chapter 11 on justification of direct discrimination, and also those in the next chapter on whether religions in themselves should be allowed to be discriminatory.

Prohibited conduct

Direct discrimination

Direct race discrimination is established if

- a person treats another *less favourably* than he treats or would treat someone else, and
- the difference in treatment is *because of race*.

This is symmetrical, so that, for example, a white person has just the same protection as a black person, and vice versa, in the same way that in sex discrimination a man cannot be discriminated against in favour of a woman. The complainant does not have to show that the employer acted from racial prejudice, as long as he can show that race was a substantial cause of the employer's actions. Segregation of people on racial grounds is also a direct discrimination. The motive for the discrimination is irrelevant, for example the *Amnesty International v Ahmed* (2009) case that was discussed in Chapter 11, where Amnesty was found to have discriminated, even though its motive was well meaning.

The comparator

The law requires a comparator, who would be someone who is not of the race in question. In order to bring a successful claim for direct discrimination therefore, a person has to show that he or she has been treated less favourably than a person of another race, etc has been treated, or would have been treated. As with other protected characteristics, the comparator can be a hypothetical person; he does not actually have to exist. It is thus sufficient to establish discrimination if it can be shown that a person would have treated someone from another racial group more favourably in the particular circumstances.

Perceptive and associative discrimination

There can also be perceptive or associative discrimination, as with most other protected characteristics. Associative discrimination has always applied in race cases. For example, in *Showboat Entertainment Centre Ltd v Owens* (1984) a white employee was instructed to exclude black youths from an amusement arcade and was subsequently dismissed for refusing to do so. Owens was successfully able to claim race discrimination.

Activity 14.3   *Redfearn v Serco Ltd* (2006)

Mr Redfearn was employed as a bus driver. His company's clients were mainly Asians who had physical and mental disabilities. His company found out that he was a member of the BNP, and indeed was elected as a BNP councillor. Following concerns expressed by the local community and trade unions, he was dismissed on the grounds that his membership and position within the BNP led to a health and safety risk to passengers, given the risk of demonstrations, etc.

He brought a claim of race discrimination before the employment tribunal, saying that it was sufficient that the reason for the treatment was in some way connected to race, or being 'referable' to race. The tribunal found that he had not been dismissed on racial grounds but instead on grounds of health and safety. He appealed successfully to the EAT, which, following the case of *Showboat* referred to above, held that the tribunal had wrongly understood the concept of racial grounds, and allowed his appeal.

His former employer appealed to the Court of Appeal. There, Mr Redfearn's claim was rejected because it agreed with the original tribunal that the grounds for dismissal were those of health and safety and that no direct discrimination had occurred. The court also rejected an argument based upon indirect discrimination, finding that the policy of dismissing members of the BNP was a proportionate means of pursuing a legitimate health and safety-related aim. Mr Redfearn's claim was therefore unsuccessful. Lord Justice Mummery said:

» In this case it is true that the circumstances in which the decision to dismiss Mr. Redfearn was taken included racial considerations, namely the fact that Serco's customers were mainly Asian and that a significant percentage of the workforce was Asian. Racial considerations were relevant to Serco's decision to dismiss Mr. Redfearn, but that does not mean that it is right to characterise Serco's dismissal of Mr. Redfearn as being on 'racial grounds'. It is a non-sequitur to argue that he was dismissed on 'racial grounds' because the circumstances leading up to his dismissal included a relevant racial consideration, such as the race of fellow employees and customers and the policies of the BNP on racial matters. Mr. Redfearn was no more dismissed 'on racial grounds' than an employee who is dismissed for racially abusing his employer, a fellow employee or a valued customer. Any other result would be incompatible with the purpose of the 1976 Act to promote equal treatment of persons irrespective of race by making it unlawful to discriminate against a person on the grounds of race.

Question

1   Do you agree with the reasoning of the Court of Appeal, or do you think that, following *Showboat*, Mr Redfearn should have won his case? Why?

 Exhibit 14.2   *Glasgow City Council v Zafar* (1998)

Lord Browne-Wilkinson said the following when making his judgment in this case:

The Act of 1976 requires it to be shown that the claimant has been treated *by the person against whom the discrimination is alleged* less favourably than *that person* treats or would have treated another. In deciding that issue, the conduct of a hypothetical reasonable employer is irrelevant. The alleged discriminator may or may not be a reasonable employer. If he is not a reasonable employer he might well have treated another employee in just the same unsatisfactory way as he treated the complainant in which case he would not have treated the complainant 'less favourably' for the purposes of the Act of 1976. The fact that, for the purposes of the law of unfair dismissal, an employer has acted unreasonably casts no light whatsoever on the question whether he has treated the employee 'less favourably' for the purposes of the Act of 1976.

I cannot improve on the reasoning of Lord Morison [*in the Scottish Court of Session*] who expressed the position as follows:

'The requirement necessary to establish less favourable treatment which is laid down by section 1(1) of the Act of 1976 is not one of less favourable treatment than that which would have been accorded by a reasonable employer in the same circumstances, but of less favourable treatment than that which had been or would have been accorded by the same employer in the same circumstances. It cannot be inferred, let alone presumed, only from the fact that an employer has acted unreasonably towards one employee, that he would have acted reasonably if he had been dealing with another in the same circumstances.'

Occupational Requirements

These used to be known as genuine occupational qualifications or requirements and are the only defence that an employer has to a charge of direct racial discrimination. The previous law set out a list of what could count as an occupational requirement, but this has been removed, and it now simply states that the requirement must be crucial to the post, and not merely one of several important factors. It also must not be a sham or pretext. In addition, applying the requirement must be 'proportionate so as to achieve a legitimate aim' (as with age discrimination). If an employer can prove this, then he can treat people differently. An example is if a director wishes to have a black man playing the part of Othello, or an Indian restaurant needs Indian waiters (although they will have to show that this is essential, etc). Another example might be where the holder of the job provides welfare services to persons of that racial group, and these can be most effectively provided by someone of a particular racial group, for example an Asian social worker for an Asian immigrant community, where the people in the community need someone who both speaks the language and understands them.

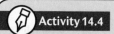 **Activity 14.4   Occupational Requirements**

Consider these two cases which were decided under the Race Relations Act:

Tottenham Green Under Fives' Centre v Marshall (1989)

A playgroup which catered to a variety of ethnic groups advertised for an Afro-Caribbean worker to replace another Afro-Caribbean who had left. The defence was that this worker was providing 'personal services' to the children, such as maintaining the cultural links with the children, dealing with the parents, reading and talking in dialect and looking after their skin and hair health.

The EAT observed that the post holder must be directly involved in the provision of the services and not merely directing others, and even if only one of the personal services provided falls within the definition then the GOQ is established. The court also stated that it should not be interpreted so narrowly that it would erect too high a fence in the way of an employer seeking to rely on the provision.

London Borough of Lambeth v Commission for Racial Equality (1990)

A local authority wanted to restrict applications for managers in their housing department to Asians or Afro-Caribbeans on the basis that they would be providing personal services.

The EAT found that this was incorrect, and that GOQs should be narrowly interpreted. The phrase 'personal services' meant cases in which direct contact was likely, mainly face-to-face and where language or a knowledge and understanding of cultural background are of material importance.

The Court of Appeal agreed and said that the use of the word 'personal' 'indicates that the identity of the giver and the recipient of the services is important'.

Questions

1 Do you agree with the EAT in the *Tottenham* case? Should a white person who had lived in the Caribbean, was married to a black person and was able to speak the dialect have been allowed to apply?

2 How do you reconcile the decision in *Lambeth* with that in *Tottenham*?

3 Do you think that these cases would be decided in the same way today?

Indirect discrimination

Originally it was not intended to include the concept of indirect discrimination in the Sex Discrimination Act 1975, which was the first full discrimination statute, but the government of the day decided to do so after becoming aware of the concept of disparate impact in American discrimination law. This was also included in the Race Relations Act and became an important part of discrimination law.

 Exhibit 14.3   *Griggs v Duke Power Co* **(1971)**

The concept of indirect discrimination, or 'disparate impact' was first recognised in the USA, in the case of *Griggs v Duke Power Co* (1971).

The USA Civil Rights Act 1964 (Title VII) states that it is unlawful for an employer '*to fail or refuse to hire or to discharge any individual, or otherwise to discriminate against any individual with respect to his compensation, terms, conditions, or privileges of employment, because of such individual's race, color, religion, sex, or national origin*'.

In *Griggs*, an employer required a high school diploma, or a successful IQ test as a condition of employment. The black complainants brought an action for race discrimination, saying that this rendered a disproportionate number of black people ineligible to apply. The American Supreme Court found in their favour.

Chief Justice Burger said:

> The objective of Congress in the enactment of Title VII is plain from the language of the statute. It was to achieve equality of employment opportunities and remove barriers that have operated in the past to favor an identifiable group of white employees over other employees. Under the Act, practices, procedures, or tests neutral on their face, and even neutral in terms of intent, cannot be maintained if they operate to 'freeze' the status quo of prior discriminatory employment practices. [*In this case whites register far better on the company's requirements*] than Negroes . . . This consequence would appear to be directly traceable to race . . . Because they are Negroes, petitioners have long received inferior education in segregated schools. . . . Congress did not intend by Title VII, however, to guarantee a job to every person regardless of qualifications. In short, the Act does not command that any person be hired simply because he was formerly the subject of discrimination, or because he is a member of a minority group. Discriminatory preference for any group, minority or majority, is precisely and only what Congress has proscribed. What is required by Congress is the removal of artificial, arbitrary, and unnecessary barriers to employment when the barriers operate invidiously to discriminate on the basis of racial or other impermissible classification . . . If an employment practice which operates to exclude Negroes cannot be shown to be related to job performance, the practice is prohibited.

Indirect discrimination therefore occurs when the practices of the employer, which apparently apply irrespective of race, form a greater obstacle for a particular racial group than for another. As a result of the European amendments to the Race Relations Act, for a time there were two definitions of indirect discrimination, depending on whether the 'racial grounds' are colour or nationality (which retained the original RRA definition) or race, ethnic origins or national origins (which were affected by the European definition, and were in line with the amended Sex Discrimination Act). This has now been harmonised by the Equality Act, and the definition is the same as for most other forms of characteristics. We set this out in Chapter 11 as follows:

(a) He applies a provision, criterion or practice to someone who has a protected characteristic.

(b) The provision, etc also applies to people who do not have the particular protected characteristic.

(c) When the provision is applied it puts (or would put) people who have the particular protected characteristic at a disadvantage compared with the people who do not.

(d) It puts (or would put) an individual person with that characteristic at a disadvantage.

(e) It cannot be shown that it is a proportionate means of achieving a legitimate aim.

This last criterion shows that indirect discrimination can be justified, which is one of the major differences with direct discrimination. An example of justification can be found in the case of *Singh v Rowntree Mackintosh* (1979).

 Activity 14.5 *Singh v Rowntree Mackintosh Ltd* **(1979)**

The complainant was a Sikh man who applied for a job at a sweet factory. The company had a policy of 'no beards'. If he wanted to work there he would thus have had to shave off his beard. He claimed that this was discriminatory, but the company sought to justify the policy on the grounds of hygiene. The EAT agreed with the employer.

Questions

1 As a Sikh, was Mr Singh covered by the Race Relations Act? Under which of the 'racial grounds'?

2 Do you think the application was made under direct or indirect discrimination? Give reasons for your answer.

3 Do you agree with the EAT that the case was justified? Why?

4 Do you think the case would be decided the same way today?

Harassment

Racial harassment can include physical abuse, offensive language, racist jokes and banter and the display of racially offensive material, such as a poster, or sending such material by e-mail. The harassment might be deliberate, but equally it might be unintentional, or even something which is meant as a joke, with no motive behind it. The main factor, however, is it makes the applicant feel himself being degraded by it and singled out because of his race, etc.

The old law did not specifically prohibit harassment on grounds of colour or nationality, but direct discrimination was used for this, although it was not ideal as a detriment had to be shown. All elements of race are now included in the harassment provisions of the Equality Act.

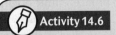

Activity 14.6

In one case heard in the tribunal, an Irishman brought a claim for harassment. He had been called a 'typical thick Paddy' by his colleagues for several weeks, and eventually complained. His employer told him to ignore the comments, because they were just jokes.

Questions

1   Do you think that this would be classed as racial harassment?

2   If it were, would it come under the new definition, or under the original 'detriment' provision of the RRA? (When answering, consider what 'racial grounds' are engaged in this case.)

3   If the Irishman were to be dismissed, in reality, as the tribunal in this case found 'because he was an Irishman who would not take Irish jokes lying down'—in other words he did not 'fit in'— would that be discriminatory?

Victimisation

This covers the situation where the employer treats the complainant unfavourably because the complainant has had the temerity to, or the employer suspects that he is about to, exercise a right under the Act, or support someone else in doing so. A comparator is now no longer necessary. Anti-victimisation protection is not given to a complainant if the original allegation made by him under the race legislation was false, or not made in good faith.

Bringing a claim

A person who has been subjected to an act of race discrimination in the employment field can bring an action in the employment tribunal if there has been an unlawful act of discrimination. He cannot bring a claim of race discrimination merely because the employer is prejudiced. Unless the employer acts upon that prejudice by causing the complainant a detriment there is no basis for a case. The claim has to be brought within three months of the discriminatory act complained of, the burden of proof being on the claimant to show that the discriminatory act took place. Once he has done that, the burden of proof transfers to the employer to show that the reason for it was not discriminatory.

Positive action

Positive discrimination, in the sense of preferring people of one race or colour for employment is not allowed. This would be contrary to the symmetrical nature of the Race Relations Act, and would be discriminatory against other racial groups. For example, if an employer stated in an advertisement for a job that only Asian people would be considered, because he wanted to reduce Asian unemployment rates, this would be discriminatory against a white person who wanted to apply. The job is closed to anyone who is not Asian. There are, however, two exceptions to this in the Equality Act which are discussed in Chapter 14.

The purpose of the first exception is set out in the Race Directive, which states in Article 5:

With a view to ensuring full equality in practice, the principle of equal treatment shall not prevent any Member State from maintaining or adopting specific measures to prevent or compensate for disadvantages linked to racial or ethnic origin.

In other words, if an employer was attempting to create the kind of environment which would encourage people of a particular racial group to thrive, and compensate for disadvantage, this would be acceptable. What is not acceptable, however, is the preferring of someone of one racial group over another, merely because of his or her race or ethnic origin, etc. This can only be done in a situation which is covered by the second exception, as set out in Chapter 11.

CHAPTER SUMMARY

- Race discrimination legislation mirrors that of other discrimination law. It covers direct and indirect discrimination, victimisation and harassment.
- Race includes colour, nationality and ethnic or national origins.
- Race does not currently include caste discrimination.
- Occupational requirements which are crucial to the post can be used.

REFERENCES

Brown, C. (1986) 'Ethnic pluralism in Britain: the demographic and legal background' in N. Glazer and K. Young (eds): *Ethnic Pluralism and Public Policy*. Aldershot: Gower.

Churchard, C. (2011) 'Legal clarity needed on "caste discrimination", say law experts' *People Management*, 19 August.

Fredman, S. (2001) 'Equality: a new generation?' *Industrial Law Journal* 30 (p145).

Hepple, B. (1992) 'Have 25 years of the Race Relations Act in Britain Been a Failure?' in B. Hepple and E. Szyszczak (eds): *Discrimination, the Limits of the Law*. London: Mansell.

Hepple, B. (2011) *Equality, The New Legal Framework*. Oxford: Hart Publishing.

Hepple B., Coussey M. & Choudhury T. (2000) *Equality: a New Framework Report of the Independent Review of the Enforcement of UK Anti-Discrimination Legislation*. Oxford: Hart Publishing.

HMSO (1975) *Racial Discrimination*. London: HMSO, Cmnd 6234.

HMSO (1999) *Report of an inquiry by Sir William Macpherson of Cluny*. London: HMSO, Cmnd 3684.

IDS (2010) *Equality Act 2010*. Thomson Publishing.

McCrudden, C. (1994) 'Racial Discrimination' in C. McCrudden and G. Chambers (eds): *Individual Rights and the Law in Britain*. Oxford: Clarendon.

Solomos, J. & Back, L. (1996) *Racism and Society*. London: Macmillan.

ONLINE RESOURCE CENTRE

A range of online resources to help you through your employment law module have been developed by the author team. These include updates, self-test questions and sources for further reading. (www.oxfordtextbooks.co.uk/orc/taylor_emir3e)

Religious discrimination

15

Learning outcomes

By the end of this chapter you should be able to:

- state why law on religious discrimination was considered necessary;

- explain the term 'religion or belief' as used in the statute;

- advise on when an occupational requirement would and would not apply under the Equality Act;

- state which exceptions and defences are available to an employer;

- discuss the tension between religious and sexual orientation discrimination.

Introduction

Religion is one of the more recent types of characteristic to be prohibited. As we saw in Chapter 12 on age discrimination, article 13 of the Treaty of Amsterdam paved the way for the Framework Directive of 2000 to be agreed. This established a general framework for equal treatment in employment and a prohibition of discrimination on the grounds of religion or belief, age and sexual orientation. Religion and belief were protected from discrimination in UK law by the Employment Equality (Religion or Belief) Regulations 2003 (which came into force at the same time as those for sexual orientation, which we shall consider in Chapter 17). The original Regulations followed the Framework Directive in outlawing discrimination only in the employment sphere, but this was later amended to include the provision of goods, facilities and services, and now the Equality Act puts it on a par with other protected characteristics.

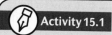 **Activity 15.1**

Read the following statements and say whether you think they are true or false. When you have finished reading the chapter come back to this exercise and see how many of your answers were correct.

1 A Catholic school wants to employ a receptionist, and advertises for one who attends church regularly. This is permissible.

2 An accountancy practice decides that an applicant who wears a full face veil would not be appropriate because it might put some clients off, and so they reject her. This is allowed by the law.

3 A petrol station manager is able to keep his station open and staffed every day of the year, notwithstanding religious holidays.

4 Following a football club can count as a 'belief' within the Equality Act.

5 A belief in global warming can be regarded as a 'belief' that can be protected.

6 An atheist is protected under the characteristic of 'religion or belief'.

7 Druidism is a religion according to the law.

Historical background

There was a debate in Britain for many years about whether religious discrimination should be prohibited. It has long been acknowledged as a right in international and European documents such as the Universal Declaration of Human Rights and the European Convention on Human Rights. It is also an established part of legislation in Northern Ireland to protect people against sectarian prejudice. It was not, however, expressly outlawed in our domestic law until December 2003, as a result of the Employment Equality (Religion and Belief) Regulations 2003, which introduced into British law the religion element of the Framework Directive. It has now been incorporated into the Equality Act as a prohibited characteristic.

Before the prohibition came into force, claimants such as Mr Ahmad found they were fighting a losing battle. He was a teacher, and education legislation at the time offered only limited protection against religious discrimination. The courts found that he had no right to have a longer lunch hour on Fridays to attend his local mosque. Lord Denning, in the Court of Appeal said '. . . *it would do the Muslim community no good, if they were to be given preferential treatment over the great majority of people. If it should happen that, in the name of religious freedom, they were given special privileges or advantages, it would provoke discontent, and even resentment . . .*'.

Lord Scarman, by contrast, was as far-sighted as ever and saw the likely future effect of such an attitude:

> When the section was enacted, the negative approach to its interpretation was, no doubt, sufficient. But society has changed since 1944; so has the legal background. Religions, such as Islam and Buddhism, have substantial followings among our people. Room has to be found for teachers and pupils of the new religions in the educational system, if discrimination is to be avoided. *This calls not for a policy of the blind eye, but for one of understanding* [our italics]. The system must be made sufficiently flexible to accommodate their beliefs and their observances, otherwise they will suffer discrimination, as a consequence contrary to the spirit of [the law], whatever the letter of that law. (*Ahmad v ILEA* (1977))

The courts did manage, however, to give protection to some religious groups, such as Jews and Sikhs, by terming them an 'ethnic group' rather than merely a religious one (as in the case of *Mandla v Dowell Lee* (1983)), and so bringing them within the ambit of the Race Relations Act 1976 (see Chapter 14). This was far from satisfactory, as the definition of 'ethnic' did not cover most religious groups (such as Muslims), and was done by means of contorting the meaning of the Race Relations Act.

During parliamentary discussions on what was to become the Race Relations Act 1976, an attempt to include religious discrimination failed because the view of the then government was that much religious discrimination would be covered by indirect discrimination and that voluntary changes would make great progress.

The government's view was, however, inaccurate and naive. Its first point, that religions are covered by indirect discrimination, is only helpful to an extent. It is true that members of religious groups can, in certain circumstances, be protected by the concept of indirect race discrimination on occasions, as happened in the case of *JH Walker Ltd v Hussein* (1996), where Asian Muslim workers were disciplined for taking a day off to celebrate Eid, a Muslim festival. It was fortunate for them that the Asian Muslim workers were also a large proportion of the workforce. If the Asians had been mostly, say, Sikhs or Hindus the Muslims would not have been able to argue race discrimination. For many years, however, even if a claim for indirect discrimination succeeded, it was a pyrrhic victory as there was originally no right to damages for indirect discrimination, and of course the perpetrator of the discrimination could also argue justification.

In relation to the second point, a report commissioned by the government from the University of Derby in the late 1990s (Weller, Feldman and Purdam, 2001) to find the extent of religious discrimination in the UK, showed that leaving things to voluntary changes had not had an enormous impact. The report, which was completed before the 11 September 2001 attacks and the rise of a perceived anti-Muslim feeling, found that:

> Ignorance and indifference towards religion were of widespread concern amongst research participants from all faith groups . . . Hostility and violence were very real concerns for organisations representing Muslims, Sikhs and Hindus . . . The majority of Muslim organisations

reported that their members experienced unfair treatment in every aspect of education, employment, housing, law and order, and in all the local government services covered in the questionnaire.(Weller et al, 2001:8–9)

This, of course, does not just affect Muslims, but members of many other religious groups, including Christians, all of whom may face prejudice and detrimental treatment in their working lives.

Before the 2003 Regulations came into force, the only real protection given to people against religious discrimination was established in the late 1990s, either by means of the criminal law, which made an assault aggravated if it were done with an anti-religious motive, or by use of the Human Rights Act 1998, Article 9 of which protects freedom of 'thought, conscience and religion' but which, as has been seen elsewhere in this book, is not particularly effective in all circumstances (see Chapter 22).

Since the Regulations came in, however, the debate has continued. The National Secular Society suggests that employers should have the right to define their workplaces as secular spaces and demand that staff leave their religion at the door. Says Sanderson, *'There should be no penalty for this, and people who are employed should understand this and not then start challenging it'* (Davis, 2008). Vickers, however, points out that *'bans on wearing religious dress will adversely affect Muslim women, and will militate against their workplace equality. In practice, rather than removing the veil in order to work, it is as likely that Muslim women will not enter the workplace at all'* (Vickers 2, 2008:25).

Peter Mooney, the head of consultancy at Employment Law Advisory Services, suggests that there can be benefits to employers encouraging religious diversity and practice. *'What it does mean is that workers feel included. This generates loyalty within the workplace and productivity doesn't go down'* (Davis, 2008).

More recently, McColgan takes up the baton and argues that, because of the conflict between religion and other protected characteristics, such as sex and sexual orientation, which we shall consider below, religion should not be protected in the way that it is (McColgan, 2009). No doubt this is a debate that will long continue.

Protected characteristic

'Religion and belief' is not actually defined in the statute, and has been left to the courts to define on a case-by-case basis. The law merely says that religion can be any religion (including a lack of religion so atheists are covered), and that belief can be any religious or philosophical belief.

The fact that it is a difficult thing to define was for many years used as one of the reasons for not having religious discrimination legislation (Hepple and Choudhury, 2001). Vickers accepts that there are advantages in having a lack of a clear definition, as the definition can be then adapted to the circumstances, and take into account modern developments. She also makes the point that it is useful not to have a demarcation between 'religion' and 'belief'. She points out, however, that not having a definition leaves courts *'acting in a vacuum, and without any principles to guide them'*. (Vickers 1, 2008:15).

The explanatory notes to the Equality Act give some help, saying that the religion must have a clear structure and belief system. They list as examples Baha'i faith, Buddhism, Christianity, Hinduism, Islam, Jainism, Judaism, Rastafarianism, Sikhism and Zoroastrianism (but this is not an exhaustive list—other religions can be also be protected if they too have a clear structure and belief system).

As for 'philosophical belief', the criteria for determining this are that:

(a) it must be genuinely held; be a belief and not an opinion or viewpoint based on the present state of information available;

(b) it must be a belief as to a weighty and substantial aspect of human life and behaviour;

(c) it must attain a certain level of cogency, seriousness, cohesion and importance; and

(d) it must be worthy of respect in a democratic society, compatible with human dignity and not conflict with the fundamental rights of others.

This final aspect is an important one, as it means that cults which are involved in illegal activities would not be protected.

The explanatory notes give as examples of belief humanism and atheism but suggest that supporting a particular football team would not be covered. The above list of criteria appears to be taken from the important case of *Grainger v Nicholson* (2009), where Burton J sitting in the Employment Appeal Tribunal held that a belief in man-made climate change, and the resulting imperatives on how people should act, is capable, if genuinely held, of being a philosophical belief. Interestingly, despite the fact that there is no mention of political belief in the legislation, the judge also said that a belief in a political philosophy or doctrine could qualify, if it has, for the person holding it, a similar status or cogency as a religious belief. He gave examples of pacifism or veganism, or possibly the political philosophies of Socialism, Marxism, Communism or free-market Capitalism. He commented, however, that a belief such as one in the supreme nature of the Jedi Knights would not count as a belief because it would not comply with the limited criteria above.

This case has led to a number of interesting decisions in tribunals, leading some legal commentators to ask flippantly 'Do you believe in fairies?' (Levine and Ford, 2011).

There have been a number of cases in employment tribunals on what does and does not count as a belief. In *Baggs v Fudge* (2005) and *Finnon v Asda Stores* (2005) membership of the BNP was held not to be a philosophical belief, but merely support for a political party. There is also the point that such support, even if held with the cogency of a religious belief, may well conflict with the fourth criterion above, '*it must be worthy of respect in a democratic society, compatible with human dignity and not conflict with the fundamental rights of others*'. In another case, *Greater Manchester Police v Power* (2009), the EAT held that a belief that mediums can communicate with the dead was capable of being a belief.

Despite the criteria above and the case law (albeit much of it only at employment tribunal level), there is still some confusion as to what counts as a protected belief and what does not, and it can make life difficult for HR and employment law professionals (Gilbert, 2010). For example, Burton J suggested above that Marxism can count, but a tribunal has found that it does not due to its extreme nature. A belief can be *capable* of amounting to a legally protected belief if it fits in with the criteria above, but whether it actually *does* or not depends on the facts of each case, and how deeply those beliefs are held. The best way of looking at this is therefore that taken by Parliament, that this is something where it is too difficult to lay down a precise list, and leave it to the courts to decide on a case-by-case basis, even if that case is one that decides someone should be protected for a real, cogent *belief* in fairies!

Activity 15.2

A member of the English Defence League is dismissed from his public sector job because he made known his beliefs, and his employer felt that this would both upset other employees and work against the employer's attempts to put in an equal opportunities and diversity policy. The sacked employee brings a claim to the tribunal alleging discrimination on the grounds of his belief.

Questions

1   What factors will the tribunal take into account?

2   What do you think the likely outcome of the case will be?

3   Would your answer be any different if he were a druid?

4   When you have read the section on the Human Rights Act (Chapter 22), consider whether he can argue a claim under that statute. If so, which articles would he use?

Prohibited conduct

Religious discrimination mirrors most of the other protected characteristics in the Equality Act, prohibiting direct and indirect discrimination (including perceptive and associative discrimination), victimisation and harassment.

Activity 15.3

May the law be with you

In 2009 Daniel Jones, who founded the International Church of Jedi-ism (which claims to have 500,000 followers worldwide) accused Tesco of religious discrimination when it ordered him either to remove his hood or be removed from a supermarket in Wales. He said that his religion required him to wear the hood in public places.

In its defence, Tesco said that the three best known Jedi Knights, Yoda, Obi-Wan Kenobi and Luke Skywalker *'all appeared hoodless without ever going over to the Dark Side and we are only aware of the Emperor as one who never removed his hood ... If Jedi walk around our stores with their hoods on, they'll miss lots of special offers.'*

1.   What questions would a tribunal ask itself when deciding whether Jedi-ism is a religion or belief (notwithstanding the views of the Attorney General)?

2.   Ask yourself those questions. What conclusion do you come to?

3.   If Jedi-ism were to count as a religion or belief, would Tesco's actions be discriminatory?

4.   If so, would they be direct or indirect discrimination?

Direct and indirect discrimination

Both direct and indirect discrimination are outlawed. Direct discrimination could be, for example, where a butcher refuses to employ Muslims and Jews because he does not like them. Indirect discrimination would be where a butcher insists that the person that he employs must be able to handle pork, and so impacts adversely on Muslims and Jews.

As with other forms of protected characteristic, direct discrimination because of religion or belief cannot be justified except where there is an occupational requirement (which is specifically defined for religion cases as we shall see below).

Indirect discrimination can be justified if it is a proportionate means of achieving a legitimate aim. In the example above, the butcher may be able to argue that the requirement was necessary as the person could not avoid handling pork.

 Exhibit 15.1

Some areas that employers should consider are:

- **Recruitment.** Apart from cases where ORs apply, it is clear that the employee's religion should have no bearing on whether or not he is suitable for the job. An employer should also consider the days that he is holding the interviews. In the case of *Stedman v UK* (1997), a Jewish woman was held not to have been discriminated against under the European Convention on Human Rights, although she had to attend an interview on a Saturday. Were she to bring her case under the current law, this is likely to be indirect discrimination unless the employer can justify it.

- **Leave.** The legislation does not require an employer automatically to accede to all requests for time off, but any refusal should be objectively justified. In one case an employment tribunal found in favour of a man who had saved up all his leave so that he could go on the Muslim Hajj pilgrimage to Mecca, but was disciplined by his employer. The defence of objective justification failed in this case.

- **Requests for time away from the employee's desk for prayer.** For example, the circumstances in the case of *Ahmad* above. The employer should see if arrangements can be made, such as a slight change in the timetable allowing him a longer lunch hour.

- **Dress codes.** For example, the banning of a female solicitor from wearing a hijab because one of the firm's clients was a large Christian organisation would probably not be justified, but insisting that a Sikh man working in food production cover his beard for reasons of hygiene would be.

- **Provision of meals.** The employer should try to have items on the menu that can be eaten by those who require a vegetarian meal, particularly, for example, if Kosher or Halal food cannot be provided.

- **Monitoring.** Although monitoring is not a legal requirement, it has been suggested that this together with training would assist in safeguarding staff against discrimination (Buchanan, 2008). Vickers supports having both monitoring and appropriate procedures, stating that '*Establishing processes which enable good practice to flourish is the best way to avoid some of the difficulties which can arise from the Religion and Belief Regulations. It is also, of course, the best way to encourage a diverse and thriving workplace, in which the overarching aims of the Regulations, to encourage equality within the workplace, can be achieved*'. (Vickers 2, 2008:54).

Associative and perceptive discrimination

The Derby report mentioned above was criticised for looking only at the religion of the victim, and not that of the perpetrator, because many religions can be discriminatory themselves. This is also a criticism that has been made of the Religion and Belief Regulations (and by implication the Equality Act), as only the religion or perceived religion of the victim is covered. For example, if a woman is treated detrimentally by her Catholic employer because she has had an abortion, and he believes that to be sinful, this will not come within the Regulations. The religion of the employer is not relevant (although she may, of course, claim sex discrimination).

The law does, however, cover *perceived* religion or belief, so if someone is discriminated against because the discriminator believes him to be a Hindu, for example, this would still be unlawful discrimination. Also covered is the religion or belief of a third party, for example, a man who is discriminated against because his wife is a Muslim will have a claim under the Regulations.

 Activity 15.4   **Cases on dress codes**

Dress codes have been amongst the most hotly contested issues since religious discrimination legislation came into force. There have been a number of highly publicised cases, which Dutt has condemned as forming part of the 'continued climate of reluctance to decide these sensitive issues in favour of the employee' (Dutt, 2006). In fact the Equal Opportunities Review showed that in 2005 only three cases of religious discrimination resulted in an award of damages (Dutt, 2006). Things have improved since then, but it still remains an uphill struggle for the claimant.

Some well-publicised examples of 'dress code' cases have been:

R (on the application of Begum) v Headteacher and Governors of Denbigh High School (2006)

This was not an employment case, but the principles apply in the employment field. Shabina Begum was forbidden from wearing the full jilbab at school. This was a more religiously conservative dress than the veil. The latter was allowed after consultation with the local Muslim community. She said that this infringed her right to manifest her religion. The House of Lords held that the school had not interfered with Begum's right to manifest her religion at all. It found that the decision to prohibit the jilbab could be justified as a proportionate means of reaching its legitimate aim of protecting the rights and freedoms of other students. The fact that a range of criteria had been considered by the school, including the pupils' freedom of religion, meant that the rule could be upheld. The case demonstrated the need for a reasoned and balanced approach to decision-making.

In his judgment Lord Bingham referred to Strasbourg authorities which:

> . . . have not been at all ready to find an interference with the right to manifest religious belief in practice or observance where a person has voluntarily accepted an employment or role which does not accommodate that practice or observance and there are other means open to the person to practise or observe his or her religion without undue hardship or inconvenience.   »

Eweida v British Airways (2010)

A British Airways check-in clerk who claimed she was religiously discriminated against for wearing a crucifix round her neck lost her case in the Court of Appeal, as it was general company policy that jewellery should be hidden, and inconvenience to a single individual did not amount to indirect discrimination under the 2003 Regulations. She is currently appealing to the European Court of Human Rights.

Azmi v Kirklees Metropolitan Council (2007)

Azmi was employed as a bilingual teaching assistant who wore a veil covering her face. Complaints were made as the children could not see her mouth and consequently found it hard to understand her. She was instructed not to wear her full veil in the classroom and was suspended when she refused. The EAT found that there was no less favourable treatment and that asking her to remove the veil was a proportionate means of achieving a legitimate aim.

Noah v Desrosiers t/a Wedge (2008)

Noah, a Muslim, was rejected for a hairstylist job because she wore a headscarf. Her claim for direct religious discrimination failed because the employer would also have turned down a non-Muslim woman who wore a headscarf. Her indirect discrimination claim was successful because the tribunal held that the employer could not justify the requirement that stylists display their hair at work.

Sahin v Turkey (2004)

On a more international level, a student at Istanbul University who was denied admission to lectures and exams because she wore a Muslim headscarf argued that this breached Article 9 of the European Convention on Human Rights. She lost her case. The court pointed out that '*in democratic societies, in which several religions coexist within one and the same population, it may be necessary to place restrictions on freedom to manifest one's religion or belief in order to reconcile the interests of the various groups and ensure that everyone's beliefs are respected*'.

It should also be noted that in France national regulations state that signs of religious observance should not be displayed in state educational establishments, thus the wearing of headscarves, etc is not allowed, and that in Germany, Belgium and Denmark restrictions on the wearing of headscarves have also been found to be lawful.

Questions

1 Consider the above UK cases. Do you agree with the outcomes? Why?

2 Do you agree with the court in *Sahin* and the French state? Why?

Occupational requirements

Occupational requirements are one of the main areas of dispute, together with dress code cases. There are two kinds of exceptions available to employers in Schedule 9 to the Equality Act (which were previously to be found in the 2003 Regulations) that apply specifically in religion cases:

1. Where the employment is for the purposes of an organised religion.
2. Where the employer has an ethos based on a particular religion.

For both these types of occupational requirement, the employer has to show that being of a particular religion or belief is in fact an occupational requirement, and that it is a proportionate means of achieving a legitimate aim to apply that requirement. We shall look at each exception separately.

Employment for the purposes of an organised religion

This exception applies where there is a religious requirement relating to the job in relation to sex, marriage, sexual orientation, etc. It can be used in the case of an organised religion, and applies where:

(a) the employment is for the purposes of an organised religion, and

(b) the post is an occupational requirement, and the requirement is applied either

    (i) so as to comply with the doctrines of the religion, or

    (ii) to avoid conflicting with the strongly held religious convictions of a significant number of the religion's followers.

The explanatory notes to the Equality Act state that this is a specific exception which is intended to cover a very narrow range of employment: ministers of religion and a small number of lay posts. It allows the employer to apply a requirement to be of a particular sex (for example male Catholic priests) or specific requirements relating to marriage, sexual orientation, etc. The requirement must be crucial to the post, and not merely one of several important factors. It also must not be a sham or pretext.

The example give in the notes is of a requirement that a Catholic priest be a man and unmarried. The notes point out that the exception is unlikely to permit a requirement that a church youth worker who primarily organises sporting activities is celibate if he is gay, but it may apply if the youth worker mainly teaches bible classes. This exception would not apply to a requirement that a church accountant be celibate if he is gay.

Employer with religious ethos

This allows an employer with an ethos based on religion or belief to require an employee also to be of that religion or belief, but only if being of that religion or belief is a requirement for the work (this requirement must not be a sham or pretext), and applying the requirement is proportionate so as to achieve a legitimate aim. It is for an employer to show that it has an ethos based on religion or belief.

The example given in the notes is of a religious organisation which may wish to restrict applicants for the post of head of its organisation to those people that adhere to that faith. This is because to represent the views of that organisation accurately it is felt that the person in charge of that organisation must have an in-depth understanding of the religion's doctrines. This could be lawful, but other posts that do not require this kind of in-depth understanding, such as administrative posts, would not be covered by this exception.

This second exception was included in the original Regulations as a result of extensive lobbying by churches and other religious organisations against the Framework Directive, fearing that, for example, religious schools would be *'forced to employ homosexuals and atheists as teachers'* (Christian Institute, 2000).

> **Activity 15.5**
>
> Consider the following situations and state whether you think that one of the two exceptions above applies. If it does, is it the first or the second kind?
>
> 1   An organisation for mentoring of Muslim youths requires that the youth worker be a Muslim.
>
> 2   The organisation above requires a cleaner.
>
> 3   A Jewish firm of solicitors which largely serves the local Jewish community requires a new solicitor to be Jewish.
>
> 4   A Muslim medical practice in a Muslim area wants to recruit a female Muslim doctor to serve its female patients.
>
> 5   A Catholic school wishes to employ a religious studies teacher.
>
> 6   The same school also has a vacancy for a geography teacher, and wants to hire a Catholic for the post.

Do some rights 'trump' others?

The specific exceptions discussed above were largely introduced to placate the pro-religion lobby when sexual orientation discrimination was brought in at the same time as religious discrimination. The difficulty is, however, how the prohibition of religious discrimination interacts with other types of protected characteristic, in particular sex discrimination, sexual orientation and gender reassignment. The question has to be asked— does one right trump the other? What factors should be taken into account in deciding which way to decide a case?

There are a number of cases where the courts have had to consider this dilemma. The three main ones will be considered here.

McClintock v Department of Constitutional Affairs

In *McClintock v Department of Constitutional Affairs* (2008), Christian magistrate Andrew McClintock stood down from hearing family cases after he was refused permission to opt out of cases which could result in an adoption by a gay couple. He lost his case in the EAT, which said that he had not indicated that his objections were rooted in any religious or philosophical belief. He was refused permission to appeal to the Court of Appeal.

Ladele v London Borough of Islington

Ladele v London Borough of Islington (2009) concerned a Christian registrar who refused to conduct gay weddings because she believed they were sinful. She originally won her tribunal case, but the EAT held that there was no discrimination. They agreed that the objectives of the council were to provide a non-discriminatory service, and that this could be appropriate justification.

Ms Ladele then appealed to the Court of Appeal. Dismissing her case, Lord Neuberger said:

> It appears to me that, however much sympathy one may have with someone such as Ms Ladele, who is faced with choosing between giving up a post she plainly appreciates or officiating at events which she considers to be contrary to her religious beliefs, the legislature has decided that the requirements of a modern liberal democracy, such as the United Kingdom, include outlawing discrimination in the provision of goods, facilities and services on grounds of sexual orientation, subject only to very limited exceptions.

The Master of the Rolls continued:

> [I]t appears to me that the fact that Ms Ladele's refusal to perform civil partnerships was based on her religious view of marriage could not justify the conclusion that Islington should not be allowed to implement its aim to the full, namely that all registrars should perform civil partnerships as part of its Dignity for All policy. Ms Ladele was employed in a public job and was working for a public authority; she was being required to perform a purely secular task, which was being treated as part of her job; Ms Ladele's refusal to perform that task involved discriminating against gay people in the course of that job; she was being asked to perform the task because of Islington's Dignity for All policy, whose laudable aim was to avoid, or at least minimise, discrimination both among Islington's employees, and as between Islington (and its employees) and those in the community they served; Ms Ladele's refusal was causing offence to at least two of her gay colleagues; Ms Ladele's objection was based on her view of marriage, which was not a core part of her religion; and Islington's requirement in no way prevented her from worshipping as she wished.

McFarlane v Relate Avon Limited

The third high-profile case in this area is that of *McFarlane v Relate Avon Limited* (2010). Here a Christian counsellor refused to offer psycho-sexual therapy to same-sex partners because he regarded same-sex sexual activity as sinful. He was, however, prepared to counsel same-sex couples where sexual issues were not involved. He was dismissed for refusing to implement Relate's equal opportunities policy. His claim for direct discrimination was rejected because the reason he was dismissed was because he was unwilling to abide by the equal opportunities policy, and Relate would have treated a non-Christian counsellor who refused in the same way. His claim of indirect discrimination was also dismissed because Relate were able to justify the requirement in order to provide non-discriminatory services, as had the council in the *Ladele* case. The EAT agreed, and Mr Mcfarlane was refused permission to appeal further by the Court of Appeal.

Both *McFarlane* and *Ladele* are, at the time of writing (autumn 2011) in the process of appealing to the European Court of Human Rights.

 **Activity 15.6   Less equal than others**

Read the following paragraphs and answer the questions that follow:

Paul and Graham work together as waiters in a large business hotel. Paul recently came out as gay. Graham is a devout evangelical Christian.

One day after work the two men, along with colleagues, attend a drinks party in a local café bar in honour of another colleague who is leaving the hotel.

An argument breaks out between them which starts in a very civilised way, but becomes ill-tempered and abusive. Graham tells Paul that homosexuality is a sin and that Paul is going to go to hell when he dies unless he renounces his sexuality and asks for forgiveness. In return Paul tells Graham what he thinks of his brand of Christianity in very colourful language.

The following day both Paul and Graham make separate complaints about the other's conduct to their manager.

Questions

1   What potential legal issues are thrown up by this case?

2   How would you advise the hotel manager to proceed, having received the complaints?

These cases therefore show that although the law protects an employee from being discriminated against because of his or her religion, it does not protect the right to manifest that religion in any way that the employee chooses, particularly if that impinges on other rights that society has deemed fit to protect, and that an employer's commitment to an equal opportunities policy can justify indirect discrimination.

The cases of *Ladele* and *Eweida* (see the 'dress code' cases above) are currently going before the European Court of Human Rights in Strasbourg. The Equality and Human Rights Commission is proposing to make a submission to the court, and in August 2011 it launched a new consultation asking for views as to whether the correct principles were applied in *Eweida* and another crucifix case to make sure that the freedom of religion and belief under the European Convention on Human Rights was properly respected.

The consultation also asks whether or not the justification tests were correctly applied in *Ladele* and the cases involving Christians working with gay couples.

The EHRC is also consulting on whether the concept of reasonable accommodation, which is currently only used in disability discrimination where employers have a duty to make reasonable adjustments, should be used in cases dealing with manifestation of religious beliefs.

REFERENCES

Carter, H. (2009) 'Jedi religion founder accuses Tesco of discrimination over rules on hoods' *The Guardian*, 18 September.

Christian Institute (2000) *Church of England Newspaper*. 2 June. Quoted in Gay and Lesbian Humanist Association response to the directive (www.galha.org/). See also discussion in House of Lords Select Committee in Europe, fourth report, 19 December 2000.

Davis, H. (2008) 'A wing and a prayer' The *Guardian*, 12 May.

Dutt, A. (2006) 'A Cross to Bear?' 156 *New Law Journal* 1900.

Explanatory Notes to the Equality Act.

Gilbert, H. (2010) 'Protected belief guidelines leave HR baffled' *Personnel Today*,12 March.

Hepple, B. & Choudhury T. (2001) 'Tackling Religious Discrimination: Practical Implications for Policy Makers and Legislators'. *Home Office Research Study 22.* London: HMSO.

Levine, M. and Ford, L. (2011) 'Do you believe in fairies?' *Employment Law Journal*, June 2011.

McColgan, A. (2009) 'Class wars? Religion and (in)equality in the workplace' *Industrial Law Journal* 38.1, March 2009.

Vickers, L. (2008) *Religious Freedom, Religious Discrimination and the Workplace*. Oxford: Hart Publishing. (Vickers 1).

Vickers, L. (2008) *Religious Discrimination at Work*. The Institute of Employment Rights. (Vickers 2).

Weller, P., Feldman, A. and Purdam, K. (2001) 'Religious Discrimination in England and Wales' *Home Office Research, Development and Statistics Directorate*, February 2001. University of Derby.

ONLINE RESOURCE CENTRE

A range of online resources to help you through your employment law module have been developed by the author team. These include updates, self-test questions and sources for further reading. (www.oxfordtextbooks.co.uk/orc/taylor_emir3e)

Sex discrimination

16

Learning outcomes

By the end of this chapter you should be able to:

- understand the reasons for the introduction of sex discrimination law in the UK;

- define the term 'direct sex discrimination' and explain its meaning in practice;

- advise when an employer can justify discriminating on grounds of sex;

- advise on the legal position vis-à-vis workplace dress codes that are different for male and for female employees;

- set out the types of harassment in relation to sex and give examples.

Introduction

Sex, or gender, was one of the first types of characteristic to be protected in English law by means of the Sex Discrimination Act 1975. It is one of the most important areas of discrimination law in terms of volume of cases. There have been a number of changes to the Sex Discrimination Act over the years, but it is now harmonised with the other protected characteristics as part of the Equality Act.

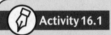 **Activity 16.1**

Consider the following situations and think about the questions posed. You should be able to answer the questions accurately when you have read to the end of the chapter.

1 A man is refused a job working on the make-up counter in a large department store. Is this unlawful sex discrimination? If it is, is it direct or indirect? If it is discriminatory, does the employer have any defence? Would your answer be any different if the job was as a sales assistant, with responsibility for a ladies' changing room?

2 A female plumber is refused a job in a plumbing firm as the employer feels there would be trouble if he had a woman amongst his all-male workforce. Is this unlawful? Would the employer's explanation be valid? What if it had been a man applying to an all-female plumbing firm, which was aimed at female clients?

3 Is it unlawful to require female employees to wear skirts while they are at work?

4 When an act of unlawful sexual harassment is committed in the workplace, is it more common for the employer or the perpetrator to end up having to defend itself in an employment tribunal? Why?

Historical background

Until the Sex Discrimination Act 1975 and the Equal Pay Act 1971 came into force, there was no sex discrimination legislation in Great Britain. Before this legislation, women had very few rights if they were given worse treatment than men, both in the employment sphere and outside it. The first step in the right direction was the Married Women's Property Act of 1882. Before this statute, once a woman married, any property that she may have possessed would become that of her husband. The Victorian woman had no right to vote, no right to custody of her children on separation or divorce, could be beaten by her husband as proper chastisement so long as he used an implement no thicker than his thumb (the origin of the phrase 'rule of thumb'). She certainly had no right not to be discriminated against in the workplace.

The suffragettes were vociferous in their pursuit of the right to vote, but it was the changes in society wrought by the First World War that started the move which eventually led, several decades later, to the formal recognition that women should not be treated worse than men just because of their sex. It was during that war that women first started to be employed

Exhibit 16.1   **Women's place in the workplace before the First World War**

The first woman to be employed by the Bank of England at the beginning of the twentieth century was Jane Elizabeth Courtney. She had a degree from Oxford in Philosophy, German and Greek, and yet, as a woman, was deemed fit only to work in the sorting office of the bank, counting banknotes, with nothing else to do but '*lay out bank notes in patterns like patience cards*' (Jane Elizabeth Courtney, 'Recollected in Tranquillity', London, 1936).

In the words of Stanley Leathes, the first Civil Service Commissioner, in 1913: '*I think it would be rather awkward to have men and women working together, shoulder to shoulder, in the same department. I do not wish to see it. If we think of employing women, we always think, is there a room we can put them in by themselves*'.

Some companies did not just provide separate rooms for the women, but also separate entrances and staircases, so that women would, literally, enter by the back door. This was done by large banks and insurance companies so that the two sexes would be completely segregated, not just so that there would be no mingling, but also so that the women could not compare their conditions and wages with those of their male colleagues.

Source: 'Office Politics' Exhibition 2004, The Women's Library

---

in large numbers in factories and businesses, taking over the jobs left vacant by the men who had gone to the front. The effect of this can be seen from the statistics: before the war, apart from those in service, women's jobs were generally restricted to housekeeping, teaching and tailoring. In 1911, women accounted for 18% of office workers; by 1921 this had increased to 46% ('Office Politics' Exhibition 2004, the Women's Library).

Women achieved universal suffrage in 1928, and more women were entering the workplace, yet the discrimination problem had not been solved. The 'marriage bar' was still in place, as it was the general attitude of employers at the time that, although they might employ a woman, once she married, then her place was in the home. It was not until the mid 1990s that female judges could even be acknowledged as such in court. Before that, Dame Elizabeth Butler-Sloss, at the time the only female judge in the Court of Appeal, was known as 'Lord Butler-Sloss'. Eventually the Lord Chief Justice issued a practice direction to say that henceforth she could be known as 'Lady' Butler-Sloss.

The Sex Discrimination Act was therefore a long-needed statute, but also revolutionary in the way that it sought to change the views of the society of the time. This was acknowledged by the Employment Appeal Tribunal when considering the case of *Peake v Automotive Products* (1977) when the Act was described by Mr Justice Phillips as follows:

a reforming Act . . . deliberately introducing new ideas and policies.

His first, instinctive reaction to the case was that there was no sex discrimination in that case, but his reasoning told him otherwise:

In truth, no guidance can be got from instinctive feelings; rather the reverse. Such feelings are likely to be the result of ingrained social attitudes, assumed to be permanent, but rendered obsolete by changing values and current legislation.

 Exhibit 16.2

According to the Employment Tribunal Statistics 2009–2010, claims of sex discrimination were higher than any other kind of discrimination. There were 18,200 claims. Most, however, were withdrawn, with successful claims only amounting to 2% of those brought to tribunal, and the number of such claims was less than the previous year.

Legal background

In the UK, as we saw in Chapter 10, the legal basis for the prohibition of sex discrimination came from domestic law, European Law and the European Convention on Human Rights. There was a particular influence of the European Court of Justice.

The two original British statutes were the Sex Discrimination Act 1975 and the Equal Pay Act 1971 (the background to which was graphically portrayed in the film 'Made in Dagenham'). Both pieces of legislation were complementary, and both came into force on the same day at the end of December 1975. The Equal Pay Act dealt with pay and benefits regarded as pay within employment. The Sex Discrimination Act covered sex discrimination, not only within the employment field, but also discrimination in the provision of goods, services and facilities. It was used to develop the law in relation to pregnancy and gender reassignment, as we have seen, and also sexual orientation as we shall consider in this chapter. All this has now been collated within the Equality Act.

Protected characteristic

The law applies equally to men and women. So, if a man has been subjected to unlawful sex discrimination, he has the same protection as a woman, and he can bring an action in exactly the same way that a woman can (apart from special treatment given to pregnant women, which is dealt with in the following chapter). In this book, however, the complainant will usually be referred to in the feminine, as she will more commonly be a woman.

Prohibited conduct

Direct discrimination

For the purposes of sex discrimination, direct discrimination is when a person treats another less favourably than he treats others and this less favourable treatment is because of his or her sex.

'Less favourably'

In order to bring a successful claim for direct discrimination, a woman has to show that she has been treated less favourably than a man in similar circumstances has been treated, or would have been treated. This man, who can be real or hypothetical, is the woman's 'comparator'.

The treatment has to be less favourable—this does not mean merely treating differently, but there has to be some element of detriment. This can be illustrated in dress code examples, such as the case of *Department for Work and Pensions v Thompson* (2004), where the EAT permitted a rule requiring men to wear a collar and tie. Tribunals generally take account even of small differences and so the extent of the detriment is generally reflected in the level of compensation awarded.

Exhibit 16.3   *Shamoon v Chief Constable of the Royal Ulster Constabulary* (2003)

Ms Shamoon was a senior police officer who brought a claim alleging less favourable treatment than two other police officers of the same rank, who were in the same force as her. Complaints had been made about her, and as a result, some of her duties had been taken away from her. She said that this was a detriment, compared with the other two officers.

The House of Lords said that the two male officers were not the appropriate comparators to choose, as no complaints had been made about their behaviour. The proper comparator would be a male police officer of the same rank (whether real or hypothetical), who had also had a complaint made against him, and who had been, or would have been, treated more favourably than Ms Shamoon.

Lord Hope said '*a comparison of the cases of persons of a different sex . . . must therefore be such that all the circumstances which are relevant to the way they were treated in the one case are the same, or not materially different, in the other*'.

So, suffering a detriment is not enough. A claimant has to show that she was treated less favourably than the comparator would have been, and he has to be someone who is in much the same circumstances as the claimant.

Occupational requirements

As we have seen, direct discrimination cannot be justified. In cases of sex discrimination, the only acceptable reason is that of occupational requirement, which in sex discrimination cases used to be known as genuine occupational qualifications or requirements. There used to be an exhaustive list set out in the Sex Discrimination Act, but now the only issue is that the requirement must be crucial to the post, and not one of several important factors, with examples given in the notes to the Act, as explained in Chapter 11.

 Activity 16.2   *Wylie v Dee & Co (Menswear) Ltd* (1978)

The complainant was directed by a job centre to a clothing store which had four vacancies. The shop already employed seven male assistants. She was told that the post was not suitable for a woman because she would have to take the inside leg measurement of the customers. She had considerable experience in men's tailoring and taking men's inside measurements.

The employer claimed that it was a genuine occupational qualification to preserve decency and privacy.

The EAT rejected this explanation, saying it was not necessary to take an inside leg measurement very often, as most men knew what their measurement was, or an experienced assistant could estimate it and, (more importantly) one of the other seven assistants, who were male, could take the measurement.

Questions

1   Do you think the same principle would apply in the case of a man applying to work in a ladies fashion store?

2   What jobs in clothes retailing might legitimately justify an occupational requirement?

Exhibit 16.4   *Buckinghamshire County Council v Ahmed* (1998)

The EAT allowed an appeal against a finding of unlawful discrimination against a man who had not been given work as a Punjabi interpreter. His name was on a list held by the council, but in fact it had only used female interpreters. The EAT ruled that the tribunal has erred in rejecting as a GOQ the council's evidence that:

in a number of the ethnic communities with which they dealt and in particular the Punjabi Muslim community, there was great delicacy in dealing with women who were concerned in various social or medical or other problems. It was said that if an interpreter were to go in to one of the homes, or see women collectively at perhaps a 'well woman' session, or women's health session or something of that sort, it would be regarded generally in the community and by the woman concerned as inappropriate that the interpreter should be a man. It was said that although if (say) a white social worker went to the house, that might be in order, if a person who was a Punjabi went there it were better, it said, that it should be a woman than a man, out of feelings of delicacy and tact.

It was not said, of course, that it was essential that it should be a woman interpreter but what was said was that the services could be provided more effectively; it would be easier for a Punjabi Muslim woman on many occasions, to explain in such matters as the case perhaps where her children had been involved in matters which had attracted the attention of the police, or where she herself had medico-social problems or something like that. It would be easier for her to speak to a woman and would not attract the sort of comment that might happen if a male Punjabi-speaker, particularly a Punjabi himself, were to go to the house.

Activity 16.3

Pauline Matthews (1996), writing before the Equality Act was conceived of, made some criticisms of the GOQs, pointing out that:

• There is no exemption for women-only services, and she asks whether the Sex Discrimination Act should consider the question of whether one sex is more vulnerable than the other. This would allow 'women-only' firms of plumbers, and such businesses.

• What about traditional women's jobs in nurseries and children's homes, and the fears about paedophiles being employed by them? Would it be a form of sexual stereotyping to avoid employing men, or is it a fear that should be legitimately recognised?

Are these covered by the Equality Act? What is your view?

Indirect discrimination

Like direct discrimination, this applies to both men and women. The definition of indirect discrimination in the Sex Discrimination Act was updated a couple of times, and of course is now harmonised with other types of protected conduct in the Equality Act.

The original definition of indirect discrimination in the Sex Discrimination Act needed a *'requirement or condition'* to which a *considerably smaller proportion of women could comply*, and to which the applicant *cannot* comply. This was an exceptionally high hurdle, as the courts interpreted it as putting an absolute bar on the ability of a proportion of women to comply, and required the court to find a 'pool of comparison'. The current definition makes indirect discrimination easier to prove. The previous definition also required that the complainant suffer a detriment, as opposed to disadvantage, which is not much different in practice. So far, this does not appear to differ greatly, but there has been very little case law. Many of the existing cases deal with the original definitions, and readers should bear this in mind when reading them.

Provision, criterion or practice

Many provisions that have been seen to be discriminatory tend to reflect the different lifestyle and childcare commitments that women have. Women tend to take time off to have children and look after them, so they may be older when they come back into the job market, and they are more likely than men to work part-time. Any provision which does not allow for this and makes working life more difficult for women than for men may be found to be indirectly discriminatory.

Some examples of how indirect discrimination has been used in cases are:

Age requirements. Before the age discrimination legislation came into force in 2006 (see Chapter 12), the use of indirect discrimination was the way in which women who were subjected to age requirements could claim for the discriminatory effect. The reason is that women are more likely than men to take out time from employment in order to have and to look after children, so this can be indirectly discriminatory, as was shown in the case of *Price v Civil Service Commission* (1978). Mrs Price replied to an advertisement for recruits to the Executive Officer grade of the Civil Service, but then discovered that there was an age requirement of 17–28. She was 35. This was found to be indirect discrimination, since far fewer women than men could comply as they were either having or bringing up children, and were therefore out of the labour market.

Unsociable hours. Because of child commitments, women will be less likely to be able to work such hours. The courts recognised this in the case of *London Underground v Edwards* (1995), where a change in shift rotas was held to be indirectly discriminatory against a female underground driver who had children (as discussed in Chapter 11).

Part-timers. Women are more likely to work part-time than men, so any provision which affects part-timers in a detrimental way compared to full-timers will probably be indirectly discriminatory (see *R v Secretary of State for Employment, ex parte EOC* (1994), below). Part-timers are also now covered by the regulations in Chapter 19.

Rewarding unbroken length of service. Again, this could be indirectly discriminatory because more women will have had time off, so their employment history will be interrupted.

Mobility requirements. Women are less likely than men to be able to move because of their childcare commitments.

Disadvantage

The threshold now is lower than for the previous definition as in the past a woman would have had to show that she could not comply with the requirement or condition, rather than it being merely to her disadvantage. *Shamoon* showed that it does not have to be physical or economic 'detriment' and that it can be construed fairly widely. Lord Hope in that case (dealing with the word 'detriment') said

> is the treatment of such a kind that a reasonable worker would or might take the view that in all the circumstances it was to his detriment?

 Activity 16.4   *R v Secretary of State for Employment, ex parte EOC* (1994)

This case showed that it is not only employment practices that can be challenged under the Sex Discrimination Act, but also statutes themselves that are discriminatory.

The Equal Opportunities Commission brought a challenge to the then requirement that those working between eight and sixteen hours a week had to work for five years before they were allowed to bring a claim for unfair dismissal or a redundancy payment, whereas those working more than sixteen hours a week only had to have been employed for two years.

It was accepted that 87% of part-time workers in the UK are women, but the Secretary of State contended that the provision was objectively justified, the purpose of the qualifying thresholds being to bring about an increase in the availability of part-time work, by reducing the incidental costs to employers of employing part-time workers.

Lord Keith of Kinkel, in the House of Lords, said at p181:

The bringing about of an increase in the availability of part-time work is properly to be regarded as a beneficial social policy aim and it cannot be said that it is not a necessary aim. The question is whether the threshold provisions . . . have been shown, by reference to objective factors, to be suitable and requisite for achieving that aim. As regards suitability for achieving the aim in question, it is to be noted that the purpose of the thresholds is said to be to reduce the costs to employers of employing part-time workers. The same result, however, would follow from a situation where the basic rate of pay for part-time workers was less than the basic rate for full-time workers. No distinction in principle can properly be made between direct and indirect labour costs. While in certain circumstances an employer might be justified in paying full-time workers a higher rate than part-time workers in order to secure the more efficient use of his machinery . . . that would be a special and limited state of affairs. Legislation which permitted a differential of that kind nationwide would present a very different aspect and considering that the great majority of part-time workers are women would surely constitute a gross breach of the principle of equal pay and could not possibly be regarded as a suitable means of achieving an increase in part-time employment. Similar considerations apply to legislation which reduces the indirect cost of employing part-time labour. Then as to the threshold provisions being requisite to achieve the stated aim, the question is whether on the evidence before the Divisional Court they have been proved actually to result in greater availability of part-time work than would be the case without them. In my opinion the question must be answered in the negative. The evidence for the Secretary of State consisted principally of an affidavit by an official in the Department of Employment which set out the views of the Department but did not contain anything capable of being regarded as factual evidence demonstrating the correctness of these views.   »

> **Questions**

1   What do you think was the decision in this case?

2   What effect did the decision have on the threshold provisions?

3   Why was the Secretary of State's argument deemed not to be justified?

Harassment

When the Sex Discrimination Act was passed in the early 1970s, there was no such concept as 'sexual harassment', and so it is not surprising, therefore, that it was not expressly defined in the Act. Until 2005, if a person wanted to claim sexual harassment, he or she would have had to prove all the necessary elements of direct discrimination, proving detriment and less favourable treatment on a case-by-case basis. The original case on this was *Porcelli v Strathclyde Regional Council* (1986), where the judges were very careful constantly to refer back to the definition of direct discrimination and ask whether a man would also have been subjected to a detriment. As Hepple points out, this often led to absurd results (Hepple, 2011: 78). The example Hepple gives is that of a woman who could not complain about pornographic displays at work, because a man might also have complained, making the displays gender neutral.

Later cases appeared to dilute the comparator aspect of it, leading to a situation where it appeared that sexual harassment, because it was directed at one sex in particular, did not need a comparator. This confusing situation was in a similar vein to the pregnancy decisions that we look at in Chapter 17.

As a result of European Law, harassment law was overhauled, and was added to the Sex Discrimination Act in 2005, and amended again in 2008 to be more in line with the Equal Treatment Directive of 2002. It is now clarified in the Equality Act in sections 26 and 40.

Where to draw the line?

Sexual harassment can take many forms, ranging from serious sexual assault to sex-based comments that one party finds amusing but the recipient feels are degrading. The existence of it can be difficult for people to accept, and they may find that they cannot draw the line between 'I was only flirting' or 'It's just a harmless bit of fun', and the affront to dignity and creation of a hostile working environment that many women feel that they are subjected to.

It can be difficult to know where to draw the line between lawful and unlawful conduct, especially when the two sides may view the same incident in different ways. What is simple flirting to a man may be viewed by the female subject of it as unwelcome and demeaning harassment. An invitation for a drink after work is hardly unlawful harassment, but it may become so if it is persisted in, or because of the language used or the manner in which it is made.

Some employers are concerned about what happens when people have a relationship at work, and it goes sour, leaving the employer liable to a claim of sexual harassment. In the USA this has been dealt with by some firms by means of a 'love contract', or consensual relationship agreements to regulate the position between co-workers and protect the employer from claims. They have taken that route as a preferable option to forbidding relationships between employees.

The Equal Opportunities Commission launched a campaign in 2002 against the 'Carry On Regardless' style of sexual harassment, which had the title 'Carry on Equality'. It was given this name in allusion to the 'Carry On' films of the 1960s and '70s, where women were regarded as sexual objects. The films may have been extremely funny and entertaining, but they were very much of their time. Society had by now accepted that women should not have to put up with such an environment at work and the law has kept apace with that view (EOC, 2002, available at www.equalityhumanrights.com). It is not just women who are harassed—Logan quotes a report by employment law firm Peninsula, which found that 77% of male workers had experienced sexual harassment by a female colleague, with many too afraid to complain to their employer, forcing them to endure silently (Logan, 2008). There is also the economic element in staff turnover and lower productivity, as well as the figures employers would have to pay in compensation following a successful harassment claim at

---

 Exhibit 16.5   **Sexism in the City**

A 2008 report by the Fawcett Society found that many firms in the City were using lap-dancing clubs for entertaining clients. It carried out a survey which found that 60% of women would be uncomfortable working for an organisation that allows its employees to use lap-dancing venues for entertaining clients. Half of the men (48%) and four in ten of the women (41%) said it was unacceptable for businesses to use lap-dance clubs as venues for entertaining clients. The report further found that '*behind the conspicuous wealth of the City lies a hidden story of disadvantage and discrimination affecting women at all levels of business*'.

Other findings were that:

- only 11% of FTSE 100 company directors are women

- only 26% of civil service top management are women

- 30,000 women lose their jobs every year in the UK simply for being pregnant

- two-thirds of low-paid workers are women

- women working full time are paid on average 17% less than men

- in 2005, 18% of sex discrimination compensation awards were for sexual harassment

- women's employment is concentrated in the five 'Cs—caring, cleaning, catering, clerical work and cashiering—and is valued less than traditional 'men's work'. The average annual pay of a mechanic is £17,700; that of a childcarer is £13,900

- UK full-time employees work the longest hours in the EU. Women, as the primary carers, cannot compete in a workplace where performance is judged according to hours put in, not quality of work produced

- traditional 'women's work' is undervalued

- nearly one in five women who work in London are at risk of poverty because they earn less than the London living wage.

Source: www.fawcettsociety.org.uk

tribunal, which Baker refers to as *'serious sums of compensation . . . secured by staff . . . who have been victims of sustained bullying and harassment'* (Baker 2008).

It should be noted that bullying is not the same thing as harassment. Bullying is a different issue, and takes place regardless of the sex, race or age, etc of the person being bullied. There is no remedy in discrimination law for that, but there is sometimes a remedy under contract law, or unfair dismissal if the person leaves and claims constructive dismissal (see Part II). Moreover, if it leads to serious ill health, particularly mental breakdown, there are potential remedies available in personal injury law (see Chapter 25).

The current law

The law is now set out in section 26 of the Equality Act, with a further prohibition on third party harassment in section 40. These have been discussed in more detail in Chapter 11. As discussed previously, the three types of harassment in section 29 are:

1. **Harassment**, which is defined as unwanted conduct which is related to a protected characteristic and has the purpose or effect of creating an intimidating, hostile, degrading, humiliating or offensive environment for the complainant or violating his or her dignity.

2. **Sexual Harassment**, which is defined as unwanted conduct of a sexual nature or related to gender reassignment which has the same purpose or effect as the first kind of harassment

3. **Harassment,** where someone has previously either submitted to or rejected conduct of a sexual nature or related sex or gender reassignment, and because of this they are treated less favourably than someone else.

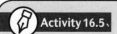 **Activity 16.5**

Can you think of other examples of harassment?
What kind of harassment would they be?

Victimisation

This applies to sex discrimination, as it does to other protected characteristics, and is discussed in more detail in Chapter 11.

Dress codes

Many people are subjected to some kind of restriction at work, whether because an employer expects certain levels of smartness from his employees or insists on a uniform being worn as part of the job. Over the years the courts have set out some principles for dealing with cases where people feel that they are being discriminated against compared with the other sex when it comes to their appearance. They have done this by using the principles of direct and indirect discrimination. The first major case was *Schmidt v Austicks Bookshops* (1977), with significant further principles being established in *Smith v Safeway plc* (1996). These are summarised as exhibits 16.6 and 16.7.

Exhibit 16.6   *Schmidt v Austicks Bookshops* (1977)

Ms Schmidt, who worked in a bookshop, complained that she was not allowed to wear trousers at work, and that she had to serve the public while wearing a skirt. Her refusal to comply led to her dismissal. Mr Justice Phillips made the following point in his judgment:

> . . . in so far as a comparison is possible, the employers treated both female and male staff alike in that both sexes were restricted in the choice of clothing for wear whilst at work and were both informed that a certain garment should not be worn during working hours. It seems to us . . . that an approach of that sort is a better approach and more likely to lead to a sensible result, than an approach which examines the situation point by point and garment by garment.

This case therefore laid down the principle that so long as both sexes were subject to restrictions in how they presented themselves, albeit not the same restrictions, given the difference between men and women, there would be no discrimination. This appears to have been followed in most of the cases since then.

 Exhibit 16.7   *Smith v Safeway PLC* (1996)

Mr Smith was dismissed because his pony tail grew too long to keep under his hat. Safeway's rule for male staff was 'Tidy hair not below shirt-collar length. No unconventional hairstyles or colouring'. The comparable rule for female staff referred to 'Tidy hair . . . Shoulder length hair must be clipped back. No unconventional hairstyles or colouring. Make up should be kept simple and to a minimum'.

The Court of Appeal rejected the claim, noting that the employers were seeking to promote a 'conventional' image.

Lord Justice Phillips said:

> 'Get your hair cut' is an instruction that I suspect most men have heard at some time, whether at school, in the armed forces or in the workplace. Usually the instruction is given not on ground of safety or hygiene [and that was not an issue in this case] but simply on grounds of appearance.

He followed the principle in *Schmidt*, and said that an appearance code which applies a standard of what is conventional to both men and women is one which is even-handed between men and women, and not discriminatory.

An interesting comment was made by one of the other judges, Lord Justice Legatt:

> Discrimination consists not in failing to treat men and women the same, but in treating those of one sex less favourably than those of the other. That is what is meant by treating them equally. If men and women were all required to wear lipstick, it could be the men who would be discriminated against. Provided that an employer's rules, taken as a whole, do not result in men being treated less favourably than women or vice versa, there is room for current conventions to operate.

Two key principles stand out from this case law:

1. Merely treating men and women differently does not necessarily mean that unlawful discrimination is occurring. Unless a man or a woman suffers a detriment because of direct or indirect discrimination, the act is not unlawful. Requiring a man to wear a tie or a woman to wear a skirt is not going to constitute a detriment in most circumstances. If someone was dismissed for not complying, however, that might constitute a detriment.

2. A key test used relates to 'standards of conventionality'. Provided men and women are required to maintain similar standards of smartness, no discrimination can be held to have occurred. So it is lawful, for example to require men to wear their hair short, while permitting women to have long hair. Similarly it is permissible to require men to wear conventional business suits, while permitting women more freedom to dress as they wish—provided a similar level of smartness is the result.

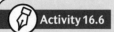 **Activity 16.6**

Consider the following real-life situations. Do you think they amount to sex discrimination?

1 A gay police officer was refused permission to wear a gold stud earring to work. His force allows female officers to wear discrete earrings, but not the men. (*Personnel Today*, 15 August 2006, Mike Berry)

2 A woman was forced to leave her job in the HMV department at Harrods because she refused to wear makeup. It was company policy to do so because of the 'washing out' effect of the store lighting. She was twice sent home and once made to work in the stockroom, but resigned when the incident escalated. (*The Guardian*, 1 July 2011, Caroline Davies)

3 A court in Germany ruled that an employer can force female employees to wear a bra, which had to be white or flesh coloured and that this was not sex discrimination. (*Daily Mail*, 12 January 2011, Allan Hall)

Questions

1 What is your view of these cases?

2 Can you think of other examples of dress codes that would be found to be discriminatory?

While the principle appears to have been laid down in *Schmidt*, and followed fairly consistently by the courts, the question remains whether it is in fact correct within the parameters of the Equality Act. As we have seen, the Act prohibits treatment of one sex which is less favourable than the treatment accorded to the other sex. Would forcing a man to wear a tie, whereas, for example, a woman is told she cannot wear pink, be equivalent? As Paul Skidmore, writing in the *Industrial Law Journal*, comments on the case of *Smith*:

> Most people have culturally conditioned, historically-specific views and expectations as to the gender connection between clothing/appearance and sex. The judiciary have in general failed to appreciate that this stereotyping of men and women could give rise to sex discrimination.

When employees have challenged employer-imposed dress requirements which differentiate between men and women, these have generally been upheld provided they impose a comparable degree of restriction on men and women.

. . . For a man to lose his job for having long hair, when a woman with hair of the same length would not have done so, should on any interpretation constitute less favourable treatment. . . . Their lordships in the Court of Appeal appear to have feared that if dress codes were not permitted to enforce conventional gender stereotypes, men might have to wear lipstick and earrings. This fantasy of their Lordships fails to consider that a more neutral dress code could be used, for example, banning jeans, t-shirts, trainers, the wearing of jewellery, etc, which could apply equally to all workers and which could achieve the aim of neatness and tidiness if that was thought to have been important.

There have been very few recent cases on sex discrimination in dress codes. Most have concentrated on discrimination because of religion and belief rather than sex discrimination, and are considered in Chapter 15.

CHAPTER SUMMARY

- Sex discrimination is symmetrical in that it can be claimed by both men and women.

- Direct sex discrimination cannot be justified unless there is an occupational requirement.

- Indirect sex discrimination can be objectively justified.

- There are two types of harassment that are specifically related to sex.

- A person who has been treated less favourably for claiming sex discrimination or giving evidence in such a matter can claim victimisation.

REFERENCES

Chamberlain, L. (2010) 'Employment Tribunal Statistics 2010: Which discrimination claims get the largest awards?' *Personnel Today* 8 September.

Employment Tribunal Statistics (2010).

Hepple, B. (2011) *Equality: The New Legal Framework*. Oxford: Hart Publishing.

London Department of Employment (1974) *Equality for Women*. London: LDE, Cmnd 5724.

Matthews, P. (1996) 'Legal Concepts of Justifying Discrimination' in J. Dine and B. Watt (eds): *Discrimination Law*. London: Longman.

Women and Equality Unit (2005) *Equality and Diversity: Updating the Sex Discrimination Act—Government Response to Consultation*. Department of Trade and Industry: London. 31 August (available at www.equalities.gov.uk/publications/etadgovtresponse.pdf).

ONLINE RESOURCE CENTRE

A range of online resources to help you through your employment law module have been developed by the author team. These include updates, self-test questions and sources for further reading. (www.oxfordtextbooks.co.uk/orc/taylor_emir3e)

Sex-related characteristics (gender reassignment, marital status, pregnancy, sexual orientation)

17

Learning outcomes

By the end of this chapter you should be able to:

- explain who is protected by the law on discrimination on grounds of marital status and civil partnership and who is not;

- understand the extent to which the law protects transsexuals from discrimination and give appropriate advice on related issues;

- set out the law on discriminatory treatment of pregnant women;

- state what is prohibited in relation to sexual orientation discrimination.

Introduction

When the Sex Discrimination Act was passed in the early 1970s the only specific type of discrimination that the UK Parliament thought necessary to outlaw specifically, in addition to general sex discrimination, was discrimination on grounds of marital status. There was no protection for the other groups that are listed in this chapter: those who have changed gender; pregnant women; homosexual and bisexual people. It was then left to the courts to try to extend that protection to these other vulnerable groups by attempting to interpret the legislation in order to confer protection. They tried to shoe-horn such protection into the definition of sex discrimination. This only worked for pregnancy and gender reassignment. Sexual orientation was eventually added into the Act with the help of European law. This has all now been collated in the Equality Act, and so discrimination because of the protected characteristics of gender reassignment, marital status and civil partnership and pregnancy and maternity are all included.

 Activity 17.1

Consider the following statements. Which do you think are correct and which are false?

1 It is quite lawful to discriminate against someone who is not married.

2 A person has to have had an operation to change their sex before the law will protect them against gender reassignment discrimination.

3 There are circumstances in which an employer can justify treating a pregnant woman less favourably.

4 A gay man has to tell his employer about his sexuality.

Return to this activity once you have read the chapter to see how many of your answers were correct.

Gender reassignment

The term 'transsexual' has been described as applying *'to those who, whilst belonging physically to one sex, feel convinced that they belong to the other; they often seek to achieve a more integrated, unambiguous identity by undergoing medical treatment and surgical operations to adapt their physical characteristics to their physical nature'* (European Court of Human Rights in the case of *Rees v UK*, 1986). The medical term is known as 'gender dysphoria', and government figures showed in 2005 that there were around 5,000 post-operative transsexuals in the UK, although other sources suggest there are more than 35,000 people who are, or will be, transsexual (Wigham, 2005 and The Women and Equality Unit, 2005). Since then the BBC have reported that it is estimated about 1% of the UK population is 'gender variant' (Summers, 2010).

There was originally no protection for transgender people against discrimination in the Sex Discrimination Act. Several non-employment cases went to the European Court of Human Rights, but did not succeed. It was not until the case of *P v S and Cornwall County Council* (1996) was decided in the European Court of Justice that transsexuals were deemed to come within the ambit of the Equal Treatment Directive. The court followed the opinion of the Advocate General, who stated:

> . . . how can it be claimed that discrimination on grounds of sex was not involved? How can it be denied that the cause of discrimination was precisely, and solely, sex?
>
> . . . I am well aware that I am asking the Court to make a courageous decision. I am asking it to do so, however, in the profound conviction that what is at stake is a universal fundamental value, indelibly etched in modern legal traditions and in the constitutions of the more advanced countries: *the irrelevance of a person's sex with regard to the rules regulating regulations in society.*

The court followed his argument and found that there had been a breach of the Equal Treatment Directive. It said that the Directive was the expression of the principle of equality, which is one of the fundamental principles of Community Law, and applies to discrimination based essentially, if not exclusively, on the sex of the person concerned.

As a result, the Sex Discrimination Act was amended and eventually prohibited direct discrimination, harassment and victimisation on the grounds that a person intends to undergo, is undergoing or has undergone gender reassignment treatment. This has now been extended by the Equality Act to all types of prohibited conduct.

Protected characteristic

Section 7 of the Equality Act protects a person who has proposed, started, or completed a process to change their sex. Originally the Sex Discrimination Act only protected those who had had medical treatment for gender reassignment, but the courts found it a difficult line to draw. The law now covers people who simply intend to live their lives as a member of the opposite sex (although it does not cover transvestites, in other words those who sometimes dress as a member of the other sex, but then revert to their own sex).

The notes to the Act give the following examples:

- A person who was born physically male decides to spend the rest of his life living as a woman. He declares his intention to his manager at work, who makes appropriate arrangements, and she then starts life at work and home as a woman. After discussion with her doctor and a Gender Identity Clinic, she starts hormone treatment and after several years she goes through gender reassignment surgery. She would have the protected characteristic of gender reassignment for the purposes of the Act.

- A person who was born physically female decides to spend the rest of her life as a man. He starts and continues to live as a man. He decides not to seek medical advice as he successfully 'passes' as a man without the need for any medical intervention. He also would have the protected characteristic of gender reassignment for the purposes of the Act.

The line for employers can appear a difficult one to tread. Lindsay J, speaking in the EAT in the case of *Croft*, encapsulated the problem for the employer, who

> . . . had to steer between the Scylla of not paying due respect to one employee's wishes, without intrusive inquiry into deeply personal matters, and the Charybdis of not respecting the wishes of other employees . . . being a manifestation of widely-held views as to a certain form of privacy or propriety.

It is a difficult situation to negotiate. The Women and Equalities Unit gives guidance on this, which is summarised by Sutton (2005). She advises that employers must tread carefully when dealing with staff undergoing gender reassignment, and suggests that there are two main areas where they should take care—when an employee decides to have gender reassignment, and when an employee has had gender reassignment in the past and the employer finds out. Sutton states that both scenarios require sensitive handling. In the first it is essential that managers discuss and agree with the employee how the process is to be handled, and in the second, the employer must ensure that the employee's confidentiality is respected and their gender status is not disclosed unless they wish it to be.

After the case of *P v S*, the European Court of Human Rights decided the case of *Godwin v UK*, a non-employment case, which led to the Gender Reassignment Bill in the UK. This came into force in April 2005 and allows people who have undergone gender reassignment to apply to have their birth certificate amended to reflect their acquired gender, and therefore to be treated legally as someone of the new gender.

 **Activity 17.2**

Chris works as a truck driver, which is a very male-dominated industry. He has always felt that he should have been a woman, and decides that he is going to start living as one. He intends to have an operation in due course, but in the meantime turns up to work in female clothing and jewellery.

His colleagues think it is both hilarious and distasteful, and taunt him for it. His managers find his way of dressing embarrassing for the company and its clients, and reduce his shifts (and therefore his income) accordingly. When Chris complains, he is told that although he will not be dismissed, he may be happier in another industry, and perhaps he should find himself another job.

1   What rights does Chris have?

2   What questions do you need to ask if you are representing him?

Prohibited conduct

The Act prohibits direct and indirect discrimination on grounds of gender reassignment, as well as harassment and victimisation. In section 16 it further specifically prohibits treating a transgender person who is absent from work for the purpose of gender reassignment less favourably than they would have been if they had been absent because of illness, for example, if the person was off work because he was receiving hormone treatment as part of his gender reassignment.

Occupational requirement

Schedule 9 allows employers to discriminate lawfully in limited circumstances where being of a particular sex, or not being a transsexual person, is an occupational requirement for the job, but the treatment must be reasonable in the circumstances. The example given in the notes is that of a counsellor working with female rape victims, who might have to be a woman by birth, and not a transsexual person (even if she has a gender recognition certificate) in order to avoid causing further distress. Other examples may be where the job involves the holder being liable to perform intimate physical searches.

The employer may also have a defence to discrimination where the employment is for the purposes of an organised religion, which was discussed in Chapter 15.

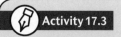

Activity 17.3

Consider the following cases, both decided before the Equality Act came into force:

1 In *A v Chief Constable of West Yorkshire* (2004) a woman who had formerly been a man applied to become a police officer. She was not appointed on the grounds that she would not be able to conduct searches of females. The Chief Constable relied on the genuine occupational requirement conditions, and said that as searching people was an intimate matter, this should only be done by someone who is of the same sex. The House of Lords said that the applicant should be treated as if she were a woman, and indeed this case would no longer come to court.

2 In *Croft v Royal Mail* (2003) an employee, who was biologically a man, intended to use the female toilets at work before she had undergone the operation. Permission to do this was refused by her employer, who said she should either use the male toilets, or a unisex disabled toilet, as female staff who had known Croft as a man were unhappy with the situation.

The Court of Appeal said that if it had been a permanent exclusion from using the female toilets, then that would have been unlawful discrimination. An employee could not, however, turn up one day as a woman and immediately demand to use the female toilets. The moment at which she would become entitled to use the female facilities depended on all the circumstances, and the employer was acting reasonably by allowing her to use the disabled facilities in the meantime. In other words, the point at which the person has changed sex is a matter of fact to be decided in the circumstances of the particular case.

Would the outcome of each case be the same or different now that the Equality Act is in force? The Act requires a comparator. Who would the comparator in each case be?

Married persons and civil partners

Prohibited characteristic

Discrimination on grounds of marital status or civil partnership was originally specifically prohibited by the Sex Discrimination Act 1975, and has been continued in the Equality Act, which makes illegal discrimination against men or women who are married or who are civil partners.

The reason for the section is that historically, when working women married, their employers then expected them to give up their job (known as the 'marriage bar', and this is why the section was needed. In the consultations before the finalising of the Equality Act, respondents were split 50/50 as to whether to retain such a provision. The government decided to keep it in case this kind of discrimination became prevalent again (IDS, 2010).

Originally this section only covered married persons, but in 2005 the Civil Partnerships Act amended this to add civil partners. Since then, the comparator has also changed. The original comparator in cases before the amendment was an unmarried person of the same sex as the claimant, but now the person should be compared to someone who is not married or not a civil partner, *irrespective* of that person's sex.

The statute is asymmetrical, in that it does not prevent discrimination against single people, those intending to get married/enter into a civil partnership or those living together, or those who are divorced. During discussions on the Equality Act, the government rejected calls to

Exhibit 17.1   **The Marriage Bar**

Although women achieved universal suffrage in 1928, and more women were entering the workplace, the 'marriage bar' was still endemic in most occupations, apart from the interwar years. The general attitude of employers at the time was that, although they might employ a woman, once she married, then her place was in the home.

In 1923, female teachers tried to have the marriage bar abolished within their profession by taking the matter to court, but the male judges, unsurprisingly given the attitudes of the time, did not agree with them—*Price v Rhondda* (1923).

The marriage bar was eventually abolished by the Civil Service in 1946, but it was not until 1968 that most companies followed suit and began to eradicate the practice. Even for companies that abolished the marriage bar early on, the discriminatory practices continued in a different form. In a 1933 memo to married women, the BBC wrote:

> Women on the staff who are already married should understand that the question of their retention on the staff or otherwise would have to be considered afresh should they contemplate having children. (BBC written archives centre, seen at Office Politics Exhibition, Women's Library, 2004)

expand protection to single people or unmarried couples. They said that in relation to unmarried couples, the legislation would have difficulty in drawing a line reflecting the permanence or otherwise of any particular relationship, and in relation to unmarried couples because there was no evidence that there was any such discrimination by prospective employers (IDS, 2010). Hepple points out that this '*exclusion of single and cohabiting persons may, sooner or later, be challenged as being incompatible with ECHR articles 8 (private and family life) and 14 (equality)*' (Hepple 2011:49). He quotes the case of *Re P: Unmarried Couple* (2008) where it was held that a provision referring to a 'married couple' should include an unmarried couple so as to comply with human rights law. It remains to be seen whether any cases come to court on this matter.

 **Activity 17.4**

The owner of a bed and breakfast advertises for a married couple to live in and run his hotel. A young heterosexual couple, who are not married, apply for the job, but are refused an interview because they are not married. It is pointed out to them that the customers, many of whom are elderly, might feel uncomfortable with the situation.

Questions

1   Is this unlawful discrimination?

2   If so, on what grounds is it unlawful discrimination?

3   If not, do you think that it should be unlawful?

4   Would your answer be any different if the couple had been homosexual?

Prohibited conduct

It is prohibited, on grounds of marital status, to discriminate against someone directly (section 13) or indirectly (section 19), or, in employment cases to harass or victimise such a person (sections 40 and 39 relating to employment).

Occupational requirement

There are no occupational requirements for married couples, but there is the exception for organised religion, which is discussed in Chapter 15.

 Activity 17.5 *Chief Constable of Bedfordshire v Graham* **(2002)**

Ms Graham was an inspector in Bedfordshire police, who married a chief superintendent in the same force. He was Divisional Commander of D division. A year later, she applied for and got a post as an Area Inspector within D division, but the Chief Constable blocked her promotion. He said it was inappropriate because of her husband's position in the same division. One reason was that criminal proceedings were to be brought against the husband, and under the criminal procedure rules a wife could not be forced to give evidence against her husband. Moreover, he thought that the officers reporting to her would be in a very difficult position if they needed to complain about her to more senior officers.

The tribunal considered whether this was discrimination on grounds of marital status, and found that the Chief Constable had treated Ms Graham less favourably on grounds of marital status than he had treated or would treat an unmarried person of the same sex. They noted that the Chief Constable had said that the principal reason for his decision was that as the spouse of a serving officer she would not be allowed to work in the same division because she could not be compelled to give evidence against him, and this applied only to people who were married to each other and so was marriage specific. The EAT agreed when the case was appealed.

Questions

1 Would this decision have been the same if the couple had been unmarried?

2 What if they had previously been married, but were now divorced?

3 Who was the comparator in this case?

Pregnancy and maternity discrimination

(For a full discussion on statutory rights to maternity leave, etc, please see Chapter 20.)

As originally drafted, the Sex Discrimination Act did not specifically prohibit discrimination against women on the ground of their pregnancy. This omission led to a number of cases both in the UK and European Court of Justice, involving a struggle on the part of the judges to try to fit pregnancy discrimination into the traditional sex discrimination model. The main difficulty was that the SDA required a comparator, and, as men could not become pregnant, there was no such thing as a pregnant male comparator, although some argued that the comparator should be a sick man.

The European Court of Justice, however, eventually set out principles in a line of cases such as *Dekker* (1991), which said that pregnancy discrimination came within the Equal Treatment Directive, and that there was no requirement for a male comparator.

This was not the end of it however, as even when Parliament amended the Sex Discrimination Act in 2005, it still decided to include a comparator in the section (the comparator being someone who was not pregnant). The Equal Opportunities Commission challenged this in the case of *Equal Opportunities Commission v Secretary of State for Trade and Industry* (2007), as it was not compliant with the Amended Equal Treatment Directive 2002/73/EC, and so the SDA was amended further. Even so, an investigation by the then Equal Opportunities Commission found in 2005 that notwithstanding the legislation, 'each year, over a half of the 440,000 pregnant women in Great Britain experience some form of disadvantage at work, simply for being pregnant or taking maternity leave. 30,000 are forced out of their jobs' (EOC, 2005).

The Equality Act does not require a comparator in pregnancy discrimination. This has been lauded by several organisations, including the Fawcett Society, which nonetheless states that there are still 30,000 women per year losing their jobs in 2011 because of pregnancy, and that the situation is becoming worse because of the recession (Fawcett Society, 2011).

Protected characteristic

A woman is protected from discrimination in the workplace from the time that she becomes pregnant, until the end of what is known as the 'protected period', which is the period of the pregnancy and any statutory maternity leave that she is entitled to. The protection is only if the employer knows that she is pregnant, or there are symptoms from which he can reasonably suspect pregnancy (*Ramdoolar v Bycity Ltd* (2005). Outside the protected period, a woman can claim sex discrimination.

The right is asymmetrical, in that it does not cover men. In addition, men cannot complain of any special treatment given to women in connection with pregnancy or childbirth.

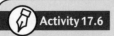
Activity 17.6

There were calls during the consultation period of the Act for parental responsibilities to be added to the list of protected characteristics. The government did not do so on the grounds that it had already done enough by extending the right to flexible working to those with children up to the age of sixteen (see Chapter 20) (IDS, 2010). Employees are also already protected from detrimental treatment for taking paternity or parental leave under section 47C of the Employment Rights Act 1996.

Question

1   When you have read Chapter 20 on family friendly policies, come back to this question: Do you agree with the government's argument that it has done enough to protect those with family responsibilities? Do the rights in the Employment Rights Act coupled with the right to request flexible working protect in the same way as the Equality Act? Give reasons for your answers.

Although pregnancy is listed in the list of protected characteristics in section 4 of the Equality Act, it is not defined in the following sections in the same format as the other characteristics. Instead, there are two sections, 17 and 18, which make it a particular prohibited conduct to discriminate because of pregnancy. Section 17 refers to non-work cases, and section 18 to work cases. There is no practical consequence to this, however, and it is to be treated as a protected characteristic in its own right.

Prohibited conduct

As with other kinds of discrimination, direct discrimination under section 13 is prohibited for pregnancy (although not associative or perceptive discrimination). There is special provision in the section that allows for special treatment of a woman because of pregnancy or childbirth. The section also emphasises that a woman must not be directly discriminated against if she is breastfeeding.

It is unlikely that the direct discrimination in section 13 will be used much, however, as a comparator is required. It is more likely that the section 18 right will be used in work cases, as this does not require a comparator, and merely prohibits 'unfavourable treatment' as opposed to 'less favourable treatment'.

The section 18 discrimination at work applies to a woman in the 'protected period'. This period starts when the woman becomes pregnant, and ends:

- If she has the right to ordinary and additional maternity leave (see Chapter 20 for explanation of these terms), at the end of her maternity leave period, or when she returns to work if this is earlier.

- If she does not have that right, then the protected period ends two weeks after the pregnancy finishes.

It protects a woman from being treated unfavourably either because of her pregnancy, or because of an illness suffered by her as a result of it within the protected period.

The specific employment-related examples given in the notes to the Act are:

- An employer must not demote or dismiss an employee, or deny her training or promotion opportunities, because she is pregnant or on maternity leave.

- An employer must not take into account an employee's period of absence due to pregnancy-related illness when making a decision about her employment.

Indirect discrimination is not specifically prohibited in pregnancy or maternity cases, although Selwyn suggests that section 18 provides sufficient protection.

Defences

There is no occupational requirement for pregnancy. Some commentators, such as Bowers and Moran, have suggested that there should be a defence of justification in some cases, as discussed in Chapter 11.

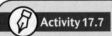

Activity 17.7

ABC and Sons is a company which employs twenty-three people. It has two female receptionists. Sandy, one of the receptionists, becomes pregnant and goes on maternity leave. Rebecca applies to fill her post as maternity cover. One week after starting work, she tells the employer that she is also pregnant.

Question

1   What options are available to ABC and Sons? What further information would you need to find out before giving your advice?

Discrimination on grounds of sexual orientation

Exhibit 17.2

In 1993 Stonewall conducted a survey of over 2,000 lesbians, gay men and bisexuals. The survey resulted in a report 'Less Equal Than Others' and showed that:

- 16% of respondents (one in six) had at least one experience of discrimination; a further 21% (one in five) suspected they had. 8% had actually been dismissed because of their sexuality.

- 48% of respondents (nearly one in two) said they had been harassed because of their sexuality.

- 24% of respondents (one in four) had avoided certain jobs, careers or employers for fear of discrimination because of their sexuality.

- Two-thirds of respondents who were working concealed their sexuality from people they worked with.

- 19% concealed their sexuality from some people. Only 11% of all respondents never concealed their sexuality at work.

Although this survey was carried out some time ago, there is little evidence that the situation has changed. Fifteen years later, a further poll carried out on behalf of Stonewall found that in the employment field, nearly one in five lesbian and gay people, almost 350,000 employees in Britain, say they have experienced bullying from their colleagues (including those junior to them) because of their sexual orientation, despite the changes in the legislation (Hunt and Dick, 2008).

It is now estimated that 6% of the UK population is gay, lesbian or bisexual (Hepple, 2011), yet Hudson, writing in *Personnel Today*, reports that many people still conceal their sexuality at work and that it has been found by Stonewall that *'concealing sexual orientation at work reduces productivity by up to 30%, and people who are out in supportive workplaces are more creative, loyal and productive'*. (Hudson, 2010)

History and background

As with religion, there was historically much debate as to whether discrimination on grounds of sexual orientation should be prohibited, and many attempts were made to 'fit' such discrimination into the framework of the Sex Discrimination Act, as was done with pregnancy and gender reassignment. They tried to argue, as transsexuals had successfully done, that the word 'sex' in the Sex Discrimination Act could be interpreted to include 'sexual orientation'. While some cases succeeded in the lower courts, they always failed on appeal to the House of Lords and the European Court of Justice. The European Court of Human Rights took a different view, but its rulings are not binding—although, where necessary, they can lead governments to make changes to statutes.

In the case of *Grant v South West Trains* (1998), a lesbian argued that her partner should have been entitled to travel concessions, as heterosexual partners were. She argued that the comparator should be her predecessor in the job, who was a man with a female partner. If the ECJ had used the same line of argument as in the transsexual case of *P v S*, this would have been correct. Instead, however, the ECJ rejected her claim, deciding that the appropriate comparator was not a man living with a female partner, but a man who had a same sex partner. The House of Lords came to a similar conclusion just before the 2003 Regulations came into force in the case of a man dismissed from the armed forces for his sexuality, saying that the word 'sex' did not include sexuality, and that the reason for his treatment was because of his sexuality.

Things changed with the signing of the Framework Directive and the introduction of the Employment Equality (Sexual Orientation) Regulations 2003. Until that date, there was no specific protection for homosexual people in British law, but it is now enshrined as a protected characteristic in the Equality Act.

Protected characteristic

The Act prohibits discrimination on grounds of 'sexual orientation', and covers heterosexual, homosexual and bisexual orientation. Importantly, it does not extend protection to those who are discriminated against because they have particular types of sexual preferences. This ensures, for example, that paedophilia is not covered.

Prohibited conduct

All the types of prohibited conduct are covered for sexual orientation discrimination. This was one of the few types of discrimination where previous legislation also allowed for associative and perceptive discrimination. This is still the case, and so a person discriminated against because of the sexual orientation of someone else, such as a man who is harassed at work because of his son's homosexuality, or someone who is discriminated against because he or she has many gay friends can claim under the Equality Act for associative discrimination.

The previous law also covered perceived sexual orientation, as does the Equality Act, so an employee who is discriminated against because the employer *believes* he is homosexual is entitled to protection, whether or not he is in fact gay. Indeed, to bring an action the person does not have to declare his sexual orientation—all he would have to show would be that he was treated less favourably than a heterosexual person by the employer because the employer believed that the applicant was a homosexual. If a person experiencing sexual orientation discrimination had to disclose his actual orientation, this may deter him from bringing a claim—it also raises all kinds of definitional difficulties that have been avoided thanks to thoughtful drafting of the legislation. In principle, the actual sexual orientation of a person is thus irrelevant, and this may increase the likelihood of affected individuals bringing claims. However, it remains to be seen whether this will in fact be the case, or whether in practice it will be impossible for an applicant to prove his case without showing his actual orientation.

In the case of *English v Thomas Sanderson Ltd* (2008) the Court of Appeal has gone further, and said that the Sexual Orientation Regulations 2003 even protect a homosexual man who is repeatedly tormented by homophobic banter (including names such as 'faggot') when (i) he is not gay; (ii) he is not perceived or assumed to be gay by his tormentors; and (iii) he accepts that they do not believe him to be gay. The banter arose purely because he had attended a boarding school and lived in Brighton. This would presumably also apply to the Equality Act.

Direct and indirect discrimination

For direct discrimination, the comparator would be a person who is not of the applicant's sexual orientation—so, for example, if a heterosexual person employed in a business run by a gay employer is not promoted, and complains, the appropriate comparison would be with a person who is not heterosexual.

Most of the examples in the section above are direct discrimination. The Act also covers indirect discrimination. These, as in the other anti-discrimination legislation, can be justified if the employer can show that a discriminatory provision, criterion or practice was proportionate and the aim was legitimate. Examples of situations that might amount to indirect discrimination here would be matters such as discriminating against parents (who are therefore mainly heterosexuals) or not employing anyone with HIV.

As seen above, the exemption allowing employers to discriminate in favour of a married couple has been amended to take account of civil partners' right to equal treatment with married partners. Employers remain free to exclude unmarried people and those not in a civil partnership from work-related benefits. If, however, a benefit is extended to unmarried partners, then the exception ceases to apply. Under the current law therefore, Ms Grant would get the travel pass for her lesbian partner.

The provisions for harassment and victimisation are very similar to those set out in other anti-discriminatory legislation. It is likely that cases of harassment on grounds of sexual orientation will be common as this is one of the major ways in which gay and lesbian people have been discriminated against over many years.

Occupational requirements

There are two types of occupational requirements. The first of these is the one that applies generally, in other words where the nature of the employment is such that a particular sexual orientation is a proportionate means of achieving a legitimate aim, and the person concerned does not meet that requirement. Such defences will apply in very limited circumstances. It is necessary to consider the nature of the work and the context in which it is carried out and, in any case, the occupational requirement should be reviewed periodically as circumstances may have changed and it may no longer be valid (this obviously applies to all protected characteristics). The example given by ACAS is that of an organisation advising on and promoting gay rights, which may be able to show that it is important that its chief executive, the public face of the organisation, should be gay.

The second type of OR covers roles which exist 'for purposes of an organised religion'. It is intended either to permit the employer to comply with the doctrines of the religion or so

Activity 17.8

An organisation which provides counselling to gay and lesbian people advertises a vacancy for a homosexual counsellor. An experienced, heterosexual counsellor applies for the job and is rejected because of his sexual orientation.

Questions

1 Does an OR apply in this case?

2 Would your answer be the same if the heterosexual counsellor had experience of counselling gay teenagers? Why?

as to avoid conflicting with the strongly held convictions of a significant number of the religion's followers. This second type of exception has been a controversial element of the law because it appears to allow religions to discriminate against people because of their sexual orientation. As such it creates a potential conflict of rights between the followers of a religion on the one hand, and those of a particular sexual orientation on the other. It was included in the original Regulations in response to opposition to sexual orientation discrimination from religious groups, and there are some very interesting cases where the two conflict, such as the case of *Ladele*.

There is an argument that it goes beyond what the EU Directive allows, but it must be remembered when applying ORs that each case should be looked at individually, and it may well be that the courts will interpret it restrictively.

Activity 17.9

A care home that is owned and run by a Catholic organisation wishes to employ a nurse. A lesbian nurse applies for the post. She is rejected because of her sexuality. The owners of the care home wish to rely on the second type of OR.

Questions

1 Would this situation come within the legislation?

2 Explain what factors would be taken into account.

CHAPTER SUMMARY

- The Sex Discrimination Act as originally drafted only prohibited discrimination on grounds of sex and marital status.
- Civil partners are now treated in the same way as married people.
- Those who live as someone of the opposite gender are protected from discrimination. They can also change their birth certificates so that their new gender is reflected there.

- Pregnant women have a right not to be discriminated against, and this is now a free-standing right. There is no need for a comparator.
- People are entitled not to be discriminated against because of their sexual orientation.
- This covers heterosexuals as well as homosexual people.

REFERENCES

Equal Opportunities Commission (2005) *Greater Expectations*. EOC.

Fawcett Society (2011) *Stop Pregnancy Discrimination*, www.fawcettsociety.org.uk.

Hudson, S. (2010) *Homophobia: Out with homophobia in the workplace. Personnel Today*, 4 February.

IDS (2010) *Equality Act*.

Summers, C. (2010) 'Have transsexuals become easy targets?' www.bbc.co.uk, 11 August.

TUC (2004) *Transgender Equality: Advice from the TUC on Trans rights in the workplace.* London: Trade Union Congress.

Ward, L. (2005) 'Pregnancy bias costs 30,000 jobs', *The Guardian*, 2 February.

ONLINE RESOURCE CENTRE

A range of online resources to help you through your employment law module have been developed by the author team. These include updates, self-test questions and sources for further reading. (www.oxfordtextbooks.co.uk/orc/taylor_emir3e)

Equal pay

Learning outcomes

By the end of this chapter you should be able to:

- state the major principles of current equal pay law;

- explain the evolution of equal pay law in the UK since 1970;

- advise on the question of who a potential claimant can and cannot choose as her comparator;

- distinguish between the three headings under which equal pay claims can be brought;

- outline the defences available to employers in equal pay cases;

- set out the principles under which compensation is determined in equal pay cases;

- advise about the practicalities of bringing and effectively defending equal pay claims;

- debate the strengths and weaknesses of the critiques of equal pay law put forward by commentators.

Introduction

One of the longest established principles of modern employment law is that men and women should be paid the same amount of money for carrying out the same jobs. The principle was first established in the Equal Pay Act 1970, and thus pre-dates UK membership of the European Community (later Union). The Act came into force in 1975 at the same time as the Sex Discrimination Act, and together they formed the basis of sex discrimination law in the UK until both were effectively subsumed into the Equality Act 2010. The two Acts were, however, designed for different purposes and were intended to complement one another rather than to form a straightforward, seamless legal code. As a result, in practice, they served rather different purposes and operated in very different ways. This remains the case now that both form separate sections within the Equality Act.

The Sex Discrimination Act dealt with situations in which a worker is treated less favourably than another of the opposite sex when decisions are being taken about who to recruit, who to promote or who to dismiss. These are not situations in which sex discrimination occurs in the contract of employment itself. The Equal Pay Act, by contrast, was concerned with contractual discrimination. While most cases brought under this Act have concerned pay and benefits, any discriminatory contractual term could form the basis of a claim under the 1970 Act. Differences in holiday entitlement or contracted hours of work, for example, regularly led to legal action.

The distinction between the two types of claim is maintained for the most part in the Equality Act 2010. However, sections 70 and 71 now make it possible to envisage rare circumstances in which a complaint relating to discrimination in the field of pay might be able to be pursued using the 'old' sex discrimination procedures—a topic we return to later in this chapter.

The equal pay clauses in the Equality Act work by implying into all contracts of employment an equality clause. Where a claimant succeeds in showing that this is being breached by an employer, the court or tribunal orders that it must be honoured in the future and makes a financial award to compensate the claimant for losses sustained in the past as a result of the clause being breached. Importantly, the principle of upward equalisation operates, so that an employer is prevented from responding by reducing the pay or value of other terms of others to bring them into line with those of the claimant.

The vast majority of equal pay claims are brought by women because in the UK, despite forty years of equal pay legislation, women's average pay remains considerably lower than that of men. In this chapter, therefore, we will generally refer to applicants as 'she' and comparators as 'he' even though in principle men have just as much right to bring claims under the Equality Act citing women as their comparators. While it is true that in the field of occupational pensions male litigants have enjoyed sustained success and have brought about the equalisation of retirement benefits, these cases represent a small proportion of the total. Moreover, of course, the chief purpose of equal pay law at both the EU and UK levels is to help bring about equality for women.

It is helpful, before discussing some of the complexities that surround equal pay law, to set out in a straightforward fashion the key rights and the manner in which they are enforced. These are as follows:

1. The major way in which equal pay claims differ from those brought under sex discrimination law is the requirement for the woman to name a 'real live' male comparator who she believes is unlawfully being paid more than she is. There is no scope for basing a claim on how a hypothetical man would have been treated as is the case with the sex discrimination provisions in the Equality Act.

2. The claimant can bring her claim under one of three headings:

   • First, she can claim that she is paid less than her chosen comparator despite both of them being employed to do 'like work'. This means that their jobs are either 'the same or broadly similar' in terms of their content.

   • The second heading is 'work rated as equivalent'. In such circumstances, although the woman is employed to carry out a job which is different in nature from that of her comparator, the two jobs have been reckoned to be of 'equal value' by their employer following a job evaluation exercise.

   • The third heading is used when a woman believes that her work is of equal value to that of a male comparator, despite being different in nature, but that this has not been established through job evaluation. If she succeeds in persuading the court that she has a good case, an 'independent expert' is appointed to carry out the requisite job evaluation exercise.

3. While there are a number of defences that employers can deploy at different stages in the proceedings, the most significant involves showing that there is a 'material factor' which does not in any way relate to gender that applies in the particular circumstances of the case. This involves showing that there is a good, 'material' reason to explain a difference in pay which has nothing to do with the difference in sex between the claimant and her comparator.

4. Equal pay law is not directly concerned with equalising the pay of men and women in general terms, nor is it concerned with unfair differences in pay rates within male and female groups of workers. It is solely concerned with providing a remedy when an employer is unable to give a good reason to explain why a particular woman (or man) is being paid less than a particular man (or woman) in terms of her pay or another contractual term.

Activity 18.1

Read the following paragraph and try to answer the questions that follow. If you return to the activity again when you have finished reading the chapter, you should be able to give full and accurate answers to the questions.

Julie and Harry work alongside one another in a software house as computer programmers. Sometimes they work on the same projects, but most of the time they are carrying out different tasks. However, they both have the same qualifications, the same job title and carry out work of similar complexity using the same systems and languages. They have worked alongside one another since 1999, but Julie has worked for the company for two years longer than Harry. »

> This month Julie discovers in a chance conversation that Harry is paid £10,000 a year more than she is. This angers her a great deal and she takes legal advice. It is suggested that her first step should be to write to her employer asking for confirmation of the difference in pay between Harry and herself, and asking for the reason.

Three weeks later she receives a reply to her letter. It says that Harry is paid more simply because at the time of his appointment it was necessary to pay a premium to recruit good programmers because so many were making good money preparing systems to deal with the 'millennium bug'. The difference in their pay has been maintained since via annual percentage pay rises.

Questions

1 On what basis might Julie be able to bring an equal pay claim?

2 How strong a defence do you think her employer could mount?

3 If she was successful, roughly how much money could Julie expect to win by way of an award?

The evolution of equal pay law in the UK

While the core principles set out in the Equal Pay Act 1970 that now form part of the Equality Act 2010 are readily understood, the precise legal position remains somewhat opaque because of the way that EU and UK law interplay with one another. The history of equal pay law is similarly complex as the UK has had over time steadily to amend principles and precedents in order to bring our law into line with that of Europe.

The complexity arises partly because the principle of equal pay for equal work as between men and women is not just part of European law, but is actually written into the founding treaties establishing the European Union. Originally it was established through Article 119 of the Treaty of Rome, the accession Treaty which the UK signed in 1973. The same principle is now set out and clarified in Article 141 of the Treaty of Amsterdam. It reads as follows:

1. Each member state shall ensure that the principle of equal pay for male and female workers for equal work or work of equal value is applied.

2. For the purposes of this article, 'pay' means the ordinary basic or minimum wage or salary and any other consideration, whether in cash or in kind, which the worker receives directly or indirectly, in respect of his employment, from his employer.

Treaty articles such as this have 'direct effect' as far as the UK courts are concerned, so any worker can use Article 141 as the legal basis of an equal pay claim irrespective of the presence on the statute books of the Equality Act. Moreover, because the EU Treaty articles take precedence over UK statutes, whenever there has been an inconsistency between the Act and the article, it is the latter that has prevailed. This situation has arisen from time to time with important consequences; notably in *Barber v Guardian Royal Exchange* (1990), when the ECJ ruled that occupational pensions were to be considered as pay for the purposes of (the then) Article 119. Deakin and Morris (2009:607–609) give numerous other examples of ways in which Article 141 has been used by litigants over the years to extend the scope of the Equal Pay Act. As a result pretty well any type of payment made by an employer to a worker, even if not conventionally seen as being a staple part of the remuneration package must now be considered as 'pay' for the purposes of equal pay law, whether it is contractual or non-contractual in nature. Occupational sick pay and maternity pay, seniority-based payment arrangements, ex-gratia payments made on retirement, redundancy pay and unfair dismissal compensation are all now considered to fall within the purview of Article 141 as result of ECJ decisions.

Further complexity derives from the presence, in addition to Article 141, of the EU's Equal Pay Directive which was originally introduced in 1975. It goes rather further in requiring member states specifically to outlaw 'job classification systems' used to determine pay which are applied differently to men and women or operate in a discriminatory fashion. It was also the first piece of law to make specific reference to the principle of equal work for equal value. As a result the UK government was required to amend the Equal Pay Act in 1983 so as to incorporate the third 'heading' described above and to allow workers to bring claims to court even when their chosen comparators were employed to carry out a wholly different kind of work. Like all directives, that covering equal pay has 'direct effect' and can be used as the basis of a legal claim in the domestic courts, but only against state employers or 'emanations of the state'—a group which includes most public sector employers and private sector companies that carry out public duties.

It is, however, important to remember that the equal pay clauses in the Equality Act cover all terms of employment contracts, whereas Article 141 and the Equal Pay Directive cover only pay and other forms of remuneration. So in some important respects UK law gives greater protection than the EU law which has been so influential in its evolution.

This legal complexity has significant practical consequences from an employer's point of view. In making decisions about pay rates and other contractual entitlements, and when deciding how to respond when faced with an equal pay claim, the employer needs to look both at the wording of the Equality Act and at Article 141. Public authorities also need to ensure that they are not breaching the Equal Pay Directive.

 Exhibit 18.1   **Key events in the history of equal pay law**

1970: The Equal Pay Act comes onto the statute books

1973: The UK joins the (then) European Economic Community and signs the Treaty of Rome

1975: The Equal Pay Act comes into force

1975: The Equal Pay Directive is agreed by the Council of Ministers

1976: The ECJ rules in *Defrenne v Sabina* (No 2) that Article 119 takes precedence over national equal pay laws.

1983: The Equal Pay (Amendment) Regulations are passed, extending the concept of equal value into UK law.

1986: The ECJ rules in *Bilka-Kaufhaus GmbH v Weber von Hartz* that employers must objectively justify practices which 'explain' differences in pay between men and women where one group is apparently disadvantaged.

1989: The ECJ rules in the *Danfoss* case that if a woman can show in an equal value claim that the average pay of a female-dominated group is lower than that of a male-dominated group, the burden of proof shifts to the employer to provide an explanation.

1990: The ECJ rules in *Barber v Guardian Royal Exchange* that occupational pensions fall within the definition of 'pay' in Article 119.   »

> **1999:** Following rulings in *Levez v TH Jennings (Harlow Pools) Ltd* the two-year limit on back-pay is extended to six years.
> **2001:** Back-pay limitations in pensions cases are extended to 1976 following rulings in *Preston and others v Wolverhampton Healthcare NHS Trust.*
> **2003:** The introduction of the equal pay questionnaire system.
> **2006:** The Court of Appeal ruling in *Armstrong v Newcastle upon Tyne NHS Hospital Trust* that employers are only required to offer objective justification for a difference in pay between a man and a woman if the reason for it is tainted by sex discrimination.
> **2010:** The Equal Pay Act 1970 is repealed and its provisions incorporated into the Equality Act 2010

Choosing a comparator

One of the most interesting areas of case law in the equal pay field relates to who it is and who it is not permissible for a claimant to choose as her male comparator when bringing her case to the tribunal. Needless to say this is a crucial decision which may well determine the outcome of the action. The choice is for the claimant to make and, once made, cannot subsequently be altered by her or by the tribunal in order to select someone more appropriate. The man in question does not have to give his permission, although practically when developing a case it is very helpful from the claimant's point of view to have the active co-operation of the male comparator. In principle it is possible for her to name more than one comparator, but the House of Lords has warned claimants against the selection of multiple comparators in the hope that one will be found to be doing work of equal value. This is seen as being an abuse of the equal value procedures (*Leverton v Clwyd County Council* (1989)).

The comparator must be employed 'in the same employment' as the claimant, a term which is defined in the Act as encompassing one of three types of situation:

1. the claimant and comparator are employed in the same establishment

2. the claimant and the comparator are employed by 'associated employers'

3. the two are employed at establishments in Great Britain at which 'common terms and conditions are observed either generally or for employees of the relevant classes'.

In most cases the first situation applies and the claimant brings her case naming as her comparator a man employed in the same workplace or group of workplaces at which she is employed. Occasionally situations arise where there is no clear workplace, for example where people work exclusively from home or where they are employed to work 'on the road'. In such circumstances the relevant establishment is taken as being that with which the claimant's work 'has the closest connection'. This principle was established by the Sex Discrimination Act (1975), but also applies in equal pay cases.

'Associated employers' are defined in employment law as being organisations which are controlled, either directly or indirectly, by the same body. The term typically refers to separate companies which form part of the same corporate group. Where one company is a subsidiary of another, a claimant employed in the subsidiary can choose as her comparator someone employed in the controlling company, or vice versa. Similarly where two companies are both controlled by a third body (even if it is not a company), they are deemed to be associated, so a claimant employed by one can name a comparator employed by the other. The same principle does not, however, apply as a rule in the public sector. This is because statutory bodies, unlike companies, are not considered to be associated in the same way. Hence, different local authorities, government departments and NHS trusts are separate employers irrespective of the extent to which they are in fact subject to a good deal of central government control.

Nevertheless, cross-employer comparisons can be made in the public sector under the third provision set out above. This is because different public sector bodies frequently observe common terms and conditions, particularly where national-level collective agreements encompass whole sectors. The same principle applies in the private sector where different employers which are not associated nonetheless choose to employ people on the same common sets of terms and conditions. If this is so, then a woman employed in one organisation can choose as her comparator a man employed by a different employer. The case law has extended this principle considerably, allowing claimants to base cases on comparisons with people who undertake different work for different employers. In *South Ayrshire Council v Morton* (2002) the Court of Session in Scotland went as far as to hear a case in which a primary school teacher employed by the local authority in Ayrshire compared herself to a secondary school teacher employed by the Highland local authority. In this case, while it was conceded that the two education authorities were not associated employers, there was '*a sufficient connection in a loose and non-technical sense between the two employers which was sufficient to allow a claim for equal pay to proceed*'. This was because they shared common terms and conditions negotiated at national level.

 Exhibit 18.2   The agency workers loophole

The well-known case *Allonby v Accrington & Rossendale College* (2004) concerned a part-time lecturer (Ms Allonby) who was employed by a college of further education. Along with several colleagues employed on a similar basis she was dismissed and then offered a contract to carry out the same work she had been doing before on a self-employed basis through an agency. Her pay and benefits under the new contract were poorer than they had been when she had been employed directly by the college. Managers at the college openly admitted that their motivation for carrying out this re-organisation was to avoid the financial impact of employment legislation. Ms Allonby then brought a series of claims under the Sex Discrimination and Equal Pay Acts, some of which were appealed right up to the European Court of Justice.

Her equal pay claim was straightforward. She chose a male full-time lecturer employed at the college as her comparator and said that she should be paid the same as him as they worked at the same establishment and he was paid more than she was. Unfortunately for Ms Allonby, although employed to work alongside her comparator doing similar work, the two were employed by different employers. He by the college, and she by an agency. These were held not to be associated employers, nor were her terms and conditions common to his. They did not emanate from a single source. So she lost her case.

This case revealed a loophole in equal pay law that has now, in practice, been plugged to a great extent by the Agency Workers Regulations 2011 (see Chapters 3 and 19). As a result, employers can no longer avoid paying people the same pay for doing the same job for a period of more than twelve weeks simply by employing some of them via an agency on different terms and conditions.

The three headings

Like work

The most straightforward equal pay cases involve the claimant using as her comparator a man who is employed by the same organisation to carry out 'like work'. Since the advent of the additional third 'equal value' heading in 1983, showing that the comparator is engaged in like work has become less crucial to a claimant's case because where their work differs in significant respects she can instead ask for her claim to be considered as being one for equal pay for work of equal value. This happens frequently in practice, the claimant simply bringing dual 'like work' and 'equal value' claims in respect of the same male comparator. But there are considerable advantages from the claimant's point of view in persuading the tribunal that the comparator's work is 'like' hers. Procedurally it is a good deal quicker, because the question of whether or not two people are engaged in like work is one of fact for a tribunal to decide itself. Equal value claims are referred on to independent experts to determine, resulting in delays of several months before the matter can be settled.

Alas, like so much else in the equal pay field, the Equality Act (like the Equal Pay Act) does not give us a clear, crisp definition of what the term 'like work' is supposed to mean. So this has had to be determined by the tribunals and judges as cases have come before them over the years. The relevant passages of the Equality Act are sections 65(2) and (3):

> A's work is like B's work if (a) A's work and B's work are the same or broadly similar, and (b) such differences as there are between their work are not of practical importance in relation to the terms of their work.
>
> It is necessary to have regard to (a) the frequency with which differences between their work occur in practice, and (b) the nature and extent of the differences.

Since the EAT's ruling in *Capper Pass v Lawton* (1976) a general consideration of the similarities and differences is the approach that tribunals have been required to undertake. They look broadly at the type of work performed by the two, at the skills and knowledge needed to do the job and at how frequently their tasks differ in practice. Provided there are no significant differences, they have concluded that the work is 'the same or broadly similar'. The emphasis is always on what tasks are performed in practice (ie, what the two people actually do on a day-to-day basis) and not on what they might theoretically be employed to do in their contracts of employment. Two people with different job titles who in practice carry out broadly similar jobs are thus considered to be employed to do 'like work' for the purposes of equal pay law.

In another leading case—*British Leyland (UK) Ltd v Powell* (1978)—the EAT focused on how great the differences between the work of the claimant and her comparator should be in order for the employer to show that the work was not 'the same or broadly similar'. In this judgment the EAT suggested asking whether or not the differences in terms of skill, knowledge or responsibility were sufficient to place the two people in different grades or categories if a job evaluation exercise were to be carried out.

It is often a difficult judgement call for tribunals. The jobs that two people do frequently vary somewhat, but the tribunal must decide whether or not these differences are sufficient to justify an employer's claim that the jobs are not broadly similar. However, some firm principles have now been established in the case law. Leslie et al (2003:101) give the following examples:

- Where two people do the same work but are paid differently because one is more highly qualified (or just differently qualified) than another it is possible for an employer to claim that they are not in fact doing like work. This occurs when they carry out the work in a different way, drawing on different skills.

- Where the comparator is paid more because he is required to perform the same role as the claimant on a more flexible basis, for example by working a greater variety of shift patterns, the work may be classed as being dissimilar. But much depends on whether or not the claimant has been denied the opportunity to work as flexibly as her male comparator. If she has not been afforded the opportunity, then the work will be judged to be broadly similar.

- Where the comparator is paid more because he exercises greater responsibility, the work may be considered sufficiently dissimilar for the claim to fail. However, when the man in question only takes on a more responsible role occasionally, the difference is not judged to be of practical importance.

- Where the only difference between the work carried out by the claimant and her comparator is the time the duties are performed (eg, where he works night shifts and she works days) then their work is generally considered to be 'like'. However, if the night shift worker carries additional responsibilities or shoulders greater personal risk, then the tribunal may say that the differences are of practical importance.

It is important to make a distinction here between judgements about whether one person's work is 'the same or broadly similar' to another's, and the question of whether the difference in pay is justified. It is easy to confuse the two because some of the factors that are considered crop up at both stages in a case. Here we are only focusing on whether the work is sufficiently similar to allow a case to proceed. The question of whether the difference in pay is or is not justified (ie, whether it is a material factor unrelated to sex) comes later. In these types of cases the employer effectively gets two bites at the cherry. It can first deploy the argument that the work of the two people is not 'the same or broadly similar', and if it fails to persuade the tribunal of this, it can go on to try to justify the difference in pay.

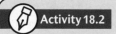 Activity 18.2

Consider the following two cases:

Electrolux Ltd v Hutchinson (1976)

Two groups of people, one predominantly male, the other predominantly female, carried out identical work in a refrigerator manufacturing plant. The first was graded more highly than the second. A group of women brought an equal pay claim, using the more highly graded men as their comparators. The employer argued that the work was materially different because the higher-graded workers could be required under their contracts to carry out other duties and to work on other shifts. »

> **Thomas v National Coal Board** (1987)

A large group of female canteen assistants were paid less than a male colleague carrying out the same duties, so they brought an equal pay claim using him as their comparator. The employer defended the claim by arguing that the man in question was employed to work on night shifts, while the women worked during the day. This involved him carrying a greater level of responsibility and meant that the work was not 'the same or broadly similar'.

In the first case the employer was unsuccessful. The difference between the two groups was found by the EAT not to be of practical importance. In the second case the employer was successful. The EAT found that the work performed by the male comparator was not the same or broadly similar to that of the claimants.

Questions

1   What factors can you identify which could explain why the EAT reached different judgments in these two cases?

2   To what extent do you consider these outcomes to have been fair, and why?

3   What other possible tests could be used by the tribunals to establish whether or not two people are engaged to carry out 'like work'?

Work rated as equivalent

The second heading under which an equal pay claim can be brought is a good deal less straightforward to grasp. Here the jobs of the claimant and her comparator may be of a completely different nature, but have nonetheless been ranked 'as equivalent' in terms of their worth through the use of a job evaluation scheme. In other words, the situation is one in which their employer has completed a job evaluation exercise which values the two jobs equally and thus places them on the same grade or point on a pay spine.

At first sight this appears rather puzzling. Surely, if the two jobs have been graded the same the two people concerned will already be being paid the same amount of money, so why would anyone ever need to bring a case of this kind? In fact such cases are not unusual, there being plenty of situations that arise in which a man doing one job is in practice paid more than a woman doing another, despite the fact that the two jobs are graded at the same level in the organisation. He may be paid a higher performance-based incentive, or be further up the spine *within* the same grade band for one reason or another. In some organisations, whatever the relative value of the two jobs concerned, a man may be graded more highly because it was deemed necessary to pay more at the time of his appointment in order to attract a better field of candidates. The employer may be able to defend itself in such circumstances, but this does not mean that the case cannot proceed and evidence be presented.

In recent years several thousand cases have been lodged with employment tribunals under the 'work rated as equivalent' heading. These relate to a common situation that has arisen in local authorities and other public sector organisations following the aggregation of several groups of employees whose pay was formerly negotiated separately, to single pay spines. Achieving this has involved using job evaluation systems to establish which new grade everyone should be assimilated to—a process which has frequently resulted in female-dominated groups being upgraded. Large numbers of women have thus found their work to have been rated as equivalent to that of men who have been paid more than them for many years simply because they were previously on different pay spines and had their pay negotiated through separate collective bargaining processes. In such circumstances the women have brought their cases to the tribunals in order to claim compensation equivalent to the difference between their pay and that of the men going back over several years.

It is also common for employers to undertake job evaluation exercises but then to hold back from implementing them for cost or other reasons. In *O'Brien v Sim-Chem Ltd* (1980) the House of Lords concluded that this was not an acceptable defence and that a claimant's case could proceed whether or not the scheme had been implemented in practice. The jobs had been rated as equivalent and that is sufficient in law to give the woman the right *in principle* to receive equal pay to that of her chosen comparator. However, this position only appears to stand once an employer has accepted that the results of a job evaluation study are in fact valid. In another case (*Arnold v Beecham Group* (1982)) a study commissioned by a firm of consultants had been completed but rejected by the employer as being deficient in key respects. As a result it was ruled that the claimant was unable to base her case on the findings of the study.

In recent years a further type of situation has arisen which has led to litigation under the 'work rated as equivalent' heading. This has occurred where competitive tendering and contracting out has occurred in public services and two groups of workers who previously received the same pay because they were graded equally move on to different terms and conditions in order to allow for effective competition against potential external providers for the right to provide a service.

 Exhibit 18.3   **Job evaluation schemes**

Job evaluation is one of the major methods used by employers to determine pay rates within an organisation. In recent years, partly because of equal pay legislation, its use has become more widespread. It involves systematically analysing the content of the various jobs in an organisation and reaching a judgement about the relative worth or size of each. Some form of scoring scheme is usually used to enable each job to be assimilated to single grading structure that accommodates all types of job however different they are from one another.

Several methods are used. At one extreme are the non-analytical approaches which rely heavily on management judgement or on negotiations between managers and staff-side representatives. Since the case of *Bromley v H&J Quick Ltd* (1988) such approaches have been considered invalid as far as equal pay law is concerned. Claimants cannot rely on them as the basis of a case, and employers cannot defend themselves with reference to such schemes.

Analytical schemes, by contrast, involve greater objectivity. Here each job is scored against a variety of factors such as 'skill', 'effort', and 'responsibility', an analysis being made of its size against pre-determined criteria. This approach is acceptable to the courts for equal pay purposes.   »

> It is often impractical for larger employers to evaluate every single job in their organisations in order to determine to which grade each is to be allocated. So a benchmarking approach is used whereby a 'typical' job from a group is chosen as the one to be evaluated and the results are then applied across all broadly similar jobs in the organisation. All in the family of jobs are thus graded the same, despite the fact that some relatively minor differences exist between them. As far as the law is concerned jobs which have been graded via benchmarking in this manner can be considered to have been 'evaluated' under an analytical job evaluation scheme as long as no evidence is produced of material differences between the work carried out by the claimant or her comparator and that of those whose jobs theirs were benchmarked against.

Aside from the requirement that the job evaluation scheme in use is analytical in nature (see Exhibit 18.3), it must also of course itself be free of sex bias. The possibility that schemes themselves might discriminate between men and women is specifically covered in the Equality Act in section 65(4) where it is stated that a job evaluation scheme must not be 'sex specific'. This means that in principle a woman can bring a tribunal claim and argue that her work should be rated as equivalent to that of a male comparator and would have been had the job evaluation scheme being used not *directly* discriminated against women in its operation. This might happen where men (or male-dominated groups of workers) were scored more highly than women (or largely female groups) on a particular factor in the scheme. For example, it is conceivable that accountants in a company (mainly male) could be given higher ratings for their professional qualifications than were given to HR managers (mainly female) for theirs. If this were so, and this was the reason that a female HR manager was graded below a male accountant, she would be able to challenge the operation of the job evaluation scheme and make her case for equal pay.

Importantly, however, it is the scheme itself which must be shown to be discriminatory and not the just manner in which it has been carried out (Deakin and Morris, 2009:618). Moreover, there is no scope under this part of the Equality Act to bring claims rooted in the concept of indirect discrimination. A scheme which favours men in general terms over women because, for example, it ascribes particular value to physical strength, cannot be challenged under this section of the Act. Instead an equal value claim would have to be brought (see Activity 18.3).

 Activity 18.3   *Rummler v Dato-Druck GmbH* **(1987)**

This case was heard by the ECJ. It concerned a German printing firm which had seven pay grades to which each job was allocated by means of an analytical job evaluation scheme. The factors used were as follows:

1 previous knowledge required

2 concentration

3 effort

4 exertion

5 responsibility

On these criteria Ms Rummler's job was allocated to Grade 3 on the grounds that it required 'medium and sometimes high muscular effort'. She argued that this was discriminatory as the scheme assumed a man was in the job. For her it was not 'medium effort', it was hard physical effort. She should therefore be re-graded to Grade 4. The employer refused, so she went to court.

Questions

1 Should women's lower average strength be taken into account in determining the amount of effort required to perform a job? Set out the arguments for and against this proposition.

2 Ms Rummler lost her case. On what grounds do you think this would have been?

Equal value

If, and only if, a claimant is not employed to do 'like work' or 'work rated as equivalent' can she bring a claim based on equal value. The situation is thus one in which the claimant carries out work which is different in nature from that of her chosen male comparator and in which no analytical job evaluation scheme (free of sex bias) has been used to grade their respective jobs, but where nonetheless she believes her work to be of equal value to his. This third heading did not appear in the 1970 Act, but was added in 1983 in order to meet in full the requirements of the (then) EC's Equal Pay Directive. The change vastly increased the number of situations in which people could bring claims and has had a major impact in practice on the management of reward in organisations. This extension has now been fully incorporated into the equal pay sections of the Equality Act 2010.

Procedurally, equal value cases can be quite lengthy and complex because of the role played by independent experts. The first question the tribunal has to consider is whether or not the claim is strong enough to proceed. It can decide for itself at the outset that the job of the claimant and that of her comparator are clearly not of equal value and can thus dismiss the case at the first hearing. In practice, according to Leslie et al (2003:113–114), this is unusual and only occurs if the employer specifically challenges the case on these grounds. Unless a case is obviously hopeless, the tribunal will not exercise its right to dismiss it on the general grounds that it is 'weak'. Moreover, where a tribunal takes such a course, the applicant may exercise her right to ask that the hearing be adjourned rather than concluded, so that she may commission a job evaluation study to prove the tribunal wrong.

Where the tribunal decides that there are reasonable grounds for determining that the two jobs are of equal value it can take one of two courses. The first is the most common. It involves the appointment by the tribunal of an 'independent expert' to carry out a job evaluation study and to report back with the results some months later. The tribunal is not obliged to accept the findings of the expert, but will in practice place great weight on them in reaching its final judgment. The second course of action involves the tribunal adjourning the case to a future date and allowing the two parties to commission their own expert job evaluation studies. In such circumstances the tribunal makes its own mind up about the case once it has read the reports of the experts instructed by the claimant and respondent respectively. The decision about whether or not to commission an independent expert is for the tribunal to make having regard to the particular circumstances of the case. Where both parties have already instructed their own experts and express no desire for a third study to be carried out, the tribunal may (but will not always) decide to continue without the services of its own independent expert. Otherwise, especially where one party has commissioned its own study and the other has not, there will be a clear need to appoint an independent expert.

Exhibit 18.4   Independent experts

Independent experts play a central role in equal value claims. They are appointed from a panel of specialists selected and maintained by ACAS. Once appointed the two parties to the case must co-operate with them fully and must disclose to them any relevant documentation. Where a party does not co-operate, the expert informs the tribunal that compliance with its request to produce an independent report will not be possible, giving full reasons. In such circumstances the obstructing party is likely to lose their case. The expert is obliged to issue progress reports to both parties and to the tribunal while the research is being carried out and can ask for additional time where this is necessary.

Once completed the report is sent to both parties and to the tribunal, the latter being then able to ask for clarification about particular points. The final report is then admitted as evidence in the case, both sides having the opportunity to accept or dispute its findings. In many cases the expert will attend the hearing as a witness to answer questions from both parties and the tribunal itself.

Independent experts are also used in other types of employment tribunal hearing, albeit in a way which is a good deal less prescribed. McGrath (2002) gives several examples of situations in which the parties to a case are in dispute about facts which can only be properly determined by the tribunal with the benefit of independent advice. Medical reports are the major examples, for example in disability discrimination cases where the existence of a disability is disputed or in stress-based personal injury claims where the extent of any psychiatric injury is disputed.

Soon after the introduction of the equal value heading in 1983 a key issue had to be decided by the courts. This concerned a situation in which a woman brought a claim naming a man engaged in a different type of work as her comparator, despite the fact that there was a man (or indeed several men) employed by the organisation doing the same job as her on the same wages. Should such a woman be entitled to bring an equal value claim? The wording of the legislation was unclear on this matter and was interpreted in different ways by the courts when faced with the first equal value claims. Eventually in 1988 the House of Lords made a definitive judgment in *Pickstone v Freemans plc*. They decided that were claims of this kind not to be allowed to proceed it would defeat the whole purpose of the equal value regulations. Employers would very easily be able to avoid their obligations simply by appointing a 'token man' to work alongside groups of underpaid women.

Equal value claims, because of the role played by experts and the need for two or more separate hearings some months apart, are often expensive for the parties. There is thus a bigger incentive than is there in many other types of claim to settle ahead of a hearing. Moreover, because many claimants bring cases on behalf of large groups of female staff who consider themselves underpaid (often with trade union backing), the financial consequences of losing a case from an employer's point of view are often very substantial indeed. It is thus common for deals to be done before a case is ever presented to a tribunal. The fact that there are relatively few equal value claims considered by tribunals each year does not therefore mean that this law is ineffective. It has in fact had a profound impact, leading to the equalisation of pay between male- and female-dominated groups in some major organisations. An example is the pay rates of checkout operators in supermarkets which was raised substantially across the industry in the early 1990s. In 1990 the trade union USDAW brought a case against Sainsbury's on behalf of the mainly female checkout operators, claiming equal pay for work of equal value with the predominantly male warehouse staff who were paid considerably more. The case was settled out of court, Sainsbury's and USDAW reaching an agreement which saw a job evaluation exercise being conducted and the rates paid to checkout staff rise by some 20%. The company's total wage bill rose by 11% as a result. Similar settlements were then reached with the other major retailers in the years that followed without the need for the threatened legal actions ever to proceed.

 Exhibit 18.5   Passing the Equal Pay (Amendment) Regulations

In 1982 the European Court of Justice ruled that the UK had failed fully to implement the (then) EEC's Equal Pay Directive by omitting the right of workers to bring claims based on the proposition that their work was of equal value to that of a named comparator. As a result, in 1983 the government introduced the Equal Pay (Amendment) Regulations to plug this gap in the law.

Unhappily, the job of presenting the government's proposed regulations to the House of Commons fell to a little-known junior minister called Alan Clark, who later achieved fame when his colourful and painfully honest diaries were published. Clark's account of the introduction of these Regulations in the House is one of the most infamous and entertaining passages in his diary (Clark,1993:28–33). It was only his second appearance at the dispatch box as a minister, the first having gone surprisingly well.

> Alas! An odious over-confidence burgeoned. Anyone can do this. Child's play. My friends encouraged me. In the dining room Tristan said 'we're selling tickets for Al's performance tomorrow...' I resolved not to disappoint them. Looking back now, I realise I was amazingly, suicidally, over-confident.

So, instead of preparing properly for his evening appearance in the House, Clark went out to dinner. He read the text of the Regulations in the car and was surprised by how long and complex they were.

> And yet this didn't seem very important as we 'tasted' the first a bottle of '61 Palmer, then 'for comparison' a bottle of 75 Palmer then, switching back to '61, a really delicious Pichon Longueville.... By 9.40 I was muzzy.... The Chamber was unusually full for an after-ten event. When I was called there was a ragged, undeferential cheer from the benches behind. But an awful lot of Labour people seemed to be in as well. Including, it seemed, every female in their parliamentary strength.   »

> ⟫ Undaunted, and still merry, Clark pushed on.

As I started, the sheer odiousness of the text sank in. The purpose of the Order, to make it more likely (I would put it no stronger than that) that women should be paid the same rate for the same task, as men, was unchallengeable. In my view, in most instances, women deserve not less than but more than the loutish, leering, cigaretting males who control most organisations at most levels. But give a civil servant a good case and he'll wreck it with cliches, bad punctuation, double negatives and convoluted apology. Stir into this a directive from the European Community, some contrived legal precedent and a few caveats from the European Court of Justice and you have a text that is impossible to read—never mind read out.... I found myself dwelling on, implicitly it could be said, sneering at the more cumbrous and unintelligable passages.

He then proceeded, instead of summarising the Regulations, simply to read them out. He was urged to 'speed up' by a backbencher. Hansard records that Clark then said the following:

In deference to the expressed wishes of my honourable friend, I will accelerate the rate at which this particular passage is delivered.

Clark then raced through the crucial passages of the Regulations at a very quick pace, tripping over his words and giving a strong impression of disinterest.

I did speed up. I gabbled. Helter-skelter I galloped through the text. Sometimes I turned over two pages at once, sometimes three. What did it matter? There was no shape to it. No linkage from one proposition to another.... Up bobbed a teeny little fellow, Janner by name, a Labour lawyer who always wears a pink carnation in his buttonhole. He asked me what the last paragraph 'meant'. How the hell did I know what it meant? I smoothed away. He started bobbing up and down as, it seemed, did about fifteen people on the other side.... This had the makings of a disaster.

The opposition backbencher, Clare Short, then made a point of order. She said that she understood she was barred from accusing a fellow MP of 'not being sober', but stated that she thought the minister was 'incapable' and that it was 'disrespectful to the office he holds' to appear in such a condition.

Fortunately for Clark, it is against the rules of the House of Commons to say this, however true it may be. The Speaker was thus obliged to order Short to withdraw her allegation. She only did so after repeated requests, and then very grudgingly. When asked if it 'would be in order for a member to address the house if he were drunk', the Speaker dismissed it as a hypothetical question and required that the debate continue. So Clark struggled on and the amendment was carried.

Employer defences

There is a variety of defences that employers can deploy at various points during an equal pay action. Some of these have already been alluded to above. They include the following:

1. In principle an employer can argue that an element of the pay package or some other entitlement neither constitutes 'pay' under Article 141, nor forms part of the contract of employment. The European case law suggests that claims based on the former are unlikely to succeed as very broad interpretation of what 'pay' means has been adopted.

2. In like work claims, the employer can show that the two jobs are not in fact 'the same or broadly similar' and that there is thus no basis for a claim. This does not, however, preclude the applicant from having her claim considered under equal value provisions.

3. The employer can seek to persuade the tribunal that an equal value claim is so ill-founded and has so little prospect of success that it should be dismissed without the need to call on an independent expert. This defence has been successfully deployed where a case which is very similar to others that have failed in the past comes before a tribunal.

4. The employer can use the findings of an existing job evaluation scheme, provided it is analytical, objectively carried out and free of sex bias, to show that the two jobs being considered are not of equal value. Importantly this defence can succeed even if the scheme has been introduced *after* legal proceedings have commenced.

However, the most important and widely used defence involves the employer satisfying the court that there is a good reason for the difference in payment between the claimant and her comparator which has nothing whatever to do with the difference in gender. This is known as the material factor defence (formerly known as the 'genuine material factor defence').

In effect this means that an employer is permitted to pay a man more than a woman for carrying out like work, work rated as equivalent or work of equal value provided the difference can be explained or justified on grounds that have nothing to do with the difference in gender. Moreover, the reason must be the genuine reason and not some coincidental factor or a distinction 'thought up' after litigation has started in order to defend the case. The statute also puts the burden of proof at this stage firmly on to the employer. It is thus assumed by the tribunal that the pay of the two people should be equalised unless the employer can persuade it otherwise.

The law on genuine material factor defences changed in 1986 following the ruling of the ECJ in the case of *Bilka-Kaufhaus GmbH v Weber von Hartz*. Henceforth where a claimant has been able to show that a pay practice has some kind of adverse impact on women in a workplace *generally* (for example by favouring a male-dominated group over one which is female-dominated), then the employer must objectively justify its practice. This was a significant change. Previously, as remains the case where no general adverse impact can be demonstrated, all the employer had to do was to 'point to' a genuine material factor in order to win its case. The extent to which such a factor was necessary and appropriate for the organisation was not considered by the courts. After *Bilka-Kaufhaus* objective justification has been necessary in many cases.

There are no examples given in the legislation to help identify what is and what is not to be considered an acceptable material factor, but over the years the courts have reached a view about many common situations. The following list consists of factors that have been accepted as valid by the higher courts and hence constitute precedents. However, it is important to remember that the same factor may be considered to be valid in one case in that it can be shown that it is the real reason for an ongoing differential in the pay of the claimant and her comparator, but as not being valid on another occasion. Where employers seek to rely on precedents but cannot show that in their case the reason is not a sham, they will lose. The facts in each individual case are thus central to the outcome. Sometimes the court needs to focus on a differential established at the time of appointment, and sometimes on pay rises occurring in the months or years that follow. Leslie et al (2003:126–137) cite the following:

- the man works longer hours than the woman
- the man works less desirable or sociable shifts than the woman
- the man works more flexible hours than the woman or works more flexibly in terms of the tasks he carries out or places that he works
- the man is better qualified than the woman in circumstances where the qualification is needed to carry out the job
- the man has longer service than the woman or greater experience of the work being undertaken
- the man's work is of higher quality than the woman's (if objectively measured)
- the man receives a London or other regional weighting unlike the woman
- economic constraints prevented/prevent the employer from paying the woman equally
- the man's job is 'red-circled', meaning that his personal pay package was/is being protected for a period following the downgrading of his job or reallocation of his duties.

All these have in the past been defences successfully deployed by employers to explain a difference in pay. Other reasons have not been accepted by the courts, the following being the major examples:

- the man asked for more money on appointment, or subsequently, than the woman
- the man and the woman are in separate groups and are thus represented in different sets of pay negotiations with trade unions
- the man was appointed to a higher grade by mistake
- the collective agreement with the union itself discriminates against women
- where a woman agrees to work on a lower rate
- where the pay offered to new starters is reduced in order to succeed in a competitive tendering exercise
- where the employer was compelled by statute to pay people at particular rates.

In some areas the position is less clear, cases having been decided in different ways over the years. The most significant concerns market forces and situations in which a man is paid more because this is deemed necessary in order to recruit and/or retain him. Typically this defence is deployed where the employer pays a market supplement to a hard-to-recruit group which is male-dominated such as computer programmers or engineers. In such cases, provided that this is the genuine reason for the difference in pay, and provided evidence can be produced to show that the higher payments are (or were) genuinely needed to recruit a group, the defence can succeed. The leading case is *Rainey v Glasgow Health Board* (1987) in which the House of Lords accepted the need to pay a higher rate where acute staff shortages had been faced by an NHS employer.

However, where there are no obvious problems recruiting a group of staff or where no compelling evidence of such a situation is presented, the use of market forces to justify pay differentials is generally unsuccessful. It is clear, for example, that the courts are unwilling to accept that a man can be paid more than a woman simply because he required more money in order to take up the job offer. They are also unwilling to accept as lawful a situation in which a woman (particularly if part of a female-dominated group of staff) has her pay lowered over time vis-à-vis that of her comparator in order to bring it down to match the perceived market rate for the job she is doing.

There is also a lack of clarity when it comes to pay which is linked to future potential. The UK case law suggests that it is acceptable in theory for an employer to pay a man additional money on appointment because it believes him to have substantial future potential (*Edmunds v Computer Services South West Ltd* (1977)). However, the ECJ in its judgments restricts this interpretation by refusing to allow employers to justify higher pay on appointment with reference to higher standards of performance once the man concerned is in post. It would appear therefore that a 'greater potential' defence can only succeed if the employer can present clear evidence to show that expectations were genuinely, unusually high at the time the male comparator was appointed.

In *Wilson v Health and Safety Executive* (2011) the Court of Appeal dealt with a long-standing issue in equal pay law, namely whether or not seniority-based pay scales can constitute a 'material factor' justifying a difference in pay between a man and a woman doing like work. In this case the pay scale continued to reward length of service with an increment for ten years. The Court of Appeal ruled that this was too long, stating that only five years was justifiable. After that, performance would be the same and reward should be too. Five years is also the maximum permitted in principle under age discrimination law. We now know that the same principle applies to equal pay law too.

In 2006, in its ruling in *Armstrong v Newcastle upon Tyne NHS Trust*, the Court of Appeal clarified a point in respect of the material factor defence which has proved to be both significant and controversial. The Lords of Appeal stated that an employer was only required to justify a difference in pay between a man and a woman *in the first place* if there was some evidence to suggest that the reason for the difference was tainted by sex discrimination. This position was later reiterated by the EAT in *Villaba v Merill Lynch* (2006). Hence it is not apparently any longer possible for a woman to challenge her lower rate of pay if the reason for the difference between it and that of her comparator is neither directly nor indirectly related to sex. This represents a major change. Previously it was enough simply to show that there was a difference in order for the employer to be required to justify it. This new position is very helpful from an employer's point of view because it reduces the likelihood that claims will be brought. Women are often paid less than men and vice versa, despite doing the same work, work rated as equivalent or work of equal value for all kinds of reasons. Some of these are often difficult to justify objectively, but are not in themselves anything whatever to do with the sex of the individuals concerned. Thanks to the *Armstrong* ruling, if the impact of this pay difference is not significantly detrimental either to women or men in general terms, then however unfair it may be, the employer is not required to justify it objectively in court.

The ruling is particularly controversial because some lawyers believe that it conflicts with the ECJ's ruling in an Austrian case called *Brunnhofer v Bank der Österreichischen Postsparkasse AG* (2001). Here it was simply stated that

> the fundamental principle laid down in Article 119 of the Treaty and elaborated by the Directive precludes unequal pay as between men and women for the same job or work of equal value, *whatever the mechanism which produces such inequality,* unless the difference can be justified by objective factors unrelated to any discrimination linked to the difference in sex.

No doubt, in time further test cases on this issue will come before the Supreme Court and the ECJ, and a definitive ruling on this key issue will be given.

 Activity 18.4   *Leverton v Clwyd County Council* **(1989)**

Mrs Leverton brought an equal pay claim against her employers citing a male comparator employed to do similar work at another establishment run by the same local authority. His work was broadly similar to hers but he was paid a higher basic annual salary.

   The employer defended itself by arguing that the difference in pay was justified because Mrs Leverton worked fewer hours and had a more generous holiday entitlement than her male comparator. The employer won the case.

Questions

1   Set out what arguments the employer's lawyer would have had to make in order to persuade the tribunal of the superiority of its case. What evidence would have had to be produced?

2   What are the major implications of this judgment for the management of compensation and benefits in organisations?

Remedies

When they find in favour of the claimant in equal pay cases, tribunals make an order requiring the equality clause in the contract to be observed. So the pay of the woman is equalised with that of her male comparator. Back-payments or payments in arrears are also ordered to compensate the woman for the fact that her pay was below his in the past. These may go back for years where the circumstances have been the same for some time, the burden of proof being on the applicant to establish for how long she has unlawfully been paid at a lower rate than her comparator. Importantly, since 1996 these back-payments have been calculated with interest (see Part VII).

   From time to time employers have argued that back-payments should be reduced to take account of the fact that some elements of the claimants' package are more favourable than that of her comparator. As in the *Leverton* case quoted above (see Activity 18.4), it is not uncommon for one person to receive lower pay than another but better benefits. This argument has now been firmly dismissed by the ECJ. When a woman wins an equal pay case her pay must be equalised irrespective of other elements in the respective remuneration packages of the claimant and her comparator. Differences of this kind may well be significant for an employer putting forward a material factor defence (as in the *Leverton* case above), but they are not relevant when a remedy is being determined.

Where the complaint is about inequality in the contract in respect of some other term than pay (eg, holiday entitlement, benefits of one kind or another) a judgement has to be made about how much compensation is appropriate. There are no set rules about this, evidence about the value of cars or staff discount schemes being brought forward by the parties. Calculations can thus be quite complex and are often disputed. When it comes to loss of pension rights, however, rather different principles are observed depending on the type of scheme (contributory/non-contributory, final salary/money purchase, etc). These are set out very effectively by Leslie et al (2003:190–192).

Until 1999 only two years' of arrears were payable under the Equal Pay Act. This was successfully challenged in *Levez v TH Jennings (Harlow Pools) Ltd* (1999). Mrs Levez won her equal pay claim at the employment tribunal, but was only awarded two years' back-pay. She appealed to the EAT who referred the matter up to the ECJ. They said that the two-year time limit breached Article 141 and referred the matter back to the UK court. The EAT then said that the limit should be six years as is standard in UK civil law under the Limitation Act, and this has now been confirmed in statute. The only exception is in the field of pensions (again!), where thanks to the House of Lords ruling in *Preston et al v Wolverhampton Healthcare NHS Trust* (2001), female part-timers who were refused access to occupational pension schemes in the past can backdate their claims to April 1976. This was when ECJ (in the *Defrenne* case) first ruled that pensions should be considered pay as far as EU law was concerned. Some sixty thousand women in the UK are potentially affected by this ruling.

 **Activity 18.5** *Evesham v North Hertfordshire Health Authority* (2000)

Mrs Evesham, a speech therapist, won an equal value claim brought against her employer using a male clinical psychologist as her comparator. Her pay was thus increased to be equal with his, full back-payments also being made. However, she was not satisfied with this outcome and appealed to the higher courts for more compensation.

Mrs Evesham's claim was based on the argument that her male comparator had six years' less service than she did. If their jobs were of equal value, her pay should therefore be six annual increments further up the scale than his.

Question

1   Mrs Evesham lost her case. On what grounds do you think this might have been?

Bringing a claim

The Equal Pay Act, unlike most other employment statutes, stipulated a six-month time limit for the bringing of a claim, and this provision continues in the Equality Act. However, this does not mean that a claimant must lodge her case within six months of discovering that she is paid less than a particular male comparator. It simply means that she must have been employed by the organisation against which the claim is being brought within the last six months. So ex-employees can bring claims against their former employers provided this is done within six months of their leaving date. This part of the Equal Pay Act was accepted as being compatible with EU law by the ECJ in *Preston et al v Wolverhampton Healthcare NHS Trust* (2000). The law also allows for an extension of the six-month time limit where the employer 'concealed a material fact' (ie, a piece of information central to a claimant's case) and the woman could not have discovered it until after her employment ceased. In such situations the six-month time limit runs only from the point at which she discovers the material information.

An interesting recent development was the ruling in *Abdulla v Birmingham City Council* (2011) in which the claimant successfully argued that because equal pay is guaranteed through an implied 'equality clause' in every employment contract, breaching the statutory right also amounts to breaching a contractual right, and this means that a claim can be taken to the High Court instead of the employment tribunal. The significance arises from the fact that the High Court can hear claims for up to six years after a point at which an unlawful pay situation is alleged to have been in place 'if the interests of justice so demand' rather than the strict six-month limit that tribunals have to observe. In practice, however, the impact may not be as significant as it first appears. This is because the losing side has to pay costs when breach of contract claims are brought before the County Court or the High Court, and this is likely to deter anyone who is not very sure indeed of the strength of their case.

Prior to April 2003 employers only had to disclose information relating to the pay levels of the applicant and her comparator once a tribunal claim had been initiated and they had been ordered by a tribunal to do so. This meant that a woman bringing a claim could not be aware of all the relevant facts before actually putting her claim into the tribunal. It also meant that employers could cover up differences in pay between staff by having a blanket pay confidentiality policy. This is no longer the case. A woman can now download a prescribed form from the Department for Business, Innovation and Skills (DBIS) website and serve it on her employer when she suspects that she is being paid less than a valid male comparator for no good reason. The employer must then reply on another prescribed form within eight weeks. A failure to do so fully is not unlawful, but can be used as evidence at a subsequent tribunal hearing. The questionnaire can be served up to twenty-one days *after* a tribunal claim has been submitted, or later still with the tribunal's permission.

The DBIS questionnaire has been carefully designed to ensure that the employer on whom it is served is not obliged to disclose confidential information about payments made to individuals and thus potentially to breach data protection regulations. It simply requires employers to state whether or not a particular individual is or is not paid more than the employee sending the questionnaire and to give reasons for the difference. Indeed, in its Code of Practice on Equal Pay, the Equality and Human Rights Commission recommends that employers do not disclose details of individual pay levels, but instead give full and frank explanations as to how decisions about pay rates have been reached.

If the employee sending the questionnaire is not satisfied with the explanation given by her employers/ex-employers, she can go on to lodge a tribunal claim using the response of the employer as evidence to support her claim. For this reason, from an employers' point of view, it is essential that any equal pay questionnaire received is treated very seriously and that any explanations given to justify differences in pay can be supported with evidence. A tribunal will not look favourably on an employer which changes its defence between the time that it responds to a questionnaire and the time it justifies its actions in court.

Exhibit 18.6 **EHRC advice to employers**

The Equality and Human Rights Commission Code of Practice on Equal Pay (developed by the former Equal Opportunities Commission) is admissible in evidence in tribunal proceedings. A failure to observe the Code does not mean that an employer is acting unlawfully, but it can be used by a claimant to strengthen her case. Conversely, an employer which can show that it has conspicuously adhered to the EHRC Code will be well placed to defend itself when faced with an equal pay claim.

The Code makes two helpful suggestions for employers:

1 It recommends that they should have a written equal pay policy and provides an example of a 'model policy' which can be adapted.

2 It recommends that employers carry out regular equal pay reviews or audits to check that their pay practices are not discriminatory. Advice on how to carry out such reviews is also provided.

Critiques of equal pay law

Equal pay law has long been criticised on several grounds and from different perspectives. However, by far the most common argument advanced is that it has proved to be ineffective in practice. It is said that despite the presence of the Equal Pay Act on our statute books for thirty-eight years, the gender pay gap (ie, the difference between the hourly earnings of male and female workers) remains unacceptably high. It follows that the law has not and is not meeting its key objective of bringing about an equalisation of pay between men and women.

Estimates of the size of the gender pay gap in the UK are similar whatever data is used to estimate its size and track progress over time. The most recent estimates using data from the Annual Survey of Hours and Earnings and the Labour Force Survey, put the figure for full-time workers at 19.9%, meaning that on average women earn 80.1% of the average hourly rate earned by men (Rogers, 2011). These studies show that the gap has narrowed considerably since 1970 when the legislation was first introduced—it then stood at 37%—but that the rate of progress in recent years has been limited. Indeed, some studies suggest that the gap widened again after the turn of the century.

The figures for part-time workers are a good deal less encouraging still. In 2007, according to Fredman (2008:194) female part-time workers earned only 61% of the male full-time hourly rate, a gap which has hardly narrowed since 1970 and has definitely widened over the past decade. Part-time workers, over 80% of whom are female, frequently suffer further by being excluded from certain types of benefits that their full-time equivalents enjoy. When both the full and part-time gender gaps are taken into account, the UK can be seen to have a poorer record on equalising pay than all other (pre-2004) EU member states. The following quotation sums up the effect over the span of a career:

> The average woman working full-time could lose out on £330,000 over the course of her working life. These aren't figures from the 1970s before equal pay came into force —they're current and show the shocking income gap that persists between men and women. The problem affects us throughout our lives because lower pay means that women face a pensions gap too—their retirement income is 40% less than men's. EOC (2007:5)

As a general rule, according to IDS (2011:5), the pay gap between full-time male and female employees is considerably greater in the private sector than it is in the public sector. The reverse is true of part-time employees, where it is public sector women who are most un-equally paid.

There are also variations between occupational groups, gender pay gaps being biggest among managerial workers and skilled trades people. There are also big geographical differences. The pay gap is widest (25%) in London and the South East.

The extent to which the law, or indeed any government intervention, could improve this situation is a question of debate, as is the extent to which it is fair to blame equal pay law in its current form for the failure of the gender pay gap to narrow further. This is because there is disagreement among commentators about what exactly causes such a wide pay gap to persist. Are women paid less simply because they are women, or are there other less easily rectified forces at work?

The major reasons for the continuing gender pay gap can be briefly summarised as follows:

1. Many women are concentrated in a relatively narrow range of female-dominated occupations which tend to be relatively poorly paid (eg, sales assistants, primary school teachers, secretaries and nurses).

2. Women are far more likely than men to take a break during their careers in order to look after children or elderly relatives. During this time those who work often undertake lower paid part-time jobs which do not draw on their skills in order to balance earning income with childcare needs. This clearly holds many women back from attaining senior and better paid positions until later, and often means that they can never successfully apply for such roles.

3. Performance-related payments, which make up an increasing portion of total pay packets, tend to favour men. More men qualify for overtime payments and productivity bonuses too, and men are more successful than women at gaining promotion into senior roles.

4. Part-time workers tend to be paid less per hour and have far fewer development and promotion opportunities than equivalent full-time staff. This reduces average female earnings because 45% of women work on a part-time basis. Similar disadvantages in pay terms apply in the case of other atypical workers such as those working at home, on a casual or temporary basis and those employed through agencies. Most of these workers are also female.

5. Even in professions where men and women work alongside each other doing the same jobs, women tend on average to be paid less in terms of a basic salary than their male colleagues and to develop their careers less quickly. This is sometimes simply due to out and out sexism, but can also be explained by the ability and willingness of men to invest greater effort into developing their careers. McColgan (1994) illustrates the point as follows:

Women doctors are frequently discouraged from entering specialisms such as surgery by the knowledge that success will require overwhelming commitment, particularly during those years which might otherwise be partially occupied with child-bearing. Many such jobs are geared implicitly to men whose wives can perform the task of help-mate and gear themselves primarily to running the household to which their husbands can return at the end of a long day.

Some of these reasons for continued pay inequity are deeply rooted in society and are not primarily caused by management decisions in workplaces. The fact that child-rearing responsibilities continue to be shouldered, in the main, by mothers rather than fathers has major consequences for pay rates and career earnings, but is not something that employers can or should be expected to control. Equal pay laws have little role to play in addressing unfairness that is rooted in such social arrangements, although it is possible that greater regulation of part-time terms and conditions might have a positive impact. In respect of other causes of the pay gap it is reasonable to argue that the equal pay legislation has failed to meet its basic aims. Its original purpose was to eliminate situations in which men and women doing essentially the same jobs were paid differently. Yet there is plenty of evidence to show that many such situations still remain. Moreover, since 1983, when equal value claims have become possible, a major aim of the legislation has been to reduce differences in pay between the male and female-dominated professional groups. Yet these are still very much with us as well.

When the Equal Pay Act was first passed it had a clear and swift impact on the earnings of full-time women. In the few years immediately before and after it came into effect in 1975 the gender pay gap narrowed significantly as employers abandoned established separate 'male' and 'female' pay scales. There was another period in which the gap narrowed more quickly in the years following the introduction of the third heading (equal value) in 1983, but progress has slowed again very considerably since 1990, and in the case of part-timers it has been negligible.

The number of equal pay cases won by claimants in tribunals remains very few. In 2010–2011 only 258 claims were successful—around 1% of those lodged. The rest were either withdrawn, settled or dismissed by the tribunals. Even if it is accepted that many cases are settled to the satisfaction of the claimant before the hearing takes place, or even before a formal tribunal claim is made, these figures show how the chances of any employer losing an equal pay action are tiny, especially where unions do not have a strong presence in the organisation.

There are thus good grounds for arguing that equal pay laws need to be reformed so that they better achieve their objectives. Increasing their scope and improving their operation might very well help to reduce the gender pay gap further. Moreover, history suggests that it is only following the introduction of major reforms in this field that employers respond and start taking the issue seriously. So what are the major faults with equal pay law as it stands now? The following points are the main ones made by its critics:

- The onus is entirely on individual women or groups of women to bring cases to tribunals. The law places no effective duty on employers to eliminate pay discrimination themselves.

- Even when an individual woman wins a claim, the employer is not obliged under law to raise pay rates for others in the same position.

- It is not possible under the existing law for trade unions to bring claims on behalf of groups of women.

- Proceedings take too long, involve too many hearings and are overly complex. Independent experts take months to complete their reports and are often impeded from reaching a firm judgment because the claimant has left the organisation at the time the report is completed.

- Winning a case can be costly for claimants. The complexity of such cases means that professional representation is usually needed, and it may also be necessary to fund a job evaluation study. Without EHRC or union backing it is very difficult for individual women to mount their own claims.

In recent years both the government and the Equality and Human Rights Commission (or its predecessor, the Equal Opportunities Commission) have appointed people to investigate these issues and put forward recommendations for reform. The Fawcett Society has also carried out reviews of equal pay law and made recommendations for reform, as have a number of trade unions.

The EOC's equal pay task force reported in 2001, while Denise Kingsmill's report for the government was published in 2002. Both made recommendations that went well beyond the confines of equal pay law into other areas of government policy such as taxation, benefits and the provision of information for employers. A particular suggestion made by these and other reviews into the law was that employers should be required (or at least given very strong incentives) to carry out their own regular equal pay audits and to act on them.

Kingsmill (2002) argued that such a policy should be restricted to start with to public sector organisations which would in effect be required to 'take the lead'. She thought that this would have a significant impact because a disproportionate number of women are employed in the public sector and because there is a strong business case for improving their pay and conditions in order to attract and retain strong performers. The Equal Pay Task force, by contrast, argued strongly for a general requirement on *all* employers to carry out regular equal pay audits. Its members suggested that trade unions as well as individual employees should be able to complain to the Central Arbitration Committee (CAC) when their employer fails to meet this duty and that the employer could thus be forced to comply.

More radical still are the suggestions made by some academic commentators such as Aileen McColgan (1994 and 1997) and Sandra Fredman (2008), who have argued for the adoption in the UK of an approach similar to that operating in Canadian provinces such as Ontario and in Denmark. This would involve not only requiring employers to carry out regular equal pay audits, but also to take action to equalise pay where largely female groups are found to be disadvantaged. In Ontario an inspectorate has been set up which operates along broadly similar lines to the Health and Safety Executive inspectorate in the UK. It carries out spot visits on samples of employers to check that they are complying with their duties under the Pay Equity Act, warns them when they are not complying, and can take further legal action if necessary.

Some progress has now been made in this direction, but it falls well short of the kinds of systems that those in favour of radical change advocate. In April 2007 a general duty on public bodies was introduced to publish an annual gender equality scheme setting out objectives that 'pay due regard to' equal pay issues and methods for tracking progress towards their achievement. Things went further with the introduction in the Equality Act 2010 of a 'public sector equality duty' which requires 'public authorities', among other things, to 'have due regard in the exercise of its functions to the need to eliminate discrimination, harassment, victimisation and any other conduct that is prohibited under this Act'.

The Equality Act also contains, in section 78, clauses which permit government ministers at a future date to introduce regulations requiring all employers with more than 250 staff to publish information about their gender pay gaps. It is, however, highly unlikely that this measure will be activated in the near future. It was one of the parts of the Act that was most vigorously opposed by the Conservative party in opposition. Moreover, it was explicitly stated in the Conservative party manifesto presented at the 2010 general election that this section of the Equality Act would not come into effect should they become the government.

 Activity 18.6   The Ontario Pay Equity Act

A model for reform of equal pay law often cited by supporters of change is the approach used in the Canadian province of Ontario, where an inspectorate has a policing role. This means that there is less need for individual women or their representatives to prepare court actions. The following are the key features of the Ontario pay equity regime:

- Employers of more than 100 are required to have written policies which identify 'female' job classes—defined as being over 60% female.

- They then have to carry out job evaluation to establish whether or not there is a discrepancy between male and female classes.

- Where there is, they have to draw up a 'pay equity plan' setting out what they intend to do to narrow the gap—that is, make pay equity adjustments—over a number of years if necessary.

- There are derogations similar in nature to the UK's genuine material factors which employers can deploy to defend unequal pay.

Aileen McColgan (1993:251) makes the following observation about the system:

> The potential of Ontario's legislation lies in its effective reversal of the burden of proof. Rather than encouraging employers to ignore issues of equal pay save in the unlikely event of an individual's complaint, the Pay Equity Act obliges them, in co-operation with any bargaining agent, to scrutinise their own pay practices for evidence of discrimination and eliminate it.

Questions

1 Aside from the wish to eliminate sex discrimination, what other arguments could be put forward by reformers in support of the establishment of this type of regime in the UK?

2 What arguments can be made against the introduction of a regime of this kind?

Other reforms that are frequently advanced to improve the operation of the Equal Pay Act, and hence to help reduce the gender pay gap, include the following:

1. The abolition of the need in equal pay cases to cite a 'real live' male comparator. Instead it is argued, women should be able to compare themselves to a hypothetical man as is the case under the Sex Discrimination Act 1975. This would make it easier for claimants to bring cases and would remove the need for independent experts. Tribunals could simply look at the evidence presented to them and establish whether it was true, on the balance of probabilities, that the woman would be paid more if she was a man.

2. The right of a tribunal to award a claimant more pay than her male comparator receives rather than just equal pay. This would encourage more claims and would allow proper compensation where women can show that they are seriously underpaid (see Activity 18.5 above).

3. Training up special tribunals to deal with equal pay cases. This would enable faster disposal of cases and would dispense with the need to appoint independent experts to carry out studies. The panel itself would effectively consist of trained experts who could make judgments on the evidence presented to them without the need for months of delay.

4. Permitting the EHRC or trade unions to bring claims directly on behalf of groups of employees. The financial consequences of losing group claims of this kind would force employers to take a proactive approach to eliminating indefensible pay inequity.

5. Extending the requirement for employers to objectively justify their 'material factors', rather than simply to point to one, across all equal pay cases. This would tilt the balance in favour of claimants and would act as a further incentive for employers to root out discriminatory pay practices.

6. A further point that is often made by people, but which has yet to find its way into government reports or academic studies, is the suggestion that the principle of 'equal pay for work of equal value' should be made generally applicable and should not just be restricted to the realms of sex discrimination law. Anyone, male or female, should be able to cite anyone else as their comparator irrespective of gender.

Bringing equal pay cases using sex discrimination statutes

The Equality Act made few substantive changes to equal pay law, and certainly did not advance equal pay rights to any significant degree. However, there is one area where there is a possibility of genuinely significant development occurring as test cases are brought forward in due course.

The wording of section 70 in the Act raises the possibility in limited circumstances for a claim that relates to pay and which before October 2010 would have to have been brought under the Equal Pay Act 1970 to be able to be brought instead under the regime that formerly applied under the Sex Discrimination Act 1975. When this occurs the woman seeking to demonstrate that she is underpaid will no longer have to cite a male comparator (or vice versa). Instead she will simply have to demonstrate that 'but for her sex she would have been treated more favourably'. In other words a hypothetical comparator could be cited instead of a real live breathing one.

Moreover, if successful, such a woman would presumably be entitled to claim an 'injury to feelings' award in addition to financial losses sustained as a result of being underpaid. This alone should have the effect of encouraging speculative claims to be made.

IDS (2010:146–149 and 159–162) provide a splendid analysis of the possibilities raised by the presence in section 70 of a clause which permits people to bring pay-related claims using the sex discrimination mechanisms when no claim *can* be founded under the equal pay sections of the Act. In other words, when there is no practical possibility of bringing a case under the equal pay procedures, and when sex discrimination in the field of pay has occurred, the Equality Act permits a claimant to challenge the employer using sex discrimination law.

The Explanatory Notes that were issued alongside the Equality Act state that this clause will only be used in two circumstances:

1. when a claimant cannot bring a conventional equal pay claim for lack of a comparator of the opposite sex

and

2. when an employer says 'I would pay you more if you were a man' or words to that effect.

However, IDS's lawyers suggest that in fact it may well be possible to sustain a claim in several other types of situation too, a key example being when a successor of the opposite gender is employed on a higher salary to do an identical job.

In *Macarthy's Ltd v Smith* (1980) the ECJ decided that a woman was entitled to bring a claim using her predecessor as her male comparator. She had replaced him and was doing the same work that he had been employed to do, despite being paid £10 a week less. In *Diocese of Hallam Trustees v Connaughton* (1996) the same principle was accepted by the EAT as applying in respect of successors. Ms Connaughton had left her job and been replaced by a man who was paid double her salary for carrying out the same job. However, this latter principle was overturned in *Walton Centre for Neurology v Bewley* (2008). It would now appear, thanks to the Equality Act, to be back at least in theory.

IDS (2010) also point out that sex discrimination law could now be used to challenge a situation in which a comparator whose work is of lower value is nonetheless paid at the same rate as a claimant, or one in which a comparator is paid an excessively greater amount for doing a job which is only of marginally greater value.

 Exhibit 18.7 **Arguments for deregulation**

Nearly all the critiques of equal pay law made by leading UK commentators call for greater regulation as a means of helping to reduce the gender pay gap. However, there are alternative views expressed from time to time which focus on the merits of deregulating this area of law.

In the USA some states have moved to regulate in this area, but most have not, and a vigorous debate has developed about the potential merits and demerits of introducing laws to enforce 'comparative worth'. As a result the UK experience is sometimes quoted in the American literature in support of arguments against regulation.

Rhoads (1993), an opponent of the introduction of equal pay laws in the USA, makes several thought-provoking observations about the position in the UK. His central argument is that equal pay law distorts the market by putting restrictions on how employers run their businesses. Over the long term this makes the economy less competitive than it would have been, reducing incomes generally and causing unemployment to rise among men and women alike. It also provides a disincentive for employers to recruit women, because it raises their wages above market levels. Rhoads is particularly puzzled by the preference of the law for job evaluation schemes over the market when it comes to setting pay rates:

»   But jobs do not have intrinsic value, and many jobs may make great demands on employees, but be worth relatively little to consumers, employers, or anyone else. Moreover, different employers will surely assign different values to the same jobs. One company may carve out its niche in a market by emphasizing sales and service. It will value good sales and repair personnel and helpful receptionists more than another company in the same line of work whose reputation is based on timely, reliable delivery. The latter company may pay inventory managers relatively more and receptionists, repair and salespeople relatively less. Rhoads (1993:155–156)

Moreover, he argues, job evaluation is not at all objective in practice. It is a highly inexact science. Different analysts always reach different conclusions about the precise worth of a particular job, leading to a situation in which the outcome of equal value claims is something of a lottery dependent on the views taken by the individual independent experts who are commissioned to advise the tribunal. This is particularly true when it comes to assessing and weighting factors which are sometimes seen as being favourable either to men or women. The tendency of equal pay law to encourage the spread of job evaluation is also a trend criticised by Rhoads on the grounds that its effect has been 'to retard the movement towards multiskilling labor contracts and performance-related pay'.

Rhoads also persuasively argues that equal pay law in the UK helps to maintain segregation between predominantly male and female jobs. The best way to tackle this, he argues, is not artificially to raise the market-determined rate for female jobs, but for women to apply for and secure the higher-paid male jobs. The role of the law should be to help ensure that this can occur by preventing sex discrimination in selection and promotion. Equal pay law, in providing women with a means of getting the higher pay without taking up more highly paid occupations, makes organisations less efficient and more likely to persist with occupational segregation.

CHAPTER SUMMARY

- The Equal Pay Act came into operation in 1975. It was amended several times in important ways after that. It was repealed in 2010, but its content was effectively transposed into the Equality Act 2010. The core principles remain the same, despite some redrafting of the language used in the statutes.

- The claimant must bring her case naming a comparator of the opposite sex who she claims is paid more than she is, without good reason, despite doing the same work, work which is broadly similar, work which has been rated as equivalent or work that is of equal value.

- Employers can defend themselves by citing a 'material factor' which is not discriminatory on gender grounds and which genuinely explains the difference between the pay of the claimant and that of her comparator.

- Equal pay law has been extensively criticised for failing to bring about equality in pay between men and women. Various reforms have been suggested including the placing of a positive duty on employers to take action to eliminate unequal pay.

For updates and further materials, please see the online resource centre at www.oup.com.

REFERENCES

Clark, A. (1993) *Diaries*. London: Wiedenfeld and Nicolson.

Connolly, M. and Townshend-Smith R. (2004) *Discrimination Law: Text, Cases and Materials*. Second Edition. London: Cavendish.

Deakin, S. and Morris, G. (2009) *Labour Law*. Fifth Edition. Oxford: Hart Publishing.

Equal Opportunities Commission (2003) *Code of Practice on Equal Pay*. Manchester: EOC.

Equal Opportunities Commission (2007) *The Gender Agenda*. Manchester: EOC.

Fredman, S. (2008) 'Reforming Equal Pay Laws' *Industrial Law Journal* 37.3, p193–218.

IDS (2010) *The Equality Act 2010: Employment Law Guide*. London: Incomes Data Services.

IDS (2011) *Equal Pay: Employment Law Handbook*. London: Incomes Data Services.

Leslie S., Hastings S. and Morris J. (2003) *Equal Pay: A Practical Guide to the Law*. London: The Law Society.

McColgan (1993) 'Equal Pay: A New Approach' in A. McColgan (ed): *The Future of Labour Law*. London: Cassell.

McColgan, A. (1994) *Pay Equity—Just Wages for Women*. London: The Institute of Employment Rights.

McColgan, A. (1997) *Just Wages for Women*. Oxford: Oxford University Press.

McColgan, A. (2003) 'Sex equality at work' in A. McColgan (ed): *Equality: Achieving Equality at Work*. London: The Institute of Employment Rights.

McGrath, P. (2002) *The Use of Experts in the Employment Tribunal*. London: EMIS Professional Publishing.

Rhoads, S. (1993) *Incomparable Worth: Pay Equity Meets the Market*. Cambridge: Cambridge University Press.

Robinson, H. (2003) 'Gender and labour market performance in the recovery' in R. Dickens, P. Gregg and J. Wadsworth (eds): *The Labour Market Under New Labour: The State of Working Britain*. Basingstoke: Palgrave Macmillan.

Rogers, S. (2011) 'International women's day: the pay gap between men and women for your job'. *The Guardian*, 8th March.

ONLINE RESOURCE CENTRE

A range of online resources to help you through your employment law module have been developed by the author team. These include updates, self-test questions and sources for further reading. (www.oxfordtextbooks.co.uk/orc/taylor_emir3e)

Atypical workers

19

Learning outcomes

By the end of this chapter you should be able to:

- advise on the extent and nature of legal protection provided by the Part-time Workers Regulations;

- explain why the Part-time Workers Regulations are necessary;

- set out the aims of the Fixed-term Employees Regulations and the methods provided for their enforcement;

- critique the Fixed-term Employees Regulations;

- give the basics of the Agency Workers Regulations;

- advise on the employment rights of ex-offenders; and

- critically analyse the operation of the Rehabilitation of Offenders Act 1974.

Introduction

In this final chapter in our section on discrimination law we focus on three further areas in which the law gives a measure of protection from discrimination to minority groups—statutes covering part-time workers, fixed-term employees and ex-offenders whose convictions have been declared 'spent'. In each case the extent of protection differs, but in all three it is a good deal less comprehensive than that provided in the case of, for example, sex or race discrimination. The law also provides protection from discrimination because of trade union membership, but this is dealt with in Chapter 27.

Recent years have seen substantial increases in flexible working. The phenomenon is partly due to government labour law policies in the 1980s and early 1990s which sought to encourage a low-cost and flexible workforce as the best means of achieving increased competitiveness and lower unemployment. It has been heralded as an opportunity for many people to take control of their lives, and have a better work–life balance, such as those who wish to work part-time so that they can continue with childcare responsibilities, further education and such matters. The EU has also seen it as a means of reducing unemployment, as by sharing work jobs go to more people on a part-time basis.

More recently, however, increasing numbers of people have been taking up part-time and fixed-term work for another reason—the recession. It has been reported that there are now record numbers of people working part time simply because they cannot find full-time work (Chamberlain, 2011).

This fragmentation of the labour market, however, whether it be part-time, fixed-term, temporary or agency work, also tends to benefit the employer and create insecurity and fluctuations in pay for the worker. As Sandra Fredman put it in 1997:

> The advantages . . . to employers are self evident: the use of casual, part-time and temporary workers permits employers to match staffing levels to peaks in demand and non-wage costs such as national insurance payments are low. The advantages for the employer, however, inevitably translate into detriments for flexible workers. (1997:339)

Fredman, writing before the relevant European legislation came into force, goes on to list those detriments: areas such as lower hourly payments, less access to overtime and training and exclusion from benefits.

Because most flexible workers are women, they were able to secure some protection from the law in the past through the indirect discrimination provisions of the then Sex Discrimination Act 1975. For example, from 1994 discrimination against a female part-time worker on the grounds that she worked part-time was treated by the courts as being unlawful sex discrimination in many situations.

Having to prove indirect discrimination, however, was not always satisfactory for those who worked part-time, or were on temporary or agency contracts. For one thing, under the old definition of indirect discrimination, the complainant would have to prove that a substantial number of her sex would be disadvantaged by an employer's practices, with all the attendant problems of identifying a pool of comparison and providing statistical evidence. Then there was the problem that only women benefited. Male part-time and fixed-term workers had no protection.

It was left to the EU social policy to come up with a number of directives to prevent discrimination against such workers, and to give them what is effectively a 'floor of rights'. It is this legislation which we shall be looking at in this chapter. We will also consider how far it has been beneficial. The chapter will also examine the issue of employing ex-offenders, and whether people who have previous convictions are obliged to disclose them to prospective employers.

 **Activity 19.1**

Consider the following statements. Which do you think are correct and which are false?

1 Until recently female part-time workers enjoyed better employment rights than male part-timers.

2 Part-timers must be paid enhanced hourly overtime rates once they start working in excess of their weekly contractual hours.

3 A fixed-term contract automatically becomes permanent after four years' service.

4 Agency workers must be treated equally in terms of pay and conditions to colleagues who are employed on a fixed-term basis.

5 People who have been sentenced to over two-and-a-half years in prison can never have their convictions declared 'spent'.

6 Ex-offenders can lawfully lie about their past convictions when applying for jobs as teachers or tax officers.

Return to this activity once you have read the chapter, to see how many of your answers were correct.

Part-time workers

The role of the part-time worker has traditionally been taken by women, as a means of earning money while still being able to care for children. As more and more women took on a role in the workforce, there were more and more part-time workers. In addition, as the economy expanded, and services started to be provided on a twenty-four hours, seven days a week basis, the traditional working hours had to be stretched to accommodate this and so the availability and number of part-time jobs increased. It is estimated that Britain has about 7.8 million part-time workers (see ONS Labour Force Survey July 2011, reported in Stewart, 2011). Of these, women constitute 80% (ONS, quoted in Bell, 2011).

In 1997, the European Union passed a directive specifically to protect part-time workers from discrimination, the Part-time Workers Directive 1997. This was incorporated into British law as the Part-time Workers (Prevention of Less Favourable Treatment) Regulations 2000, and came into force in July of that year. It was hoped that this would protect part-time workers and create a better working environment. During the consultation process before the coming into force of the Regulations, the Department of Trade and Industry said that the new law would bring advantages not only in pay and other benefits, but that in addition:

> [t]here should be wider benefits to employers and society. Greater confidence about equal treatment could help increase movement between full time and part time jobs (increasing labour market flexibility) and increase attachment to the labour market. Employers will gain if this results in an increase in the labour supply. The economy and society will gain as a whole if people are able to achieve a better balance between work and family responsibilities.

It was also stated by the then Secretary of State, Stephen Byers, that:

> Part-time work is valued by both employers and employees, and for good reasons. It means companies can have a flexible, cost-effective, experienced workforce and employees can balance their life at work with other commitments.

An investigation by the Equal Opportunities Commission in 2005 found that part-time work was still regarded by many as having a 'stigma' which can 'scar' an individual's employment prospects for life, particularly in terms of pay. This is still the case now—a comparison of gross hourly earnings of full-time and part-time workers between 2000 and 2010 demonstrates relatively little change; part-time workers' median hourly pay is now 64% of that of full-time workers, slightly up from 59% in 2000 (Bell, 2011).

There are advantages, however. In the light of the current economic downturn, Philips finds that there has been a rise in demand for part-time experienced staff as many firms look towards cost-effective recruitment. She quotes Women Like Us, a social enterprise that was set up to support women with children to find flexible work, which recorded a 121% increase in employer enquiries in July 2008, compared with July the previous year. The view of employers is that taking on high-calibre part-time workers was 'a less risky strategy' than employing experienced people full time, particularly as female returnees who wanted part-time work were preferable to those who were seeking full-time positions as they were more likely to remain in their job when the economy recovered. Employers were doing this for business reasons, as it gave them the flexibility to employ the right people without being committed to a full-time salary (Phillips, 2008).

 Exhibit 19.1 *R v Secretary of State for Employment, ex parte Equal Opportunities Commission* **(1994)**

This was an important case, in which the House of Lords confirmed that discrimination against part-timers was indirect discrimination against women.

It concerned the requirement that, in order to bring an unfair dismissal or redundancy payment claim within the then two-year period for both, the applicant had to have worked at least sixteen hours a week. If the applicant worked only 8–16 hours per week, he or she had to wait five years before being allowed to bring such a claim.

The Equal Opportunities Commission assisted the applicant, a female part-time cleaner who worked for eleven hours a week, and who was therefore denied a right to make a claim under the legislation.

The Secretary of State accepted that, as 87% of part-time workers at the time in the UK were women, this could amount to indirect discrimination, but argued that it was justified, as the purpose of the qualifying threshold was to encourage employers to provide part-time work, by reducing the costs to employers of employing such workers.

The House of Lords decided that the argument would apply equally if the employers were allowed to pay the part-timers less than the full-timers, which would be a gross breach of the principle of equal pay. It also found that there was no evidence before the court to prove that the different threshold provisions had in fact resulted in a greater availability of part-time work than would have been the case without them. The court therefore held that the Secretary of State had not proved justification. The law was thus changed so that there was no lower limit of hours worked per week before a person could claim unfair dismissal after the two-year qualifying period. (Note—the qualifying period for unfair dismissal is now one year, and two years for a redundancy payment, although the government are considering whether to increase it back to two years for unfair dismissal.)

In an article written in 2000, Aileen McColgan (at p265) explains that the Regulations are problematic for other reasons:

> (they) simply fail to address the disadvantage experienced by part-time workers. The problem for such workers is that the jobs, occupations and workplaces in which they are found are characterised by low pay. Where part-time workers are given access to the same jobs as full-time workers, they usually share the same terms and conditions. The fact is, however, that they are not given such access. Thus, while some part-time workers are low skilled, and remain low skilled because of the failure of the employer to train them, many more are working in jobs for which they are over-skilled (this is because of discrimination against part-time workers in access to 'better' jobs). Yet others are underpaid not because their skills or their jobs are of low quality, but because they are in a poor bargaining position.

The debate was continued in 2011 by Ellis, who writes that of the two aims of the Directive, namely removing discrimination against part-time workers and promoting the flexible organisation of working time, the British implementation of the Directive has been skewed towards the first of these two objectives. Notwithstanding that, he suggests that the regulations themselves are not as effective as they could be, partly because of the difficulty of finding a full-time comparator. He quotes McColgan on this, who noted that when introducing the Regulations the government accepted that the restrictive nature of this test would mean that only around one-sixth of part-time workers would be able to locate a comparator (Ellis, 2011).

The law

The Part-time Workers (Prevention of Less Favourable Treatment) Regulations came into force in July 2000, implementing the EU Part-time Workers Directive 1997. The aim of the Regulations was to ensure that part-time workers are treated no less favourably in their employment conditions than comparable full-timers, unless this is justified on objective grounds.

Regulation 5 of the Part-time Workers (Prevention of Less Favourable Treatment) Regulations reads as follows:

(1) A part-time worker has the right not to be treated by his employer less favourably than the employer treats a comparable full-time worker—

    (a) as regards the terms of his contract; or (b) by being subjected to any other detriment by any act, or deliberate failure to act, of his employer.

(2) The right conferred by paragraph (1) applies only if—

    (a) the treatment is on the ground that the worker is a part-time worker, and (b) the treatment is not justified on objective grounds.

Workers

The Regulations apply to all 'workers', so they cover employees as well as those who do not count as employees, such as casual, freelance or agency workers. This does not apply to the self-employed.

What does part-time mean?

A part-time worker is someone who works fewer hours a week than recognised full-timers do in the organisation in question. The Regulations do not set out a full definition of what a part-time worker is, effectively saying that a part-time worker is someone who is not a full-time worker, depending on the employer's business. In other words, there is no specific formula, and each case depends on its own facts. Thus, in some companies, workers who work thirty hours and above might be customarily regarded as full-time, whereas in another company it might be only workers who work more than, say, forty-five hours a week.

What is protected?

As a result of the Regulations, part-time workers are protected in the following areas:

- rates of pay (including overtime pay, once they have worked more than the normal full-time hours)
- access to pension schemes and pension scheme benefits
- access to training and career development
- holiday entitlement
- entitlement to career break schemes, contractual sick pay, contractual maternity and parental pay
- treatment in the selection criteria for promotion and transfer, and for redundancy.

Part-time workers who believe that they are being treated less favourably than a comparable full-time colleague can request a written explanation, and if this is not satisfactory, can then take the matter to an employment tribunal. There is also a right of protection against victimisation. So workers who take action to enforce these rights should not be treated adversely for having done so.

The only area in which discrimination against part-timers generally remains lawful is in respect of overtime payments. Part-timers only have the right to enhanced hourly rates when they work more hours than is usual for full-timers in the organisation concerned. It is important to note, however, that this exception only applies to overtime payments and not to other forms of payment such as overtime allowances. These like all other forms of payment must be paid on a pro-rata basis to part-timers (*James et al v Great North Eastern Railways*, (2005)).

The comparator

In order for a claim to be made, part-timers will need to identify a comparable full-timer who is receiving more favourable treatment. There are several tests to establish who is a comparable full-timer. The full-time worker (who can be of either sex) must:

- work for the same employer
- be engaged in the same or broadly similar work (taking account experience and skills where relevant). In the House of Lords case of *Matthews v Kent & Medway Towns and Fire Authority* (2006) it was said that it was vital to give a broad interpretation to the 'same or broadly similar' test. It said the comparison is different from that under the Equal Pay Act, and that the work must be looked at as a whole
- the part-time worker can also be compared to himself when he worked full-time, if that is relevant.

Objective justification

The guidance notes to the Regulations state that differential treatment of part-time workers compared to full-timers can be objectively justified by employers where it:

- is to achieve a legitimate objective, for example a legitimate business objective;
- is necessary to achieve that objective; and
- is an appropriate way to achieve that objective.

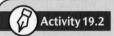 **Activity 19.2**

Mr Hughes is employed by Norris Holdings. He works twenty-five hours a week on quality control in their factory in Sunderland. He wishes to go on a training course that many of the other employees (both full- and part-time) are attending. But it is usually held on a Tuesday when he is not working, as he shares childcare responsibilities with his wife. The employer does not therefore send him on the course. Mr Hughes argues that he has been discriminated against.

Questions

1   Is this unlawful discrimination?

2   Would your answer be different if the courses were held on different days, but the one that the employer had chosen for his staff (for reasons of work and productivity) was the Tuesday course?

3   What legislation would Mr Hughes rely on if he wished to bring a claim?

4   Would your answer have been any different if he had been a woman?

Fixed-term workers

Part-time work is not the only type of flexible working to have been addressed by European directives. A further EU directive, extending a fair measure of protection to fixed-term workers (and indeed to all employed temporary staff), has also been introduced into UK laws. The European Fixed-term Workers Directive 1999 had two main aims:

• to improve the quality of fixed-term work by removing discrimination against fixed-term when compared with permanent workers

• to prevent abuse arising from the use of successive fixed-term employment contracts or relationships.

The law

The Fixed-term Employees (Prevention of Less Favourable Treatment) Regulations 2002 incorporate the 1999 EU Directive on fixed-term work, and provide a right for fixed-term employees to be treated no less favourably than comparable permanent employees, unless the difference in treatment can be objectively justified. Significantly, unlike the Part-time Workers Regulations, these apply only to employees. Those who work under contracts for service are thus excluded, a category which incorporates many fixed-term and temporary staff (eg, agency workers, apprentices and those doing work experience). This has been criticised by a number of commentators, not only because it gives no protection to 'workers', but also because it is argued that it does not fully transpose the provisions of the Directive which applies to 'fixed-term workers' as well as 'employees'.

It should also be noted that in October 2008 the European Parliament voted to support the introduction of the Agency Workers Directive, which led to the Agency Workers Regulations 2010. These came into force in October 2011, and give temporary and agency workers rights comparable to permanent employees after twelve weeks, such as equal pay and working conditions (excluding sick pay and pensions).

What is a fixed-term contract?

A fixed-term contract is defined in the Regulations as including:

- A contract made for a specific period of time that is fixed in advance, such as a shop assistant hired for the Christmas period.

- A contract that terminates on the completion of a particular task or project, such as the setting up of a new database.

- A contract that terminates on the occurrence or non-occurrence of a specific event, such as the return to work of another employee after maternity leave, or the non-renewal of funding for the post in question.

What is prohibited?

The Regulations prohibit less favourable treatment afforded to an employee on the grounds that he is employed on a fixed-term contract, rather than a permanent one, either as regards the terms of his contract; or by his being subjected to any other detriment by any act, or deliberate failure to act, of his employer. The rights include the same opportunity to receive training, to secure any permanent position in the establishment, including the right to be informed of any such vacancy, as a permanent employee. In order to comply with this duty, the employer must either advertise all vacancies internally in such a way that fixed-term employees have the opportunity to see them, or expressly notify fixed-term employees of available permanent vacancies. The employee also has the right to a written statement of reasons for any less favourable treatment.

The Regulations also allow for a pro-rata principle to be applied, that is *'where a comparable permanent employee receives or is entitled to pay or any other benefit, a fixed-term employee is to receive or be entitled to such proportion of that pay or other benefit as is reasonable in the circumstances having regard to the length of his contract of employment and the terms on which the pay or other benefit is offered'.*

The comparator

The comparator for a fixed-term employee is a permanent employee who is:

- employed by the same employer
- engaged in the same or broadly similar work having regard, where relevant, to whether they have a similar level of qualification and skills
- working at or based at the same establishment. Where, however, there is no permanent comparator working at or based at the same establishment, the fixed-term employee may compare his or her treatment with a permanent employee working at or based at another of the employer's establishments.

The result of this is that a fixed-term employee can only compare his or her treatment with someone who is engaged in similar work at a similar level, and who is working at or based in the same workplace (or a different workplace if there is no comparable permanent employee in the fixed-term employee's own workplace). There is no provision for a comparison to be made with a hypothetical employee, nor can a former employee be a comparator.

McColgan (2003:196) describes the approach to the definition of a comparator in the Regulations as 'narrow', particularly compared with other discrimination legislation, such as sex and race, which allow for a hypothetical comparator. She also refers to the fact that a former employee cannot be a comparator, and points out that *'If the purpose of the Regulations is to avoid discrimination against fixed-term workers [employees] they ought, it might be thought, to apply in the case where an employer chooses to replace permanent workers [employees] with fixed-term workers [employees] employed on lesser terms and conditions'.*

Limitations

As with most cases of direct discrimination, a case will only succeed if the differential treatment is *on grounds of* the fact that the employee is on a fixed-term contract. If the treatment were for any other reason, this would not be discrimination within the terms of the Regulations.

The other point to note is that less favourable treatment of a fixed-term employee will be justified on objective grounds if the terms of his or her contract, taken as a whole, are at least as favourable as the terms of the comparable permanent employee's contract of employment. This means, therefore, that if one of the terms of a fixed-term employee's contract is less favourable than the equivalent term in the comparator's contract, it can be offset by the provision of another benefit or more advantageous term in the fixed-term employee's contract, so long as the overall package of benefits is no less favourable than that of the permanent comparator.

The employer can also generally justify his treatment of the fixed-term employee, so long as this is done on objective grounds. This means that the employer must show that he has considered and balanced the rights of the employee against business objectives. As long as he can show it is a genuine objective and that the treatment was necessary and appropriate to achieve that objective, then the treatment will be justified.

Successive fixed-term contracts

A major change in British law, which potentially affects a large number of fixed-term workers, is the provision in the Regulations for the contract of a fixed-term employee who has been employed on a single fixed-term contract or a series of consecutive contracts with the one employer to become permanent after four years. This applies unless the employer has an objective reason that justifies extending or renewing the employee's contract on a fixed-term basis only. The employer is allowed, however, to modify the application of these provisions through a collective agreement or workforce agreement. Such an agreement could instead, for example, place a different limit on the total duration of successive fixed-term contracts or limit the number of successive fixed-term contracts.

 Exhibit 19.2   **Criticisms of the legislation**

The TUC and others have criticised the Regulations, not only for failing fully to implement the European Directive, but also for a number of other reasons:

- The fact that the Regulations are limited to employees not workers.

- The failure of the government to include agency workers within the ambit of the Regulations. Employers can thus effectively undermine the impact of the law by deliberately employing agency workers (NB: Agency workers have since been given their own set of regulations which came into force in October 2011, but these only protect once a worker has been with an employer for twelve weeks). »

- The 'overall package' approach of the Regulations does not sit comfortably with other discrimination legislation, whereby if a person is treated less favourably on one point, discrimination is made out.

- The narrowness of the comparators allowed.

- The TUC believes that four years is too long for successive contracts to be regarded as permanent, as it would benefit relatively few people, and suggests that two years would be fairer.

Agency workers

The Agency Workers Regulations (2010), which implement the Agency Workers Directive, came into force on 1 October 2011, and were agreed by the then government effectively as a sweetener to keep the working-time opt-out (see Chapter 26).

The Regulations apply to workers supplied by temporary work agencies, who are protected when they have been employed in the same role for twelve continuous calendar weeks.

The Regulations state that an agency worker is entitled to the same basic working conditions and employment conditions as he would have if he had been recruited by the hirer directly.

The comparator is someone who also works for the end user, is engaged in broadly similar work, having regard to whether they have a similar level of qualifications and skills and is based at the same establishment.

The twelve-week period has been a major criticism of the Regulations, with some fearing that end users will terminate contracts or move temporary staff to new roles before the time limit, so avoiding the application of the Regulations. According to a report by solicitors' firm Allen and Overy in 2011, it is estimated that the Regulations could threaten up to 500,000 temporary employment contracts (Chamberlain 2, 2011).

Ex-offenders

Many of the above reforms have had as part of their impetus a desire for freedom within the labour market. At times employers have difficulty in recruiting the right staff, even in a recession, so it is as important that they can find employees from a wide choice of people, as it is for people not to be hindered from applying for jobs that they are suitable for.

One group that is at risk of being marginalised from employment is that of ex-offenders. Many employers naturally have concerns about employing a person with a criminal conviction, and indeed there are some employers who have a legal duty to make sure that they do not do so, such as those who work with children, and who need to make sure that the prospective employee does not have a record for sexual offences. However, there are a significant number of people in this country who have a criminal record, and if such people were denied the right to employment as a result, this would have a severe knock-on effect not only for them, but for the labour market as a whole.

Not all of these people, of course, have serious criminal records or have spent time in custody. Many people have convictions for relatively minor offences, often committed in their youth. There is also evidence to show that being in employment can reduce re-offending by between a third and a half. If people have access to jobs, there is more of an incentive to stay away from committing further offences.

The Rehabilitation of Offenders Act was passed in 1974 as a means of addressing these issues. The aim of the Act is to help those who have been convicted of an offence, but have since stayed on the right side of the law. It helps such people to 'wipe the slate clean', by specifying a certain period of time that an offender has to disclose previous convictions. After that period, a conviction becomes 'spent', and the person is afforded two rights by the Act (although there are certain exceptions, as will be discussed below).

The two basic rights are:

- the right to stay silent/not to reveal a conviction after it is deemed to be 'spent'
- protection from dismissal, exclusion (ie, not being appointed) or any prejudicial act by an employer on account of a spent conviction.

A conviction is deemed to be spent once a certain amount of time has elapsed after the conviction (not after the end of the sentence). This rehabilitation period depends on the sentence that was given, not the offence committed. The times operate on a sliding scale (see Table 19.1).

There are certain points to note in relation to the Rehabilitation of Offenders Act:

- It is the length of sentence that counts, not the time actually served.
- A suspended sentence is treated as if it has been served.
- After this time has elapsed, provided no further offence is committed, the convicted person can lawfully keep the conviction secret.
- When a further offence is committed before the period has elapsed, the two periods run concurrently. They are not added together.
- A person whose conviction is spent can also lawfully answer 'no' if asked on an application form or in an interview if they have a criminal record. The question can be treated as if it does not refer to spent convictions.
- Referees are not obliged to share their knowledge of a past conviction in job references. However, they are not prevented from doing so provided the disclosure is made 'without malice'. Referees are free of legal liability in this respect.

Table 19.1 When does a criminal conviction become spent?

Sentence	Under 18 when convicted	Over 18 when convicted
imprisonment over thirty months:	never spent	never spent
imprisonment six to thirty months:	five years	ten years
less than six months' imprisonment:	three and a half years	seven years
fine or community punishment/ rehabilitation/community service order:	two and a half years	five years
detention in a detention centre:	three years	three years
conditional discharge:	one year	one year
absolute discharge:	six months	six months

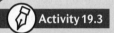

Activity 19.3

James is applying for a job in advertising. He is twenty-nine years old, but was convicted of theft when he was eighteen. He was sentenced to 100 hours' community service. The application form asks him to declare any convictions that he may have.

Questions

1 Does James have to declare the conviction?

2 When does/did his conviction become spent, if at all?

3 After he has been employed there for two years, his employer finds out about his conviction, and dismisses him on the basis that he cannot trust him, both for not declaring the conviction, and also because it was an offence of dishonesty. Does James have any recourse?

Although the above provisions of the Act allow many people to get on with their lives after being convicted of an offence, there are exceptions. These are there to protect the vulnerable and to ensure the reputation of certain professions. Such professions and occupations include doctors, nurses, midwives, dentists, barristers, solicitors, accountants, teachers and police officers. It is interesting to note that there are no exclusions on tax officers, company directors or army personnel. There is also an additional, general exception that covers any employment or work which is concerned with providing services to those under eighteen, where the person involved would have access to such children. A person who comes within these exceptions would have to declare any conviction, no matter how old it may be, spent or unspent, provided the employer states clearly in the application form or at the interview that the job applied for is exempted from the Act. There are also provisions for certain employers to obtain a criminal record certificate for certain sensitive occupations.

In 2002, the government commissioned a report reviewing the Rehabilitation of Offenders Act, on the basis that it is now an old statute, and has been criticised for being too complicated and for not helping ex-offenders to put their past behind them. It has been said that the rehabilitation periods are too long, and therefore limit the prospects of the resettlement of ex-offenders. The report, 'Breaking the Circle' made a number of recommendations, many of which the government accepted, but no changes have yet been made.

In 2011 the Act was criticised again, this time by Nacro (originally called the National Association for the Care and Resettlement of Offenders). It says that the Act has been a success, but that this is qualified. The main problem according to Nacro is that the Act is so old. In a recent report, Nacro states that 'The Act ... is being undermined by the increase in sentence length which has occurred since the Act was implemented. Many offenders who would have received sentences of two and a half years or less in 1974 are receiving sentences of between three and four years today. This means that many offenders who would have previously been helped by the Act now find that their offences will never become spent.' In addition to this, the list of exemptions to the Act (which are regularly updated on www.crb.homeoffice.gov.uk) has also grown by 50%, all of this making the Act less generous than those which apply in other European countries (Nacro, 2010). There are no plans to amend it at present.

CHAPTER SUMMARY

- At present, most flexible workers are women, but this is a growing sector of the workforce, as more people take on non-traditional methods of working.
- Before this legislation came in, women could use discrimination law, but this was unsatisfactory for a number of reasons, and did not protect men.
- Part-time workers should not be treated less favourably than full-timers, unless this can be objectively justified.
- Fixed-term workers should not be treated less favourably than full-timers, unless this can be objectively justified.
- A fixed-term employee who has been with the same employer for four years is entitled to a permanent contract.
- An agency worker is entitled to comparable terms and conditions as a permanent employee after twelve weeks.
- Ex-offenders are entitled not to refer to their convictions in certain circumstances, depending on what they were sentenced to.

REFERENCES

Bell, M. (2011) 'Achieving the objectives of the Part-Time Work Directive? Revisiting the Part-Time Workers Regulations' *Industrial Law Journal* 40.3.

Chamberlain, L. 1 (2011) 'Workers forced into part-time roles hits record high' *Personnel Today*, 17 August.

Chamberlain, L 2 (2011) 'Agency workers regulations could threaten 500,000 temporary jobs' *Personnel Today*, 13 September.

Equal Opportunities Commission (2005) *Part time work is no crime—so why the penalty?* EOC interim report. Manchester: Equal Opportunities Commission.

Francesconi, M. & Gosling, A. (2005) *Career paths of part time workers. EOC 2005 working paper number 19.* Manchester: Equal Opportunities Commission.

Fredman, S. (1997) 'Labour law in flux: the changing composition of the workforce' *Industrial Law Journal* 26.4 (p337).

Home Office (2003) *Breaking the Circle: A Summary of the Views of Consultees and the Government Response to the Report of the Review of the Rehabilitation of Offenders Act 1974.* London: HMSO.

McColgan, A. (2000) 'Missing the point? The Part Time Workers (Prevention of Less Favourable Treatment) Regulations 2000 (SI 2000, no 1551)' *Industrial Law Journal* 29.3 (p260).

McColgan, A. (2003) 'The Fixed-Term Employees (Prevention of Less Favourable Treatment) Regulations 2002: fiddling while Rome burns?' *Industrial Law Journal* 32.3 (p194).

Nacro (2010) 'The Rehabilitation of Offenders Act 1974 and the Rehabilitation of Offenders Act 1974 (Exceptions) Order 1975', Nacro Communications.

Phillips, L. (2008) 'Downturn means more demand for women who work part time' *People Management*, 21 August.

Stewart, H. (2011) 'Part-time jobs are the only option for millions of British workers', *The Guardian*, 13 July.

TUC (2002) *Response to DTI Consultation on rights for Fixed Term Employees.* April 2002 (available at www.tuc.org.uk).

ONLINE RESOURCE CENTRE

A range of online resources to help you through your employment law module have been developed by the author team. These include updates, self-test questions and sources for further reading. (www.oxfordtextbooks.co.uk/orc/taylor_emir3e)

Employment policy and practice

PART IV

Family-friendly statutes

Learning outcomes

By the end of this chapter you should be able to:

- describe a woman's entitlement to time off for ante-natal care;

- state what kind of precautions an employer should take for the health of a pregnant or nursing woman;

- set out how much maternity leave a woman can take;

- explain the rules relating to statutory maternity pay;

- distinguish between paternity and parental leave, and explain the rights for each;

- advise on whether someone has a right to work flexibly and what the employer has to consider when faced with such a request; and

- debate the arguments for and against extensive family-friendly regulation.

Introduction

In recent years there has been a rapid expansion of so-called 'family-friendly employment laws'. While women have had an entitlement to maternity leave for some time, this has been extended further, and other rights created, such as that of paternity leave for fathers after the birth of a child, a right to parental leave for both parents, and emergency time off for dependants, adoption leave, and a right to request flexible working. The amount of regulation concerning these rights has been criticised and the extent of each right can be complicated to work out. This chapter will look at these laws and break each down into its component parts. It will also consider whether it is appropriate that the statute book should reflect a commitment to a 'work–life balance', or whether this kind of legislation in fact ignores the needs of business and therefore has a deleterious effect on the economy.

It is important to remember when reading this chapter that it is concerned with statutory rights. These are the basic minimum rights which employers are obliged to grant their employees under statute. In practice many employers operate contractual schemes which provide more generous entitlements. These can be legally enforceable, but only in the context of breach of contract or constructive dismissal claims. Here we are solely concerned with basic, minimum statutory rights.

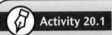 **Activity 20.1**

Monica has been employed by Steele Enterprises for six years, and is expecting a baby in four months' time. She is married to Daniel, who also works for the same company, and has been there for three years.

Questions

1   She wants to have one afternoon off each fortnight so that she can go to ante-natal classes run by the local midwives, but her employer refuses. Is he allowed to do so?

2   Is Monica entitled to take maternity leave? If so, how long can she take?

3   Will Monica have any income if she takes maternity leave?

4   Daniel wishes to stay at home for a while after the birth so that he can look after Monica and get to know the new baby. Does he have such a right? If so, how long can he take? Will he be paid?

5   Monica is concerned because she wants to return to work after any maternity leave, but the local nursery only has a place for the baby for three days a week. She has therefore decided that she wants to work part time. Can she do this?

Return to this activity once you have read to the end of the chapter, to see how many of your answers were correct.

Background

The current law relating to maternity and parental leave was introduced relatively recently. The old scheme for maternity leave for mothers was very complex, and created many problems for both employers and employees. Fathers had no rights and there was no scheme for those who needed time off for family emergencies, or wished to work in a more flexible manner. Most of this legislation applies only to employees and there are some exclusions, such as the armed forces, the police and those employed in share fishing.

Additional rights were brought in by the Employment Relations Act 1999, and the Maternity and Parental Leave, etc Regulations 1999, which came into force in December 1999. These were:

- a new framework for maternity leave and maternity pay
- the right to parental leave
- the right to time off to care for dependants.

As part of the government's emphasis on family-friendly policies, the law was further extended by the Employment Act 2002, the measures coming into effect in April 2003. The new rights consisted of:

- longer periods of paid maternity leave
- higher rates of maternity pay
- the introduction of paid paternity leave
- a right 'to apply' for flexible working.

Since then, the Work and Families Act 2006 further extended paid maternity leave, and regulations now provide the option for fathers to share some of the mother's maternity leave. These will be considered later in this chapter.

Ante-natal care

When a woman becomes pregnant, she will need to take time off, not only to have the baby, but also for necessary checks and visits before the baby is born. There are likely to be appointments to see the midwife and doctor, visits to the hospital and ante-natal classes. The right to time off for ante-natal care is part of the package of measures designed to assist women both to be able to have children and to be part of the workforce. This right is contained in sections 55–57 of the Employment Rights Act 1996, and consists of:

- the right not to be unreasonably refused time off to attend ante-natal care appointments during working hours; and
- the right to be paid for this period of absence.

The right to have time off for ante-natal care applies only to employees and so does not extend to casual workers and other 'non-employees'. Although it only applies to employees, it can be used by all employees irrespective of length of service or number of hours worked.

There are three conditions before the woman can take advantage of the right:

1. the woman must be pregnant
2. the appointment must have been made on the advice of a registered doctor, midwife or health visitor
3. if she is asked for it, the employee must be able to produce evidence of the appointment by means of a letter or appointment card.

'Ante-natal care' is not actually defined in the legislation, and some commentators have suggested that this leaves a grey area as to whether or not relaxation and parentcraft classes are included. In *Gregory v Tudsbury Ltd* (1982), an employment tribunal decided that relaxation classes were part of ante-natal care, although other tribunals have ruled differently. In the absence of a definitive ruling from the EAT or the Court of Appeal, the only direction we have to go on is that provided by the government on the Businesslink website (www. businesslink.gov.uk), which states that pregnant employees are entitled to time off for both relaxation classes and parentcraft classes.

The pregnant employee has to seek permission from her employer before she takes the leave for ante-natal appointments. She cannot just attend the appointment and later inform the employer that it was for an ante-natal purpose. The employer can refuse to give permission for time off only if it is reasonable to do so. If the employer refuses permission when requested, the employee cannot go ahead and take the time off because she could then risk disciplinary action. If the refusal is unreasonable, however, she can go to the employment tribunal to seek a remedy, as detailed below.

An example of a refusal that might be reasonable is if the woman only works two days a week and is able to make a non-urgent appointment outside working hours, but this does depend on whether she has a say in the timing of the appointment. It must be remembered, however, that the right is to time off during *working hours*. This means that the employer cannot try to rearrange her working hours, or insist that she make up for lost time. She also has a right to be paid for the time off, and a schedule to the statute sets out how the hourly rate should be calculated. The time off includes time taken to travel to the appointment.

If an employer unreasonably refuses a woman time off for an ante-natal appointment, she can complain to an employment tribunal, which can make a declaration that the right has been unreasonably refused and order that any unpaid work be recompensed. Moreover, it is automatically unfair to dismiss someone for a reason connected with pregnancy, irrespective of length of service. This would cover any dismissal that occurred as a result of a woman who had been unreasonably refused paid time off taking that time to attend an appointment. Any disciplinary action taken against a pregnant woman in such a situation would amount to sex discrimination.

 Activity 20.2

Sarah has been employed as a full-time PA by Mitchell & Co for five months. Her working hours are 9am–5pm. She is pregnant, and has been allowed by her employer to have time off for visits to the midwife.

As a result of her pregnancy, she has been suffering pain in her legs and back, and her midwife has recommended that she attend pregnancy yoga classes. These start at 5pm, which means that Sarah will have to leave work an hour early every Wednesday, in order to get there in time. This is in addition to her visits to the midwife, which take place every two weeks.

Questions

1 Is Sarah entitled to take time off for ante-natal care?

2 Can Mitchell & Co refuse to allow her to attend the class? Give reasons for your answer.

3 Does a yoga class count as 'ante-natal' care?

Health and safety issues

There can be dangers in the workplace for pregnant women and new mothers, from their working conditions or the environment in which they spend their working hours. In 1992, the EC Pregnant Workers Directive set out measures to avoid risk at work to the health and safety of three groups of women:

- pregnant workers;
- those who have given birth in the last six months; and
- those who are breastfeeding and their babies.

The reasoning behind this part of the Pregnant Workers Directive is that 'particularly sensitive risk groups must be protected against the dangers which specifically affect them', and that pregnant workers and new mothers form such a group. The Directive justifies it by reference to the Equal Treatment Directive, and the need not to treat women on the labour market unfavourably and place emphasis on equal treatment for men and women.

The UK law is contained in the Management of Health and Safety at Work Regulations 1999, and places an onus on the employer to minimise any threat to such women's health and safety. This area of law covers all workers and not just employees. (The situation in respect of factory workers is covered in UK law by the Public Health Act 1936 which is more stringent in some respects than the EU law.)

Risk assessment

The law expects employers periodically to undertake risk assessments of the risks to the health and safety of all employees (see Chapter 24). In so doing, they must take specific account of women who fall into one of the three categories set out in the above paragraph. This is particularly important where hazardous substances are in use. The Directive sets out examples of the types of things that may cause a risk, such as vibration, noise, biological and chemical agents, and certain work practices which may be of danger to women in such a condition. If the employer does not do this, it could amount to sex discrimination.

The health and safety obligations that employers face refer not only to women who are already pregnant, or who have recently given birth, but also to all women of childbearing age. This is because women may often not know that they are pregnant at a time that they are exposed to particular risks and certain working conditions may harm the unborn child. When carrying out a risk assessment, an employer should consider matters such as:

- physical problems with a woman's workstation and equipment
- lifting/carrying heavy loads
- stretching and bending
- standing or sitting for long periods of time
- long working hours
- excessively noisy workplaces
- working in a stressful environment or with a heavy workload
- rest periods and access to sanitary facilities
- working with hazardous substances or chemicals.

Exhibit 20.1   *Day v T Pickles Farms Ltd* (1999)

This was a case in which the EAT considered an employer's obligations in relation to the health of pregnant women.

Ms Day worked in a sandwich shop where food was cooked on the premises. She became pregnant and had to leave work because the smell and handling of food in the shop made her morning sickness much worse. Her doctor certified her as unfit for work.

The employment tribunal said that the requirement to carry out an assessment only arose if there was actually a pregnant worker in employment, but the EAT said that this was wrong. The employer should, at the very least, have carried out the assessment when Ms Day, a woman of childbearing age, had been employed. It was not necessary for the woman to become pregnant in order to trigger the need for an assessment, but rather the duty arose because there was a woman of childbearing age employed in the undertaking. A woman is not usually aware that she is pregnant to begin with. The only way, therefore, to ensure that risk is avoided, is to anticipate it by carrying out the assessment before she is aware that she is pregnant.

The EAT also said that not carrying out this assessment may have amounted to a detriment under sex discrimination legislation.

When employers have completed their risk assessments they must communicate its results to female workers. If the assessment shows any risk to their health or safety, a way must be found to protect them. Details of the preventative and protective measures must be communicated and reviewed regularly. If the risk assessment shows a risk to the health and safety of a new or expectant mother, the employer has to take reasonable measures to avoid the risk. For example, if a pregnant woman is serving in a shop, and spends a long time standing, causing her to be at risk of varicose veins, the employer could provide her with a chair. If the risk cannot be avoided, he must alter the woman's working conditions or hours of work, if it is reasonable to do so and if this would avoid the risk. Where, as in the case of a woman who works in a chemical factory, there is no suitable alternative to the work that she is doing, then the employer must suspend her from work on full pay for as long as is necessary to avoid the risk.

The Regulations also specifically protect such women from having to do night work. If a woman is a new or expectant mother, and a doctor or midwife certifies that performing night work would pose a risk to her health and safety, she is entitled to be offered alternative work such as doing a day-time shift, or if necessary must be suspended on health grounds.

The risk assessment is for the benefit of all female workers of childbearing age, but the employer only has to take action such as altering a woman's working conditions, or suspending her on health and safety grounds if she has given written notice that she is pregnant, breastfeeding, etc.

A woman can make a complaint to the employment tribunal, and get a declaration of her rights, or if it is the kind of case that would amount to sex discrimination (for example if the employer does not carry out the risk assessment) the woman may be entitled to damages. If the employer dismisses the woman rather than carry out his obligations, this would be automatically unfair dismissal. The woman would also, of course, be able to make a formal complaint to the Health and Safety Executive (see Chapter 24).

Activity 20.3

Jemima started a job at EasyKlean, a chain of dry cleaners, four weeks ago. She works in a small shop and does not do the dry cleaning herself (although this is done on the premises). She works behind the till, taking the clothes from the customers and handing out tickets.

She has just found out that she is pregnant, something that she did not know about when she started work. Her doctor says that it would not be good for her health or her pregnancy if she continued in her current role as the fumes from the dry cleaning fluid could have a bad effect.

When she tells her manager of the pregnancy, he gets angry and says that if he had known that she was pregnant he would not have given her a job.

Questions

1 What obligations does EasyKlean have in these circumstances?

2 What rights and remedies are available to Jemima?

Maternity leave

Statutory maternity rights have been in existence in the UK since 1974, but have been greatly expanded and clarified in recent years. There are three different types of maternity leave:

1. compulsory maternity leave (CML)

2. ordinary maternity leave (OML)

3. additional maternity leave (AML).

The law is contained in the Maternity and Parental Leave, etc Regulations 1999 (which were later amended), the Employment Rights Act 1996 and the Work and Families Act 2006.

All pregnant employees are now entitled to up to fifty-two weeks' maternity leave, no matter how long they have worked for their employer. The purpose of maternity leave is to allow the mother to give birth and to recover from giving birth, as well as to bond with and care for her new child. If an employee has a contractual right to maternity leave in addition to the statutory right set out in this guidance, she may take advantage of whichever is the more favourable to her.

Compulsory maternity leave

CML is straightforward; it is the two weeks after the birth (four weeks for those who work in a factory), during which there is a compulsory period of maternity leave. The onus is on the employer to make sure that no work is done during this period. This covers any work done for the employer, so the woman must not even work from home. Normally this forms part of the OML, so CML only applies where a woman decides she does not wish to exercise her right to OML.

Ordinary maternity leave

The length of the OML, which used to be eighteen weeks, was extended in 2003, and is now twenty-six weeks (ie, six months). It starts on the day that the employee notifies that she wishes it to begin, but there is an exception to this. This is if, within the four weeks before she wishes the leave to start, she is absent because of illness due to pregnancy. In such a situation the start of the OML is automatically triggered, even if she is ill for only one day. If the employer wishes, it can agree to waive this, and in the BERR guidance on the subject (now available on the BERR archive), it is stated that '*odd days of pregnancy-related illness may be disregarded at the employer's discretion . . .*'. However, the trigger is not set off if the absence is due to a routine ante-natal appointment (as discussed above). Of course, if the baby arrives early, then the OML will start then.

 Activity 20.4

McColgan (2000) criticises the illness trigger, saying that '*it is difficult to ascertain the reason behind this rule, and its retention. The ERA entitles women to time off for ante-natal care, and ante-natal appointments become increasingly frequent as the due date approaches . . .*', and therefore there should be no difference if a woman takes time off to see a doctor for an ante-natal appointment, or if she takes time off because she is unwell.

It does appear to be difficult to reconcile this rule with the arguments discussed in Chapters 16 and 17 on sex discrimination and pregnancy-related illness. If it is discriminatory to take detrimental action against a pregnant woman if she becomes ill as a result of her pregnancy, then why is it not discriminatory to force her to start her maternity leave because of a pregnancy-related illness?

The guidance also begs the question that, if the government thought that it was a good thing for employers to ignore odd days of illness, why is this left to their discretion, and not spelt out in the legislation? The Working Families (www.workingfamilies.org.uk) website advises employers that it is considered good practice not to trigger maternity leave for the occasional day off in that period, although obviously it is at the employer's discretion.

Questions

What is your view? Why?

To take maternity leave an employee should inform her employer no later than the end of the fifteenth week before the week the baby is due (or as soon as is reasonably practicable) of:

- the fact that the woman is pregnant
- the expected week of childbirth (EWC)
- the date on which the OML is due to start (this can be any time after the eleventh week prior to the EWC).

The employer then has a duty, within twenty-eight days of being given the woman's notice of when she wishes to start the OML, to notify her of the date when that leave will *end*. Unlike the old (pre-2000) scheme, this information does not need to be given in writing, nor are any statements of intentions about taking further leave or returning to work required. The employer no longer has the right to insist on being given a date when the woman intends to return to work.

She can change the date she starts her maternity leave as long as she gives twenty-eight days' notice to her employer.

During OML the contract of employment continues in all respects except for pay. All benefits continue to accrue (including holidays). Company cars, portable computers and mobile phones are kept, health insurance is retained and all duties owed by employers and employees (mutual trust and confidence, etc) continue. There is a general right of return to the same job on the same terms and conditions following OML, all pay rises and other improvements to terms and conditions being honoured. After the return to work the contractual situation should be as if the maternity leave had not happened.

The employee's right to return from ordinary maternity leave is a right to return to the same job in which she was employed before her absence, with her seniority and other rights as they would have been had she not been absent, and on the same or better terms and conditions as if she had not been absent. The only exception is where the job becomes redundant during OML, in which case the right is to return to a suitable alternative job with similar terms and conditions. It is important to remember that the right is to return to the same job and not necessarily to the same work. It may be that changes have been made in her absence that mean the work the woman does on her return may be somewhat different. It only becomes a different job where the content is substantially altered. At present there is no general right for a woman to return on a part-time basis or on different working hours unless this is provided for in the contract of employment. There is just a right to request flexible working (see below).

The woman is entitled to return to work before twenty-six weeks have been completed, but she must give twenty-eight days' notice of this. There is no longer a requirement to give notice of the intention to return after twenty-six weeks. The assumption must be that she will return.

Additional maternity leave

Since April 2007, all employees, regardless of service, have been entitled to an additional period of twenty-six weeks maternity leave. Before then, only those who had twenty-six weeks' service could take additional maternity leave (AML).

During this period her contract of employment continues. Until October 2008 this was only the case to a limited extent, but since then employees taking AML have retained the same contractual benefits as for OML. They keep the same terms and conditions of employment, save for salary. The main difference with OML is that for AML the right to return is to the same job *if reasonably practicable*. Otherwise it is to a suitable job on no less favourable terms and conditions.

This means a woman can be away from her job on maternity leave for fifty-two weeks in total. When an employer writes to the employee—setting out her return date—it will assume, if she is eligible for additional maternity leave, that she will be taking it. If an employee wishes to change the return date she must give twenty-eight days' notice. As with OML there is no longer a requirement for the woman to give notice of her intention to return at the end of her AML, she just turns up for work on the day concerned. However, twenty-eight days' notice must be given if she wants to return earlier than the end of the twenty-six weeks.

Keeping in touch

During her maternity leave, the legislation states that an employee can do up to ten days' work under her contract of employment without losing her right to SMP, as long as both she and her employer have agreed for this to happen, and agree on what work is to be done and how much she will be paid for it.

The employer may make contact with the employee (and vice versa) while she is on maternity leave, as long as the amount and type of contact is not unreasonable, to discuss a range of issues—eg, to discuss her plans for returning to work, or to keep her informed of important developments at the workplace. The employee should be informed of any relevant promotion opportunities or job vacancies that arise during maternity leave.

Return to work

If she returns at the end of her full fifty-two weeks of maternity leave and has not told her employer that she wishes to come back at any other time, she does not need to provide any further notice. The employee can change the dates of her return to work as long as she gives eight weeks' notice to her employer. If the employee decides not to return to work at the end of her maternity leave she is entitled to continue to receive her full amount of statutory maternity leave and pay. She must give the employer at least the notice required by her contract or, where there is none, the statutory notice.

 **Activity 20.5**

Consider the following two cases:

The Home Office v Holmes (1984)

Ms Holmes was a civil servant in the Home Office. She took maternity leave following the birth of her second child. As she was a single parent, she asked her employer if she could return to work part-time. This was refused on the grounds that she had the right to return only to the same contractual terms as before and it was departmental policy not to allow part-time posts in her grade. She claimed that the requirement to work full-time was indirectly discriminatory.

The tribunal accepted evidence that, despite changes in the role of women in modern society, the raising of children placed a greater burden on women than on men. It decided that the requirement to work full-time was a detriment and that the employer had failed to justify its policy that full-time working was necessary in her grade.

The EAT upheld the tribunal's finding that there had been an unlawful indirect discrimination, though it emphasised that this case stood very much on its own facts and that other circumstances would not necessarily produce the same result.

Greater Glasgow Health Board v Carey (1987)

Ms Carey was a health visitor. She requested to return to work part-time, working two or three days a week when she returned from maternity leave.

Her employer refused, because it said that it needed her to work five days per week in order to maintain continuity of care to clients.

An employment tribunal decided that the requirement was unlawfully indirectly discriminatory.

Overturning the tribunal decision, the EAT held that the tribunal had not given sufficient weight to the Board's evidence that an efficient and effective service could not be provided on the basis suggested by the employee, and that continuity of care would be in jeopardy. The Board was therefore justified in imposing the five-day week requirement.

Questions

1 How can these cases be reconciled?

2 When you have read the section on the right to request flexible working, return to this exercise. These are old cases, which were heard before the current legislative framework was in place. Do you think that the decisions would be any different if heard today? Why?

Maternity pay

If a woman has been employed by her employer for at least twenty-six weeks, ending with the fifteenth week before the expected week of childbirth, and earns more than £102 per week (the lower earnings limit 2011–2012) then, although she is not entitled to be paid her salary, she will receive statutory maternity pay (SMP) for the first thirty-nine weeks of her maternity leave (this increased from twenty-six weeks in October 2007).

There are two levels of SMP. The 'higher rate' is paid for the first six weeks. This is equivalent to 90% of the woman's salary. After this she is paid at the 'lower rate' (which is £135.45 per week in 2012–2013) for the remaining thirty-three weeks. This is reviewed every April, and the current level can be found on the DirectGov website. If the woman earns less than the lower rate of SMP, then she will be given 90% of her earnings for the whole thirty-nine weeks. SMP is payable by the employer, but is partly (or, for small firms wholly) reimbursed by the state through reduced employer national insurance contributions.

Women who do not qualify for SMP have to claim state maternity allowance from the DWP from the start of their leave. This is currently paid at £135.45 per week for employed women earning above the lower national insurance limit. Lesser sums are paid to those on lower earnings. If the employee suffers detriment or dismissal because she has exercised her right, or does not receive the SMP that she is entitled to, then she can complain to an employment tribunal. For further discussion of the discrimination aspect of treatment of women while on maternity leave, see Chapter 17.

Paternity leave

Ordinary paternity leave

The right for a man to take a short period of time off after the birth of a child so that he can care for the child or support the mother was introduced by the Employment Act 2002, and detailed in the Paternity and Adoption Leave Regulations 2002. The original right, now called ordinary paternity leave, is to take one or two weeks' leave. This came into force in 2003, and only applies to employees. Ordinary paternity pay can be claimed during the period of leave. In order to be eligible, an employee must:

- have or expect to have responsibility for the child's upbringing
- be the biological father of the child or the mother's husband or partner
- have worked continuously for his employer for twenty-six weeks ending with the fifteenth week before the baby is due
- inform his employer of his intentions by the end of the fifteenth week prior to the EWC
- state whether one or the full two weeks are going to be claimed
- complete a self-certification form if requested to by the employer confirming that he meets the eligibility criteria
- if the child is born early or late, the employee must give notice of the variation as soon as is reasonably practicable.

The Regulations allow an eligible employee to take either one week or two consecutive weeks' paternity leave. He has to take the time off within fifty-six days of the birth, and has to take it in a chunk of one week or two weeks; he cannot take random individual days, or odd periods of less than one week. He can start his leave:

- from the date of the child's birth (whether this is earlier or later than expected); or
- from a chosen number of days or weeks after the date of the child's birth (whether this is earlier or later than expected); or
- from a chosen date later than the first day of the week in which the baby is expected to be born.

Leave can start on any day of the week on or following the child's birth but must be completed:

- within fifty-six days of the actual date of birth of the child; or
- if the child is born early, within the period from the actual date of birth up to fifty-six days after the first day of the expected week of birth.

Only one period of leave is available to employees irrespective of whether more than one child is born as the result of the same pregnancy. The same right to leave exists for stillbirths if born after twenty-four weeks of pregnancy.

Ordinary paternity pay

The rate of statutory ordinary paternity pay is the same as the standard rate of statutory maternity pay. As of April 2011, this is £135.45 a week or 90% of average weekly earnings if his usual income is less than this. Employees who have average weekly earnings below the lower earnings limit for national insurance purposes (£107 a week from April 2012) do not qualify for SPP. Return to work arrangements and contractual entitlements are as for ordinary maternity leave (OML). An employee can make a complaint to an employment tribunal if he is denied his entitlement to paternity leave, if he is victimised for asserting his rights under the Regulations, or if he is denied payment of SPP.

Additional paternity leave

In April 2011, the much-awaited right to Additional Paternity Leave and Pay was introduced. The scheme is in addition to ordinary paternity leave and pay, and mirrors that of AML, including keeping the same terms and conditions, and allowing keeping in touch days.

It provides fathers with a right to take up to twenty-six weeks leave to care for their child during the first year of its life. This leave has been described as leave 'shared' with the mother—if the mother has returned to work, then additional paternity leave can be taken between twenty weeks and one year after the child is born or placed for adoption, and the father has to give eight weeks' notice of when this leave will start and finish. There will therefore be no overlap with the mother's maternity leave or pay. Additional statutory paternity pay will also mirror that of SMP, and be 90% of earnings. In effect, the provision will allow the mother to share some of her leave and pay with the father. Government research indicates that initial take-up of this new right is likely to be modest—between 10,000 and 19,000 fathers per year, a figure which is likely to increase as fathers begin to take a larger role in early childcare (IDS, 2009:236). Keeble (2006) makes the point, however, that '*the scheme is likely to be very attractive for parents where the mother earns substantially more than the father as she will be able to return to work at her higher salary while the father stays at home with the child and receives some income in the form of ASPP'*. In addition to this, employers have concerns about the complexity and administrative burdens involved in such a transfer of leave, particularly as the mother and father are likely to work for two different employers. If, however, the scheme becomes flexible, then there may be more take-up. In response to this fear by employers, Roberts and Joffe, writing in *The Times*, state that:

> shared parental leave could benefit employers, in much the same way as flexible working arrangements. The burden of leave would be spread across employers, rather than the mother's employer taking the entire hit. And employees who are able to create a decent work-life balance are likely to be more loyal and productive and more likely to return to work. (Roberts, J. and Joffe, N. (2011))

 Exhibit 20.2

Research from uSwitch.com reported in March 2011 and relating to paternity leave found that 26% of fathers are concerned that taking such a prolonged period of time off work would damage their career, while 16% expressed concerns about losing their job.

Nearly half said they just wouldn't be able to get the time off in their current position, while 52% said they would not be able to afford it.

However, 80% of the men questioned said the changes were a good thing, with 61% stating they would not mind if a colleague took six months' paternity leave. Ann Robinson, director of consumer policy at uSwitch.com, said the Coalition has recognised that fathers are now more hands-on than in the past, but she added that putting legislation in place to support dads is only part of the battle.

The biggest fight will be to change social opinion, fears and prejudices and this is not going to happen overnight.

Source: www.uswitch.com

 Activity 20.6

The spate of legislation in the area of family-friendly policies has led to some criticism. In separate articles in the *Industrial Law Journal*, James and Di Torella make the following points:

1. The legislation is piecemeal, '*applying the small step approach to an issue that perhaps requires a complete overhaul and rethink appears to have a little to offer all interested parties, but does not fully satisfy any*'. James (2006: 277)

2. The '*piecemeal increases in the length of SMP are a safe way of appearing to be family-friendly whilst, in practice, failing to address the real needs of families in 21st century Britain*'. James (2006: 273)

3. Paternity leave—'*. . . offering leave only to men who have the stipulated length of service required . . . introduces a divide between fathers who can take leave and those who cannot . . . It also has damaging ideological ramifications because it reinforces the notion that the mother has (and should have) the main responsibility for childcare (as her eligibility is not dependent upon length of service), suggesting that the father's role is secondary. This is at best a missed opportunity . . .*'. James (2006: 275) »

4. Paternity leave—'*The main problem is that the legislation is drafted in such a way to reinforce the idea that mothers rather than fathers are the primary carers.*' Di Torella (2007: 322)

5. Keeping in touch days—'*On the one hand, if sympathetically handled, KIT days could provide a useful tool enabling employees to maintain connections with the workplace . . . On the other hand, KIT days might, if handled unsympathetically, be perceived as a requirement rather than an option (either by employers or employees) and may add to the stresses and strains of women's daily lives during what is already an intense period of re-adjustment.*' James (2007: 316)

Questions

1 Do you agree with these comments? Why?

2 If not how would you change the law and why?

Parental leave

The right to parental leave originated in the EU's 1996 Parental Leave Directive 96/34/EC. It has the aim of promoting:

- the balancing of work and family life
- equal opportunities for men and women
- women's participation in the workforce
- the assumption of a more equal share of family responsibilities by men.

The Directive did not originally apply to the UK when it was adopted, because of this country's opt-out from the Agreement on Social Policy. When the Labour Party came into power in 1997, the opt-out was reversed, and the UK signed the Social Chapter of the Maastricht Treaty. Following this, the Maternity and Parental Leave, etc Regulations 1999 (amended in 2002) were put into place, with the stated aim of the government to '*make a real difference to families, making it easier to balance the demands of family life and work*'.

In the consultation before the Regulations were drafted, the government said that the regulation of this area would be carried out with a 'light hand', hoping that employers and their employees would reach agreement, by means of workforce agreements, collective agreements, or individual agreements which are incorporated into the contract of employment. If none has been agreed, there is a default scheme which applies and which sets out minimum provisions.

Parental leave, which is unpaid, applies to employees, whether they are men or women. The employee is eligible to take the leave if he or she has been continuously employed for at least one year. The person claiming the leave must have caring responsibilities for a child who is under the age of five. In other words, the person must be the mother or the father of the child, as registered on the birth certificate, or otherwise have 'parental responsibility', which is a legal responsibility that can be granted by a court. Adoptive parents also have the right to take periods of parental leave. The leave that is taken must be for the purpose of caring for that child. If it is not, and is in fact taken for another purpose, this may be treated by the employer as an act of misconduct. Legitimate reasons why an employee might wish to take advantage of this right could be:

- to spend more time with a child in the early years
- to accompany a child during a stay in hospital
- to look at new schools
- to settle a child into new childcare arrangements
- to enable a family to spend more time together, for example taking the child to stay with grandparents.

The default or fallback scheme

If there is agreement between the parties, whether by collective agreement, workforce agreement, or individual agreement, further matters can be set out. These can be elements such as how much notice the employee should give before taking parental leave, whether the employer can postpone the leave if the business cannot cope or could be harmed by the employee's absence, and for how long that postponement should be, and how much leave can be taken in any one go.

The employer may also be prepared to extend the right to step-parents, grandparents or foster parents; he might waive the one-year qualifying period, and perhaps allow parents of older children to take some parental leave.

If there is no agreement, the fallback scheme will automatically apply. In addition, if the employee reaches an individual agreement with the employer (in other words, not a collective or workplace agreement), and the fallback scheme is more favourable, then he will still be entitled to rely on the fallback scheme if it is more favourable than the arrangement in his contract. All schemes, whether by agreement, or under the fallback scheme, must have at least the following elements:

- The leave must be taken within the first five years of a child's life (or the first five years after an adoption, up to the age of eighteen). If the child is disabled the right is for eighteen weeks' leave during the first eighteen years of the child's life.

- Up to thirteen weeks' (three months) parental leave can be taken in respect of each child. This is unpaid leave in respect of the birth or adoption of a child, and the parent (or person with responsibility for the child) is entitled to thirteen weeks per child. So, people who have two children can take thirteen weeks for each child. It must, however be taken before that particular child reaches the age of five. Multiple births give multiple rights, so if a couple have twins, they are entitled to two lots of thirteen weeks. This is expected to change to four months from March 2012, following the signing of a European Directive. There is also a possibility that some of the leave might be allowed to be shared between the parents.

- Employees remain employed whilst they are on leave and they are entitled to return after leave to the same job if the leave taken is less than four weeks. If the leave lasts longer than four weeks, and it is not reasonably practicable for them to return to the same job, then they should be offered another job which is both suitable and appropriate. The right is to return to the same, or more favourable, terms and conditions as if he or she had not been absent.

- The leave has to be taken in chunks of one week, or multiples of a week; if less than a week is taken, it is rounded up to count as a whole week, and so the remaining time is lost to the employee (unless the child is disabled).

- There are pro-rata rights for part-timers (so, for example, if a woman works two days a week, then a week's leave is two days' leave).

- Up to four weeks' leave per child can be taken in any one year.

- Employees have to give twenty-one days' notice before taking parental leave, and must inform the employer of how long they wish to be away from work. Because of this, parental leave is not usually taken in an emergency; it is generally taken as planned leave. If an emergency arose, then 'time off for dependants' can be taken (see below).

- The employee has to be prepared to show the employer proof of entitlement, such as proof that he is the father, or has parental responsibility, or of the age of the child.

Within seven days of the notice, the employer can write to the employee and postpone the leave that he or she wishes to take by up to six months. An employer can postpone if it considers that its business would be 'unduly disrupted' if the employee took leave during the period intended in his notice. The BERR guide (available from the archived BERR website) gives an example, where:

> the work is at a seasonal peak, where a significant proportion of the workforce applies at the same time or when the employee's role is such that his or her absence at a particular time would unduly harm the business.

If the leave is postponed, the employer must agree to permit the employee to take a period of leave of the same duration as that specified in the notice, within six months, and before the child's eighteenth birthday. The date for this should be arranged in consultation with the employee. The employer should not, however, postpone parental leave that the employee wants to take immediately following the birth or adoption of a child, in circumstances in which the employee has given twenty-one days' notice of the EWC.

Employees have the right to go to an employment tribunal if their employer prevents them from taking parental leave or postpones the leave unreasonably. An employee who takes parental leave is also protected from victimisation, including dismissal, for taking it. Any dismissal for asserting a statutory right is, of course, automatically unfair (see Chapter 6).

The parental leave scheme has been criticised for several reasons. The fact that at least a week, or multiples of a week have to be taken is seen as inconvenient, and the fact that the Directive gave governments the option of allowing the leave to be taken until a child reached the age of eight, but that this has not been followed in the UK, has been described as 'not . . . generous' (McColgan: 2000). Also criticised is the lack of a right to return to the same job if a lengthy block of leave is taken.

A further, and more entrenched, criticism is the fact that parental leave is unpaid. As the then Equal Opportunities Commission pointed out to the Select Committee on Social Security during the 1998–1999 sessions (quoted in McColgan 2000:140–141):

> When a child is born, family resources are usually fully stretched, and men's hours of work tend to rise to increase family income. In these circumstances, few men are likely to opt for unpaid leave. If men are unable to take parental leave, responsibility for children will continue to be carried mainly by women. The objective of increasing equality of opportunity between the sexes by encouraging a more equal sharing of family responsibilities between men and women will not be achieved.

This was the view with which a House of Commons Select Committee, in making its report, concurred. It stated that:

> the payment of leave in some form would increase the take-up of the new entitlement'; 'the experience of other countries . . . suggest that there is a strong case for parental leave being paid, if it is to be widely used and provide parents with a genuine choice'; 'if unpaid, leave is unlikely to be taken up in sufficient quantities to make a real difference to people's lives and is highly unlikely to be taken up by single parents, the low-paid, or fathers.

Despite these criticisms, there have been no proposals to make any payments for parental leave, but it may be that the introduction of additional paternity leave may go some way towards allaying such concerns.

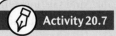

Activity 20.7

How far do you think that the aims of the Parental Leave Directive that are set out above have been achieved in the way that the UK has implemented it? Give reasons for your answer.

Time off for dependants

This right to 'dependants' leave' is a right for employees to be permitted to take a reasonable amount of unpaid time off work during working hours in order to deal with a variety of unexpected or sudden events affecting their dependants, and in order to make any necessary longer-term arrangements for their care. This right also originated in the Parental Leave Directive (1996), which describes the right as one to take time off work for 'urgent family reasons in cases of sickness or accident making the immediate presence of the worker indispensable'. The UK law is contained in the Employment Rights Act 1996 (inserted by the Employment Relations Act 1999).

The time off is available to employees, male and female, irrespective of their hours of work and whether they are full or part time and employed on temporary or permanent contracts. No qualifying period of employment is required and the right is therefore available to employees from the very first day of their employment. Armed forces, police and share fishermen are included.

The circumstances in which the leave can be taken are set out in section 57A of the ERA. They are:

- To provide assistance when a dependant falls ill, gives birth or is injured or assaulted (even if not injured). The injury does not have to be a serious injury, and can be mental or physical, and can also be a deterioration of an existing condition.

- To make arrangements for the provision of care for a dependant who is ill or injured.

- In consequence of the death of a dependant. This can include time off to make arrangements for a funeral.

- Because of the unexpected disruption or termination of arrangements for the care of a dependant, for example if a nursery closes unexpectedly.

- To deal with an incident which involves the child of an employee and which occurs unexpectedly during school hours, for example if the child becomes ill during the school day, or is being suspended from school.

A 'dependant' is defined as a spouse, child, parent or person who lives in the same household as the employee (but not lodger). Also included is any person who reasonably relies on the person concerned for assistance on an occasion when the person falls ill or is injured or assaulted, or to make arrangements for the provision of care in the event of illness or injury. This person does not have to be related, for example it could be an elderly neighbour who has a fall and the employee is the nearest person who can help.

The right is to time off that is necessary and reasonable. This is a matter of fact for the tribunal, and depends on the circumstances of the case. There are no limits on the number of times when time may be taken off in any one period. However, because this right is generally one that is intended to be exercised in an emergency, it is often impossible for employees wishing to take leave to inform their employer in advance. They must therefore inform the employer of the reason for their absence as soon as reasonably practicable, and say how long they expect to be absent (unless it is an emergency where this can not be complied with until after they have returned to work).

The employer may refuse permission if a spouse or partner is available, but any refusal has to be reasonable. If an employee abuses the right, they can risk disciplinary proceedings. The employer is not permitted to rearrange working hours to make up for lost time.

An employee can make a complaint to an employment tribunal for a declaration if the employer has unreasonably refused to permit him or her to take time off. If a person is dismissed for exercising the right to take time off in these circumstances, it would be an automatically unfair dismissal.

 Activity 20.8

Do you think it is appropriate that the word 'dependant' is so widely defined? Why?

It may be reasonable for an employer to refuse permission for an employee to leave work if a spouse or partner is available to deal with the situation. Do you think that this is fair?

What decision would you make as an employer if a father gets a phone call at work to say that his child has been badly injured at school, and his wife does not work, but she is very upset about it and needs him to be with her? Why?

 Exhibit 20.3   *Qua v John Ford Morrison Solicitors* **(2003)**

Ms Qua was employed as a legal secretary. During the first nine months of her employment with the respondents she took a total seventeen days off work—in separate two to four day absences—in order to care for her sick son. He had a long-term illness which led him to have to miss school regularly. This caused considerable disruption at the solicitors' firm, as the absences made it impossible for them to provide consistent secretarial support for the particular solicitor with whom Ms Qua worked.   »

» The employment tribunal found that on a number of occasions Ms Qua did not contact her employers, and that on several occasions she made some contact but did not specify with any sort of precision her anticipated length of absence, and then did not clarify on subsequent days an update to the position. She was dismissed because of her bad attendance record before completing twelve months' service.

The tribunal said that '*We find as a fact that she could have and ought to have reasonably been able to make better arrangements for the short-term problems which she knew at all times she was likely to have to face on an ongoing basis. We find that she never seriously faced up to the problem of making arrangements for short-term care for [her son]*'.

Ms Qua appealed against the tribunal's finding that her dismissal was not automatically unfair. The EAT agreed with the tribunal, and said that this was a right to take a reasonable amount of time off to deal with unexpected events, not a right for an employee to take time off herself to provide care, beyond the reasonable amount necessary to enable her to deal with the immediate crisis.

Mrs Recorder Cox QC said:

The statutory right is, in our view, a right given to all employees to be permitted to take a reasonable amount of time off work during working hours in order to deal with a variety of unexpected or sudden events affecting their dependants, as defined, and in order to make any necessary longer-term arrangements for their care.

The right to time off to '. . . provide assistance' etc. in subsection (1)(a) does not in our view enable employees to take time off in order themselves to provide care for a sick child, beyond the reasonable amount necessary to enable them to deal with the immediate crisis. Leave to provide longer-term care for a child would be covered by parental leave entitlement if the employee has responsibility for the child and is entitled to parental leave (that is, has at least one year's service). That does not arise in the present case because the Appellant had only been employed for 9 months at the time of her dismissal. Section 57A(1)(a) envisages some temporary assistance to be provided by the employee, on an occasion when it is necessary in the circumstances specified. Under subsection (1)(b) time off is to be permitted to enable an employee to make longer-term arrangements for the care of a dependant, for example by employing a temporary carer or making appropriate arrangements with friends or relatives. Subsection (1)(d) would include, for example, time off to deal with problems caused by a child-minder failing to arrive or a nursery or playgroup closing unexpectedly.

The right is a right to a 'reasonable' amount of time off, in order to take action which is 'necessary'. In determining whether action was necessary, factors to be taken into account will include, for example, the nature of the incident which has occurred, the closeness of the relationship between the employee and the particular dependant and the extent to which anyone else was available to help out.

We consider that, in determining what is a reasonable amount of time off work, an employer should always take account of the individual circumstances of the employee seeking to exercise the right. It may be that, in the vast majority of cases, no more than a few hours or, at most, one or possibly two days would be regarded as reasonable to deal with the particular problem which has arisen. Parliament chose not to limit the entitlement to a certain amount of time per year and/or per case, as they could have done pursuant to Clause 3.2 of the »

Directive. It is not possible to specify maximum periods of time which are reasonable in any particular circumstances. This will depend on the individual circumstances in each case and it will always be a question of fact for a tribunal as to what was reasonable in every situation.

Where an employee has exercised the right on one or more previous occasions and has been permitted to take time off, for example, to deal with a dependant child's recurring illness, an employer can in our view take into account the number and length of previous absences, as well as the dates when they occurred, in order to determine whether the time taken off or sought to be taken off on a subsequent occasion is reasonable and necessary.

Adoption leave

Adoption leave was introduced as part of the same legislation as paternity leave, and also came into force in April 2003. It applies to *'an employee (whether male or female and whether married or single) who is the adoptive parent of a child newly placed for adoption'*. It does not apply to step-family adoption or adoption by a child's existing foster carers as these do not involve the new placement of a child. To qualify, as with paternity leave, the employee must have at least twenty-six weeks' continuous service by the week in which he or she is notified of being matched with a child for adoption.

The leave mirrors that of maternity leave, having a period of ordinary adoption leave (OAL) for twenty-six weeks and additional adoption leave (AAL) for a further period of twenty-six weeks. Where a couple adopts a child, only one of them is entitled to take adoption leave. It is up to the couple which parent takes the adoption leave. The other adoptive parent may be entitled to take time off equivalent to paternity leave if he or she meets the relevant statutory criteria. Payments, notification procedures, contractual entitlements and keeping in touch are as for maternity and paternity leave.

The right to request flexible working

In 2001, the Work and Parents Taskforce produced a report at the behest of the government. Its brief was to *'consider how employers and working parents can be encouraged to adopt a constructive dialogue to find working patterns that suit them both'*. Such patterns that a parent might choose are:

- job sharing
- compressed working hours
- annual hours working
- term-time working
- homeworking
- extended leave
- part-time work.

Instead of heavy regulations, the Report recommended a 'light touch' approach to flexible working, and the emphasis in the Regulations is on employers and employees resolving the situation by discussion and negotiation. This led to the passing in 2000 of the right to request flexible working. The statutory right is now contained in the ERA 1996, the Flexible Working (Eligibility, Complaints and Remedies) Regulations 2002 and the Flexible Working (Procedural Requirements) Regulations 2002.

 Exhibit 20.4   Arguments for flexible working

Many mothers and fathers want to work flexible hours. They say greater opportunities to work flexibly will help them better balance the responsibilities they have caring for their children with those they have at work.

The benefits of flexible working are not confined to parents. Businesses find that flexible working arrangements enable them to retain skilled staff and reduce their recruitment costs, to lessen absenteeism, and to react more readily to changing market conditions.

It is a key message of the Government's Work-Life Balance Campaign, promoted by employers, that flexible working can benefit employers and employees alike.

Professor Sir George Bain
Chairman, Work and Parents Taskforce
(Forward to the 2001 Report)

The legislation now allows employees to ask for a one-off variation in the contract of employment if they:

- have been continuously employed for at least twenty-six weeks
- are either the mother, father, adopter, guardian or foster parent of a child under the age of seventeen (eighteen if the child is disabled), or are married to, or are the partner of, such a person, and have, or expect to have, responsibility for the upbringing of the child
- alternatively that they are the carer of an adult who lives at the same address.

The right is one only to request a change to the contract, such as hours of work or location, and to have the request considered seriously. Only one request can be made per year. The purpose of applying for the change is to enable the employee to care for the child. The application has to be made before the fourteenth day before the day on which the child reaches the age of seventeen, or the age of eighteen if he or she is disabled and is entitled to a disability living allowance. There is a form on the Directgov website for making the application, which is useful, as there are several elements that have to be complied with. The application has to specify:

- what change is being requested
- the date it is proposed it should become effective
- what effect, if any, the employee thinks that making the change would have on the employer and how it might be dealt with, and
- how the employee meets the conditions as to the relationship with the child.

If an employer wishes to refuse the change, it has to hold a meeting to discuss the application within twenty-eight days. The employee has a right to be accompanied at this meeting, and has to be notified of the decision within fourteen days. The employee also has a right to appeal against the decision. If the employer agrees, then the change can be made. The employer cannot try to revert back to the former pattern of work when the child reaches the age of seventeen.

As explained above, the right to request flexible working is simply that: a right to request. It is not a right to have the request granted. The only obligation that an employer has is to consider the request seriously. The eight grounds set out in the legislation for refusing are:

1. Burden of additional costs to the business which clearly outweigh the gains, and which overall are detrimental to the business (eg, if the employer has recently trained the employee to undertake certain work, which can only be done during certain hours, and the employee asks not to work those particular hours).

2. Detrimental effect on ability to meet customer demand (the example given by BERR is a hairstylist who applies to reduce her full-time hours from 10am to 3pm. This is refused because the beginning and end of the working day are the busiest times for the salon).

3. Inability to reorganise work among existing staff.

4. Inability to recruit additional staff.

5. Detrimental impact on quality (eg, a skilled furniture finisher applies not to work on a Friday, but this would affect his employer's ability to quality check the furniture before it is despatched to stores for the weekend, and the employee is the only person who can do this).

6. Detrimental impact on the performance of the business (eg, if the employee wishes to have a day off on the busiest day of the week for a curtain-making business, and is required to be on hand when the fabric is delivered, as all the staff have to help to move it into the store room, so that the machinists can start work).

7. Insufficiency of work during the periods the employee proposes to work (eg, if the employee wishes to work on a Monday, when there is very little work, instead of a Saturday, which is the busiest day for that particular employer).

8. If the change is incompatible with planned structural changes (eg, if a waiter who wishes to work on a Sunday instead of a Monday, but the owner of the restaurant, whose customers are mainly weekday office workers, has decided to close the premises at the weekends).

Remedies

The employee can complain to an employment tribunal if the employer breaches the procedural regulations, if the decision to reject the application to work flexibly was based on incorrect facts or if the reason given for refusal was not one of those listed above. If the tribunal finds that the complaint is well founded, it can make a declaration to that effect, and may make an order for reconsideration of the application and make an award of compensation to the employee. It cannot force the employer to grant the request. An employee must not be treated to a detriment or dismissal because he has made such an application. This would also entitle him or her to apply to the tribunal. As an alternative to going to tribunal, the parties have the option of asking an arbitrator to deal with the case under the ACAS flexible working arbitration scheme. Arbitration is discussed in more detail in Chapter 30.

Activity 20.9

A study of the first year of the 'right to request legislation' found that it had helped many parents. But many employers still do not understand it, or are deliberately flouting its requirements.

The research, by pressure group Working Families, found that 60% of parents who had asked to work flexibly had been allowed to do so. But several respondents were told that they could not work flexibly unless they gave up management or supervisory roles. One was even threatened with redundancy. Half the reasons employers gave for refusing requests fell outside the grounds allowed by the legislation.

Some of the barriers to flexible working that parents cited included high childcare costs and their employers' attitudes.

Working Families has called for a new right to flexible working, as opposed to simply the right to request it. The charity also wants to see stronger remedies under the legislation.

Questions

1   Do you think that the legislation goes far enough in allowing only a 'right to request' flexible working, or should there be a 'right to flexible working'?

2   What do you think the arguments would be for extending the right?

3   What would the arguments be for keeping the right as it is?

Source: Carrington and Holmstrom (2004:29)

The right to request time off for training

The right to request unpaid time off for study or training came into force in April 2010. It applies to employees with 26 weeks' service, and operates in the same way as the right to request flexible working. The proposed training can only be training which either leads to a qualification, or which helps the employee develop skills relevant to his job, workplace, or business.

This right currently only applies to organisations which employ over 250 people. A plan to extend this to smaller employers has been put on hold indefinitely.

Future changes

At the time of writing (Summer 2011), the government are holding a consultation regarding the future of family-friendly policies and legislation (BIS, 2011). Under the proposed new system, while the initial block of maternity leave will still be taken by the mother, the remainder of the existing maternity leave would be renamed parental leave. Each parent would have four weeks' paid leave exclusive to them, with the remaining weeks available for either parent on an equal basis.

The consultation also covers whether parental leave should be extended to children over five, and whether to give fathers the right to attend ante-natal appointments.

PART IV EMPLOYMENT POLICY AND PRACTICE

There is also a proposal that there should be a duty for employers to consider requests for flexible leave reasonably. The plan extends to a code of practice for employers when faced with such a request, and considers the provision for allowing an employee to make a second request per year, if the original request was for a temporary change only. The outcome of this consultation will be found on the BIS website in due course.

Debates

The regulation of so-called 'family-friendly' policies is often portrayed as primarily supporting the 'work–life' balance, and making it easier for those with children to juggle their opposing obligations at work and at home. However, this is not the only intended outcome of such legislation. There is a business case for it too, as the 1998 government paper 'Fairness at Work' (5.1–5.2) states:

> Competitiveness depends on the UK making the best use of the talents of as many people as possible. The larger the number of people—particularly skilled people—to which business can look, the better. We also need to ensure that as many people as possible who want to work should have the chance to do so . . .
>
> But work and parenthood can create conflicting pressures . . . Helping employees to combine work and family life satisfactorily is good not only for parents and children but also for businesses.

As with the debates relating to working time, therefore, there are both social and economic arguments underpinning regulation of this area.

Social arguments

We live in a changing society, one in which people are realising that they can be employed, yet still have a life outside work; a society which aims to have equality between men and women, and which tries to have laws that achieve that end. With the recognition of women's rights and the increase in the proportion of women who go out to work, problems have arisen when people seek to balance their obligations towards their families, while still remaining part of the workforce and earning money to support that family. It is this dichotomy that lies at the heart of the 'work–life balance' debate. Until the 1990s there were very few laws that supported the work–life balance, and people had to juggle as best they could. As we saw in Chapter 16 it was not until then that sex discrimination law was interpreted in such a way as to outlaw discrimination on the grounds of pregnancy, and the expansion of family-friendly laws has been a recent phenomenon supported by the Labour government. The expectation is that if employees (both men and women) are given the opportunity to spend more time with their families then this will underpin social cohesion. The result will be fewer breakdowns in marriages and relationships, thus indirectly benefiting society as a whole.

Such an emphasis on the rights of employees, however, has been criticised for limiting the rights of employers and leading to an economy which is less able to compete globally with others. As Lea (2001:1.6) puts it:

> employees . . . have obligations as well as rights towards their employer . . . Life, for everyone, is full of 'hard choices'. And it is a sentimentalist retreat from life's harsh realities to imply that hard choices can somehow be 'washed and wished away' by bringing in more work-life balance regulations.

She goes on to quote Marrin (2000):

> one of the many awkward facts of life that progressives refuse to confront is that some problems are truly insoluble. Some conflicts of interest cannot be resolved. Some irresistible forces do come up against immovable objects. One of those conflicts is between work and children for mothers. (Lea, 2001:4.2.1)

and Phillips (2000):

> [People] are refusing to make such choices [between career and children] and insisting that they must have it all, loading the consequences on to employers instead. The government is encouraging this selfish and irresponsible attitude. Constantly exhorting employers to produce 'family-friendly' working, it cavalierly brushes aside the impact on job performance of working fewer hours and expects employers to make good any deficiencies. How sad it is too that a movement that started in legitimate pursuit of equity for women in employment should be descending into such farcical unfairness. How it tarnishes those many working-women who have not lost sight of the reasonable limits to self advancement as they struggle to reconcile work and family. And ultimately, since this increasingly intolerable burden will make more and more employers reluctant to employ women at all, how stupidly self-defeating. (Lea 2001:4.3.2)

It is not just mothers who feel that the legislation does not assist them, however. Fathers, too, have complained that the law does not go far enough in its aims of allowing them to spend more time with their families. In a critique of family-friendly legislation, Di Torella states that because the emphasis is that the father can use the leave to '*care for the child and support the mother . . . this does little to promote the idea of equal parenting, rather it reinforces the message that mothers need to be supported*' (Di Torella 2007:322).

These issues emphasise not only the unfairness of such policies to employers, but also to other employees, who do not have family responsibilities and feel resentful that they are having to work harder to make up for their colleagues' 'extra privileges'. Lea argues that there is nothing wrong in having such policies, so long as they stay merely policies and are brought in on a voluntary basis by employers and are not turned into regulation which is thrust upon them from above.

Economic arguments

Is Lea correct, or has society moved on to the extent that employers realise that if they do not have such policies they will lose valued personnel? One employer, quoted by Carrington and Holmstrom (2004), said:

> There's a clear business rationale—its about valuing your people . . . If young men have been with us as apprentices or graduates, we have put a lot of investment into them, and we want them to remain with us. Ultimately it's about intangibles such as morale and motivation.

This is echoed in the government paper, Fairness at Work (1998:5.3):

> Many successful modern companies, both large and small, have . . . adopted a culture and practices in support of the family. To the mutual benefit of the employee and the business, they allow flexibility over hours and working from home allowing parents to spend more time with their children. They provide time off for family crises. Some provide childcare facilities or fund employees' use of nurseries. They know how important it is to retain staff in whom they have

invested and on whom they depend . . . In the future it will become increasingly important to enable employees to balance satisfactorily family responsibilities and work, and children to benefit from parental care.

It is this which provides the economic rationale for 'family-friendly' legislation—it is not just social legislation, but regulation which has a firm foothold in economic theory. If employers do not keep their staff happy, then they will lose them to another employer. In order to compete effectively in today's employment market, employers have to become family-friendly themselves. It appears that many employers are keenly aware of this. In response to the publication of proposals by the government which were eventually incorporated into the Work and Families Act, the Director General of the Institute of Directors, Miles Templeman (quoted at www.iod.com), said:

Our members, by and large, support family-friendly policies. Three out of four believe that it is actually morally right for society to have family-friendly policies in the workplace. They realise that these policies aid staff recruitment and retention and ultimately boost morale.

There is still, of course, the problem that employers may think twice about hiring a woman of childbearing age, but this is a problem that can be dealt with by means of the sex discrimination legislation. Phillips (2000) calls family-friendly policies self-defeating because of this.

The debate refuses to die down. Phillips' line has recently been taken up with much controversy by Nicola Brewer, the chief executive of the Equality and Human Rights Commission. She has suggested that it is 'an inconvenient truth' that employers thought twice about employing women because of the additional costs and inconvenience incurred. (*The Times, Personnel Today*). This view has been supported by Kevin Green, the head of the Recruitment and Employment Confederation, who admits that recruiters were often asked by employers not to put forward women of childbearing age or those that were pregnant. Indeed, REC research in 2005 found that 78% of recruiters had been told by firms that they would prefer not to hire women likely to have children in the near future. The research also revealed that one in eight recruiters had bowed to pressure and discriminated against women when registering or putting applicants forward for jobs (Berry, 2008).

To counter Phillips' and Brewer's assertion, however, it could be said that it is self-defeating to admit defeat before one has even started, and to refuse to change anything because one expects to be defeated. In addition, family-friendly policies have moved on. They no longer just deal with pregnant women and maternity leave; there are now also rights for fathers and some for carers of adults.

In addition to the above arguments, there is also the difficulty of administering such regulation, particularly for small employers. For the types of leave which have an element of payment, such as maternity leave, the employer pays the employee and then recoups a portion of it from the state. This creates a lot of paperwork, which is resented by many small employers in particular. There have been calls for these administrative burdens to be eased and for such payments to be made directly by the state. However, instead of simplifying it, the new legislation relating to paternity leave promises to make things even more complex for employers, who may have to liaise with the employers of the other parent to administer the right to take time off.

 **Activity 20.10**

The IOD has come up with a recent twenty-four-point plan to help employers in the current economic climate. The aim of the plan is to make the labour market much more employer-friendly. 'We need to make it easier and cheaper for companies to employ people,' the Director General of the IOD is quoted as saying. Elements of this plan include scrapping the right to request both flexible working and time off for training, on the grounds, say the IOD, that both create extra red tape, and don't really work anyway.

Do you agree with the IOD's plans? Give reasons for your answer.

CHAPTER SUMMARY

- The creation and extension of a broad range of family-friendly employment rights has been one of the most significant recent developments in UK employment law. New rights have been introduced over time in slices every two or three years.

- Longer-established rights include the right for women who are pregnant to have paid time off to attend ante-natal appointments, to take a period of maternity leave, and to be paid a set weekly sum during much of that leave. There are also extensive health and safety regulations that deal specifically with the rights of pregnant workers.

- Aside from substantial extensions to minimum leave and maternity pay periods, other recent changes have included the introduction of paid paternity leave, unpaid parental leave, a right to take time off to deal with family emergencies, adoptive leave and a right for some parents and carers to request formally to work on a more flexible contract.

- Further changes are expected in the future. These include an extension of the right to request flexible working to all parents of children under the age of eighteen and the sharing of a portion of maternity leave between mothers and fathers.

REFERENCES

Berry, M. (2008) 'Childbearing age women screened out by recruitment agencies' *Personnel Today*, 18 July.

BIS (2011) Consultation on Modern Workplaces, May 2011.

Carrington, L. and Holmstrom, R. (2004) 'Signs of Change' *People Management*, 3 June.

CIPD (2004) *Flexible working and paternity leave: Survey report*. October. London: CIPD.

Di Torella, E.C. (2007) 'New Labour, new dads—the impact of family friendly legislation on fathers' *Industrial Law Journal* 36.3 (p318).

DTI (2005) *Work And Families: Choice And Flexibility*. February.

HMSO (1998) *Fairness at Work*. White Paper, May 1998, Cm 3968. London: HMSO.

IDS (2009) 'Maternity and Parental Rights' *Employment Law Handbook*. London: Incomes Data Services.

James, G. (2006) 'The Work and Families Act 2006: legislation to improve choice and flexibility?' *Industrial Law Journal* 35.3 (p272).

James, G. (2007) 'Enjoy your leave but 'Keep in Touch': help to maintain parent/workplace relationships' *Industrial Law Journal* 36:3 (p315).

Keeble, S. (2006) 'Additional paternity leave' *Personnel Today*, 21 March.

Kennedy, S. (2008) 'Paid maternity leave does us no favours either, say fathers' *The Times*, 15 July.

Lea, R. (2001) *The 'Work-Life Balance'. . . and all that—The re-regulation of the labour market*. IOD policy paper. London: Institute of Directors.

McColgan, A. (2000) 'Family friendly frolics? The Maternity and Parental Leave etc Regulations 1999' *Industrial Law Journal* 29.2.

Marrin, M. (2000) 'The arrogant folly of trying to nationalise parenthood' *Daily Telegraph*, 9 December.

Phillips, M. (2000) 'Farce of the working women who have too many rights' *Sunday Times*, 17 September.

Roberts, J. And Joffe, N. (2011) 'Why working mums work' *The Times*, 30 May.

Taylor, J. (2011) 'IOD ruffles feathers with radical growth plan' *Management Today*, 7 February.

Walsh, I. (2008) *The right to request flexible working: A review of how to extend the right to request flexible working to parents of older children*. BERR: London. May 2008.

Work and Parents Taskforce (2001) *Report on Flexible working*. Available at www.dti.gov.uk. London: HMSO.

ONLINE RESOURCE CENTRE

A range of online resources to help you through your employment law module have been developed by the author team. These include updates, self-test questions and sources for further reading. (www.oxfordtextbooks.co.uk/orc/taylor_emir3e)

Wages and benefits

Learning outcomes

By the end of this chapter you should be able to:

- advise on which employees must be paid the national minimum wage;

- calculate whether or not an individual worker was paid the national minimum wage in a particular pay period;

- explain how enforcement authorities ensure that all are being paid the national minimum wage;

- administer statutory sick pay records in an organisation;

- advise on when an employer can and cannot make deductions from wage packets;

- brief colleagues on the fundamental principles of pension scheme regulation;

- debate the merits and demerits of the UK's regulatory regime for occupational pensions.

Introduction

In this chapter we look at a number of distinct areas of law that regulate the payment of wages and benefits. We start by focusing on the national minimum wage legislation, describing how it works in practice and assessing the many debates that still surround its effectiveness and impact. We go on to explain the situations in which employers can and cannot lawfully make deductions from pay packets, the right for all employees to receive an itemised pay statement and the administration of statutory sick pay (SSP). Finally we briefly introduce a major topic which is increasingly important, but which we only have space to touch on in this book. That is the regulation of occupational pension schemes.

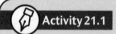

Activity 21.1

Consider the following statements. Which do you think are correct and which are false?

1 All workers regardless of age and status are entitled to receive pay that is equal to or greater than the national minimum wage.

2 The NMW must be paid over and above any fringe benefits or payments in kind that employees receive.

3 Workers who are on-call but asleep are entitled to receive the NMW for these hours.

4 Employers are obliged to pay employees who are off sick a minimum weekly rate.

5 As a general rule, employers are not permitted to discipline employees by fining them.

6 Employees have the right to be paid in cash if they wish to.

7 Occupational pension schemes have been deregulated in recent years.

Return to this activity once you have read the chapter, to see how many of your answers were correct.

The national minimum wage

The National Minimum Wage Act was passed in 1998 and came into effect on 1 April 1999. On the face of it, it provides a clear, universal and straightforward right. The statute simply says that no one, worker or employee, can lawfully be paid less than the hourly rate set down as being the minimum by the Secretary of State for Business, Innovation and Skills. The rate itself—or set of rates—are actually set after consultation with the government's Low Pay Commission. This body includes representatives from different sectors, economists, managers and trade unionists. The commission recommends a rate which will not to any substantial degree have the effect of increasing unemployment. The NMW is not index-linked. Increasing or decreasing it is entirely within the power of the Secretary of State. The level of the rate is reasonably well publicised by the DBIS, and evidence suggests that the vast majority of people (97% according to one survey) know that they cannot lawfully be paid at a lower rate. Indeed, a far greater proportion of the public appear to be aware of their employment rights in this area than in any other (Pollert, 2005).

The main adult rate of the NMW was initially set at £3.60 and has been raised several times since. In recent years we have seen annual rises implemented each October, employers being given plenty of advance warning about impending increases (see Table 21.1). At the time of writing (2011) the rates are as follows:

- basic adult rate of £6.08 per hour
- rate for those aged 18–22 of £4.98 per hour
- rate for those aged 22 + who are in training in a new job of £4.98 per hour
- rate for 16–17 year olds of £3.68 an hour
- apprentice rate of £2.60 an hour

The advent of age discrimination legislation from October 2006 had no impact on the national minimum wage. So for the time being at least, the age differentials remain. The only complexity as far as basic entitlement arises in the case of the training wage. Here the law sets the following conditions:

- The person must be in their first six months working with an employer.
- They must be spending at least twenty-six days of the first six months in training.
- They must be undertaking some form of nationally accredited training—ie, NVQ, SVQ or other form of government training scheme.
- They must have formally entered an agreement with the employer to this effect.

Where these conditions are not met, the employee is entitled to the full adult rate of £6.08 (as of October 2011).

An important apparent principle of the NMW is its universality, many believing that it covers everyone across the country whatever their employment status. In fact this is not the case. The NMW is by no means universal, hundreds of thousands of people in various categories not being covered. The following are the exempt groups:

- workers under the age of twenty-six who are working under a contract of apprenticeship AND are in the first year of that apprenticeship,
- everyone under eighteen working as an apprentice,
- people undertaking periods of work experience as part of a course of higher education (provided it is for one year or less),
- people working in sheltered work schemes run for homeless persons,
- voluntary workers,
- share fishermen and fisherwomen,
- people engaged in family work (eg, au pairs and paid companions),
- prisoners.

Is someone being paid the national minimum wage?

Where people are paid a straightforward hourly rate and work a fixed number of hours each day, there is not much problem ensuring that they are paid at the NMW level. Complexities

Table 21.1 National Minimum Wage—Hourly Rates

Date of change	Adult Rate	Development Rate
April 1999	3.60	3.00
June 2000	3.60	3.20
October 2000	3.70	3.20
October 2001	4.10	3.50
October 2002	4.20	3.60
October 2003	4.50	3.80
October 2004	4.85	4.10
October 2005	5.05	4.25
October 2006	5.35	4.45
October 2007	5.52	4.60
October 2008	5.73	4.77
October 2009	5.80	4.83
October 2010	5.93	4.92
October 2011	6.08	4.98

occur where people are paid an annual or monthly salary and are expected to work whatever hours are required to complete their jobs, to satisfy customers or to meet targets. As a result, the National Minimum Wage Act is a lengthy and highly technical piece of legislation. The Act set out two separate calculations that must be made in order to ascertain whether or not an individual was in practice paid at or above the NMW rate in any one period of work:

1. working out what payments have been received, and

2. working out the number of hours worked.

The one figure is then divided by the other to check that the right rate is being paid in practice. The reference period over which you must work out the average number of hours worked is whatever the pay reference period is (ie, weekly for a weekly-paid worker, monthly for a monthly-paid worker etc). You add up the hours worked and divide this into the weekly pay. If, between October 2011 and October 2012, the figure for any pay reference period is below £6.08 an hour, then the law is being broken. Where there is no regular pattern of payment, the averaging should be done over a month.

In calculating the total remuneration received in a month employers must include all money payments paid to the employee by the employer in respect of work undertaken in that month. The figure also includes any payments made at a later date that form part of the remuneration for the week or month in question, all bonus payments and commissions. Benefits in kind are not included. So employers cannot add in extra payments to take account of company cars, meals in the staff canteen, mobile phones or laptops. The only exception to this rule is 'live-in' accommodation. Here a 'charge' can be made and taken into account when calculating the NMW, but only to the tune of £4.73 a day (as of October 2011). In practice this means that employers providing free accommodation can add £33.11 to the weekly pay packet before calculating the hourly rate being paid.

For NMW purposes 'pay' does not include other payments that do not specifically relate to work undertaken in that month (or week) (ie, pension contributions, advances on wages, loans made by the employer, etc). The following are also excluded:

- sick pay or strike pay,
- overtime payments/shift premia (this is significant as it means that overtime payments must be over and above the NMW),
- on-call payments,
- regional weighting payments,
- tips
- expenses.

The rules for calculating the number of hours worked in the relevant pay reference period vary depending on the type of work the worker is doing. The Act sets out different types of work and, for each, specifies what is and what is not included for the purposes of counting hours. The categories identified are as follows:

- time work (straightforward with weekly hours specified in the contract),
- salaried work (where an annual salary is paid for undertaking a job and hours worked in a year are discernible),
- output work (where hours vary—the worker is contracted to produce x amount of product),
- unmeasured work (like salaried work but where there are no discernible annual hours).

These parts of the Act are highly complex, providing different methods of calculation for each category. The same basic principles apply in each case, but in some categories it is a good deal harder to make an estimate of time worked than in others. Included are:

- hours when a worker is on call, and
- hours when a worker is travelling on business but not commuting.

Excluded are:

- hours when a worker is absent or on strike, and
- time spent on rest breaks.

Record-keeping requirements for NMW purposes are not hugely stringent. The requirement is simply that sufficient records are kept to enable one to establish that the NMW is being paid. Contracts and collective agreements are acceptable for this purpose. It is not necessary in law to keep weekly records of time actually worked. However, where records of this kind are kept, there is a requirement to retain them on file for three years.

Exhibit 21.1   **On-call hours and the national minimum wage**

An important issue in certain types of jobs is whether or not the job holder should be considered to be at work for the purposes of calculating the national minimum wage when he or she is on call rather than actually working. Sometimes people are obliged to be on an employer's premises for long periods, ready to respond to phone calls or the demands of clients, but are free to watch TV, read or even sleep during these periods. Their activities thus fall into a grey area between working and not working. Should this time be paid at the level of the national minimum wage or not? And what is the position if they are at home but on call, and ready to be called out if necessary? The answer has been provided by a number of cases that have been appealed up to the higher courts in the years since the NMW Act first came into effect.

Much appears to depend on which category of work a particular job is placed in. Where it is 'time work' with weekly working hours specified in the contract, on-call time counts as far as the NMW is concerned provided the worker concerned is available to work throughout the period. Hence, in *Scottbridge Construction Ltd v Wright (2003)* the Court of Session in Scotland ruled that a nightwatchman must be paid the NMW for all the hours he was at work, despite the fact that he spent much of the time he was on his employer's premises sleeping. Central was the finding that because he might have to get up to respond to an alarm system at any time, he was 'at work' even if he was also snoring away in his bed.

A similar judgment was reached by the Court of Appeal in *British Nursing Association v Inland Revenue* (2002). This case concerned the position of duty nurses employed on a bank. After office hours an agency designated some of its nurses to be on duty. They went home during this time, but emergency calls from nursing homes were diverted through to their home numbers and they might be called on to organise the supply of cover when a colleague was unable to work a shift. Even though they were in their own homes with their families watching TV, eating dinner or carrying out domestic chores, they were still 'at work' and were entitled to the NMW for this time.

Less fortunate was Mrs Walton (in *Walton v Independent Living Association* (2002)), whose job was to provide twenty-four-hour care for a patient who suffered from epilepsy. She carried this work out on a 'three days on, three days off basis', being present in her client's home or accompanying her outdoors for stretches of seventy-two hours at a time. Clearly she was not physically working throughout this time. She slept, read and watched TV for a lot of the time, but she always had to be present in case the client suffered a fit. In her case the Court of Appeal decided that she was not entitled to the NMW for all seventy-two hours. This was because her work was categorised as 'unmeasured work' under the Act. Her contract stipulated that she would spend around seven hours a day actually working *on average*, although the precise amount of time would vary from day to day. This meant that only those seven hours could be taken into account for the purposes of calculating the national minimum wage.

Source: Simpson (2004)

Output Work

From the outset, one of the biggest problems with the NMW was its application in situations where people work on a piece-work basis. There is no hourly rate for such jobs, because the workers concerned are paid per widget produced, per call answered, per sale made or per kilogram of strawberries picked. The more experienced and skilled a worker is, the more he or she gets paid. In 2004, following a great deal of lobbying about the unfairness of its original approach, the government introduced a new method of calculating the NMW in such circumstances.

The current approach is that the employer must pay pieceworkers the full amount of the NMW for the hours they actually work unless certain conditions are in place. These are as follows:

1. there must be no fixed hours of work

2. the workers must have received written notice of their legal rights under the new 'rated output work system'

3. the worker is paid the right number of 'deemed hours' for the work they carry out.

Deemed hours are calculated by the employer carrying out what is known as a 'fair test' to establish the rate at which the typical worker carries out the task for which piecework rates are being paid. This is done by working out how long it takes an average performer to reach a pre-defined target (100 widgets or whatever target is chosen). This figure is then multiplied by 120% to establish the number of deemed hours. The additional time is built in to help ensure that poorer performers are paid the national minimum wage and not just those who work at average speed or faster.

The approach is best illustrated with an example. Let's assume that in a widget factory the average worker takes two hours to manufacture ten widgets. The two hours must then be multiplied by 120% to allow the calculation of deemed hours. That means that for NMW purposes ten widgets take 144 minutes or 2.4 hours to make. We then multiply 2.4 by the national minimum wage. This gives us 14.59 with an NMW of £6.08 an hour. The resulting figure is then divided by the number of widgets (ie, 14.59 is divided by 10) to calculate the fair piece rate. In this case it means that the minimum amount that can be paid per completed widget is £1.46.

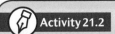 **Activity 21.2**

Paul works as a barman in a large seaside hotel. He is paid monthly in arrears at an annual salary of £12,800 at a time at which the national minimum wage is set at £6.08. He lives in accommodation provided by the hotel for which he is not charged a rent. He is thirty years old.

In October Paul completed twenty-three shifts of nine hours. On twenty of these he took a half hour rest-break, on the other three he worked through without a break as no one else was available to cover for him.

One morning he was asked if he would cover for a porter who had a dental appointment. This amounted to a further three hours' work. He was not paid for this but happily agreed as he knew he would be given substantial tips by customers whose luggage he carried up to bedrooms. He ended up taking home £57 in cash that morning.

Paul's October pay statement contained the following:

Gross pay: £1069.37

Assuming that the hotel wishes to take advantage of the NMW rules governing live-in accommodation, calculate whether or not Paul was paid the national minimum wage rate in October?

This system has the virtue of approximating to fairness, although the very slowest workers still get paid beneath the level of the national minimum wage, as do those who are prevented from working at average speed for any reason. As such it represents a compromise between the legitimate interests of the workers and those of employers who wish to provide an incentive to maximise productivity. The problem is that the system is complicated and not easy in practice for workers themselves to appraise. As a result, there remain examples of unscrupulous employers who are able to set 'deemed hours' which are in reality very difficult or impossible to meet. Piece rates thus continue to be set, especially for home workers who are not unionised and are unaware of their rights under the NMW Act, which result in hourly payments that fall well below those that should be paid by law (Hari, 2004).

Enforcement

The national minimum wage is enforced through three mechanisms:

1. by making a claim in the employment tribunal,
2. by bringing a case to the County Court,
3. via a complaint to a compliance officer employed by HM Revenue & Customs (HMRC).

The second of these possibilities is only rarely used because of the expense involved in bringing civil actions in the County Court and the possibility of having costs awarded against you if you lose. However, because cases can be brought up to six years after the employee concerned has left a job that paid below the NMW, it is a course taken by some. The usual limit of three months applies in the case of employment tribunals, meaning that former employees must put their claims in within three months of leaving a job for which they were paid below the level of the NMW in order to claim the back-pay that they are owed.

HMRC's compliance officers issue thousands of enforcement notices each year, requiring employers to increase pay rates and to pay back-pay to people who are found to have been paid at rates blow the NMW. If an employer fails to comply with an enforcement notice, the Inland Revenue can issue a penalty notice which requires an additional sum to be paid to the employees concerned equivalent to double the current rate of the NMW per day of non-compliance. In addition a fine is levied which is calculated according to the following formula:

> Twice the rate of the minimum wage at the time of the charge multiplied by the number of employees who has been paid below the level of the NMW multiplied by the number of working days they have not been paid the NMW.

Employers can appeal against these to an employment tribunal, but their rate of success has been very poor (Simpson, 2004). Since April 2009 back-pay has been paid at the current rate of the NMW and not at the rate it was at the time it was not paid.

The Act also gives workers the right to see records kept on hours worked and wages paid so that they can themselves ascertain whether the NMW is being paid. However, this right only applies where they reasonably believe they are not being paid the NMW and an application must be made to the employer in writing. Where this right is infringed or where a worker is actually being paid less than the NMW, a complaint can be taken directly to an employment tribunal. Where an employer is found to have prevaricated, not to have given access to data, or has falsified data, the tribunal can order that a sum of eighty times the NMW is paid to the worker concerned. If a claim that less than the NMW has been paid is substantiated, the tribunal simply orders that the money owed should be paid. There are no punitive damages. The courts assume that there is an implied term in every contract that the NMW will be paid, and where it is not the relevant monies must be reimbursed.

Assessing the impact of the national minimum wage

The introduction of a national minimum wage was politically controversial from the time that it was first mooted by the Labour Party in the 1980s. Opponents cited the experience of other countries where similar interventions had apparently led to increased unemployment and to damaging wage inflation. Unemployment can be caused by minimum wages if employers respond to their introduction by reducing the number of people they employ or if the costs force them out of business. Wage inflation occurs when workers who see themselves as being of higher status or 'worth more' than people whose wages are increased to minimum wage level demand higher wages themselves in order to maintain differentials. This then has a spillover effect up the organisational pay hierarchy leading to higher pay all round. Employers wishing to maintain a positive reputation in the labour market also increase wages so that they are clearly above NMW level, allowing them to recruit and retain good people (the so-called 'mezzanine effect'). Costs are then passed on to customers and the result is price inflation. Such arguments are commonly made in countries where the national minimum wage is set at levels that are high enough to generate these economic effects (eg, Gaski, 2004) and they were made by Conservative politicians and many business representatives prior to the introduction of the UK's NMW in 1999.

The general consensus, however, is that the introduction of the NMW in the UK has little if any general adverse impact. Numerous studies have been carried out by economists looking for evidence of negative economic effects (eg, Metcalf, 2004; Stewart, 2004) and by sociologists focusing on the practical responses of managers after April 1999 (eg, Arrowsmith et al, 2003). These all conclude that, except in one or two industries, the introduction of the national minimum wage created little or no new unemployment and that there was no major impact on inflation. About 1.2 million people benefited from the NMW when it first came in, although in some cases they simply lost in state benefit payments what they gained in higher wages.

The NMW has had no major adverse economic effects for several reasons. First, it was introduced at a low level initially so as to ensure that it did not create unemployment. Secondly, it was introduced at a time when the UK economy was booming, when there were skills shortages and when unemployment was at a historically low level. And thirdly, in the view of a number of critics, the enforcement mechanisms were too weak to provide sufficient incentive for employers to comply. As a result, many continued to be paid below the NMW level in practice. The only industries in which the impact has clearly been negative are those which are facing other major difficulties in addition to any created by the NMW—care homes which have suffered from severe cuts in government funding, agriculture which is suffering because of intense international competition and the forcing down of prices by supermarket chains, and small retailers who are being forced out of business by the same chains. The other employers of large numbers of low-paid workers (eg, hotel and catering, contract cleaning, hairdressing, textiles) appear in the main to have absorbed the costs associated with the NMW without needing to contract their workforces. Only time will tell whether or not further rises in the level of the NMW will have more pronounced adverse effects, and whether the positive impact will be found to have continued through the years in which the economy has not been expanding. In the meantime, however, the NMW can generally be regarded as having been successful in achieving its aims.

Statutory sick pay

Statutory sick pay (SSP) is the minimum level of pay that employers are required to pay employees through the payroll when they are sick. In practice many larger employers operate schemes which are a great deal more generous, but in the absence of such approaches the SSP system sets minimum standards and effectively provides a safety net for people who would suffer greatly in financial terms were their employers to pay them nothing at all when they are sick. The rate of SSP is set by the Chancellor of the Exchequer in his annual budget statement. It is increased each year in line with inflation, the new rate coming into effect every April. At the time of writing (2011) the level of SSP is £81.60 per week.

Employers used to be able to claim back most money paid in SSP from the government, but this system was steadily withdrawn in the 1980s and 1990s. Effectively it is now only smaller employers who can claim any compensation from government funds. This is because the current rules stipulate that SSP payments can only be reclaimed once they exceed 13% of the total employers' national insurance payments made in a particular calendar month. This is done by reducing subsequent employers' NI contributions. A very substantial proportion of a large employer's workforce would have to be off sick at the same time for them to breach the 13% threshold, but where an employer has just a handful of employees it can happen easily when one or two people are away for reasons of illness. SSP is treated for tax purposes in the same way as any other income paid by an employer.

At the time of writing employees (ie, not all workers) qualify for SSP provided they are earning more than the national insurance 'lower earnings limit' (currently £102 per week). New starters only qualify for SSP once they have actually begun working. Someone who calls in sick on their first day of work is not entitled to SSP.

SSP starts on the fourth consecutive day of a 'period of incapacity for work' and is paid in respect of days on which an employee is normally required to work under his/her contract of employment. A period of incapacity can include days on which an employee does not normally work such as a weekend. So someone could be off sick on a Friday, remain ill over the weekend and start being paid SSP on the following Monday (ie, on the fourth day of sickness). It is then paid for up to twenty-eight weeks of incapacity for work. After that employees are obliged to make a claim for state incapacity benefit. SSP is paid from the first day of sickness (as opposed to the fourth) when an employee becomes sick again within fifty-six days of a previous period in which SSP was paid. If a woman falls ill during the last four weeks prior to her expected date of confinement her maternity leave is automatically triggered. She thus gets paid statutory maternity pay (if entitled to it) and not SSP (see Chapter 20). An employer's liability to pay SSP ceases after twenty-eight weeks, whether the period of sickness is a single block or a series of linked periods of incapacity with fewer than fifty-six days in between.

Employers are under a legal obligation to retain records of SSP paid and the days for which it was paid for three years. Employers are also supposed to issue 'leavers' statements' using a SSP1 form when someone leaves within eight weeks (fifty-six days) of being paid SSP. This is then passed to the new employer who is obliged to pay SSP from the first day of sickness under the fifty-six-day linking rule. Employers can withhold SSP payments when they have good reason to believe that someone is not genuinely incapacitated. Moreover, after seven days it is possible to insist that a doctor's note is produced by an employee as a condition of continued payment.

When employees consider that they have unlawfully been denied SSP payments they have to complain in writing to the relevant officer at their local tax office. The complaint must be made within six months of the first day on which a supposed SSP payment was due and not paid. The Inland Revenue then investigate and issue an order requiring the employer to pay if they find in favour of the employee concerned. Employees are also entitled to write to their employers asking for a written explanation of any failure to pay SSP. In addition, inspectors employed by the Department of Work and Pensions have the job of undertaking spot checks on employers to see SSP records. A range of criminal sanctions are available where employers are found not to have complied with the expectations of the law, the maximum fine that can be levied being £5000.

Unauthorised deductions from wages

The right not to have unauthorised deductions made from your pay packet applies to all workers, not just to employees. Members of the armed forces are the only major exempt group. We have a long history of regulation in this area going back to the Truck Acts of the nineteenth century. The relevant body of law used to be contained in the Wages Act 1986. It now forms section 2 of the Employment Rights Act 1996, but people still regularly refer to these as 'Wages Act matters'. Unfair deductions from wages constitutes a small and simple area of law, but it is one which accounts for around 20% of all employment tribunal cases.

Essentially, the law lays out clearly the circumstances in which an employer *can* make deductions from pay without the consent of the worker. It follows that it is unlawful to make deductions in any other situation. The term 'wages' is defined broadly to include the whole range of salary payments, bonuses and benefits owed under the contract of employment. Expenses are the only obvious omission from the law in this area. The situations in which deductions in wages can lawfully be made are as follows:

1. where a court orders payment from employee to employer (compensation for damaged property, etc),

2. where a court issues an attachment order requiring an employer to pay a fine or a debt out of one of its employee's wages,

3. in a strike situation or other industrial action,

4. where it is authorised by legislation (eg, tax and national insurance payments),

5. where it is authorised by contract (eg, trade union dues),

6. where there has been an overpayment of wages.

The interesting cases are in the area of overpayment of wages. These deal with situations in which an employer pays an employee too much by accident—something which occurs surprisingly often. The rule here is that the recovery must not cause hardship. Repayments must be spread over several months if necessary so that the employee is able to maintain a reasonable standard of living. It is thus necessary, where substantial sums are involved, to spread repayments with agreement. Case law has also determined that there are circumstances in which recovery is not possible. The main one is where the employee has been led to believe they can keep the money (ie, where the employer changes his mind).

There are special rules for retailers to deal with cash shortages and stock deficiencies. They say that deductions can be made to recover monies from those on duty at the time that a shortage occurred, but only to a maximum of 10% of a single week's or month's gross pay. The major exception concerns final pay packets paid when someone leaves. Here it is possible to exceed the 10% limit. The Act also stipulates recovery of monies must start within twelve months of the shortfall occurring. After that date the employer has no right to make the deductions.

In other circumstances fines cannot be levied (ie, for lateness, misconduct, damage to property, etc) unless:

1. there is an express term of contract saying it is permitted

2. the employee has agreed in writing *in advance* of the incident.

Complaints about breaches of rights in this area are taken directly to employment tribunals, a time limit of three months applying. So the case must be sent to the tribunal office within three months of the date at which an unlawful deduction occurred; subject of course to the requirement to make a formal grievance to the employer first and then wait for twenty-eight days. If a case is found to be well founded, the tribunal simply orders that repayments are made. No punitive damages are recoverable. Instead the worker is simply put back financially where he or she would have been had no unlawful deduction been made. An alternative is to go to the County Court and sue the employer for breach of contract. No three-month time limit applies in such cases, but there is a risk of having to pay costs if you lose the case.

 Exhibit 21.2   *Canada Life v Gray* **(2004)**

Under the Working Time Regulations 1998 it is unlawful for employers to pay workers money in lieu of holiday. Rather, there is a duty on the employer to encourage workers to take their twenty-eight days of statutory holiday entitlement, although it is lawful for employers to carry leave over from one holiday year to the next. The only exception is where someone leaves a job before they have had an opportunity to take leave that they are owed.

This case concerned two salesmen who worked for Canada Life on commission-only contracts from 1975 until the termination of their contracts on 31 October 2002. They received no salaries and no holiday pay or holiday entitlements. Their contracts described them as 'self-employed consultants'. The two men were paid final commission payments in December 2003.

They brought tribunal claims alleging that they were owed unpaid holiday pay going back to 1 October 1998 when the Working Time Regulations first became law. The claim was made under the Unfair Deduction in Wages Regulations.

The employer argued that the two men were self-employed and thus not covered by the relevant statute, and that in any case their claims for holiday pay in the years before 2002 were out of time. Moreover, the Working Time Regulations prevent employers from paying money in lieu of holiday, so how can a failure to do so be unlawful?

The employer lost this case at both the employment tribunal and later at the EAT on all three legal points. The two men were not genuinely self-employed and were thus 'workers' for the purposes of the unfair deduction from wages legislation. Their claims were not out of time because the failure to pay holiday pay in 2002 was the last of a series of deductions and not a one-off occurrence. On the third point the EAT decided that the employer had failed to provide the men with statutory paid holiday and that it was just that they should be compensated for this.

Source: Underwood (2004)

Itemised pay statements

It is now a universal statutory right for employees (not all workers) to receive an itemised pay statement at the time that they are paid. The slip must set out gross pay, all fixed deductions, all variable deductions and net pay. Remedy is via an employment tribunal which may order compensation to be paid, but will usually simply issue a declaration stating that itemised pay statements must be provided in the future.

There used to be, under the Wages Act, a right for certain groups of workers to be paid in cash. This was not included in the equivalent sections of the Employment Rights Act 1996 and does not now apply, except where employees have a contractual right dating from before 1996.

The regulation of occupational pension schemes

Around 45% of all employed people in the UK are members of occupational pension schemes provided by employers. The regulation of these schemes is now very complex indeed and would take two or three chapters to explore properly. In a book that covers employment law generally this would neither be possible, nor, we would anticipate, hugely popular among readers for whom occupational pensions are of only marginal interest. We are thus restricting ourselves to a brief overview of the subject.

Until twenty-five years ago, subject to Inland Revenue rules and the principles of the law of trusts, employers had a wide degree of discretion as to how they ran their occupational funds:

- employees could be compelled to become scheme members as a condition of employment
- major groups (such as part-timers) could be excluded from membership as a matter of policy
- funds need not be transferred from one pension scheme to another when an employee resigned and wished to join another scheme
- there was little requirement to communicate details about the scheme or its investments to employees
- there were no restrictions on employers who wished to invest their pension funds in their own businesses
- there was very little supervision of scheme trustees on the part of government agencies.

Since 1985 this situation has changed radically. In a series of Social Security, Finance and Pensions Acts governments have step by step built a huge regulatory edifice which, in a short space of time, has transformed the way that occupational pension schemes are run and has made them a great deal more costly from an employer's point of view. Several significant rulings by the European Court of Justice have also played a role in restricting the employer's freedom of manouevre in this field. Moreover, pension funds are subject to greatly increased taxation and have recently been the subject of significant new accounting standards.

Early leavers

Employees who have completed two years' service now have the option of transferring any accrued pension to another occupational pension scheme or to a personal pension plan, the transfer value being calculated according to standard conventions. Alternatively they may leave their pensions in the original employer's scheme where their value will be 'preserved' or revalued in line with inflation (to a maximum of 5% per annum). This restricts very considerably the ability of employers to use pensions as a form of deferred pay to discourage employee turnover—one of the main reasons for the establishment of pension schemes in the early twentieth century.

Voluntary membership

Employers are at present unable to require employees to join their schemes or even to advise them to join. It is also now possible for an employee to leave a pension scheme while remaining employed in the organisation and to request that it be preserved or transferred to a personal pension plan. This will change after 2012 when a series of new measures are due to be introduced to encourage higher levels of pension saving and participation in occupational schemes.

Disclosure of information

Trustees of occupational pension funds are now required to disclose a large amount of information concerning their schemes to members, potential members, retired members and their spouses, and also to recognised trade unions. Some classes of information must be disclosed on request, while others must be provided automatically in rule books, annual statements and other forms of regular communication. As a result, no one should be in the position of not knowing what their level of benefits is, what the rules of the scheme are and what is its overall financial health.

Self-investment

Organisations are now barred from investing fund assets in property, companies or other ventures controlled by the sponsoring organisation. From 1992 pension fund trustees were banned from investing any more than 5% of a scheme's total assets in employer-related shares or property, but this was changed to a total ban in the Pensions Act 1995 which also banned the practice of funds giving loans or loan guarantees to the sponsoring employer. The collapse of the Maxwell Group of companies and the discovery that £248 million of pension fund assets had been used to secure loans to failing private Maxwell companies led to public demand for this change to the law.

Sex discrimination

In 1990, following the applicant's victory in the European Court of Justice in *Barber v Guardian Royal Exchange* (see Chapter 8) all occupational pension scheme benefits had to be equalised as between men and women. This was a complex and costly operation because most schemes mirrored the state pension system in providing benefits for men from the age of sixty-five and women from the age of sixty. Problems have arisen from the fact that, on average, women in the UK live for seven years longer than men and thus require additional funding if they are to enjoy pensions of equal value. Equalisation of access to pension scheme membership for predominantly female groups, such as part-time workers, has also had to be introduced.

Minimum funding requirements

Under the Pensions Act 1995 employers are required to ensure that their schemes are solvent. The minimum funding standards require that trustees obtain actuarial valuations at set intervals to establish whether or not a fund's assets are sufficient to meet its liabilities. Where assets fall below this minimum funding level employers now have five years to restore the level of assets. Where assets are judged to have fallen below 90% of the minimum funding level, they must be restored to the 90% level in one year.

Regulatory bodies

Three regulatory bodies now oversee different aspects of occupational pension provision. All are funded through levies on pension funds:

- The Occupational Pensions Regulatory Authority
- The Pensions Compensation Board
- The Pensions Ombudsman

In addition a government-run compensation fund has now been set up, also funded by levies, which compensates pensioners when company pension funds are insolvent.

The abolition of tax credits

Since 1997 employers have no longer been able to claim tax credits on advanced corporation tax paid to pension funds. These had been central to pension fund taxation for decades. They allowed pension funds to reclaim a rebate from the Inland Revenue for most of the tax automatically paid on the share dividends they received. In effect they allowed pension schemes a substantial amount of tax relief on their investments. Tax was paid only once when the pension was paid out. Now the funds pay tax on their profits and the pensioners also pay tax once they receive their benefits after retiring. Most analysts agree that the change has benefited the Treasury to the tune of around £5 billion of additional taxation per year.

Accounting standards

As of 2005 employers have been required to use the new accounting standard FRS17 when compiling annual accounts, the purpose being to bring the UK into line with much international practice. This means that pension fund assets and liabilities must be valued in annual accounts on a market-related basis. As pension fund assets fluctuate this will show up in the annual accounts and gives (or may well give) a picture of volatility. This may well influence the propensity of investors to buy shares in particular organisations.

Critiques of pension fund regulation

While most would agree that a certain amount of pension fund regulation is necessary to prevent abuse by employers, many analysts have come to the conclusion that the regulatory regime is now too strict and that it has become counterproductive as a result. It is now much more expensive for employers to provide occupational pension schemes and they are far more restricted than once they were in how they run their funds. They no longer operate effectively as a tool of employee retention and represent an increasing financial risk.

For these reasons many in the pensions industry blame 'over-regulation' for the declining willingness of employers to provide pension schemes and to fund them sufficiently. In particular, regulation is blamed for the increasing preference of employers to offer membership to staff on a defined contribution rather than a defined benefit basis. This means that the employer no longer even pretends to guarantee a particular level of pension to members when they retire. Instead the investment risk is increasingly being passed entirely to employees whose pension is then determined by the value of their individual 'pension pot' and prevailing annuity rates at the time of their retirement.

Activity 21.3 Stakeholder pensions

A new form of government sponsored pension arrangement known as 'the stakeholder pension' was introduced in October 2001. It was intended to supplement rather than replace occupational pensions, although many fear that it will, over time, in practice operate as a less satisfactory alternative.

Stakeholder pensions are aimed particularly at middle income earners who do not have other private or occupational pension arrangements. Around 5 million people in the UK earn between £10,000 and £25,000 a year and do not currently have access to an occupational pension scheme. Many are employed in small businesses and they are the main target group.

All employers with more than five employees who do not operate their own occupational scheme are obliged by law to provide access to a stakeholder pension, although they are not obliged to make any contributions themselves. The hope is that trade unions and insurance companies will set up plans, that people will join and that employers will then pay monthly sums directly into the fund from the payroll. Stakeholder pensions run according to government-mandated rules, so administration charges are kept low.

Over three million stakeholder plans have been set up, but the vast majority of these (over 80% according to most surveys) are 'designation only'. This means that employers have set group schemes up, as they are required to by law, but that no money is being saved in them by employees (see Blake et al, 2005 and Taylor, 2008).

Questions

1 Why do you think the government is keen for employees to save into pension schemes provided by employers?

2 Why are employees so reluctant to save towards a pension?

3 What more could be done via regulation to increase pension saving?

4 In what ways might de regulation play a positive role?

Future pension policy

The increase in the dependency ratio (ie, the proportion of people who are of working age compared to those who are retired) as a result of population ageing has major implications for pensions. Unless change is introduced the economy will struggle to support retired people financially in the future. If a situation is to be avoided in which older people are required to live on substantially lower incomes than they currently do or in which taxes rise very considerably, working lives will have to be extended somewhat and much higher levels of saving for pensions will have to be achieved.

In May 2006 the government published a white paper entitled 'Security in Retirement: towards a new pensions system' setting out its proposals for long-term, fundamental reform of state pensions. This drew heavily on the recommendations of the Turner Commission which reported in 2005 after having undertaken a lengthy, in-depth investigation of the whole issue. The relevant legislation is found in the Pensions Act 2008. The major changes will be as follows:

- From October 2012 (later for small businesses) everyone who is employed will either have access to an occupational pension scheme or the government-sponsored 'personal pension account scheme'.

- People will be able to opt out if they wish, but they will be automatically enrolled into one scheme or the other when commencing a new job. Employers will not be able to opt out.

- In the case of personal pension accounts employees will contribute 4% of earnings and employers 3%. Tax relief will mean that a further 1% is effectively contributed.

- Rules for accessing the state pension and state second pension will be simplified and the system made more accessible to people who take periods out of the workforce for the purposes of raising families and caring for elderly dependants.

- The male state pension age will rise from sixty-five to sixty-six in 2016 and the female age from 2020, and then further to sixty-seven and sixty-eight at dates yet to be set.

CHAPTER SUMMARY

- Since 1999 a national minimum wage has operated in the UK. Its level is increased by the government each October. There are separate, lower rates for young workers and those in training.

- When employees are absent due to sickness employers must, as a minimum, pay them the current rate of statutory sick pay. This is payable for up to twenty-eight weeks of sickness.

- Long-standing regulations restrict the extent to which employers can make deductions from their workers' wages without prior agreement.

- The extent to which occupational pension schemes are regulated has increased vastly in recent years. Many argue that it is the costs associated with these changes which have led to the decline in the coverage of such schemes.

- The government is currently implementing major reform of the UK pensions system. After 2016 state pension ages will rise, while from 2012 all employees will have to be enrolled in pension schemes automatically on commencing employment.

For updates and further materials, please see the online resource centre at www.oup.com.

REFERENCES

Arrowsmith J., Gilman M.W., Edwards P. & Ram M. (2003) 'The impact of the National Minimum Wage in small firms' *British Journal of Industrial Relations* 41.3 (435).

Blake D., Byrne A. & Harrison D. (2005) 'Barriers of pension scheme participation in small and medium-sized enterprises' *Pensions Institute Discussion Paper PI-0505*. London: The Pensions Institute.

Gaski, J.F. (2004) 'Raising the Minimum Wage is Unethical and Immoral' *Business and Society Review* 109.2 (p209).

Hari, J. (2004) 'How some of Britain's poorest women are being cheated out of the national minimum wage' *The Independent*, 15 December.

Metcalf, D. (2004) 'The impact of the national minimum wage on pay distribution, employment and training' *The Economic Journal* 114 (pC84).

Pollert, A. (2005): 'The unorganised worker: the decline in collectivism and new hurdles to individual employment rights' *Industrial Law Journal* 34 (p217).

Simpson, B. (2004): 'The National Minimum Wage Five Years On: Reflections on Some General Issues' *Industrial Law Journal*, 33 (p22).

Stewart, M.B. (2004) 'The employment effects of the national minimum wage' *The Economic Journal* 114 (p110).

Taylor, S. (2008) 'Occupational Pensions' in G.White & J.Druker (eds): *Reward Management: A Critical Text*. Second Edition. London: Routledge.

Underwood, K. (2004) 'Holiday pay, recent cases: more questions than answers' *Employment Law and Litigation* 9.6.

ONLINE RESOURCE CENTRE

A range of online resources to help you through your employment law module have been developed by the author team. These include updates, self-test questions and sources for further reading. (www.oxfordtextbooks.co.uk/orc/taylor_emir3e)

Privacy and confidentiality

(**22**)

Learning outcomes

By the end of this chapter you should be able to:

- set out the principles of the Data Protection Act;

- describe what rights are granted to an employee by that Act;

- advise in what circumstances employers can monitor the telephone, internet and e-mail usage of their employees;

- explain the importance of the Human Rights Act in relation to the right to privacy and the law on confidentiality;

- evaluate the law relating to whistleblowing and protected disclosures;

- outline how an employer should approach the task of giving a job reference; and

- set out the methods that an employer can use to protect a business from competition from former employees.

Introduction

There are various pieces of legislation which relate in one way or another to the subject of privacy and confidentiality in the workplace. Records may be kept which contain personal information about employees; employers may have reasons to monitor their employees' telephone conversations and e-mails; they may wish to protect confidential processes when the employee leaves, and the employee may have reason to 'blow the whistle' on some wrongful action of his employer.

There are four statutes which relate directly to issues of confidentiality in the workplace:

- the Data Protection Act 1998
- the Public Interest Disclosure Act 1998
- the Regulation of Investigatory Powers Act 2000
- the Telecommunications (Lawful Business Practice) (Interception of Communications) Regulations 2000.

We will look at each of these in this chapter as well as at two other areas of law which are also influences in this area:

- the law on job references,
- the law on restricting the activities of past employees.

Drew and Vause describe the law in this area as a complex web of regulation which requires careful consideration in order to ascertain what conduct is permissible. In analysing the separate requirements, it is important to realise that it is often not enough simply to comply with one set of obligations. To the extent that they overlap, they must all be observed. So, for example, if an interception is permitted by the Telecommunications Regulations, it must also comply with the requirements of the Data Protection Act and the Human Rights Act (Drew and Vause, 2007).

Activity 22.1

Cliff begins working as a senior salesman in a small company, XYZ Ltd, retailing specialised audio equipment in July.

At the end of August he receives his first pay. This is presented to him in a brown envelope and consists entirely of cash. It is explained to him that he will be paid in cash, because the firm receives a great deal of its income in cash. Some senior employees have always been paid this way.

After a further month spent observing the organisation's managers, and after receiving a further brown envelope, Cliff comes to believe that the cash payments are a means used by the firm to avoid paying employee national insurance contributions. He therefore telephones HM Revenue & Customs and raises his concerns with its representatives. His concerns are noted.

At the end of October he receives a pay cheque instead of cash. He is pleased with this development, but believes that the firm must have listened into his call to the Revenue or recorded it. He decides to take more care in future when making calls from his desk.   »

>> In October Cliff decides to apply for a part-time magistrate's post—a long-term ambition. He completes the forms and waits to be informed about the interview date. Instead after three weeks he is sent a letter of rejection. He calls the Lord Chancellor's Department and is told that one of his references was unsatisfactory.

He becomes convinced that the managing director of XYZ Ltd has written a poor reference for him or has impugned his character in some way. He therefore goes to see the MD and asks to see the reference. This request is refused on grounds of confidentiality. He then asks to see his personal file. This request is also turned down.

A month later he is called to the managing director's office and presented with copies of documents from his personal file. This bundle contains nothing but letters of appointment and a copy of his original application.

In the second week of November Cliff resigns to take up a job offer with a rival firm. He leaves on a Friday. The following Monday he receives a letter from the former employer stating that he must not take up the new job and that if he does legal action will be taken. A clause in his offer letter is cited. It reads as follows:

> The employee undertakes that for one year after leaving his employment, he will not work for a direct competitor of XYZ Ltd.

Questions

1 What different legal issues are raised in this case?

2 If you were to advise Cliff on his position, what advice would you give?

Return to this activity once you have read the chapter, to see if your answers were correct.

The Human Rights Act

The UK signed up to the European Convention on Human Rights on its inception in the 1950s. The Convention gave citizens rights which are set out in a list of articles. These are listed in the Convention and are fundamental human rights such as the right to privacy; freedom of expression; the right to a fair trial, etc. A problem with the Convention for many years was that it was not directly enforceable in the UK courts. If people wanted to enforce their Convention rights they had to undergo the lengthy and expensive process of taking a case to the European Court of Human Rights in Strasbourg in order to do so. The Human Rights Act 1998, which came into force on 2 October 2000, changed that by directly incorporating the Convention into UK law. As a result the rights that have been ratified by the UK are now part of domestic law, and:

- UK citizens no longer have to present human rights cases at Strasbourg: they can do so in UK courts
- there is a duty on public authorities to act in a manner compatible with the rights and freedoms contained in the Convention.
- UK courts (which are also public authorities) are obliged to interpret other legislation in the light of the Convention; that is, with an eye to the principles set out in the Convention.

Although the Human Rights Act allows people to bring a claim in the UK courts, there are some restrictions on this. A claim for one of the Convention rights (eg, privacy) can only be brought directly against a public body. So, if a person employed by a public employer wanted to claim that their privacy had been breached by the employer, they could bring an action specifying that. If, however, the person wanted to bring a claim against a private employer, another action would have to be found to add the HRA claim on to. For example, in a privacy case, the person concerned could resign, make a claim for constructive dismissal and then add the breach of privacy claim on to the dismissal claim. You cannot bring a straightforward Convention-based privacy claim on its own against a private employer.

When the HRA was first passed, commentators predicted that it would have a profound effect on many areas of employment law. This has not been the case and its effect so far has been minimal, but there is yet potential for it to have an impact, particularly when courts and tribunals are asked to interpret statutes in a way that is in accordance with the Act. An area where this is considered to be a strong possibility is in the field of privacy and confidentiality, where Article 8 of the European Convention sets standards of conduct for public authorities.

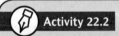 Activity 22.2

Maria is dismissed from her job as a local authority librarian because she comes to work one day wearing a 'Troops out of Afghanistan' t-shirt, and this offends her manager. There is no dress code that employees in her library have to abide by.

Maria is furious. She believes that her manager has infringed her right to freedom of expression. However, she is advised that she cannot bring an unfair dismissal claim because she has completed less than a year's service.

Questions

1   What other route might be open to Maria as a means of challenging her dismissal?

2   How would her position be different if she were to have been dismissed from a job as a librarian in a commercial organisation such as a private college or a media organisation?

Data protection

In the past, employers would have held limited information on their workers, such as their addresses, job title and salary. The amount of information has, however, exploded with the rise of computer and internet use. As Lorber (2004:180) points out:

> [I]n a typical office, computerised data are recorded and processed from the moment an office worker arrives. Arrival at work is recorded on CCTV; use of a swipe card or pass to gain entry [is] recorded; logging onto a PC is recorded. He or she then starts work, perhaps sending and receiving emails . . . accessing the Internet, using a telephone and leaving voicemail messages, all of which are likely to involve recording of data. Recording of data continues unabated until the worker goes home.

In practice, therefore, employers collect a large amount of wide-ranging information on their staff, which is held on personnel records and elsewhere, and relates to all sorts of issues, minor and major. As Ford (1999:57) states, *'the potential for abuse is clear. Information may be collected for purposes which are irrelevant to performance at work; it may include private facts; it may be collected for one purpose but be used for another; it may be inaccurate; and it may be disclosed to third parties without the knowledge or consent of the worker.'* The Data Protection Act 1998 is intended to deal with these aspects of the collection, storage and use of information.

The original Data Protection Act, in 1984, was passed at the same time as the use of computers became more widespread, and dealt predominantly with electronic data, to counteract the *'threat to personal privacy that rapid manipulation of data potentially posed'* (Carey, 2004:1). In 1995, the European Community adopted a new directive on the processing of personal data. The aim of this directive was to protect the privacy of those about whom the information was stored, and the Data Protection Act 1998, which came into force in March 2000, implements this directive into domestic law. It extends the original Data Protection Act by broadening the definition of 'data', to include information held both electronically (whether on computer or other electronic means) and in manual or paper-based filing systems, and deals with the processing of personal data by employers. It has significance well beyond the world of employment. We will focus on the employment-related aspects here, but it is important to remember that decisions in cases that have nothing whatever to do with employment may have significance for workers' rights, such as the *Durant* case discussed below. Under the Act, employers are permitted only to process personal data which is 'necessary' and 'justifiable' and must only keep it for as long as is strictly necessary. Adequate security measures must be taken, and the employer must designate a person to be the 'data controller', who has responsibility for the collection and processing of data.

Part of the objective of the law is to encourage employers to think carefully about what kind of information they ask of their workers. What is the purpose of such information? Who is to have access to it and under what conditions? The worker is given rights to access his or her personal records and demand rectification of errors, and can claim compensation for damage caused by any breach of the Act and also for distress in certain circumstances. Individuals can also see all manual files held on them and make complaints, seek correction or claim recompense. Part of the complaint of employers is the cost, particularly for large organisations which have thousands of databases, of searching for the required data. Data is defined in section 1 of the DPA as information which falls into one of the following categories:

- is being processed automatically by equipment which is operating automatically in response to instructions (this can be computerised, or otherwise, such as voice-activated telephone recording systems and certain CCTV devices),
- is recorded with the intention that it should be processed by means of such equipment (for example a manual record that is made with the intention of being scanned into a computer system),
- is recorded as part of a relevant filing system, or with the intention that it should form part of such a system (this means paper records, and is discussed below, under the *Durant* case),
- forms part of an accessible record (such as a health record, an educational record or an accessible public record),

- is recorded information held by a public authority (this was inserted by the Freedom of Information Act 2000).

The first three of these are likely to be the most important in an employment context, and the last will also apply to public sector employees. It is important to remember that the Act only applies to personal data, which is defined as data relating to a living individual who can be identified from that data. The major rights under the Act are as follows:

- the right of access to personal data,
- the right to know the purposes for which that data will be used,
- the right to prevent processing which is likely to cause damage or distress,
- the right not to be subjected to certain categories of decisions based solely on the automatic processing of data.

The DPA applies to workers, not just employees. The code of practice related to the Act states that it also covers former workers, applicants, former applicants, volunteers and those on work placements.

Data protection principles

The Act applies to 'data processing', which means obtaining the data, recording it, holding it, or doing anything with it, such as consulting it or disclosing it. Schedule 1 of the Act sets out eight 'principles' which apply to such processing:

- personal data shall be processed fairly and lawfully,
- personal data shall be obtained only for specified and lawful purposes, and used accordingly,
- personal data shall be adequate, relevant and not excessive for the purpose proposed,
- personal data shall be accurate and up to date,
- personal data shall be kept for no longer than is necessary for the purposes for which it is processed,
- personal data shall be processed in accordance with the rights of the person to whom the data relates,
- personal data shall be safeguarded against unlawful processing and accidental loss, destruction or damage,
- personal data shall not be transferred to a country outside the European Economic Area unless that country has similar rights for data protection.

Sensitive data

Stricter rules apply to 'sensitive data', which is broadly defined as information that includes a person's:

- racial/ethnic origins
- religious beliefs
- political opinions

- trade union membership
- health
- sex life
- criminal convictions.

In addition to the data protection principles set out in Schedule 1, at least one of the following conditions, which are found in Schedule 3, must also apply to sensitive data:

- that the processing is necessary for performing or exercising a right or obligation imposed by or in connection with employment,
- that the processing is necessary in connection with legal proceedings or for the purposes of obtaining legal advice,
- that the processing is necessary for the administration of justice or statutory duty, or
- the processing of racial or ethnic origin information is necessary for the purposes of monitoring equality of opportunity or treatment.

Sensitive data should not be processed or revealed to a third party without the employee's express consent (unless needed for legal purposes). There are many legal purposes which may require sensitive data to be held (eg, notice of pregnancy for health and safety reasons, illnesses which may affect the job such as epilepsy, insulin dependence, past convictions in certain occupations, etc).

Code of practice

The statute also established the office of the Information Commissioner, who acts as an independent official to oversee the Act. He reports annually to Parliament and can, in certain circumstances, enforce a person's rights under the Act. The Information Commissioner has issued a code of practice giving guidance on how employers should act on the principles of the Act. The current Code is a consolidation of four earlier guides relating respectively to:

- recruitment and selection
- employee records
- monitoring at work
- medical information.

The Code sets out how the Commissioner will interpret the eight principles in terms of their practical application in the workplace and can be obtained from the Information Commissioner's website. Although the Code contains guidance and is not legally binding, it provides the benchmarks that the Commissioner will use when deciding whether or not to enforce the Act.

The *Durant* case

Durant v Financial Services Authority (2003) is not an employment law case, but in it the Court of Appeal gave guidance on important data protection principles, such as what constitutes 'personal data' and which manual files are covered.

Mr Durant was a customer of Barclays Bank who complained about them to the Financial Services Authority and subsequently sought disclosure from the FSA of all personal data it held on him. He got some of the computerised records, but in heavily edited form. He was refused disclosure of documents kept in the authority's manual records system. The court said that the purpose of allowing a person to check the data that is held on him was to enable him to check whether a data controller's processing of personal data infringed his privacy, rather than being an automatic key to information in which the individual is named, or a surrogate for the litigation disclosure process.

It therefore concluded that 'personal data' had a narrow meaning, and that mere mention of a person's name did not necessarily mean that data was personal. It became personal if it was 'biographical in a significant sense', and if it focused on the subject, who is the person concerned. Data which merely mentioned the individual's name or concerned him in some way, but which was not *focused* on him and which 'did not affect his privacy' was not to be considered as 'personal data'. The court pointed out that 'the protection given is for the protection of personal data, not documents'.

The other aspect of the Court of Appeal's judgment concerned to what extent manual files came within the scope of the Act. It decided that the European Directive envisaged that it should be interpreted narrowly, and that the Act only applied to manual records if they were of '*sufficient sophistication to provide the same or similar ready accessibility as a computerised filing system*'.

This effectively means that the Act only applies to a filing system in which the files forming part of it are structured or referenced in such a way as to indicate clearly at the outset of the search whether personal data is held on it, and which has a sufficiently sophisticated and detailed means of readily indicating where files can be found. A file with a name on the front arranged in date order would not normally fall within the definition, whereas files with '*any clear systematic internal indexing mechanism*' probably would.

In the light of this case, the Information Commissioner clarified the position, pointing out that:

- where an individual's name appears in information the data will only be 'personal data' where its inclusion in the information affects the named individual's privacy

- it is likely that very few manual files will be covered by the provisions of the DPA.

Importantly for employers, the Commissioner states that personnel files which are subdivided to allow retrieval of personal data without a manual search (such as sickness, absence, contact details, etc) are likely to be held in a 'relevant filing system' for the purposes of the DPA. He also points out that as far as public sector employers are concerned the Freedom of Information Act 2000 (which came into force in 2005) requires all personal data to be readily accessible, thus bringing many items of data back within the scope of the DPA.

The *Durant* case above appears to restrict the scope of the Data Protection Act significantly. It has been welcomed by employers, as it makes the life of the data controller much easier, but it has also been criticised for perhaps limiting the DPA to such an extent that it may no longer properly implement the European Directive. For example, Lorber (2004:183) comments that:

> the Court's narrow view of the meaning of 'personal data' significantly reduces the protection which the legislation gives to privacy in contexts other than subject access. If the Durant approach is correct, data controllers could collect considerable amounts of unfocused personal information without any of the protections offered by the legislation and, in particular, the data protection principles. There would, for example, be no constraints on the use of CCTV or webcams other than in circumstances in which privacy is obviously affected.

In relation to manual files, Carey (2004:16) argues that '*a set of manual personnel files, each relating individually to a specific employee, containing structured records on the employee and stored alphabetically according to each employee's last name, clearly falls within the definition . . . A single ring-binder containing an individual's personal data may not be a structured file, and therefore would not form part of a relevant filing system. It is unlikely that the provisions would catch an unstructured collection of papers which only incidentally contain personal data.*' He goes on to say that there has been much concern in the employment field about the impact of extending data protection legislation to manual data, as it has proved to be one of the most costly and time-consuming aspects of the DPA for businesses.

This restriction by the Court of Appeal of the legislation relating to manual files has been welcomed by businesses, but as Lorber (2004:186) comments, '*Arguably, rather than looking for equivalence in search techniques, the Court's focus should have been equivalence in protection*'. By effectively narrowing the access to information that is kept on an individual, it could be argued that the judgment in fact goes against the spirit if not the letter of the legislation.

The spirit of the legislation is, as the Directive originally pointed out, to protect the privacy of the individual. There is, however, tension between the rights of the individual to have limits on the information that is processed about him, and to be able to access that data, and the rights of the employers who have to foot the bill for the cost of complying with the legislation:

> In 2003, the Government, in its reply to a questionnaire from the European Commission on the Directive, said that 'Technological developments have had a huge impact on the way in which the exercise of [subject access rights] affects data controllers. It is no longer the case that data controllers can discharge their obligations by simply downloading data from centrally held databases . . . Data controllers' task in dealing with subject access requests [is] immeasurably more complex, time-consuming and costly.' The Commission, however, was not convinced that 'the implementation of the provision is in fact posing serious practical problems'. (Lorber 2004:180–181)

There is therefore, the pull, which is seen in so much of employment law, between the rights of workers and those of employers. The right to privacy of the worker is put against the costs of compliance and time involved for the employer, who sees it as an unworkable and unnecessary law.

Enforcement

Two methods of enforcement are provided by the DPA. The first relates to the Information Commissioner, to whom a person may apply for an assessment whether any processing concerning that person is being carried out lawfully. The Commissioner will assess the case, and decide if it is proportionate to take action, having regard to matters such as the seriousness of the breach, the damage and distress to the worker, the costs of compliance.

The main powers of the Information Commissioner are:

- to serve notices requiring information
- to ask an organisation to give an undertaking on a particular course of action to improve its compliance
- to serve enforcement notices and 'stop now' orders where there has been a breach, requiring employers to take specified steps to make sure they comply with the law

- to conduct audits (either by consent or compulsory ones)
- to issue monetary penalty notices, fining employers up to £500,000 (these are issued only where there has been a 'serious contravention' of the data protection principles, in other words, one which is deliberate or reckless, and which is likely to cause substantial damage, or substantial distress)
- to prosecute those who commit criminal offences under the Act
- to report to Parliament if there are data protection issues of concern.

It is a criminal offence for the controller not to respond to these notices. It is also a criminal offence to obtain personal data unlawfully. The other option that a person has is to bring proceedings in the County Court against the data controller/employer for compliance with a request for access to his personal data, and/or seek compensation if he has suffered damage as a result of unlawful processing. In the *Durant* case, the court set out some guidance on how it exercised its discretion in deciding not to order compliance:

- the information Mr Durant sought was of no '*practical value*' to him
- the purpose of the Act was to ensure that individuals know what records say about them so as to have '*an opportunity of remedying an error or false information*' not '*to fuel a separate collateral argument*'.
- the FSA had acted at all times '*in good faith*'. Mr Durant's argument was with Barclays Bank, not with the FSA.

Monitoring and privacy

We now move on to the question of privacy within the workplace, and whether there is a sphere of privacy that surrounds the employee that cannot be taken away, or whether employers are within their rights to monitor their employees' activities and correspondence. Oliver (2002) argues that having a right to privacy is important to maintain a person's autonomy, dignity and personal well-being, and further that privacy-invasive practices may inhibit independence of thought and creativity, as people are not be able to think properly if they know or think that they are being watched. She also states that '*there is . . . substantial evidence that privacy-invasive practices in the workplace, particularly pervasive surveillance, can cause actual psychological damage and stress-related illness*' (Oliver 2002:325). On the other hand, it could be said that when employees are at work, there is no such thing as privacy. They are being paid for being there and are there on their employer's time, using equipment and telephone lines that the employer has paid for. The private rights of the employee are therefore in conflict with the property rights of the employer. The European Court of Human Rights, however, has held otherwise, as we shall see below.

There are a number of reasons why an employer might wish to use monitoring: in order to assess the quality and quantity of a worker's performance; to make sure that work is being done during working hours; for security reasons (for example in financial services organisations); to check compliance with an employer's rules, among others. Until the matter was specifically legislated for, there was really no protection of the privacy of workers. As Ford (2002:148) points out, the common law gave '*almost absolute priority to management prerogative and almost no recognition to workers' private interests*'. Now, however, the privacy of workers is subject not only to the DPA, and the HRA, but also the Regulation of Investigatory Powers Act 2000 (RIPA) and the Telecommunications (Lawful Business Practice) (Interception of Communications) Regulations 2000 made under it. We shall look at the monitoring aspect of each of these.

The Data Protection Act

As we saw above, the Data Protection Act applies to monitoring of employees by employers, and there is guidance relating to it in the third part of the Information Commissioner's Code. It will not apply if there is merely interception of, for example, telephone calls. But it does apply if they are recorded because, as stated above, the DPA applies to the *processing* of information. The DPA does not stop an employer from monitoring and recording the communications of his staff, but any such activity should be consistent with the principles of the DPA, which are set out earlier in this chapter.

By its very nature, monitoring may intrude on a worker's private life, and so should be no more than is absolutely necessary, and should only take place after the employer has carried out an 'impact assessment' and considered an alternative to monitoring. If an employer wishes to monitor, it should be clear about the purpose of the monitoring and, unless covert monitoring is clearly justified, the workers should be made aware of the nature, extent and reasons for it. Covert monitoring should only be authorised if there are grounds to suspect criminal activity, or similar, should be strictly targeted to obtaining evidence within a specific period, and should not continue once the investigation has finished. More detailed guidance about this can be found in the Code of Practice on the Information Commissioner's website.

 Exhibit 22.1   **The Employment Practices Data Protection Code**

There were originally two codes, covering recruitment and selection and employee records. The second two parts of the code covering monitoring at work and medical information were added later. All four codes have now been consolidated into a single code in four parts, named the Employment Practices Code.

Part 1: Recruitment and selection

This includes the following:

- make a staff member responsible for compliance,
- make serious data protection breaches a disciplinary offence,
- only request data about an applicant that is relevant to recruitment,
- only request details of criminal convictions if justified for the role,
- ensure job applicants sign a consent form if documents are needed from a third party,
- inform applicants if automated short-listing is the sole basis of decision,
- retain interview notes,
- establish a retention period for recruitment records based on business need,
- destroy information on an individual's recruitment within six months,
- dispose of salary information from previous employers,
- only ask for sensitive personal data for successful applicants.

»

» The Code also makes it clear that job references for candidates and interview notes are *not* generally exempted from the Act and can be seen by employees once they have started in their new jobs. However, exemptions do include information being used in the process of negotiations, promotion planning or during criminal investigations.

Part 2: Employment records

This clarifies the above position on job references and also includes the following key points:

- employers should be open with employees about what records they hold and for what purpose,
- sickness and accident records should be 'kept separately' from absence records and treated as 'sensitive data',
- in merger and acquisition situations consent must be obtained from employees before information about them can be disclosed to potential buyers/merger partners,
- formal steps must be taken to check that information held is up to date—annual checks of files by employees themselves are recommended,
- the Code emphasises the importance of strict security measures,
- equal opportunities monitoring data should be anonymised,
- disciplinary and grievance records should be kept only for a limited period (ie, spent after so many months),
- notes of disciplinary investigations from which no action was taken should be destroyed.

Part 3: Monitoring at work

This is less precise. It allows employers a great deal more room for manoeuvre than the first two parts of the Code. Key points are as follows:

- employers should not monitor workers as a general rule,
- monitoring should only occur for a specified and justified purpose,
- workers should be made aware of the nature, extent and reasons for any monitoring—except where covert monitoring is justified,
- employers must carry out an impact assessment before monitoring—this should set out why it is strictly necessary.

Part 4: Information about workers' health

This is intended to cover data gathered from pre-employment medical questionnaires, information held about the needs of particular disabled employees, copies of doctors' notes and letters and results of eye, breathalyser or blood tests. It is fairly lengthy, but the key points can be summarised as follows:

- employers should only gather medical information when strictly necessary,
- employers should keep all such data private,
- employers should make sure workers are aware that they are collecting/holding such data and why,
- interpretation of the data should only be carried out by a suitably qualified health professional.

»

Additional practical points include the following:

- never ask workers/job applicants to disclose their entire health record,
- never monitor calls made to occupational health services by employees,
- record the business purpose for which any form of medical testing is being carried out,
- employers should only test job applicants if they have a genuine intention of appointing them,
- permanently delete/destroy all records that are no longer required for a legitimate business purpose.

Exhibit 22.2   Monitoring in the EU v monitoring in the USA

Wugmeister and Bevitt contrast the two systems, observing that the EU has an 'omnibus' data protection directive, whereas the USA federal and state privacy laws address specific instances of abuse, or protect particularly sensitive information, such as health or financial information, and groups in need of special protection, such as children. They suggest that both the EU and the USA recognise the need for employee privacy. However, the degree to which they recognise that need differs. In the USA, collecting personal information about employees is generally seen as a legitimate activity, provided that it is carried out for non-discriminating, legitimate business purposes. By contrast, EU employers generally have to justify why they need to collect personal data from their employees. Certain data may not be collected at all, and some monitoring activities are prohibited as a matter of law.

The Human Rights Act

The HRA establishes a right to privacy in Article 8, which is known as the right to 'respect for private and family life'. There are two specific clauses in Article 8:

1 Everyone has the right to respect for his private and family life, his home and his correspondence.

2 There shall be no interference by a public authority with the exercise of this right except such as in accordance with the law and is necessary in a democratic society in the interests of national security, public safety or the economic well-being of the country, for the prevention of disorder or crime, for the protection of health or morals, or for the protection of the rights and freedoms of others.

The first part of the article establishes the right; the second part sets out a partial defence for a public authority that has breached that right.

There are two parts to the defence. The first is that the action taken by the employer is 'in accordance with the law', in other words what the employer is doing should not be something illegal and prohibited. If the action is allowed by law, then the second part of the defence comes into play. This is if the action fits into one of the reasons set out in the article, such as for the prevention of crime, or the protection of the rights of others (which can be the rights of the employer), etc. Such a defence means that there is a measure of proportionality, a balance between the rights of the worker and those of the employee. Oliver's view is that the test of proportionality should apply to any interception of a worker's communications made by an employer (Oliver, 2002).

 Exhibit 22.3   **Social media sites**

There is a concern among employers about the effect of the growing use of social media sites in the UK. While two-thirds of organisations in the UK ban access to such sites while at work (Chalton, 2010), there are still a number of risks that are faced by employers. As well as time-wastage, these can relate to defamatory comments and damage to brands, potential breaches of security and confidentiality and the risk of cyber-bullying. Chalton summarises the ten main social media risks for employers as:

1 Employee posts derogatory comments about employer.

2 Employee posts video clips on a social media site that may bring employer into disrepute.

3 Employees leak confidential information about their employer via a social media site.

4 Employee airs controversial views on blogs in which his/her employer is named.

5 Rejecting an applicant because of the content of their Facebook profile.

6 An employee takes lists of contacts they have built up from social media sites accessed in work and their own time and then leaves to work for a rival.

7 Employees post user-generated content on internal sites without checking copyright status or accuracy.

8 Employees spend too much time at work on social media sites.

9 Using information posted on blogs when making recruitment decisions.

10 Cyber-bullying of other employees.

Employers will need to have policies in place to deal with such issues, always balancing the privacy of the employee with the right of the employer. There is guidance on how to develop such a policy on the ACAS website at www.acas.org.uk.

Two important cases in this area have been heard by the European Court of Human Rights: *Halford v UK* and *Copland v UK*. Both cases were brought before the HRA came into force in the UK, so the complainants could only argue the point in the European Court, and were able to do so because their employers were public bodies.

Halford v UK (1997)

Alison Halford was a senior police officer in Merseyside Police who brought a sex discrimination claim against her employer. During the course of these proceedings, her employer allowed her a private telephone in her office so that she could make phone calls relating to the claim (this was in the days before widespread use of mobile phones).

She had reason to believe that, despite what the employer had told her, the private telephone was being intercepted, and brought another claim for breach of privacy. This was eventually heard by the European Court of Human Rights.

The government, which was the respondent in the case, argued that telephone calls made by Ms Halford from her workplace fell outside the protection of Article 8, because she could have had no reasonable expectation of privacy in relation to them. At the hearing before the court, counsel for the government expressed the view that an employer should in principle, without the prior knowledge of the employee, be able to monitor calls made by the latter on telephones provided by the employer.

The court said:

In the Court's view, it is clear from [previous] case-law that telephone calls made from business premises as well as from the home may be covered by the notions of 'private life' and 'correspondence' within the meaning of Article 8 para. 1.

There is no evidence of any warning having been given to Ms Halford, as a user of the internal telecommunications system operated at the Merseyside police headquarters, that calls made on that system would be liable to interception. She would, the Court considers, have had a reasonable expectation of privacy for such calls, which expectation was moreover reinforced by a number of factors. As Assistant Chief Constable she had sole use of her office where there were two telephones, one of which was specifically designated for her private use. Furthermore, she had been given the assurance, in response to a memorandum, that she could use her office telephones for the purposes of her sex discrimination case.

The court then went on to consider Article 8(2), and found that there was no law in the UK at the time which allowed the employer to intercept calls in this way, and so the infringement of the right could not be justified as it was not 'in accordance with the law'. In summary, this decision shows that the right to privacy does exist at work. It must be remembered, however, that this is a decision based on a very specific set of facts.

Copland v UK (2007)

Ten years later, the European Court went on to consider the case of Lynette Copland. Ms Copland was a PA to the principal of Carmarthenshire College, which was a public body. She became aware that the deputy principal had suggested that she was having a relationship with one of the directors. He had instigated monitoring of her telephone, e-mail and internet usage to ascertain whether she was making excessive use of college facilities for personal purposes. The college argued that it had not intercepted any telephone calls but had simply reviewed its phone logs and checked Ms Copland's e-mail and internet history.

The court held that even monitoring the date and length of telephone conversations and the numbers dialled could give rise to a breach of a right to privacy. Although the college could have obtained the same information legitimately by reviewing the relevant telephone bills, this was not a bar to a finding of interference with Ms Copland's rights. Furthermore, simply storing data relating to Ms Copland's private life was a breach of her rights and it was irrelevant that the information was not disclosed to her or used against her in any disciplinary proceedings. In reaching its conclusions, the court took account of the fact that Ms Copland had not been given any warning that her telephone calls might be subject to monitoring. As a result, she had a reasonable expectation as to the privacy of calls made and e-mails sent from work.

Activity 22.3

Questions

1 What do you think was the deciding factor in the court's finding in each of the above two cases?

2 Do you agree with these decisions? Why?

3 Should a worker have a 'reasonable expectation of privacy' while at work? Give reasons for your answer.

RIPA and the Lawful Business Practice Regulations

In the case of *Halford*, it was found that there was no basis in law for the kind of interception that took place, and so it was not 'in accordance with the law', as required by Article 8(2). The Regulation of Investigatory Powers Act 2000 (RIPA) was therefore passed, so that such monitoring would be allowed in certain circumstances. If the sender and recipient of a telecommunication (telephone call, e-mail, etc) have consented, or if the employer believes that there is consent, then it becomes lawful to monitor the exchange. If there is no consent, or the employer believes otherwise, then the person intercepted can bring a court action for damages. This is a 'more traditional approach' than the Human Rights Act, as it is *'deferential to management prerogative, with its defence of consent to interceptions'* (Ford, 2002:151). It should be noted that at the time that Ms Copland brought her claim, RIPA (see below), had not yet come into force. Even if it had, however, it is likely that the decision would have been the same, as the college had not expressly told her that her calls and e-mail/internet usage were being monitored.

RIPA allows for regulations to be made in this area, and so the Telecommunications (Lawful Business Practice) (Interception of Communications) Regulations 2000, which came into effect on 24 October 2000, were brought in. These are generally known as the Lawful Business Practice Regulations, and they list broad categories of lawful interception and/or re-cording of telecommunications by employers. The Regulations allow employers to intercept *and* record e-mails, text messages and phone calls in order to:

- establish the existence of facts relating to the business;
- ascertain compliance with employer regulations, whether internal or imposed by an external body;
- ascertain compliance with standards (eg, telesales people);
- prevent or detect crime;
- investigate unauthorised use of phones or e-mail; or
- protect a system, for example against viruses.

The employer has the right to intercept/monitor, but *not* to record messages:

- to check whether or not a call or e-mail is business-related (for example to make sure that a large number of e-mails are not being received from outside organisations for personal use)

- where calls are made to a confidential, counselling or support helpline (this is intended for charities whose staff work on helplines, so that they can receive supervision and support).

The Regulations have been very controversial, because they *'have watered down the restrictions placed on employers by RIPA to such a large extent that it could now be said that RIPA hardly limits employer monitoring practices at all'* (Oliver, 2002:339). The problem with the Regulations, as some commentators see it, is that there is no requirement of proportionality, of balancing the rights of workers against those of the employers—the rules are weighted in favour of the employer. It could be argued, however, that, if one uses the Regulations in conjunction with the HRA, a court must read them in the light of the HRA. Thus a need to balance arises, as Article 8 brings in the required element of proportionality. This has not yet been argued in court, however.

The draft regulations were originally based on the Telecommunications Data Protection Directive, the aim of which was to protect personal privacy and which do emphasise the need for proportionality. They were strongly criticised by employers' groups, and, in response to their concerns, the government substantially changed the final wording of the Regulations to reflect those concerns. Ford (2002:151) sees no conflict between the Regulations and the HRA test of proportionality. He says that *'The Regulations merely confer a power on management without specifying how the discretion should be guided by Article 8 and the Data Protection Act. On that basis the Regulations are neutral in effect'*.

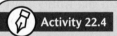

Activity 22.4

1 If the Regulations and RIPA were brought in to make monitoring 'in accordance with the law', does that mean that they are acceptable within the HRA, or should they have a specific test of proportionality?

2 Under the HRA, judges have to interpret statutes in a way that is consistent with the HRA. Does that mean that they have to imply a test of proportionality under the Regulations? If they do this, will the impact of them be diluted?

Whistleblowers' rights

In July 1999, the Public Interest Disclosure Act 1998 (PIDA) came into force. Until that date, there had been no protection for those who 'blew the whistle' on practices of their employers. Indeed, Lewis (2000:170) says that *'a conventional view . . . of whistleblowers was that they are troublemakers who deserved to be punished for disloyalty'*.

Workers who disclose information about their employer can face punishment or dismissal, and have not been well protected by courts in the past. When people made disclosures before 1999, and were dismissed, or disciplined for it, it was unlikely that they would have had any remedy. Indeed, the employer may well even have had a right to bring breach of contract claims against them, because, as we saw in Chapter 5, an employee owes to his employer a duty of trust and fidelity, which is implied into the contract of employment. Disclosures of this nature when made to outside bodies would be likely to breach that duty, if it were not for PIDA.

The pre-1999 position inevitably led to a culture of secrecy, where people would feel obliged to keep quiet, no matter what illegal practices were happening at their place of work. There have been a few cases where the courts have considered this, and used the common law to allow disclosure where there is *'any misconduct of such a nature that it ought in the public interest to be disclosed to others'* (eg, *Initial Services v Putterill* (1968)). The test for public interest is a high one, and it effectively only allowed the disclosure of a breach of statutory duty to a relevant regulatory body. It was not an area of law that had any clear guidelines, and certainly not enough to give proper protection to someone who wanted to disclose something.

The public perception of whistleblowing changed somewhat after a series of scandals, such as the Maxwell pensions crisis, and of disasters like those that occurred on the *Herald of Free Enterprise* car ferry and the Piper Alpha oil platform. These scandals and disasters resulted in a number of public inquiries, which found that people in the organisations often knew of the potential dangers or malpractice, but had felt unable to raise the matter internally or to pursue them externally. The inquiry into the Piper Alpha tragedy, for example, found that *'workers did not want to put their continued employment in jeopardy through raising a safety issue that might embarrass management'* (Lewis, 2001:170). A charity called Public Concern at Work was formed and campaigned for statutory protection for whistleblowers. It eventually succeeded when the PIDA 1998 was brought into force.

PIDA adds the new law into sections 43A–L of the ERA 1996. It gives a measure of protection to 'whistleblowers' who take action when they become concerned about the activities of their employer. However, in practice, the Act does little more than give whistleblowers protection in limited circumstances, giving them a right not to suffer a detriment or to be unfairly dismissed for blowing certain types of quite narrowly defined whistles. A dismissal in these circumstances, as we saw in Chapter 6, is considered automatically unfair. The Act sets out under what circumstances whistleblowers who are dismissed or suffer some other detriment can claim redress in the courts. These too are quite narrow, the burden of proof at each stage being on the employee.

There is no qualifying period of employment, and the law applies to all workers and not just employees (see Chapter 3). Interestingly the definition of worker in PIDA is wider than in other parts of employment law, as it specifically includes agency workers and independent contractors. Excluded from the scope of the protection are those who work in the security services, and the police.

Although there has been some criticism of the way that PIDA has been drafted, in 2010 the Council of Europe widely praised it as an example of comprehensive whistleblower legislation and adopted a resolution that all member states should have in place whistleblower protection (www.pcaw.co.uk).

Qualifying disclosures

The Act protects only certain kinds of disclosure, known as a 'qualifying disclosure'. This is central to the Act. The disclosure must concern, or be reasonably believed to concern one of the following:

- a criminal offence
- a failure to comply with legal obligations
- a miscarriage of justice

- a danger to the health and safety of any person
- environmental damage
- information showing that there has been, or is likely to have been concealment of any of the above matters.

Straightforward incompetence or dishonesty are not included, nor is abuse of power unless one of the above is also involved.

To whom can the whistle be blown? The law is quite complicated in this area, but in summary, the disclosure can be made to one of the following:

- the employer concerned (ie, a senior manager)
- a legal advisor
- a minister of the Crown
- a prescribed person (in other words, an authority such as HM Revenue & Customs, HSE, etc a list of these prescribed persons being set out in Regulations which accompany the Act).

Importantly in these circumstances the disclosure can only be valid (ie, protected under PIDA) if:

- it was made in good faith

and

- the person making the disclosure reasonably believes that the information disclosed and any allegation made is substantially true.

In the case of disclosure to a third party or a representative of a media organisation three additional conditions apply:

- the disclosure is not made for personal gain;
- the 'failure' (ie, subject matter of the disclosure) is an exceptionally serious one; and
- it is reasonable to make the disclosure in all the circumstances of the case.

This third condition might, for example, cover situations where whistleblowers reasonably believe that they will be subjected to a detriment if they make their disclosure to their employer, or to a prescribed person. Alternatively, there may be no prescribed person with authority relating to a particular kind of disclosure, or the employer might destroy evidence of the failure. Sometimes there will be a justification for a media disclosure when someone has previously made the same disclosure to an employer or to a prescribed person, but no action has been taken in response.

The impact of PIDA

It can be seen from the above that it can be very complicated to decide if a disclosure actually comes within the scope of PIDA. The case of *Fecitt & Ors v NHS Manchester* (2011) puts the burden of proof on the whistleblower to show that they have made a protected disclosure and suffered a subsequent detriment, then the burden shifts to the respondent to prove, on the balance of probabilities, that the treatment complained about was not done because of the protected disclosure. There are numerous defences that an employer can deploy when faced with a PIDA case in the tribunal. As a result, in practice, the law is only likely to be used in cases where employers act illegally, ignore the protests of individuals *and* then punish them in some way for making a disclosure. The extent of the impact can be seen from the statistics: in a review in 2010 Public Concern at Work (PCAW) found that:

- The number of PIDA claims to employment tribunals increased from 157 in 1999/2000 to 1761 in 2009.
- Employees lodged over 9000 claims alleging victimisation for whistleblowing up to 2009.
- Two-thirds of these claims were settled or withdrawn without any public hearing.
- Of the remaining third 68% lost, 27% won and in 6% of cases the claim was either settled or withdrawn before the tribunal made a judgment.
- Eight out of ten claimants first raised their concern with their employer.
- 8% of claimants raised their concern with a regulator.
- Only 1% of individuals who initially raised their concern with their employer or a regulator subsequently went to the media.
- 87% of individuals said they would raise a concern about possible corruption, danger or serious malpractice in the workplace.
- 38% of individuals said their employer had a whistleblowing policy (up 9% from 2007) (PCAW, 2010).

It therefore appears that while workers are feeling more able to raise issues, employers still have some way to go to make things easier for their staff to do so. Syal comments that the figures for employment tribunal cases 'will increase fears among campaigners that whistleblowers are being deliberately undermined or removed from their workplace, despite repeated promises to protect them.' (Syal, 2010).

Lewis, in considering the report by PCAW, takes it one step further. He points out that in bringing in the statute, Parliament did not set out to *encourage* whistleblowing, as some other countries have done, but rather to *protect* those who raise a particular type of concern in a specified way.

He suggests that if Parliament now feels that it is in the public interest to encourage people to report wrong-doing, a number of amendments could be made to the law, such as:

- the existing law might be amended to require 'reasonable suspicion' instead of the current convoluted formula of 'reasonable belief . . . tends to show'.
- the 'good faith' requirement could be dropped so that attention would focus on the message rather than the motive of the messenger. In exchange, it might be made a criminal offence to knowingly make a false allegation.
- a public interest disclosure agency could be established. This would not only be a symbolic gesture about the value of whistle-blowing in today's society but such a body could be given a broad range of functions including investigating concerns, advising both sides of industry, representing whistle-blowers, monitoring and reviewing the impact of the legislation and educating the public generally about the importance of reporting concerns to the appropriate authorities (Lewis, 2011).

Exhibit 22.4   ***Street v Derbyshire Unemployed Workers' Centre* (2005)**

Mrs Street made allegations of misuse of funds against her manager. Although she had followed the procedures, she had not done so in good faith, as she was primarily motivated by personal antagonism towards her manager against whom she had had a long-running vendetta.

The EAT, finding against her, said that disclosures should be made in the public interest, and that advancement of personal motives was 'inimical to that purpose'.

The Court of Appeal agreed with the decision, and said that good faith must have something over and above a reasonable belief in the truth of the allegations, and that a tribunal should enquire into the motive of the worker for making the disclosure. It accepted that a worker will often have mixed motives in making a disclosure, but said that a tribunal must find that a disclosure was not made in good faith when the main purpose of making it was something other than the public interest.

It could be argued that this decision undermines the aim of the PIDA, which is to get things out into the public domain, and to encourage employers to address and remedy failures in the workplace. Public Concern at Work in fact made such submissions to the court as part of the case, saying that the requirement of good faith should mean only that the disclosure must be made honestly, and that it could be satisfied even if accompanied by ulterior motivation, such as a personal grudge. The decision of the Court, however, stands.

One of the main problems that has emerged in terms of making the law effective as a genuine protector of whistleblowers is the use by employers of a defence based on the notion that the worker was not acting in good faith when he or she blew the whistle (see Exhibit 23.4 on the case of *Street v Derbyshire Unemployed Workers' Centre*). The report by Dame Janet Smith arising from the Harold Shipman inquiry recommended that the good faith requirement should be removed from the legislation, but this was not followed. The Committee on Standards in Public Life has also emphasised that the Act should be seen as the back-stop to, and not a substitute for, effective whistleblowing procedures.

Another criticism of PIDA relates to the way that the law is drafted. Some argue that this is misguided and that it should simply be modelled on mainstream anti-discrimination law. This would simplify it, while also placing the onus of proof on the employer. One of the proponents of this view is Lewis (2005:241). He points out that anti-discrimination case law is applied to the assessment of compensation for injury to feelings in protected disclosure cases (except where a dismissal has occurred and no injury to feelings award can be made). In *Virgo Fidelis School v Boyle* (2004) the EAT indicated that the detriment suffered by whistleblowers should normally be regarded as a very serious breach of discrimination legislation. He goes on to argue that discrimination against whistleblowers is not very different from that against trade union officials. Both are different to other forms of discrimination in that they are based on choices rather than inherent characteristics, but trade unionists are a group that are protected from discrimination, and by analogy one could apply the same reasoning to whistleblowers. He states that '*there is considerable evidence that whistleblowers are stigmatised and made to feel less valued as citizens'* (Lewis, 2005:243). He suggests that an anti-discrimination model would be more effective than the present regime because protection could extend beyond the field of employment and thus *'send an important general message about the importance of having an open culture'* (Lewis, 2005:244). In addition, such a model would mean that *'workers might be given the right not to suffer detrimental treatment before, during and after employment'*.

The most important advantage of putting whistleblowers under the umbrella of a general Equality Act, however, would be access to the Commission for Equality and Human Rights and its resources. This would mean that whistleblowers would not have to rely just on voluntary bodies and trade unions for assistance, and the benefit of this would increase even further if the Commission became a prescribed person to whom a disclosure could lawfully be made. Such a move would allow the Commission to offer advice and support and, as it has both investigative and enforcement powers, this *'might encourage potential whistleblowers to feel that disclosures in the public interest were valued rather than the subject of opprobrium'* (Lewis, 2005:252). The drafters of the Equality Act 2010, however, did not take the opportunity to include whistleblowing as one of the protected characteristics.

Former employees and job applicants are not covered by the present legislation, but the EAT in the case of *BP v Elstone* (2010) may have paved the way for such protection. In this case, Mr Elstone worked for a company called Petrotechnics. He made disclosures to one of their clients, BP, regarding safety and was dismissed for gross misconduct by Petrotechnics.

He then took up consultancy with BP, who, once they found out from Petrotechnics that the claimant had been dismissed for disclosing confidential information, terminated his contract. BP therefore subjected him to a detriment for making a protected disclosure while he was employed by someone else. The EAT said that didn't matter, so long as he had been a worker at the time of the protected disclosure, and found in Mr Elstone's favour. The EAT looked at the purpose of the whistleblowing legislation and decided that the central issue was the protection of workers rather than the identity of employers, and so a worker's protection should not be lost simply because they have changed employers.

Job references

Wallace Bruce (1997:462) points out that *'it is a reality of contemporary employment that the use of the reference in the workplace is so common that most employees take it for granted they will be granted one on request and even more significantly prospective employers expect that as a matter of course the employee would provide a reference or give his or her consent to one being obtained from the employer'*. Despite this, problems can arise when an employer either refuses to provide a reference, or provides one which is inaccurate—either unfavourable, when the employee deserved a good reference, or a misleadingly favourable reference for a bad employee whom the employer wished to see the back of.

Until the case of *Spring v Guardian Assurance plc* (1994), there was really no adequate remedy that employees had when references were written about them that were unjustly poor. They could bring discrimination claims if there was an element of unlawful discrimination in the reference, or they could be very brave and bring a claim of libel against an employer in the County Court. But libel cases are notoriously difficult to prove and can be very costly indeed. Now, however, thanks to the House of Lords judgment in *Spring*, the law of contract has provided a possible route for litigants to take. Here, it was decided that if an employer decides to provide a reference, then it is under a duty both to the employee and the prospective employer to take reasonable care to make sure that what is said is fair and accurate. If the original employer does not take such care, then it will be liable in negligence for any economic loss that the employee or prospective employer suffers as a result. Care must therefore be taken by the employer to provide a true, accurate and fair reference, and the reference must not give a misleading impression. So long as reasonable care is taken in its preparation, the reference does not have to be full and comprehensive.

There is no legal obligation for an employer to provide a reference at all, and indeed some large organisations have a policy of not providing one, or just providing the dates of employment and job title. It is rare, however, that an employer will refuse, as there may be grave consequences for the employee if he is not given one. Moreover, a failure to provide a reference can lead to proceedings in a court or tribunal too. Furthermore, in the *Spring* case, Lord Slynn indicated that although there may be no legal obligation to provide a reference, there is a moral obligation to do so.

When an employer *does* decide to write a reference, a consistent approach has to be taken. If he usually does give references, but refuses for a particular employee, that employee may then have a claim against him. For example, in the case of *Coote v Granada Hospitality* (1999), an employer refused to provide a reference to a female employee because she had brought a sex discrimination claim against the company. This was deemed to be victimisation under the then Sex Discrimination Act and a very substantial pay-out was the result. It was significant in this case that other employees who had asked for references were not treated the same way.

It is also important to point out that although an employee does not have a right to a reference (unless this has previously been agreed as part of the contract of employment, which is not common), a reference may affect the outcome of a tribunal case. Good references are often used in evidence by employees whose employer tries to justify a dismissal on grounds of incompetence or misconduct. Conversely, the writing of a good reference may be an offer by an employer which will help to settle a claim.

References and the Data Protection Act

The second influence that has led to recent expansion in this area of law has been the Data Protection Act, because it makes it possible for employees to see references written about them once they have started in a new job. Because a reference contains personal information, this brings it within the ambit of the DPA.

This subject is dealt with in the second part of the Information Commissioner's Code, 'Employment Records'. The Code distinguishes between references given in a personal capacity, and those given on behalf of an employer. The original employer does not have to give a worker access to the reference that is written. Once the reference is with the prospective employer, however, the worker is allowed to see it. The identity of the author of the reference can still be protected, but in 99% of cases this will be irrelevant because the worker will know only too well who has written the reference. As matters stand, failed job applicants do not always have the right under the DPA to see references written about them. Here it is possible to refuse to disclose references on the grounds that doing so might damage the interests of a third party (ie, the writer of the reference), but if the Information Commissioner requires disclosure then the reference must be disclosed. Moreover, in any event, it is important to remember that where these references are disclosed, legal action can follow.

Activity 22.5   *TSB Bank plc v Harris* **(2000)**

Ms Harris was a financial advisor employed by the TSB. She developed a bad relationship with her manager and, as a result, decided to apply for a new job at Prudential. She was interviewed and offered the new job subject to references. However, when Prudential received the reference from Ms Harris's boss at TSB it was not favourable. It simply said that seventeen complaints had been made against her, four of which had been 'upheld' and another eight of which were outstanding. No general assessment of her work record or character was provided. As a result, Prudential refused to employ Ms Harris. When she asked them why not, they told her. She thus resigned from her job at the TSB anyway and claimed constructive dismissal. She was particularly angered by the fact that she had only been informed about two of the seventeen complaints, and that in both cases she had been able to answer the points made satisfactorily.

The employer made the following points in its defence:

- nothing in the reference had been inaccurate
- the reference complied with the minimum standards set at the time by LAUTRO (a financial services regulatory body)
- in focusing on formal complaints the reference was similar in terms of its content to all the others that TSB gave at this time
- it was standard practice across the sector at this time to give short, factual references that revealed only what was necessary under law (ie, complaints).

Ms Harris won her claim at the employment tribunal, and again subsequently when the employer appealed to the EAT.

Questions

1 On what legal basis do you think Ms Harris was able to win her constructive dismissal claim?

2 To what extent do you agree that employers should be limited by law as to what they can and cannot say in a confidential reference?

3 What lessons can employers learn from TSB's experience when formulating policies on reference writing?

Employment law post-termination

When an employee leaves an employer, that employer may wish to safeguard its business against the former employee taking his knowledge or contacts to a direct competitor, or setting up his own business in direct competition. The subject of restraint of trade, use of confidential information and intellectual property is a very complex area of law, and will only be dealt with briefly in this chapter.

Restrictive covenants

One of the ways that an employer has of protecting trade secrets or other confidential information is by including a restrictive covenant in the contract of employment. This can offer a degree of protection from unfair competition by preventing the employees from making use of privileged knowledge. This is usually done by making it a condition of the contract that employees do not leave to take up work with direct competitors for a specific period of time after their employment ends. If a former employee then acts in breach of such a covenant, the former employer would have grounds to bring an action against him or her. However, a restrictive covenant is only enforceable if it is specific and reasonable. Otherwise it will be seen as a restraint of trade, which is unlawful. A general blanket covenant restricting an ex-employee from working for any competitor for a number of years would not thus be acceptable. The factors that are taken into account in deciding whether a covenant is reasonable are:

- The type of work done by the employee, for example if he is brought into contact with confidential information which can only be properly protected by the use of a covenant.

- How widely the class of 'prohibited' customers is defined. A covenant that states that employees may not approach those who were customers of the employer a long time ago, or those with whom they normally have dealt, would be unreasonable.

- How long the restraint lasts for—anything over a year is likely to be difficult for an employer to justify. Periods of less than a year are more reasonable, but it depends on the circumstances.

- The activities that an employee is prohibited from doing.

Confidentiality

An employer can also bring a legal action based on the common law duty of fidelity. This is an implied term in the contract of employment which can be enforced against both former and current employees. The matter was considered in the splendidly named Court of Appeal case of *Faccenda Chicken v Fowler* (1986), in which a former sales manager set up his own company and hired some of his ex-employer's salesmen. They made use of the previous company's sales routes and identities and needs of its customers. The court held that this knowledge was not a trade secret, and that, when deciding if that was the case, the following questions should be taken into account.

- What was the nature of the information?
- Did the employee work in a job where he regularly handled such information?
- Did the employer impress upon the employee the confidentiality of the information?
- How restricted was the circulation of the information within the business?
- Could the confidential information be readily isolated from other information that the employee was free to use?

 Activity 22.6 **The secret ice cream recipe**

Jessica runs a long-established family business. The firm's main activity is the manufacture of speciality ice creams which are only sold in a limited number of retail outlets in the seaside town in which the factory is based. The town is more famous for its delicious ice cream than it is for its other tourist attractions and Jessica's business is very successful as a result. Everyone who visits tries the ice cream, and most are so impressed that they come back again and again to sample scoops in different flavours.

>> One day Jessica receives an anonymous letter. It warns her that one of her longest-standing employees, a man called Clive, has recently been overheard in a restaurant discussing taking up employment with a well-known local businessman who plans to enter the town's ice cream market with his own range. Jessica is very alarmed because Clive is a senior technician who has intimate knowledge of the recipe and special ingredients that have made her family's business so successful for three generations.

Questions

1   What different types of action should Jessica now consider taking?

2   What further information would you need to give her accurate advice?

3   What course of action would you advise, and why?

CHAPTER SUMMARY

• The Human Rights Act allows people to argue human rights points in cases in British courts, rather than having to go to the European Court of Human Rights in Strasbourg.

• The Data Protection Act gives workers a right of access to personal data held about them and the right to know the purpose for which that data will be used.

• There is a code of practice about how data should be processed and stored, issued by the Information Commissioner.

• An employer can monitor his workers within reason, but he should make them aware that this is being done, otherwise he breaches their privacy.

• There is now legal protection for whistleblowers, but this has been criticised for not being effective enough.

• Employers have to take care that any job references that they provide are accurate.

• An employer can protect trade secrets or other confidential information by including a restrictive covenant in the contract of employment.

REFERENCES

Carey, P. (2004) *Data Protection: A Practical Guide to UK and EU Law*. Oxford: Oxford University Press.

Chalton, J. (2010) 'Ten social media legal risks' *Employers' Law*, 10 November.

Drew, D. and Vause, A. (2007) 'Monitoring and surveillance—lessons from America' *Compliance Monitor*, February 2007, CM 19 5 (24).

Ford, M. (1999) 'The Data Protection Act 1998' *Industrial Law Journal* 28 (p57).

Ford, M. (2002) 'Two conceptions of worker privacy' *Industrial Law Journal* 31 (p135).

Information Commissioner's Office (2006) *The Durant case and its impact on the Data Protection Act* at www.ico.gov.uk.

Information Commissioner's Office *The Employment Practices Code* at www.ico.gov.uk.

Lewis, D. (2001) 'Whistleblowing at work: on what principles should legislation be based?' *Industrial Law Journal* 30 (p169).

Lewis, D. (2011) 'Ten years of Public Interest Disclosure Act claims: what can we learn from the statistics and recent research?' *Industrial Law Journal* (39) 3 (p325).

Lorber, S. (2004) 'Data protection and subject access requests' *Industrial Law Journal* 33 (p179).

Oliver, H. (2002) 'Email and internet monitoring in the workplace: information privacy and contracting-out' *Industrial Law Journal* 31 (p321).

Public Concern At Work (2010) 'Where's whistleblowing now? Ten years of legal protection for whistleblowers', www.pcaw.co.uk.

Syal, R. (2010) 'Tenfold rise in whistleblower cases taken to tribunal' *The Guardian*, 22 March.

Wallace-Bruce, N.L. (1997) 'Employers beware! The perils of providing an employment reference' *Journal of Business Law* (p456).

Wugmeister, M. and Bevitt, A. (2008) 'Comparing the US and EU approach to employee privacy' *Privacy and Data Protection*, March 2008.

ONLINE RESOURCE CENTRE

A range of online resources to help you through your employment law module have been developed by the author team. These include updates, self-test questions and sources for further reading. (www.oxfordtextbooks.co.uk/orc/taylor_emir3e)

TUPE

Learning outcomes

By the end of this chapter you should be able to:

- set out the core rights that employees have as a result of the TUPE legislation;

- advise about when TUPE applies and in what ways;

- advise about the requirement to consult employees in TUPE situations;

- distinguish between dismissals that are fair, automatically unfair and potentially fair when they occur for reasons related to a transfer;

- explain in what circumstances employers can and cannot lawfully alter contracts of employment following a merger, acquisition or any other kind of relevant transfer;

- appreciate the TUPE rights that apply in conditions of insolvency.

Introduction

TUPE (pronounced 'tupey') stands for Transfer of Undertakings Protection of Employment. The aim of TUPE Regulations is to protect the interests of employees when the business they work for changes hands, or when their part of an operation is acquired or transferred to another business. They also apply in merger situations, when in-house processes are outsourced, when a contract to provide a service transfers from one provider to another and when a public sector body such as a local authority 'contracts out' services, or indeed, brings formerly contracted out services back in house. They form a specialised corner of employment law, but one which can be very important for large numbers of people. The TUPE Regulations originate in the European Union's Acquired Rights Directive of 1977, so have been with us for many years. But they have long been considered by everyone with any knowledge of them as being overly complex and highly unsatisfactory. In 1999, when giving judgment in a case, the EAT said 'there is no doubt that the position in law in relation to transfers of undertakings is in a mess'. This was a very honest assessment of the position. In 1998 the European Union agreed a new Acquired Rights Directive, largely as a result of pressure from the UK government. The aim was to clarify some of the more significant issues, to take account of European Court rulings and generally to move some way towards sorting out 'the mess'. This new directive was supposed to be given effect by the national parliaments of all member states by June 2001. As a result the UK government undertook an extensive, wide-ranging consultation. The complexity of the issues meant that the timescale for implementation had to be adjusted first to the summer of 2002 (Sargeant, 2002), and then postponed again to Spring 2004 (Aikin, 2003). Draft regulations were finally issued in March 2005, the new Transfer of Undertakings (Protection of Employment) Regulations 2006 being introduced the following April. These wholly replaced the former 1981 Regulations and now provide the statutory basis of our law in this area. In many respects they have served to clarify matters while also bringing statute in to line with established case law. They also introduced some significant changes, particularly in respect of situations in which an insolvent firm is taken over. This whole area of law, however, remains highly complex and uncertain in important respects. It will thus unquestionably continue to be the source of much litigation in the future.

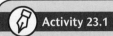

Activity 23.1

Read the following paragraphs and try to answer the questions that follow. If you return to the activity again when you have finished reading the chapter, you should be able to give full and accurate answers to the questions.

A carpet retailer used to employ several hundred people to fit the carpets that customers purchase in its chain of showrooms. It then cut costs dramatically by moving instead to a situation in which it employs no carpet-fitters, but instead contracts this work out to specialist carpet-fitting companies and to self-employed fitters who compete with one another to secure year-long contracts to serve stores in different parts of the country.

» The first annual contract to fit carpets purchased at the Birmingham showroom was won by a new firm (ABC fitters Ltd) set up by two former employees of the company with the generous redundancy payments they had recently received. Most of their employees are former colleagues. The contract was then renewed for a second year.

After two years the firm is obliged to compete with another much larger supplier (PQS fitters Ltd) to secure the contract for a third year. They are undercut in the bidding process and lose the contract to PQS. PQS pays its workers a lower hourly rate and has a less generous benefits package than ABC.

Questions

1   Is PQS obliged to take on the employees of ABC who work for 100% of their time on the contract described above?

2   If PQS refuses to take on ABC's employees what might the penalty be?

3   Can PQS take on ABC staff but then make changes to their contracts of employment?

Core TUPE rights

The Acquired Rights Directives and the UK's subsequent implementing legislation establish a number of rights that apply in TUPE situations. These are as follows:

1. Employees affected by a transfer have the right to be consulted formally before, during and after the transfer by both the transferor and transferee organisations.

2. Transferred employees have the right to have their continuity of service recognised by their new employer.

3. The content of contracts of employment transfer with the employees to whom they apply. It is usually unlawful to force changes to contracts as a result of a TUPE transfer.

4. Employment-related liabilities and benefits as well as collective agreements transfer along with employees in TUPE situations.

5. It is often unfair in law (or at least potentially unfair) to dismiss an employee for a reason related to a TUPE transfer.

6. There are obligations placed on transferors to give specific information to transferees about the employees who are transferring.

TUPE is usually seen as providing important legal rights protecting the interests of employees. It is important to remember, however, that in one very major respect they favour the interests of the employer. This is because they deny employees the right to object to being transferred across to another employment except where the regulations are not fully complied with. If an employee does object and resigns at the point of transfer, however many years' service he/she has, there can be no case for unfair dismissal or constructive dismissal unless there has been a change made in the level of terms and conditions (ie, TUPE is not followed) after the transfer.

On the surface the rights established under TUPE seem straightforward and comprehensive, even if they mainly apply to employees and not to all workers in an organisation (see Chapter 3). In fact 'straightforward' is the last word that should be used to describe the practical application of TUPE. In respect of most of the above rights there have long been major uncertainties that have left employers and employees unsure about whether any rights apply to their particular situation and if they do, exactly which and in what way. At root the uncertainty has derived from the fact that the original Acquired Rights Directive 1977 and the subsequent enacting legislation in the EU member states was overly simplistic, failing to take into account the complex reality of different types of transfer situation. As a result it has been necessary over the years for the courts (including on many occasions the ECJ) to decide when and how TUPE applies in particular situations. Unfortunately, the complexity of the situations often led different courts to come to apparently diverse conclusions. The result has been confusion, a tendency for employers to fight cases rather than to settle them, a deterrent for employees who are not certain of their rights and are thus reluctant to litigate, a need for specialist lawyers to be employed to advocate cases and a tendency for employers to avoid complying with the law (either knowingly or not knowingly) and to get away with it. There is no question that the 2006 Regulations have made an important contribution to reducing the uncertainty in some areas, but there remains plenty nonetheless, and they have certainly done little to reduce the complexity of the law.

 Exhibit 23.1

The extent to which employers, in practice, can avoid their obligations under TUPE and effectively ignore them is extraordinary. A few years ago a major international hotel company took over a smaller chain of hotels based exclusively in the UK. The UK company had formerly been owned by a brewery and was sold in its entirety. Thousands of employees were affected.

No consultation with staff took place either before or after the takeover, although it was no secret that talks about a possible takeover were taking place. Following the transfer, a number of senior managers were dismissed and their places taken by long-standing employees of the international hotel group. All staff were then issued with new contracts of employment. These were no less generous than their former terms and conditions, but they were standardised and thus did not allow for any local flexibility of the kind that had been practised in the UK hotels previously.

The vast majority of staff signed the new contracts. Some people decided to leave and look for new employment instead, but no one brought any legal action. The TUPE Regulations were apparently avoided entirely with no adverse consequences either to the purchaser or the seller of the company.

When does TUPE apply?

One of the most intractable issues with the TUPE Regulations has always been how to establish exactly when they apply and when they do not (tupe or not tupe, that is the question?). Various similar but slightly different legal tests have been applied over the years, including the 'going concern test', the 'business identity test', the 'test of the stable economic entity' and the 'organised group of workers test' (Sage, 2002). These are not alternatives and one does not override another. Rather all have been formulated by the ECJ when faced with different cases and all can be applied singly or together.

As a result of the case law and the (UK's) 2006 Regulations we can be clear about certain principles. For example, it is clear that TUPE does not apply when mere assets are sold. So, it is possible to sell a building, either with or without the equipment inside it, without the new owner needing to employ the people who work there at the time of the sale. TUPE only applies when a 'going concern', an 'economic entity' or 'an organised group of workers' is transferred along with the assets. This makes it possible for a business to sell on some premises to another owner without TUPE applying, but if the new owner continues to carry on the same business in those premises the Regulations do apply. The distinction, however, is not always so clear cut. What happens, for example, if an Italian restaurant is sold, but is then re-branded and redecorated, before being opened a few weeks later as an Indian restaurant? Do the same staff have to be re-employed on the same terms and conditions? The answer is apparently yes if the new owner continues to run the Italian restaurant for any length of time before effecting the re-branding exercise. It is also the case that no relevant transfer occurs when one individual or corporation simply sells shares in a company to another, resulting in a change of control. This is distinguished from a situation in which one company takes over another, because the same company remains the employer and no formal change of ownership takes place. In other respects the 2006 Regulations brought much needed clarity to the question of what is and what is not to be considered a 'relevant transfer', although important question marks remain (see Cavalier & Arthur, 2006; McMullen, 2006 and IDS, 2011 for a discussion of some of these).

It is helpful when trying to understand the law in this area to make a clear distinction between 'standard transfers' where a business/organisation or part of one changes hands and a 'service provision change' where a contract to provide a service switches from one provider to another.

Standard transfers

A number of conditions need to be in place here for TUPE to apply. First there must be a transfer of 'an economic entity'. The 2006 Regulations define these as *'organised groupings of resources which have the objective of pursuing an economic activity, whether or not that activity is central or ancillary'*. The requirement for this economic entity to be 'stable' as used to be the case, and remains the case in many EU countries, is no longer a requirement in the UK. The definition covers more or less any situation in which an enterprise or organisation exists with assets and people which carries out some kind of economic activity. Importantly, it can apply where only one person is employed in a relevant job.

Secondly the 'economic entity' must retain its identity following the transfer. This means, in practice, that after the transfer has taken place the new owners/management must continue to run it as a going concern, even if only for a short period. TUPE does not apply when it is just assets that are being sold—such as a list of customers or a brand name or a factory building. Transfers within a group of companies do generally amount to a TUPE transfer as do transfers that take place between separate public sector bodies such as NHS trusts or local authorities. However, the 2006 Regulations make it clear that transfers of staff between separate government departments should not be considered to constitute TUPE transfers.

Finally, in order for the UK's TUPE Regulations to apply the entity which is being transferred must be 'situated' in the UK immediately prior to the transfer taking place. Sales of subsidiary companies (or parts of them) based overseas, even if owned and controlled from the UK, are not therefore covered. Sales of UK-based entities to overseas-based entities are, however, covered in so far as rights are enforceable in the UK courts.

Over the years different ECJ rulings have carried weight in the UK courts. In the last few years, however, it has become apparent that the leading case ('seminal' according to IDS, 2011:22) in this field is a Dutch one called *Spijkers v Gebroeders Benedik Abbatoir CV* which was originally decided in the ECJ in 1986. Under the *Spijkers* approach most transfers of a going concern are effectively covered by the TUPE Regulations—and this situation is now reflected in our statutes, thanks to the 2006 Regulations.

Spijkers sets out a 'shopping list' of factors for tribunals to consider when deciding whether an economic entity has or has not been transferred for the purposes of TUPE. This 'shopping list' approach involves looking at various factors *immediately* before and *immediately* after the transfer in order to establish whether or not 'an economic entity' has in fact been preserved. The list is as follows:

- the type of business or undertaking concerned
- whether the business's tangible assets are transferred
- the value of the intangible assets at the time of the transfer
- whether or not the majority of the employees are taken over by the new employer
- whether or not its customers are transferred
- the degree of similarity between the activities carried on before and after the transfer
- the period, if any, for which those activities are suspended.

The 2006 Regulations are also framed in such a way as to close a loophole that used to exist whereby employers simply avoided TUPE obligations by taking on no staff from the past entity at all. In *Cheeseman and others v R Brewer Contracts Ltd* (2001) and *ADI (UK) v Willer* (2001) the EAT and the Court of Appeal established that a transferee company cannot avoid its obligations under the TUPE Regulations *simply* by refusing to transfer the majority of the staff engaged in the relevant activities. In assessing such cases tribunals have been obliged, according to these authorities, to check the reason why the staff have not transferred. If it is concluded that the reason why the incoming employer is refusing to accept a transfer of staff is to avoid obligations under TUPE, then the fact that the staff have not transferred will not prevent the existence of a transfer. The staff (or the liability for them) will transfer in any event. The 2006 Regulations enshrine this position in statute by stating that it is a relevant transfer whenever a group of employees is organised to carry out a body of work *immediately before* a transfer takes place.

Service provision changes

The 2006 Regulations clarified the position here by stating that provided the following conditions are in place TUPE *does* apply where:

- prior to the transfer there is an organised grouping of employees assigned to carry out service activities on behalf of a particular client,
- this is the principal purpose of the grouping.

BUT that TUPE *does not* apply in the following situations:

- where the transfer is between two 'public administrative authorities',

- where there is no organised grouping of staff or resources with the principal purpose of serving the needs of one particular client,
- where there is no on-going relationship between the contractor and the client (including situations where a client purchases one-off services on a number of occasions),
- where the contract is mainly to supply goods to a client rather than services (eg, a company which provides sandwiches to be sold in a canteen).

Importantly in the case of service provision changes, unlike standard transfers, there is no need for there to be a retention of an entity's identity. By creating a distinct category of transfers called 'service provision changes' the 2006 Regulations have effectively extended the number of situations in which TUPE does apply very considerably. For example it is now the case, as it was not before, that where a professional services firm employs a person or group of people to work for most of their time on a single client's account, and that contract is lost, the new provider is obliged to take on the employees concerned.

 **Activity 23.2**

Organisation A (Large-Org) takes over Organisation B (Small-Org). It is accepted that this is a 'relevant transfer' and that the TUPE Regulations apply in respect of all Small-Org's employees. Small-Org is solvent at the time it is taken over. However, after the transfer has taken place some TUPE-related issues arise which managers think could be legally significant. They ask your advice about the following:

1 It becomes clear that three former Small-Org employees have outstanding employment tribunal claims awaiting a hearing. They are alleging that a senior manager of Small-Org, who has since left, sexually harassed them at last year's Christmas party. Managers of Large-Org were not told about this outstanding case prior to the transfer taking place.

2 Following the takeover managers decide that henceforth they will exclusively use Large-Org's established providers of services across all operations. This involves terminating contracts with the following:

- Small-Org's lawyers (two solicitors there work 100% of their time on Small-Org's affairs)
- Small-Org's caterers (they have delivered 500 sandwiches each day to Small-Org's premises for ten years)
- Small-Org's courier firm (they have delivered all Small-Org's high-value parcels and packages for three years).

3 A month after the takeover managers decide to terminate three contracts with immediate effect:

- Small-Org's finance director on the grounds that they do not need two FDs
- A florist employed by Small-Org on a casual basis to provide fresh flower displays each week for the public areas of their premises
- A marketing administrator formerly employed by Small-Org who has been absent on grounds of 'stress' since negotiations about a possible takeover first took place three months ago.

Question

What advice would you give managers of the newly merged company about each of these outstanding issues?

Consultation requirements

The requirement for employers to share information and to consult with employees collectively both before and after a transfer has taken place has always been a feature of the TUPE Regulations. Obligations in this respect are placed on both the transferor and the transferee organisation. Until 1995, however, in UK law the need to consult was restricted to situations in which trade unions were recognised and there was only a need to consult with their representatives. The position was changed in 1995 and again in 1999 to ensure that the UK met its obligations under the Acquired Rights Directive. The ECJ had earlier found that the UK was in breach of the Directive in not providing a general, universal right to information and consultation. The Collective Redundancies & Transfer of Undertakings (Protection of Employment) (Amendment) Regulations 1999 constitute the current statute governing this area of law.

In many respects consultation rights prior to the transfer of an organisation to new owners are similar to those in the case of redundancy (see Chapter 6). The differences are as follows:

- there is a duty to inform representatives of any employees to be affected by the transfer, consultation is only required with those representing employees who will be affected by 'new measures' related to the transfer, and
- there are no minimum time periods in which consultation must take place and the maximum protective award is thirteen weeks' pay.

Where there is a recognised trade union it must be the body consulted. Where there is no trade union recognised, consultation must be with other employee representatives. In such circumstances elections must be organised by the employer to identify representatives with whom consultation can take place, sufficient numbers being elected to represent the interests of all employees who are likely to be affected by the proposed transfer either directly or indirectly. All of the people in these categories must then be entitled to vote. Those elected must be allowed reasonable paid time off to attend training events designed to help them in their role. Moreover, victimisation provisions apply in the case of anyone taking part in an election (ie, voters as well as candidates). So employers cannot lawfully cause anyone a detriment because they have sought to exercise these legal rights.

Irrespective of whether or not representatives are elected, for whatever reason, the employer is obliged in any case to inform employees individually and in advance of the transfer of:

- the proposed date of the transfer,
- the reason for the transfer,
- the legal, economic and social implications for employees,
- any measures that it is envisaged may be taken which will affect employees.

Employment tribunals have the discretion to award up to thirteen weeks' gross pay to each affected employee in cases where an employer is found not to have fulfilled the above obligations—a so-called 'protective award'. The 2006 Regulations made a significant change in this area by making it possible for a case to be brought 'jointly and severally'. This makes both parties to a transfer (ie, the transferor and the transferee) liable in principle for the payment of a protective award following a failure to consult or inform sufficiently.

Exhibit 23.2

TUPE law is especially complex on the question of with whom employers should provide information and consult with and when.

The requirement vis-à-vis information sharing is to include 'all affected employees' or their representatives. This is a broad category that will encompass people who are not themselves to be transferred, but whose work may in some shape or form be affected.

With consultation it is a narrower group who are included. The Regulations here refer to those who will be subject to measures taken by the employer in connection with the transfer. This is generally taken to mean people whose conditions or working practices may change. It will largely be people who are themselves to be transferred.

On the question of when consultation and information sharing should begin, the law is not entirely clear. In *BIFU v Barclays Bank plc* (1987) it was established that the obligation to consult applies even if a transfer does not actually ever take place, yet in *IPCS v Secretary of State for Defence* (1987) it was found that the obligation to consult only kicks in when the employer has 'formulated some definite plan or proposal' which it intends to implement. Merely contemplating the possibility of a TUPE transfer is not sufficient to mean that the need to consult or share information is triggered.

It thus appears that consultation starts when there is a definite identifiable plan on the table and must take place even if the likelihood of the plan ever being put into action is limited.

Source: Deakin and Morris (2009:817–818)

Contractual rights

This part of the TUPE Regulations is intended to ensure as far as is practicable that the terms and conditions enjoyed by employees at the time of the transfer continue afterwards and are recognised by the new employer. In practice, the law is framed rather more broadly to cover the contract of employment itself as well as *'all the transferor's rights, powers, duties and liabilities under or in connection with any such contract'*. This means that it is not only express terms of contract which transfer with employees (hours, pay, holiday entitlement, job title, etc), but also generally job descriptions, notice periods, bonus schemes, discretionary rights, benefits and, as a general rule, liability for unpaid wages, unpaid holiday, etc. The only time when these last liabilities may not sometimes transfer is in the case of takeovers of insolvent companies (see below).

Occupational pension rights are the only exception to the principle that contracts transfer along with businesses or any other 'stable economic entities'. For many years this posed a major problem for employees who lost out when being transferred from an employer with a good, generous occupational scheme (eg, a local government department) to a transferee which offered inferior pensions or no scheme at all. Indeed, the absence of pension obligations on the part of transferees provided a financial incentive to contract out established in-house services because payroll costs were lowered as a result. The Pensions Act 2004, which came into force in April 2005, for the first time ensured that a transferee employer must offer transferring staff pension benefits which are comparable to those offered by the former employer. This had been the situation in local government transfers to private sector contractors for some time, but since 2005 has applied to all transfers. However, the extent to which the pensions arrangements offered are actually comparable is sometimes questionable. It is still in practice the case that people end up with less satisfactory pensions if they are transferred—although they do not lose their pension rights altogether as they often used to.

Prior to 2006 collective agreements did not transfer with employees except insofar as they determined individual terms and conditions of employment. This is no longer the case. The transferee must now honour any collective agreement made by the transferor—although that does not preclude future changes being negotiated with representatives provided the result does not conflict with the right of individual employees to have their contracts honoured. Generally union recognition must now transfer too, although the new Regulations do provide that this should not happen/should cease once any transferred group of employees ceases to maintain a separate identity from other employees following the transfer.

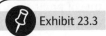

Exhibit 23.3   *Parkwood Leisure Ltd v Alemo-Herron* **(2010) and** *Worrall et al v Wilmott Dixon Partnership Ltd* **(2010)**

These two cases concern situations in which collectively agreed terms and conditions transferred with employees at the time of a TUPE transfer because the relevant collective agreement had been incorporated into their individual contracts of employment. They both involved situations in which private sector organisations had taken over part of the activities of public authorities.

In both cases, the Court of Appeal and the EAT respectively, decided that a 'static' approach needed to be taken, whereby only the elements of a collective agreement that were in force at the time of a transfer need transfer with the employees. Subsequent changes made by the former public sector employers in negotiations with trade unions do not apply once people have transferred.

It is frequently and understandably the case that employers who have received employees from another employer in a TUPE transfer wish to harmonise terms and conditions so that all employees are employed on equal terms. It is commonly believed by employers that they are 'safe' to force through contractual changes to bring about harmonisation two years or so after the TUPE transfer has taken place. In fact this is most definitely not the case. TUPE specifically exists to prevent transferees from doing this. Its purpose is to protect employees' contractual rights and there is no 'safe' time. The longer the period that passes, the easier it becomes to convince a tribunal that a contractual change is for reasons other than the transfer, but the extent to which this can be argued inevitably varies depending on individual circumstances.

Contracts can only be changed in two specific situations—both of which require employee consent (or that of trade union representatives) in any event:

1. where the changes are for a reason unconnected with the transfer (ie, incidental to it)

2. where the changes are for a reason connected with the transfer, but are due to an 'economic, technical or organisational reason' (known as a valid ETO reason).

This latter provision was introduced in 2006 in order to make it somewhat easier for employers to make changes, with agreement, post-transfer. As yet little significant case law has been made to help define exactly when these ETO reasons will and will not apply. It is, however, likely that the scope will be narrow as it has long been in the case of dismissals following TUPE transfers. Here it is only permissible when there are changes '*in job functions or numbers of the workforce as a whole*'.

In practical terms, therefore, employers must take great care when trying to harmonise terms and conditions following a TUPE transfer. It is wise for them to ensure that the harmonisation involves no reduction in pay or any other rights and that some form of financial inducement is offered to boot so as to reduce the risk of claims. It is definitely very unwise to seek to force through changes using heavy-handed tactics of the kind that are used sometimes to effect contractual changes in non-TUPE situations and which we discussed in Chapter 7 (time-limited offers, threats not to increase the pay of those who do not accept new terms, threats to dismiss/rehire etc).

It is important to note that continuity of employment must also be honoured following a transfer and that all policies and procedures which are contractual transfer along with the staff. Hence if people's pay is performance-related, the new employer must continue the system and pay performance-based bonuses relating to the whole review period, even if that includes months prior to the transfer having taken place. The same is true of profit-sharing schemes, stock option plans and any other contractual bonus schemes (Aikin, 2003:116–120). The principle of continuity also applies to contractual disciplinary and grievance procedures. If a particular employee is mid-way through a procedure it continues on the same timescale following the transfer. Redundancy procedures are particularly significant in many TUPE situations because rounds of redundancies often follow transfers. Here too it is important to remember that contractual procedures transfer with employees and have to be honoured.

 Activity 23.3   Abolition of the 'two-tier' code

Under UK Transfer of Undertakings (TUPE) Regulations special rules apply to private sector organisations which take over services previously provided by a public sector agency (ie, public to private outsourcing). These help ensure, for example, that a 'broadly comparable pension scheme' is provided by the new employer.

Under a 'two-tier workforce code' introduced in 2003, even after the transfer any new employees hired had to be employed on 'no less favourable conditions' than their former public sector colleagues.

The statutory code for central government organisations was withdrawn in December 2010 and replaced with a voluntary code which merely urges reasonableness and consultation with recognised trade unions. In March 2011 the equivalent two-tier local government code was withdrawn.

At the time of writing (summer 2011) consultation is ongoing about the future of provisions which require private sector transferees to provide high-quality pensions for staff transferring across to them from public sector organisations.

Questions

1   Why do you think the Blair government introduced a binding 'two tier code' for organisations which take over functions that were formerly carried out by central or local government employees?

2   Why do you think the Coalition government has decided to replace the binding code with one of a voluntary nature?

Unfair dismissal rights

Just as it is generally unlawful to alter a contract for a TUPE-related reason, it is considered unfair in law to dismiss an employee for a TUPE-related reason. The precise position here changed in 2006 with the abolition of the rather unsatisfactory situation whereby TUPE dismissals were listed as 'automatically unfair' but in practice could be fair in limited circumstances. The position is now clearer, but not hugely more helpful from an employer perspective. Here, as is the case for contractual changes, the term 'ETO' is used meaning 'economic, technical or organisational' reasons. The position basically stated is now as follows:

1. Dismissals which are principally due to the transfer itself or a reason connected with the transfer which does not fall into the ETO category are *automatically unfair*. This means that they are effectively outlawed in the case of employees with more than a year's service. There is no defence.

2. Dismissals which are for a reason connected with the transfer but one which does fall into the ETO category are considered *potentially fair*. Like dismissals on grounds of redundancy or misconduct, they are thus fair if the employer can convince a tribunal that they were carried out reasonably.

3. Dismissals which take place after the transfer has occurred but are not for reasons connected to the transfer will be *fair* in law, provided of course that in all other respects they meet the expectations of unfair dismissal law.

Importantly, and often not appreciated, is the continuation since 2006 of the established rule which only permits unfair dismissal claims to be brought by employees who have completed a year's service (likely soon to be two years) even in cases of automatically unfair dismissals for a TUPE reason. So employers are 'safe' to dismiss recent starters who transfer even if the reason is TUPE-related and there is no ETO reason. This is not of course the case for those who do have more than a year's service as employees. It is also important to appreciate that all employees affected are potentially covered in this situation and not just people who have actually transferred. Non-transferring employees in either the transferor or transferee organisations who are nonetheless dismissed for a transfer-related reason are equally entitled to bring claims provided they have a year's continuous service. Crucially, and again often unappreciated, this includes people who are dismissed shortly before a transfer goes through.

There is nothing new in principle with the situation in which an employer can lawfully dismiss for a transfer-related reason and where there is a valid ETO reason. There is voluminous case law on this subject and it is not straightforward always to be sure whether or not a particular situation does or does not fall within or outside the law. Generally, however, it is wise to play safe. The courts have long had a tendency to construe 'ETO' narrowly and are reluctant to create new precedents in this area which help employers to dismiss lawfully. The actual wording of the Regulations on this point is as follows:

> where the sole or principal reason for the dismissal is an economic, technical or organisational reason entailing changes in the workforce of either the transferor or the transferee before or after a relevant transfer.

This places the onus on the employer to show that a genuine ETO reason existed to justify the dismissal. Moreover, of course, even if they do so successfully, the dismissal will only be fair in law if they are further found to have acted reasonably in the manner in which the dismissal was carried out. There thus remains a big legal gap here which will be filled only once test cases are decided in the higher courts—namely the question of how a reasonable employer should deal procedurally with a dismissal that is transfer-related but for an ETO reason. The case law in this area is complex covering various situations in which employers have sought to argue that an ETO reason did apply and where dismissed employees argued that there was no valid ETO reason. Employers are therefore advised to take legal advice whenever they are in doubt before dismissing. What is clear, however, is that in order for an ETO reason to apply there must be a change in the content of jobs carried out by the workforce or a reduction in overall numbers—and preferably both.

 Activity 23.4   **What is a valid economic reason?**

In *Wheeler v Patel & J Golding Group of Companies* (1987), Mrs Wheeler ran a shop on behalf of its owner, Mr Golding. He wanted to sell the shop to Mr Patel, but Mr Patel was reluctant to buy the shop if he had to employ Mrs Wheeler. He was prepared to go ahead with the purchase in these circumstances, but would offer a good deal less money. In the event Mr Patel did buy the shop at the higher price. This was achieved by Mr Golding dismissing Mrs Wheeler three days before the completion of the sale.

Mrs Wheeler brought a tribunal claim naming both Mr Golding and Mr Patel as respondents. She had, she claimed, been dismissed because of a transfer and that was unfair. Mr Patel claimed that he was not legally liable because Mrs Wheeler had not been employed in the shop 'immediately before the transfer'. Mr Golding said that his decision to dismiss was justified for an ETO reason. In this case it was economic. A higher price was paid for the shop without Mrs Wheeler than would have been paid had she remained an employee.

Mrs Wheeler lost her claim at the employment tribunal, but then went on successfully to appeal to the EAT. Mr Patel was not liable. Mr Golding, however, was. The EAT decided, importantly, to make a distinction between economic reasons that relate to the conduct of the business (eg, insufficient funds to pay to keep someone) and economic reasons that did not. In this case the reason for the dismissal was a desire on Mr Golding's part to get a better price for the sale. That did not relate to the conduct of the business itself, so no ETO reason applied. It was an unfair dismissal.

By contrast, in *Whitehouse v Chas A Blatchford and Sons Ltd* (1999) Mr Whitehouse was one of thirteen employees working on a contract to supply prosthetic appliances to a large hospital. When the contract came up for renewal Mr Whitehouse's employers were unsuccessful, losing the work to a company called Blatchfords.

Blatchfords won the contract after assuring the hospital that they would provide a less expensive service by reducing staff costs. As a condition of winning the contract they were required to reduce the number of employees from thirteen to twelve. Mr Whitehouse thus transferred to Blatchfords but was soon made redundant. He lost his case at the Court of Appeal. The reason for the dismissal was fair because it was 'economic'. Blatchfords would not have won the contract had they not agreed in advance to reduce the headcount from thirteen to twelve.

Questions

1 How do you think the Court of Appeal was able to distinguish the circumstances that prevailed in Mrs Wheeler's case from those which applied in Mr Whitehouse's case?

2 Do you think the distinction is a valid one?

3 What are the main arguments for and against allowing employers to dismiss for economic reasons very close to the time of a transfer?

Sharing of information between transferors and transferees

An innovation introduced by the 2006 TUPE Regulations was the placing of a positive legal duty on transferors to provide transferees with classes of information about transferring employees ahead of the completion of a transfer. The purpose is to ensure that transferees are fully aware of any outstanding liabilities that they may be taking on in respect of employees, including outstanding grievance disputes or pending employment tribunal cases. The information to be provided includes the following in respect of each transferring employee:

- name
- age
- particulars of employment (ie, the same as must be given to the employees when they start employment)
- details of all grievance and disciplinary actions within the past two years
- information about outstanding tribunal or other court claims and any resolved in the past two years
- information about any collective agreements which will continue to have effect following a transfer.

This information needs to be provided either 'in writing' or in some other 'readily accessible form' at least fourteen days prior to the transfer date. Where this new duty is not complied with, the transferee can complain to an employment tribunal provided the claim is lodged within three months of the transfer. Transferors who are found not to have fully complied will be ordered to do so and 'may' also be required to pay compensation to the transferee where a loss has been sustained as a result of the failure to comply.

Insolvency

The 2006 Regulations introduced several quite complex changes to the existing TUPE Regulations in respect of the takeover of insolvent businesses. As matters stood, the fact that a business was insolvent when taken over did not reduce liability in any way as far as TUPE responsibilities to employees were concerned. The transferee had to make redundancy payments and pick up the tab for any unpaid wages, holiday pay, employers' national insurance contributions, etc—indeed all debts passed to the transferee. It was also the case that the new employer was liable for unfair dismissal claims made by employees even if they were dismissed by the transferor before the transfer took place. In insolvency cases this can be a large sum of money as it is not uncommon to dismiss people quickly (if unlawfully) as a means of helping to shore a business up financially before it becomes insolvent. This was widely believed to discourage would-be purchasers from stepping in to rescue insolvent businesses before they were wound up by receivers.

The new Regulations address these issues by stating that most payments of this kind which are statutory and employment-related (labelled 'relevant debts') do not now transfer when an insolvent business is purchased. This includes pay in lieu of notice, unpaid holiday pay and outstanding redundancy payments. The details, however, are quite complex. For example, with redundancy payments, employees who are made redundant just before the transfer of an insolvent firm takes place will claim the statutory figure from the National Insurance Fund, but have to claim any amount that is owed to them contractually over and above the statutory minimum from the transferee company. More significantly, in many respects, it is now possible for transferor, transferee or receivers to negotiate changes to terms and conditions that are transfer-related and are not for an ETO reason where a firm that is insolvent is being transferred.

 Exhibit 23.4   *Longden and Paisley v Ferrari Ltd and Kennedy International* (1994)

This case shows how an important distinction is made between dismissals that are undertaken in order to make the sale of a solvent business more attractive, and those which take place when a company is insolvent.

Ferrari was placed into receivership in 1991. The receivers negotiated the sale of the company to Kennedy International Ltd, who in turn provided them with a list of the employees they wished to retain following the transfer. Mr Longden and Mr Paisley's names were not on this list.

Two weeks before the sale, the two men were dismissed by the receivers, the reason being given that they were redundant. They subsequently brought tribunal claims alleging unfair dismissal.

The EAT ruled that the men had not been employed immediately before the transfer and that Kennedy International could not thus be liable. On the question of the dismissal it was found that it was fair. The main reason that the two men had been made redundant was the fact that Ferrari was insolvent. The transfer itself was not the main reason. Whether the sale had gone ahead or not, the two men would have lost their jobs.

CHAPTER SUMMARY

- The Transfer of Undertakings Regulations originate in Europe. They are intended to extend a good measure of protection to employees whose jobs are affected when the entity they are employed by is taken over by or merges with or is subcontracted to another organisation.

- The TUPE Regulations also apply when one contractor loses the contract to provide an organisation with services to another contractor.

- The Regulations require both the transferor organisation and the transferee to consult extensively with workforce representatives both before and after a TUPE transfer has taken place.

- Contracts cannot be changed by the transferee for a reason related to the transfer unless there is a valid economic, technical or organisational (ETO) reason. Continuity of employment must also be observed following a transfer.

- It is automatically unfair to dismiss someone simply because of a transfer. However, it is considered to be potentially fair if there is a valid ETO reason.

- When companies take over insolvent organisations some TUPE Regulations no longer apply. This is true of the extent to which the new employer is responsible for paying employment-related debts accrued by the insolvent employer.

- For updates and further materials, please see the online resource centre at www.oup.com.

REFERENCES

Aikin, O. (2003) *Tolley's Managing Business Transfers*. Edited by Murray Fairclough. Croydon: Reed Elsevier.

Cavalier, S. & Arthur, R. (2006) *Providing a Service? The New TUPE Regulations 2006*. Liverpool: Institute of Employment Rights.

Deakin, S. & Morris, G. (2005) *Labour Law*. Fourth Edition. Oxford: Hart Publishing.

IDS (2011) *Transfer of Undertakings: Employment Law Handbook*. London: Incomes Data Services.

McMullen, J. (2006) 'An analysis of the Transfer of Undertakings (Protection of Employment) Regulations 2006' *Industrial Law Journal* 35.2.

Sage, G. (2002) *TUPE: A Practical Guide*. London: The Law Society.

Sargeant, M. (2002) 'New transfer regulations' *Industrial Law Journal* 31 (p35).

ONLINE RESOURCE CENTRE

 A range of online resources to help you through your employment law module have been developed by the author team. These include updates, self-test questions and sources for further reading. (www.oxfordtextbooks.co.uk/orc/taylor_emir3e)

Health and safety

PART V

Health and safety— the criminal law

$$24$$

Learning outcomes

By the end of this chapter you should be able to:

- identify the different sources of law in the field of health and safety;

- distinguish between the impact of the criminal and civil law arms of health and safety law;

- outline the main provisions of the Health and Safety at Work Act 1974;

- advise about the meaning of the term 'as far as is reasonably practicable' in health and safety law;

- explain the significance of risk assessments and policy statements;

- identify the major roles and responsibilities of the two health and safety inspectorates;

- advise on the management of trade union health and safety representatives;

- set out the major duties placed on employers in health and safety regulations;

- contribute to the major public policy debates on the proper role of the criminal law in health and safety management.

Introduction

The amount of health and safety law that UK employers must contend with is very substantial. It grows each year and changes regularly. It is also the subject of a great deal of criticism both from those who consider the UK to be over-regulated and those who think that more regulation, or at least more effective sanctions, are needed in order to give a more acceptable and effective level of protection. Health and safety is often seen as being a specialised area of legal practice, separate from (though related to) employment law. Moreover, of course, it covers obligations owed by organisations that spread well beyond employees and others who work on their sites to customers and the public in general. For all these reasons, it is often given cursory treatment in texts on employment law or, in some cases not mentioned at all except in passing or where it relates to other employment rights such as unfair dismissal or pregnancy.

It is impossible in three chapters to cover the field of health and safety law in great depth. Most of the regulations are specialised in nature and concern only particular industries, so we have confined our analysis to three core areas. In this chapter we introduce health and safety law in general terms, before describing and assessing those aspects which fall under the jurisdiction of the criminal courts. In Chapter 25 our attention turns to claims for compensation of the kind which injured workers bring against employers who they consider to have breached a legal duty or acted negligently. Finally, in Chapter 26 we focus in detail on the most significant and highly contested recent development in the health and safety field, namely the Working Time Regulations.

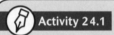 **Activity 24.1**

Consider the following statements. Which do you think are correct and which are false?

1 The criminal law plays a marginal role in the enforcement of health and safety standards in UK workplaces.

2 The Health and Safety at Work Act 1974 sets out in considerable detail what employers must do if they are to avoid prosecution under health and safety statutes.

3 Trade union-appointed health and safety representatives enjoy a number of significant legal privileges.

4 A great deal of health and safety law has a European origin.

5 Health and safety inspectors have the power to close down workplaces they consider to be unsafe.

6 Many commentators question the extent to which the criminal law on health and safety serves a useful purpose in practice.

7 It is generally agreed that the Health and Safety at Work Act and the current regime of inspection achieves its objectives effectively and efficiently.

Return to this activity once you have read the chapter, to see how many of your answers were correct.

The structure of health and safety law

The first and most important point to make by way of introduction to health and safety law is that it is clearly divided into two parts. Both are equally significant from an employer's perspective and seek to achieve the same outcome over the long term (ie, a safe and healthy working environment). They also share some core principles in common, but they operate in very different ways. On the one hand there is a 'criminal law arm', on the other a 'civil law arm' (see figure 24.1). The criminal law, as was explained in Chapter 2, is enforced primarily by agencies of the state, and if found guilty a defendant is punished in some way as a means of deterring others. In the case of health and safety law the principal enforcement agencies

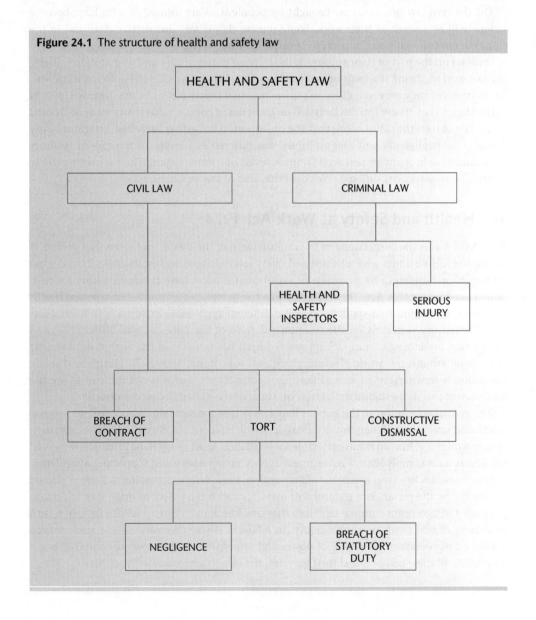

Figure 24.1 The structure of health and safety law

are the health and safety inspectorates operated by local authorities and, at a national level, by the Health and Safety Executive. Their inspectors undertake regular visits to premises and can require that changes are made to procedures and practices if they are unhappy with what they find. A failure to make such changes is one of two situations in which an organisation (or sometimes its senior directors) can find itself in the dock of a criminal court. The other is where a major incident, usually (but not always) resulting in death or serious injury, occurs as a result of an organisation's failure to abide by the principles of health and safety law. In such cases the Director of Public Prosecutions (or the Procurator Fiscal in Scotland) may bring the case against the organisation concerned. Criminal liability for health and safety issues is the subject of this chapter.

On the civil law side cases are brought by people who are injured or who have become seriously ill as a result of their work. Some pursue claims for constructive dismissal in the employment tribunal (see Chapter 25) because they have resigned due to a supposed breach of contract on the part of their employer, the implied duties of care and to maintain safe systems of working being the basis of most such claims. Where people have suffered more serious detriments they are more likely to pursue personal injury claims in the County Court or in the High Court. These too can be based on breaches of contract, but many more are rooted in the law of tort, the claim being that the organisation has either breached a statutory duty or has acted negligently and that an injury was suffered as a result. In the case of fatalities such claims are brought by bereaved families, levels of compensation rising according to the extent of any detriment suffered. We cover this area of law in Chapter 25.

The Health and Safety at Work Act 1974

The HSWA forms the cornerstone of the criminal arm of the health and safety law system. It sets up the regime under which health and safety law is policed and establishes all the central principles that underpin its governance. Subsequent statutes have taken the form of regulations issued under this Act. The 1974 Act effectively replaced a number of separate health and safety regulations that applied somewhat different approaches in different industrial sectors. The Act draws heavily on the recommendations of the Robens Committee (1972) and has formed something of a model approach which has influenced the evolution of similar systems all around the world (Gunningham and Johnstone, 1999:6–7). Health and safety legislation is now largely an area of European competence, but it is not difficult to see the influence of this well-established UK law on some of the EU's more recent directives.

The central conclusion of the Robens Report was that the state should not seek to regulate health and safety through lengthy, detailed codes which set out exactly what is expected in each type of workplace. Instead it was preferable for legislation to set out general principles which all employers must comply with, a government agency giving advice and supporting a regulatory regime that relies to a great extent on self-regulation. Compliance, according to Robens, should be ensured by the presence of government inspectors with the power to make spot checks on premises and significant criminal sanctions that could be applied when a serious lapse in health and safety caused death or serious injury. In addition it was necessary to give trade union-appointed representatives a degree of power and responsibility to encourage compliance at a local level. All these points found their way into the Health and Safety at Work Act.

Reasonableness

Fundamental to the HSWA is a general requirement on all employers to act reasonably vis-à-vis the health and safety of their employees. Failing to to so may result in criminal prosecution; successfully doing so provides the basis for a defence in situations where a serious injury has occurred. The precise formulation is set out in section 2:

> It shall be the duty of every employer to ensure, as far as is reasonably practicable, the health, safety and welfare at work of all his employees.

The Act then goes on broaden this general statement with some more specific requirements:

- to maintain plant and equipment and to provide safe systems of working
- to ensure safe arrangements for handling, use, transport and storage of hazardous equipment and/or substances
- to provide all necessary information, training and supervision in the use of hazardous equipment/substances
- to ensure that entrances and exits to buildings are safe and maintained
- to provide adequate facilities and arrangements to ensure welfare at work.

Later sections of the Act place employers under a similar duty, though set out in less detail, to take reasonable steps to protect sub-contractors, self-employed people and anyone else working on a premises who is not actually employed by the employer who controls the workplace.

Section 2 of the HSWA has the advantage of incorporating wording that can apply in every workplace. This was new in 1974 because many workplaces including hospitals, hotels and schools had not been covered by safety laws prior to that (Whincup, 1997:304). But the wording can also be criticised for being so vague as to prevent any employer from being certain that it is complying with the law. What managers consider to be 'reasonably practicable' can easily differ from what judges think. Over time Health and Safety Commission codes of practice (now issued by the Health and Safety Executive) and a large body of case law have helped to provide further information, but at the end of the day using a general test of 'reasonableness' is always going to leave a lot of room for different interpretations. For example, as Kloss (2010:143–144) points out, we still have no definitive ruling on the extent to which smaller employers with limited resources are lawfully able to adhere to less stringent safety requirements than large PLCs or public sector corporations operating similar workplaces.

What has been established through the case law about the term 'reasonably practicable' is the following:

- employers are expected to do what is feasible in the light of current knowledge to protect the health and safety of their employees
- steps must be taken unless it would be unreasonable to expect them to be taken
- decisions must be taken with reference to formal risk assessments and comparison of any risk with the costs involved, actions being considered reasonable unless there is a gross disparity.

> **Activity 24.2   *R v Swan Hunter* (1981)**
>
> Swan Hunter ran a shipyard in which a tragic accident took place. Eight men, including employees of the company, were killed when a fire broke out in a confined space on a ship that was being constructed. The fire was caused when an employee of Swan Hunter ignited some leaking oxygen with his welding torch. However, it was accepted that he had not himself acted at all negligently. The fire had in effect been caused by another man who had failed to turn off an oxygen supply when he left work the previous evening. This second man, however, was not employed by Swan Hunter, but by a sub-contractor.
>
> Both Swan Hunter and the sub-contractor, (a company called Telemeter) were convicted of breaching section 2 of the Health and Safety at Work Act and fined accordingly. Telemeter accepted its portion of the blame because it had not trained its employee about the flammability of oxygen. Swan Hunter, however, appealed against its conviction. It had trained all its employees in the safe use of oxygen and welding equipment and had thus complied with its duties under the Act. It did not believe that it was under a duty to take similar steps in respect of sub-contractors' employees. Swan Hunter lost its appeal.
>
> **Questions**
>
> 1   Is it fair to expect employers to take responsibility for the H&S training of all sub-contractors who work on their premises, even if only for a short time?
>
> 2   On what legal basis can it be argued that Swan Hunter were criminally liable in this case?

Risk assessments

Reasonableness on the part of an employer is in large part demonstrated by the provision of evidence that risk assessments have been carried out and acted upon. This idea is present in the HSWA 1974, but was subsequently formalised in the Management of Health and Safety at Work Regulations 1992. Since then all employers have been placed under a specific duty to carry out risk assessments covering all potential health and safety issues across their operations. Wherever more than five people are employed, the requirement is now to record both the findings of the risk assessment and to identify in this written report any groups of employees who are identified as being 'especially at risk'.

An approved code of practice issued alongside the regulations in 1992 (subsequently updated in 1999) gives detailed guidance on what needs to be done in order to comply with the regulations:

> A risk assessment should usually involve identifying the hazards present in any working environment or arising out of commercial activities and work activities, and evaluating the extent of the risks involved, taking account of existing precautions and their effectiveness

All employers should therefore take care to ensure that they have gone through this process and recorded the results. All potential risks to health and safety should be identified, and the likelihood of their causing any harm, the nature of the risk and the number of people who could be exposed to the risk stated. It is clearly necessary to update a risk assessment whenever new processes, machines or substances are introduced, but it should be regularly reviewed in any event.

Of course, carrying out a risk assessment in itself is not enough. The employer also has to show that it has responded by putting in place management systems, communication programmes and training arrangements appropriate to the level of risk identified. In some situations health surveillance measures might also need to be taken. All depends on the nature of the risks identified, and these are clearly going to be of a completely different order on a construction site or in a chemical plant than in an office building or shop.

Policy statements

Risk assessments serve to inform the content of health and safety policy statements. Under the HSWA all employers employing more than five people must have a written health and safety policy, the master copy of which is signed and dated by a senior manager. Stranks (2001:21) gives excellent advice about the appropriate content of such a policy. He suggests three sections:

1. A general statement of intent setting out the organisation's health and safety 'philosophy' and the major responsibilities vis-à-vis health and safety that each member of staff carries.

2. A section setting out exactly who is responsible for health and safety matters in the organisation—who monitors what, who is accountable for what and the chain of command in terms of management responsibility.

3. A statement of arrangements that are in place for the management of health and safety in the workplace—training systems, precautionary measures, systems for recording accidents, supervision, storage arrangements, etc.

Stranks stresses the importance of a policy statement being seen to be a 'living document', continually being reviewed and updated. As new hazards become apparent or risks to health increase, the policy should be adapted. A failure to do so is evidence that an employer is not acting 'reasonably' and is thus breaching the HSWA.

Health and safety representatives

Kloss (2010:156) shows that involving employees in the management of health and safety at work either directly or via trade union representation has a long-established history in well-managed workplaces. The Robens commitee identified it as being a key feature of good practice, and since 1974 it has been a statutory duty. The HSWA required employers to consult with health and safety representatives appointed by recognised trade unions, but charged these people with the task of representing the interests of the whole workforce, and not just union members. In 1996, following a European Court ruling, the law was amended via the Health and Safety (Consultation with Employees) Regulations to ensure that all employers consulted with workforce representatives even if they did not recognise a trade union.

The role of the trade union health and safety representative is to investigate hazards and accidents, to investigate any complaints from members about health and safety matters, to carry out regular inspections, to liaise with health and safety inspectors and to attend meetings of H&S committees.

A Health and Safety Commission code of practice recommends that they should not have been employed at the premises for less than two years on appointment. The number of reps which is appropriate is not stipulated in the relevant regulations, but is a matter of judgement depending on the circumstances. Factors of relevance are:

- size of premises/numbers employed
- variety of occupations
- shift patterns
- rapidly changing circumstances
- number of peripatetic workers
- nature of the risks.

Management are not permitted to prevent H&S reps from carrying out independent inspections, but may insist on being present. Reps are to be permitted paid time off for duties and necessary training and must be given any information they need in order to carry out their duties (eg, accident reports, information about planned expansion or changes that may affect safety). They also have a right to inspect any health and safety documentation that the employer is required to keep by law, except where it concerns an identifiable individual. Health and safety representatives must also be provided with reasonable facilities and assistance. This is not specifically defined in law, but is generally accepted to indicate a desk, access to a private meeting area, secure filing, telephone access, photocopying facilities and a notice board.

Since 1992, managers been specifically obliged to consult with their reps about proposed changes which have health and safety implications 'in good time', while the Trade Union Reform and Employment Relations Act 1993 (TURERA) included regulations aimed at protecting reps from victimisation for carrying out their duties. Importantly, reps cannot be relieved of their duties by management unless they leave their jobs. They are appointed by the union and remain in post until the union executive decides otherwise.

Two or more union safety reps can require an employer to establish a health and safety committee which meets regularly to keep track of health and safety developments and to monitor the effectiveness of policies, training and communication arrangements. HSE guidance suggests that such committees should be relatively small and contain at least as many employee representatives as managers. Health and safety representatives who are not appointed by unions, but who have volunteered (or possibly been elected) to serve in non-union workplaces do not have the same rights of inspection or information. The duty here is simply on managers to consult regularly with them about all the major health and safety issues, present and future. Holding regular meetings of a representative health and safety committee is clearly an effective method of achieving these objectives.

Further requirements of HSWA

There are one or two other specific duties placed on employers by the 1974 Act that are worth mentioning briefly:

- to maintain an accident book
- to display a notice of insurance on a staff notice board
- to register premises with appropriate inspectorate
- to display a poster summarising the main provisions of the HSWA 1974 on a staff noticeboard.

Other major health and safety regulations

In the years since 1974 a great number of further regulations have been issued under its broad framework. We have already made reference to the most significant of these (the Management of Health and Safety at Work Regulations 1992) but there have been hundreds more. Many, of course, relate to specific industries, and are beyond the scope of this chapter, but others have more general relevance to employers. The following are the major examples.

The First Aid Regulations

The Health and Safety (First Aid) Regulations 1981 require all employers to ensure that they provide adequate first aid equipment on their premises and that they employ a sufficient number of staff trained in basic first aid skills. The Health and Safety Executive approves training courses and issues certificates in first aid for this purpose. First aiders are required to refresh their knowledge by attending courses at least every three years.

There is no specific requirement included in the Regulations about precise numbers, but a related code of practice suggests one first aider for every fifty employees as a general guide in low-risk workplaces. This clearly needs to be a good deal higher in workplaces where risks of injury are high and/or where people work on shifts, so as to ensure that there is always someone present with the required first aid qualifications. Moreover, where there are particular hazards it is necessary to train first aiders in specialist care as well as general first aid.

COSHH

The Control of Substances Hazardous to Health Regulations 1988 (always pronounced as 'Cosh' came into force on 1 October 1989. These comprised the first major EU intervention in the field of health and safety law. The statute comprises nineteen specific regulations and four codes of practice. They apply to all organisations, but are more significant in some than others.

In respect of all potentially hazardous substances, including everyday cleaning fluids, the regulations require organisations:

- to carry out risk assessments
- to have written policies on usage of substances
- to control access to substances
- to carry out appropriate health surveillance
- to give users full and proper training.

The regulations are a great deal more detailed in respect of substances which contain carcinogens or that are especially toxic. Substances containing biological agents or ingredients which have been genetically modified are also covered at length.

Noise

1989 saw the introduction of specific regulations aimed at protecting employees' hearing by regulating their exposure to noise. These were replaced with new more restrictive law which was then introduced in stages following the issuing of the Control of Noise at Work Regulations (2005). They have only applied in the music and entertainment industries since April 2008. The Regulations require employers to measure noise levels, to assess their likely impact, to take steps to reduce exposure and to carry out health surveillance (ie, hearing tests) where there is a risk to workers' hearing as a result of their exposure over time. There are two levels of noise exposure identified:

- the lower level (daily or weekly exposure to noise levels of 80 decibels and a peak exposure of 135 decibels)
- the higher level (daily or weekly exposure to noise levels of 85 decibels and a peak exposure of 137 decibels).

In the case of the former there is a need to record exposure, reduce it to the lowest reasonably practicable level, undertake specific risk assessments and provide staff with information and training about the risks. Ear protection equipment must be provided on request. In the case of the higher level it is compulsory that ear protectors are worn and warning signs posted establishing 'ear protection zones'. Moreover, employers are obliged to have in place a 'planned programme of noise control'. This may well have to include making sure that employees are limited in how much time they can spend working in the noisiest areas. In any event, there is now an absolute limit of daily or weekly average exposure of 87 decibels. No worker can lawfully be exposed to more.

It is a common misconception to assume that noise levels only reach these 'actionable levels' in specialised types of workplace where particularly noisy equipment is used. This is not so. As Whincup (1997:328) helpfully points out 'the first action level is reached as soon as it is necessary to shout to be heard' (see Table 24.1).

Table 24.1 Decibel levels

Noise	Decibel level
Faintest audible sounds	0–20
Quiet library	20–40
Conversation	40–60
Primary school classroom	60–80
Night clubs	80–100
Chainsaws	100–120
Jet aircraft taking off 25 metres away	120–140

Source: HSE (2005)

The six pack

The biggest single set of developments on the criminal side of health and safety law since 1974 came into effect on 1 January 1993. Commonly referred to as the 'six pack' these comprised five separate sets of regulations which gave effect in UK law to the EU's Framework Directive on health and safety at work and also to five further 'daughter directives' dealing with more specific issues.

The six sets of regulations are as follows:

- The Management of Health and Safety at Work Regulations 1992
- The Workplace (Health, Safety and Welfare) Regulations 1992
- The Provision and Use of Work Equipment Regulations 1992 (known as PUWER)
- The Personal Protective Equipment Regulations 1992
- The Manual Handling Operations Regulations 1992
- The Display Screen Equipment Regulations 1992.

To an extent these can be seen as comprising something of a return to more detailed and specific regulation following the establishment, post-1974, of a regime that places general duties of reasonableness on employers. But in practice the 1992 six-pack regulations actually do little more than put some flesh on the bones already established in 1974, for example by making it explicit that employers must carry out formal risk assessments, record these and put in place appropriate action to reduce levels of risk. Specific groups requiring particular attention are named—such as pregnant women and young children—while minimum standards are established in fields such as room temperatures and the provision of separate male and female toilet facilities.

The latter two sets of regulations have had the greatest impact on the greatest number of workers. The Manual Handling Regulations seek to reduce the number of back injuries sustained at work (over 25% of all injuries) by requiring employers to train people in safe lifting techniques and ensuring that tasks that require lifting are allocated to appropriate staff. The Display Screen Equipment Regulations are designed to reduce damage to sight and injuries to arms and necks resulting from excessive use of computer screens and/or badly placed equipment. They require all workstations to be assessed, training to be given in the minimisation of risk and the provision of regular rest breaks and eye tests.

Smoking bans

Bans on smoking in enclosed public places have now been introduced via separate sets of regulations in England, Scotland, Wales and Northern Ireland. The English legislation is contained in the Health Act 2006, the other relevant statutes being The Smoking (Northern Ireland) Order 2006, the Smoke-free Premises (Wales) Regulations 2007, the Smoking, Health and Social Care (Scotland) Act 2005 and the Prohibition of Smoking in Certain Premises (Scotland) Regulations 2006. The content of each is largely similar but differs on some minor points of detail.

The smoking ban in England applies to all workplaces, including any areas which are 'substantially enclosed', meaning areas that comprise more walls and ceiling than they do open space. So a typical bus shelter, for example, would normally be covered. The smoking of tobacco, products containing tobacco or the smoking of 'any other substance' are covered by the ban. Not inhaling is no excuse, the act of lighting up in an enclosed space being sufficient to break the law. Company cars are included, unless they are convertibles, if they are or might be used by more than one person. The only exemptions relate to parts of workplaces which also have a residential purpose, such as rooms provided for live-in staff, prison cells, rooms in residential care homes etc—but the exemption only applies to occupants of the room, not to anyone else who happens to want to smoke indoors. This provision was introduced to help ensure, for example, that old Mrs Peacock's room in a nursing home does not, by default, become a smoking room for staff and patients generally.

Organisations are now under a legal obligation to ensure that 'No-Smoking' signs are displayed prominently at each entrance to their premises. They must be compliant with regulations that require them to be at least A5 size, to display a no-smoking symbol and to state that 'it is against the law to smoke here'. Signs also have to be attached inside all vehicles that are covered by the ban.

This is criminal law enforced by local authority-trained inspectors, most being environmental health officers who are able to enter premises without warning to check that managers are observing these Regulations. A range of fixed penalty fines can be levied on organisations who fail to comply:

- £200 for failing to display a prominent 'no smoking' sign
- £1000 for failing to pay the £200 fine
- up to £2,500 for failing to take all reasonable steps to prevent smoking.

The phrasing of the last part here is particularly tough, putting the burden for policing firmly on the employer/management:

> It is the duty of any person who controls or is concerned with the management of smoke-free premises to cause a person smoking there to stop smoking.

In addition individual employees or visitors to workplaces who smoke in enclosed spaces are subject to a fixed penalty fine of £50 if caught smoking in an unlawful location by an inspector. The fine can rise to £1000 if it is not paid within a specified period of time. There are three defences available:

1. that all reasonable steps were taken to stop the person from smoking
2. that the accused did not know, or could not reasonably have been expected to know, that a person was smoking
3. that for other reasons it was reasonable not to comply with the duty.

From an employment perspective these are similar to the defences deployable in cases of sexual harassment (see Chapter 11), so it is likely that it will be very helpful in showing reasonableness to be able to produce written policies on smoking, evidence that appropriate training has taken place and evidence that sufficient disciplinary sanctions have been applied. A decision thus needs to be taken in workplaces about whether or not a breach of the smoking ban is to be treated as gross misconduct, leading to the possibility of summary dismissal, the alternative being ordinary misconduct punishable by a formal warning (see Chapter 5).

 Exhibit 24.1   **Violence at work**

One of the more startling recent developments in health and safety law has been its necessary response to the rising number of cases of violence in UK workplaces. According to official crime statistics recent years have seen the number of incidents more than double, shopworkers, social workers and door-to-door sales people being increasingly subjected to serious verbal and physical abuse. While around 15,000 retail employees in the retail sector suffer actual physical violence each year, over 100,000 suffer from threats and well over 300,000 have to cope with verbal abuse of one kind or another.

»

> The response of the enforcing authorities has been to expect employers to incorporate violence at work into their risk assessments and to take action to reduce its incidence and the fear that it induces in workers. Preventative measures thus need to be taken wherever 'reasonably practicable' and full training given to staff who are at risk in how to deal with potentially violent situations. A failure to take such action in situations where a risk exists can lead to the issuing of prohibition or improvement notices by health and safety inspectors.
>
> It is also worth noting that under the terms of the Employment Rights Act 1996 employees have a right not to be subjected to any detriment if they refuse to work in unsafe conditions. This applies to situations in which an employee believes himself or herself to be in imminent danger of being on the receiving end of a violent assault.
>
> *Source:* Ishmael (1999)

Enforcement of health and safety regulations

The principal method by which the criminal law on health and safety is enforced is through the activities of inspectorates. In the UK the work is divided between local authority environmental health officers and inspectors working from one of the Health and Safety Executive's (HSE) thirteen regional offices. Employers are required to register with whichever of these two agencies is responsible for the relevant type of premises. As matters stand the division of responsibility between the two agencies is determined by the type of premises concerned. The Health and Safety (Enforcing Authority) Regulations 1998 set out in detail who is responsible for expecting what, but the general rule appears to be that local authority inspectors have the privilege of visiting more desirable types of workplace than their colleagues in the HSE. The premises for which local authority inspectors take responsibility are as follows:

- places of leisure and entertainment
- hotels and restaurants
- offices
- storage and wholesale depots/warehouses
- places of worship
- zoos and veterinary practices
- mobile vending vans
- massage parlours.

HSE inpectors, by contrast, focus on manufacturing plants, construction sites, farms and laboratories—indeed anywhere where specialist expertise is required. The HSE also look after schools, hospitals and government buildings.

Whichever agency an inspector is employed by, their powers are the same and these are quite extensive. Inspectors have the power, for example, to seek an injunction to have a place of business closed down and they can bring charges of manslaughter against an organisation where someone is killed in a workplace accident. However, the approach that the inspectorates take is one of seeking to work with employers rather than against them and to positively encourage compliance with the law and with good practice rather than to threaten. The more draconian powers are only used as a last resort. Section 20 of the HSWA 1974 lists the powers that are exercised on a regular basis. These include the following:

- to enter premises without the permission of the occupier, with a police escort if necessary
- to examine whatever equipment or documentation they believe to be necessary
- to take measurements, recordings and photographs
- to direct that an area is left undisturbed while an examination or investigation proceeds
- to take samples and substances away for further examination
- to inspect and take away copies of documentation
- to require managers and staff to answer questions, and to sign to say that answers given are truthful.

In practice this means that inspectors turn up at a workplace without prior warning and can insist on inspecting any areas that they wish to. They will typically focus on areas which are considered to be relatively high-risk as far as health and safety is concerned such as kitchens, storage areas or factory floors. They will also want to look at risk assessments, accident books and written health and safety policies. If they then come across a practice that they consider to be dangerous or any apparent contravention of a health and safety statute they prefer to consult with employers and advise them informally before taking formal action. But they have the power to issue one of two types of notice:

1. An improvement notice specifying what remedial steps the employer must take and by when.
2. A prohibition notice ordering that an activity is discontinued until remedial steps are taken.

Improvement and prohibition notices come into effect as soon as they are issued. There is a right of appeal to an employment tribunal, and onwards up to the High Court, but it is very rare indeed that a health and safety inspector's judgement is overturned on appeal. In practice between 10,000 and 20,000 enforcement notices are issued each year (see HSE, 2010).

Contravention of an improvement or a prohibition notice is a serious criminal offence. Magistrates can fine offenders up to £20,000, while fines in the Crown Court are unlimited. Prosecutions can also be brought more generally for wilful, flagrant or reckless breach of health and safety regulations. This generally occurs following a death or serious injury that is judged either by an inspector, by the Director of Public Prosecutions or (in Scotland) by the Procurator Fiscal to have been avoidable. There are around 1500 prosecutions each year, resulting in an average fine (in 2009/2010) of £15,817. This indicates that most of the fines levied are of a relatively small amount, but each year there are several very heavy fines imposed on some employers. Fines of £250,000–£750,000 are not uncommon in cases where very serious lapses on the part of a large, well-resourced organisation led to death or serious injury.

Corporate manslaughter

As a rule it is corporations rather than individual managers who are prosecuted under the health and safety statutes, but occasionally individual directors are personally prosecuted and fined or even imprisoned for offences committed under the HSWA 1974 or when found personally guilty of manslaughter. This occurs where it can be shown that they are person-ally responsible in some way because they neglected to fulfil their statutory duties or con-sented to a decision which resulted in serious injury or death.

The Corporate Manslaughter and Corporate Homicide Act 2007 came into force in April 2008. It did not create any new legal duties, but increased the ease with which criminal charges can be successfully brought against corporations (not individuals) when a person dies as a result of gross failures in the way that activities are managed or organised. The Act extended the existing offence of 'corporate manslaughter'. To be found guilty senior figures in the corporation concerned now have to be culpable of *a gross breach* of any duty of care they owed to the deceased person. The Act thus covers all situations in which a corporation, through gross negligence or carelessness on the part of senior directors, causes an employee or a member of the public to die. Crown immunity in this area was lifted by the new Act so public authorities, with some significant exceptions, are now included on the same basis as private companies. Partnerships, sole traders and other non-incorporated bodies are also included, but only in their capacity as employers. Unlimited fines are possible under the new law, but no other additional penalties were created. However, a significant change was a measure permitting courts to impose 'remedial orders' requiring the guilty party to address the issue that caused the fatality, and to impose 'publicity orders' requiring a guilty organisa-tion to publicise details of its conviction and fine.

 Activity 24.3   *West Bromwich Building Society Ltd v Townsend* **(1983)**

This case concerned a building society branch in Wolverhampton that was subjected to a routine health and safety inspection by a local authority environmental health officer called Mr Townsend. Following his inspection, Mr Townsend took the decision to use the branch as a test case and to issue an improvement notice requiring the building society to install 'anti-bandit screens' to protect staff from the possibility of a violent robbery. The notice stated that it was Mr Townsend's opinion that the employer was contravening the Health and Safety at Work Act 1974 by not providing such screens:

> The reasons for my said opinion are that staff engaged in the handling of money and in general office duties in the premises are not protected as far as is reasonably practicable from the risk of attack or personal injury from persons frequenting the area of the premises normally open to the general public and I hereby require you to remedy the said contraventions or, as the case may be, the matter occasioning them by September 22nd 1982, in the manner stated in the schedule which forms part of this notice.

The employer appealed against the improvement notice to an industrial tribunal (now an em-ployment tribunal). In doing so it made the following points:

1   The building society had considered how it could best protect its employees and included such considerations in risk assessments that were regularly kept under review.

2   The cost of installing protective screens in all its eighty-six branches would be over £500,000, yet the amount of cash kept on any one of its premises at any one time was only £3,500 maximum.

3 The improvement notice merely stated that it was Mr Townsend's opinion that the building society was in contravention of the HSWA 1974. No particulars were given about which clause in the Act was being contravened and no justification given to back up the general opinion.

4 The improvement notice was not really concerned with bringing about necessary improvements in health and safety at the particular branch concerned. Its real aim was to create a precedent that would apply to all building society branches across the whole country.

The West Bromwich Building Society lost its appeal to the industrial tribunal, but subsequently won a further appeal to the High Court.

Questions

1 To what extent do you agree with the judgment of the High Court in this case, and why?

2 How do you think the building society was able to show that it was not in fact contravening the 1974 Act?

3 How far do you agree that this case reveals underlying weaknesses in the approach to health and safety law that was established in the HSWA 1974?

Debates about criminal liability in health and safety law

We will end this chapter by briefly outlining three of the major debates about the role of the criminal law in promoting health and safety at work and some of the more prominent critiques of the existing approach.

Is a criminal law arm necessary at all?

The most fundamental debate concerns the extent to which criminal sanctions play any real useful role in promoting health and safety. Barrett & Howells (2000:219–221) argue that the toughening up of the law we have witnessed in recent years has been due to 'popular demand' rather than to any genuine belief on the part of experts in health and safety that any constructive outcomes will result. In fact, there is in their view only a weak argument in favour of the proposition that heavy penalties in this field act as a deterrent, leading employers to take greater care with the health and safety of their employees and customers. This is because except in a small minority of cases no wrongdoing is ever intended. Breaches of the law occur by mistake following 'breakdowns in systems which, on the face of it, are satisfactory'. The problem is that such breakdowns occur all the time, but the chances of any one leading to serious injury are slim. As a result, according to Barrett and Howells, *there is no correlation between the degree of wrongfulness of behaviour and the amount of harm done*. A bad employer who deliberately puts its employees' welfare at risk in order to increase profits may well never see any injuries occurring at all, while by contrast, a good employer who tries hard to look after health and safety can easily wind up facing criminal sanctions because an accident occurs. So much is in the hands of employees themselves and so much down to minor lapses of judgement that are never going to be avoided altogether however harsh the sanctions regime that is imposed.

Moreover, as we will see in Chapter 25, in many ways the criminal law regime does little more than mirror what goes on in the civil law. When someone dies or is injured seriously at work, the employer (if culpable) already has to pay very large sums in damages to injured parties or their families. There is thus already a strong legal deterrent built into the system. Why impose additional criminal sanctions on top? What purpose does it serve? Could it not be seen as just a layer of government bureaucracy eating up public money to no really positive effect? For those who find these arguments attractive, it follows that public money should be focused on providing advice to employers about how to avoid injuries, rather than on policing their activities through a regime of inspection underpinned by threats of fines for non-compliance. Because it is in employers' economic interests to run safe and healthy operations, the focus of government should thus be on facilitating effective self-regulation.

A wholly different view is taken by those who are unpersuaded by this 'business case' for self-regulation. Carol Boyd (2003) has reached a fundamentally different conclusion following her programme of research into health and safety practice in call centres, airlines and nuclear power stations. She found evidence of a sizeable gap between the rhetoric of HRM policy statements and the reality of health and safety practice. She asserts that in a highly competitive market economy there will always be pressures on managers and their employees to cut corners with health and safety, to minimise spending and to hope that no serious consequences result. Because the risks are small, the temptation to take a greater profit and lapse on health and safety is always going to be strong. Indeed, even where the risks are great there is evidence that organisations tend to turn a blind eye rather than invest the necessary money in minimising them. Just as the tobacco industry successfully managed to 'bury' the evidence linking smoking to lung disease for a generation, so modern organisations opt for the most limited level of compliance they can get away with when confronted with evidence of risks by inspectorates. Her view is that there is no alternative than better resourced and more effectively empowered enforcement agencies. She thus calls for *'significant support and funding from government as well as an ideological shift towards greater levels of intervention in employer's activities'*.

Something of a 'third way' in this debate is proposed by Gunningham and Johnstone (1999) in their comparative study of health and safety enforcement regimes in different countries. Their analysis derives from the proposition that some organisations—especially smaller ones—are only willing (or perhaps able) to adhere to basic minimum standards of health and safety management, while others genuinely do move beyond this and have developed a 'safety culture' in which safety considerations are 'built in ... at every stage of the production process'. In other words, some organisations do effectively self-regulate, while others do not. They therefore propose the evolution of 'next generation regulatory and enforcement instruments' based on the notion that genuine incentives should be given to organisations to encourage movement away from minimal compliance to the development of a genuine safety culture. Heavy-handed enforcement fails, in their view, because many employers always find ways of complying with 'the letter of the law rather than its spirit'. The result is a good deal of public spending and no real positive outcome. Light touch regimes fare equally poorly because they fail to provide any genuine encouragement to employers to self-regulate in situations where there is a choice to be made between spending on health and safety and enhancement of profits. Gunningham and Johnstone thus propose a two-track approach in which most employers (in track one) are regulated by enforcement agencies and must submit to regular inspections. However, those that can show that they genuinely have developed a safety culture, with effective employee involvement and a philosophy of continuous improvement, should be able to apply for 'track two status'. This would free them from such regular inspections and would free them up to develop their own methods of improving health and safety without the need to comply with burdensome regulation. There would have to be a mechanism in the hands of inspectors to demote track two organisations back down to track one if their commitment lapsed, but it would be hoped that the benefits of self-regulation would be so attractive to employers, that the risks of this occurring would be slim. Were the twin-track approach to work, organisations would seek to improve their own practices in order to gain accreditation as a 'track two member'. This would then serve to free up inspectors to focus their attentions on those employers with the poorest records and whose operations pose the greatest risk to health and safety. The end result should be a genuine all round improvement of standards and a real reduction in the level of risk.

How effective is the current UK regime?

The clear purpose of the criminal law regime on health and safety is to minimise the number of avoidable workplace injuries and illnesses. The extent to which our current regime achieves this, and even the extent to which it has resulted in improved statistics are matters of considerable controversy.

In 1972 the Robens Report stated that at that time around 1000 people in the UK were killed each year in workplace accidents and a further 500,000 injured. Industrial accidents and diseases of one kind or another resulted in the loss of around 23 million working days per year at a cost of £200 million (approximately 1% of the gross national product) (Whincup, 1997:301). If we look at the equivalent figures produced each year by the Health and Safety Executive nowadays, we see evidence of a very substantial decline. In 2009/2010, for example, only 152 fatalities were reported and 121,430 other industrial injuries. However, on days lost the figures appear to have moved in the opposite direction. According to HSE statistics, 1.3 million workers were suffering from illnesses they attributed to their work causing the loss of 28.5 million working days due to work-related ill health and workplace injury (HHSE, 2010).

So what conclusions can be reached about the effectiveness of thirty-eight years of the HSWA? First of all it is important not to take the figures at face value. The measurements used and the methods of collecting the statistics have changed a number of times since 1972, so we should only look at them as broad guidelines. Barrett (2000:265) points out that Robens omitted from his statistics injuries and illnesses sustained in the service industries because this data was not collected at that time. So the real figures for injuries, illnesses and days lost were actually considerably higher in 1972. Moreover, of course, the past four decades have seen huge shifts in the nature of the work that most people do, as well as a considerable rise in the size of the UK workforce. Far fewer people are employed in the manufacturing, agricultural, extractive and construction industries (ie, the high risk areas) and many many more are employed in white collar occupations and in the service sector more generally. In many respects therefore a convincing argument can be put forward that the figures on death and injury in the workplace would have come down dramatically in any event since 1972, irrespective of legislative intervention.

The government and the Health and Safety Executive take the view that the post-1974 regime has been broadly successful and that no major changes are necessary. A strategy document published in 2000 (Revitalising Health and Safety) called for some switch of emphasis and for the setting of more ambitious targets, but concluded that no major changes were needed as far as the law is concerned:

> The Government considers that the basic framework of the 1974 Act has stood the test of time. This provides for goal setting law, taking account of levels of risk and what is 'reasonably practicable', with the overiding aim of delivering good regulation that secures decent standards and protection for everyone.(Department of the Environment, Transport and the Regions, 2000:8)

In 2010 a government review by Lord Young also concluded that the existing system worked well. His recommendations as far as criminal enforcement is concerned mostly involve reducing the complexity of information issued by the HSE by consolidating it into one place and making it more readily understandable for small businesses. He also recommended that self-employed people working in low hazard environments as well as employers of home-workers should be relieved of the requirement to undertake full risk assessments.

This rosy view is heavily criticised by James and Walters (2004). Their conclusion is that the 1974 Act has, in fact, not lived up to expectations, that far too much avoidable ill health is caused by the experience of employment and that the 2000 revitalising health and safety strategy was 'big on words but short on action'. Moreover, their analysis of the annual figures published by the Health and Safety Executive since 2000 leads them to argue that at best there has been no improvement in rates of workplace injury and illness, and at worst a substantial increase. In particular, they draw attention to an apparent year on year increase in the number of incidences of work-related ill health and the number of days lost from work-related injuries and ill health. Their pamphlet ends with a robust call for extensive legal reform, additional funding for the inspectorates and measures to facilitate more effective worker representation.

 Exhibit 24.2 **Crown immunity**

One of the more controversial aspects of health and safety law over the years has been the presence in the statutes, including the Health and Safety at Work Act 1974, of clauses which do not apply to central government functions due to the doctrine of Crown immunity. This means that unless Parliament specifically extends the effects of criminal legislation to the Crown, they do not apply across the civil service and in other central government offices. Health Authorities lost their Crown immunity in 1990, but many government organisations including the prison service and the armed forces retain it.

Crown immunity applies as far as the inspection regime set up by the HSWA 1974 applies. This means that in theory, HSE inspectors cannot do any more than advise government on health and safety lapses in their own offices. They can issue prohibition notices and improvement notices, but cannot prosecute these organisations if they fail to comply. This means, for example, that the Home Office cannot be prosecuted if it operates an unsafe system of work in a prison.

The new law of Corporate Homicide introduced in 2008 does not contain Crown immunity. The government's original intention was that it should, leaving deaths in prisons and police custody outside the regulations. A debate about this issue formed the basis of a dispute between the House of Commons and the House of Lords in the summer of 2007 which almost led to the Corporate Manslaughter and Corporate Homicide Bill being dropped. In the event, however, ministers conceded to the demand of the House of Lords and amended the Bill so that the doctrine of Crown immunity does not apply in cases covered by the Act.

CHAPTER SUMMARY

- A clear division exists in health and safety law between the criminal arm, enforced by health and safety inspectorates, and the civil arm which is concerned with compensating people who have been injured at work.

- The Health and Safety at Work Act 1974 is central to the operation of the criminal side of health and safety law. It places various key duties on employers, requiring them to undertake risk assessments, to develop health and safety policies and to take sufficient precautions in the face of possible health and safety hazards.

- Over the years several specific sets of regulations have been issued under the HSWA 1974. These include regulations on first aid, manual handling, noise and smoking in public places.

- Criminal charges can be brought against corporations if notices issued by health and safety inspectors are not fully complied with. They can also be brought if death or serious injury occurs when an employer is to blame. In the case of deaths, corporate manslaughter charges can be brought against corporations and/or their senior directors.

For updates and further materials, please see the online resource centre at www.oup.com.

REFERENCES

Barrett, B. (2000) 'The impact of safety legislation on the contract of employment' in H. Collins, P. Davies & R. Rideout (eds): *Legal Regulation of the Employment Relation*. London: Kluwer.

Barrett, B. and Howells, R. (2000) *Occupational Health and Safety Law: Text and Materials*. Second Edition. London: Cavendish Publishing.

Boyd, C. (2003) *Human Resource Management and Occupational Health and Safety*. London: Routledge.

British Medical Association (2002) *Towards Smoke-Free Public Places*. London: BMA.

Department of the Environment, Transport and the Regions (2000) *Revitalising Health and Safety: Strategy Statement*. London: HMSO.

Gunningham, N. & Johnstone, R. (1999) *Regulating Workplace Safety: System and Sanctions*. Oxford: Oxford University Press.

HSE (2005) *Noise at Work: Guidance for employers on the Control of Noise at Work Regulations 2005*. London: Health and Safety Executive.

HSE (2010) *Health and Safety Statistics 2009/10*. London: Health and Safety Executive.

Ishmael, A. (1999) *Harrassment, Bullying and Violence at Work*. London: The Industrial Society.

James, P. & Walters, D. (2004) *Health and Safety Revitalised or Reversed?* London: Institute of Employment Rights.

Kloss, D. (2010) *Occupational Health Law*. Fifth Edition. Oxford: Blackwell.

Stranks, J. (2001) *A Manager's Guide to Health and Safety at Work*. Sixth Edition. London: Kogan Page.

Whincup, M. (1997) *Modern Employment Law: A Guide to Job Security and Safety*. Ninth Edition. Oxford: Butterworth Heinemann.

ONLINE RESOURCE CENTRE

A range of online resources to help you through your employment law module have been developed by the author team. These include updates, self-test questions and sources for further reading. (www.oxfordtextbooks.co.uk/orc/taylor_emir3e)

Health and safety— the civil law

Learning outcomes

By the end of this chapter you should be able to:

- explain why most injured employees seek compensation through negligence claims rather than claims based on allegations of breach of contract;

- advise about the doctrine of vicarious liability and its significance for employers;

- set out the key legal tests used to establish whether or not an employer has acted negligently;

- outline the major defences that employers use in personal injury cases;

- consider when an employee might find it beneficial to bring a claim of breach of statutory duty, breach of contract or constructive dismissal when injured or made ill as a result of a job;

- give advice about the recent evolution of the law in the area of stress-based personal injury claims;

- debate the merits of moving towards a no-fault compensation system in place of our existing tort-based approach.

Introduction

In Chapter 24 we outlined the basic structure of health and safety law in the UK, going on to look in detail at the sanctions applied by the criminal courts as a means of punishing organisations which breach their statutory duties. The aim of this body of law, along with the inspectors who enforce it, is to prevent workplace injuries and illnesses from occurring in the first place. In this chapter we move on to look at the 'other half' of health and safety law—the civil law arm—which like most employment law serves to provide compensation to employees or ex-employees who have suffered a detriment because of the unlawful actions of their employers. The situation is complicated somewhat, however, by the ever present doctrine of vicarious liability which means that an entirely blameless employer can nonetheless end up paying compensation to someone who has been injured due to the actions or inactions of a fellow employee.

In some jurisdictions, such as the USA, compensation for injuries sustained while at work is gained through the law of contract. There is a duty of care implied into all contracts, and if this is breached by the employer, an injured party can sue for damages. This can happen in the UK too, but it is far more common in practice for claimants to bring their cases using the law of tort, alleging either negligence on the part of their employer, breach of statutory duty, or both (see figure 24.1). According to Deakin and Morris (2009:296) this has arisen due to an 'historical accident' whereby satisfactory remedies under the law of tort developed faster in the UK than equivalent rights under the law of contract. Most of this chapter will thus focus on personal injury claims brought to the County and High Courts and the defences that are available for employers to deploy when faced with such litigation. It is, however, important to remember that breaches of health and safety law can also amount to breaches of implied terms of a contract of employment (the duty of care, the duty to maintain safe systems of working, etc), and that remedies can also be sought using that route. Such is particularly true of constructive dismissal actions in the employment tribunal based on a failure of an employer to meet its health and safety obligations.

As is true of any constructive dismissal case, a claimant can only win if he/she is first able to show that the employer repudiated the contract through its actions. Later in the chapter we focus particularly on stress-based personal injury claims. This is the area of the law which has developed fastest in recent years and which has been the subject of many important recent cases brought before the higher courts. Finally we turn to the major critiques of UK personal injury law as it relates to employment, briefly setting out the case for and against substantial reform.

 Activity 25.1

Anna works as a performer at a funfair based in a seaside resort. One of her roles involves standing with her back against a wooden board, blindfolded, while a colleague known as Blackdagger throws twelve knives at her. These land at various points around her body and between her legs, after which, to tremendous applause from the audience, she steps forward, removes the blindfold and takes a bow.

» One day, having successfully performed this act with Blackdagger several times a day for a number of months, a terrible accident occurs. Just as Blackdagger is taking aim with a knife which is supposed to land in the area beneath Anna's left arm, there is an almighty explosion some distance away which is strong enough to cause the ground to shake under everyone's feet. Blackdagger momentarily loses his concentration and the knife lands in Anna's chest, causing her a very serious injury.

Her doctor tells her that she is lucky to be alive, but after two operations and a long period of rest she makes a full recovery. During this time she resigns from her job at the funfair and takes her former employer to court seeking substantial damages. Blackdagger decides to take early retirement as he is too stressed to contemplate throwing knives at another assistant.

Questions

1 What would Anna have to prove in order to win her case?

2 What possible defences might the funfair use in order to reduce the amount of damages or to avoid paying her damages altogether?

3 What chances would Blackdagger have of gaining any compensation for the stress he suffers as a result of this accident?

Return to this activity once you have read the chapter, to see how many of your answers were correct.

Negligence

In a landmark judgment passed in 1937 the House of Lords decided in *Wilsons & Clyde Coal Co v English* that all employers owed all employees a general duty of care in tort in respect of their health and safety at work. In doing so the law lords provided a new avenue to employees who suffered injuries at work to claim compensation from their employers. Until that time it was rare for employees to win personal injury claims because most accidents at work were caused at least *in part* either by another employee or by the victim him/herself, and that was sufficient (under a now defunct doctrine known as 'common employment') to absolve the employer of blame, and hence the need to pay any damages. As a result, since 1937, the tortious route has generally been followed by employees who are injured or become ill as a result of their work, and we have a great deal of case law to guide us in respect of the torts of negligence and breach of statutory duty. The major alternative available avenue—basing claims on breaches of implied terms of contract—has been taken less frequently, and is a good deal less well developed in the case law in consequence.

The tests used to determine whether an employer is guilty of negligence are similar to those used in the criminal law to establish reasonableness. Everything depends on the facts of the particular case. Central is the extent to which the risk of injury or illness was foreseeable and whether or not the employer's response was reasonable given the probable costs associated with its reduction. Negligence is summed up by Kloss (2010:194) as '*a failure to take reasonable care which causes foreseeable damage*' and by Stranks (2005:21) as '*careless conduct injuring another*'.

In order to win damages for negligence, the claimant must prove three separate points:

1. that the employer owed a duty of care to the employee,
2. that the employer's conduct breached that duty,
3. that a detriment (damage, loss or injury) was caused as a result.

The standard of proof used is 'that which an ordinary prudent employer would take in all the circumstances'. Importantly this means that the court does not judge the case with hindsight and the knowledge that an injury has in fact been sustained. Instead the judge puts him/herself in the position of the employer before the accident or illness in order to ascertain whether what was done was reasonable in all the circumstances. Central is the concept of reasonable forseeability. If the accident, illness or injury was not reasonably foreseeable, the employer was not negligent.

Reasonableness on the part of the employer is judged in very similar ways in the civil courts as it is in the criminal courts, although the precise facts of the individual cases tend to vary. So, for example, where there is a Health and Safety Executive code of practice published on a particular aspect of health and safety, that provides the basis for judging whether the employer acted reasonably just as it does in the criminal courts. The same broad approach is also taken in respect of risk assessments. The employer who has carried out a detailed risk assessment, and reviewed it regularly, as required by the Management of Health and Safety at Work Regulations 1992 (essentially a criminal law statute), will be far better placed to defend itself from a personal injury claim than an employer who has not done so.

Vicarious liability

It is always important to remember that in cases of negligence, as in any common law action, the doctrine of vicarious liability applies. This means that the employer takes legal responsibility for the actions of employees while they are at work—the precise term used being 'acting in the course of employment'. In this context this means that the employer is sued when one of its employees acts negligently, even if the employer itself is wholly blameless. This long-established legal doctrine is justified on the grounds that if an employer is prepared to take a profit from the work its employees carry out, it should also be prepared to take responsibility for their mistakes. In other words, an employer cannot have all the benefits associated with employing people, while avoiding the disadvantages.

Vicarious liability applies automatically in the case of employees. It can, however, also apply in the case of negligence on the part of people working for the employer under contracts for services (casual workers, trainees, agency temps, etc) and sub-contractors working on its premises, provided the employer can be shown to be at fault 'personally' to some degree. This might happen if an employer failed to warn someone other than an employee about a significant risk or failed to give proper supervision in a risky environment. A good example is the case of *R v Swan Hunter* (1981) discussed in Chapter 24.

Plant and equipment

Many of the leading cases dealing with negligence relate to injuries sustained because the environment in which someone works or the equipment they are provided with is unsafe in some shape or form. So if a workplace is too hot or too cold or too noisy, if a floor is slippery or the air toxic in any way, and an injury or illness results, the employer is responsible and must pay damages. Only if an employer was found to have taken all reasonable precautions, an accident occurring despite this, would it win the case. For example, in *Latimer v AEC* (1953), the employer had decided that it would be safe to continue operating a plant after a flood had caused the floor to become slippery. By spreading sawdust around, it was considered that employees would be sufficiently protected. Mr Latimer slipped and fell despite this and brought a claim for damages. The court found in favour of the employer on the grounds that it had taken all reasonable precautions. The only alternative would have been to close the plant altogether. Taking account of all the facts, it was decided that closing down the factory would have been too 'drastic' a step to have taken, and that the employer had in fact acted as 'a reasonably prudent man' would have done.

Injuries arising from the use of faulty equipment are also the employer's responsibility, even if the fault lies with the manufacturer of the equipment and not the employer whose employee was injured as a result. There is nothing to stop the injured person from suing both his/her employer and the manufacturer of the equipment in such circumstances, but the norm is simply to sue the employer. This may seem unfair, but the courts have decided that expecting an employee to pursue a claim against a manufacturer who may be based overseas is too much to expect. There is of course nothing to stop an employer who loses such a case itself taking action against the manufacturer to recover the damages paid out to the injured employee.

Over the years employers have sought to avoid responsibility by arguing that the term 'equipment' relates only to the tools or machinery an employee uses in carrying out their job. The courts have taken a very employee-friendly view in such cases, arguing that 'every article of whatsoever kind furnished by the employer for the purposes of his business' can be construed as being equipment (*Knowles v Liverpool City Council* (1993)). In this case the definition was extended to include a paving stone in a street. In another, the ship which someone worked on was said to consitute 'equipment'.

Systems of work

Another major source of litigation has been accidents that occur because there is no safe system of work in operation, either because none has been devised or because employees do not in practice operate the systems as they are supposed to. Here too the judges have high expectations of employers. It is not acceptable to argue that the injured employee him/herself was to blame because they did not act with basic common sense or because they did not do what they were told to do. Where proper supervision or training should be given and it was not, then the employer is liable. An important House of Lords ruling was that in *General Cleaning Contractors Ltd v Christmas* (1952). Here a window cleaner fell and injured himself while cleaning an office window. He had made the mistake of relying on holding a sash window frame and balancing his foot on a window sill when working at height. The sash window gave way and he fell, causing significant injury. The employer argued that Mr Christmas was an experienced window cleaner and was well aware of the risk he was taking by relying on the support of a sash window. In giving judgment the House of Lords said that this was not relevant:

> It is the duty of an employer to give such general safety instructions as a reasonably careful employer who has considered the problem presented by the work would give to his workmen. It is, I think, well known to employers ... that their workpeople are very frequently, if not habitually,

careless about the risks which their work might involve. It is my opinion, for that very reason that the common law demands that employers take reasonable care to lay down a reasonably safe system of work. Employers are not exempted from this duty by the fact that their men are experienced and might, if they were in the position of an employer, be able to lay down a reasonably safe system of work themselves.

The conclusion was that a reasonable employer would have done more to reduce the likelihood of such an accident occurring by providing instruction on safe window cleaning and by providing wedges to reduce the chances of a sash window giving way.

Another group of cases concerns protective clothing. Here too it is clear that the employer must not only provide adequate protective clothing (eg, goggles, ear protectors and gloves), but also explain to employees why it is necessary for them to comply with safety arrangements and wear the protective clothing. Just issuing it is not enough. Hence in *Pape v Cumbria County Council* (1991), a former cleaner won damages of £22,000 after she developed a skin disorder. She had not worn the rubber gloves provided to her, but the employer had never explained to her the risks associated with not using them when working with commercial cleaning fluids.

Exhibit 25.1   *Paris v Stepney Borough Council* (1951)

Mr Paris was employed to maintain council vehicles. One day, when removing a bolt from a chassis he was unfortunate to cause a metal particle to splinter and hit him in the eye. He was not wearing goggles. The accident had particularly serious consequences because Mr Paris was already blind in one eye. The splinter had entered his good eye and this had left him totally blind.

The employer argued that it was a freak accident that could not have reasonably been forseen. Moreover, goggles were never provided for the kind of work that Mr Paris was engaged in because the risks were so low. Both sides won the case at various stages, but ultimately the House of Lords found in favour of Mr Paris. In doing so they found that the level of risk associated with his job varied between people who had two good eyes and people such as Mr Paris with his one blind eye. In the case of the former the level of risk was low and it was reasonable for the employer not to provide goggles. In Mr Paris's case, however, the risk was considerably greater because he only had one functioning eye. The employer was fully aware of this situation and acted unreasonably in ignoring the special dangers faced in his case. Goggles should have been provided for him. This case is important because it places a higher duty of care on employers in the case of employees with relevant disabilities. Where, for particular individuals, a risk is higher, then the employer must respond.

In practice a similar approach is taken in cases where an employer employs people who are very experienced alongside less experienced staff. There is a differential level of risk, because the less experienced staff are more likely to injure themselves or others than their more experienced colleagues. This needs to be taken account of in risk assessments and differential action taken in response.

Another interesting group of cases concern situations in which scientific evidence of a danger to health and safety associated with certain industrial practices only comes to light after someone has been working 'unsafely' for some time. Examples include (1) the 'discovery' in the 1960s that working in a very noisy environment over many years could lead to hearing loss, (2) the discovery in the 1970s of a condition known as 'vibration white finger' which affects people who work over a prolonged period with vibrating tools, and (3) the finding in the 1980s that repetitive strain injury could cripple people who use keyboards in their jobs to excess (see Kloss 2010:197–199). A question the courts have to decide in such cases is at what point an employer ceased to be acting 'reasonably' in failing to take precautions to protect employees from these conditions. This is often a difficult call because the first published evidence raising the possibility of a risk to health often pre-dates the issuing of regulatory guidance by many years. But it matters a great deal because someone may have largely developed loss of hearing, painful upper limb disorders or numb fingers before the date at which it was known that such conditions could develop as a result of unsafe workplace systems. Moreover, where someone has moved from employer to employer in an industry, it may determine which of a number of employers must share the burden of paying damages to the injured employee. The leading cases state that the date chosen should reflect that at which an ordinary prudent employer would have become sufficiently aware of the possibility of a risk to take action. This will often be before an official regulatory pronouncement is made. For example, in the case of vibration white finger, it has been fixed at 1973 by *'when the condition had been examined in a large number of medical publications, and had been the subject of two reports from the Industrial Injuries Advisory Council'*.

It is highly likely that a similar judgment will have to be made in the future about when it is reasonable to have expected an employer to take account of the dangers associated with passive smoking. At the time of writing the evidence that cancer can be caused by inhaling others' cigarette smoke is mounting substantially. Employers with any sense will thus look to the judgments in the vibration white finger cases and take action now to ensure that no employee is put in this position. Many employers are relying on government advice and regulation on the question of passive smoking, assuming that there are no legal risks to them unless and until they are told to make changes to reduce their employees' exposure. This is not prudent. While it may remain lawful in terms of the criminal law to allow employees to smoke passively in many situations, the civil courts may very well reach a different view if presented with a case in which a non-smoker has developed lung cancer after many years' exposure to tobacco smoke. Here it is scientific evidence which drives judgments about what is 'reasonable' as much as government action.

Defences

Having pointed out that judges are inclined to find against employers when they have before them employees who have sustained disabling injuries or bereaved families whose suffering could have been avoided had an employer taken greater care, it is important also to stress that there are defences that employers can successfully deploy. Some of these result in the employer having to pay no damages at all because they are found not to have been liable. Others lead to a situation in which the amount of damages is reduced to reflect the fact that the employer is only in part to blame for the injury or illness that has developed.

A common defence used in negligence claims is that of 'contributory fault'. Here it is argued that while the employer is prepared to shoulder some of the blame, the injured employee is also in large part to blame because he/she acted recklessly or carelessly. Fault is then assigned on a percentage basis (eg, 30% employer, 70% employee) and damages reduced accordingly. It is not uncommon for damages to be reduced to zero on the grounds that an employee has acted so recklessly as to be entirely responsible for his/her own fate. This happened in the tragic but often quoted case of *Jones v Lionite Specialties Cardiff Ltd* (1961) in which an employee fell into a tank of noxious liquid and died. The court held that the individual was wholly to blame as he had put himself at risk in order 'to take big whiffs of the liquid's vapour to which he had taken a liking'. As a result the man's widow received no compensation at all.

It is difficult to see any obvious pattern of principle from a reading of the leading cases on contributory negligence. The extent to which courts reduce damages varies considerably depending on their reading of the facts in any particular case. It is clear, however, that recklessness on the part of an employee reduces damages paid a lot more than mere carelessness, and that a certain amount of routine carelessness is judged as being something that employers must expect and build in to their risk assessments. As long ago as 1940 in *Caswell v Powell Duffryn Collieries*, the House of Lords established the principle that '*it is not for every risky thing that a workman in a factory may do that he ought to be held guilty of contributory negligence*', because tiredness, pressure to work quickly and other features of the working environment inevitably lead people to take less care of health and safety matters than they would in an ideal world. Another determining factor appears to be the extent to which a danger is obvious. Where it is not, it is harder for an employer to show that the injured employee acted negligently. Whincup (1997:271–275) illustrates this point by contrasting the leading cases of *Crookhall v Vickers Armstrong* (1955) with *Qualcast v Haynes* (1959). In the former case, the employer provided protective masks to protect their employees from inhaling particles of dust from their foundry's 'sandy floor' and periodically checked to see that masks were being worn. In the second, protective boots were provided to stop employees' feet being damaged if the molten metal they worked with was spilt, but no checks were carried out to ensure that employees actually wore the protective boots when ladelling molten metals. Yet in the first case (*Crookhall*) the employer was held mostly liable, and in the second (*Qualcast*) the employee was found to be 100% to blame for his own injury. The reason, according to Whincup, is that the dangers associated with inhaling dust over a long period of time are less obvious to an employee than the more immediate dangers associated with spilling hot metal on unprotected feet. Even though both employees were experienced and skilled workers, Mr Haynes was obviously acting recklessly, whereas Mr Crookhall was merely being careless.

A related, but distinct defence is based on 'voluntary assumption of risk'. Here it is argued by the employer that injured employees were warned very explicitly and in good time that they would be putting themselves at risk by accepting an assignment or agreeing to work on a particular project, and that they nonetheless assumed that risk. Often, this occurs in circumstances where the employee stands to earn a good deal of money because of the voluntary assumption of risk. Importantly, the courts will not accept the argument that an employee voluntarily assumed a risk just because he/she knew about it. People often know that there is a risk, but feel compelled to carry on working for fear of being sacked. This defence only applies therefore where an employee is made fully aware of a risk, is given full training, proper supervision and all necessary equipment, but nonetheless decides to take on the risk in any event. It is not difficult to think of examples; bomb disposal experts, war reporters, circus performers and cinema stuntmen all potentially fall into this category.

A third defence concerns situations where an injury is originally sustained outside work or in another employment, but is worsened in some way through the job that someone does. A fourth concerns risks that are categorised as being 'unforeseeable' such as Acts of God. Employers are not liable for injuries sustained by freak weather conditions, for example, situations in which people are struck by lightning or injured in unexpected terrorist attacks. A fifth defence relates to the time limits that exist on a claimant's right to bring a personal injury case. In most cases, thanks to the Limitation Act 1980, the time limit that applies is three years. This means that the case must be lodged within three years of the date of the accident, or from the date at which the claimant first learns that he/she may have the basis of a claim (eg, where an illness develops over time). In the case of a death, the family of the deceased also have three years to bring the claim. After this, the employer can argue that the claim is out of time and that the court cannot therefore hear it.

The final defence relates to vicarious liability and the expression we referred to above— *'acting in the course of employment'*. It is open to an employer to argue that the injury occurred or that the illness was caused by events or actions that took place outwith 'the course of employment'. The defence is deployed in two types of situations:

1. when an employee is injured when doing something beyond or outside the duties they are employed to carry out

2. when an employee is injured by another employee who is acting outside the duties he/she is employed to carry out.

There is a considerable case law on this issue, not all of which relates to employees. For example, the leading case of *Lister v Helsey Hall Ltd* (2001) concerns the sexual abuse of boys at a boarding school by a warden. The school argued that it was not vicariously liable because the abuse took place outside working hours and not in any case during the course of the warden's employment. The House of Lords decided in favour of the claimants on the grounds that there was sufficient 'closeness' between the nature of the warden's employment and the abuse. The warden was employed to look after the children in the boarding school and he had been the cause of substantial harm.

Some important principles relating to vicarious liability are now well established. For example, it is clear that employers cannot be liable for injuries sustained in car accidents while employees are commuting to and from their normal places of work. However, once someone is on the road during the working day and carrying out their work duties, it does become the employer's responsibility if they suffer an injury in a car accident. Here, as in all cases of vicarious liability, accidents during working hours are only not the responsibility of the employer where employees go off on 'frolics of their own', for example by deviating from a journey for personal reasons (Kloss, 2005:233). Case law has also established that employers are liable for accidents that occur during rest-breaks when employees slip or trip while walking to the toilet or to the staff canteen. These are deemed to be injuries sustained 'during the course of employment'.

An interesting area of law concerns vicarious liability for injuries that occur when practical jokes are played that go wrong. Employers will often seek to defend themselves in such situations by claiming that they are not vicariously liable because practical joking is outside the job description of employees and cannot thus be described as taking place 'during the course of employment'. Such defences often succeed, particularly where an employer is wholly unaware of the joke or its attendant risks and could not reasonably have anticipated the injury. However, vicarious liability does apply when an employer can be shown to have been aware of a particular employee's propensity to play jokes that carried a risk and did not act to stop them from being played.

 Activity 25.2   *Iqbal v London Transport Executive* **(1973)**

Mr Iqbal sustained serious injuries while working in a bus depot run by the London Transport Executive. He was hit by a bus that was being driven out of the depot and into the street.

The bus was not, however, being driven by a qualified driver. Instead, a bus conductor took it upon himself to move the bus, despite being aware that he should call an engineer to carry out such duties in the absence of any qualified drivers. Mr Iqbal sued his employers (the LTE), but lost his case.

Questions

1 Why do you think Mr Iqbal was not able to claim compensation from his employer in this case?

2 What legal arguments could be advanced in support of Mr Iqbal?

Breach of statutory duty

Breach of statutory duty, like negligence, is a tort developed by judges in the common law courts over many decades. Sometimes cases are brought under this heading as an alternative to a negligence claim, but it is not at all unusual for injured employees to bring a 'double-barrelled action' and to sue their employer both for negligence and breach of statutory duty simultaneously (see Stranks, 2005:23). The purpose in doing so is to increase the chances of success. An employer may be able successfully to defend itself against a claim of negligence, but not in respect of a breach of statutory duty claim—or vice versa.

Damages for breach of statutory duty are won where a claimant is able to show that an employer has failed to act in accordance with a relevant health and safety statute or regulations issued under a statute. However, not all the health and safety statutes can be relied upon because some explicitly exclude the right. Importantly this includes most of the Health and Safety at Work Act 1974, which states at section 47 that:

> Nothing in this part shall be construed as conferring a right in any civil proceedings in respect of any failure to comply with any duty imposed by sections 2–7 or any contravention of Section 8.

The same type of exclusion clause is also found in the Management of Health and Safety at Work Act 1992, ensuring that for the most part these regulations are first and foremost part of the criminal law.

Despite this restriction, there are situations in which it is advantageous for an injured employee to bring a breach of statutory duty claim. This is especially so where a statute imposes a very clear and specific obligation on an employer which goes beyond the more general conception of reasonableness we have been focusing on in our analysis of criminal health and safety actions and negligence cases. There are fewer injuries and illnesses that fit into this category, but where one does it is much harder for an employer to defend its actions as being nonetheless reasonable in the circumstances. The significance of this point is best illustrated with an example:

An important set of statutory regulations which do not contain any exclusion clause precluding civil actions are the Control of Substances Hazardous to Health Regulations 1988 (see Chapter 24). Regulation 7 reads as follows:

> Every employer shall ensure that the exposure of his employees to a substance hazardous to health is either prevented or, where this in not reasonably practicable, adequately controlled.

This is more specific and detailed than the general requirement to do what is reasonably practicable we find in the Health and Safety at Work Act. Under the COSSH Regulations employers either *shall* prevent exposure to hazardous substances or *adequately control* exposure. A failure to meet these obligations amounts to a breach of statutory duty, even if it would be possible in some circumstances for an employer to defend itself from a claim of negligence using one of the defences outlined above. Kloss (2010:208) cites the case of *Dugmore v Swansea NHS Trust* (2003) to illustrate this point. Ms Dugmore was a nurse who suffered from an allergy to latex protein and developed a serious allergic reaction when she wore powdered latex gloves in her work. The condition was diagnosed after a particularly unpleasant attack and vinyl gloves provided to her instead. Some years later, however, she picked up an empty box at the hospital which had previously been packed with latex gloves and suffered a further attack. She was unable to return to work, and brought a claim of breach of statutory duty, winning damages of £354,000. A claim of negligence would not have succeeded, because the hospital could have claimed that her allergic reaction to latex could not have been reasonably foreseen. But her claim of breach of statutory duty succeeded because the wording of the COSSH Regulations is so precise ('every employer shall ensure') and the duty thus extends beyond a general requirement on employers to act reasonably in the circumstances.

Kloss (2010:208) also cites the case of *Stark v Post Office* (1999) which concerned a postman whose bicycle brake snapped and got stuck in the front wheel. As a result he was catapulted forwards and sustained some serious injuries. He was unsuccessful in his claim of negligence because the bicycle had been regularly inspected and repaired by his employers. They had, in fact, done everything they practically could have done to maintain the bike and could not have reasonably been expected to spot the 'metal fatigue' that ultimately caused the accident. However, Mr Stark won his claim for breach of statutory duty. This is because, as with the COSSH Regulations discussed above, strict liability is imposed on employers under the Provision and Use of Work Equipment Regulations 1992:

> Every employer shall ensure that work equipment is maintained in an efficient state, in efficient working order and in good repair.

The duty is very precise and specific, and is not qualified by any reference to reasonable practicability. As a result a breach of statutory duty was found to have occurred in Mr Stark's case and he won substantial damages from his employer.

Exhibit 25.2   Calculation of damages

When a claimant wins a claim of negligence or breach of statutory duty the compensation that they are paid is intended to put them back financially to where they would have been had the injury not occurred. But in practice, especially in the case of more serious injuries, this is very difficult to calculate accurately.

What are known as 'special damages' are awarded to compensate a victim for quantifiable losses sustained up until the date of the court hearing. This will typically include loss of earnings, medical expenses and the cost of any specialist care the injured person may have been required to pay for during a period of recovery.

'General damages' are paid on top of these. Here the court has to make estimations about likely loss of future earnings and damages to compensate for pain, suffering and loss of bodily functions. Inevitably the courts have to make informed guesses here, taking account of the medical evidence available to them and other evidence concerning, for example, the likelihood that an individual would have achieved promotion and gone on to earn a good deal more than was being earned at the time of the accident. Possible future inflation is not taken into account, the courts assuming that lump sums will be prudently invested and thus will be inflation-proof.

Sometimes, when the extent to which someone will recover in the future is unclear, a court will make a provisional award. The individual can then return later to ask for further damages if the prognosis turns out to be less rosy in practice.

In the case of deaths, the court is obliged to make an estimation about how long the victim would have lived naturally in deciding what widows and widowers should be awarded. Additional fixed lump sums are payable in such circumstances under the Fatal Accidents Act 1976 and the Administration of Justice Act 1982.

Breach of contract and constructive dismissal

The vast majority of personal injury claimants come to court alleging either negligence or breach of statutory duty, or both. This is simply because the law in these areas has developed extensively over the past sixty or seventy years and provides a very adequate route whereby injured employees can gain extensive compensation from their employers. However, there are circumstances in which employees prefer to bring a claim based on breach of contract rather than the torts of negligence or breach of statutory duty. One is where the employee wishes to continue working for his/her employer, is concerned about a health and safety provision, and is thus seeking a declaration of contractual rights rather than just compensation for injuries or illnesses sustained in the past. Another is where an employee resigns for a reason relating to health and safety and wishes to pursue a relatively cheap and quick claim for constructive dismissal in the employment tribunal. In either situation the approach used is to claim that the employer has breached one of the implied duties that all employers owe to all employees as part of their fundamental contractual relationship (see Chapter 8). The two of most relevance to health and safety at work are:

- the general duty of care
- the duty to maintain safe systems of working.

The first of these was relied upon in the often quoted case of *Johnstone v Bloomsbury Health Authority* (1991) which concerned a junior doctor who believed that his hours of work were so great as to constitute a breach of the duty of care. It is important to note that the case pre-dates the Working Time Regulations 1998, but this does not mean that the legal principles it established are no longer of any relevance. Mr Johnstone was employed as a senior house officer at University College Hospital in London. His contract of employment stated that his hours of work were forty per week, although he would also be required to be 'on call' for a further forty-eight hours a week 'on average'. This is what happened, but in some weeks he was asked to work in excess of 100 hours a week, with inadequate periods of sleep and, in consequence, suffered from stress, depression, exhaustion and a diminished appetite. He argued that the contractual requirement to work eighty eight hours a week 'on average' breached the employer's implied duty of care. He sued for damages and applied for a declaration that he could not be asked to work more than seventy-two hours in any one week.

Dr Johnstone won his case in the High Court and again when his employers appealed to the Court of Appeal. It was held that damage to his health from working such excessive amounts of time was reasonably foreseeable. What makes the case interesting, however, are the grounds the judges employed to deal with the employer's main defence; namely that no express term of the contract had been breached. In Chapter 8 we explained that as a rule express terms 'trump' implied terms when the two conflict. So in this case the employer quite reasonably sought to argue that in signing a contract which stipulated eighty-eight hours work a week 'on average', Dr Johnstone effectively waived his right to claim that this constituted a breach of the duty of care. The *Johnstone* judgment is not wholly clear on this point because different Lords of Appeal said slightly different things in finding for the claimant, but the fact that the contract separated working time into forty basic hours and a further forty-eight 'on average' is crucial. It allowed the Court to hold that the employers could exercise discretion in how they applied the contract, and that the breach of duty of care arose in their decision to use this discretion to put their employee's health in danger. Compensation was thus paid to Dr Johnstone and a general declaration made that in future he should not be asked to work hours which might reasonably injure his health.

An example of a constructive dismissal claim which is often quoted is *Waltons and Morse v Dorrington* (1997). Mrs Dorrington worked for Waltons and Morse in an old, poorly ventilated building. In the area she worked several colleagues were heavy smokers. Although she had no medical condition that made it difficult for her to breathe, she feared the effects of passive smoking and complained to management. On their refusal to address the issue, she decided to resign. She then brought a case of constructive dismissal, arguing that the employers had breached their implied duty of care in failing to address the issue. In response, Waltons and Morse provided strong evidence of the impracticability of installing the necessary ventilation in such old premises. Mrs Dorrington won her claim in the employment tribunal and again subsequently at the EAT. It would have been perfectly possible for the employer to have provided a separate smoking area or to have prohibited smoking altogether in the poorly ventilated rooms. In failing to do so the employer had breached implied terms in Mrs Dorrington's contract. It had failed to provide a suitably healthy working environment for her to work in, and she was thus entitled to resign and claim for compensation under the law of constructive dismissal.

Stress-based claims

Undoubtedly the most important recent development in the field of employment-based personal injury claims concerns stress-related conditions. In Chapter 24 we described how the issue has increasingly moved up the Health and Safety Executive's agenda and is hence finding a place in the criminal law arm of health and safety law. We now need to consider its impact on the the civil law side.

Sufficient case law now exists for us to reach considered conclusions about the extent to which employers should fear stress-based personal injury claims and hence about how these situations should be handled in practice. From the outset we can say that there are a number of widely believed myths about the way the law treats stress which have tended to make employers over-cautious and act as something of a barrier to the effective and fair management of stress cases in the workplace. In fact the case law is very helpful to employers, and only those who act in a clearly unreasonable way need have any real fear of paying out large amounts of compensation.

As with all personal injury claims, the preference of those suffering from stress caused by their work has been to use the law of negligence. Here, the big breakthrough came in 1995 when the High Court awarded a social worker called James Walker damages of £175,000 against Northumberland County Council after he suffered two nervous breakdowns. The *Walker* case was new in that it was the first time that a personal injury award was made for psychiatric injury following prolonged stress due to workload. Previously the awards had all been in trauma cases where a sudden shock of some kind had caused the illness. This case gained a great deal of press coverage, and in the following years several high sums have been reported in the press as having been paid out to employees who have suffered breakdowns due to occupational stress. Importantly, however, most of these have in fact been out-of-court settlements. Few cases have actually gone through the full legal process, although in some cases a settlement has been reached when it has become clear that the employer is likely to lose the case. For example, in *Ingram v Worcester County Council* (2000) a settlement of £203,000 was made after the employer had been found to have acted negligently when a warden responsible for the regulation of travellers' sites suffered two work-related breakdowns. He had, according to the court, suffered 'prolonged and unremitting stress' and had also been undermined in his job by senior council officials.

Understandably, the result of the publicity in these cases and others where high settlements were made has been to make employers cautious in the way that they handle stress-related absences, particularly where there is a clear link between the stress suffered and the job carried out. There is a tendency, particularly in the public sector, to allow people to take many months of absence due to stress and not to treat it managerially in the same way as any other illness or cause of absence. There is a fear of acting in such a way as to induce further stress and hence to end up having to pay out large sums by way of compensation.

In fact it must be remembered that the *Walker* and *Ingram* cases were unusual in important respects, that there are few examples of other similar claims succeeding in the courts and that there are substantial procedural obstacles facing people wanting to bring these claims. Earnshaw, and Morrison (2001) argue strongly that employers do not need to worry about these cases as much as they do for a number of reasons:

- James Walker had two work-related breakdowns, he won because the employer ignored the first one and overloaded him again to cause a second.

- The burden of proof is on the employee. This is not easy to show without witnesses to back up the claimant's story.

- There is no legal aid available. So claimants either have to be quite well off to pursue a claim, or persuade a solicitor to take them on on a 'no win/no fee' basis. Even then they have to pay around £1000 for an initial assessment by the solicitor.

- Claimants have to show that the stress-related illness was 'reasonably foreseeable'. This is much harder than with a physical injury as there is no objective definition of a 'reasonable workload' or 'a stressful situation'.

- Claimants have to show that the work was the main factor causing the stress and that other factors outside work were not responsible.

- Claimants have to be supported by a doctor who is prepared to certify that they have a psychiatric illness identifiably caused by work.

The *Ingram* case was similar to the *Walker* case in that the employer's duty was breached only after a breakdown was suffered in circumstances in which it was clearly foreseeable by the employer.

These principles have since been confirmed in a series of other cases. Moreover, in the process, other principles which are helpful from an employer's point of view have also been clearly established. In 2002, ruling on four separate stress-based personal injury claims (usually referred to as *Hatton v Sutherland*—one of the four) the Court of Appeal found against three ex-employees who had earlier won large amounts of damages in the lower courts. They found in favour of the fourth. The grounds varied. In one case they said that the risk of further injury had not been reasonably foreseeable, in another they found that the workload had not been excessive. In the third the illness was found to have been 'readily attributable to causes other than workplace stress'. In the process the Court set out guidance which is very helpful from an employer's point of view. It included the following:

- employers are not obliged to make searching enquiries to establish whether an individual is at risk,

- employees who stay in stressful jobs voluntarily are responsible for their own fate if they subsequently suffer stress-based illnesses,

- there must be indications of impending harm arising from workload in order for an employer to take action,

- the employer is only in breach where the risk is foreseeable *'bearing in mind the size of the risk, the gravity of the harm, the costs of preventing it and the justification of running the risk'*,

- there are no occupations which should be regarded as intrinsically dangerous to mental health,

- employers who offer confidential counselling services with access to treatment are un-likely to be found in breach,
- the illness must clearly be caused by breach of duty and not just by occupational stress,
- damages must be reduced to take account of pre-existing disorders or the chance that the claimant would have fallen ill anyway.

In 2004, the House of Lords endorsed the above principles in *Barber v Somerset County Council*. In this case, however, they found for the claimant on the grounds that his breakdown had been foreseeable and the employer had failed to act to prevent it. So employers are by no means let off the hook by these recent rulings. They simply apply the existing law on neg-ligence to the apparently 'new' situation of psychiatric injury suffered due to workload and the working environment. The test set out in the *Barber* case is clear and balanced:

> The conduct of a reasonable and prudent employer, taking positive thought for the safety of his workers in the light of what he knows or ought to know.

Only if this principle is broken, is an employer likely to face a stress-based personal injury claim and a sizeable bill for damages. It is essential to appreciate that employees are not en-titled to receive compensation just because they are injured or become ill as a result of their work. With stress-based claims, as with other more 'traditional' types of industrial injury there is a need to show that the employer knew of the risk and clearly acted negligently in failing to take sufficient steps to reduce it.

 Activity 25.3   *Hartman v South Essex Mental Health and Community Care Trust* **(2005)**

Mrs Hartman was employed as a nursing auxiliary at a children's home. At the date of her retire-ment in 1999 she had worked at the home for ten years. Mrs Hartman had a long history of personal problems, having been sexually abused as a child, suffered domestic violence in her first marriage and seeing her child die from meningitis. Throughout the 1970s and 1980s she consulted a psychia-trist and was prescribed anti-depressants and tranquillisers. In 1988 she suffered a serious nervous breakdown, but appeared to recover well.

She was appointed to the job at the children's home in 1989 after being passed as fit for full-time employment by the trust's occupational health department. On her confidential health screening questionnaire she had disclosed the breakdown suffered in 1988 and said that she was taking tran-quillisers and sleeping tablets. In 1991 she ceased taking tranquillisers.

In 1996 one of the children who lived in the home died after being injured in a car accident. Mrs Hartman administered first aid to this child, accompanied her to hospital and had to deal with the trauma suffered by the family on her death. This incident triggered a further depres-sive episode, but she was able to return to work after a few weeks and appeared to be back to normal.

In 1997 the number of hours Mrs Hartman worked increased due to staff shortages. The manager of the children's home wrote to her boss complaining about the stress that her staff

»

» were suffering due to this situation, and these concerns were conveyed on to the director of primary care. Four staff left the home citing stress as their reason for resigning, but no immediate action was taken.

In 1998 Mrs Hartman developed bonchitis and went off on sick leave. She subsequently suffered from panic attacks and sleeping problems. She made an application for ill health retirement which was supported by the trust's occupational health department. Her condition was diagnosed as 'a mood disorder of moderate severity characterised by depression and anxiety'.

She then brought a negligence claim against her former employers, and won her case in the High Court. She was awarded £52,000 by way of damages. The judge made the following points:

- But for the accident and pressures at work, Mrs Hartman's condition would have been less severe and would have lasted less time.
- The trust knew that Mrs Hartman had had a depressive illness in 1988 and that she was taking tranquillisers when she started working for them.
- The trust had received a complaint from the manager of the children's home concerning staffing levels and overwork, yet had not acted to improve the situation.
- A number of staff employed at the home had resigned for reasons of stress during this period.

The case was appealed to the Court of Appeal, and in 2005 they found against Mrs Hartman. The key points in the judgment are the following:

- Mrs Hartman had disclosed details of her illness to the occupational health department and not to her managers. The questionnaire she completed was clearly marked 'confidential' and for use by the occupational health service only.
- The car accident occurred eighteen months before Mrs Hartman's breakdown and there was no sign after this that she was particularly vulnerable to psychiatric injury.
- Mrs Hartman had not taken up the offer of counselling made to all staff following the accident.
- At the time that she became sick for the final time, Mrs Hartman appeared to be coping well personally with the stress caused by understaffing.

In short, the Court of Appeal decided that 'it was not reasonably foreseeable to the trust that Mrs Hartman would suffer psychiatric injury and, accordingly, they were not in breach of duty to her'.

Questions

1 Did the High Court judge and the Lords of Appeal apply different legal tests when deciding this case?

2 To what extent do you agree that the Court of Appeal applied the same, long established, legal tests used to determine negligence claims relating to physical injury?

3 Which aspects of the ruling in the *Hatton* case worked to the advantage of the employer in this case?

The Protection from Harassment Act

A significant new development in the law on stress and mental breakdown caused by bullying at work was introduced as a result of the case of *Majrowski v Guy's and St Thomas's NHS Trust* (2006). Here the claimant chose not to rely on established routes of litigation—harassment on grounds of sexual orientation, constructive dismissal or stress-based personal injury law. Instead he brought his claim under the Protection from Harassment Act 1997, which is not primarily about employment situations at all. It had not been used to tackle workplace harassment in the past, because it does not contain any clauses relating to vicarious liability. It was thus widely thought only to be relevant when one individual is harassed to an unacceptable degree by another (eg, in disputes between next-door neighbours, in stalking situations or when unpleasant threats are made by animal rights campaigners, etc). In this case, however, the House of Lords approved an earlier Court of Appeal ruling by agreeing that employers can be vicariously liable for breaches of the Act by their employees. As Mr Majrowski had been seriously bullied by his manager, his employers were therefore responsible. The test is that a harasser must have knowingly caused serious distress or alarm on at least two occasions.

The precedent established by *Majrowski* was nonetheless used in July 2006 by Helen Green in her high-profile and well-publicised High Court victory over Deutsche Bank, the case being notable because of the very substantial sum awarded in damages—£828,000 (£35,000 for pain and suffering, £25,000 for disadvantage in the labour market, £128,000 for lost earnings and £640,000 for loss of future earnings and pension). After costs were also taken into account the employer's total bill exceeded 1.5 million. Helen Green's case concerned, on the face of it, a stress-based personal injury claim of a similar nature to the *Walker* case described above. Ms Green had been bullied by colleagues, had a breakdown as a result, returned to work, had been bullied again and had a further breakdown. This had happened over a four-year period and involved Ms Green suffering unpleasant verbal abuse from five separate colleagues. Eventually, when it became clear that she would not be returning to work in the foreseeable future, the bank dismissed her. Significantly, Ms Green relied on the *Majrowski* judgment as well as on longer-established stress-based precedents in bringing her case, and this allowed the High Court to award her the very substantial amount of damages she ended up with.

The extent to which substantial numbers of people will bring future cases using the *Majrowski* route is, however, uncertain. There are advantages. First, because the case is heard in the County Court or in the High Court and not the employment tribunal, there is a six-year time frame in which to bring the case, rather than three months (see Chapter 2). Secondly, there is no need for the harassment to be based on a personal characteristic that is covered by the law of discrimination (sex, race, disability, age, etc), nor is the employer able to defend itself by showing that reasonable steps were taken to prevent harassment from occurring. Thirdly, in theory at least, a resignation is not required as it would be were the case to be brought under the law of constructive dismissal. Fourthly, in addition to compensation, the winning side can claim full costs from the losing side. Fifthly, damages for 'anxiety' are available and there is no need to prove that negligence has occurred or that any actual injury has been sustained.

On the negative side, however, there is a risk that the claimant will lose and will themselves be required to pay costs. This last point may well in practice ensure that relatively few claimants bring cases against their employers under the Protection of Harassment Act and it should certainly ensure that weak, speculative claims are not commonly brought. It is also necessary to point out, as is explained by Rajgopal (2008) in his review of more recent cases, that there has been a clear tendency for the judges to raise the bar somewhat when considering the strength of claimants' cases. In *Sunderland City Council v Conn* (2008), for example, it was held that in order to be covered by the Protection from Harassment Act, the conduct the employee was complaining about had to be 'oppressive and unacceptable' and not merely 'unattractive or unreasonable'. Moreover, the Court of Appeal also held that 'the gravity of the misconduct must be of an order which would sustain criminal liability'. It is highly questionable whether claims such as Helen Green's in the *Deutsche Bank* case would have been successful had these more recent tests been applied when she brought her claim.

Debates about the personal injury claims system

What happens in practice when someone suffers an injury at work, or becomes ill as a result of their work, and has to give up their job as a result? The answer is that they first apply to the Department for Work and Pensions in order to claim employment and support allowance. This is not intended to compensate for loss of earnings in any way, but merely to provide a basic level of income on which to subsist. In addition the person may qualify for industrial injuries disablement benefit paid by the government, the amount of money received depending on the severity of the disability. But this benefit also serves more to help an injured person to subsist than it does to compensate for lost earning power. At the time of writing (summer 2011) for those over the age of eighteen who are assessed as being 100% disabled and in need of constant care the sum paid is only £150.30 per week (£7,815.60 a year). The figures for people with lesser injuries or illnesses are far lower, however much income has been lost as a result. If the person is a member of their employer's occupational pension scheme, it should be possible to draw a pension following an industrial injury or the contraction of an industrial disease. But fewer than half of all employees in the UK are members of such schemes, and the resulting income, even if enhanced considerably, is unlikely to compensate someone fully for the loss of income and quality of life that they are suffering. So most people will seek further compensation from their former employers in the form of a lump sum.

Since 1969 all private sector employers have been required by law to take out comprehensive employers' liability insurance, so any payments made in a settlement or by order of a court are made by insurance companies and not by employers themselves. It is clearly in the interests of the insurance companies and the employers who pay the premiums to them for settlements to be as low as possible when employees are injured or develop illnesses at work. Moreover, of course, they will try not to pay any compensation at all if they believe there is a chance that a court would rule that the employer is not liable (ie, has not acted negligently or breached its statutory duty). As a result injured parties are often faced with a choice between accepting a relatively low offer from their former employer's insurers or taking the case before the courts. The latter course of action can be costly in terms of legal fees and will usually take several years. Whinchup (1997:352) shows that most claims take at least four years to settle in court and that it is not unusual for more complex cases to take ten years. It takes a further two or three years if the case is subsequently appealed.

Litigation takes so long because there is often a great deal of detailed evidence to be amassed and because insurance companies have no incentive to respond quickly. Moreover, doctors are necessarily obliged in many cases to avoid committing themselves about the likely speed and extent of an injured person's recovery. So there is often a case for waiting to see what happens before making a full and final settlement. Not only does this practice result in further delays, it also gives the injured person no incentive whatever to take steps to hasten recovery and get back into work. Even when a case proceeds to court relatively quickly, delays are inevitable simply because of the large volume of personal injury claims that are made and which clog up the court system. Success rates are also low. At the end of the day, only 6% of accident victims end up recovering damages in the court room (Whincup, 1997:353). Another extraordinary statistic is that for each pound won by claimants in tort damages, at least 85 pence is spent on legal costs (Kloss, 2005:257). It is not difficult to conclude that insurance companies and lawyers are bigger winners in this system and not employees or employers.

The major alternative approach that is used in some other countries is to have a state-run no-fault approach to the compensation of injured and ill employees. Contributions are made into a central fund and this then pays out compensation to all who suffer serious accidents or develop serious illnesses as a result of their jobs. There is no need for the employee to prove that the employer acted negligently, or that there was a reasonably foreseeable risk that was not confronted sufficiently strongly. Conversely there is no requirement for an employer to prove contributory fault or voluntary assumption of risk in order to reduce compensation levels. The big advantage of such schemes, examples of which run successfully in New Zealand and Sweden, is that adequate compensation reaches victims much more quickly. The ordeal of lengthy legal actions is avoided in the vast majority of cases, resulting in a scheme which is much less costly to administer. A far greater proportion of the money awarded to victims is made up of compensation, while far less is taken up with legal costs. The outcome is reduced insurance costs for employers, and speedier and more satisfactory compensation for those left incapacitated.

The major argument against the adoption of a centrally administered, no-fault scheme is that it provides little incentive to employers to improve health and safety arrangements in their workplaces. Insurance premiums are determined according to the type of industry, meaning that employers who invest heavily in health and safety pay the same premiums as those who take risks with that of their employees. There is thus a chance that preventing accidents from occurring in the first place would move down rather than up employer agendas. Against this a number of points can be made:

- It can be argued that the presence of the criminal sanctions we discussed in Chapter 24 provides sufficient incentive for employers to improve health and safety in their workplaces.

- Because under the tort system compensation payments are made by insurance companies and not by employers, the civil law already provides relatively little incentive to improve health and safety.

- The UK already operates a no-fault scheme of this kind under the Consumer Protection Act 1987 for situations in which customers are injured as a result of purchasing defective goods.

- It would be possible to devise a system which required increased premiums to be paid by employers who wished to employ higher-risk systems of working.

The second major argument against moving towards a no-fault system is that it would encourage people who have in reality suffered only very minor injuries and who have recovered quickly to exaggerate the seriousness of their condition in order to claim compensation from the fund. This would be of no great advantage to anyone and might end up leading to a situation in which premiums paid by employers increased further so as to keep the central fund solvent. Even if the employees who exaggerated their injuries were ultimately unsuccessful, their claims would take up time and would create unnecessary worry for employers in the short term. Moreover, lawyers would still have to be employed by both sides to advise and conduct cases where there was a dispute. There would also have to be some form of court-based appeal system, so the extent to which public money could be saved is questionable.

 **Activity 25.4   The Pearson Commission**

In 1973 the then government appointed a commission under Lord Pearson to look into the whole area of personal injury claims and to make recommendations for change. The commission considered the New Zealand approach and the merits of no-fault schemes generally. They found considerable opposition to such approaches existed on the part of lawyers, insurance companies and trade unions.

Their recommendations were moderate rather than radical. Instead of establishing a general no-fault compensation scheme, they recommended increasing the level of benefits paid to injured workers by the government, including earnings-related supplements to reflect the fact that the loss in income suffered was greater for some people rather than others. They also argued for more generous state benefits for widows following industrial accidents, including self-employed people in the disablement benefits scheme and permitting people to claim when they were injured in commuting accidents.

None of these recommendations was in practice taken up by the then government or by any of its successors. As a result many commentators have criticised the Pearson Commission as constituting 'five years of wasted effort' and 'a great lost opportunity'.

(*Source:* Whincup, 1997:358–359)

Questions

1 Why do you think trade unions might have objected to proposals for a no-fault approach to personal injury compensation?

2 Why do you think governments since 1978 have been so reluctant to implement the proposals made by the Pearson Committee?

3 To what extent do you agree that the Pearson Commission report represented a lost opportunity?

In 2010 Lord Young's report on behalf of the government entitled 'Common Sense, Common Safety' made a range of recommendations for reform of personal injury law. On the question of a no-fault scheme, he recommended that it would be appropriate for lower value claims. At the higher end he recommended that recommendations made in another report, by Lord Jackson, be implemented. These include the radical suggestion that in no-win-no-fee cases lawyers' fees should no longer be recoverable from the losing party following a case. The winning lawyer would instead claim fees from the party being represented, but these should be capped at 25% of any settlement or award. In order to make this possible, Jackson recommended that the value of awards made by the courts should be increased by 10%.

CHAPTER SUMMARY

- In the UK most personal injury claims in the employment context are brought under the law of negligence (a tort), the injured person alleging that the employer's negligence led to the injury.

- There are several defences that can be deployed by employers. The most significant involves showing that the injury was not reasonably foreseeable.

- Sometimes cases are brought under different headings such as breach of the duty of care or breach of statutory duty. It is also possible for an employee to resign for health and safety reasons and to pursue a constructive dismissal claim in the employment tribunal.

- The most significant recent development in this area of law is the bringing of cases that relate to stress, mental breakdown and bullying at work. Substantial amounts of damages have been won by claimants pursuing cases of this kind where the employer has acted negligently.

- Commentators have long argued that the UK system of personal injury law is unsatisfactory from the point of view of both employers and injured employees. Legal action tends to be costly, lengthy and overly risky. Many thus argue for the establishment of a simpler, national, no-fault insurance scheme.

For updates and further materials, please see the online resource centre at www.oup.com.

REFERENCES

Deakin, S. and Morris, G. (2009) *Labour Law*. Fifth Edition. Oxford: Hart Publishing.

Earnshaw, J. and Morrison, L. (2001) 'Should employers worry? Workplace stress claims following the John Walker decision' *Personnel Review* 30.4.

IRS (2000) '£203,000 award for single breakdown' *Employee Health Bulletin, 13*. Industrial Relations Services.

Kloss, D. (2005) *Occupational Health Law*. Fourth Edition. Oxford: Blackwell.

Kloss, D. (2010) *Occupational Health Law*. Fifth Edition. Oxford: Blackwell.

Rajgopaul, C. (2008) 'Protection from Harassment Act claims' *Tolley's Employment Law Newsletter*. April.

Stranks, J. (2005) *Health and Safety Law*. Fifth Edition. Harlow: Pearson Education.

Whincup, M. (1997) *Modern Employment Law: A Guide to Job Security and Safety*. Ninth Edition. Oxford: Butterworth Heinemann.

Young, Lord D. (2010) 'Common Sense, Common Safety'. London, HM Government.

ONLINE RESOURCE CENTRE

A range of online resources to help you through your employment law module have been developed by the author team. These include updates, self-test questions and sources for further reading. (www.oxfordtextbooks.co.uk/orc/taylor_emir3e)

Working time

Learning outcomes

By the end of this chapter you should be able to:

- describe the background to the implementation of the Working Time Regulations;

- say to whom the Regulations apply, and advise about which groups are exempt;

- set out the rules that apply to rest breaks and holiday leave;

- outline the maximum hours that an employer can ask a person to work;

- explain the use of the opt-out, and suggest how this area of the law may develop in the future; and

- debate the economic and social arguments for and against the legislation.

Introduction

In the previous two chapters we considered health and safety and its interaction with employment law and practice. One of the most controversial pieces of legislation that formally comes within the ambit of health and safety is that which tries to limit working time.

The aim of the European 1993 Working Time Directive is to ensure that employees are protected against adverse effects on their health and safety caused by working excessively long hours, having inadequate rest or disrupted work patterns. The issue has, however, generated much heated debate on whether such law is in fact needed. The arguments surrounding the regulation of working time relate not only to the health and safety of workers, but also include the economic and social aspects of such legislation and whether, as a result, the country benefits from it or not.

To some, the Working Time Regulations 1998 (which gave effect to the EU directive in the UK) represent a wholly unnecessary and unwelcome opportunity for the state to meddle in private employment matters. For others they are a long-needed means of protecting employees from sustaining damage to their health by working excessive hours. A third group thinks that this is just 'bad law': poorly drafted, imprecise, overly complex and designed to satisfy the EU while actually making no real impact on UK workplaces. The one thing that is not generally contested is the view that the Working Time Regulations have been one of the more complex and controversial bodies of new employment legislation introduced in recent years.

In this chapter we will look at the background to the Working Time Regulations, and the specifics of the law. We will then move on to consider some of the arguments that have been raised both for and against such regulation.

Activity 26.1

Consider the following statements. Which do you think are correct and which are false?

1 The Working Time Regulations apply to workers, not just employees.

2 The Working Time Regulations do not allow a person to work (including doing any overtime) in any circumstances for more than forty-eight hours a week.

3 British workers have the same limit on their working time as other European countries which are members of the European Union.

4 It is generally agreed that the Regulations have had a great impact on British working practices.

5 The ability to opt out of the maximum weekly working hours is widely used by other European countries.

Return to this activity once you have read the chapter, to see how many of your answers were correct.

Background

The origins of working time legislation lie in the brutal conditions faced by workers in the factories of the industrial revolution, which led to the British factories legislation in the nineteenth century. As early as 1818, the philanthropist Robert Owen was petitioning for the regulation of working hours. Employers at the time were opposed to such legislation, fearful of international competition.

It was these concerns, together with the fear of industrialised countries that they would face a revolt by workers similar to that of the Soviet October Revolution, that eventually gave rise, in 1919, to the birth of the International Labour Organisation. This was supported by employers as a way to dilute international competition by establishing minimum conditions that applied across the board.

Some of the original aims of the ILO were to ensure an eight-hour day, or a forty-eight-hour week, and a weekly rest of twenty-four hours. The eight-hour day was implemented by France the same year, and a forty-hour week in 1936. Germany also had the same eight and forty-hour regulations by 1938 (although these limits have since changed). Britain, by contrast, fought fiercely against having any such law imposed upon it by Europe in the 1990s, and it was not until 1998 that we had any formal regulation of working time. This is ironic, as Britain was one of the drafting members of the original ILO convention.

In Britain, working time had traditionally been the subject of voluntary measures and collective agreements in the many unionised industries, but, as the influence of the unions diminished, the impact and coverage of such agreements was greatly reduced. There was some regulation of sectors such as transport, where drivers were subject to driving limits and rest periods, but nothing that applied to the workforce as a whole.

In 1993 the European Union passed the Working Time Directive. The aim of this legislation was stated to be:

> To adopt minimum requirements covering certain aspects of the organisation of working time connected with workers' health and safety.

The Conservative government of the day questioned the validity of the Directive on the basis that it was made under Article 118 as a health and safety measure, rather than Article 100, which relates to the rights of employed persons. It brought a case in the European Court of Justice arguing the point. If the UK government had been successful, it would have meant that in order for it to be adopted, the Directive would have required a unanimous decision rather than a majority decision, and as such the UK would have been able to block it. Until the outcome of this case, the government made no attempt to comply with the 1996 deadline. The ECJ decided against the UK, and so the Directive had to be implemented. This was done in 1998 by means of the Working Time Regulations. The UK did, however, manage to retain an opt-out clause, whereby individuals could agree with their employer to work for longer hours. The issue of whether this opt-out should be kept has still not been resolved. As will be seen below, there have been various attempts between the European Union and the UK to come to some compromise, but this has come to nothing. The British Regulations have attracted criticism, not only because of the policy behind the introduction of working time limits, but also because they are extremely lengthy and complicated. In the following section we will look at the main elements that make up the law.

 Exhibit 26.1   Arguments for regulating working time

During a debate in the House of Lords in November 1998, shortly after the Regulations came into force, Lord McKintosh of Haringey said:

> We are proud to have implemented the working time directive because we believe in a flexible labour market, but one which is underpinned by fair minimum standards. Throughout the centuries there has been an imbalance in the relationship between workers and employers. That is the whole basis on which the labour movement grew in the first place. Some employers still seek to take advantage and to abuse this, and so workers need support. It is not right that employers should be able to force workers to work excessive hours against their will, for fear of getting the sack . . . [The rights] exist in most other countries in Europe and it is right that workers in this country should have them as well . . . .

> . . . there are [also] benefits to business from this measure. It is an old fashioned idea that business should involve the exploitation of workers. All modern business nowadays recognises that agreement, collaboration and co-operation between employer and employee are the secret of success.

Source: Hansard, 4 Nov 1998 (Column 358–359)

Core working time rights

The UK law is contained in the Working Time Regulations 1998, which have since been amended in relatively minor ways.

In general, the law applies to workers, not just employees, and the basic 'headline' entitlements as set out in the Regulations are:

- a limit of forty-eight hours per week
- all workers to receive twenty-eight days' paid annual leave each year (including eight bank holidays)
- twenty minutes' rest in any period of work lasting six hours or more
- eleven hours rest in any one twenty-four-hour period
- twenty-four hours rest in any seven-day period
- night workers limited to eight hours work in any one twenty-four-hour period
- free health checks for night workers
- special regulations restricting working time of young workers (ie, 16–18 year olds).

On the face of it this looks very clear cut and straightforward, but this is very far from the case. The Regulations themselves are very complex, and run to more than 100 pages in length, with numerous situations in which there are exceptions. We shall consider first to whom the Regulations apply.

Who is covered?

The Regulations apply to all workers, not just employees. A 'worker' is defined in these Regulations as a person who works under a contract of employment, or any other contract, where he or she undertakes to do or perform personally any work or services for the 'employer'. This is discussed further in Chapter 3. Agency workers are specifically included in the Regulations, but they do not apply to self-employed people. There are exceptions to the Regulations (although often they still apply to young workers). The sectors entirely excluded from their scope are:

- sea transport
- sea-going fishing vessels
- mobile workers in inland waterways and lake transport.

Moreover, there are some sectors which are only partially excluded (so some of the Regulations apply):

- civil protection service (such as the armed forces, the police, ambulance service, etc)
- mobile workers in civil aviation (such as flight crew and cabin crew), but they are entitled to four weeks' paid annual leave and health assessments for night workers
- mobile workers in road transport (such as coach drivers and lorry drivers) are entitled to four weeks' paid annual leave and health assessments for night workers
- domestic servants.

Many of these sectors have their own regulations which differ from the Working Time Regulations and which are outside the scope of this chapter. They also have their own enforcement authorities, other than the HSE. There is also a right for a worker to opt out of the forty-eight-hour working week, which will be considered below, and a further exemption for those who have control over their working hours, known as the 'unmeasured' working time exemption.

Unmeasured working time

The Regulations state that a worker falls into the category of unmeasured working time if *'the duration of his working time is not measured or predetermined, or can be determined by the worker himself'*. This rule would generally apply to managing executives or other persons with autonomous decision-taking powers, who can decide when to do their work, and how long they work.

Until 2006, there was also a further exemption introduced in 1999 after employers lobbied the government. This was for those workers who have an element of their working time predetermined, for example under the terms of their contract, but who choose to work longer hours on a purely voluntary basis. This was known as the 'partly unmeasured' working time exemption. This has now been repealed, subsequent to a complaint by Amicus to the European Commission (which subsequently went to the ECJ) that the UK had not properly implemented the Directive, and is therefore no longer an option. Such workers will now come fully within the scope of the Regulations. It will not, however, make much difference in practice, as such workers are still able to opt out of the forty-eight-hour week.

What is working time?

Working time is described in the Regulations as the time when someone is '*working, at his employer's disposal and carrying out his activity or duties*'. This means that whenever a person is at work, or is doing something for their employer, then they are at work. So, if an employee has to go to a business lunch, this would be working time, as it is being done for the employer. It also covers workers travelling as part of their work, such as travelling salespeople, and time spent doing job-related training.

It does not, however, include time where the worker can do his own thing, such as during rest breaks, or training which is not related to the job (eg, when a worker goes on a day-release course at a local college). The guide to the Regulations by the former Department of Business, Enterprise and Regulatory Reform (BERR) states that they do not cover travel outside working hours, nor routine travel between home and work, much as weary commuters may wish them to!

The ECJ has considered the status of on-call time, and decided that this would count as working time when a worker is required to be at his place of work while on call, even if he is asleep. When a worker, however, is permitted to be away from the workplace when 'on call' and accordingly free to pursue leisure activities, on-call time is not 'working time' (*SIMAP v Conselleria de Sanidad y Consumo de la Generalidad Valenciana* (2001)).

Activity 26.2

Safe and Sound plc provides security services to a variety of corporate clients on a sub-contracted basis. It employs 2,000 security guards and maintains a headquarters office staffed by a further fifty employees. Concerned at press reports concerning the Working Time Regulations, the company's HR director carries out some research to discover how many employees are working over forty-eight hours a week. She finds that two distinct groups regularly work such hours—security staff employed to work night-time shifts and managers.

Given your knowledge of the Working Time Regulations, what action would you advise the HR director to take in the case of these two groups?

Rest periods and rest breaks

The aspect of the Working Time Regulations that most people will be familiar with is that of the maximum forty-eight-hour week. The Regulations also provide, however, for rest breaks and daily rest.

Daily rest

A worker is entitled to a rest period of eleven uninterrupted hours between each working day.

Weekly rest

In addition to this, he or she is entitled to one whole day off a week. Days off can be averaged over a two-week period, meaning workers can take two days off a fortnight.

Rest breaks

During the working day, if it is more than six hours long, the worker is entitled to a rest break of at least twenty minutes. (For young workers a thirty-minute break is required for four and a half hours of work.) This must be part of a rest period (in other words, it should not come at the end of the working day), and it is time for the employee to do what he or she pleases. In the case of *Miller v Lambert* (2000), an employment tribunal case, a woman who was usually the only person on duty in a service station, had to lock the door if she wanted to go to the toilet, leaving the customers waiting outside. The tribunal said that the employer would not have found it acceptable if she had taken a break of twenty minutes, and there was no room in which she could have taken her rest away from her workstation, and so they decided that the company was in breach of its obligation to allow her to take her rest break. There is a further entitlement of 'adequate' rest breaks where the pattern of work is such as to put the worker's health and safety at risk, such as where the work is monotonous. It is not clear how these differ from ordinary rest breaks.

Obligation or entitlement?

The Regulations only provide a remedy when the employer 'refuses' to permit the worker to take his or her rest break. So there have been a number of tribunal cases, where the worker has been unable to take the rest, but has failed at tribunal because the employer has not actually 'refused'.

There is thus a question whether the right to take rest is an obligation or entitlement. In other words, if a worker forgoes the rest voluntarily, would this still bring it within the wording of the European Directive? The view of the government is that this is acceptable, but there is an argument that this does not reconcile with the fact that the Directive was intended to be a health and safety measure. If workers therefore choose not to have their breaks they might be putting their own health and safety, and perhaps that of others, at risk.

The trade union Amicus, in the *SIMAP* case referred to above, also complained that the Directive had not been properly implemented in that, for health and safety reasons, rest breaks should be obligatory and employers should be responsible for ensuring that they are taken. The European Commission agreed with Amicus. The matter then went to the European Court of Justice, which considered the UK guidelines to the Regulations available from what was then the Department for Trade and Industry (now BIS). (*Commission of the European Communities v United Kingdom of Great Britain and Northern Ireland, Case C-484/04*).

The guidelines at the time stated that '*Employers must make sure that workers can take their rest, but are not required to make sure they do take their rest*'. The ECJ held that this statement does not comply with the Directive because it gives the impression an employer is not required to ensure that workers take their rest breaks, and therefore renders the rights meaningless. It stated that workers' rest should be treated as a basic right, rather than an option for workers to take if they choose. The guidance was later amended to say: '*Employers must make sure that workers can take their rest*'.

Weekly limits

The general time limit that is set out in the Regulations is forty-eight hours a week. In order to keep some flexibility, however, this is averaged out over a period of seventeen weeks (known as the 'reference' period), although this can be longer in some situations, such as that for doctors in training (who have a twenty-six week period), or as part of a workforce or collective agreement which can extend the reference period up to fifty-two weeks.

The average weekly working time is calculated by dividing the number of hours worked by seventeen (or twenty-six, etc). If the worker is away during the reference period because he or she is taking paid annual leave, maternity leave, or is off sick, then this time will need to be made up for in the calculation. This is done by adding up the hours worked during the days which immediately followed the seventeen-week period, using the same number of days as those when work was missed.

 Exhibit 26.2   **Averaging**

A summary of an example of averaging given in the government guidance on the Directgov website is as follows:

A worker has a standard working week of forty hours (eight hours a day) and does overtime of eight hours a week for the first twelve weeks of the seventeen-week reference period. Four days' leave are also taken during the reference period.

So, during the reference period of seventeen weeks, the worker has done sixteen weeks and one day (forty hours a week and eight hours a day) and twelve weeks of eight hours of overtime.

This makes the actual hours worked as:

$$(16 \times 40) + (1 \times 8) + (12 \times 8) = 744$$

To this has to be added the time taken on leave, taken from the first four working days after the reference period. The worker does no overtime, so four days of eight hours should be added to the total.

$$4 \times 8 = 32$$

His average, therefore is (total hours divided by number of weeks):

$$\frac{744 + 32}{17} = 45.6 \text{ hours per week}$$

The average limit of forty-eight hours has been complied with.

 Exhibit 26.3   **Doctors' hours**

The Working Time Regulations did not fully apply to doctors working in the NHS until 2009. They are now subject to the same limits on working hours as other employees. This has been the source of some debate, as doctors, particularly junior ones, had been known for their long-hours culture. A survey quoted by Woods referred to it as a 'ticking time bomb' (Woods, 2010) because doctors believed that they had less time to train. It has since been indicated that the Regulations might be looked at again to consider whether the on-call aspect of doctors' hours might be changed (Bloxham, 2010).

The opt-out

Workers can agree to work longer than the forty-eight-hour limit. An agreement must be in writing and signed by the worker. The agreement has to be entered into on an individual basis and not through a workforce or collective agreement. This agreement is known as an opt-out, and can be for a specified period or an indefinite period. The opt-out agreement can be cancelled by the worker at any time, upon giving at least seven days' notice, or longer (up to three months) if this has been agreed. A worker cannot be unfairly dismissed because he refuses to sign the opt-out—it has to be with his agreement. A worker can only opt out of the maximum forty-eight-hour week; he cannot opt out of any other part of the Working Time Regulations.

Even if a worker has signed an opt-out, there is an argument to say that he or she still cannot be required to work excessively long hours if this would give rise to a reasonably foreseeable risk to health or safety. In a case decided before the Working Time Directive came into existence (*Johnstone v Bloomsbury Health Authority* (1991)), the Court of Appeal decided that, in relation to the working hours of a junior doctor, notwithstanding the express provisions of the contract, the employer could not lawfully require the doctor to work so much overtime in one week as would foreseeably damage his health (see Chapter 25).

The opt-out was added to the Directive at the request of the then UK government, and so far, has been used almost exclusively in the UK. It has been an extremely controversial part of the Regulations, and there are ongoing discussions within the EU as to whether it should continue or not. The TUC, in its response to the 1998 consultation document on the original regulations said:

> It cannot be right for the Government to accept that the 48 hours is a reasonable limit in line with the requirements of health and safety at work and then suggest that individuals should be free to work more than 48 hours without limit. Indeed, it is contrary to the general principles of health and safety law to allow people to 'volunteer' to adopt an unsafe system of work. (IDS, 2005:37)

In 2004 the European Commission published a ten-year review of the Working Time Directive, focusing in particular on the opt-out provision. The opt-out was supposed to be implemented only under certain conditions and there was some concern that workers were being coerced into 'volunteering' for longer hours, and that some workers were feeling forced to sign the opt-out as a condition of being offered employment.

The then Labour government's response was that:

> The opt-out, properly operated, allows workers to choose whether or not they wish to have their hours limited. Provided workers freely choose to work long hours, and are subject to appropriate health and safety regulations, we feel strongly that their right to choose should be respected. (IDS, 2005:37)

This is still the view of the current government, with the Liberal Democrat MEP Liz Lynne further arguing that the removal of the opt-out would push people into illegal work where they would no longer be covered by health and safety legislation (Haurant, 2009).

In 2008, the UK managed to secure the temporary continuation of the opt-out by agreeing to more rights for agency workers (see Chapter 19). Later that year, the European Parliament voted to end the opt-out. Since then, there have been negotiations, but no agreement, and it is still not clear at the time of writing (early 2011) what the outcome will be.

The UK's view is that labour market flexibility promotes economic growth and lowers unemployment, but countries such as France, Spain, Italy, Greece and Cyprus argue that the opt-out is bad for workers' health, and gives UK employers an unfair competitive advantage. As the TUC has said, it is difficult to see how, if the limits on hours are set in order to protect the health and safety of workers, such workers can opt out, and still be 'subject to appropriate health and safety regulations'. Its view is that long hours cause stress, illness and lower productivity. And when many employers are moving to short-time working, the need for an opt-out of the forty-eight-hour week is even more out of date (Haurant, quoting TUC General Secretary Brendan Barber).

Annual leave

All workers, outside the excluded sectors, are entitled to twenty-eight days' paid leave per year (calculated on a pro rata basis for part-timers). This includes the eight bank holidays, although the worker is not entitled to have the actual days of the bank holiday off, unless this is expressly stated in his contract.

The worker cannot be given payment in lieu, except where the employment is terminated, and the leave can only be taken in the leave year to which it relates. There is nothing, of course, preventing an employer and his worker agreeing more leave than the twenty-eight days, and the extra leave can be forwarded to the following year if the agreement allows for this.

The leave should be paid and there should be payment in lieu for any unused leave when the employment comes to an end. Rolled-up holiday pay is not permitted—workers have to be paid for the leave at the time that they take it.

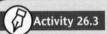 **Activity 26.3**

You are hired to work as an HR manager by a Canadian hotel company (Sleepwell Holdings) that is opening a chain of motel-style operations in the UK for the first time. Five 100-room units are being constructed in the north-west of England and staff are now being sought through recruitment advertisements placed in local newspapers and at job centres.

The company has been highly successful in Canada by keeping staffing costs to a minimum, despite paying reasonably high hourly rates. A key feature of its HR strategy has been its policy of hiring staff to undertake a number of different operational roles (room attendant, receptionist, bar worker, waiter, ground staff, etc). This has enabled it to operate more flexibly than its rivals, deploying staff as and when they are needed. Management are obviously keen to adopt the same highly flexible working practices in its new UK operations.

In Canada efficiency has been substantially enhanced by providing staff with live-in accommodation within the motels. The major reasons are as follows:

1 Because staff do not have to commute to work, they can be employed on split shifts (eg, four hours in the morning and four hours in the evening). This means that they can be deployed when the motels are at their busiest. »

> **2** An on-call system can be operated. Off-duty staff are designated as being 'on-call' for certain periods of the week. During this time they must not leave the premises and can be called upon to work for short periods if the motel suddenly gets very busy.
>
> **3** School leavers are particularly attracted to the jobs Sleepwell offers because accommodation is provided. The company prefers to employ younger people because it finds that their lifestyles permit them to work more flexibly than older people with family commitments.
>
> **4** Sleepwell has found that it is far easier to staff their motels late at night and early in the morning where live-in accommodation is provided.
>
> You are charged with the task of adapting these established Canadian practices for use in the five new UK motels. You want to maintain as much of the Canadian approach as you can, while also ensuring that the company complies with the Working Time Regulations (1998).
>
> In which areas is there a potential clash between established company policy and the requirements of the Working Time Regulations? What steps might the company be able to take in order to reconcile these differences? Write a short paper for Sleepwell's operations director setting out the options and justifying your recommendations.

If a worker is absent, for example on maternity leave, her entitlement to paid annual leave must be ensured. So when a woman exercises her right to take a year's maternity leave, she is entitled to add twenty-eight days' annual leave. The same is true of people who are away owing to sickness for a lengthy period. Holiday continues to accrue in these circumstances. The cases of *Stringer v HMRC* (2009) and *Pereda v Madrid* (2009) also paved the way for allowing workers who fall ill while on annual leave to take the missed holiday another time.

An employee should give notice of his or her intention to take annual leave. This should be twice as long as the amount of leave to be taken; so leave of two days requires four days' notice. But just as for rest breaks and rest periods, workers do not *have* to take their annual leave. This also formed part of the Amicus complaint to the European Commission referred to above. The Commission did not, however, choose to pursue this element of the complaint in its case to the ECJ.

Rolled-up holiday pay

In 2006 the ECJ made a significant judgment in three linked cases, all originating in the UK (*Robinson-Steele v RD Retail Services Ltd*, *Clarke v Frank Staddon Ltd* and *Caulfield and others v Hanson Clay Products Ltd*). The decision made a definitive ruling about an issue that the UK courts had failed to resolve over a number of years, leading eventually to a situation in which the Court of Appeal in England and the Court of Session in Scotland had reached completely different conclusions about the same legal point.

Where UK workers are employed to work irregularly, particularly on a regular-casual basis, it was common for them to receive rolled-up holiday pay as a means of complying with the EU's Working Time Regulations. Where people work irregular patterns it is administratively difficult for an employer to identify exactly when someone is taking annual leave and must therefore be paid, even though they are not working. As a result it became common for employers to include within pay packets an additional sum added to hourly rates which was designated as 'rolled-up holiday pay'. When workers took holiday, they were then not paid for that time. More money was received when they did work to take account of the fact that they were entitled to statutory paid leave each year. Some, however, questioned the legality of this approach, arguing that it de-coupled payment for holidays from the time the worker was actually on holiday. There was also concern that it served to discourage people from taking their full entitlement in terms of holiday each year because they could earn more by continuing to work on the enhanced hourly rates.

In giving judgment on these three cases the European Court found that the practice was unlawful. They said that all workers must take their designated holiday, inform their employer of the days and be paid a wage equivalent to what they would have worked during that period. The fact that rolled-up holiday pay was clearly labelled as such and understood by the workers to be compensation for holidays did not make the practice lawful.

However, the European Court did also rule that where rolled-up holiday pay has been paid in a clear and transparent way, workers affected cannot then claim further monies in respect of the weeks they are on holiday. In other words, the ECJ ruled that rolled-up holiday pay systems are unlawful under the Working Time Directive, but that no compensation was payable to the workers who had brought the case to court. All the claimants got effectively was a declaration of their rights. Many employers have thus decided to continue with their rolled-up systems, taking extra care to ensure that they are fully transparent, understood and that sums are labelled clearly on pay slips. They calculate that if there is no financial gain to be had, workers will not choose to take their cases to tribunal.

Night work

A night worker is someone who normally works at least three hours at night (unless a collective agreement etc, provides otherwise), and night time is between 11pm and 6am. There is a limit of eight hours' night work in twenty-four, calculated over a seventeen-week period. If, however, the work involves special hazards or heavy physical or mental strain, the hours must not exceed eight in *any* twenty-four-hour period. A night worker cannot opt out of the night work limit. A night worker is entitled to a free health assessment before his or her assignment, and thereafter at regular intervals. Night workers suffering from health problems connected with the fact that they perform night work should be transferred whenever possible to suitable day work.

Young workers

There are special limits set for young workers, that is, those who are above school leaving age, but under eighteen. These are that they may not work more than eight hours a day or forty hours a week. These hours worked cannot be averaged out and there is no opt-out available. Young workers should not do night work.

However, they may work longer hours on particular days where this is necessary to either maintain continuity of service or production, or to respond to a surge in demand for a service or product and provided that there is no adult available to perform the task and the training needs of the young worker are not adversely affected. Young workers who are employed on ships or as part of the armed forces are excluded from the working time limits under the Working Time Regulations.

Workforce agreements

These allow an employer to seek to vary working time regulations in various ways if it first secures acceptance by its workforce through a workforce agreement. Effectively this means that whole workplaces can adapt their interpretation of the Working Time Regulations to suit their needs.

If there is a union recognised, the agreement must be concluded with its officers. If there is no union there are two options for employers:

1. The employer organises the election of representatives with whom it then consults and concludes a local agreement.

2. The employer draws up its own workforce agreement and persuades over 50% of its workforce to sign up in agreement.

Remedies

When the government introduced the Working Time Regulations in 1998 it included two rather unsatisfactory enforcement mechanisms. Since then the courts have effectively added a third which is far more potent.

If a worker believes that his working time rights are being infringed he can complain to the Health and Safety Executive who may or may not decide to investigate the case. If it finds in favour of the worker, it issues a legally binding 'improvement notice' on the employer concerned. The HSE is responsible for the enforcement of the maximum weekly working time limit and night work limits and health assessment. It does not, however, enforce annual leave or rest entitlements.

If a worker is dismissed or suffers 'action short of dismissal' because he has challenged his employer's failure to comply with the 1998 Regulations he can complain to an employment tribunal and can get compensation, a declaration of his rights or both. If workers believe that their employer has failed to comply with the provisions relating to rest or annual leave, they can also bring a complaint to a tribunal, provided of course that the claim is brought within three months of the employer's failure to comply.

There was originally no general provision for a worker simply to go to a tribunal to complain that he or she was being required to work too many hours. In 1999, however, the High Court decided the case of *Barber v RJB Mining Ltd*, in which the court said that Parliament clearly intended that all contracts of employment should be read so as to provide that an employee should work no more than an average of forty-eight hours a week during the reference period. In other words, the forty-eight-hour limit became an implied term present in all contracts of employment. This effectively means that:

1. If the employer denies a worker his or her rights it is a breach of contract and a complaint can be made to an employment tribunal or a civil court.

2. If the employer denies a worker his or her rights, the worker can resign and claim constructive dismissal.

Activity 26.4

Assume that you are employed as an HR manager in a large city centre hotel. In two weeks' time a major international conference is due to be held in the city which will receive a great deal of high-profile media coverage. Your hotel will be one of the main conference venues. Sessions will be held in your conference rooms, a large exhibition set up in your public areas and three big dinners hosted in your restaurant. The hotel will be far busier during the conference week than it is at other times of the year. Moreover, because there is a great deal of preparation required, staff will have to work very hard indeed in the two weeks leading up to the start of the conference. Consequently the general manager has stated that no staff can take any annual leave for the next three weeks and has warned everyone that they can expect to work at least sixty hours per week. Overtime payments (at time and a half) will be made for any hours worked over and above the standard forty-hour working week. All contracts of employment state that weekly hours worked are 'as required by the needs of the hotel'.

Three employees come to see you stating that they are not prepared to work sixty hours during the coming three weeks. They state that it is 'against the law to make us work more than forty-eight hours a week' and say that they will refuse to stay for any longer. Since 2000 it has been the policy of the hotel to require all new starters to 'opt-out' of the forty-eight-hour week limit imposed by the Working Time Regulations by signing individual agreements. You check the files to see if these employees have signed such agreements.

Relevant information about the three employees is as follows:

1   Janet O'Sullivan has been employed as a room attendant/chambermaid for five years. She is thirty-six years old. She was appointed before the Working Time Regulations came into effect and has not signed an opt-out agreement.

2   Leo Gruber has been employed as a kitchen assistant for six months. He is seventeen years old. He signed the standard opt-out agreement on his appointment.

3   Tom Ewing has been employed as a night porter for two years. He is fifty-seven years old. He also signed a standard opt-out agreement on his appointment.

You ask each of these three employees to come to your office separately the following morning to discuss their positions. What would you say to each of them? What further information would you need to ensure that your responses were legally accurate?

The effectiveness of the Regulations

It has now been almost fifteen years since the Regulations came into force, and it is interesting to look at the effect that they have had on the working time of the British workforce. Hardly a week seems to go by without newspapers reporting that people are working longer hours than ever. Have the Regulations had any effect?

Union leaders had thought they were winning a battle to change Britain's long-hours culture. Between 2000 and 2006 the number of people working more than forty-eight hours fell from 3.8 million to 3.1 million. The Labour Force Survey and research for the TUC showed that the total crept up in the second half of 2007 and jumped sharply to 3.3 million in the first quarter of 2008 (Carvel, 2008). Carvel quotes the TUC as saying *'This is due to the challenging economic climate, which has made employers more reluctant to recruit new staff and instead work existing employees harder'.* Indeed a poll has shown that more than a quarter of UK workers are so short of time that they are now eating breakfast at their desks as well as missing out on their lunch break (Thomas, 2006). The worsening of the recession since 2008, however, has meant that employers perhaps do not have sufficient work to give their employees, and so the hours have gone down, with some workers even being forced to take on part-time work instead of full-time (see Chapter 19).

Although the hours worked by UK workers have shown a decline, in 2008 they were still the longest in Europe (Scott, 2008). *The Guardian* quotes Paul Sellers, a TUC spokesman, as saying that many workers were given no choice about working long hours: *'We have 3.75 million people working more than 48 hours a week. Our incidence of long hours is 3.5 times the European average'* (Seager, 2004). This is seen by some to be a reflection of the numerous derogations that are contained within the Working Time Regulations. For many commentators, they will not have the full effect that was originally intended by the EU until the opt-out is removed. As Rodgers comments, in relation to the fact that many workers 'agree' to opt out of the working time limits, *'many doubt whether the social objectives of the [Working Time Directive] ... are being achieved'* (Rodgers, 2010).

Debates about the Working Time Regulations

The question whether limits should be placed on the hours that people work is an old and contentious issue; it is an argument that has been with us from the days of the Industrial Revolution, and there still seems to be no agreement between the very opposite camps. As Taylor and Lucas (2006) point out, *'there is always pressure from trade unions to reduce hours . . . and there is always resistance from employers'.*

The question of working time has, however, gained in importance in recent years because of changes in working patterns and in the expectations of society. Taylor and Lucas (2006) summarise the position as follows:

> Customers expect to get what they want, when they want at the lowest possible price. Gone, for many businesses, are the days when they could open from 9 to 5, Monday to Friday. There are now requirements to have someone available at work around the clock in many sectors. This is taking place at the same time that people have realised that they *can* try to have more time with their family, or doing other things, as well as having a job, a change in society apparently reflected in the Government's slogan of achieving a 'work-life balance'.

Barou (2001) suggests that that *'the old model, in which employees adapted to a prescribed work schedule, was key to the way that we structured our lives, but is now over. New expectations are giving rise to new challenges'.* He says that three key trends are changing our concept of, and approach to, working time. He specifies these as:

- the historic tendency towards greater productivity, which allows people to work less but to produce the same amount
- the general movement towards individual work schedules, which, for the first time, make it possible to reconcile social, family and school-related demands (called 'temps choisi' in France)
- the larger number of women in the labour force (he says that this is related to the above).

As we have seen above, the original purpose of the EU in passing the Working Time Directive was to ensure the health and safety of workers. The health and safety aspect is not, however, the only perspective that can be taken. There are a number of issues that are raised by the existence of the rules, and arguments both for and against. For ease of discussion, these can be divided into 'social arguments' and 'economic arguments'. Although most proponents of placing limits on working time tend to cite social arguments as the major factor in support, we shall later see that France, when legislating in favour of a thirty-five-hour week, did so with the stated objective of reducing unemployment.

Social arguments

There are two elements that come within this heading. One is the health and safety argument, the other is that related to work–life balance.

The health and safety argument in favour of having such legislation is that, if workers work for too many hours, this will lead to stress. Not only is stress a big issue in itself for both employers and employees, resulting in a number of court cases, as we have seen in Chapters 24 and 25, but it can also then lead on to other, even more serious illnesses, such as heart disease, drug and alcohol addiction and high blood pressure. Against this, there have been points made such as the fact that, for some people, not working enough is stressful. This is not just because they enjoy being at work, but also, overlapping with the economic argument, if people are deprived of the right to earn more by working overtime, this may lead to financial difficulties, which are extremely stressful in themselves.

The work–life balance argument is different, but no less compelling. One of the aims of having such regulation is to enable employees to strike a better balance between work and home. The theory is that if employees can spend more time with their families, then this, by leading to fewer breakdowns in relationships, will lead to better cohesion in society as a whole. Against this, it is argued that some people do not want to have this balance thrust upon them. Some people live to work, and others wish to have an opportunity to earn as much as they can by working as much as they can. If they are deprived of the ability to do so, this can also lead to unhappiness, and the breakdown of relationships. The work–life balance arguments are further discussed in Chapter 20.

Economic arguments

The world is a fast-changing place, and the growth of globalisation, together with the emergence of a consumer-led society has necessitated changes to working practices. Those who argue against having regulation of working time do so predominantly because it is seen as a hindrance on the ability of businesses to compete in a flexible and efficient way, and hence on their productivity. This is seen as then having an adverse effect on the economy of the nation as a whole, which leads to greater risk of recession. Another element of the economic case against regulation of working time derives from the view that the regulations themselves are very costly to implement and maintain. The British Chambers of Commerce report 'Burdens Barometer 2008' estimated that employment regulation cost business billions of pounds a year, of which the biggest cost comes from the Working Time Regulations. According to the BCC, these accounted for a huge cumulative £16 billion by 2008; a figure which rises year on year by about £18 million (BCC, 2008).

On the other hand, economic arguments in favour of working time can also be deployed. One is rooted in the idea that when people work very long hours they tend to become tired and may therefore make mistakes (which can be costly in themselves), or simply not be able to do as much, or as well, as they can when they are working fewer hours. The quality of the work will probably not be as good as the work that can be achieved if they are feeling fresh, keen and better motivated to give their best.

Another economic argument is more controversial and it is one that the then socialist French government used when reducing working hours in France to thirty-five hours per week in the late 1990s. Unemployment levels in France were extremely high, and the government needed to find some measure to reduce them. It decided that the best option would be to reduce working time from its then limit of thirty-nine hours to thirty-five hours (albeit on an annualised basis). This was put forward on the basis that, if working hours were to be reduced in this way, then, not only would people have a better quality of life, but there would be more work to go around. Employers would be forced to take on more people. This decision was rescinded in 2008. The box below discusses the situation in France in more detail.

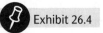 Exhibit 26.4   **The French experiment**

The thirty-five-hour working time limit was originally introduced in France on a voluntary basis in 1998, and made compulsory two years later (although there were a number of exemptions, such as doctors and lawyers, and another amendment in 2005 weakened the law further). In 2008, however, this was abolished.

The primary aim of the legislation was to reduce unemployment, by sharing work. A secondary objective was to improve the population's work–life balance, the French government arguing that '*a society's contentment cannot just be measured in a GDP index*' (Thornhill, 2005).

Lichfield (2001) says that those opposed to '*the principle of a state-imposed reduction in the working week*' insisted that it '*would be ruinous to French competitiveness . . . It would discourage foreign investment. It would increase taxes and social charges because the government would have to compensate employers. It would destroy more jobs than it created.*' He goes on to point out that '*none of that has happened, yet*'.

He quotes a report by Le Plan, the French State's strategic planning body, published in 2001, which said that the thirty-five-hour week, and its voluntary predecessor, had created 285,000 jobs within five years. Lichfield suggests that this is '*far fewer than the number of jobs forecast by the government four years earlier, but by no means the calamity forecast by business leaders and orthodox market economists*'.

He continues, saying that the report establishes that the shorter working week '*has increased consumer confidence and consumer spending—boosting rather than crippling the French economy. Foreign investment in France is booming . . . in return for shorter annual hours, workers have agreed to more flexible hours; to work longer days or to come into the office or factory on weekends, even, miraculously, to work during the month of August. The result has been a windfall of productivity.*'

»

>> This is supported by Barou (2001), who states *'since the changes were introduced, 5 million French employees have had their working time reduced. France has also moved from a vicious economic spiral of rising unemployment and welfare charges to a virtuous growth circle. The measures to reduce working time have played an important part, accounting for the creation of 200,000 jobs, 130,000 in 2000 alone . . .'*

The critics, however, argued that the concept of 'sharing work is illusory'. Unless wages are cut, it is more expensive for a company to employ two part-time workers than one part-timer, because of additional overhead costs. Also, although up to 300,000 more jobs may have been created, it is difficult to say for sure, as France, like the rest of Europe at the time, was experiencing an economic upswing' (Evans-Pritchard, 2005).

Ultimately, the critics won, and the strict limit of thirty-five hours has proved to be nothing more than an experiment. Although credited with creating up to 350,000 jobs between 1998 and 2002, the strict limit cost France about £10 billion a year in state aid, and was effectively abolished by President Sarkozy, who criticised it for damaging France's economic effectiveness (Pitcher, 2008). A law passed by the country's Parliament allowed French employers to strike individual deals with unions on working hours, leading to overtime being allowed.

Notwithstanding this, Hollinger still refers to it as a totem of French working life (Hollinger, 2011), even though she admits it is not actually practised. She says that, *'in the private sector at least, the 35 hour week has been so emptied of any real substance in a series of reforms ... that the average working week in France is now 39.4 hours.'*

The debate still rages, however, with French politicians continuing to debate whether they should have a 35-hour limit at all.

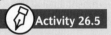 Activity 26.5

Below are brief details of the working hours laws relating to three countries, taken from the ILO database:

SINGAPORE

Daily limit: eight-hour day. Individual employers and workers who work not more than five days per week can agree that the hours on one or more days will be less than the eight-hours limit and that it will be exceeded on the remaining days to a limit of nine hours or forty-four hours per week.

Weekly limit: forty-four hours per week. Individual employers and workers can agree that the number of hours in every alternate week will be less than forty-four hours and the limit be exceeded in the other week. The employee cannot work for more than forty-eight hours in one week or more than eighty-eight hours in any two-week period. There are some exceptions, such as urgent work on machinery or plant, or industrial work essential to the economy.

Annual leave: seven days in respect of the first twelve months of continuous service, and one day's annual leave for every subsequent twelve months of continuous service up to fourteen days (in addition to the rest days). Plus public holidays.

>>

JAPAN

Daily limit: eight-hour day. Where there is a temporary need, due to a disaster or other unavoidable circumstances, employers can extend working hours beyond the eight-hour limit, with the permission of the competent government authority.

Public servants in public offices are permitted to work more than ten hours per day in the event of a temporary need, for the purpose of providing a public service.

Weekly limit: forty hours. This does not apply to certain groups, including managerial or supervisory workers; intermittent work; watch keepers.

Employers can introduce monthly or annual hours averaging schemes.

Annual leave: ten days. After two years of service, one day is added, to a maximum of twenty days' annual leave.

GERMANY

Daily limit: eight-hour day. A ten-hour limit is permitted, provided an eight-hour average is maintained over a six-month or twenty-four-week period. Regulations are permitted that provide for a limit of less than eight hours for certain sectors, work or groups of workers, if particular dangers to workers' health are expected.

Weekly limit: forty-eight hours, including overtime.

Annual leave: twenty-four days.

Questions

1 What are the main advantages and disadvantages of the regulatory systems used in Germany, Japan and Singapore?

2 Would you like to see similar approaches introduced in the UK?

3 Given that other industrialised nations have limits on working hours, and indeed, all other European member states have the same, or more stringent, rules (none of them having the opt-out that the UK relies upon), do the economic arguments still hold? Give reasons for your answer.

CHAPTER SUMMARY

- The Working Time Regulations originated in Europe. They are regarded as health and safety legislation. They regulate daily rest, weekly working time, weekly rest, annual leave, among other matters.

- The maximum weekly working time is forty-eight hours, but the UK has retained an opt-out to this, so a person can agree to work more hours. The opt-out remains extremely controversial amongst fellow European member states.

- Britons still work some of the longest hours in Europe. For many years there was a decline in hours worked, but this has reversed again since 2007.

REFERENCES

Barou, Y. (2001) 'Careers a la carte' *Financial Times*, 27 March.

Bloxham, A. (2010) 'Doctors' hours could change as European Working Time Directive reviewed' *The Telegraph*, 22 December.

British Chambers of Commerce (2008) Burdens Barometer 2008, available at www.britishchambers.org.uk.

Carvel, J. (2008) 'Long-hours culture is returning, warns TUC' *The Guardian*, 6 June.

Department for Business, Enterprise and Regulation (2008*) Your Guide to the Working Time Regulations*: London: HMSO.

Department of Trade and Industry (1999) *Your Guide to the Working Time Regulations*. London: HMSO.

Evans-Pritchard, A. (2005) 'France to abandon the 35-hour week' *The Daily Telegraph*, 24 March.

Hari, J. (2003) 'Britain's burnt out workers could benefit from some French lessons' *The Independent*, 10 September.

Haurant, S. (2009) 'Working time opt-out remains as talks collapse' *The Guardian*, 28 April.

Hollinger, P. (2011) 'French debate on 35-hour week misses point' *Financial Times*, 6 January.

IDS (2009) *Working Time. Employment Law Handbook*. London: Incomes Data Services.

Lea, R. (2001) *The 'Work-Life Balance'. . . And All That: The Re-Regulation of the Labour Market*. Institute of Directors: London.

Lichfield, J. (2001) 'The French miracle: a shorter week, more jobs and men doing the ironing' *The Independent*, 19 June.

Logan, G. (2008) 'EEF warns that 48-hour working time opt-out war is far from won' *Personnel Today*, 13 June.

Lucas, R., Mathieson, H. & Lupton, B. (eds) *Human Resource Management in an International Context*. London: CIPD.

Lunn, J. (1996) 'Working time' *New Law Journal*, Vol 146: 6773, 20 December.

Pitcher, G. (2008) 'France scraps 35-hour working week limit' *Personnel Today*, 25 July.

Rodgers, L. (2009) 'The notion of working time' *Industrial Law Journal*, Vol 38.1, no 1 March 2009.

Scott, A. (2008) 'UK's working week still among "longest in Europe" *Personnel Management Online*, 5 September.

Smith, D. (2004) 'Strangled' *The Sunday Times*, 7 March.

Taylor, S. and Lucas, R. (2006) 'Comparative Employment Law' in R. Lucas, H. Mathieson & B. Lupton (eds): *Human Resource Management in an International Context*. London: CIPD.

Thomas, D. (2006) 'Breakfast eats into working time as more Brits snack at desk' *Personnel Today*, 19 January.

Thornhill, J. (2005) 'Comment and analysis: labour market reforms' *Financial Times*, 15 February.

Woods, D. (2010) 'Working Time Directive has had an adverse effect on junior doctors' career development opportunities' *HR Magazine*, 13 April.

ONLINE RESOURCE CENTRE

 A range of online resources to help you through your employment law module have been developed by the author team. These include updates, self-test questions and sources for further reading. (www.oxfordtextbooks.co.uk/orc/taylor_emir3e)

Collective employment law

PART VI

Freedom of association

Learning outcomes

By the end of this chapter you should be able to:

- understand the most important concepts in collective employment law;

- explain which collective employment rights apply in which circumstances;

- define the term 'freedom of association';

- set out how freedom of association is protected in UK labour law;

- appreciate the extent of the law preventing dismissal and action short of dismissal on trade union grounds;

- state how the law preventing discrimination on grounds of union membership operates in employee selection processes;

- advise about when union members and officials should be granted requests for time off to undertake their activities;

- determine when an individual has the right to be accompanied by a union official at a disciplinary or grievance hearing.

Introduction

In this and the following two chapters we introduce collective employment law. Many of the principles that we have explored earlier in the book apply here too, but there are also important new concepts to come to grips with. In this first chapter we introduce the subject in general terms, before focusing on rights of freedom of association. This is the way that the law seeks to protect the right of employees to form trade unions, to join them and to take part in their activities. In Chapter 28 we move on to look at the regulation of collective bargaining and at ways in which employers can, in certain circumstances, be required in law to recognise trade unions and to consult collectively with their workforces. In Chapter 29 we look at the law on strikes and industrial action.

In recent years collective employment law has become increasingly marginal from the perspective of many managers and employees. This is because the number of people who join trade unions has declined markedly, because there are fewer strikes than there used to be and because trade unions have no presence whatever in so many organisations. But it remains highly relevant in organisations which are unionised and which determine terms and conditions through collective bargaining processes. It also remains a subject which attracts a great deal of attention from academics who specialise in employment law, and hence is a topic about which a great deal of research is carried out. It also the subject of many interesting debates which we will introduce.

Unfortunately it has not been possible for us to include a chapter on one of the most controversial topics in collective employment law, namely the regulation of internal trade union affairs, funding arrangements and the election of trade union officials. Notes on this topic are available on our companion website.

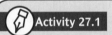 **Activity 27.1**

Display Stands Ltd is a small manufacturing firm based in Leeds. It is a family business which has grown rapidly in recent years. The total number of staff has increased from 50 to 150 since 2007. The managing director, Mr Paul Banks, has run the firm for several years using a personal style of management. His approach has involved getting to know his employees well and dealing with them in an honest and straightforward way. However, the recent expansion of the firm has made the traditional approach difficult to maintain. Mr Banks spends more and more time travelling to meet potential clients and has had to delegate much of the day-to-day management to his foreman. As a result he is no longer able to put a name to each face on the factory floor, let alone deal with each worker on an individual basis.

Recently Mr Banks has learned that a group of employees are trying to establish a trade union presence in the firm. The ring leader is a recent recruit called Mick Joynt who was formerly a part-time steward in a local brewery. Paul Banks is concerned as he wishes to avoid the » development of what he calls 'a them and us' employee relations culture. He therefore instructs his foreman to take the following steps:

- to avoid hiring trade union activists in the future,
- to warn Mick Joynt informally that his union activities are unwelcome and that he would be wise to desist if he wishes to be considered for promotion,
- to hold a staff meeting in order to remind everyone of the advantages of management's existing approach to employee relations and of the consequences of 'putting it at risk' through trade union activity.

At this stage you are asked to advise Mr Banks on his actions.

1 What advice would you give about the steps he has taken to date?

2 What approaches would you recommend were adopted in the future?

Return to this activity once you have read the chapter, to see how many of your answers were correct.

Introducing collective employment law

Collective employment law protects and to an extent promotes the position of trade unions in UK workplaces. In some respects it provides clear positive rights (eg, the right to disclosure of information for collective bargaining purposes) in others a right has effectively been created, but it is not directly or clearly expressed. There is, for example, no positive right to join a trade union in the UK. But in practice for most employees, most of the time, such a right exists because employers are deterred from using any available means to stop them from joining. Similarly, within quite strict legal parameters there is, in practice, a right to take strike action in support of a grievance against your own employer. But this too is achieved in law through a number of different statutes which restrict an employer's ability to resist. There is no straightforward right to take industrial action set out clearly in any statute. As a result collective employment law is complex and imperfect. There are plenty of holes which serve to ensure that for some people and in some circumstances employers can lawfully deter trade union activity and avoid the consequences that would apply were there a clear, universal legal right.

Before we go on to look in detail at freedom of association, it is useful to summarise up front some important concepts within collective employment law. These often create confusion among students who are new to the topic.

Trade union status

Trade unions hold a privileged place in UK employment law. The same is true of union members who enjoy a range of rights that are not open to members of other kinds of association. As a result central issues in collective employment law are the definition of a 'trade union', when a body becomes a union and under what circumstances it ceases to enjoy this legal status.

In recent years we have seen a great number of union mergers. In each case the new body must satisfy various conditions before it can enjoy the legal privileges associated with union status.

The approach used is that an official known as the Certification Officer is charged, among other things, with the duty to maintain an approved list of trade unions operating in the UK. The current Certification Officer is David Cockburn, a former solicitor and academic. He has been in post since 2001. There are two key criteria he uses to decide whether or not an organisation qualifies as a 'bona fide' trade union:

- the organisation concerned must be independent
- its principal purpose must be the regulation of the relationship between a body of workers and an employer or an employer's association.

This means that several prominent bodies which call themselves 'unions' are not in fact trade unions for the purposes of collective employment law. Examples are the Writer's Union, the National Farmers' Union and the National Union of Students. They do not qualify because their principal purpose is not the regulation of an employment relationship. The other major group which are left off the list are company unions or staff associations which often carry out the functions of trade unions, but are not considered sufficiently independent to be listed by the Certification Officer.

Interestingly, effectiveness is not a criteria. Nor, in principle, is size. Hence, in 1982 a little known teachers' association called the British Association of Advisers and Lecturers in Physical Education (BAALPE) successfully won a legal challenge to its presence on the Certification Officer's list of trade unions mounted by the National Union of Teachers. The NUT argued that BAALPE was too small and ineffective to play a useful role in collective bargaining on teachers' terms and conditions. The larger organisation lost the case. Effectiveness was irrelevant. BAALPE was independent and had as its principal purpose the regulation of relations between workers and employers.

In legal terms the Certification Officer's decisions matter a great deal because key collective employment rights are only available to listed unions, their officials and members. The most important are as follows:

- the right to organise industrial action while enjoying some legal protection
- the right to make an application for compulsory recognition
- a range of other rights such as a favourable taxation regime and limits on the amount of money that the body concerned can be sued for.

Appeals against his decisions are made to the Employment Appeals Tribunal.

 Exhibit 27.1   *Squibb UK Staff Association v Certification Officer* **(1979)**

In 1979 representatives of Squibb & Sons Staff association brought a claim against the Certification Officer, who they claimed had wrongly decided that they did not qualify as an independent trade union. The association had been in existence for a number of years and had a membership of 230.

> » In his ruling the Certification Officer concluded that while the association undertook the tasks and responsibilities of a trade union, it was too small and too reliant on the company to qualify for union status. While it was in many ways independent, it remained vulnerable to interference and would not survive were the company to withdraw good will and facilities. The fact that the company fully supported the application was irrelevant. The Employment Appeals Tribunal agreed with the Certification Officer's judgment.

Official union approval

The second fundamental concept in collective employment law is 'officialness'. Legal protection for union members is very often dependent on their actions being 'official'. This means that what they are doing in the union's name is sanctioned (officially) by the union hierarchy, which in practice means that it is clearly approved of by the relevant trade union executive committee.

Unofficial union activity carried out locally by members acting 'off their own bats' frequently means that legal protection is lost. The three main examples are as follows:

- there is no protection available from unfair dismissal law for workers who take unofficial industrial action (see Chapter 4)
- protection from dismissal for a trade union reason only applies if the person concerned is acting with the approval of their union
- union officials only have the right to take paid time off for training purposes if the course in question is provided or approved by their union executive.

In the case of industrial action, a strike or other form of action is considered to be official unless the union executive issues a repudiation notice stating that it is not legally responsible.

Recognition by an employer

Some important collective employment rights are only available to bodies/officials/members which are *both* listed as independent trade unions *and* recognised by employers for collective bargaining purposes. The most important are:

- the right to disclosure of information for collective bargaining purposes
- the right to be consulted on issues such as redundancy and transfer of undertakings
- the right for officials to have reasonable time off work to undertake their duties
- the right for union members to have reasonable time off for union activities.

The test used here by the courts is a simple and pragmatic one. There is no requirement for there to have been any formally signed recognition deal. If an employer is, in practice, negotiating with a trade union about one of a range of the following topic areas, then as far as the law is concerned that union is recognised by that employer:

- terms and conditions of employment
- recruitment or dismissal policy
- the allocation of work

- discipline
- trade union membership issues
- facilities for TU officials
- negotiation or consultation machinery.

Recognition is not, however, necessary in order for litigants to access other important collective employment rights:

- a union does not have to be recognised by an employer in order to organise a lawful strike
- individuals who belong to unions which are not recognised, or who are not members of a union at all are lawfully able to join a strike organised by a trade union
- protection from dismissal on trade union grounds extends to all employees irrespective of whether or not a union is recognised
- workers have the right to be accompanied and represented by a union official at significant disciplinary and grievance hearings whether or not the union is recognised by the employer concerned.

Introduction to freedom of association

The right to form trade unions and to join them has for many years been considered a fundamental human right. According to Deakin and Morris (2009:676), it is widely seen as being 'the hallmark of a democratic society'. It is thus present in many international treaties and conventions including:

- the United Nations Universal Declaration of Human Rights,
- the International Covenant on Economic, Social and Cultural Rights,
- the International Covenant on Civil and Political Rights,
- the European Convention on Human Rights,
- the European Social Charter, and
- the Charter of Fundamental Rights of the European Union.

Moreover, membership of the International Labour Organisation (ILO) is conditional on a country agreeing to respect the principles of freedom of association.

In the UK, there is no single statute which gives a clear, unambiguous right protecting freedom of association. Instead there are a number of separate statutes which act together to discourage discrimination by employers for trade union reasons and which give some significant positive rights to trade unions, their officials and their members. The key areas of law are the following:

- protection from dismissal on trade union grounds,
- protection from action short of dismissal on trade union grounds,
- protection from exclusion from a job on trade union grounds,
- 'time off rights' for union officials and members,
- the right to be accompanied and represented by a union official at serious disciplinary and grievance hearings.

Protection from dismissal on trade union grounds

This is the most important way in which UK law protects people who engage in trade union activity. On the surface it is straightforward and comprehensive. Now found in the Trade Union and Labour Relations (Consolidation Act) 1992, the right was first established in the Industrial Relations Act 1971 and has not been substantially amended since then. It is simply considered *automatically* unfair to dismiss someone for a trade union reason. There is thus no requirement to have been employed for a year before the right kicks in, and importantly no defence of reasonableness that an employer can deploy. The right covers:

- being a trade union member
- joining a trade union
- taking part in union activities
- proposing to join a trade union
- proposing to undertake union activities.

In more recent years equivalent protection has been extended to employees who choose not to join a trade union or wish to leave a trade union. This was done as part of a range of measures introduced in the 1980s and 1990s to outlaw, step-by-step, the operation of closed shops (arrangements whereby membership of a particular trade union was a condition of employment in an organisation).

Moreover, additional special procedural rules favouring the dismissed employee apply only in the case of dismissals for these trade union reasons. The most significant is the fast-tracking of such cases so that a partial hearing takes place in the employment tribunal within seven days of an application being lodged. Where a tribunal decides that the claim is likely to succeed it can order that the claimant is re-engaged pending a full hearing. Although in practice this means suspension on full pay in most cases, it is a far more favourable position from an employee's perspective than the legal system affords to others who are unlawfully dismissed. As such there is much stronger disincentive built into the law vis-à-vis trade union-related dismissals than is the case, for example, for pregnancy dismissals or dismissals caused by a claimant's assertion of any other statutory right. There are also enhanced levels of compensation payable to applicants who win dismissal claims in these circumstances (see Chapter 4).

However, despite these significant legal rights, there are 'holes' in this body of law, that many argue mean that the UK is in breach of the various international conventions and treaties listed above to which we are signatories:

1. In redundancy cases it is necessary for the ex-employee to show that someone else in a similar position in terms of their job and who *did not* engage in union activity was not dismissed. This is difficult to achieve in practice.

2. Where someone has less than a year's service (soon likely to be two years) at the time he or she is dismissed, the burden of proof for showing the reason for the dismissal is on the employee and not, as is the case once twelve months' service have been completed, on the employer.

3. Protection only extends to people who are dismissed for taking part in 'the activities of an independent trade union at an appropriate time'. This is a key phrase and it has been interpreted controversially in the courts over the years.

The phrase 'activities of an independent trade union at an appropriate time' has been the subject of much case law:

- you have to be a member of a body that is listed by the Certification Officer as being a trade union,
- the activities you engage in must be *officially* sanctioned by the trade union in question,
- this law excludes participation in any kind of industrial action (that is covered by the separate body of law we assess in Chapter 29),
- 'at an appropriate time' is taken to mean when the employer has given permission.

The test used is one of 'substantial inconvenience'. So if union activity goes ahead without permission and causes 'substantial inconvenience' then protection from automatically unfair dismissal on trade union grounds is lost.

Over the years case law has determined that most types of general trade union activity are covered by this statute and do count as 'activities of an independent trade union at an appropriate time':

- preparing for industrial action
- internal union meetings
- union recruitment activities
- contacting union officials for advice
- in the case of officials, all activities set out as the reasonable basis for time off in ACAS's Code of Practice 3 (*Time Off for Trade Union Duties and Activities*).

Until 2004 there was no equivalent protection accorded to people in the 'worker category' (see Chapter 2) who were not employed under a contract of service. This meant that major groups such as casual workers and agency temps could be lawfully dismissed for trade union reasons. In some cases this still may be the case because some people in these categories may not be able to persuade a tribunal that they are even 'workers' for the purpose of this legislation. But most would now appear to have sufficient legal protection. The reform was introduced in the Employment Relations Act 2004. Interestingly, however, it is not linked—as is the case with employees—to the law of unfair dismissal. The rights of workers who are not employees in this regard are more broadly framed. There is a straightforward right for them not to suffer a detriment for a trade union reason, the remedy being compensation to a level that is considered just and equitable by the tribunal. According to Deakin and Morris (2009:713), because this sum can include an element of compensation for injury to feelings, awards made by tribunals to 'workers' who are dismissed on trade union grounds may well be greater than those made to 'employees' in equivalent circumstances. This is because in the case of employees compensation is restricted within the limits imposed by unfair dismissal law. It follows that it will be in the interests of some employees to bring cases as 'workers'—a rather unusual situation in UK employment law.

Assume that you have recently started working as an HR manager at Southington College of Further Education. Your predecessor left at a difficult time citing stress as her major reason for resigning.

The college has been running a deficit for the past two years and senior management decided six months ago that there was no alternative but to sanction a round of compulsory redundancies among administrative staff. Ten people were made redundant two weeks prior to your arrival. One of these, Guy Turville, has now put in a tribunal claim alleging unfair dismissal on trade union grounds. He is requesting reinstatement in his previous job.

The principal of the college summons you to a meeting at which she gives you the following information:

- Guy Turville is a member of the UNISON trade union which is recognised by the college for collective bargaining purposes. At the time of his dismissal he had been employed at the college for ten months in a general administrative role.

- There being no UNISON official employed by the college, Mr Turville took it upon himself to represent administrative staff when the decision to make compulsory redundancies was made.

- When it was announced that the college would not be seeking volunteers for redundancy and that recent performance appraisal scores would be used as the major selection tool, Mr Turville stated that he was going to organise industrial action to force a change of policy.

- In the event Mr Turville was unable to generate sufficient support and no industrial action occurred.

- Mr Turville was selected for redundancy on the basis of a poor formal performance review undertaken by his manager three months ago.

- Of the ten people made redundant, Mr Turville's appraisal scores were the highest. He was thus the last person to be selected, being tenth on the list of ten.

You leave the meeting having been given the task of writing a briefing paper for the principal on this case by the following morning. She wants to know what chances the college has of winning the tribunal case, on what legal points the outcome will depend and what the consequences of losing might be.

Questions

1 What major points would you make in your briefing paper?

2 What further information would you require in order to give accurate legal advice?

Action short of dismissal

Not only is it unlawful to dismiss for a trade union reason, it is unlawful to inflict any kind of detrimental treatment on an employee because they have engaged in union activity or joined a union. The law therefore seeks to ensure that employers do not seek to discourage union activity in their organisations using any kind of negative means. The core principles are very much the same as for dismissals on trade union grounds. The same criteria are used by the tribunals in judging cases, the same groups are covered and the phrase 'activities of an independent trade union at an appropriate time' is interpreted in exactly the same way. However, in cases of action short of dismissal the following applies:

1. the burden of proof is effectively on the employer to show that the reason the action was taken was other than a trade union reason

2. compensation for victorious applicants is whatever the tribunal considers to be 'just and equitable in the circumstances'.

A range of different types of cases have been brought before the tribunals over the years, allowing precedents to be set concerning the major situations that arise in workplaces when managers try to discourage trade union membership or to deter union activity. What, for example, is the position when an employer takes action which has the effect of deterring union activity, but which was not done primarily for that purpose? The leading case here is *Gallacher v Department of Transport* (1994), in which a careers advisor suggested to a union official that he would enhance his promotion prospects if he curtailed his union activities somewhat. The employer was found not to have acted unlawfully because the *purpose* of the advice had not been to deter union activity. Importantly, however, in such cases the tribunals expect employers to be able to show that there was some other legitimate purpose underlying their actions. Otherwise they tend to assume that the reason was to deter union activity.

A more common situation is where an employer seeks to use essentially *positive* methods which have the effect of deterring union activity in a workplace. The main example is the use of sweetener payments to encourage staff to move over on to individual contracts of employment and hence to contract themselves out of existing collective bargaining pay-determination mechanisms. In 1995 the House of Lords made rulings sanctioning this kind of activity in certain circumstances in the cases of *Associated Newspapers v Wilson* and *Associated Ports v Palmer*, the Employment Relations Act 1999 effectively backing up their interpretation. Subsequently, however, the Lords' judgment was criticised by the European Court of Human Rights, and in response, the government amended the law in the Employment Relations Act 2004. It is therefore now unlawful to offer inducements of any kind aimed at persuading people to refrain from union membership or participation in union activities such as collective bargaining where a trade union is recognised or is seeking recognition. Where some accept and others do not, the latter can bring cases alleging that they have suffered a detriment for not having agreed to move onto individual employment contracts.

Another relatively common situation occurs where two unions are competing for members in the same organisation and bargain separately with the employer. This can lead to a situation in which the employer strikes a more generous deal with one union than another—thus favouring its members and hence, in theory at least, causing a detriment to members of the other union. This has happened extensively in the coal industry over recent years where the employer has tended to favour the Union of Democratic Mineworkers over the National Union of Mineworkers. NUM members have complained that their treatment (eg, poorer terms and conditions) amounts to action short of dismissal on union grounds (Barrow, 2003:186). In *NCB v Ridgeway* (1987) this was found not to be the case. This law is intended to protect individual trade union members/activists from poor treatment on grounds of their *unionism*. It is not about protecting the right to join a particular trade union.

Finally, it is important to point out that causing someone a detriment for a trade union reason can also amount to a breach of contract (a breach of either express or implied terms). It can therefore form the basis of a constructive dismissal claim as well as a claim for compensation based on action short of dismissal. As a result an employer can easily find itself trying to defend an automatically unfair dismissal on union grounds when a rather lesser sanction was in fact meted out. So, for example, management might want to 'punish' a union activist for being awkward by withdrawing a company car or by moving him/her to a less interesting job. If in doing so the contract of employment is breached, the victim can resign and claim constructive dismissal.

 Exhibit 27.2   *Bass Taverns v Burgess* (1995)

Mr Burgess was employed as a pub manager by the Bass brewery group. He was also a shop steward and received additional pay for making the union presentation on induction courses for new managers.

On one occasion he used the union presentation, designed to recruit new members, to make a series of candid but disparaging remarks about the company. Using colourful language he told the new managers that the company was only interested in profit and had no interest in the safety of its workforce. On his own admission he went 'over the top' in his remarks.

The company responded by barring him from making such presentations in the future. This involved a demotion from his position as an approved trainer and some loss of pay. Mr Burgess resigned and claimed that he had been constructively dismissed on account of his trade union activities.

Mr Burgess won his case at the EAT and then again at the Court of Appeal. His remarks had not been made in bad faith and it was unreasonable for the employer to expect a union recruitment campaign not to be uncritical. Mr Burgess had been constructively dismissed and the reason was automatically unfair.

Refusing access to employment

The third major way in which the law protects freedom of association in the UK is by making it unlawful to fail to recruit (or re-recruit) someone for a reason related to their membership or non-membership of a trade union. This dates from 1990 and was primarily introduced with the purpose of protecting people who were denied employment opportunities in closed-shop organisations because they were not union members and did not wish to join. In the process, however, the then government introduced an equivalent right for union members who were denied employment on that account. The relevant statute now forms part of the Trade Union and Labour Relations (Consolidation) Act 1992, which in this respect is thoughtfully drafted. Ministers appear to have anticipated possible ways round a generally framed right and thus included a list of specific types of situation in which exclusion for a trade union reason is unlawful. These include refusing to answer enquiries from an individual about a job or failing to send application details, misleading people about the number of vacancies available or even offering a job on such poor terms and conditions that the individual is obliged to turn down an offer of employment. The burden of proof is on the failed candidate to show that the reason they were not appointed was their union membership status. This is difficult to achieve in practice without some clear evidence that one's unionism or non-unionism played a part in a recruitment decision.

At present the law in this area only covers trade union *membership*. Employers can still refuse to employ people because of their past record of trade union *activity*. This distinction allows employers lawfully to turn down applications, for example, from known union 'trouble-makers' or from people who are not union members but who have nonetheless been engaged in some union activities in the past (like joining a strike). This right is thus construed a good deal more narrowly than the more general rights for existing employees not to be dismissed or to suffer action short of dismissal on trade union grounds. It is also interesting to note that the law on exclusion only applies when people are denied access to *employment*. Turning people down for jobs which fall into the wider worker category would thus appear to remain lawful—although employment agencies are specifically included insofar as they might wish to refuse to offer work to a union member (or be told to by a client).

The Employment Relations Act 1999 gave the Secretary of State the right to issue regulations prohibiting the maintenance of blacklists of union troublemakers by employers or employers' associations. Until recently this right was not exercised, ministers taking the view that it was not necessary to extend the law as blacklisting has ceased to be a problem in the UK. However, the situation changed in 2010 following a finding by the Information Commissioner against the maintenance of a 'secret blacklist' by a group of employers in the construction industry.

Time off rights for union officials

So far in this chapter we have focused on legal interventions which seek to prevent employers from discriminating against workers and job applicants for trade union reasons. These make a central contribution to the presence in the UK of a de facto 'right' to freedom of association. But other more positive measures are also present in the law. We now turn to focus on the three main examples:

- the right for trade union officials to take paid time off to undertake their duties,
- the right for trade union members to take unpaid time off to take part in union activities,
- the right for people to be represented at grievance and disciplinary hearings by trade union officials.

Once a union is recognised its officials gain the right to take reasonable *paid* time off during contracted working hours to carry out their role. What is and what is not reasonable is determined by employment tribunals having taken into consideration the size and resources of an organisation. However, tribunals are guided by two documents in making their decisions:

1. The Employment Act 1989 makes it clear that the right extends only to include activities which relate to matters for which a union is recognised.
2. The ACAS Code of Practice 3 (*Time off for trade union duties and activities*) (2003) sets out what is normally to be considered 'reasonable' in these cases.

Central here is the notion that time off can only be taken with an employer's permission. As a result, the majority of complaints to employment tribunals consist of claims that an employer has acted unreasonably in refusing to allow permission after a request has been made. The remedy is usually a straightforward declaration of the applicant's rights, but compensation can also be paid to whatever level the tribunal considers is 'just and equitable in the circumstances'. In practice this commonly amounts to reimbursement of wages that have not been paid because an official has taken unpaid time off (or used annual leave entitlement) to carry out union duties. The ACAS Code states that the following are normally reasonable:

- preparing for negotiations
- informing members of progress
- explaining outcomes to members
- preparing for disciplinaries, grievance hearings, employment tribunals, etc.

Paid time off for training purposes is also permitted. Here reasonableness is determined with reference to the following:

- the extent to which management was given notice
- the amount of time taken in any one period
- the relevance of the training to the official's duties
- the extent to which the employer can practicably cover during the employee's absence
- the need to maintain adequate public service
- safety considerations.

Another important condition concerns the fact that the training concerned must be approved by the TUC or the official's own union. Union learning representatives (ULRs) have to undergo a set course of training before they gain the right to take reasonable paid time off to carry out their duties. The case law in this area has tended to take a broad view of whether or not there is a great deal of proximity between a union official's duties and the relevance of the training. Hence in *Young v Carr Fasteners* (1979) it was found to be reasonable for a union official to have been paid to attend a training course relating to occupational pensions even though pensions were not at that time a matter of negotiation between the relevant union and employer. The fact that they were likely to become so in the future was sufficient for the request for time off to have been reasonable.

A common misconception is that union officials have a legal right to be provided with office facilities by employers. This is not the case. When an organisation recognises a trade union it makes sense from the point of view of maintaining good industrial relations to provide some form of basic office facilities for its officials. Desks, phone lines, notice boards, access to private meeting rooms and photocopying are usually provided as a minimum, and indeed must be by law in the case of union health and safety reps (see Chapter 24), but there is no legal right to these facilities for ordinary shop stewards, whether they work on a part-time or on a full-time basis.

Activity 27.3

Saw & Plane Ltd is a Timber Yard employing 150 people. A good majority are members of the Transport and General Worker's Union, but there is no formal recognition agreement in place. No general collective bargaining occurs, but the manager (Sidney Brown) does negotiate agreements on an ad hoc basis with an elected union official (Fred Smith). To date these have only concerned work allocation and the length of break times.

Yesterday Fred went to see Sidney to say that he was going on a negotiation skills training course for shop stewards which is being organised by his union. As a consequence he will be absent from work for a whole week in three weeks' time. At their meeting Sidney said that this was not convenient as workload is expected to be exceptionally busy that week. Fred disputed this, stating that his colleagues would be quite able to cope in his absence. Moreover, he maintained to Sidney that he had a right to be paid for the week he was going to be away as he was not prepared to take the time off as part of his holiday entitlement. Sidney said that this was wholly unacceptable. He is not prepared to give Fred permission to attend and is certainly not prepared to pay him for doing so.

Questions

1 What advice would you give to Sidney Brown on the basis of the information provided above ?

2 Were the matter to come to court, what would be the central legal issues that would have to be considered ?

Time off rights for union members

Legal protection is also given to ordinary union members in organisations where their union is recognised to take *unpaid* time off for union activities. The ACAS Code of Practice sets out guidance as to what is normally reasonable activity:

- discussions and votes as collective bargaining processes proceed
- voting in union elections
- meeting full-time officials to discuss workplace issues.

The other criterion is that the activities must relate to the employment relationship. General union business or action of an essentially political nature is excluded. So members have no right to time off, for example, to attend their union's annual conference or to take part in a political protest which does not relate to their work. Strike activity and other forms of industrial action are covered elsewhere in the legislation and are specifically excluded from the right to unpaid time off.

The same formulation of 'reasonable in all the circumstances' that applies in the case of union officials is used here too. So where the employee's absence would be seriously disruptive to business, where too little notice is given or where an individual asks for an excessive amount of time off for union reasons in a short time, the employer is within its rights to refuse.

Also, as with the rights of union officials, complaints are taken to employment tribunals, an individual employee claiming that he or she has been unreasonably refused unpaid time off to engage in legitimate union activities. If a case is well founded the tribunal will issue a declaration to that effect and may also order that compensation is paid. This is whatever is considered to be 'just and equitable in the circumstances'. As there has not generally been any financial loss suffered, a small sum to compensate for injury to feelings is all that a tribunal will award (Barrow, 2002:174). Sometimes, however, a collective agreement will give employees a contractual right to paid time off for some union activities. In such cases there can be financial loss, because an employer may allow the activity to take place but not pay employees. If so, the tribunal can order that payments are made by way of compensation.

Exhibit 27.3   *Luce v Bexley London Borough Council* **(1990)**

Ms Luce was a teacher. In 1988 prior to the passing of the Education Act which introduced the 'national curriculum', she and five colleagues formally asked their head teacher for time off to attend a rally in central London to demonstrate against the Act, after which MPs would be lobbied in Westminster. Permission was refused. Ms Luce claimed that this amounted to unreasonable refusal for unpaid time off to carry out union activities. The EAT found against the union members on the grounds that the lobby they had intended to take part in was concerned with government educational policy generally and did not relate to employment policy or terms and conditions. There was thus an insufficient link between the subject of the political demonstration and the employment relationship. The ruling suggests that had the Act been concerned with teachers' pay or conditions of employment, attendance could have been reasonable provided the other tests relating to disruption and notice given to the employer were met.

Accompanying rights

The Employment Relations Act 1999 introduced a right for workers to be accompanied by a union official or a work colleague at serious disciplinary and grievance hearings. This right was clarified, and in important respects effectively extended, in the Employment Relations Act 2004. Importantly it applies irrespective of whether or not an employer recognises the worker's union, or indeed any worker. Interestingly, according to Deakin and Morris (2009:450) there is no requirement that the union concerned be 'independent' and thus listed by the Certification Officer. This appears to mean that the right to accompany also extends to officers of staff associations and presumably other non-listed 'unions'.

A 'serious' disciplinary hearing is defined as a formal meeting at which a formal warning or other disciplinary may either be issued or confirmed. A 'serious' grievance hearing is defined as a meeting at which an employee alleges that the employer has breached some kind of legal duty—either contractual or statutory. This means that employees do not have the right to be accompanied at meetings which will not result in the issuing of a disciplinary warning—investigatory hearings, for example—however much a worker might need support and assistance in such circumstances.

When the law on companions at grievance and disciplinary hearings was first established in 1999 the right was only for companions to *accompany* and not to *represent* the worker. The role was very considerably widened in the Employment Relations Act 2004. Companions are now essentially representatives in the tradition of established practice in organisations which recognise trade unions. Companions can confer with the worker during the meeting, can make statements and ask questions, and also respond to points on the worker's behalf.

It is for the worker and not the employer to choose the companion. The worker can postpone the meeting to a time acceptable to the employer within five days of the original date to enable the chosen companion to attend. The ACAS Code of Practice on discipline at work states that an employer might be acting reasonably in some circumstances if it refuses to allow a particular individual to act as the companion. The examples given are someone who has a conflict of interest or someone who is based at a distant location when there are suitable alternative people based closer to home.

The remedy is via an employment tribunal, two types of cases being brought:

1. unreasonable refusal to allow accompaniment, and

2. detriment suffered because the right to accompaniment was exercised.

In the first case compensation of up to two weeks' pay can be awarded. In the second, compensation is whatever is considered just and equitable in the circumstances. Importantly, where a dismissal goes ahead, a breach of accompanying rights is not used by tribunals to judge an employer's decision to dismiss as being outside the band of reasonable responses (see Chapter 5).

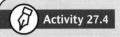 **Activity 27.4**

Assume that you work as an HR officer for Sound Precision Instruments Ltd (SPI), a small company which designs and manufactures high-tech medical equipment on a site near to Cambridge. There are 150 staff employed. No trade union is recognised for any purpose and no staff have made it known that they are union members.

Three months ago a technician called Tony Hawk-Ward was appointed to a post in one of the company's development laboratories. His starting salary was £18,000 a year (Grade F). Two weeks ago Tony was asked if he would take on some additional duties. These included some staff training, responsibility for ordering new equipment and representing the laboratory staff on the company's health and safety committee. He agreed to take on the new responsibilities and was informed that he would be rewarded with a promotion to Grade G (£20,000 a year) with immediate effect.

Last week SPI's chief executive attended a dinner organised by the Cambridge City Chamber of Commerce at which he sat next to the finance director of another local firm (Hi-tech Laboratories Ltd). During their conversation it emerged that Tony Hawk-Ward was previously employed by ⟩⟩

>> Hi-tech and that managers there had been delighted when he resigned. He had apparently developed an 'anti-managerial attitude' during his time there, refusing to accept instructions from his supervisor, 'sabotaging' a new computerised clocking-in procedure and organising a half-day strike in opposition to the introduction of new shift patterns.

The chief executive came to work the next day and asked you to do the following:

1 Formally warn Tony that disciplinary action will follow if he 'gets up to any of his old tricks' while employed at SPI.

2 Inform Tony that his recent promotion is being revoked for the time being. It will be reconsidered in six months' time, dependent on satisfactory conduct.

Tony Hawk-Ward responds by lodging a formal grievance, the first that SPI has ever had to deal with. A date for a hearing is set, but Tony says he wishes to postpone it until the following Thursday afternoon at 3.00pm, because his trade union official is unable to attend at any other time.

He is told that the meeting will go ahead as planned at the original time.

Questions

1 What possible legal issues arise from this situation?

2 What further information would you need to have in order to respond to the chief executive's requests?

3 What course of action would you recommend was taken in order to ensure that legal action was avoided?

CHAPTER SUMMARY

- Collective employment law concerns the regulation of the relationship between trade unions and employees in their capacity as trade union members. In order to be able to enforce these rights it is often necessary for a union to be listed by the Certification Officer, recognised by an employer or for its members to be acting 'officially' in the name of the union.

- Freedom of association is protected by laws which deter employers from dismissing employees or taking action short of dismissal against them for a trade union reason. Further law offers protection to those who are refused work in an organisation because they are trade union members.

- The law gives equal protection to people who suffer the same detriments because they are not union members or because they have left a union.

- Trade union officials working for employers who recognise their union are entitled to reasonable paid time off in order to train and to perform their duties. Their members are entitled to unpaid time off in order to participate in appropriate union activities.

- Irrespective of whether or not a union is recognised, members are entitled to be accompanied, and to a considerable extent represented, by union officials at serious disciplinary or grievance hearings. Alternatively they may be accompanied by a work colleague.

For updates and further materials, please see the online resource centre at www.oup.com.

REFERENCES

ACAS (2003) *Code of Practice 3. Time off for trade union duties and activities.* London: Advisory, Conciliation and Arbitration Service.

Barrow, C. (2002) *Industrial Relations Law*. Second Edition. London: Cavendish Publishing.

Deakin, S. & Morris, G. (2009) *Labour Law*. Fifth Edition. Oxford: Hart Publishing.

ONLINE RESOURCE CENTRE

A range of online resources to help you through your employment law module have been developed by the author team. These include updates, self-test questions and sources for further reading. (www.oxfordtextbooks.co.uk/orc/taylor_emir3e)

Consultation and bargaining

28

Learning outcomes

By the end of this chapter you should be able to:

- put the arguments for and against making collective agreements legally enforceable;

- explain the role, function and approach to cases of the Central Arbitration Committee (CAC);

- advise about when it is and when it is not a requirement in law that information is disclosed to a recognised trade union for collective bargaining purposes;

- explain the circumstances that must apply in order that an employer may be forced to recognise a trade union and bargain with its representatives;

- critique the statutory trade union recognition regulations contained in the Employment Relations Act 1999;

- explain the requirements of the European Works Council Directive and comment on its practical impact;

- discuss the major elements that make up the Information and Consultation of Employees Regulations 2004.

Introduction

Until relatively recently the law almost stayed out of the way completely when it came to collective bargaining between employers or employers' associations and trade unions. Its role is still marginal when compared with common practice in most industrialised countries, but there is a great deal more legal intervention than there once was. The same is true of collective consultation with either union representatives or some other body representing employee views and interests. Here though European law has helped to ensure that formal consultation occurs in a variety of situations. Indeed we have already discussed some earlier in the book, redundancy, TUPE and health and safety being the major areas where a degree of consultation and information-sharing is required. Larger pan-European organisations are required to operate European Works Councils or some equivalent arrangement, while all organisations of any size may need to consult on a wide range of employment issues if there is sufficient demand for the establishment of such arrangements among their workforces.

This is an area of law where UK traditions and those of most EU countries tend to jar against one another. The established workplace norms in Germany, France, Italy and elsewhere are so different from those of the UK when it comes to legal intervention in collective bargaining and consultation that a degree of tension between governments about the appropriate way forward as far as EU-level regulation is concerned is inevitable. To date UK governments have been successful in ensuring that the prevailing European models are not extended wholesale across the English Channel, but in the process a degree of compromise has been necessary. The result is regulation in the UK which is pretty limited in its effect, providing some meat for commentators to chew on, but little that has had, or is likely to have, a truly significant impact on the conduct of employment relations.

After briefly considering why the UK maintains a tradition of voluntarism as far as collective bargaining and collective agreements are concerned, the chapter goes on to assess the work of the Central Arbitration Committee—the authority which has the major enforcing role in respect of what law we do have in this field. This is followed by an analysis of four distinct, but interrelated areas of regulation—disclosure of information for collective bargaining purposes, compulsory union recognition, European Works Councils and the Information and Consultation Regulations.

 Activity 28.1

Consider the following statements. Which do you think are correct and which are false?

1   Collective agreements are legally enforceable in UK courts.

2   When adjudicating disputes the Central Arbitration Committee takes a different approach to that taken by employment tribunals.

3   Trade unions are empowered to require employers to disclose detailed pay information ahead of pay negotiations.

> **4** Since 2000 all employers have been required to recognise trade unions and bargain with them in good faith if a majority of a workforce votes in favour of such an arrangement.
>
> **5** The European Works Councils Directive has had little practical impact on the conduct of employee relations practice in large European corporations.
>
> **6** All organisations employing over fifty people now have to consult formally with their workforces about major employment-related issues where there is a clear demand for such arrangements to be established.
>
> Return to this activity once you have read the chapter, to see how many of your answers were correct.

The legal status of collective agreements

Were this book to be concerned with employment law in almost all other major industrialised economies there would have to be a number of lengthy chapters devoted to the law on collective bargaining and collective agreements. This is because in a good majority of jurisdictions including the USA, most other European countries, South Africa and Canada, collective agreements are legally enforceable. Their status in law is thus similar to that of the individual contract of employment in UK law. If one side breaches the agreement, the other can seek damages or apply for a declaration that an unlawful breach has occurred. Indeed in the USA, the term 'contract' is actually used to describe a collective agreement negotiated between a union and an employer. The UK is thus highly unusual in preserving the position whereby in the vast majority of cases collective agreements are 'binding in honour only'.

The reasons for this are several and are widely debated among historians of employment law. It is partly, as we showed in Chapter 1, simply because the UK has a tradition of minimal state involvement in industrial relations. While this position has changed considerably over the past thirty years, the regulatory edifice we call 'employment law' has been built pragmatically in response to evolving circumstances. The absence of any overarching strategy or of a central drive towards regulation for its own sake has meant that most UK governments have pursued a policy effectively described by the epithet 'if it ain't broke don't fix it'. In the absence of any good reason for moving towards the enforceability of collective agreements, governments have thus seen no reason to include it in their programmes. A second important reason is the cautionary tale of what happened when the Heath government briefly broke with this approach and tried to introduce legal enforceability along with other controversial reforms in the early 1970s. The result was farcical in many ways because neither the unions nor the employers wanted to alter their established approach to industrial relations. In response they thus agreed to write into their agreements a clause making quite clear that they were *not* intended to be legally enforceable. Within three years the law was repealed and collective agreements were assumed in law (once again) to be binding in honour only. In 1991 the then Conservative government flirted with the idea of re-introducing legal enforceability, largely in order to help encourage overseas investment from countries where it is the norm, but in the event they did not pursue the idea (Barrow, 2002:152).

The current position is set out in the Trade Union and Labour Relations (Consolidation Act) 1992. The presumption is that a collective agreement cannot be enforced in a court unless it contains a clause which clearly states that it *is* intended to be legally enforceable. This leaves employers and trade unions free to establish for themselves what status their agreements are to have, and in practice few have opted for legal enforceability. The exceptions tend to be Japanese and American-based corporations who wish to run their UK employee relations policies along similar lines to those that prevail in their operations at home.

It is easy to understand why employers would want collective agreements to be 'binding in honour only'. Why submit to further employment regulation if it can be avoided? Why reduce flexibility of manoeuvre when it is not necessary to do so? But it is harder to understand the long-standing trade union objection. It partly appears to result from a general resistance to state interference in 'free collective bargaining' and partly from a belief that employers will be less likely to recognise unions and bargain with them if the agreements they make might be subject to interpretation by the courts. Moreover, unions like employers wish to avoid the need to phrase collective agreements in the very clear, precise terms that would be necessary in order to render them legally enforceable. Not only would this require the employment of lawyers (at considerable expense) to advise on drafting, it would also make agreements harder to make because ambiguous wording of the kind which is currently common in UK collective agreements would have to be avoided.

There is, however, a strong argument that can be made in favour of enforceability from an employee/trade union perspective. This relates to the Transfer of Undertakings regulations we discussed in Chapter 23. Under TUPE law when a business or part of a business changes hands, or when part of a public sector organisation is contracted out to the private sector, any collective agreement covering the affected workers transfers with them. The new employer is thus obliged to honour the contents of the former employer's collective agreement. In all the other major EU countries this has profound significance because a breach of the agreement on the part of the new employer constitutes an unlawful act. Those who suffer a detriment as a result are able to gain redress in the courts. In the UK, by contrast, this is not the case. Here it is only the contents of individual contracts that cannot lawfully be breached by new employers following a transfer. As far as the law is concerned, they can do what they like when it comes to collective agreements because they are binding in honour only. As a result, the absence of legal enforceability in the UK weakens the position of employees in transfer situations vis-à-vis that of counterparts in other EU countries (Doyle, 1986:116). One would have thought that union objections would have mellowed somewhat with the introduction of compulsory collective bargaining measures from 2000. Because employers who are reluctant to recognise them can now be forced to do so by law, a key part of the traditional trade union case against enforceability has been removed. But this does not appear to be the case, and no serious campaign for change has been established.

Having grasped the points made above, it is equally important to appreciate that where terms of collective agreements are incorporated into individual contracts of employment (see Chapter 8) they may well be legally enforceable. Bargaining, dispute resolution and consultation procedures cannot be incorporated this way, but substantive terms frequently are. Hence, where pay is negotiated collectively, and a reference to this fact is made in offer letters or in written employment contracts, individuals can take their employers to court and sue for breach of contract where pay rates that have been agreed collectively are not honoured.

The Central Arbitration Committee

Responsibility for enforcing such law that we do have on collective bargaining, as well as that on collective consultation, mainly rests with the Central Arbitration Committee (CAC) rather than with the employment tribunal system. The CAC was established in its current form in 1976, but it is the direct descendant of the Industrial Court which acted as an independent arbitrator in industrial relations disputes from 1919 until its abolition in 1976 (Rideout, 2002). Like ACAS, the CAC is independent of government but publicly funded. It has a council which controls its affairs and which seeks to ensure that it fulfils its statutory obligations. The current chairman is Sir Michael Burton (a High Court judge). He is assisted by ten part-time deputy chairmen who are either academics with an industrial relations background or employment judges, and over sixty members with experience of industrial relations practice either as union or management negotiators.

CAC hearings usually take place before a three-strong panel consisting of Sir Michael or one of his deputies, one staff-side member and one employer-side member. This, however, is as far as any similarity with an employment tribunal goes. The CAC takes a very different and much less legalistic approach to bringing disputes to a satisfactory conclusion. The first major difference is that each panel is, to a very considerable extent, able to conduct its proceedings as it thinks fit. There is thus a good deal of variation between the approaches taken by different panels. Moreover, they operate without being required to take account of precedents set by other panels. So a considerable variety of outcomes is possible too. The second major difference is the CAC's preference for 'a flexible and problem-solving approach' (Deakin and Morris, 2009:86). Instead of simply sitting back and listening to the two sides put their case at a formal hearing, CAC panels prefer to encourage a jointly agreed settlement between the parties to a dispute. They will only make a binding adjudication once this has proved to be unattainable. The panels can undertake the conciliation work themselves, but nowadays they prefer to delegate it to ACAS officers. This encourages the disclosure of confidential information that can assist in bringing about a successful conciliation, but which might influence any ultimate adjudication by the CAC. The third difference is the informality of proceedings. They often take place at an employer's premises or in a nearby hotel, rather than in a formal court setting. The presence of lawyers to act as representatives is not encouraged (although inevitably where the stakes are high top QCs are employed) and no costs can be awarded against a 'losing' party. The CAC has no power to order that documents are disclosed ahead of a hearing and no power to insist that any witness attends. An inquisitorial approach is taken, evidence being read and heard from both sides along with any legal arguments. Once an adjudication is made, a dissatisfied party can apply for judicial review of the decisions if it believes that the CAC has misdirected itself in law or has applied the law wrongly. Such cases are heard in the High Court or in the Court of Appeal.

The CAC has responsibility for dealing with the following types of disputes:

- statutory recognition and derecognition of trade unions
- disclosure of information for collective bargaining purposes
- the establishment and operation of European Works Councils
- information, consultation and participation of employees when a European PLC is formed

- the Information and Consultation Regulations 2004.
- The European Co-operative Regulations 2006
- the Companies (Cross-Border Mergers) Regulations 2007.

The remainder of this chapter explains the principles of the law in the most important of these areas.

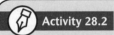

Activity 28.2

Evidence from surveys of users of the CAC show high levels of satisfaction with its approach. Rideout (2002) argues that it provides an immensely valuable service effectively and cheaply, being 'free to reach decisions based on informed common sense'. Reviews of the employment tribunal system are rarely so complimentary.

Which of the following approaches taken by the CAC in adjudicating disputes would you like to see adopted by employment tribunals hearing other types of employment law cases? Which would you not like to see tribunals adopt? Give reasons for your answers.

- promotion of/involvement in settling a dispute without the need for a formal hearing
- holding hearings at an employer's premises
- discouraging legal representation
- refusing to take account of precedents set by former panels
- procedural informality.

Disclosure of information for collective bargaining purposes

Since 1971 recognised trade unions have had the right to require disclosure of certain information prior to and during collective negotiations. The law in its current form dates from 1975 and is now set out in sections 181, 182 and 183 of the Trade Union and Labour Relations (Consolidation) Act 1992. Its purpose is to help ensure that collective bargaining between employers and recognised trade unions can proceed effectively. It aims to deter employers from stymieing open discussions by preventing trade union officers from having access to information that is relevant to the negotiations they are conducting. But the right only extends to areas of an organisation's policy and practice for which a union is recognised, so partial recognition gives partial disclosure rights. If a union does not undertake pay negotiations, it has no right to have details of payment arrangements disclosed to it. Moreover, the right is limited to:

- information 'without which the trade union would be to a material extent impeded in carrying out collective bargaining',

and

- which it is 'in accordance with good industrial practice to disclose'.

Essentially this means that information which is outside the scope of negotiations can be legally withheld. The statute goes on to exclude further classes of excluded information:

- information which would be against the interests of national security to disclose
- information which it would be unlawful to disclose (eg, under data protection laws)
- information which has been communicated to the employer in confidence
- information which relates to a specific individual (eg, a salary figure)
- information which if disclosed would cause substantial injury to the undertaking (eg, sensitive commercial information)
- information which relates to ongoing legal proceedings.

In addition, employers are not required to disclose information which could only be compiled or prepared with a 'disproportionate amount of work', and there is no right for a union to request disclosure of a specific document. Further guidelines are laid down in an ACAS Code of Practice which gives examples of four classes of information that should *normally* be disclosed:

1. current levels of pay and benefits
2. redundancy and recruitment policies
3. promotion and staffing plans
4. investment and financial information.

Despite these restrictions, the right to disclosure of information for collective bargaining purposes remains extensive. If information does not fit into one of the above categories, and is genuinely necessary to help a union prepare a reasoned bargaining position, it should be disclosed.

The CAC is responsible for hearing complaints from trade unions in disclosure of information cases. They only hold a formal hearing to make a binding adjudication after ACAS has first tried and failed to conciliate. Sanctions can be imposed once an employer refuses to disclose information after having been required to by the CAC. Even then though, ultimately, the CAC cannot force disclosure. If an employer refuses to do so unreasonably, it can instead be ordered to make improvements to the terms and conditions of employment of the relevant employee groups. In practice fewer than a dozen cases a year are handled by the CAC, of which the majority are settled or withdrawn without the need for a formal declaration to be made. It is very rare indeed for an award to be made.

Critics of the law argue that it is too restrictive and that it takes too long to dispose of cases. As a result, by the time a union gets a declaration of its right to have certain classes of information disclosed, it is too late for it to have a meaningful purpose because the relevant round of negotiations has long been completed. That said, of course, such a declaration should mean that similar classes of information are disclosed in the future. Gospel and Lockwood (1999) argue for a far broader formulation of the law. In their view disclosure should not only be required for collective bargaining purposes, but also in order to facilitate effective joint consultation between managers and unions.

Activity 28.3

UVW Ltd is a fast-growing company based in South Wales. Its business involves the provision of telephone-based information services for other organisations. Instead of setting up their own call centres to undertake this work, the company's clients sub-contract UVW to undertake this work on their behalf to an agreed set of standards. UVW's call centre employs a total of 450 staff on a variety of shift patterns.

Two months ago UVW signed a partnership agreement with UNITE, thus recognising a trade union for the first time. It has been agreed that the scope of bargaining will be restricted to the field of pay and benefits for the first year. Over half of the company's employees are members of the union, many having joined in recent months. The agreement requires management to meet with union representatives once a month for consultation and collective bargaining purposes. The need to negotiate a new pay settlement is high on the agenda for the first few meetings.

So far no agreement on pay rates or pay determination mechanisms has been reached. The union has put in a bid for a rise of 5%, but is not in a position to back up its demand with a coherent or persuasive case. The company has so far just rebutted the bid as 'totally unaffordable in the current climate'.

Yesterday the HR Director, Valerie McDonald, received a letter from the union's senior official at UVW asking formally for various pieces of information that it says it needs in order to conduct effective collective bargaining. Most are uncontroversial and straightforward for the company to provide, but Valerie is concerned about the following seven items which she does not wish to disclose:

1   details of the company's current succession planning activities

2   full details of the pension scheme rules and its current financial situation

3   a print-out showing what each member of staff, including managers, was paid during the last financial year

4   definite confirmation or a denial of rumours that the company is about to increase its client charges by 10%

5   details of the company's job evaluation scheme

6   a copy of the agreement the company recently signed with a provider of lease cars for use by managers and sales staff

7   information about ongoing discussions with a major client which is seeking to renegotiate its contract with UVW.

Valerie McDonald asks you to advise her about her legal position. She wants to know which of these requests for information from UNITE she can lawfully withhold and why. She also asks for information about how the law in this area is enforced and what the chances are of her having to defend her actions in front of a tribunal. What would you write?

Compulsory trade union recognition

The Employment Relations Act 1999 had as its centrepiece the introduction of compulsory trade union recognition. This part of the Act came into effect in the summer of 2000. The schedule to the Act covering this area is 110 pages long, supplemented by lengthy guidance notes, making it difficult adequately to summarise in a few paragraphs. Basically the Act forces an employer to recognise a trade union and to bargain with it in good faith where it can be established that a majority of employees in a defined bargaining group wish this to be so. Central, however, is the notion that recognition can only be required by law if the parties themselves fail to sign a voluntary agreement, the law only intervening as a last resort. The statute applies to all workplaces employing more than twenty workers (not just employees).

An independent trade union kicks off the recognition process by formally requesting recognition from an employer. Bodies which have not been listed as independent trade unions by the Certification Officer cannot make use of the procedure. The request must identify the bargaining group the union wishes to represent and state that it is made under the terms of the Act. The bargaining group must be coherent and distinct. At this point the employer has three choices:

- accept the request
- accept it in principle but disagree with the bargaining unit
- refuse the request.

Where there is disagreement on the details, the employer and union are expected to negotiate an agreement—with the help of ACAS if needs be. Where the employer refuses the request, the union can apply to the CAC for a decision and, if needs be, a requirement that a ballot is held.

Where there is a disagreement about the bargaining group defined by the union, CAC makes a ruling with reference to 'effective management', 'existing bargaining agreements' and 'the desirability of avoiding fragmented bargaining units within an undertaking'. In practice therefore a bargaining group must be relatively large as a proportion of the organisation and coherent.

Where the CAC is satisfied that 50% of members of the bargaining group are union members, a recognition is made *unless*:

- it decides that a ballot should be held 'in the interests of good industrial relations'
- a significant number of union members write to inform CAC that they do not wish the union to bargain on their behalf
- other evidence is produced which leads it to the same conclusion (eg, where there are question marks over the reasons/circumstances in which members have been signed up).

In such circumstances CAC will appoint someone to organise a secret ballot, the costs being shared equally between the union/unions concerned and the employer. Where the union does not enjoy 50% membership of the bargaining group it can nevertheless seek to persuade the CAC that a majority of the workforce would be likely to support recognition by providing compelling evidence to back up its claim. A petition containing the signatures of over 50% of the bargaining group is the type of evidence that is required. In practice the union has to have the membership of at least 10% of the relevant workforce and to be able to show that it would be more likely than not to win a recognition ballot. Where CAC is satisfied with the evidence produced by the union it orders that a ballot must be held.

The Act contains provisions putting a duty on employers to co-operate with the balloting process (eg, by providing names and addresses to the union) and to give unions the right to put their case to the workforce. Where CAC is satisfied this has not occurred it can simply make a recognition order. The union side wins if a majority of those voting *and* at least 40% of the workers constituting the bargaining unit support the recognition proposal. The CAC makes a formal declaration of the result either way, its declaration lasting for three years. Where a ballot goes the union's way, employers have thirty days to commence collective bargaining unless some longer period is agreed. Collective bargaining must cover pay, hours and holidays as a minimum.

If a re-organisation subsequently occurs and either side believes the defined bargaining unit is no longer appropriate they are supposed to negotiate. If they fail to agree they can go to CAC for a ruling. If it sees fit, CAC can terminate a declaration in these circumstances. It can also designate a new unit or can require a ballot to be held to ascertain the level of support for the union in the new unit. Otherwise employers cannot derecognise for three years unless the number of employees falls below 20. Thereafter derecognition can only occur if the employer goes through the procedures laid down:

- formally writes to the union concerned requesting derecognition
- seeks a negotiated settlement
- applies to CAC for a derecognition ballot.

If CAC concludes that there are grounds for believing a majority of workers favour derecognition a ballot is held. Such a ballot can also be triggered by workers approaching CAC to say that they wish to end collective bargaining arrangements. Derecognition ballots are then run according to the same rules used in recognition ballots (ie, the management would need to secure the support of a majority plus 40% of the votes).

Assessment

In practice relatively few formal claims have been made to CAC to date (742 by August 2011) and many of these were withdrawn before a formal order was made because voluntary agreements were reached. However, a great many more voluntary settlements have been reached in the years following the introduction of compulsory recognition law in recent years (over 2000), many being new-style partnership agreements. It is widely believed that the threat of possible future compulsory recognition has caused employers to seek out such deals. It is thus reasonable to state that, at least from the government's perspective, this legislation has met its objectives and is working reasonably well. The Employment Relations Act 2004 made one or two minor amendments to the 1999 Act, but for the most part simply clarified terms and interpretations of the original statute. It also introduced penalties for employers who are found to have intimidated workers ahead of recognition ballots.

There remain, however, two major criticisms of the legislation which continue to anger trade unions and disappoint commentators. First, many are opposed to the twenty-worker limit which remains in place and ensures that owners and managers of smaller workplaces can never be required to recognise unions or to negotiate with representatives of their work-forces even if 100% of the workers are members of a union and would like to see their terms and conditions determined through collective bargaining processes. Secondly, there remains in the legislation something of a 'loophole' which prevents formal applications being made to CAC where an organisation already 'recognises' (however partially) either a union or another collective body. As a result, an employer can effectively avoid being forced fully to recognise a union, whatever the proportion of staff it has as members, by negotiating with it over a limited range of topics (eg, discipline and grievance procedures) or by negotiating with a staff association which it has itself set up. This loophole has provided a useful 'get out clause' for some of the country's most notorious non-recognisers of unions—such as News International—and may well effectively put the UK in breach of the International Labour Organisation's convention on freedom of association (Ewing, 2000).

 Exhibit 28.1 **The *Mirror Group* case**

Until 2000, the Mirror Group Newspapers Group did not recognise any union representing journal-ists working in its sports division, despite the fact that over 50% of these employees were members of the National Union of Journalists (NUJ). Management decided that they would head off the possibility of compulsory recognition by pre-empting any claim that the NUJ might make. They did this by concluding a recognition agreement with another union, the British Association of Journal-ists (BAJ), of which just one journalist in the sports division was a member. Subsequently, when the NUJ did make an application for recognition to the Central Arbitration Committee it was ruled to be 'inadmissible' because the employer had already entered into a recognition agreement with another union. The fact that no negotiations between the Mirror Group and the BAJ had actually taken place was irrelevant. Unless the BAJ agreement had been abandoned, the CAC could not even hear the claim that the NUJ was bringing. In 2005 the case went to judicial review, where the decision went in favour of the CAC.

 Activity 28.4

XYZ Ltd is a large warehousing and distribution company based on a single site on Wearside. It cur-rently employs 300 staff broken down as follows:

    20 managers

    40 administrative employees

    120 drivers

    120 shop floor staff

Fifty shop floor employees are members of the Shop Workers' Union (USDAW) and eighty driv-ers are members of the Transport and General Workers Union. No other employees are union members. There is currently no trade union recognition or collective bargaining. »

> » The managing director, Mr Gordon Bennett, is keen to avoid recognising any union. He fears that the consensual approach to management he has fostered would be put at risk if pay and conditions were to be collectively negotiated.
>
> Mr Bennett has recently read an article about the union recognition law introduced under the Employment Relations Act 1999. He is unsure of its relevance for XYZ Ltd and asks you for advice.
>
> Assume that you have been asked to write a report for Mr Bennett on the legal position and its possible implications for XYZ. What would you include in your report and what recommendations would you make?

European Works Councils

Rarely can such a simple and relatively insignificant piece of employment regulation as that relating to European Works Councils (EWCs) have given rise to so much debate and occupied so many column inches in newspapers. This happened because during the 1990s the question of European social regulation was the subject of a major political division in UK politics and because the European Works Council Directive was the first major piece of social policy introduced by the EU after the signing of the Maastricht Treaty in 1993. In the absence of other actual regulation to focus on (although much more has since been planned and come into existence) the ire of those opposed to increased EU integration was necessarily focused on European Works Councils.

The EWC Directive was agreed in 1994 between all the then member states of the EU except the UK; because of the UK's then 'opt-out' from the social chapter of the Maastricht Treaty, it did not apply here until 2000 after the Blair government took the decision to opt in. In practice, however, the coming onto the statute book of the Transnational Information and Consultation of Employees Regulations (TICER) 2000 has had little practical impact and has yet to give rise to any significant litigation. The Central Arbitration Committee's annual report for 2010–2011 states that no cases related to these Regulations were presented to it at all during the course of the year (CAC, 2011), a situation that is typical.

The Directive is concerned with information and consultation arrangements in 'community scale undertakings'. These are companies or groups of companies which employ over 1000 people, including at least 150 in two or more member states of the European Economic Area (ie, the EU plus Norway, Iceland and Liechtenstein). Surprisingly only just over 2000 companies meet this requirement, the number having increased from 1800 with the accession of ten new member states in 2005. Over a fifth of these are actually based in the USA. The number of UK-based corporations that are affected is around 260 (DBERR, 2008:8), and in practice a good number of these were fully complying with the Directive before 2000 (Carley and Hall, 2000). Some already ran a joint consultation committee at corporate level which complied with the Directive's requirements, while others started complying earlier because they were obliged to do so in respect of their European employees. It seemed absurd to run a works council for employees in France and Spain, but to exclude the majority of UK-based workers, so everyone was included. As of 2008 113 UK-based companies operate EWCs (DBERR, 2008:8).

A common myth about the EWC Directive is that it obliges affected companies to set up European Works Councils. This is not actually the case. Management are only under an obligation even to initiate negotiations with the purpose of establishing an EWC if asked to do so by 100 employees based in at least two member states or their representatives. This is unlikely to happen if existing arrangements are considered satisfactory. Moreover, the regulations allow for the establishment of an alternative 'information and consultative procedure' where it is agreed that a fully-blown EWC arrangement is unnecessary. Where a request by 100 people or union representatives from two or more countries is received, a 'Special Negotiating Body' must be set up to agree the arrangement that will be established. This should be representative of the whole workforce, including at least one person from each country in which the company employs people. It then convenes to try to agree community-scale consultation and information-sharing arrangements. In the event of a failure to agree, a fall-back or default position automatically applies. This requires the establishment of a European Works Council consisting of between three and thirty employee representatives who meet at least once a year to be consulted about the financial position of the organisation and any future plans which might affect terms and conditions or the number of jobs. There is also provision for additional 'exceptional meetings' to discuss proposed redundancies, relocations or plant closures. As far as UK-based corporations are concerned, complaints about an unlawful failure to negotiate EWC arrangements are taken to the Employment Appeals Tribunal. Complaints relating to the running in practice of an EWC or equivalent body are taken to CAC.

The EWC Directive (and thus TICER) place all employee members of an EWC, an equivalent body established under the Directive or a Special Negotiating Body under a duty not to reveal any confidential information they may be entrusted with as part of their duties. It also absolves management of the need to disclose information which would seriously harm or be prejudicial to the company. So no confidential information of any great significance need be disclosed to members of a works council or equivalent at all, and where it is, members can be required to keep it to themselves.

For the above reasons the EWC Directive has had a very modest impact in practice. Across the whole of the European Union, in 2008, of 2278 companies that were covered by the Directive, only 820 had actually established EWC arrangements (DBERR, 2008:8). According to the Confederation of British Industry, in practice they serve little purpose either for employers or employees and can cost over £250,000 per company per year to run.

The Information and Consultation Regulations

New rights came into being in a series of three slices after 2005 requiring large and medium-sized employers to inform and consult with their employees on a collective basis where there is sufficient demand from a workforce. This law originates in the European Directive on Informing and Consulting Employees which was finally agreed by the Council Of Ministers in 2001 and by the European Parliament in 2002. Early drafts of the Directive envisaged extending arrangements similar in nature to European Works Councils to every employing organisation of any size across the EU. These proposals were watered down very considerably in the face of opposition from the UK government and one or two smaller countries. The Directive is given effect in UK law by the Information and Consultation of Employees Regulations 2004 (ICER). The Regulations have been introduced in stages:

- April 2005—undertakings with 150 plus employees
- April 2007—undertakings with 100 plus employees
- April 2008—undertakings with 50 plus employees.

It does not apply to smaller businesses at present.

It is worth remembering that UK employers are already under a duty to consult collectively with workplace representatives on redundancies, TUPE matters, health and safety issues and some pension issues. The new regulations do not replace these, instead requiring additional information-sharing and consultation over and above these specific existing duties. The scope of the Directive is expressed as follows:

> the right to be informed and consulted about the business you work for, including the prospects for employment and substantial changes in work organisation or contractual relations.

It is important to remember what the term 'consultation' means in employment law. It falls between information-sharing and negotiation. When an employer is obliged to consult, it is required to discuss issues with workforce representatives *with a view to reaching agreement*. Agreement does not actually have to be reached. The employer is discharging its legal responsibilities provided it seeks agreement in good faith. The main features of the I & C Regulations are as follows:

- The Central Arbitration Committee has the major enforcing role and not employment tribunals.
- Quite substantial financial penalties for non-compliance (up to £75,000) are payable. But these are exacted by the government. No benefit goes to the employees or unions bringing the case.
- Negotiations only have to be initiated and new arrangements put in place where 10% of the workforce request their establishment.
- Where employees wish to force negotiations with a view to enforcing the regulations, but do not want to reveal their names to their employer, a petition can be sent to CAC who then have the power to require the employer concerned to disclose to it the information necessary to establish whether 10% of the workforce have made the request.
- Where there is already in place a *written* pre-existing agreement on consultation covering a whole workforce, either with representatives or directly with employees, more than 40% of the workforce must request that negotiations start to establish new arrangements.
- Balloting of employees in such circumstances takes place with the same rules as exist currently for union recognition—ie, a majority vote including at least 40% of the electorate.
- Negotiations about new arrangements do not even begin until the workforce have rejected existing arrangements in a ballot. If the ballot goes in favour of existing arrangements, three years must pass before another can be held.
- There is freedom for organisations to set up joint arrangements and to run different types of arrangements for separate divisions, departments or sites, etc.

The Regulations set out the default arrangements that apply where management and workforce are unable to reach agreement about a system. This may well be the model that is adopted in most workplaces, as is currently the case with working time and parental leave which also permit local variation from a default scheme. The major features are as follows:

1. Appointment to an information and consultation committee is via election, a secret ballot of all employees being held.

2. The maximum number of representatives is twenty-five, one person being elected for every fifty employees.

3. Management are required to provide information to the committee in three areas:

   - the recent and probable development of the undertaking's activities and economic situation

   - the situation, structure and probable development of employment—and about any threats to employment

   - decisions likely to lead to substantial changes in work organisation or contractual relations

4. Management are also required to consult the committee on the last two items listed above, namely employment and work organisation.

5. Once established the committee itself determines how and in what way, if any, it wants to move away from the default scheme. This could be achieved if management and a majority of members agreed.

As in the case of European Works Councils, there are additional provisions concerning the disclosure of confidential information. Other regulations deal with the right of members of consultative committees to be given paid time off normal duties to attend meetings and not to be dismissed or subjected to a detriment on account of these activities.

Assessment of the Information and Consultation Regulations

Opinion about the practical impact of the Information and Consultation Regulations is divided, largely because the Regulations themselves are so complicated that they leave huge amounts of room for interpretation of their possible future practical impact.

Prior to their introduction there was a tendency for lawyers and consultants to talk up their significance at conferences and in publications in a bid to frighten managers into employing their services as advisors. The presence of a possible £75,000 fine for non-compliance was given much more prominence in these submissions than the fact that:

- negotiations only needed to take place at all once 10% of a workforce had formally requested them

and

- that the figure was 40% where pre-existing consultation arrangements were in place.

The overselling of the Regulations' practical significance was compounded by government advisors misleadingly talking about 'groundbreaking changes' and the Regulations constituting 'a red letter day in the history of industrial relations' (Hall, 2005). There was also a failure to highlight the fact that employers can themselves put in place 'pre-existing' arrangements at any time prior to a formal request being received for negotiations and hence lift the threshold for employees to force changes from 10% to 40% of the workforce. What is more, of course, employers wishing to avoid enhancing the position of trade unions in their organisation, can institute direct consultation with employees ahead of any request to establish alternative arrangements. These can then only be replaced by union-friendly structures if a ballot is forced and a wish for change subsequently endorsed by over 40% of the workforce. That is not a practical proposition in most organisations where unions do not already have a strong enough presence to enjoy consultation rights. Welch (2006) is very critical of these aspects of the Regulations, arguing that they serve little real purpose from the point of view of workers or unions. Instead he believes that new regulations should be issued which complement and facilitate union recognition and force employers to consult with a works council as a matter of course.

IRS (2004) reported a survey of larger employers which found that 66% considered their existing consultation arrangements to be adequate under the legislation and that 84% were not anticipating a request from employees to negotiate new arrangements. This and other evidence caused Hall (2005) and Tostivin (2007) to conclude that change would largely be restricted to the smaller organisations coming within the purview of the Regulations after 2007 and 2008 because they are less well placed to appreciate methods of reducing their impact by establishing employer-friendly pre-existing arrangements. Moreover, simply because of their size, they are more likely to be subject to requests from 10% of the workforce. On the other hand, of course, it is far easier for a small organisation to formalise existing informal consultation arrangements and thus be in a position to resist attempts to, on the part of a workforce, move towards a more comprehensive and costly approach. As yet there is no evidence to suggest that the extension of the Regulations to smaller organisations has had any major practical impact. In 2010–2011 the CAC reported dealing with only one dispute arising from these Regulations (CAC, 2011).

 Activity 28.5

Assume that you are appointed to the new post of human resources manager at WideNet Ltd a fast-growing internet services provider employing 300 people. The firm is highly successful and intends to expand five-fold during the coming two years. This will involve acquiring a similar sized internet company based in the Republic of Ireland.

On your arrival you find that there are no HR policies in place and that HR matters are managed in an ad hoc manner by various senior managers. There is inconsistency in the way that people are treated and a failure to comply with much employment legislation.

No trade union is recognised and there are no formal consultation arrangements in place. It is clear that employees are not happy with this situation. A substantial minority have joined the UNITE trade union in recent weeks and it can only be a matter of time before someone wins an employment tribunal claim.   »

> **» Questions**
>
> 1 What steps would you now wish to see taken as far as consultation arrangements are concerned?
>
> 2 What arguments would you deploy as a means of seeking to persuade senior managers of the need for change?

CHAPTER SUMMARY

- The UK is unusual among industrialised countries in that collective agreements here, as a general rule, are not enforceable in court. Instead they are 'binding in honour only'.

- Employers who recognise trade unions are obliged in law to disclose to them the information they need in order that meaningful collective negotiations are possible.

- Where a majority of a workforce is in union membership or would probably vote for union recognition in a ballot, employers can be required to recognise the relevant union and to negotiate with it in good faith for a minimum period of three years about pay, hours and holidays. Alternatively a ballot may be required to be held to establish whether or not there is widespread support for recognition.

- Companies with a sizeable workforce in other EU countries may be required to set up a European Works Council to inform and consult with about significant issues.

- In certain defined circumstances managers of workplaces employing more than fifty people may be required in law to consult with and inform workplace representatives about issues of significance.

For updates and further materials, please see the online resource centre at www.oup.com.

REFERENCES

CAC (2011) *Annual Report 2010–11*. London: Central Arbitration Committee.

Carley, M. and Hall, M. (2000) 'The implementation of the European Works Councils Directive' *Industrial Law Journal* 29 (p103).

CIPD (2008) 'European Works Councils'. CIPD Factsheet. London: Chartered Institute of Personnel and Development.

Deakin, S. and Morris, G. (2009) *Labour Law*. Fifth Edition. Oxford: Hart Publishing.

Department for Business, Enterprise & Regulatory Reform (2008) *Proposal to amend the European Works Council Directive*. London: DBERR.

Doyle, B. (1986) 'Legal Regulation of Collective Bargaining' in R. Lewis (ed): *Labour Law in Britain*. Oxford: Blackwell.

European Works Council Bulletin (2003) 'Latest EWC Figures'. EWCB 43.

Ewing, K. (2000) 'Trade union recognition and staff associations—a breach of international labour standards?' *Industrial Law Journal* 29 (p267).

Gospel, H. and Lockwood, G. (1999) 'Disclosure of information for collective bargaining: the CAC approach revisited' *Industrial Law Journal* 28 (p233).

Hall, M. (2005) 'Assessing the Information and Consultation of Employees Regulations' *Industrial Law Journal* 34 (p103).

IRS (2004) 'Learning to talk the hard way: information and consultation' *IRS Employment Review* 809.
8 October.

Rideout, R. (2002) 'What shall we do with the CAC?' *Industrial Law Journal* 31 (p1).

Tostivin, M. (2007) 'Information and Consultation—are you ready?' *Tolley's Employment Law Newsletter*, 12.8.

Welch, R. (2006) *The Information and Consultation Regulations—Whither Statutory Works Councils?* Liverpool: Institute of Employment Rights.

ONLINE RESOURCE CENTRE

A range of online resources to help you through your employment law module have been developed by the author team. These include updates, self-test questions and sources for further reading. (www.oxfordtextbooks.co.uk/orc/taylor_emir3e)

Industrial action

Learning outcomes

By the end of this chapter you should be able to:

- appreciate the significance of trade union immunities in the development of the law on industrial action;

- advise about which torts do and which do not attract immunity for trade unions and their officials;

- explain the significance of the 'golden formula' in determining the lawfulness of a strike or other form of industrial action;

- set out the circumstances in which strikes are unlawful in the UK; advise about the procedure and legal tests used when employers seek injunctions to halt episodes of industrial action;

- understand the legal position of individual employees taking industrial action in terms of their contracts and their rights under unfair dismissal law;

- critique the law on picketing in the UK;

- debate the rights and wrongs of the whole body of law on industrial action in the UK.

Introduction

The law in the UK concerning industrial action is complex and contains a number of uncertainties. It has been fashioned over the past century through common law judgments and statutes which have been the subject of regular judicial re-interpretation, leaving us with a situation in which strikes and other forms of action are only lawful if they meet a wide range of different qualifying criteria. Some argue that governments have deliberately refrained from simplifying the law because its very complexity acts as a deterrent to would-be organisers. It suits governments, employers and many consumers (ie, voters) for the law to act in this way. Another major criticism of the law is that in failing to provide a universal 'right to strike' the UK is in breach of several international conventions and treaty commitments to which we are signatories.

The law on the organisation of industrial action is now mainly contained in one place—the Trade Union and Labour Relations (Consolidation) Act 1992—but it remains difficult to summarise succinctly. Our aim in this chapter is to sketch out the broad principles and their practical implications. We will look separately at three distinct topics:

1. the law relating to trade unions and trade union officials organising industrial action;

2. the law relating to individual workers taking industrial action;

3. the law relating to picketing (ie, demonstrating support for a strike outside an employer's premises).

It is important to remember that while most case law concerns strikes, all forms of industrial action are covered by the same law. That includes overtime bans, go-slows, working to rule, refusal to carry out parts of one's job and short protests, as well as one-day stoppages and lengthier periods of strike action.

 Activity 29.1

Assume that you have just started working in an HR role at a road haulage company. Over 400 staff are employed, the vast majority as heavy goods vehicle (HGV) drivers. Most are members of the Transport and General Worker's section of UNITE, which is recognised for collective bargaining purposes.

You arrive in your new job three days before the first of a series of one-day strikes is due take place. Within two hours of your arrival, you are called in to see the managing director (Mr George Rake), who is clearly in a state of considerable stress. He is has just been informed by a full-time officer that the strike will definitely go ahead later in the week unless he accedes to the union's demand for an immediate 5% pay increase.

In a very angry manner he tells you that the result of the strike will be a revenue loss of £80,000, plus longer-term damage to well-established customer relationships. He tells you that he intends to fight the union 'tooth and nail', employing every tactic he can to break the strike. He says that ⟫

»   he has been negotiating for weeks and that this 'softly-softly' approach has got him nowhere at all. He wants to examine the possibilities of carrying out the following:

1   getting the strike declared unlawful in court

2   threatening the ring leaders of the strike with disciplinary action

3   hiring and training a team of 100 new HGV drivers who are not union members, before making 100 of his existing employees redundant

4   suing the union for £80,000 (ie, to compensate for expected losses arising directly from the strike).

You have two hours to write a paper setting out the legal position and making recommendations. What would you say in your paper? What further information would you need to have in order to give full and accurate advice?

    Return to this activity once you have read the chapter, to see how many of your answers were correct.

The position of unions and union officials

The law in this area is more complicated and uncertain than it is in any other area of employment regulation. This is because, despite the presence of clear statutory guidance on the core principles, to gain an understanding of its detailed application it is necessary to study large numbers of judgments made in the courts over a century or more. Not only are these complex and inevitably concerned with the facts of particular cases, they also leave room for difference of interpretation. This law is both fascinating and historically and politically important, but it is only of marginal interest to most students of employment law today. It will thus only be summarised here briefly. Excellent fuller accounts are provided by Deakin and Morris (2009), Barrow (2003), Lockton (2010), Pitt (2011) and Morris and Archer (2000).

    The best means of gaining an understanding of the current law on industrial action is to grasp the main contours of its historical development. A good starting point is the case of *Taff Vale Railway v Amalgamated Society of Railway Servants* (1901), one of the most important (some would say *the* most important) in the history of UK employment law. Here the House of Lords determined for the first time that a trade union could be sued by an employer when it organised industrial action which caused damage to that employer's business. Until that time, employers had been able to sue individual union officials, but had not generally done so simply because they rarely had the means to pay the damages even if the employer won the case. *Taff Vale*, however, altered this position fundamentally by effectively making it impossible for a union to organise meaningful industrial action. Any strike, by definition, involves the union concerned in the commitment of one or more torts (ie, civil wrongs), the main examples being inducing others to breach their contracts and conspiring to damage someone's business. If it can be sued for damages caused as a result of these acts, it cannot realistically risk organising the strike for fear that its funds will be quickly sacrificed. However, the *Taff Vale* case ultimately proved something of a godsend to British trade unions. This happened because the public outcry about it was so great that it made the right to strike into a major political issue of the day, fuelling membership of trade unions and their recently formed Labour Party. As a result, in 1906 the recently elected Liberal government made the issue a priority, resulting in the passing of the Trade Disputes Act 1906. This established the principles on which the contemporary law on industrial action is still based (see Ewing, 2006).

The key feature of the Trade Disputes Act was the creation of a system of legal immunities for trade unions and trade union officials when organising industrial action. As a result, rather than giving a positive right to strike as happened in most European countries, in the UK employers who suffered losses due to industrial action were not able to sue the unions or union officials who were responsible. As far as the trade unions themselves were concerned, the Act gave them 'wholesale' immunity from actions in tort. For trade union officials, immunity was granted from such legal actions when they were 'acting in contemplation or furtherance of a trade dispute' (the so-called 'golden formula'). This remained the position to all intents and purposes until 1971 when the Heath government, responding to the increase in the amount of industrial action taking place at that time, passed the Industrial Relations Act to put the law on industrial action on a wholly different footing. The new law, however, was short lived, and in 1974 a newly elected Labour government under Harold Wilson used its Trade Union and Labour Relations Act to return the law to the original 1906 position.

Following the election of the Thatcher government in 1979 the position changed again, but the approach to reform taken this time was a good deal less radical. Instead of replacing the principles established in 1906, the law was modified in a step-by-step fashion through a series of Employment Acts passed during the 1980s and early 1990s. Trade union immunities remained the bedrock, but steadily, over time the number of situations in which unions and their officials could claim immunity was reduced. The resulting 'settlement' was codified in one Act—the Trade Union and Labour Relations (Consolidation) Act 1992—which is where most of the law on industrial action is found today. The Blair and Brown governments made very few substantive changes to this body of law, so the position remains one in which unions and union officials cannot be sued when organising strikes and other forms of industrial action provided the action they are organising meets a variety of legal criteria.

How then have we moved from a situation in which unions had blanket immunity in 1906, to the far more restricted position that statutes have established applies today? It is helpful to answer this question by focusing on three separate means that have been used: narrowing the scope of tortious immunity, restricting the definition of the 'golden formula' and prescribing conditions for lawful industrial action. We will briefly explore each of these in turn.

Torts which attract immunity

The Employment Act 1982 made important changes to the scope of immunities enjoyed by trade unions and their officials. There were two main elements. First, the position established in 1906 whereby employers could never bring actions in tort against trade unions was removed. Henceforth, unions were placed in the same position as union officials, being immune only when acting 'in contemplation or furtherance of a trade dispute'. In return, restrictions were placed on how much by way of damages a trade union could be sued for in any one legal action. The amounts vary depending on the size of a union's membership, but for unions of any size the figure is £250,000.

Secondly, the number of torts which attract immunity was reduced significantly. Gone was blanket immunity for unions and their officials in respect of 'any tortious act' (including negligence, trespass, nuisance and defamation), and in its place came the following formulation, now found in section 219 of the 1992 Act:

> An act done by a person in contemplation or furtherance of a trade dispute is not actionable in tort on the ground only—
>
> a) that it induces another person to break a contract or interferes or induces another person to interfere with its performance, or
>
> b) that it consists in his threatening that a contract (whether one to which he is a party or not) will be broken or its performance interfered with, or that he will induce another person to break a contract or interfere with its performance.

In practice, as matters stand, this means that immunity only applies in respect of four torts. These are known as the 'economic torts' and are those which it is difficult to avoid committing when organising most forms of industrial action. Commentators often remark that the current legal position leaves unions vulnerable to judges creating new torts that restrict their freedom but which fall outside the statutory formulation; but to date this has not happened. The four economic torts are as follows:

1. **Inducing a breach of contract**. Actually breaching a contract is a matter for the law of contract, not the law of tort, but seeking to persuade someone else to breach their contract is a tort. By its nature organising industrial action nearly always involves a union through its officials persuading people to breach their contracts of employment.

2. **Interference with contract using lawful means.** This involves taking action which hinders or prevents a contract from being fulfilled. Examples include pickets acting to deter delivery of goods to or from an employer's premises.

3. **Intimidation.** In law this concerns any situation in which a threat is made to damage another party's interests. It is not just about physical violence. Threatening industrial action would often be covered were immunity not to be given.

4. **Conspiracy.** Most of us would be open to prosecution for conspiracy if we formed an organisation or a plan which was aimed primarily at damaging someone else's economic interests. Most industrial action involves a group of people conspiring to damage a business in some shape or form.

The golden formula

Central to the Trade Disputes Act 1906 and to all subsequent legislation on industrial action is the expression 'in contemplation or furtherance of a trade dispute'. This has become known as 'the golden formula' because it describes the situation in which immunity under the law of tort applies to trade unions and their officials. Interpretation of the golden formula has developed over the years, partly through case law and partly through statutes which have clarified the position.

The term 'trade dispute' is now clearly defined in section 218 of TULR(C)A 1992. This lists seven subjects which enable a dispute to qualify under the definition. When the dispute is *wholly or mainly* about one of the following it thus *does* qualify unions and their officials for immunity:

- terms and conditions of employment
- recruitment, dismissal and suspension of workers
- allocation of work
- matters of discipline
- membership or non-membership of trade unions
- facilities for trade union officials
- procedural matters relating to recognition, negotiation or consultation of/with trade unions.

If the major reason for the industrial action does not fall into one of these categories, it is not a trade dispute and there is no immunity for the union or union officials organising the industrial action. This means that industrial action which is essentially political in nature (ie, aimed at damaging a government rather than an employer) is not covered. Hence in *BBC v Hearn* (1977) the union lost its claim when TV technicians refused to transmit the FA Cup Final to South Africa. This was a political protest and not a trade dispute. It is of course lawful for public sector unions to organise action against the government in its role as an employer.

The other requirement set out in section 218 of the Act is that the term 'trade dispute' in the context of the Act 'means a dispute between employers and workers, or between workers and workers'. The courts always interpret the former as meaning a dispute between workers and their own employer, which can have important consequences. For example in *Dimbleby & Sons v National Union of Journalists* (1984) it was ruled that the union concerned could not retain immunity when taking action against a parent company when the workers concerned were employed by a subsidiary company. Provided the subsidiary company has been created for genuine commercial reasons its workers can only strike against it and not a controlling organisation—even if this is where the power really lies. Other cases (notably *Examite Hire Ltd v Whittaker* (1977)) ensure that this position does not apply when an employer creates a subsidiary company for the purpose of making a union liable. The same is true of attempts to cause the removal of a union's immunity by employing workers indirectly through an agency.

 Exhibit 29.1   *University College London NHS Trust v UNISON* **(1999)**

This is a relatively recent case which illustrates how restrictive the right to enjoy trade union immunities has become. Here an NHS hospital had entered into negotiations with a consortium of private sector companies with a view to them building and subsequently running a new hospital financed by the government's Private Finance Initiative (PFI). The UNISON trade union was »

>> concerned that terms and conditions of employment would be less satisfactory for workers transferring from the NHS hospital to the new PFI hospital. Its officials thus demanded that managers include in any contract a clause guaranteeing that workers who transferred would be re-employed on no less favourable terms and conditions. The trust's management refused to do this, in the process provoking a ballot for industrial action.

The case came to court because the employer claimed that this was not, in truth, a dispute between it and its workers. Instead it related to possible future terms and conditions that might or might not be introduced by a new employer which had yet even to be clearly identified. There should thus be no immunity for the union or its officials. The Court of Appeal found for the employer. Later UNISON took the case to the European Court of Human Rights, arguing that UK law breached the European Charter. Their case was ruled 'inadmissible' so no clear ruling was ever given.

In 2004 the government introduced new guidelines covering transfers to private providers in the NHS and in local government which seek to ensure that employees are guaranteed new conditions which are no less favourable than those they currently enjoy, but this does not alter the legal position vis-à-vis taking industrial action in such situations before the transfer has occurred.

Further conditions

During the 1980s and early 1990s a range of additional restrictions were introduced in successive Employment Acts which narrowed further the number of situations in which full immunity was enjoyed by unions and their officials. These formed part of the then government's strategy to reduce the number of strikes and other episodes of industrial action taking place. With the exception of one or two minor changes made in the Employment Relations Act 1999, all of these restrictions were retained by the Blair/Brown governments. The major examples are as follows:

1. **When secondary action takes place**. This is industrial action taken in support of workers who are employed by another employer. It is not thus directed at the workers' own employer (eg, miners coming out in support of ambulance drivers).

2. **When lawful balloting arrangements have not been followed**. Industrial action is now only 'lawful' (ie, attracts immunity) if it occurs following a balloting procedure that is in accordance with statutory requirements. This means that all union members who are to be asked to take action are given the opportunity to vote via a secret postal ballot. Employers must be given at least seven days' notice of the ballot and vote counting must be overseen by an independent scrutineer. Ballot papers must contain the statement 'if you take part in industrial action you may be in breach of your contract of employment'.

3. **When proper notice has not been given to the employer**. Following a ballot in favour of industrial action, seven days' notice must be given to the employer of the date that action will commence. This provides for a 'cooling off period' in which negotiations aimed at averting action can take place. Moreover, industrial action then has to commence within four weeks of the ballot which authorises it having taken place. After this time has passed a further ballot has to be held.

4. **When the dispute concerns one of the prohibited reasons**. Certain types of trade dispute are no longer considered acceptable in law and cannot attract immunity for unions or their officials. These are actions which have as their main purpose enforcing a closed shop, securing the reinstatement of dismissed strikers and exerting pressure for trade union recognition.

5. **When unlawful picketing has occurred**. Where a union organises picketing which fails to meet legal requirements, immunity for it and the officials concerned can be lost. The major examples of situations in which picketing is unlawful include those where pickets are not employed at the workplace concerned and situations in which picketing ceases to be 'peaceful'. The law on picketing is explored in greater detail below.

Activity 29.2

Assume that you are employed on a consultancy basis to give HR advice to members of a magazine publisher's association. You are approached to advise two of the association's members about a related issue. The two companies concerned are ABC Publishing and XYZ Magazines. Both publish and print mass circulation television listings guides on a weekly basis and employ several hundred staff. Both also recognise UNITE for collective bargaining purposes.

Managers at ABC Publishing have been in dispute with staff for some weeks now over their proposal to consolidate a variety of allowances and bonus payments into one simplified scheme for all workers. While the net effect on the wage bill will be neutral, some employees may lose out under the new system. After several months of negotiation with union representatives (resulting in a failure to agree), the company imposed the new arrangements unilaterally. As a result, shop stewards balloted their members with a view to organising an all-out strike. The result went in favour of industrial action and the union has now given ABC Publishing formal notice of their members' intention to commence striking next Monday for an indefinite period. Unless a resolution can be found, this means that ABC's TV listings magazine ('What's on the Box?') will not appear on newsstands from next week.

Management at XYZ Magazines have been following the dispute at ABC Publishing with interest. On hearing about the proposed strike they immediately put in place plans to double the print-run of their television listings magazine ('TV-Tonight') from next week.

XYZ shop stewards are unhappy about this proposal which they believe will lead to large profits being made on the back of a wholly justified dispute being organised by fellow workers at ABC publishing. Why, they argue, should XYZ shareholders benefit while ABC employees are being made to suffer so unfairly? They thus give notice to XYZ management that their members will refuse to print the planned additional copies of 'TV-Tonight'. For the duration of the strike at ABC Publishing, they will stop work after printing the normal weekly print-run.

You are approached by managers at ABC Publishing and XYZ Magazines to give advice on the legal avenues that may be open to them as a means of stopping both cases of industrial action from going ahead. What further information would you seek? What advice would you give to each company?

Remedies

Unions who organise action that does not attract immunity in tort can be sued by the employer affected, by a union member or by members of the public who suffer a detriment as a result of the action. Employers can apply to the courts for damages after a strike has taken place, but because there are limits on the amount of money that can be awarded against a trade union in respect of any one legal action, this approach is rarely used. It might serve more purpose where multiple employers are the victims of the same strike and can thus bring separate actions, but it only happens very rarely indeed. This is because the long-term industrial relations consequences for an employer which bankrupted a trade union in such circumstances would not be at all rosy, and because there is a better alternative method available—namely, preventing the action from occurring in the first place.

In practice, the approach used is for the employer to seek an interim interlocutory injunction in the High Court either to stop action from going ahead or to halt it once it has already started. Technically this is an emergency remedy provided by the court pending a full trial to be scheduled at a later date. In practice, however, because it serves to stop the industrial action concerned in its tracks until such time as a full hearing can take place (ie, several months later), to all intents and purposes it brings it to an end.

As a result, where there are balloting irregularities, where a proposed strike involves secondary action, where it does not fall within the legal definition of 'a trade dispute' or where there is some doubt about these matters, an employer instructs its lawyers to apply for an interlocutory injunction. The tests used by the High Court in such cases are widely criticised for being too employer-friendly in that it is no longer necessary (as it used to be) for the employer to present the court with a convincing prima facie case to support the granting of an injunction. The employer is not now required to present evidence which shows that it would be likely to win a full trial. Instead it merely has to convince the court that there is 'a serious question to be tried'. Effectively this simply means showing that the employer's case is not trivial or vexatious in any way. Having established that this is so, the court goes on to consider the issue of the 'balance of convenience' in the case. Barrow (2003:356) sums this approach up as follows:

> It means that the court should balance the extent to which the plaintiff would not be compensated by damages if the injunction were not granted and if he won at trial, against the loss the defendant would suffer if the injunction were granted, if he won at trial.

As the defendant in industrial action cases (the union) inevitably nearly always stands to lose less financially than the employer (the claimant) in an industrial dispute, it is not difficult for an employer to get its injunction and for the industrial action to be stopped—provided of course there is some legal irregularity.

The consequences for a union of failing to abide by an interlocutory injunction are very serious. Senior officials may be fined for contempt of court (as happened to Arthur Scargill the miner's leader in 1984) and the union itself can be fined too. More commonly a court will order that the union's assets be sequestrated. This means that union bank accounts are frozen for the period for which the contempt lasts (ie, the duration of the industrial dispute) and until such time as a judge considers the union to have 'purged' the contempt (eg, by issuing an apology). Assets are later returned minus any fines that have been levied and, of course, legal costs.

An important distinction has to be made in this context between official and unofficial industrial action. In the case of the first a union is liable in law for the consequences, in the case of the second it may not be. The position is set out in section 20 of TULR(C)A 1992. Here it says that an action (eg, calling a strike) will be considered to have been authorised and endorsed by the union if it is carried out by an official of the union, the principal executive committee, or any other person or committee authorised to do so under a union's rules. In effect, this makes trade unions vicariously liable for the actions of all their officials, and means that industrial action organised by any of them is considered, in principle, to be official. However, there is a method by which a union can escape liability when its officials and members act locally and off their own bats to organise unofficial industrial action. This involves the principal executive committee, union president or general secretary of the union issuing a repudiation notice. Until 1990 that was all that was required, but since then the regulations have been tighter. It is thus now necessary for the union to repudiate the action 'as soon as is reasonably practicable' and to confirm that it has done so to the employer concerned. Moreover, a statement must be issued at the earliest possible opportunity to all union members who may be affected warning them that their action has been repudiated by the union, is thus unofficial and may put them at risk of dismissal.

 Exhibit 29.2   *Metrobus v Unite the Union* **(2009) and** *British Airways v Unite the Union* **(2010)**

There have been a number of instances over recent years in which employers have successfully applied to the High Court for interlocutory injunctions which have the effect of postponing strike action due to balloting irregularities. High profile cases have involved railway engineers, airline cabin crew and even university lecturers. In each case managers successfully petitioned the High Court to issue an injunction which, in effect, prevented strikes from going ahead. These cases all followed on from the *Metrobus* case which was decided in July 2009. Here the union appealed the decision to the Court of Appeal and lost, in the process helping to ensure that the High Court is in future likely to take an even stricter line than was the norm before this case.

In the *Metrobus* case there were minor defects in the information provided on ballot papers and some irregularities in the provision to the employer of the names of those going on strike. They had also delayed twenty hours before formally informing Metrobus of the ballot result. These were pretty minor infringements, but the Court of Appeal found that they were sufficient to justify an interlocutory injunction.

Importantly, in presenting its case, the union had sought to invoke the Human Rights Act using Article 11 of the European Convention on Human Rights—the right to freedom of assembly and association as the basis for its major legal argument. In other words, it was asking the Court to rule that UK law as it currently stands breaches the Convention.

In passing judgment the Court stated that in its view the provisions in the law on balloting and notice to employers 'are not so onerous or disproportionate as to be incompatible' with Article 11.   »

>> The impact of this ruling has been very substantial, allowing the High Court to grant injunctions where there have been minor infringements by unions which were unintended and also of no consequence whatever to the final outcome of ballots.

However, one recent case bucked the trend and went in favour of the union. This happened in one of a number of battles between British Airways and Unite, representing cabin crew. In May 2010 the Court of Appeal overturned an earlier High Court ruling to award an injunction against the union whose only failure was to have communicated the result of a strike ballot by text and through e-mail rather than by letter, and to have failed to include information on the number of spoiled ballots.

The Court of Appeal decided that these breaches of the Regulations were mere 'technicalities' and that they should not be allowed to prevent staff from taking strike action—the ballot had shown over 80% to be in favour of taking industrial action.

The position of individual employees

Aside from legal sanctions that can be taken against the union that is organising industrial action, employers can seek to deter individual employees from joining a dispute. Two of the ways in which this commonly occurs are as follows:

1. By refusing to pay the employee for those hours or days that they are not working.

2. By threatening and/or carrying out a dismissal.

Both these courses of action are restricted to an extent by the law. Others, by contrast, are not. So employers still have at their disposal a range of tools that they can draw on to try to persuade individuals that it is not in their interests to join a strike or another form of industrial action.

In Chapter 27 we considered the law on freedom of association. Here we established that employers could not lawfully dismiss employees or take action short of dismissal against them for a trade union-related reason. It is important to remember that these rights do not apply once industrial action is being taken. A separate body of law regulates the rights of individual employees engaged in such circumstances.

Breach of contract

When employees take industrial action they are normally breaching their contracts of employment. When they give notice of their intention to take action they are telling their employers that they intend to breach their contracts. The only common form of industrial action which does not involve breaching a contract is 'working to contract', which involves employees only carrying out the duties that are strictly required under their terms and conditions of employment.

This means that an employer is quite within its rights not to pay employees (either in part or fully) for hours not worked or duties not carried out because they were taking industrial action. The only exception is where some form of strike pay arrangement has been agreed which is contractual.

Exhibit 29.3   *Wiluszynski v London Borough of Tower Hamlets* **(1989)**

Mr Wiluszynski was employed as an estates officer in the council's housing department. Along with colleagues he took limited industrial action for a period of one month, coming into work but refusing to carry out one aspect of his duties—answering telephone enquiries from councillors.

At the start of the period the council wrote to employees stating that the action they were taking amounted to breach of contract and that they would not be paid any salary unless they carried out all their duties. Despite the fact that Mr Wiluszinski and his colleagues carried out all their other duties, they were not paid at all in the month in which the action took place.

The case went to court and the employer won the case. At the Court of Appeal the following often quoted point was made:

> He cannot blow hot and cold, he cannot eat his cake and have it, he cannot approbate and reprobate.

You cannot therefore partially breach your contract of employment any more than you can partially burst a balloon. A breach is a breach.

Unfair dismissal

Unofficial industrial action gives no protection whatsoever for the employees involved as far as dismissal is concerned. It is considered an 'automatically fair' reason for dismissal under unfair dismissal law, irrespective of length of service or mitigating circumstances. If the main reason for a dismissal is taking part in unofficial action the tribunal will not consider the reasonableness of the circumstances. Indeed it will not even hear the case. This means that it is quite lawful for employers to dismiss people taking unofficial action selectively. There being no requirement to treat people consistently, employers can 'pick off' the ring leaders, get rid of poorer performers and generally dismiss whoever they want to for whatever reason. The consequences may be problematic as far as future relationships at work are concerned, but legally selective dismissal is entirely possible.

With official industrial action the position now changes after twelve weeks of the dispute commencing. The period was eight weeks between 2000 and 2004, there having been no qualifying period before then. This does not mean after twelve weeks of an all-out strike, it means twelve weeks from the date at which industrial action of whatever kind began. Until that time the dismissal of an employee taking official action is considered to be automatically unfair. This means that no defence can be deployed by the employer because reasonableness is not considered and no qualifying period in terms of continuous service with the employer applies for people wishing to pursue tribunal claims.

After twelve weeks dismissal of people taking official action becomes potentially fair, so it can be lawful provided the employer acts reasonably. Since 2000 no cases have reached the higher courts, so we cannot be certain about how exactly they will judge reasonableness when dismissals of this kind occur. However, it is likely that the courts will retain their long-standing practice of applying a consistency rule in considering cases in which official strikers have been dismissed. This means that all dismissed employees must be treated alike. There can be no selective dismissal or selective rehiring soon after a dismissal.

In addition, the Employment Relations Act 1999 requires an employer to show that it took 'all reasonable steps' to resolve the dispute if it wants its action in dismissing the employees concerned to be judged as reasonable. The tests used are entirely procedural. They do not require the tribunal to consider the merits of the industrial action itself:

- Did the employer comply with procedures laid down in a collective agreement?
- Did the employer offer to commence/resume negotiations after the start of the dispute?
- Did the employer unreasonably refuse a request for conciliation or mediation services to be used in an attempt to settle the dispute?

The aim of this law is to deter situations arising in which employers deliberately provoke strikes as a means of avoiding making redundancy payments, a situation which is believed to have occurred in some of the newspaper workers' cases during the 1980s.

Reinstatement and re-employment orders are more common in industrial action cases than in other types of unfair dismissal case, compensation being the outcome where the employer has hired a replacement workforce before the case is heard by a tribunal. The case law has been complex on the question of whether or not the tribunals should take account of an employee's 'contributory fault' when determining appropriate levels of compensation. The current position, set out by the House of Lords in *Crosville Wales Ltd v Tracey* (1997), is that the merits of the industrial action itself should not be a matter for the tribunal to consider. However, deductions from compensation should be made if an individual has engaged in unlawful picketing or has acted in a particularly inflammatory way.

It is important to note that there is no equivalent provision in the law on industrial action to protect employees from 'action short of dismissal' or 'any other detriment', should an employer wish to punish those who took action in some way. It is also important to note that because protection from dismissal for taking part in industrial action is provided through unfair dismissal law, it cannot apply to people who are not 'employees' working under 'a contract of service'. A good proportion of the UK's workforce (ie, those in the 'worker category' who are not employees) are thus not protected from dismissal in these circumstances. Both these legal gaps have understandably been criticised by trade unions and other commentators for many years.

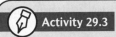 **Activity 29.3**

Southington College of Further Education employs 250 staff to teach a range of academic and vocational qualifications. Tight budgets for the forthcoming year have led the college's principal, Mrs Margaret Chopper, to make substantial cuts so as to ensure that her budgets balance. Her actions include making three members of staff redundant, failing to renew the contracts of two staff who are employed on temporary contracts and re-allocating some work from administrative to »

> teaching staff. The reaction of staff is varied. People in some departments accept the changes and agree to take on the additional work. In Arts and Design it is agreed that staff will protest by carrying out only those duties which are listed on their current job descriptions. Staff in the Information Technology Department agree that they will continue to work normally in most respects, but will not participate in any way in the processes for admitting students on to next year's courses. This will involve a refusal to handle admissions documentation, to respond to telephone enquiries or to interview candidates. By contrast, staff in the Manufacturing Department decide to approach their trade union with a view to organising a series of one day stoppages. A letter is sent to Mrs Chopper giving notice of an intention to call a ballot for strike action by the union's full time steward with responsibility for Southington College.
>
> The principal is unsurprised by the threats made by these three groups of staff, but is unsure of the legal position and wants to ensure that it informs her response.
>
> What advice would you give to Mrs Chopper if you were asked? What additional information would you need in order to give effective advice?

Picketing law

The law on picketing is divided into two distinct parts—that covered by the civil law and that covered by the criminal law. Both are guided by the content of the 1980 Code of Practice on Picketing issued by the Department of Employment (this was updated, but not substantially altered in 1992). The Code sets out the standards which are used by the police when assessing what action they should take and by the courts in assessing the legality of police actions. The Code is also used by the civil courts in deciding whether or not to award damages or to grant injunctions to people or organisations that are caused a detriment by pickets. It states that picketing needs to be 'peaceful' and should not intimidate. Pickets must be employees of the workplace concerned, accompanied if necessary by a full-time union official. It also states that, as a general rule, the number of pickets posted on each entrance to a place of work should be limited to six. At the time it was introduced, the Code of Practice was widely derided as unworkable. In an era of mass picketing during major national disputes it seemed absurd to think that the number of pickets could be limited to six—even if this is a 'general rule' and not an absolute requirement. The Code has, however, stood the test of time. The Blair government kept it in place, and today there is a widespread political consensus that it provides a reasonable basis for determining the lawfulness or otherwise of a picket.

Civil law

Under the common law it has been possible since 1982 to sue any trade union under whose banner an unruly picket assembles using the torts that no longer attract immunity. The major examples are:

- trespass (where pickets assemble on a private road or on privately owned land adjacent to a workplace entrance)

- private nuisance (where pickets are constitute a nuisance to people/firms who are nothing to do with the dispute but are prevented from carrying out their lawful business by a large picket)

- public nuisance (where 'public health, safety, comfort or convenience' are affected by pickets blocking roads, dropping litter, etc).

Deakin and Morris (2009:958) suggest that there is now a fourth example in the form of tortious liability created under the Protection from Harassment Act 1997. This is primarily aimed at stalkers who repeatedly harass victims, but the definition of harassment contained in the Act could also be applied to pickets. Aside from creating criminal offences, the Act also provides for victims of repeated harassment to seek an injunction restraining the perpetrator. As yet there have been no examples of the Act being used in a picketing scenario, but in theory it could be.

It is important to point out, however, that when a picket is peaceful and consists of workers demonstrating outside their own place of work, those who are inconvenienced (the employer, staff wishing to work, suppliers, customers, etc) have no basis for bringing any kind of legal action, even if they suffer financial loss as a result. This is because picketing is covered by the sections in the Trade Union and Labour Relations (Consolidation) Act 1992 which relate to trade union immunities. The law thus effectively provides for a right to picket. It is only when the picketing ceases to be peaceful (ie, goes beyond communicating a message and seeking to persuade in a peaceful fashion) that immunity is lost. Only at this stage, therefore, can the employer apply for an interlocutory injunction to stop the strike from continuing.

Of course the question of what is and what is not 'peaceful' is a matter of interpretation. Some judges have shown a willingness, when applying the law, to expect strict adherence to the limit of six pickets on any one entrance, while others have seen this as constituting general guidance and not legal writ. In recent years there have been few cases, but commentators argue that in the future it is likely that rulings will be less restrictive from a trade union point of view. This is because since the Human Rights Act came into effect in 2000, judges have been obliged to interpret the law in accordance with the European Convention on Human Rights (see Chapter 22). It is plausibly argued that Article 10 (on freedom of expression) and particularly Article 11 (on freedom of assembly) could be invoked in the context of picketing to ensure that breaching the guideline of six pickets was not in itself sufficient to render a strike unlawful (see Deakin and Morris 2009:962).

Criminal law

There are also a range of criminal offences which pickets can find themselves committing if they do not take care (Barrow 2003:361–366). This can lead to their arrest and, on occasions, the dispersal of a picket by the police. The major examples are as follows:

1. **Obstruction of the highway**. This includes any action which disrupts 'ordinary and reasonable use of the highway'. Local bye-laws, for example around airports, can be stricter, but generally just stopping a vehicle and seeking to persuade the driver not to enter a premises is entirely lawful. A criminal act is only committed if pickets unreasonably obstruct, for example by lying down in front of a vehicle or physically preventing it from proceeding in some way.

2. **Obstructing a police officer in the execution of his duty**. The police have a duty to 'maintain the peace' and can disperse a picket, require pickets to go home or prevent them from assembling in the first place if they believe that a 'breach of the peace may occur'. Refusal to comply is a criminal offence.

3. **Offences under the Public Order Act 1986**. Passed in the wake of the miners' strike of 1984–1985, and of tragedies caused by crowds in football stadia, this Act created a new hierarchy of criminal offences ranging from 'disorderly conduct' through 'intentionally causing harassment' and on to 'threatening behaviour', 'affray', 'violent disorder' and 'riot'. It permits the police to determine where a picket should assemble and to maximise its numbers where they believe a breach of the Act is likely to occur.

4. **Offences under TULR(C)A 1992**. These were originally part of the Conspiracy and Protection of Property Act 1875, but were included in the 1992 Act as a means of signalling their modern significance to picketing situations. They relate to situations in which one person intimidates or stalks another in order to compel that person to abstain from something they have every right to do (ie, going to work). It also covers situations where a striker might hide tools or clothes, or perhaps disable a car, in order to deter someone from going to work.

Debates about the law on industrial action

The body of law we have briefly described in this chapter is unquestionably the most politically contentious in employment law. People hold very strong views both in favour of it and against it, there being few who argue for any kind of a middle way. On the one hand there are those who argue that the right to take industrial action must be limited in law to prevent a minority being able to 'hold to ransom' a majority (of workers, consumers, taxpayers or citizens of the country in general) through the use of industrial muscle. On the other hand there are those who fiercely defend the right of workers through trade unions to withdraw their labour, either completely or partially, in order to prevent employers from exploiting them unreasonably or treating them unfairly. The former position is the one to which successive UK governments have broadly held, the latter is the one which underpins most international treaties and conventions on labour rights. At the heart of the debate is a relatively simple disagreement about whether or not workers in the UK should or should not be accorded in law a generally applicable 'right to strike'.

The main arguments in favour of our existing laws are a pragmatic mix of the economic and the political (see Hanson, 1991 for an accessible and positive account of the law's impact). Strikes and other forms of industrial action damage the economy over the long term. Their aim is to prevent businesses from implementing what their managers believe are necessary changes or to reduce profitability by supporting unaffordable pay increases. In the public sector they interfere with the delivery of essential public services or render them less efficient than they could be. They also have the potential to interfere with the achievement of a government's legitimate economic objectives in terms of inflation control, international competitiveness and taxation. They should therefore be discouraged, in part through

Table 29.1 Average number of working days lost due to strikes

1970–1974:	14.1 million
1975–1979:	11.6 million
1980–1984:	10.5 million
1985–1989:	3.9 million
1990–1994:	0.8 million
1995–1999:	0.6 million
2000–2004:	0.8 million
2005–2009:	0.6 million

Source: adapted from Monger (2005) and EIRO-online (2010)

regulation, so that they can only occur when absolutely necessary. Moreover, the use of industrial action to achieve political ends, or to defend indefensible industrial practices like closed shops, should not be permitted at all because they harm the human rights of others as well as hindering economic performance. The situations that occurred in 1974 and 1979 whereby governments were effectively brought down in large part by trade unions engaging in industrial action should not be able to occur again—and this requires tough anti-strike legislation.

Seen from this perspective, the law on industrial action that was created between 1979 and 1993 can be seen as a success. Necessary economic restructuring has been able to proceed unimpeded, along with substantial reform of the public sector. Industrial relations problems have moved from the top of the political and managerial agendas to being matters, in the main, of specialist interest. And, most important of all, the number of strikes has declined hugely. The extent of this trend is shown in Table 29.1. What is more, this has been achieved not by banning legitimate strikes, but by introducing sensible, workable reforms. The biggest cause of reduced strikes is the requirement to ballot a workforce and then to wait seven days before starting the industrial action—a modest reform which gives everyone an opportunity to avert a strike by going back to the negotiating table after a ballot has gone in favour of action.

The opposing view questions some of these assertions. The number of strikes has reduced generally across most of the industrialised world and would have happened in the UK in any event during the post-1980 period. All that the law has done is make it difficult for trade unions to organise perfectly legitimate strikes in support of workers whose livelihoods have been threatened by unnecessary and damaging privatisations, by restructuring and downsizing programmes that benefit shareholders at the expense of workers and by unfair pay deals which have served to increase inequality in the UK to far too great an extent. The position of women at work, of ethnic minorities and those whose health and safety is put at risk is worse than it would be were unions permitted to exercise greater economic muscle. UK productivity rates have not improved vis-à-vis those of our competitors to any great extent, while great injustices have been allowed to proceed under the banner of 'management's right to manage'.

Aside from rebutting the economic and political arguments put forward by those who approve of the law on industrial action, opponents also deploy arguments that are rooted in a belief in fundamental human rights—one of which is the right to strike. The Institute of Employment Rights (2002:89–97) puts this case concisely. The key points are as follows:

- All workers should have a basic right to strike, in failing to provide this the UK is in breach of international treaty obligations.
- It should be unlawful to sack a worker (not just an employee) for taking strike action, and it should be a requirement that employers reinstate those they have sacked unlawfully in such circumstances.
- It should be lawful to take industrial action to protest about matters of economic and social policy. It is unacceptable to limit the 'right' to trade dispute issues.
- Secondary action (labelled 'solidarity action') should be permissible, if the primary action it supports is lawful.
- Pickets should be able to assemble at any place of work whether they are employed there or not to demonstrate peacefully.
- The technical requirements required of unions organising pre-strike ballots are too costly and in practice serve to impair the right to organise legitimate industrial action. It is for workers, not legislation, to determine how best their views are ascertained.
- An employer should only be able to get an injunction to halt a strike if it genuinely has a stronger case in law than that of the opposing union.

 Activity 29.4

Assume that you have recently started working in an HR role for an American computer company (XYZ Technologies) which is establishing a presence in the UK for the first time. Your first major project involves reviewing and, where necessary, rewriting the company's HR policies to bring them into line with UK legislation. The staff handbook contains the following passage:

Industrial action

- It is the policy of XYZ Technologies to establish constructive relations with a single labour union at each of our workplaces. Consultation with union representatives about employment policy and practice is continual. Disagreements are resolved in a spirit of co-operation around the negotiating table.
- XYZ Technologies considers industrial action of any kind to be unnecessary. In all circumstances, employees who take such action will be considered to be acting in breach of their contracts of employment.
- It is the policy of XYZ Technologies to withhold pay for any day during which an employee takes any form of industrial action. »

> • XYZ Technologies reserves the right to take formal disciplinary action against employees who engage in industrial action, and if it so determines, to terminate their contracts of employment without notice.
>
> Write a memo to the operations director setting out *from a legal perspective* what is and what is not acceptable in this existing policy statement. What are the principal points of law that need to be taken into account in drawing up a new policy statement for the company's UK operations?

CHAPTER SUMMARY

- The law relating to trade unions organising industrial action in the UK is complex and difficult to summarise. It is based around the concept of immunities in tort for unions and their officials while they are planning and organising such action.

- Where a union organises industrial action without fully complying with the law (for example by not holding a secret postal ballot of all members in a workplace) an employer can ask for an injunction in the High Court to prevent a strike from going ahead or continuing. Failure to observe the terms of such an injunction leads to the union's funds being sequestrated.

- Individual union members, if they are employees, enjoy considerable protection under the law of unfair dismissal when participating in official industrial action. No such protection exists when they participate in unofficial action.

- It is entirely lawful for employers to dock some, or even all, of an employee's pay on days when industrial action is being taken.

- The criminal law on picketing restricts the number of pickets who can demonstrate outside a workplace entrance at any time, and acts as a disincentive to unruly or overly aggressive picketing. These laws have often been strictly enforced by the police.

For updates and further materials, please see the online resource centre at www.oup.com.

REFERENCES

Barrow, C. (2002) *Industrial Relations Law*. Second Edition. London: Cavendish Publishing.

Deakin, S. and Morris, G. (2009) *Labour Law*. Fifth Edition. Oxford, Hart Publishing.

Eiro-online (2010) 'Developments in industrial action 2005–2009' European Industrial Relations Observatory.

Ewing, K. (ed) (2006) *The Right to Strike: From the Trade Disputes Act 1906 to a Trade Union Freedom Bill 2006*. Liverpool: Institute of Employment Rights.

Hale, D. (2007) *Labour Disputes in 2006*. London: Office of National Statistics.

Hale, D. (2008) *Labour Disputes in 2007*. London: Office of National Statistics.

Hanson, C. (1991) *Taming the Trade Unions: A Guide to the Thatcher Government's Employment Reforms, 1980–90*. Basingstoke: Macmillan.

Institute of Employment Rights (2002) *A Charter of Worker's Rights*. Edited by K. Ewing & J. Hendy. London: IES.

Lockton (2010) *Employment Law*. Sixth Edition. Basingstoke: Palgrave Macmillan.

Monger, J. (2005) 'Labour Disputes in 2004'. *National Statistics Feature* at www.statistics.gov.uk.

Morris, G. & Archer T. (2000) *Collective Labour Law*. Oxford: Hart Publishing.

Pitt, G. (2011) *Employment Law*. Eighth Edition. London: Sweet & Maxwell.

ONLINE RESOURCE CENTRE

A range of online resources to help you through your employment law module have been developed by the author team. These include updates, self-test questions and sources for further reading. (www.oxfordtextbooks.co.uk/orc/taylor_emir3e)

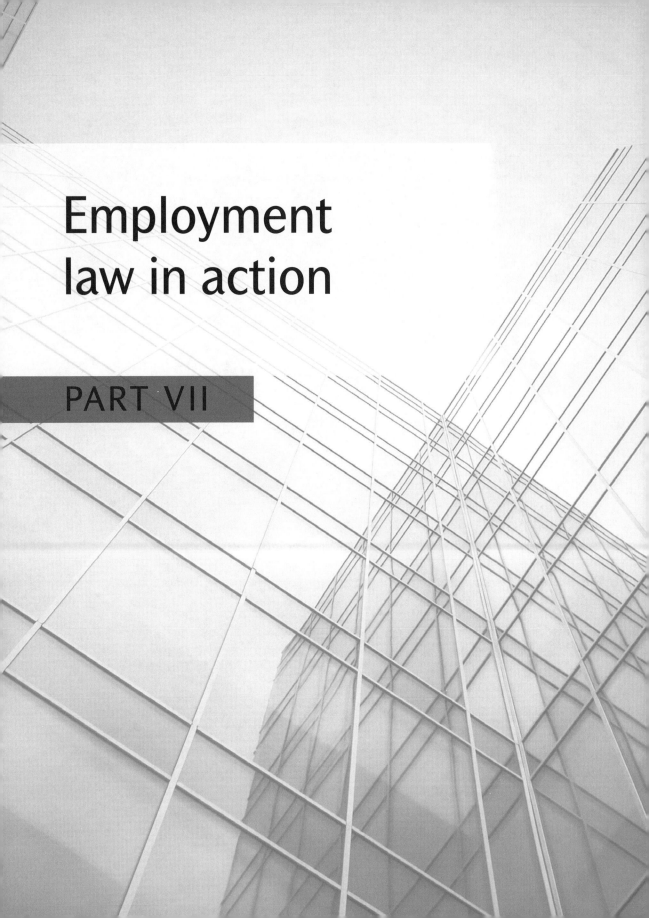

Employment law in action

PART VII

Employment tribunal procedure

Learning outcomes

By the end of this chapter you should be able to:

- describe the various steps in bringing a case in an employment tribunal;

- state the overriding objectives of the tribunal panel;

- understand the dispute resolution steps that have to be taken before a party should bring a case;

- identify the time limits for bringing various types of claim;

- be aware of the work of ACAS and the ways in which a case can be settled;

- understand the difference between case management discussions, pre-hearing reviews and the final hearing;

- say what disclosure means, and how to get documents that are relevant to a case;

- be familiar with the usual procedure of a main hearing; and

- state the types of remedy that can be granted by a tribunal.

Introduction

This chapter and the one which follows deal with the practicalities of bringing a case in an employment tribunal. We will first look at tribunal procedure and at the steps that are generally taken before a full hearing takes place. In Chapter 31 we will conclude by considering how to carry out the role of advocate or representative of one of the parties in a tribunal. These two chapters on employment tribunals necessarily provide only a short introduction to preparing a case. If a case is being taken to tribunal, one must be aware of the possibility of further matters cropping up. For a fuller account on tribunal procedure there are two very helpful and practical guides: Isobel Manley and Elaine Heslop's *Employment Tribunals: A Practical Guide* (2008) and Naomi Cunningham and Michael Reed's *Employment Tribunal Claims: Tactics and Precedents* (2009). A more legalistic approach to the subject is provided by *Tolley's Employment Handbook*, which is updated frequently (the latest edition at the time of writing is the 2011 one), and by the employment lawyer's 'bible', *Harvey on Industrial Relations and Employment Law* (loose-leaf), which sets out the full rules of procedure and the relevant case law.

 **Activity 30.1**

Consider the following statements. Which do you think are correct and which are false?

- Claimants and respondents are obliged to state their cases on prescribed forms provided by the Employment Tribunals Service.

- Tribunals will extend the three-month time limit that applies in unfair dismissal cases when they consider it to be just and equitable to do so.

- A majority of claims made to tribunals are either withdrawn or settled ahead of a full hearing.

- In more complex cases tribunals hold case management discussions before a full hearing in order to determine preliminary legal points that the parties dispute.

- Claimants have the right to request that respondents send to them copies of any documents that are of direct relevance to the case.

- Before deciding whether or not to bring a case, would-be claimants can serve a detailed questionnaire on their employers to which honest and full answers must be given.

- At the main hearing the claimant always presents his or her case first.

- If the tribunal finds that following the correct procedure in the case would have made no difference to the outcome, the dismissal will still usually be deemed unfair, and the claimant will be entitled to full compensation.

- Leading cases have set clear precedents which help tribunals determine the amount of compensation they will award.

Return to this activity once you have read the chapter, to see how many of your answers were correct.

History and background

The employment tribunal system exists as part of the legal system, together with the County Court and the High Court. Appeals are to the Employment Appeal Tribunal, and then to the Court of Appeal and the Supreme Court. The work of the court system is described in Chapter 2. Employment tribunals, which were known as 'industrial tribunals' until the mid 1990s, were created by the Industrial Training Act in 1964. They were originally intended to hear appeals relating to industrial training levies, but their jurisdiction has gradually been extended, with the first claims of unfair dismissal being heard in 1971. They now hear a wide variety of matters relating to employment statutes. These include unfair dismissal, redundancy, discrimination in employment (non-employment-related discrimination claims are heard in the County Court), equal pay and unpaid wages, and many others. A list of these can be found on the Courts and Tribunals Service website (www.justice.gov.uk). This chapter and the next will concentrate on procedure in employment tribunals rather than in the High Court and the County Court, but many of the principles are the same, even if the procedure is slightly different.

The Donovan Commission, which reported in 1968, stated that labour tribunals should ideally be 'easily accessible, speedy, informal and inexpensive' (Donovan Commission, 1968: 578). They are certainly much less formal than courts, with parties sitting around tables instead of being in a traditional courtroom with a dais for the judge, and legal representatives do not wear wigs and gowns. That informality does, however, tend to vary a lot in practice, depending on the nature of the claim, whether the parties are legally represented, and the legal and factual complexity of the case before the tribunal.

The Employment Tribunals (Constitution and Rules of Procedure) Regulations 2004 ('the Tribunal Rules'), which were slightly amended in 2005 and 2008, set out the procedure to be used by employment tribunals. The Tribunal Rules state that the overriding objective of the tribunal is for the tribunal members and the chairman to deal with cases 'justly'. This means that, as far as practicable, they should:

- ensure that the parties are on an equal footing
- deal with the case in ways that are proportionate to the complexity or importance of the issues
- ensure that it is dealt with expeditiously and fairly
- save expense.

These objectives can be seen in action even from the initial stages of a claim. Apart from the claim and response forms (which are set out in a prescribed format), most things can be dealt with by letter, until the final hearing (although there are occasions when there will be a need for the tribunal to have a shorter interim hearing beforehand, as will be seen below).

In 2007, however, a review by Michael Gibbons into the now-discredited compulsory grievance procedure found that tribunals were still not as simple or cheap to use as they could be. He urged the government to make them simpler to use, and to redesign the tribunal application process, so that potential claimants can access it through a telephone helpline, and receive advice on alternatives when doing so (Gibbons, 2007).

At the time of writing (autumn 2011) the government is in the process of consulting on proposed changes to the tribunal system, such as introducing fees for making a claim to prevent spurious claims, and also to allow single judges to hear cases and so speed up the tribunal process (BIS, 2011) For updated information on this please see our related website, the link to which is found at the end of each chapter.

The panel

The tribunal panel is made up of three people, all of whom are impartial and have nothing to do with the case they are hearing. The employment judge (formerly known as the 'chairman' until 2007), who sits in the middle of the panel, is a solicitor or barrister of at least seven years' standing. The two 'wing members', as they are known, come from opposite ends of the employment spectrum: one is an employer representative, the other an employee representative. They are there to balance the panel, and to bring an element of industrial relations knowledge that the lawyer judge may not have. At times, it may be unavoidable that there is only the judge and one member of the tribunal panel available, in which case the judge will have a casting vote.

Time limits

The time limit for most types of case is three months from the date of the act complained of (or six months for equal pay and redundancy pay claims). Therefore, if someone is dismissed, the time limit will be three months from the date that his or her contract of employment was terminated. The date of the act complained of counts as the first day of the three months, so, for example, if a person is dismissed on 2 May, his claim form has to be received by the tribunal office by 1 August. If there is a series of acts to be complained of, such as in a case of discrimination, this can be complicated. The usual rule is that the time limit applies from the earliest act complained of, but in some cases it can be argued that the series of acts was in fact a continuing course of conduct (eg, a campaign of racial harassment or sex discrimination).

If it appears that the claimant will not be able to submit on time, or if he has not been able to do so for a very good reason, such as the fact that he was in hospital at the time, then an application can be made to the tribunal to exercise its discretion to extend the time limit. If the claim is for unfair dismissal, the test that the tribunal will apply when considering whether to extend the time limit is whether it was not reasonably practicable for him to present his proposed claim on time. If the claimant is claiming discrimination, then the tribunal will ask itself whether it is 'just and equitable' to extend the time limit. The time limit for bringing an appeal from a decision of the employment tribunal to the Employment Appeal Tribunal is forty-two days from the date of the judgment, or the date that the written reasons were sent to the putative appellant.

Claim and response forms

In order to start a claim in the employment tribunal a claimant has to fill in a claim form known as an 'ET1'. This is a prescribed form and can be found on the Courts and Tribunals Service 'Justice' website). Claimants have to fill in the relevant details about their employment and also state the legal grounds on which they are making a claim to the employment tribunal. It is important that a claimant states all the relevant grounds on the form where more than one is being claimed (eg, unfair dismissal and discrimination), as the tribunal may decide not to allow subsequent amendments to the claim at a later date.

Once accepted, the claim is sent by the Employment Tribunals Service to the respondent, who then has twenty-eight days to respond, assuming he or she wishes to resist the claim. This too must be done using the prescribed form (which is also available on the Justice website). It is known as the 'ET3', and in it the respondent is required to summarise the full grounds on which he or she intends to resist, as the tribunal may not allow an amendment later.

Default judgments

If a response is not received within the time limit or fails to supply the necessary information, it will not be accepted, and the judge may issue a default judgment without a hearing. A respondent can apply to the tribunal to review this within fourteen days of the date the judgment was sent in the post.

Negotiation and settlement

Taking a case to court or tribunal, or contesting one, is not only stressful for all involved, but also means taking a risk. The outcome is never certain, however strong a claimant or respondent believes their case to be. Even if the law is apparently on one party's side, there are many factors which may make the case go the other way. For example, witnesses may not 'come up to proof' in that they may not say what one expects them to say and so the evidence that is presented is different from what the party expected in the earlier stages of the case. Alternatively, the tribunal panel may not believe a witness, and there are many other unknown factors that add to the uncertainty of outcome. In addition to this, much tension is created between people who in some cases may have to continue working with each other in the future, whatever the outcome.

It is therefore wise for all parties at least to consider settling a claim. Not only will this save on the legal costs of preparing and presenting a hearing for those parties who are represented, but the parties will have more control over the outcome and any sums paid. The agreement can cover not only whether any money is paid, but also whether there is reinstatement and anything else agreed upon by the parties, such as the provision and wording of a reference.

ACAS and COT3

One of the main ways that a case is settled once a claim is made is through ACAS (the Advisory, Conciliation and Arbitration Service). Conciliation is one of the main purposes of ACAS, and a statutory scheme for the organisation to help employers and employees settle their differences at an earlier stage of the proceedings was set up by the Employment Protection Act 1975. A party does not have to submit to the conciliation process if it does not wish to do so. A great many cases, however, are successfully settled by ACAS or with the support of ACAS conciliators. In its 2010–2011 annual report, ACAS states that it conciliated in over 74,000 employment tribunal claims (ACAS, 2011). Many claims are helped to settle by ACAS, and thus reduce tribunal times and cost.

ACAS procedures, which are set out in the Tribunal Rules, used to start only when a claim form was received by the tribunal office. Since 2009, however, ACAS have had the power to conciliate in cases *before* a tribunal claim has been brought. The annual report shows that this is a service which is increasing markedly in uptake (ACAS, 2011).

For conciliation after a claim has been brought, the tribunal office will send copies of the documents in the case to ACAS.

Once the matter has been referred to ACAS, the tribunal should not hold a final hearing until the relevant time limit has run out. The ACAS officer will be impartial and will attempt to help the parties to reach a settlement. If the ACAS officer does manage to resolve the parties' differences and agree on an amount of compensation to be paid, this will be set out in a binding agreement called a 'COT3'. Once such an agreement has been signed it will generally bring the tribunal proceedings to an end.

Compromise agreements

Compromise agreements allow for parties to contract out of the tribunal process and agree not to go to tribunal or court at all for the dispute. They can only do this under the special compromise agreement provisions set out in the Employment Rights Act 1996, which provide certain safeguards for the potential claimant. These include requirements such as having an independent advisor, for example a solicitor, union official or someone who works for an advice centre. The name of the advisor must be in the agreement, which must be in writing.

If either party does not keep to his or her side of the agreement, the other person will not be able to take the original claim to a tribunal, as the agreement not to do so will be binding. In such circumstances, however, it is possible to go to the County Court to claim breach of contract (ie, breach of the compromise agreement). If the agreement is done with the help of ACAS then it will be a COT3 rather than a compromise agreement.

 Activity 30.2

Andrew is employed as a cleaner for a contract cleaning company. He believes that he is being passed over for promotion because he is a man and wishes to complain about his employer's sex discrimination. He has stayed in his job, but has made a complaint to the tribunal.

Both he and his employer agreed to have ACAS's help in reaching a settlement. They came to an agreement, which was drawn up in a COT3, and the employer paid Andrew an agreed sum by way of compensation.

A few weeks later, Andrew was reading in the newspaper about a discrimination case where the claimant was awarded a much larger amount of money than he had settled for. He wishes to change his mind about the agreement, and to go back to court.

Questions

1 Is he able to do so?

2 Would your answer be any different if the agreement reached had been a compromise agreement?

Other settlements

The above methods are not the only ways of settling a case. It is very common for cases to be settled between the parties, generally with the help of legal advisors, right up until the case is heard, and even, on occasions, during a break at the time of the hearing. If the settlement occurs on the day of the hearing (often referred to as an agreement made at the 'door of the court'), then the tribunal will still make an order, which will have the same effect as if the tribunal had reached a decision itself, although obviously the terms of the order will be the ones that the parties agreed to themselves rather than terms imposed on them by the tribunal.

Case management

In the late 1990s, the civil courts faced a change in the way that cases were conducted, following what became known as the 'Woolf Reforms' (named after Lord Woolf, the author of the report on the matter). There was more emphasis placed on efficiency and more input from judges in managing cases, particularly complicated ones, so that the civil court system functioned more smoothly. This ethos has filtered down to the employment tribunal system, so judges now have powers to give directions to parties, such as setting out timescales for cases. They can also make orders in relation to disclosure of documents and information to the other side, witness statements and preparation of the claimant's schedule of loss. Another order that the judge makes is to allocate a case to the 'fast track' if it is a short, uncomplicated one, or the 'standard' procedure if it is more complex. These are known as 'case management orders', and their purpose is to make sure that the preparation for the hearing progresses smoothly and that as much information as possible is exchanged. One benefit of this may well be that once the parties are in receipt of all the information in the case, they will be more likely to settle.

In the great majority of cases, the directions are given by the judge by letter from the tribunal without a hearing being held. This fits in with the tribunal's overriding objective of dealing with cases expeditiously and saving expense. There will be occasions, however, where it makes more sense to have the parties present so that any directions can be discussed before directions are given and the judge will therefore hold a 'case management discussion (CMD)' (formerly known as a 'directions hearing'), which is often held by telephone. Judges themselves can make the decision to hold a CMD, or one of the parties can request that one is held. This may happen, for example, if a party feels that the other side is not co-operating in disclosing documents, or in complex cases where exchange of further information at an early stage is necessary to allow each side to be fully aware of the details of their opponent's case.

Case management discussions are heard by a judge sitting alone. Orders are frequently made at the end of such discussions, dates for exchange of statements being agreed and often dates for a full hearing settled. Increasingly, CMDs take the form of telephone conferences, the judge speaking simultaneously to the representatives of both parties in the case. This saves time and expense as the need to appear before the judge in person is avoided.

In summary, case management discussions are held to:

- clarify the issues in the case;
- decide what orders should be made about issues such as documents and witnesses; and
- decide the time and length of the main hearing.

They will normally be held in private, before a judge sitting alone, or over the phone.

Pre-hearing reviews

The case management discussion is precisely that, a discussion where the management of the case and its preparation takes place. Sometimes, however, there are preliminary legal issues which need to be discussed before the main hearing takes place and so a pre-hearing review is held. Examples of such issues may be whether the claim was submitted within the relevant time limits, whether an amendment should be allowed, whether there should be a striking out of the claim or response forms, or whether an order for disclosure has not been obeyed by one side or the other. Explanations of these terms are provided below. There could also be more substantial preliminary matters heard at this hearing, such as whether the claimant was in fact an employee or a worker and hence whether the claim can proceed at all.

In summary, pre-hearing reviews are held to:

- decide whether the claim or response should be struck out;
- decide questions of entitlement to bring or defend a claim;
- decide, if either side's case appears weak, whether a deposit needs to be paid.

Striking out

A tribunal has the power to 'strike out' a claim or response. This is a rarely used power and means that the case or response is in effect 'thrown out', for reasons such as the tribunal finds that the claim is misconceived, or that the claimant is vexatious in bringing the action.

Amending forms

The parties have to set out their cases clearly and fully in the ET1 and ET3, albeit in summary. A claimant, for example, has to state the legal basis of his or her claim—is it for unfair dismissal, race discrimination or both? If it is both, then this must be made clear on the form. However, sometimes matters come to light later, perhaps as a result of legal advice that was not available when the form was filled in, when further information becomes available or when a relevant event (such as a dismissal) occurs after the original claim has been submitted.

In such cases claimants may want to add something to the ET1 or to amend it in some other way. The same is true of respondents and the ET3. If so, the tribunal's permission has to be sought to make the amendment. If it is a simple amendment, such as changing the spelling of the respondent company's name, it can be done during the case management process. A more substantial amendment, however, such as adding a new ground to the claim or response forms, would be heard at a pre-hearing review, as the parties will probably want to argue the matter in front of the judge before a decision is made. It is entirely at the judge's discretion (or that of the full tribunal panel, if the hearing is before them) whether to allow the amendment or not. Occasionally, the need for an amendment will crop up at a late stage of the proceedings, such as at the final hearing. In general, the later the request for an amendment is made, the less likely it is to be granted, but it is still within the discretion of the tribunal, who will weigh the arguments for both sides and try to deal with the issue fairly.

Disclosure of documents and information

Before a case can be heard, both parties need to see any documents in the possession of the other side that are relevant to the case. Most documents tend to be in the possession of the employer, such as personnel files, minutes of meetings, e-mails, etc, but the claimant may also have documents that would be disclosable. The disclosure of these documents can either be done voluntarily or, if a party does not do this, the other party can request documents by letter. If the other side does not respond appropriately, then the party that has made the request can apply to the tribunal for an order for disclosure. Disclosure can only be required in relation to existing documents. It is not used to require that the other side creates a new document, such as compiling statistics.

In addition, a request for additional information can be made by each side. This used to be known as a request for 'further particulars', and that is exactly what it is—a request for further information about something in the claim or response forms which requires clarification or elucidation. For example, if the respondent states in his response form that there was a meeting held to discuss a claimant's maternity leave, which she disputes, she could request details about the meeting, such as the date on which the respondent says it was held and who was present. A party can also ask that the other side provide a written answer to a particular question, even if it is not clarifying something specifically in the claim or response form.

There is a fine line in judging whether such requests should be made, or whether it is something that should be saved for cross-examination. Cunningham and Reed (2009) summarise the position as follows:

> As a rule of thumb, if the question is designed to elicit hard information that cannot easily be fudged or falsified [such as how many women of a certain grade are employed by the respondent], it is best to make it the subject of a request for additional information or written answers. If the aim is to embarrass a witness or give him the opportunity to say something foolish, it is best to save for cross-examination [such as asking a dismissing manager what factors he took into account before deciding to dismiss—in this case, do not give him the chance to prepare the answer].

Discrimination questionnaires

Discrimination cases are often difficult to prove and so questionnaires can be invaluable in providing information that will help a claimant bring a case. Questionnaires are available in discrimination cases only, and are an opportunity for the claimant to ask the respondent questions, for example about equal opportunities policy and profiles/statistics of the workforce, such as what proportion of employees are women and at what level they are employed. The respondent does not have to answer them, and the tribunal has no power to order any employer to do so, but where the questions are not answered fully and properly, the tribunal can draw an inference against the respondent when deciding the case. This can be of great assistance to a claimant.

Questionnaires are also important because they can be sent before legal proceedings begin, so the potential claimant in a discrimination case can use one to decide if it is worth bringing a claim, particularly in a case where an applicant for a job has been refused a place and feels that discrimination took place, but has no information to prove this. A questionnaire has to be sent within twenty-one days of the ET1 being presented to the tribunal office. The respondent then has eight weeks in which to give answers.

In general with disclosure, 'fishing expeditions' are not allowed. In other words, claimants cannot use the disclosure process to trawl for evidence that they are unaware of. Discrimination questionnaires are an exception to this. Examples of questionnaires can be found on the website of the Equality and Human Rights Commission www. equalityhumanrights.com.

The main hearing

A party does not have to attend the hearing. It is possible simply to submit written representations. Before this decision is made, however, it is advisable to be very sure that these representations are sufficient, particularly in a case where there is a dispute as to the facts. If the tribunal does not have a witness giving live evidence, it cannot make a proper judgment as to whether it accepts his or her evidence, and is highly likely in consequence to ascribe greater credibility to the opposite side's witnesses. As a result, any witness whose evidence is likely to be central to the outcome of a case is well advised to appear in person before the tribunal.

Once in the tribunal building, the parties will be asked to wait until they are led into the room where the hearing is to be held. There are usually two waiting rooms: one for claimants and one for respondents. Each party can then feel free to discuss the case with his or her legal representative, if he or she has one. This waiting period is often used to undertake last-minute negotiations. Once in the main hearing room, the claimant and any legal advisor will sit at the table on the right-hand side of the room, and the respondent on the left. The judge (who should be referred to as 'Sir' or 'Madam') has great discretion as to how the case will be conducted. He or she often starts by clarifying what the issues in the case are and by confirming what legal points will be raised during the proceedings.

In some tribunals, representatives or the parties themselves (when not represented) are permitted to make opening statements setting out the broad contours of their case. But this stage is now more often dispensed with and the judge asks that the evidence is presented straight away. Where the claimant's side goes first, proceedings thus start with the claimant taking the oath and reading out their witness statement. After this, the claimant's representative has an opportunity to ask questions. This is known as 'examination in chief'. This stage is followed by the cross-examination stage, in which the respondent's representative asks questions. Finally, if they have not already done so, the tribunal members ask the claimant questions.

After this, any other witnesses who are present to support the claimant take the stand and read their statements. They too are then questioned by the claimant's representative, the respondent's representative and the tribunal. Once the claimant's case has been presented, the reverse process occurs. The respondent's witnesses take the stand one after another and submit to examination in chief, cross-examination and questions from the tribunal.

Finally, once both sides have presented all their evidence, closing submissions are made. The rule here is usually that the party who started first 'has the last word', and makes their submissions second. These submissions should refer both to the evidence that has been given and how it fits into the legal framework. If there is any legal argument this is the point at which it is made, unless there were any preliminary points of law that were heard before the first witness took the stand.

 Exhibit 30.1   Who starts?

The rule as to who starts in a case depends on who has the burden of proving it. In general, in an unfair dismissal case where dismissal is admitted, it is the respondent who starts, as he will have the burden of satisfying the tribunal that there was a potentially fair reason for dismissal. This tends to be the most common type of case. In a discrimination claim, a breach of contract, or an unpaid wages case, it is the claimant who starts. The claimant also starts if there is a dispute about employment status or when a dismissal is not admitted.

The claimant goes first:

- if there is a dispute as to whether he or she was an employee or had sufficient length of service
- in unfair dismissal cases if there is a dispute as to whether he or she was dismissed
- in discrimination cases
- in breach of contract cases
- in unpaid wages claims.

The respondent goes first:

- in unfair dismissal cases where it is agreed that there was a dismissal, and the issue is whether or not it was fair.

If there is more than one cause of action, then it is best to ask the judge which party should start, as it is at the judge's discretion. It will usually be the respondent to start, but if, for example, the case is a joint discrimination and unfair dismissal case, it is more likely that the claimant will go first.

If there is time, the tribunal will then retire to decide the case. In most cases, there will have been a conflict of fact, and the tribunal has to decide which witnesses it believes. The panel then applies its understanding of the law to a conclusion as to whether the case has been proved within the legal framework or not. If there is not enough time, because it is late in the day or because there are other cases waiting to be heard that day the tribunal 'reserves' its decision, setting it out in writing together with its reasons and sending it by post. This is usually done within twenty-eight days. Often a tribunal will state which side has won and move on (if the claimant has won all or part of his case) to discuss remedies. However, the tribunal will give detailed reasons later in a written judgment.

Remedies

When claimants bring a case they are seeking something, whether it be compensation, a declaration of rights, reinstatement in the original job or re-engagement by the employer albeit in another role. These are the remedies that a tribunal has the power to award.

If the tribunal finds in favour of the claimant, it will need to decide what remedy to give. If judgment has been given on the day of the hearing, the tribunal may well continue to have the remedy hearing there and then, but if there has been a reserved judgment, or if there is not enough time, then a separate remedies hearing has to be held at a later date. This is where the schedule of loss and any mitigating factors become important. We will look at these in more detail in Chapter 31.

Reinstatement

A reinstatement order allows the employee to return to his or her previous job, as if there had not been a break in his or her employment. Pay, conditions and length of service will be the same.

Re-engagement

An order for re-engagement instructs the former employer to take back the claimant.

A tribunal will not order reinstatement or re-engagement unless the successful claimant has stated a preference for this outcome. Otherwise, as is the case in the vast majority of cases, the tribunal will go on to consider how much should be given by way of compensation.

In making either a reinstatement or a re-engagement order, the tribunal should consider:

- whether the claimant wishes to be reinstated or re-engaged
- whether it is practicable for the employer to comply with such an order (it is not just a question of whether or not it is physically practicable, but also whether the relationship between the parties has irretrievably broken down and that reinstatement would not therefore be an appropriate remedy)
- whether, if the claimant has caused or contributed to the dismissal, it would be just to make such an order.

Compensation

In an unfair dismissal case, the compensation consists of two parts: the basic award and the compensatory award. The process of calculating such an award is set out by the Employment Rights Act 1996. The claimant should set out how much he or she is seeking in a schedule of loss, which is prepared in advance of the hearing. The tribunal will usually order a schedule to be prepared as part of the case management process. The next chapter will look in more detail at how to prepare the schedule of loss.

The award in discrimination cases is less easy to quantify than that in an unfair dismissal case, as there is no set procedure and no maximum amount that can be awarded. The tribunal will use as a guide the awards made in previous cases, the usual headings being as follows:

- financial losses sustained owing to the act of unlawful discrimination
- an award for injury to feelings
- compensation for any psychiatric damage
- aggravated damages.

Vento v Chief Constable of West Yorkshire (2003)

In this important case (which was updated by the EAT in *Da'Bell v NSPCC* (2009)), the Court of Appeal set out some clear guidelines to determine awards in discrimination cases.

(a) Awards for injury to feelings are compensatory. They should be just to both parties. They should compensate fully without punishing the wrongdoer. Feelings of indignation at the wrongdoer's conduct should not be allowed to inflate the award.

(b) Awards should not be too low, as that would diminish respect for the policy of the anti-discrimination legislation. Society has condemned discrimination and awards must ensure that it is seen to be wrong. On the other hand, awards should be restrained, as excessive awards could be seen as the way to 'untaxed riches'.

(c) Awards should bear some broad general similarity to the range of awards in personal injury cases.

(d) In exercising their discretion in assessing a sum, tribunals should remind themselves of the value in everyday life of the sum they have in mind. This may be done by reference to purchasing power or by reference to earnings.

(e) Tribunals should bear in mind the need for public respect for the level of awards made.

The court then went on to set out guidance for tribunals in assessing how much compensation to award for injury to feelings in a discrimination case:

Employment Tribunals and those who practise in them might find it helpful if this Court were to identify three broad bands of compensation for injury to feelings, as distinct from compensation for psychiatric or similar personal injury.

(i) The top band should normally be between £18,000 and £30,000. Sums in this range should be awarded in the most serious cases, such as where there has been a lengthy campaign of discriminatory harassment on the ground of sex or race. Only in the most exceptional case should an award of compensation for injury to feelings exceed £30,000.

(ii) The middle band of between £6,000 and £18,000 should be used for serious cases, which do not merit an award in the highest band.

(iii) Awards of between £500 and £6,000 are appropriate for less serious cases, such as where the act of discrimination is an isolated or one-off occurrence. In general, awards of less than £500 are to be avoided altogether, as they risk being regarded as so low as not to be a proper recognition of injury to feelings.

There is, of course, within each band considerable flexibility, allowing tribunals to fix what is considered to be fair, reasonable and just compensation in the particular circumstances of the case.

A decision about whether or not to award aggravated damages and, if so, to what level must depend on the particular circumstances of the discrimination and on the way in which the complaint of discrimination has been handled. Common sense requires that regard should also be had to the overall magnitude of the sum total of the awards of compensation for non-pecuniary loss made under the various headings of injury to feelings, psychiatric damage and aggravated damage. In particular, double recovery should be avoided by taking appropriate account of the overlap between the individual heads of damage. The extent of overlap will depend on the facts of each particular case.

Costs

In most employment tribunal cases, each side will pay its own costs. However, in certain circumstances, the tribunal may order one side to pay costs to the other. Those circumstances can include if one side has behaved unreasonably in the way it has carried out the case or if a tribunal thinks that a claim was so weak that it should not have been brought.

CHAPTER SUMMARY

- Employment tribunals are less formal than other courts.
- The tribunal is made up of a judge and two lay members.
- A case has to be brought on a standard ET1 form, and a response on a standard ET3 form.
- Full details have to be given, and permission is rarely given to amend.
- There are various preliminary hearings that can be held to sort out issues such as disclosure.
- There is an emphasis on settlement if possible.

REFERENCES

ACAS (2009) *Code of Practice. Grievance and Disciplinary Procedures.* April 2009. London: Advisory, Conciliation and Arbitration Service.

ACAS (2011) *Annual Report and Accounts.* London: Advisory, Conciliation and Arbitration Service. Available at www.acas.org.uk.

BIS (2011) 'Resolving Workplace Disputes: A Consultation'.

Cunningham, N. (2005) *Employment Tribunal Claims: Tactics and Precedents.* London: Legal Action Group.

Cunningham, N. and Reed, M. (2009) *Employment Tribunal Claims: Tactics and Precedents.* London: Legal Action Group.

Gibbons, M. (2007) *Better Dispute Resolution: A review of employment dispute resolution in Great Britain.* London: Department of Trade and Industry.

Harvey on Industrial Relations and Employment Law. London: Butterworths (1972–present) (loose-leaf).

Hepple, B. & Morris, G. (2002) 'The Employment Act 2002 and the crisis of individual employment rights' *Industrial Law Journal* 31 (p 245).

Manley, I. & Heslop, E. (2008) *Employment Tribunals: A Practical Guide.* London: The Law Society.

Royal Commission on Trade Unions and Employer Associations 1965–1968 (1968) *(Donovan Commission) Report*, London: HMSO, Cmnd 3623.

Slade, E. (2011) *Tolley's Employment Handbook 2007*. London: Tolley Publishing.

WEBSITES

Courts and Tribunals Service www.justice.gov.uk

ACAS www.acas.org.uk

Businesslink www.businesslink.gov.uk/

ONLINE RESOURCE CENTRE

A range of online resources to help you through your employment law module have been developed by the author team. These include updates, self-test questions and sources for further reading. (www.oxfordtextbooks.co.uk/orc/taylor_emir3e)

Preparing and presenting a case

Learning outcomes

By the end of this chapter you should be able to:

- outline the procedure of an employment tribunal hearing;
- organise a case in readiness for a hearing;
- prepare claim and response forms;
- draft a witness statement;
- understand how to negotiate a settlement;
- prepare a schedule of loss;
- understand the different types of questioning technique for examination in chief and cross-examination; and
- prepare and present a hearing in the employment tribunal.

Introduction

In this final chapter we aim to provide practical guidance to help you prepare and present a case before an employment tribunal. Although primarily written from the point of view of the advocate at such a hearing, the material is also relevant to advisors, witnesses and the parties to a case. If witnesses are familiar with the procedure for a hearing, and know what to expect, they are much more likely to be relaxed and give evidence effectively. So throughout this chapter, where the word 'advocate' is used, it can also apply to people representing themselves or their employer at tribunal hearings.

We will use one set of facts to illustrate the various stages of taking a case to tribunal. Let us assume that this case is called *'Grumble v Robinson Coaches'*.

 Exhibit 31.1   *Grumble v Robinson Coaches*—The Facts

Mr Grumble, a fifty-nine year-old minibus driver, was employed by Robinson Coaches for some five years. His duties were to drive a school minibus in the morning and afternoon, and he could do what he liked for the rest of the day. When he was not driving his employer allowed him to take the vehicle home and to use it as if it were his own.

He was a well-liked employee and there had never been any problem with him, although it had been noticed that he had seemed a little short-tempered since he came back from a recent holiday. He had been overheard to say that he could not wait to retire.

In March, two weeks after he came back from holiday, there was a brake problem with the vehicle that he normally drove. A replacement was brought out to the job for him, and the vehicles exchanged. The next day the second vehicle broke down and the manager of Robinson Coaches, Mr Flair, drove a third vehicle out to Mr Grumble.

The following day this third vehicle developed a fault with the starter motor. The only way to drive it was to keep it running and not to switch it off. When Mr Grumble complained, Mr Flair told him that there was no choice but to keep it running and to do his best as there were no spare vehicles left and there was no time to hire one. Mr Grumble believed that using the vehicle in this condition was illegal.

When he came back at lunchtime, he was told to leave the vehicle in the yard, and that someone else could do his journey for him in the afternoon. This meant that he would not be able to take the vehicle home overnight. Mr Grumble got annoyed and started swearing. He demanded that the bus be repaired that afternoon so that he could drive it home. Mr Flair refused, saying that it could not be done. An argument ensued in the course of which Mr Flair told Mr Grumble to 'Get lost!'.

Mr Grumble picked up his bag to leave and said 'You told me to get lost, so I am getting lost'. He went to Mr Robinson's office and asked for his P45. Mr Robinson was very surprised, but was busy and asked no questions. He said he would post it to him, which he did the following day.

Mr Grumble has brought actions for unfair dismissal and constructive dismissal.

Fact management

Good management of facts leads to a case which is well prepared and is therefore much more likely to be well presented. Effective preparation before a case begins can make the difference between a case where all the facts are put before the tribunal in a clear manner, with all the relevant points being made, and a case that is chaotic and in which important points are missed.

When taking on a case, it is important to go through all the paperwork and organise the facts. This can be done, for example, by:

- Deciding what has to be shown by each side. You need to know not only what your own side has to show, but also what the other side are hoping to prove, so that you can be prepared to answer the points that they might make.

- Making a list of the witnesses for each side. You will need to note what points each witness will show and the order in which you think you want to call your witnesses (you can always change your mind about the order up to the last minute).

- Noting the arguments for and against each point and any discrepancies in the evidence.

When preparing the case, it is essential to think about the strengths and weaknesses of the points that both sides will be making. This involves putting oneself in the position of the opposite side so that points they are likely to make can be anticipated and dealt with. It is important to avoid being taken by surprise at the hearing.

The whole case should be prepared before the hearing starts, from the opening, through all the topics for questions, and down to the final speech. This does not mean, however, that everything should be written out verbatim. That is a bad idea because it can take the spontaneity out of the advocacy. If everything is read out, particularly if this is done in a monotone fashion, tribunals are likely to find evidence unconvincing. It may also prevent the advocate from thinking on the spot, especially if a new point arises during the hearing. It is best, therefore, to have 'bullet points' for each point to be made, rather than write out all the questions, or the whole closing speech.

 Activity 31.1

Read the facts of *Grumble v Robinson Coaches*. Before you read the rest of the chapter, consider how you would go about the fact management of the case.

Questions

1   What will each side have to show?

2   What is the relevant law in the area?

3   Who will be the witnesses on each side?

4   What will each witness say?

When you have read to the end of the chapter, return to your answers to see how you did.

Understanding the law

It is beyond the scope of this chapter to go into the details of the law applicable in the *Grumble v Robinson Coaches* case. We discussed unfair dismissal law and constructive dismissals in Part II. But it is vital when presenting a case that you thoroughly research the relevant statutes and the leading cases in preparing for a hearing.

Grumble v Robinson Coaches is an unfair/constructive dismissal case. In this case, as dismissal is not admitted, the burden of proof is on the applicant to show that he was dismissed. If this is established, the burden is then on the respondent to show that the dismissal was not unfair. The first step in the fact management would be what each side wants the tribunal to accept. In this case, one way of doing this would be as follows:

The claimant wants to show:

- that the words used by Mr Flair would be understood by a reasonable bystander to constitute a dismissal,
- alternatively, that he was constructively dismissed by having to drive defective vehicles and/or by being sworn at by his manager,
- that the dismissal was substantively and procedurally unfair.

The respondent wants to show:

- that the words used did not amount to a dismissal,
- that Mr Grumble in fact resigned,
- that there was no constructive dismissal as it did everything it could to get the vehicles fixed, and no implied or express term was breached,
- if it is found that he was dismissed, that the dismissal was a fair one, given the behaviour of Mr Grumble towards Mr Flair.

Starting the process—claim and response forms

Before bringing a claim, certain matters have to be checked. The most important of these are:

- Is the claimant an employee? (If he is not an employee, then the employment tribunal will not have jurisdiction in this type of case.)
- If so, is there a written contract of employment, and have you seen it? (If there is a written contract, you need to see it to make sure you know the details of the employment agreement between the parties and can prove the relevant dates.)
- Is the claimant still within time to bring a claim? (If he is out of time, he will not be able to bring a claim unless a successful application to extend the time limit is made to the tribunal.)

These points should be checked by both the claimant, to see if he can bring a claim, and also the respondent so that he can confirm that the claimant has the right to bring a claim.

Activity 31.2

Let us assume that Mr Grumble clearly was an employee and that there was no written contract of employment, as the agreement had been made orally.

If Mr Grumble's last day at work was 9 March, what is the final date on which his claim form should arrive at the tribunal office?

Claim and response forms can be found at the Employment Tribunals section on the Justice website (www.justice.gov.uk). Claims can either be submitted online or by post. There are personal details to be filled in, and the relevant dates, and then the claimant should set out the details of the claim. The legal basis and main facts should be summarised on the claim form, but this is not a witness statement which has to include all relevant matters. The details set out in the claim should therefore be brief and to the point. The claim should say exactly what is being claimed. If, therefore, a case is for both indirect and direct sex discrimination, or direct race discrimination plus unfair dismissal, it should clearly say so on the form.

Exhibit 31.2

Details of claim

The claim must be on the form obtained from the employment tribunal (or on additional sheets attached to it). For an unfair/constructive dismissal case, the section where the case must be detailed is section 5.2, where Mr Grumble (or his advisor) can write something along the lines of:

1   The claimant was a driver employed by the respondent company, Robinson Coaches. He has driven a school minibus morning and afternoon since July 2001.

2   On 7 March 2006, there was a brake problem with the vehicle that he normally drove. A replacement was brought out to the job for him and the vehicles exchanged.

3   The next day, the second vehicle also broke down and a further vehicle was provided.

4   On 9 March 2006, the third vehicle developed a fault with the starter motor. The only way to drive it was to keep it running and not to switch it off. When the claimant complained, he was told by Mr Flair to keep it running and to do his best, as there were no spare vehicles left and there was no time to hire one.

5   The claimant believed that using the vehicle in this condition was illegal. When he brought this to the attention of Mr Flair, and asked that the vehicle be repaired urgently, Mr Flair swore at him, pointed to the gate and told him to leave. This amounted to an unfair dismissal.

6   Further, or alternatively, by expecting the claimant to drive an unroadworthy and illegal vehicle, the respondent put the claimant in an impossible situation. The dismissal therefore amounted to a constructive dismissal.

7   The claimant therefore claims unfair dismissal and, alternatively, unfair constructive dismissal.

The respondent, if he wishes to contest the case, must respond to each allegation in the claim form. So, if the claim is for both direct disability discrimination and unfair dismissal, and the respondent denies both, then he should specifically say that it is neither. If the facts are disputed, the respondent should set out in brief what he says the facts are. It is useful to use the same format as is used on the claim form and respond to each allegation in turn.

 Activity 31.3

Mr Robinson has given you instructions that Mr Flair accepts that he said 'Get lost', but that they were words said in the heat of the moment and were certainly not intended to be a dismissal of Mr Grumble. He also says that the defects in the vehicles were not illegal.

Draft the details of the response form for Robinson Coaches.

Schedule of loss

In unfair dismissal and constructive dismissal claims the tribunal has the power to award re-instatement, re-engagement or to make an award of compensation. In this case, Mr Grumble is only seeking compensation. He does not wish to go back to work for Robinson Coaches. When claimants seek monetary awards they should draw up a schedule of loss setting out exactly what award they are seeking. This is then sent to the respondent some weeks or months ahead of the hearing. If the matter subsequently proceeds to a full tribunal hearing, the schedule of loss is updated and presented again at the hearing.

The schedule of loss not only serves to show the tribunal how much is being claimed so that it can use it as the basis of making an award if it finds for the claimant, but also assists the respondent when it comes to deciding whether to settle or not. It helps to indicate if it is worth contesting the case and whether a settlement is likely or possible. Offers made with a view to settling can then be tailored accordingly. In a case of unfair dismissal or constructive dismissal, the schedule of loss is calculated as follows:

Basic award

The basic award is intended to compensate the employee for the loss of job security. The method of calculation is set out in section 119 of the Employment Rights Act 1996. The factors taken into account are the employee's length of service with the employer and his or her weekly pay.

- The pay is gross pay.
- There is a limit to the weekly pay. As at 1 February 2012, this was £430. This is raised periodically. The up-to-date amount can be found on the Businesslink website (www.businesslink.gov.uk).
- The period for which he was employed ends with the effective date of termination. This is defined in section 97.
- A maximum of twenty years' employment can count.
- Only complete years are counted.

The basic award can be reduced for the following reasons:

- If there has been a redundancy payment, or a contractual payment specifically for dismissal.
- Where the employee's conduct before the dismissal means that it would be 'just and equitable' to reduce the basic award.
- Where the employee has unreasonably refused an offer of reinstatement.

Compensatory award

This is to compensate the employee for the loss that he has suffered as a result of the unfair dismissal, and the calculation is set out in section 123 of the Employment Rights Act 1996. There are two parts to the compensatory award:

- loss of earnings between the dismissal and the tribunal hearing
- future loss of earnings.

Actual loss of earnings is calculated by taking the net weekly pay and calculating it from the effective date of termination up until the date of the tribunal hearing.

If the claimant has found a job before the hearing, and the job pays as much as or more than his previous job, the compensatory award would only be calculated up until the date that he started the new job.

 Exhibit 31.3   Calculating Mr Grumble's loss of earnings

If Mr Grumble had not found a job as at the date of the hearing, his loss of earnings would be:

Net pay × number of weeks between the effective date of termination (EDT) and hearing

Let us assume that the hearing takes place twenty weeks after the EDT, and that weekly net pay is £190. Mr Grumble's loss of earnings would be:

190 × 20 = £3,800

If the claimant has not found a job by the date of the hearing, the tribunal has to decide when he is likely to find a job and what the wage is likely to be. In making this decision, the tribunal takes various factors into account, such as the type of job, the local job market, the employee's age and relevant skills.

Let us assume that Mr Grumble has not found a job by the date of the hearing. The market for coach drivers is very good, as they are in short supply and the respondent will be able to come to the hearing with evidence that this is the case. The tribunal will listen to arguments for both sides as to how long it is likely to take the claimant to find a new job, and then make a decision on the balance of probabilities.

If the claimant has found a job by the date of the hearing, but is earning less than in his previous employment, the tribunal will multiply the weekly deficit in wages by a reasonable estimate of how long the shortfall will last. The loss of benefits, such as company car, medical insurance, etc, would be quantified and added to the compensatory award. This does not apply to Mr Grumble. If an employee is unfairly dismissed and finds a new job, he will no longer have the qualifying period to claim for unfair dismissal or redundancy in his new employment. It is usual, therefore, for a tribunal to make an award for 'loss of statutory protection', which is usually about £250. Expenses, for example, travelling to find a new job, can also be added to the compensatory award.

From February 2012, the maximum that can be given by way of a compensatory award is £72,300. However, there is no limit where the employee is dismissed unfairly or selected for redundancy for reasons connected with health and safety matters or whistleblowing.

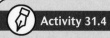 **Activity 31.4**

If you are drafting the schedule of loss for Mr Grumble, how long would you say is reasonable to expect him to find another job, given his age, skills and the local job market?

Using your answer to the above, work out Mr Grumble's future loss.

The compensatory award can be reduced for the following reasons:

- The claimant's contributory fault. Where the tribunal finds that the dismissal was caused or contributed to by the claimant, it can reduce the award by the percentage that it finds was his fault.

- The claimant's failure to mitigate. The employee has a duty to take reasonable steps to find another job. If he does not do so, then this is a failure to mitigate his loss and the tribunal can reduce his award.

- Recoupment. Part of the compensatory award in unfair dismissal cases compensates an employee for the loss of earnings up to the date of the tribunal hearing. However, some employees may have already received Jobseeker's Allowance benefit or income support for the same period. If this has been the case, the tribunal will make a recoupment order, and the Jobcentre Plus local office will take from the employer the relevant amount before it is paid to the claimant, to avoid 'double payment'.

 Exhibit 31.4   **Award limits (from February 2012)**

Limit on a week's pay: £430

Maximum basic award for unfair dismissal (30 weeks' pay): £12,900

Minimum basic award for dismissal on trade union, health and safety, occupational pension scheme trustee, employee representative and on working time grounds only: £5,300

Maximum compensatory award for unfair dismissal (there is no limit where the employee is dismissed unfairly or selected for redundancy for reasons connected with health and safety matters or public interest disclosure ('whistleblowing')): £72,300

Amount of award for unlawful inducement relating to trade union membership, activities or services, or for unlawful inducement relating to collective bargaining: £3,500 »

Minimum amount of compensation where individual excluded or expelled from union in contravention of section 174 of the Trade Union and Labour Relations (Consolidation) Act 1992 and not admitted or re-admitted by date of tribunal application: £8,100

Maximum award in breach of contract cases heard in the employment tribunal: £25,000

Source: The Employment Rights (Increase of Limits) Order 2010 (check Businesslink website for annual updates)

Additional award

If a tribunal orders reinstatement or re-engagement and the employer does not comply, the tribunal can make an additional award on top of the basic and compensatory awards. The additional award will be between twenty-six and fifty-two weeks' pay, subject to the £430 limit on a week's pay.

Negotiating a settlement

When it comes to negotiating a settlement, each party will be hoping to get the best out of it for his or her side. The claimant will want to obtain as much money as possible, while the respondent will want to pay out as little as possible. The art of negotiating a settlement is to arrive at a figure that keeps both parties happy and is somewhere in between the two extremes. It is very common for cases to be settled, and even cases that come to the tribunal for a hearing may still settle just before or even during the hearing. Before negotiating a settlement, it is necessary to be aware of the strengths and weaknesses of the case for each party.

 Activity 31.5

The sticking point in negotiating the settlement for this case is likely to be the period that he will remain unemployed. Mr Grumble says that he has not found a job because of his age, and expects it to take him another six months before he obtains one. Mr Robinson disagrees. He finds it very difficult to find good coach drivers and knows that staff shortages are a problem throughout the industry. He thinks that Mr Grumble has failed to mitigate his loss and that he should have found a job a long time ago. He is prepared, however, to say that Mr Grumble should find a job within the next four weeks.

Questions

1 What are the strengths and weaknesses of the case for Mr Grumble and the case for Robinson Coaches?

2 Calculate the total figure that Mr Grumble is seeking in compensation.

3 What would be a reasonable figure for both parties to settle for?

Witness statements

When preparing a witness statement it is important to remember that the statement is likely to be used as the witness's main evidence. Each witness reads his or her statement out in the tribunal before being questioned about it. The witness statement is therefore an important document and must contain all the relevant facts that the witness is able to give evidence about.

There are two main points to be made about the above sentence. One is the word 'relevant'. The statement should not contain matters that have no bearing on the issues before the tribunal. An example in Mr Grumble's case might be a description of where he had gone on holiday or what he had done the evening before the termination of his employment (unless, of course, they have some relevance to the issues at hand). The other part of the sentence above that should be noted are the words 'that the witness is able to give evidence about'. The witness giving evidence simply means the witness telling the tribunal what he or she knows about a particular matter. This will usually be first-hand knowledge. In civil courts, such as the County Court, witnesses are not generally permitted to give what is known as 'hearsay' evidence (ie, information that someone else has given them). An example of this would be if Mr Jones, a friend of Mr Grumble, came along to the tribunal and wanted to say that Mr Grumble had met him in the pub the evening following the events in question and had told him what Mr Flair is alleged to have said, or had told him that he was sacked. These are not facts that Mr Jones knows about himself. They are 'facts' that he has been told by Mr Grumble. On the other hand, if Mr Jones had overheard what happened between Mr Grumble and Mr Flair, or perhaps seen Mr Flair shouting and pointing to the gate, then that would be 'direct' evidence from Mr Jones of the events.

In employment tribunals, the hearsay rule is more relaxed than in the civil courts, but it is still something to bear in mind. A manager can come to tribunal and give evidence about the outcome of a meeting involving his team even if he was not there. If, however, there is a dispute as to what was actually said at the meeting, his evidence will not be particularly helpful, as he will not be able to say truthfully that he knows exactly what was said. To prove what was said at the meeting, someone who was present needs to come to the tribunal to give evidence, and if they do not, the tribunal may well decide not to put much weight on what the manager is saying. Hearsay can be complicated, but it is not a rule that is strictly observed in an employment tribunal.

Fact not law or opinion

A witness statement is a document that sets out what the witness wants to say about what happened. It is not a document in which to present legal argument. In his witness statement, therefore, Mr Grumble would give his side of what happened. He would not say 'and it was constructive dismissal because . . .' and start quoting cases and statutes. That would be legal argument and is for the advocate to develop at the end of the case. As well as not presenting legal arguments, witnesses should also avoid expressing opinions. They should stick to the facts as they know them. The only time that a witness should express an opinion is if he or she is an 'expert witness', such as a medical expert in a disability discrimination case, who is there to give an expert opinion as to the claimant's disability.

Drafting witness statements

When it comes to drafting a statement, all the above points should be borne in mind. If possible, the statement should be drafted chronologically (ie, in the order that events happened) and in subject areas. The paragraphs should be numbered, as this makes it easier to refer a witness to particular sentences when asking further questions about the statement, and legal practice is to have the statement in double-spaced lines. The statement should be in the witness's own words, and should refer to any relevant documents that the witness created or saw. Most of all, however, the witness statement should tell a story.

A witness statement is usually structured as follows:

- identity of witness
- brief details of the claimant's job
- story of the complaint
- what has happened since
- statement of truth, declaring that 'this statement is true to the best of my knowledge and belief'.

When the statement has been completed and the witness has checked it through, he or she should then sign and date it.

 Activity 31.6

Before reading the section below, go back to the facts of *Grumble v Robinson Coaches* and consider the following questions.

Questions

1   Who will be the witnesses on each side?

2   Assume that you are on the same side as each witness. What do you want this witness to say?

3   Draft a statement for Mr Grumble.

Witnesses for the claimant

On the facts that we have above, the witness for the claimant will be the claimant himself, Mr Grumble. The evidence that he is likely to give, and which should therefore be in his witness statement, is as follows.

His name, date of birth, address, his occupation (or former occupation), and his date of employment. This information will already be on his claim form, but it serves to identify him before the tribunal.

He should then go on to give his story chronologically:

- what his job was and what his duties were
- how he got on in his job and his relationship with his employers
- the details about the vehicles breaking down

- his belief that the employer should have provided him with another vehicle and not expected him to drive a faulty vehicle
- details about the argument with Mr Flair
- what he had understood the words 'get lost' to mean
- his current situation (this may need to be updated by oral evidence). This is important because of his 'duty to mitigate' his losses by trying to find another job, as will be explained below
- statement of truth
- signature and date.

Witnesses for the respondent

On the facts that we have above, the witnesses for the respondent will be Mr Flair and Mr Robinson. The evidence that they are likely to give, and which should therefore be in their witness statements, is as follows.

Statement of Mr Flair

He should give his name, date of birth, address (this can be his business address), and his occupation/role in the respondent organisation.

He should then go on to give his story chronologically:

- brief details of Mr Grumble's dates of employment and his duties
- how Mr Grumble got on in his job and his relationship with his employer
- the fact that the company allowed him to take the vehicle home and do his own thing when not driving
- that it was noticed there was a change in him when he came back from holiday
- the details about the vehicles breaking down
- his assertion that the vehicle Mr Grumble was expected to drive was not dangerous
- details of the argument with Mr Flair
- what Mr Flair had understood the words 'get lost' to mean—just part of the argument
- the current situation (this may need to be updated by oral evidence)
- statement of truth
- signature and date.

Statement of Mr Robinson

He should give his name, date of birth, address (this can be his business address), and his role in the respondent organisation.

He should then go on to give his story chronologically:

- when the business employed Mr Grumble, in what role and how Mr Grumble got on in the job
- the fact that the company allowed him to take the vehicle home and do his own thing when not driving
- a change in him was noticed when he came back from holiday. (It is not necessary to repeat what Mr Flair has said unless there is anything extra that Mr Robinson could add.)

- what happened when Mr Grumble came to see him and he agreed to give him his P45
- why he gave him the P45 (because he thought Mr Grumble was resigning)
- statement of truth
- signature and date.

Disclosure

Once the witness statements are signed and dated they will be exchanged with the other side. This is usually done simultaneously, each party disclosing the statements of its witnesses to the other side, together with other documents, as described in Chapter 30. It is common for documents to be exchanged some weeks before witness statements, but both should be exchanged several weeks before the hearing takes place.

Bundles

When the documents have been exchanged and the case is ready for the hearing, the bundles have to be prepared. These are the paginated bundles of all the papers that are used in the hearing, together with an index and a chronology. There should, at least, be a copy for each of the three tribunal members, a copy for each advocate and one for the witness stand. It is also helpful to have one for the claimant and one for the respondent, so that they can easily follow the proceedings.

It is expected that the party who has the burden of proof in a case will prepare the bundles, but in practice it is usually the respondent who does so as he has better resources to do it. Often there will be an order made in the judge's directions as to who will prepare the bundles and when they should be submitted. Whenever a document contained in the bundle is referred to in the hearing, whether in a speech or during the questioning of witnesses, the page number should be referred to, and the advocate should wait until everyone has found the relevant paragraph.

Advocacy

The hearing will take place at one of the Employment Tribunals Service's tribunal centres. The parties should attend about an hour before the stated hearing time so that there will be time for any final discussions and any last-minute negotiations towards a settlement.

There is often more than one hearing listed in the same room so the parties may have to wait for their case to be called. There are usually separate waiting rooms for claimants and respondents so that discussions can take place without worrying that the other side can hear what is being said. When the case is called, the clerk will switch on the recording device and introduce all the parties. The judge will make some opening comments, and perhaps summarise the issues, and then the party who goes first will start.

 Activity 31.7

In the case of *Grumble v Robinson Coaches*, the respondent does not accept that Mr Grumble was dismissed. Who, therefore, should go first?

Note taking

Advocates should be thinking about their closing speeches at all times during the case. This final speech should be in the advocate's mind whenever a point is made, whether favourable or not. Everything that is said lays the ground for the final speech, and the advocate should be continually fashioning it, both mentally and as bullet points on a piece of paper. It is important therefore to make a note of what is said during the hearing. There are several reasons for this. First, it assists in questioning the witnesses if an advocate has at hand a note of what the witness has just said, particularly if it contradicts something that was said earlier, or there is a discrepancy with what another witness has said. Secondly, it would be very difficult to do a closing speech which refers to the evidence without having a note of what was said during the hearing. Thirdly, having a ready note of the evidence and what was said by the witnesses and the tribunal members is useful when considering whether to appeal or not as it takes time before an official transcript can be obtained.

The judge will also be taking a note of the evidence, so it is important to 'watch the judge's pen' and not speak too quickly. When questioning a witness, the advocate should ask him or her to pause while the judge catches up with his or her note of what is being said.

Opening statements

In most cases, an opening statement will be unnecessary and is nowadays very much the exception. If in doubt, ask the judge if he or she wishes the case to be opened. Even if there is an opening statement, it should be very short and should merely summarise the issues so that the tribunal knows what it should focus on. In many cases, the judge starts by summarising his or her understanding of the key issues. It is, however, polite to check that the tribunal has received copies of the bundle if one has been prepared and submitted, and briefly mention the contents and chronology. The judge should be referred to as 'Sir' or 'Madam'.

Examination in chief and types of question

When an advocate calls a witness to give evidence and asks him or her questions, this is known as 'examination in chief'. The usual practice is that the witness statement 'stands' as his or her evidence. When calling the witness, the tribunal should be told that there is a statement. The page in the bundle should be referred to, and the judge asked whether he or she wishes the statement to 'stand' as the evidence in chief for that witness.

The way that a witness should be called is as follows:

Advocate: Sir, I call Mr Grumble

[Mr Grumble is sworn in and takes his seat—in employment tribunals all parties are seated—in the witness's chair]

    A: Are you James Grumble?

Witness: Yes

    A: Please can you turn to page 10 of the bundle. Can you confirm that that is your statement?

    W: Yes

    A: At page 12 of the bundle, is that your signature?

    W: Yes, that is my signature

    A: Can you confirm that the contents of the statement are true to the best of your knowledge and belief?

W: They are

A: Do you wish the statement to be used as your evidence?

W: Yes

A: Sir, may the statement stand as Mr Grumble's evidence in chief?

If the judge agrees (and this is usually the case), Mr Grumble should then be asked to read out his statement. If there are any aspects of the statement that need to be clarified, or updated, the advocate can ask Mr Grumble to pause when he reaches that point and ask him the relevant question.

When Mr Grumble has finished reading the statement, the advocate should then ask him about what has happened since the statement was completed so that the tribunal can be updated as to his current situation. This will often involve giving the witness an opportunity to comment on points that have been made in the opposing side's witness statements. If the judge does not wish for the statement to stand as the evidence in chief, or if there is no statement to be read out, then the advocate should ask questions to elicit the story from the witness.

When asking questions in chief, the advocate should not, as far as is possible, ask leading questions about matters that are in dispute. A 'leading question' is a question to which the answer can *only* be 'yes' or 'no'. Doing so gives the impression that words are being put into the witness's mouth. More generally, however, witnesses give a better impression and will come over as more credible when they express themselves in their own words.

Let us assume that there is a dispute as to whether Mr Jones gave the keys of a vehicle to Mr Grumble in the morning or the afternoon. Mr Grumble says it was the morning, Mr Flair says it was the afternoon. A leading question would be: 'Did Mr Jones give you the keys to the coach *in the morning*?' This is not appropriate, as it is putting the words into Mr Grumble's mouth. The correct, non-leading question would be: '*When* did Mr Jones give you the keys to the vehicle?'

The rules that apply to witness statements also apply to evidence in chief, so, for example, Mr Grumble should not be asked about the law, nor should he be asked to give his opinion. He should not, therefore, be asked 'was the dismissal unfair?' When the advocate has finished asking questions of each witness it is the turn of the advocate for the other side to cross-examine.

Cross-examination and types of question

Cross-examination is when an advocate asks questions of the other side's witnesses. The purpose of cross-examination is to elicit information that would help the advocate in proving his or her case or to weaken the case of the other party. It does not provide an opportunity to examine the witness crossly!

In any kind of questioning, and even more so during cross-examination, it is essential to listen to the answer and look at the witness. The types of question used in cross-examination are the opposite of those used for examination in chief. An advocate should use mainly closed questions, to which the witness would find it difficult to give an answer other than 'yes' or 'no'.

Let us assume Mr Grumble's advocate wishes to cross-examine Mr Flair about what type of vehicle Mr Grumble was driving on a particular day. He would not ask 'What type of vehicle was Mr Grumble driving?' because it would leave the answer open. Instead, he should say 'Mr Grumble was driving a sixteen-seat minibus, wasn't he?'

Asking a closed question puts the advocate in some control of the evidence that is given. It can be quite fatal to a case in some circumstances to ask a wide open question, such as 'why?', unless the advocate is fairly sure of the answer, as it would give the witness the opportunity to say things that the advocate may not have expected and which could be damaging to the advocate's case. One motto of advocates is 'never ask a question to which you do not know the answer'. This is not always workable in practice, but is useful to follow as a general rule. Cross-examination should be structured chronologically and in subject areas, as jumping about weakens the force of the questioning.

The advocate who is cross-examining is expected to 'put his case'. This means that if there are any points on which the parties differ, the advocate has specifically to ask the witness for the other side about them. So, for example, if the parties disagree where Mr Flair was standing when he allegedly pointed to the gate and told Mr Grumble to 'get lost', the advocate cross-examining Mr Grumble would not say 'Where was Mr Flair standing?' That is an open question which would just give Mr Grumble an opportunity to give his version again. It does not put forward the evidence that the advocate wishes to hear, which is that Mr Flair was in fact sitting having his lunch in the common room. The question that should be asked, therefore, is 'Mr Flair was in the common room when you approached him, wasn't he?' Mr Grumble may well deny it, but the advocate has 'put his case'.

It may seem like a pointless exercise, as the witness is likely to deny the points made by the advocate and reiterate any evidence about it that he has already given in chief, but it is necessary to give him an opportunity to comment on what the advocate's client asserts.

 Activity 31.8

Before you continue to read the rest of the chapter, re-read the statement that you drafted for Mr Grumble.

Assume that you are the advocate for Robinson Coaches. Plan what you wish to ask him in cross-examination.

Some notes of the main areas for cross-examination of each witness are as follows:

- The fact that they had always got on well.
- The company had always treated him well; it allowed him time to himself and allowed him to drive the vehicle home.
- The company did try to replace and fix the vehicles.
- There was no other vehicle to give him.
- The vehicle he was asked to drive was not dangerous.
- It would have been fixed when brought back to the yard.
- It was a stressful time for the company too, having vehicles breaking down in quick succession.

- The words used were part of an argument.
- He decided to leave of his own accord.
- Was it really because he was near to retirement and had had enough?

Mr Flair

- He had never had a problem with Mr Grumble in the past.
- Mr Grumble was well liked and a good worker.
- The problems with the vehicles—he put Mr Grumble in a difficult situation by saying he had to continue the journey with a defective vehicle, which Mr Grumble believed to be illegal.
- Deny that Mr Grumble was swearing and arguing.
- The words used were intended to tell him to leave.

Mr Robinson

- He did not ask Mr Grumble why he wanted his P45.
- He made no effort to find out what had happened or to clarify the situation.
- Was it because he was aware that Mr Grumble had been dismissed?

Re-examination

When the cross-examination has finished, the advocate who originally called the witness has a chance to clarify any matters that arose in cross-examination. He or she should not ask about any new issues, and, as in examination in chief, should not ask leading questions. If the advocate has forgotten to ask something which should originally have been asked about in examination in chief, then permission to ask this should be requested. If it is granted, the other side will be allowed to cross-examine on the new matter.

Closing speeches

The closing speech is the advocate's opportunity not just to summarise the evidence, but to persuade the tribunal to find in his or her party's favour. This is done by making reference to the evidence and to the law, and showing how one fits into the other. The advocate should only refer to the evidence which has actually been given. If there was something that the advocate hoped that a witness would say but did not in fact do so, then this is not evidence and should not be referred to.

It is at this stage that the law, both statutes and case law, will usually be referred to, unless there have been any earlier legal applications such as those for amendment. The advocate must bring to court copies of any cases that he is referring to in any detail and should provide these to the panel.

Again, structure and relevance are important, as it is for any type of advocacy, as a speech that meanders will lose its force and bore the listener. Advocates never interrupt one another during closing speeches, however much they may disagree with what is being said. It is recognised that each side has the right to put their case and legal argument forward in the way that they wish. Judges, however, often do interrupt closing statements to ask for clarification of points. Where one advocate believes that the other has made a glaring error, then they need to wait until the speech is completed before politely pointing the matter out to the tribunal.

This is also a point that applies to 'objections'. The reader will be familiar with American courtroom dramas from television, where advocates jump up and down shouting 'Objection, your Honour!' Things are much more sedate in this country, and the advocate should catch the judge's eye and make his or her objection in a calm and polite manner.

The end of the case

The advocate's job will then be almost done. The decision will be handed down (and if the tribunal gives its reasons on the day, a full note of this must be taken by the advocate). If the claimant is successful, the tribunal will often ask the parties to see if they can reach agreement on the remedy. If this cannot be done, remedies will be argued about and then decided upon by the panel. The case will then be over, unless there is an appeal.

CHAPTER SUMMARY

- Prepare the case properly, using bullet points.
- Anticipate what the other side will say and pre-empt it.
- Listen to what the witness has to say.
- Relevance is very important.
- Ask open/non-leading questions in chief.
- Ask closed/leading questions in cross-examination.
- Prepare most of your closing speech even before the hearing starts.

ONLINE RESOURCE CENTRE

A range of online resources to help you through your employment law module have been developed by the author team. These include updates, self-test questions and sources for further reading. (www.oxfordtextbooks.co.uk/orc/taylor_emir3e)

INDEX

References such as "178–9" indicate (not necessarily continuous) discussion of a topic across a range of pages. Wherever possible in the case of topics with many references, these have either been divided into sub-topics or only the most significant discussions of the topic are listed. Because the entire work is about 'employment law' the use of this term (and certain others which occur constantly throughout the book) as an entry point has been minimised. Information will be found under the corresponding detailed topics.